W9-BCJ-784

Varieties of Visual Experience

Edmund Burke Feldman

PROFESSOR OF ART, UNIVERSITY OF GEORGIA

Varieties of Visual Experience

SECOND EDITION

Prentice-Hall, Inc., Englewood Cliffs, N. J.

Harry N. Abrams, Inc., New York

TO MERRILL
1928–1972

Second Edition 1981

Library of Congress Cataloging in Publication Data
Feldman, Edmund Burke.
  Varieties of visual experience.
  Bibliography: p.504
  Includes index.
  1. Art—Psychology.   2. Composition (Art)
I. Title.
N71.F4 1981   701   80–16414
ISBN 0–13–940585–2

Library of Congress Catalog Card Number: 80–16414

Published in 1981 by Harry N. Abrams, Incorporated, New York

Printed and bound in Japan

CONTENTS

Color sections are marked with an asterisk (*)

PREFACE AND ACKNOWLEDGMENTS

This book is meant to stimulate thought and discussion about art as it enters our private lives and our common existence. At a time when splendid works of specialized scholarship abound, only this purpose seemed a valid reason for adding to the list of books on the subject. My guiding assumption has been that works of art illuminate life as nothing else can. Therefore I have tried to talk about the recurring features of human affairs as they are known through visual form. So this book deals with the thematic and utilitarian values of art before taking up stylistic, formal, and technical considerations. This approach seemed best for gaining the interest of the reader who wants to know how art is useful in daily life, how it speaks, and what it means.

Readers may wish to differ with some of my observations, or with the way they have been expressed. If so, I shall be pleased that they have found material stimulating enough to provoke questions, alternative views, or dissent. Art is too important, and we should care too much about it, to be content with bland acceptance or plain indifference to any serious discussion of its uses and merits. As a teacher, I would be disappointed if students had little to say or think about following any presentation I had made. Consequently, I hope my written commentary and visual comparisons will stimulate inquiry about the issues which have been raised. Indeed, many works of art were selected because their presentation at a particular place in the text would make a critical point, or test the reader's understanding of some theoretical position while leading to an appreciation of the meaning and quality of the work itself.

A book that tries to initiate a kind of humanistic dialogue necessarily grows out of many such dialogues carried on over the years with teachers, colleagues, and students. I was fortunate as a boy to study with artists who liked to talk about art while trying to teach me the rudiments of painting and drawing; hence, many important questions were raised for me in conversation long before I realized their significance in the world of scholarship. Afterward, I acquired labels for those early questions and categories for their answers. Now I submit them in book form after they have passed through the crucible of so many conversations that I cannot honestly say who is responsible for the ideas that I, following a common delusion of authors, believe to be my own. Here let me thank them—teachers, students, colleagues, and friends—for what they have given me in countless ways.

PREFACE TO THE SECOND EDITION

The acceptance of this book by so many different readers—artists and teachers, critics and historians, specialists and generalists—has encouraged us to retain its overall plan while adding two new chapters, a Glossary, and four Time-Line Charts. In the first of these new chapters, *The Image of Woman in Modern Painting*, I have tried to demonstrate the pertinence of visual art to an important contemporary concern. The discussion shows, I trust, that art criticism, through its analysis of visual form and style, can uncover many of the attitudes underlying our personal and social behavior. Another new chapter, *Photography*, stresses the cultural and aesthetic rather than the technical features of the medium. It also attempts to provide a critical scheme for judging photographs, keeping in mind the distinctive features of photographic art while evaluating its products according to the same, broadly humanistic criteria that are applied to the other, well-established mediums of visual expression.

The preparation of this new edition has entailed the collaborative labors of many able professionals in two fine publishing houses. At Prentice-Hall, I have been indebted to Norwell (Bud) Therien, and at Harry N. Abrams, Inc., to Margaret Kaplan and Adele Westbrook for editorial guidance, as well as to Dirk Luykx for the design of the book (immensely difficult when there are hundreds of illustrations to be considered). Let me thank them all for their counsel and their hard work.

EDMUND BURKE FELDMAN

PART ONE

THE FUNCTIONS OF ART

Introduction

THE FUNCTIONS OF ART

FOR MANY OF US, THE IDEA THAT ART FUNCTIONS, that it is useful in human affairs, may be greeted with skepticism. We have been taught to believe art is the product of surplus energy and wealth. Moreover, we think of the fine arts as *uniquely* useless—unnecessary for meeting the fundamental requirements of organized living. Nevertheless, the visual arts have existed throughout human history and they appear to be thriving today. How can we explain art's survival for so long among so many peoples? Do human societies tolerate art because of some blunder in the organization of social life? Or is art prized because it satisfies vital personal and social needs? Clearly, this book is written in support of the latter premise. I hope to show that the visual arts—painting, sculpture, architecture, industrial design, the crafts, photography, films, and television—are employed usefully in the lives of everyone.

Contemporary art, which we often encounter in its exotic and abstruse manifestations, performs the same functions today as its historic antecedents. Art continues to satisfy (1) our individual needs for personal expression, (2) our social needs for display, celebration, and communication, and (3) our physical needs for utilitarian objects and structures. However, if art provides us with effective advertising designs, for example, and soaring airport terminals and handsome refrigerators, we nevertheless wonder how contemporary "extravagances" in paint, metal, stone, and plastics affect the quality of our lives. We realize that manufacturers need designers to create packages and displays that can attract buyers. But what function is performed, or what need satisfied, by paint splashed on a canvas which is then exhibited for the amazement of honest men and women?

Is there any reason why we should spend our time trying to understand the works of artists who have not taken the trouble to make their meaning clear? Furthermore, what connection, if any, is there between today's art and the masterpieces of the past? Answers to these questions—or attempts to answer them—are what the following pages are about.

1

PERSONAL FUNCTIONS OF ART

ALTHOUGH MAN IS A SOCIAL BEING WHO MUST LIVE IN groups and communities to survive, he does have a private and separate existence. He can never escape the consciousness of other persons and their relation to him, but he also feels that thoughts occur to him uniquely, that there are things he feels that are his alone. Inside each of us many events take place, and it appears to be our nature to tell others about them if we can. To communicate our ideas and feelings we use many kinds of languages. Art constitutes one of those languages.

As an instrument of personal expression, art is not confined solely to self-revelation; that is, it does not deal exclusively with the private emotions of an artist's life. Art also embodies personal views of *public* objects and events. Basic human situations like love, death, celebration, and illness constantly recur as themes, but they can be saved from banality by the uniquely personal comment the artist makes. For example, adolescence is shown in a new light by the sculpture of Wilhelm Lehmbruck; the expectation of death hovers over every painting by Edvard Munch; and there is an irrepressible love of living in the people painted by Frans Hals. It does not matter whether Hals's subjects were in fact somber or dreary; when he paints them they are cheerful. For the robust citizens he portrayed, Hals's pictures served as signs of prosperity. For the artist, they were *opportunities* to display a personal outlook: all in all, when the satisfactions of life are weighed against its hazards and pain, it is better to enjoy the pleasure in each moment.

Perhaps all works function as avenues of personal expression for the artist. That does not prevent them from serving other purposes. As we look at the examples in this volume, however, it should be clear that some works are thoroughly devoted to their official pur-

pose. Some cannot avoid being vehicles of the artist's private vision. In the modern world, this personal element has been treasured above all others. Consequently, the personal functions of art may seem to constitute the very essence of art for artist and viewer.

Art and Psychological Expression

Visual images preceded written language as a means of communication. Here, however, we are not primarily interested in art as a vehicle for imparting information, since other languages have evolved as more precise instruments of communication. But we are interested in visual art as a means of *expressing* the psychological dimension of life.

Why is it necessary to distinguish between communication and expression? One reason is that art is not merely a language for translating thoughts and feelings inside of people into conventional signs and symbols outside of them; that constitutes communication in the sense that a street sign is communication. Art does this, but it also involves forming lines, colors, and shapes so that they mean something significant to the artist; that constitutes expression in the sense of painting a picture as opposed to lettering a sign. The materials and techniques of art become the artist's mode of expression; they *embody* his meaning since they help create it and give it objective existence. Without art—without the use by man of particular materials in particular ways—there would be no way of finding expression for certain states of feeling. Poems or songs cannot have the same meaning as paintings or sculptures about the same subjects; they embody a different set of meanings because they are made of different materials and

ALBERTO GIACOMETTI.
Man Pointing. 1947. The Museum
of Modern Art, New York. Gift of
Mrs. John D. Rockefeller III

The tragedy of Giacometti's man is that he wants to communicate with others but cannot because of his spiritual isolation—that is, they won't listen. Richier's man is a tragic victim or antihero, an ineffectual creature who seems predestined to fail.

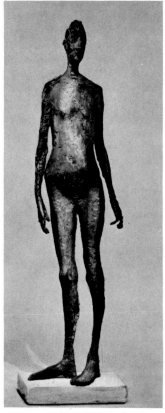

GERMAINE RICHIER.
Leaf. 1948.
The Hirshhorn
Museum and Sculpture
Garden, Smithsonian
Institution, Washington, D.C.

employ different techniques. In other words, a painting *of* a tree, like a poem *about* a tree, is an objectification of feelings and states of consciousness stimulated by the tree and given existence by special materials and techniques. Without words, syntax, rhyme, and rhythm, there would be no poem. Without colors, shapes, lines, and textures, there would be no painting.

In *Man Pointing* by Alberto Giacometti (1901–1966), we see the expression of loneliness, of the individual who is physically and spiritually remote from other men. In a similar vein is Germaine Richier's (1904–1959) *Leaf*. The elongation of the figure in both works, the indistinctness of the bodily parts, the attenuation of the forms, and their general lack of corporeality suggest the difficulty we would encounter in attempting to communicate with the individual, to relate to him personally. The figures seem surrounded by silence. The discovery of feelings such as these in sculpture, and of the ideas they imply, illustrates how art can be the vehicle for an exceedingly intimate kind of expression. Because the sculpture is not of an individual but rather of a generalized type, we might conclude that the artist is not dealing with the problem of a particular person but is commenting about a universal problem: we multiply media of communication, but are not able to *reach* each other; we are all isolated.

The feelings expressed by Giacometti and Richier may have more or less universal validity, but they are clearly derived from an individual, psychological appreciation of loneliness and remoteness. The portrait of a specific person, on the other hand, has fewer universal implications; it provides an artistic opportunity to probe the personality of an individual. At the same time, a portrait reveals the values of the artist in his choice of subject and treatment. In *The Poet Max Hermann-Neisse* (1927), George Grosz (1893–1959) presents the "map" of a man. The artist's linear style and powerful draftsmanship, highly developed in his career as a German newspaper satirist, give us a painfully truthful account of the bones of the skull, the veins of the temple, and the worried wrinkles of the face and forehead. The carefully drawn hands, although folded, present in themselves a portrait of agitation. The quality of intense brooding is further accentuated by the rumpled clothing, whose folds seem to be in turbulent motion. Any painter can ennoble his subject, minimize his defects, or exhibit the ideal aspects of a person. But Grosz was a brutally honest reporter; he seemed to enjoy dwelling on the fact that man is, after all, a peculiar-looking creature. He was obsessed with the moral ugliness of his country; he used art to express the far from ideal character of everything he saw. Art can embody distaste. Even in a man Grosz presumably liked (the situation here is intimate), he could not help seeing the frightening countenance of sickness, ugliness, and perhaps cruelty as well.

The *Portrait of Max Jacob* by Juan Gris (1887–1927) shows a subject of about the same age in a similar pose. But the effect is much more placid. Indeed, the Grosz seems to express the restless Gothic or Germanic temperament, while the Gris exhibits the more relaxed and classic qualities of the Mediterranean world. The drawing is excellent, too, but the

GEORGE GROSZ.
The Poet Max Hermann-Neisse.
1927. The Museum of Modern Art,
New York

JUAN GRIS. *Portrait of Max Jacob.*
1919. The Museum of Modern Art,
New York.
Gift of James Thrall Soby

artist is unwilling to approach caricature; the gentleness of the sitter is emphasized. The artist does not idealize his subject; he seems to be making a chart of the convolutions of his face, hands, and body, as if in preparation for a painting. Nevertheless, a quality of gentle humanity emanates from the portrait, a work of accuracy, delicacy of feeling, *and* penetrating psychological insight.

The portrait is plainly suited to the expression of personality, but the landscape presents a different psychological problem. Still, in *An April Mood* by Charles Burchfield (1893–1967), we see the anthropomorphic possibilities of Nature when man projects his moods upon her. The trees, stripped of leaves, give Burchfield the opportunity to characterize them as witches or druids, and by exaggerating the heavy character of the dark clouds which frame the illuminated forms in the center, the artist creates a dramatic, emotionally charged stage. Nature provides theatrical occasions, of course, but only because men see in them the working out of their own private dramas of menace and threat, fear and resistance, deliverance and jubilation. In this painting, the upraised arms of the trees seem to be joined in a weird, natural imitation of primitive sun worship.

An intriguing example of art as psychological expression is seen in George Segal's *The Dinner Table.* Mr. Segal (born 1924) makes sculptures by placing plaster-soaked rags on the bodies of his models. After the plaster sets, the rags are taken off and assembled into cast-plaster figures. His final forms, therefore, are replicas of living forms without the exaggeration or simplification which would result if the sculpture were carved or modeled. The artist then installs props to create a "real" environment. Segal finds his creative role in the identification of commonplace people in commonplace situations; he does not display sculptural virtuosity. The whiteness of the plaster figures, which are naturalistic in all respects except color, is

contrasted with the realism of the materials and objects used as props. This whiteness usually suggests the purity of form and idealization of type we associate with classical Greek sculpture. Instead, we are presented with rather grubby, ungraceful figures. They are neither ugly nor handsome, strong nor weak; neither friendly nor hostile. The artist's theme is *the ordinariness, the artlessness of our everyday environ-*

CHARLES BURCHFIELD. *An April Mood.* 1946–55.
Whitney Museum of American Art, New York.
Gift of Mr. and Mrs. Lawrence A. Fleischman and purchase

VINCENT VAN GOGH. *Landscape with Olive Trees.* 1889.
Collection Mr. and Mrs. John Hay Whitney, New York

Two versions of the animation of nature. The
Burchfield is theatrical: we feel that the trees are
being asked to *impersonate* people. But Van Gogh
truly believes the universe is alive.

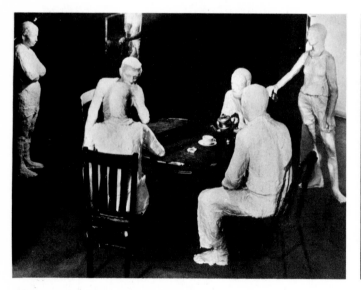

GEORGE SEGAL. *The Dinner Table.* 1962.
Schweber Electronics, Westbury, New York

LOUIS LE NAIN. *Peasants at Supper.* 1641.
The Louvre, Paris

There is a frozen quality about both groups of
diners. But the immobility of Le Nain's peasants
is intended to suggest their fundamental dignity
and self-respect. Segal's people are immobile because they seem to have nothing important to do.

ment and of the people in it. His technique results in a lumpy, torpid quality. The forms lack precision and distinctness, and we ascribe the lack of these qualities to the people the artist represents. He expresses their indistinctness, colorlessness, and indifference; he stresses their placid, vegetable-like character.

Love, Sex, and Marriage

In addition to expressing the varieties of personality and the interaction of personality and culture, art also deals with the themes of love and sex, marriage and procreation. The treatment of love varies from the physical embrace of Auguste Rodin's *The Kiss,* to the maternal affection conveyed by Mary Cassatt's painting *La Toilette,* to the motherly pride displayed in Jacob Epstein's *Madonna and Child.*

The female figure is commonly used for expressing personal feelings about love and sexuality. And the work of a single sculptor, Gaston Lachaise (1882–1935), illustrates two interesting variations on a sexual theme. In the *Standing Woman* of 1912–27, the ele-

AUGUSTE RODIN. *The Kiss.* 1886–98.
Rodin Museum, Paris. Love as tender eroticism.

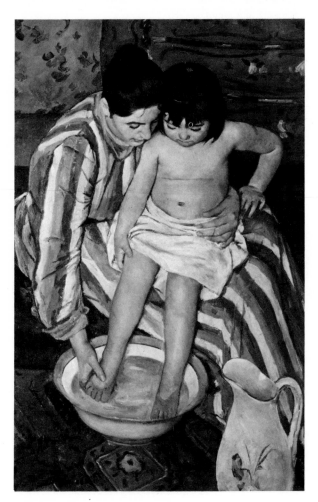

MARY CASSATT. *La Toilette.* c. 1891.
The Art Institute of Chicago. Robert A. Waller Fund.
Love as protective concern.

JACOB EPSTEIN. *Madonna and Child.* 1927.
The Riverside Church, New York.
Love as maternal pride.

19

gance of the hands and feet is combined with idealization and exaggeration of the fleshy forms associated with procreation. The sexual theme is closely related to the maternal; the eroticism of the whole is tempered by the lightness and agility of the feet, the buoyant grace of the hands. By contrast, the *Standing Woman* executed in 1932 reveals a greater exaggeration and stylization of form, with an almost athletic emphasis on childbearing and fecundity. The feet are solidly planted in the earth, and the muscles of the shoulders and abdomen constitute an aggressive assertion of the female biological role. With less gentleness in the transitions between forms than in the early bronze, the late figure expresses procreative arrogance; this emphasis diminishes its ability to suggest any of the tender meanings of love. In *Reclining Nude* by Amedeo Modigliani (1884–1920), we see, in contrast to the fleshiness of Lachaise, a sinuous and elongated version of the female. She is regarded as an object of pleasure. Her very sleep is an expression of sexual fulfillment, of the subordination of all functions and meanings to the erotic. Finally, we encounter the ultimate abstraction of the female form in *Torse Gerbe* by Jean Arp (1887–1966). In the Arp, almost all aspects of personality are denied in favor of a kind of impersonal sexual or biological meaning. He carries abstraction of organic form as far as one can go without losing contact with what is, biologically and psychologically, human.

left: GASTON LACHAISE. *Standing Woman.* 1912–27. Whitney Museum of American Art, New York

right: GASTON LACHAISE. *Standing Woman.* 1932. The Museum of Modern Art, New York. Mrs. Simon Guggenheim Fund

Our culture abounds with references to love in marriage, many of them attempts at cynical humor. Much of this humor revolves around the difficulty of sustaining the romantic meanings of love after a couple have

JEAN ARP. *Torse Gerbe.* 1958. Collection Arthur and Molly Stern, Rochester, New York

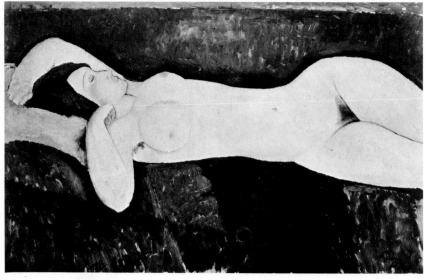

AMEDEO MODIGLIANI. *Reclining Nude.* c. 1919. The Museum of Modern Art, New York. Mrs. Simon Guggenheim Fund

MARC CHAGALL. *Birthday*. 1915–23. The Solomon R. Guggenheim Museum, New York

OSKAR KOKOSCHKA. *The Tempest (The Wind's Bride)*. 1914. Kunstmuseum, Basel

come to know each other so well that they cannot easily hold on to the mystery and illusion that feed romance. Love as romantic transcendence is most popularly expressed in the work of Marc Chagall (born 1887), as in *Birthday*, which is so much in the spirit of our notions of perpetual courtship: the exchange of gifts on anniversaries; the perpetuation of courtesies and gallantries practiced before marriage. The charm and popularity of Chagall are in good mea-

sure traceable to our belief that the substance of love consists of just such rituals as the one celebrated in *Birthday*.

A more cynical view of the marital relation is expressed by Oskar Kokoschka (1886–1980) in *The Tempest,* or *The Wind's Bride*. The pair is shown swirling in space before a moonlit mountainscape. Love for them, as for Chagall's couple, has performed the miracle of levitation. But while Chagall's people

CARL HOFER. *Early Hour.* 1935.
Portland Art Museum, Portland, Oregon.
Love as a domestic quandary.

JOHN KOCH. *Siesta.* 1962.
Private collection,
Durham, North Carolina.
Love as an extension of upper-class leisure.

BARBARA ADRIAN. *Bed of Stones.* 1964.
Collection Mrs. Alexander Rittmaster,
Woodmere, New York.
Love as a proletarian triumph over
the requirements of comfort.

are magically lifted up, Kokoschka's are *swirled.*
Words in both titles for the Kokoschka—"tempest"
and "wind"—suggest the *sturm und drang,* the storm
and stress, of a Germanic conception of human relations. As the bride sleeps, wrapped in tender and
trusting emotions, the groom stares—starkly and stiff-
ly awake. Although he is also levitated and swirled
by the power of love, he remains incapable of sup-
pressing feelings of gloomy foreboding.

Carl Hofer (1878–1955) in *Early Hour* carries the
theme of *The Wind's Bride* one step further to disillusioned domesticity. The crisp morning light reveals
the husband, already awake, dispassionately contemplating the form of his wife. The dog asleep at the foot
of the bed completes the picture of familial routine.
The face of the man is not one of apprehension as in
the Kokoschka; rather, its leanness, combined with
the man's baldness, creates an impression of asceticism, of intellectual resignation to the dilemma of
marriage. It is interesting that in both Germanic works
the wife is shown in contented sleep, while the husband is apprehensively awake in the moonlight or
skeptically contemplating the plain truths of domesticity in the clear light of morning. In the American
conception of love, at least in films, the husband
suffers neither qualms nor regrets; neither does he
indulge in dark speculation about the fate of manhood under the constraints of domesticity. In paint-

ROGER DE LA FRESNAYE. *Conjugal Life*. 1912.
The Minneapolis Institute of Arts

EDOUARD MANET. *Le Déjeuner sur l'herbe*. 1863.
The Louvre, Paris

ing, this attitude is expressed by the sophisticated realism of John Koch (1909–1978) in *Siesta*. Unlike his continental counterpart, the American male apparently experiences love as a casual, uncomplicated episode in the normal routine of everyday life.

Another version of the marital theme is seen in *Conjugal Life* by Roger de la Fresnaye (1885–1925). Here, in a work by a follower of Cubism, the process of breaking up figures and converting them into geometric forms has begun; it is most visible in the treatment of the hands and faces. But correspondence to visual reality remains strong, sufficiently strong to resist the depersonalizing effects of a fully developed Analytic Cubism. There is about this couple a casual,

comradely quality which is accentuated by the matter-of-factness of the woman's being nude while her clothed husband reads the newspaper and enjoys his pipe. Their relationship exhibits a kind of mutual indifference based on the comfortable intimacy of the long-established marriage. The composition strengthens this idea through the way the figures lean on each other: the principal lines and masses seek the center and lock the figures into a tight formal structure. There is a slight resemblance between the female figure in this work and the one in *Le Déjeuner sur l'herbe* (*Luncheon on the Grass*) by Edouard Manet (1832–1883), where we also find a scene of relaxation in which clothed male figures are juxtaposed with the female nude. The Manet painting, executed in 1863, caused a great scandal because of this association and because of the contemporary, as opposed to classical or allegorical, treatment of the subject matter. However, the work of La Fresnaye is less shocking since the subject is *conjugal* life and the Cubist style has shifted emphasis from eroticism to the manner of organizing forms in space.

Clearly, the meanings of love find varied expression in contemporary art. If one quality characterizes the modern approach, it is candor and, with notable exceptions like Chagall, a refusal to sentimentalize romance. On the contrary, a bitter comment on marriage, as in *Couple* by George Grosz, is probably a more accurate, if exaggerated, expression of our attitudes toward the institution St. Paul said was preferable to burning.

In summary, the attitudes artists express toward women and marriage can serve as an interesting index of the values of their particular cultures. Their work is also evidence of the capacity of art to deal with intimate psychological themes in all their variety and subtlety. In Lachaise we found the sexual-reproductive attributes of woman glorified, but at the expense of her femininity and completeness of personality. In Modigliani we saw frank admiration for the sexual-

hedonic qualities of woman: she was a useful *thing*, but not a person. For Chagall she was a little girl; for Kokoschka and Hofer an enigma, a source of puzzlement; for La Fresnaye a comfortable article to have around the house. These attitudes are not new; they confirm what we have always known—that the holy bond has its problems. The contemporary artist, however, has been candid enough, tactless enough, to say so.

Death and Morbidity

Death has always fascinated and frightened man. He has never been able to solve its mystery: how vitality and personality can inhabit matter in one instant and depart from it in another. From the Paleolithic portrayal of dead animals in dark recesses of caves to the African tribal sculptures of departed chiefs (see the figure of a chief from the Belgian Congo), art has given form to man's attempt to understand, if not to master, the fear and enigma of death. While science advances in its ability to control the causes of death, art expresses the anxiety of man about its finality. Art has always done so. Indeed, sculpture, particularly, had its origins in ancient efforts to provide lifelike bodies for departed souls to inhabit. The monuments of Egyptian art were, in their principal motivation, enormous state-supported enterprises aimed at overcoming the anxiety which attends the death of a king who is revered as a god. It might be said that the modern treatment of mortality represents an extension of the anxiety which everyone feels, but which in ancient times was given expression mainly for the benefit of chiefs and kings.

ARTISTIC EXPRESSIONS OF MORTALITY

A lithograph by Käthe Kollwitz (1867–1945), *Death and the Mother,* expresses the almost insane terror which grips a mother whose child is about to be taken. The imagery gains some of its symbolic force from medieval personifications of the devil as the emissary of death. Notwithstanding our emergence from such superstitions, this work is disturbing since it exploits fears which we find difficult to suppress. An impersonal phrase like "infant mortality" is given powerful emotional content; one experiences dread and the impulse to strike out against the death symbol.

A strange portrayal of mortality and fate occurs in *Death on a Pale Horse* (*The Race Track*) by the American painter Albert Pinkham Ryder (1847–1917). Here death carries his conventional attribute, a scythe, as he rides a white horse around a racetrack. No one is present to view the sinister race, which curiously involves no competitors. Like other paintings by Ryder, this looks as if it were dreamed. (It *appears* to have been dreamed. Actually, the painting was a response to the death of a waiter Ryder knew, a man who gambled his savings on a horse race, lost his

GEORGE GROSZ. *Couple.* 1934.
Whitney Museum of American Art, New York

Figure of a chief, from Bena Lulua,
Belgian Congo. 19th century.
Copyright 1973 by The Barnes Foundation,
Merion, Pennsylvania

KÄTHE KOLLWITZ. *Death and the Mother*. 1934.
Collection Erich Cohn, New York

ALBERT PINKHAM RYDER. *Death on a Pale Horse
(The Race Track)*. c. 1910.
The Cleveland Museum of Art.
Purchase, J. H. Wade Fund

money, and committed suicide. But we should not let
the motivation of the painting interfere with any reasonable interpretation we can make of the result—see
Chapter Seventeen for a discussion of interpretation.)
Although the figure is unmistakably the specter of
death, the question remains, how does he accomplish
his grim task? Perhaps the artist's mythic imagination
is at work. The ancients, for example, believed in
myths of a world held by a thread, or supported by a
brawny god condemned or tricked into taking it as
his burden. Does Ryder's painting mean that death
takes souls so long as his mysterious figure races
around the track with his scythe held aloft? Is the
track a symbol of the circle of the lands, the world?
If so, we have a magical *explanation* of death, a primitive use of cause and effect which operates in
dreams and in myth but which our waking minds will
not accept. Unlike the Kollwitz, this work lacks vivid
realism; the victims of death are not seen—they are an
absent multitude. If my interpretation of the painting
is correct, the rider, the horse, and the track represent
an inevitable cycle—the necessary passing away of
lives due to the race of Death around a magic circle.

The Dead Mother by Edvard Munch (1863–1944)
is a work of infinite pathos in its feeling, not so much
for the mother, who is beyond suffering, but for the
child, who holds her hands to her ears as if to
stop the *sound of death*. This is a work whose psychological realism is more thoroughgoing than that of
Kollwitz, who employs conventional death symbols.
Munch presents the actual death scene and studies its

EDVARD MUNCH. *The Dead Mother*. 1899–1900.
Kunsthalle, Bremen

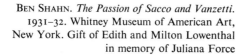

BEN SHAHN. *The Passion of Sacco and Vanzetti.*
1931–32. Whitney Museum of American Art,
New York. Gift of Edith and Milton Lowenthal
in memory of Juliana Force

impact on a child. The child is not too young to understand death, yet she does not have adult mechanisms for protecting herself, for softening the blow. The date of this painting is 1899–1900, a time when harsh reality and strong emotion was not encouraged in art, and was avoided, if possible, in life. In Munch we have a model of the heroic artist who, like Ibsen, is unafraid to examine real life, using the tools of psychological analysis to carry out the task.

The Passion of Sacco and Vanzetti by Ben Shahn (1898–1969) deals with the death of two men convicted of participating in an anarchist bombing. The mourners are represented as "respectable" members of society who have somehow played a role in a miscarriage of justice leading to the execution of innocent men. The background shows the courthouse and a portrait of a jurist taking the oath. In a scene heavy with irony, lilies, symbols of resurrection, are carried over the open coffins of the dead men, illiterate but not ignorant immigrants who were tried by a prejudiced judge. Shahn reveals Sacco and Vanzetti in death as defenseless, foreign-looking, harmless. Their mourners look guilty and hypocritical. The picture is a work of bitterness and indignation: outrage at a society which takes cruel vengeance, and compassion for the two "little" men caught up in large events that destroyed them. In this work, death is not a mystery or an adversary to be overcome. It is understood as the matter-of-fact, logical consequence of social and political

hypocrisy. Our emotions are mainly enlisted against the entire human and social apparatus which kills. But the fact of death itself is treated objectively and dispassionately.

In *Girl Before a Mirror,* Pablo Picasso (1881–1973) represents some of the morbid anticipations of a young girl as she becomes aware of her biological role in womanhood. A kind of X-ray representation of the actual figure on the left and its reflection in the mirror on the right shows the spinal cord and the shapes of internal organs related to reproduction and nurture. The innocent face of the girl is reflected in the mirror by a dark, hollow-eyed visage, surrounded by black and blue moon-shaped crescents. The head on the left is surrounded by a bright halo, a sunny nimbus, with a bright yellow passage on the side where a shadow would be expected. This clear-eyed "sun-face" can be seen as a symbol of unclouded youth; the "moon-face" in the mirror presents the fearful aspect of death. The girl's arm is shown reaching across to the mirror and the apparition which holds the image of her fears. Since the painting is divided vertically into two equal parts, the arm moving across the picture serves to unite the halves compositionally and psychologically. It is a gesture which represents the end of innocence, a touching expression of sympathy for that other self—the self which may die in the act of bringing life into the world. The painting constitutes a remarkable achievement of sympathetic imagination

PABLO PICASSO.
Girl Before a Mirror. 1932.
The Museum of Modern Art,
New York.
Gift of Mrs. Simon Guggenheim.
Anticipating her womanly role,
a girl confronts a premonition
of her own death.

EDVARD MUNCH. *Puberty.* 1895.
National Museum, Oslo.
The crisis of adolescence
experienced as biological dread.

on the part of a man into the apprehensions of a girl
emerging from adolescence. It should be compared to
the more naturalistic treatment of the same theme by
Munch in *Puberty*, an equally haunting work, and
to the lithograph *Adolescence* by the English artist
Gerald Brockhurst (born 1890).

ARTISTIC EXPRESSIONS OF ILLNESS

Just as the modern expression of love tends to be
characterized by candor and skepticism, the art of
our time also confronts illness and disease frankly,
almost clinically. The artist, of course, is not interested
in pathology from a medical standpoint but only as
part of the human condition. He is not fascinated with
morbidity for its own sake but he refuses to ignore a

GERALD LESLIE BROCKHURST. *Adolescence.* 1932.
Syracuse University Art Collection.
The onset of womanhood is discovered in
a magical awareness of the body's opulence.

THÉODORE GÉRICAULT. *Madwoman.* c. 1821.
The Louvre, Paris

of Soutine's woman bespeak her illness but also transcend it; we recognize in her a fellow human being who is suffering.

The Frugal Repast, an etching Picasso executed when he was himself young and poor, portrays a gaunt, emaciated couple. The man is blind. The drawing emphasizes their almost starving condition and it offers the artist an opportunity to attenuate their hands and bodies, giving them a languid, skeletal quality. Although the man is handicapped and both are plainly undernourished, the couple seem resigned to their situation; the artist does not tax our normal sympathies. They have some food and each other. The etching is thus a highly civilized tribute to romantic love; it does not degenerate into mawkish sentimentality. What appears to be a morbid interest in the effect of malnutrition on lovers becomes a human triumph over serious deprivation. The weakness caused by hunger is converted into tenderness; the artist discovers a peculiar kind of amorous beauty in their withered bodies.

dimension of experience which helps to define our humanity.

An early nineteenth-century treatment of mental illness is seen in the *Madwoman* of Théodore Géricault (1791–1824). The artist scrutinizes the woman as carefully as she herself examines some real or imagined threat. She seems to be terrified and deluded at once. But without our knowledge of the subject of the painting, would we interpret this work as a study of character, as the portrait of a somewhat suspicious, possibly eccentric French peasant woman? The Géricault should be compared with *The Madwoman* by Chaim Soutine (1894–1944), which was painted in 1920, approximately one hundred years later. Here the artist attempts to convey the *experience* of the sick person. She trembles with fear; there is no question in our minds that she is mentally ill. Géricault maintains his objectivity whereas Soutine enters into the life of the subject. The earlier painter is classified as a Romantic because his choice of bizarre and emotionally laden subjects constituted an effort to deal with the intensity of man's inner life by describing his abnormal behavior, his reactions in emergencies, his loss of rational control under stress. Soutine is called an Expressionist because of his subject matter and because of the agitated style he used to render his theme. The Expressionists took the Romantic interest in violent and extreme themes and directed it toward the act of painting itself, which became a record of the convulsions of form. The frightened eyes and tortured hands

CHAIM SOUTINE. *The Madwoman.* 1920.
The National Museum of Western Art, Tokyo.
Presented by Mr. Tai Hayashi, 1960

PABLO PICASSO. *The Frugal Repast*. 1904. The Museum of Modern Art, New York. Gift of Abby Aldrich Rockefeller

It should not be thought that works like *The Frugal Repast* are attempts to gloss over the reality of poverty, to minimize the need for social and economic reforms by appearing to mitigate its consequences. Some artists create works designed to *encourage* changes in social life. It is nevertheless an abiding trait of art, as opposed to politics, to reveal the values people can create in any situation or condition in which they happen to find themselves. Puccini's romantic opera *La Bohème* deals with a theme like Picasso's, the composer creating aesthetic values out of the love of a consumptive, dying girl for an impoverished poet. Picasso's etching,

29

IVAN ALBRIGHT. *Self-Portrait*. 1935.
Collection Earle Ludgin, Chicago

Photograph of Melvyn Douglas as he appeared
in the CBS Television Network presentation
"Do Not Go Gentle into That Good Night." 1967

The institutionalization of aging in our culture leads to a variety of
indignities: segregation of old people, organized games for grandparents, and the horrid bureaucratic designation "senior citizen."

KARL ZERBE. *Aging Harlequin*. 1946.
Collection Dr. Michael Watter,
Washington, D.C.

DOMENICO GHIRLANDAIO.
An Old Man and His Grandson. c. 1480.
The Louvre, Paris

made in 1904 when he was twenty-two and presumably as ardent a votary of tragic love as any hero of Puccini, followed by eight years the first performance of *La Bohème.* Both of these men succeeded in creating works which depend on the idea of love sustained and carried to intensity *because of* affliction and *in spite of* the world's indifference.

There is an aesthetic—which is to say, a system of ideas about art—based on the experience of illness and the general decline of vitality. In Géricault and Soutine, we saw this interest as part of a concern with the total human condition. In Munch, death constituted a permanent fact of life. In Shahn's *Passion,* we encounter death as part of a satiric-ironic statement about injustice. Although the work as a whole belongs to the tradition of social protest, it also expresses personal outrage at the destruction of two simple men. In Picasso's etching we see the outcome of an aesthetic development in which the signs of affliction have acquired a sympathetic, even erotic, significance. In Ivan Albright's *Self-Portrait* and Karl Zerbe's *Aging Harlequin,* decline and a certain ugliness associated with senescence (compare Ghirlandaio's *An Old Man and His Grandson*) are recorded in fascinating detail. Zerbe (1903–1972) enlists compassion for the harlequin, viewing him in a noble light despite his ravaged countenance. Albright (born 1897) presents himself with familiar personal objects, drinking champagne and calmly contemplating the fate which is clearly detailed in his face. This artist portrays aging not so much as a psychological or spiritual condition but as a stage of life in which the processes of disease and deterioration have grown stronger than the forces of vitality and renewal.

Perhaps the ultimate depiction of deterioration is seen in the work of Hyman Bloom (born 1913) and of Alberto Burri (born 1915). Bloom, an American painter, reveals in *Corpse of an Elderly Female* a fascination with death and decay unmitigated by any artistic device which might soften its clinical accuracy. Bloom's interest in cadavers can be interpreted as a reaction to the slaughter which took place during World War II. The carnage of recent history, added to a fascination with the painting of flesh, as in Rembrandt's *Slaughtered Ox,* may account for Bloom's choice of theme. Working abstractly, and with a different clinical emphasis, is the Italian artist Alberto Burri. His *Sacco B.* is made of burlap sacking stretched and sewn around what appears to be an open wound or incision. Burri, who was a military doctor, creates compositions which seem to be visual variations based on surgical operations, the dramatic focus of which is the opening in the flesh. One can view them as organizations of gauze, burnt wood, burlap, and other materials, but their arrangement seems to have a hidden purpose. When the tears in the sacking are seen as the result of some mysterious surgery, Burri's surfaces become animated with meaning: they are related to disease; wounds and surgery are presented as a kind of primitive handicraft; a rather disorderly

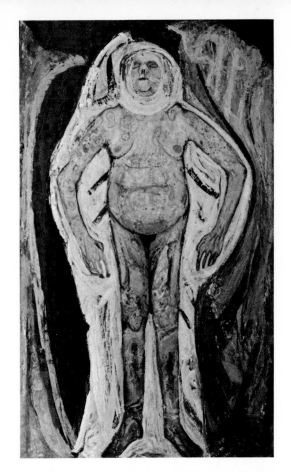

HYMAN BLOOM. *Corpse of an Elderly Female.* 1945. The Chrysler Museum, Norfolk, Virginia

REMBRANDT VAN RIJN. *Slaughtered Ox.* c. 1655. The Louvre, Paris

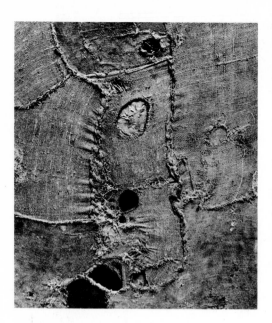

ALBERTO BURRI. *Sacco B.* 1953.
Collection the artist.
The clinical ritual of surgery converted into
aesthetic drama.

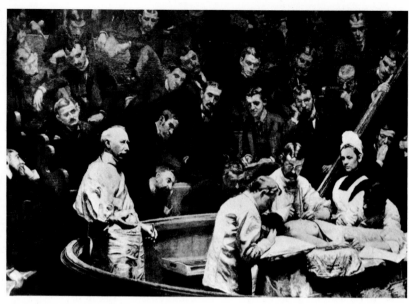

THOMAS EAKINS. *The Agnew Clinic.* 1889.
The University of Pennsylvania, Philadelphia.
The ritual of surgery portrayed as a triumph of mind over flesh.

death seems to hover over the whole. It is a far cry
from the Thomas Eakins painting of modern surgery
in 1889, *The Agnew Clinic,* with its progressive and
optimistic presentation of surgical technique.

Examples could be multiplied. We have seen how
one of the personal functions of art—now as in the
past—is the confrontation of death and all its attendant feelings. If art does not help us postpone death
or the decline of our powers, it *does* help us to face
the experience, to see it as part of the gamut of living.
Art expresses our fears, curiosities, and aversions concerning mortality; it helps us to see life in terms of its
physical conclusion.

Spiritual Concern

We should distinguish between religious art and an
art of spiritual concern. Usually, religious art is the
expression of collective ideas about man in his relation
to divinity. Sometimes it possesses spiritual qualities.
At other times, it functions as education or history or
as a kind of visual preaching. Nonreligious art may
evince spiritual qualities, as in Van Gogh's *The Starry
Night*; yet ostensibly religious art may have little spirituality, as in *Christ Preaching at Cookham Regatta* by
Stanley Spencer (1891–1959). Rouault's works, in
contrast, possess spiritual content whether the subject
matter is sacred as in Rouault's *Christ* or secular as in
his *Three Clowns.*

What accounts for this paradox? Religious art tells
a sacred story, enjoins right behavior, or endeavors to
sustain faith. But spiritual art tries to reveal the divine

in everyday human nature. That is, spiritual art tries
to declare the immanence of the divine in the world,
often finding it in unexpected places. It does not come
with appropriate labels, and its creators may not
necessarily think of their work as having a spiritual
quality. Furthermore, spiritual art expresses the *questions* an artist may have about man's place in the
universe, whereas religious art tends to deal with
answers which have been institutionally established.
We might define spiritual concern as *the search for ultimate values through art.*

For a certain kind of artist, work is an effort to discover meaning in the world through the materials,
processes, and language of art. Particularly now, the
artistic enterprise is identified with search and inquiry.
In the past, artists, like others, were more certain
about the meanings and purposes of life; hence, they
tended to concentrate on giving expression to the
commonly accepted conceptions of man and existence.
But the modern era has witnessed a profound change
in the artistic expression of values. The industrial,
scientific, and political revolutions of the eighteenth
century ultimately caused an almost universal questioning of traditional dogmas and philosophies about
the nature of man, the purposes of his existence, his
relations to other men, and his relation to the divine.
But while these assumptions have been questioned or
abandoned, our era has not been especially successful
in providing alternatives which remain tenable even
for the period of one lifetime. That is why the intellectual, spiritual, and artistic activity of our time has
been devoted to questioning and searching. Hence,
works of art dealing with personal values are char-

STANLEY SPENCER. *Christ Preaching at Cookham Regatta:*
Series No. VI: Four Girls Listening. 1958.
Arthur Tooth & Sons, Ltd., London

GEORGES ROUAULT. *Christ.* 1937. Private collection

GEORGES ROUAULT. *Three Clowns.* 1917.
Collection Joseph Pulitzer, Jr., St. Louis

SEYMOUR LIPTON. *Menorah*. 1953.
Temple Israel, Tulsa, Oklahoma

The useful and the secular often converge in the spiritual: Van Gogh's painting begins with an everyday theme and culminates in a mystical statement; Lipton begins with liturgical function and ends by expressing spiritual concern.

VINCENT VAN GOGH. *The Starry Night*. 1889.
The Museum of Modern Art, New York.
Lillie P. Bliss Bequest

acterized by the expression of doubt and uncertainty more than by conviction and the assumption that artist and public share some orthodoxy.

It is common to contrast the religiously centered art of the Middle Ages with the secular, "religiously indifferent" art of the present era. But this contrast is misleading. One could cite the considerable artistic effort which is expended today in the design of sacred buildings and in the creation of liturgical art objects to enhance and facilitate religious worship. It is obvious that Le Corbusier's chapel at Ronchamp and the *Menorah* by Seymour Lipton (born 1903) constitute examples of religious art because of their use in worship. But it is less evident that works without plain religious utility are expressive of the artist's spiritual aspiration.

The Starry Night of Vincent van Gogh (1853–1890) is evidently a picture of a village at night, with prominent cypresses in the foreground and exaggerated concentric and spiral emanations of light from the stars and the moon. The flamelike shapes of the trees and the brushwork in the hills and sky tend to animate the entire scene so that everything appears to be alive and in motion. Only the houses and the church are relatively at rest. The artist endows the features of the landscape with a kind of life they do not normally possess. This sense of the aliveness of all things, not excepting inanimate objects, characterizes Van Gogh's

work even when he paints a chair or shoes. For him, the distinctions between organic and inorganic, animate and inanimate, or void and mass do not exist: all of creation exhibits the divine presence. For those who do not possess the spiritual gifts of Van Gogh, the experience of his paintings constitutes a glimpse into a hallowed world—an opportunity to share in his "God-intoxicated" perception.

In *Christ* by Georges Rouault (1871–1958), we have a religious subject which also exhibits the distinctive spirituality of this artist's work. It is noteworthy that there is very little iconographic material in the painting—no conventional symbols or gestures or details of dress which might identify Jesus and his Apostles. We have only the downcast countenance of Christ and the vaguely Middle Eastern head clothing of the disciples. As men, they are characterized by intensity and a certain plainness if not coarseness of feature. They are crowded together very closely, as in photographs of very humble people. Rouault's use of heavy black lines serves not only to bind the composition together and strengthen the impact of the forms but also to emphasize the sorrowful quality of this close-knit group.

What qualities of the work account for its spiritual character? The first is the similarity, with minor differentiations, of the three men. They are thus able, collectively, to symbolize all men, humanity. Although the Christ figure is the most highly individualized, we view the men as a group rather than as a series of distinct personalities. The second is the lack of refinement of the features, the deliberate avoidance of physical beauty. The result is an emphasis upon the nonmaterial. The colors are intense, the features are rough, the transitions from light to dark are harsh; we are shocked out of our conventional expectations of harmony of color and elegance of shape and proportion. Third is the passive, accepting expression of the face of Jesus. This not only expresses the ethos of Christianity but also describes the body of humanity as suffering. Fourth is the huddled arrangement of the figures: they symbolize the oppressed, frightened, and victimized condition of those who are weak.

These factors, working together, express the wretchedness of the human condition. Obviously, they do not describe the power and mastery of man, his technological mastery, his commercial avidity and materialistic prowess. Certain themes at the heart of Christianity—the virtue of humility and the significance of suffering—are expressed so as to give them universal application. Since the moral status of man, as seen in the work of Rouault, is very different from the condition of man as we commonly see him—in the midst of his prosperity and aggressiveness—we conclude that the artist is attempting to reveal the authentic nature of human beings, what humanity is *really* like as opposed to what man thinks he is.

Whereas the spirituality of Rouault grows essentially out of one insight—the moral inadequacy of mankind—the sculptor Henry Moore (born 1898) expresses spiritual affirmation and renewal. His UNESCO sculpture casts humanity in a monumental role. Monumental sculpture is usually employed to celebrate military triumphs, to idolize a god-emperor or a hero—to commemorate victories of one sort or another. But Moore, if he celebrates any victory, celebrates *the durability* of man. The massiveness of the figure creates a powerful sense of stability, and the large forms abstracted from the thighs and torso are like the shapes of old hills and eroded mountains. The positive forms are punctuated, so to speak, with openings and hollows and surmounted by a head which seems to symbolize the dominance of intelligence over matter. The openings and deep hollows are not merely "negative shapes." They are positively conceived and permit the environment to become a part of the sculpture as it interacts with it. Without any dramatic devices this figure suggests resurgence after having been struck down, penetrated, and submerged. The forms, although taken from nature, have a certain arbitrary quality. They represent the outcome of human will and intelligence working on materials provided by art and by life. The image of man is Promethean: man suffers and is defiant. He is not morally squalid, and although his reclining position can be taken as one of defeat, as in the *Dying Gaul,* he is capable of physical and spiritual renewal. Compared with Rouault, Moore seems less theological, less affected by knowledge of the sinfulness and corruptibility of man. Rather, his sculpture expresses the forces of human defiance, of an earth creature which slowly rebuilds itself, whether it knows or not that the powers of the universe will strike it down again.

Since spiritual concern in our time is expressed through questioning, uncertainty, and restlessness, it is not surprising that *motion* and *agitation* should characterize many contemporary works. Certainly

HENRY MOORE.
Sculpture for UNESCO
Headquarters,
Paris. 1958

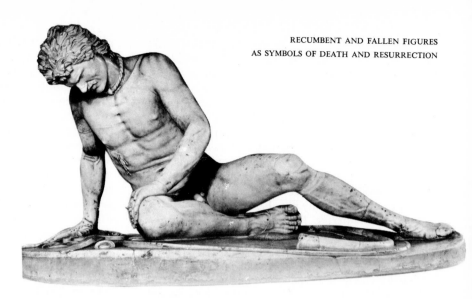

Dying Gaul.
Pergamum. c. 225 B.C.
Capitoline Museum,
Rome

Van Gogh used the motion of patterned brushstrokes to express the aliveness of everything. Rouault and Moore, on the contrary, employ stable forms, possibly because the image of man is for them less uncertain. However, in Umberto Boccioni (1882–1916), perhaps the best-known of the Italian Futurists, we see motion described as the essential characteristic of modern man. *Unique Forms of Continuity in Space,* executed in 1913, constituted both the culmination of many studies of movement and Boccioni's personal adaptation of the lessons of Cubism. It is, of course, an optimistic work, and it possesses a gracefulness and embellishment of form which we do not see in the more cerebral works of the French Cubists. This sculpture may not be entirely successful in the expression of spirituality since it surrenders readily to the desire to create surfaces of fascinating beauty. But the artist did aim at dematerialization; he sought to convey something of the spirit of man by identifying him as a being whose solidity and stability are an illusion—an illusion which, incidentally, this sculpture fails to break down. Notwithstanding the fact that the figure is not enclosed by a single continuous skin and that the movements of muscles and tendons have been permitted to break through, we have a work which remains whole and coherent; it refuses to dissolve at its boundaries and merge with the environment. Despite his obsession with motion and dematerialization, Boccioni cannot escape the physical unity and corporeality of man.

A different, if more poignant, expression of the spiritual quandary of modern man is found in the work of Jackson Pollock (1912–1956). *Number 1* (1948) shows the typical paint surface of his mature style: tangled skeins of pigment dripped and spattered on the canvas, creating an almost infinite labyrinth of pattern and movement. Seeing the work as a whole, one is aware of an overall texture as well as a repetition of black, somewhat calligraphic marks overlaid with splashes, unstructured white drippings, and knots and spots of color. Because it is a huge canvas, nine by seventeen feet, we feel drawn into details of the maze. The impact of Pollock's work derives from the kinetic power of the paint application and is best experienced directly. Devoid of representational elements, the painting inevitably refers the viewer back to the artist's act of executing it. Its imagery is of paths of motion, at once dancelike and trancelike, more purposive in the blacks, spotted at random with

UMBERTO BOCCIONI.
Unique Forms of Continuity in Space. 1913.
The Museum of Modern Art, New York.
Lillie P. Bliss Bequest

some of the colors, and enmeshed and trapped with the whites. No single movement is fathomable in terms of an intentional origin, departure, journey, and return. We seem to be looking at a multitude of voyages amid various kinds of terrain and conflicting fields of force. The movements seem to be aimless. If the viewer sees beyond the picture as a continuous texture, he cannot fail to be excited by its release of energies and its repetitious, restless, antigraceful action. If we pursue particular passages, we cannot fail to feel entrapped, enmeshed. Summoned to a spectacle here or there, the viewer is shunted aside before arriving, cast into mazes and vortices from which he can be extricated only by turning away. The experience of the work, which begins as visually intriguing, leaves us frustrated and disturbed.

The disturbing features of Pollock's work would not have attracted such wide interest if they did not constitute so faithful a reproduction of the spiritual landscape of our time. Perhaps all personal biographies would reveal similarities to Pollock's "voyages" if we could know the lives of others from the inside. However, the lack of culmination and coherence in Pollock may be a feature of some but not *all* interior landscapes. We may from time to time believe that our biographies contain minor fruitions and hints of fulfillment. Such intimations in our personal existence would not invalidate Pollock's relevance to the spiritual condition of modern man. He remains the painter of our energetic and industrious failures.

Aesthetic Expression

Aesthetic needs and impulses are not the specialized interest of a small group. Everyone is concerned with what is beautiful or pleasing in the visual world. We are interested in beauty wherever it can be found—in people, in nature, and in objects of daily use. Some artists specialize, however, in making things which are beautiful or aesthetically satisfying *in themselves,* apart from any utility they may have. Objects created to be beautiful or intrinsically pleasing are nevertheless useful because they help to satisfy our aesthetic interests and needs. In his earliest days, man may have been concerned about colors or shapes only if they were signs of danger or opportunity. Since his life depended on how accurately and intelligently he could see, vision was a matter of supreme importance. We still possess remarkable visual equipment and outstanding capacity for interpreting optical experience. However, the conditions of contemporary life may not demand as much of our perceptual capacities as we are equipped to supply. Hence, some forms of visual art appear to have evolved in complex cultures as a means of engaging unused perceptual capacity. Perhaps aesthetic pleasure is, in fact, the satisfaction experienced in employing to the fullest our innate capacities for perception.

An elementary aesthetic pleasure might be called "the thrill of recognition." Obviously, recognition has always played an important role in human survival. Its significant role in all human affairs accounts for the popularity of art which is easily recognized, which provides many cues to its origin in reality. When we *recognize* something in a work of art, we are in a sense rehearsing our survival technique, sharpening our capacity to distinguish between friend and foe. It is only a short step from the ability to perform such discriminations to the ability to enjoy perception itself, suspending impulses to fight or flee. Rather, we learn to linger over visual events and to maximize our delight in them.

Georges Braque (1882–1963) devoted his life to

JACKSON POLLOCK.
Number I. 1948.
The Museum of Modern Art, New York

37

GEORGES BRAQUE. *The Round Table.* 1929.
The Phillips Collection,
Washington, D.C.

making painting a source of pure visual delight. An early associate of Picasso in the creation of the intellectual austerities of Analytic Cubism, Braque employed the principles of Cubism to paint surfaces of immense sensuous appeal and decorative ingenuity. *The Round Table* shows his mastery of shape and texture and his droll wit in exploiting optical and pictorial conventions for pleasure and humor rather than reliable cognitive cues. One recognizes the room and the table easily enough, with the top tilted forward to reveal a number of ordinary objects: a mandolin, a knife, fruit, a magazine, a paper, a pipe, an open book, and so on. The objects in themselves are unimportant; they have shapes and colors and textures which Braque can rearrange. He can show the top and side view of an object at the same time; he can paint opaque objects as if they were transparent; he can reverse the expected convergence of lines in perspective; he can exaggerate ornament with white lines, arbitrarily exchange light areas with shadow areas, or paint shadows a lighter and brighter color than the objects which cast them. The purpose of these "violations" and surprises is not to create a painting *of* something; the painting must *be* something, a kind of organism which lives according to its own cockeyed law. And that law seems to state that any twisting, slicing, distortion, or reversal of shape, color, and texture is justified if it can increase our delight in

looking. The logic of the painting is based on the obligation to surprise or please the eye rather than reproduce a set of relatively innocuous objects.

But how does an artist please the eye? Once the logic of reproducing appearances is abandoned, the possibilities are infinite. The painter becomes a kind of intuitive investigator of the shapes and colors and textures which singly or in combination are somehow appealing. His artistic conscience does not permit him to exploit the literary associations one has with objects. Any satisfactions one takes in the work must derive from pictorial organization and painterly technique. He tries to arrive at just the right quantity and shape of, say, dark brown imitation wood graining. He surrounds the table shapes with thick and thin white outlines: they flatten out the shape and destroy the illusion of deep space which has been mischievously suggested by shadows cast into the corner of the room. Three-dimensional effects are created and then flattened or penetrated, pressed into two dimensions. The viewer is forced to "read" the painting as if the walls and floor were in the same plane as the table base. There is a certain visual humor or, at least, trickery going on in Braque's painting—humor which, because it is very subtle, does not result in laughter, but which fully challenges our capacity to enjoy ourselves visually.

The development of abstract and nonobjective art has been almost identical to the development of an art of *purely* aesthetic purpose in the modern era. As painting and sculpture have departed (some would say have been "liberated") from historical and didactic functions, they have increasingly been devoted to the problems of creating forms and experiences which would be valid in themselves. Thus, in the sculpture of José de Rivera (born 1904), *Construction "Blue and Black,"* we have a work of almost absolute precision and geometric beauty. The sculpture "works" only in an aesthetic frame of reference. Practical objects may, of course, resemble the Rivera sculpture and even derive their design inspiration from it. But we have reached the point where it is not necessary to ask what this work *symbolizes;* the theme or subject

JOSÉ DE RIVERA.
Construction "Blue and Black." 1951.
Whitney Museum of American Art,
New York

ALEXANDER CALDER.
Spring Blossoms. 1965.
The Pennsylvania State University,
University Park

matter of the sculpture is the formal organization of the thing itself.

Alexander Calder (1898–1976) invented an entirely new sculptural genre—the mobile—which delights us by the variety of movement of its abstract shapes. His *Spring Blossoms* is a whimsical work in which the slightest movement of air in the space around it imparts a comic, rollicking motion to the intricately balanced parts. They shift into an infinite number of constellations, arriving at temporary periods of equipoise by trembling, wriggling routes. Although mobiles do not obviously resemble people or trees, their movement may suggest the sway of branches or the complex maneuvers of exotic dancers. But these are only associations of the viewer, stimulated if not encouraged by this truly original and often comic artist. His art is highly intellectual and controlled, even in the latitude it provides for seemingly random motion. Moreover, it is sculpture which "uses" the atmosphere and light of the place where it is located: the climate of the room collaborates with Calder, helping to carry out his compositional intention.

The *Juggler* by David Hare (born 1917) is another work in which a playful abstraction of motion is the principal theme. But motion is not intended here, as it was in Boccioni, to transcend man's physical being to reach a spiritual condition. Rather, the balance and skill of the juggler become an excuse to fashion a curious steel "thing." It is important to understand this recurrent practice in contemporary art: unlike the arts of tradition, in which materials were fashioned so they might imitate appearances, the contemporary arts often reverse the relationship. They try to find phenomena in life which seem to suit what can be done with materials. Thus, the juggler provides the theme or the opportunity for

DAVID HARE.
Juggler. 1950–51.
Whitney Museum of
American Art,
New York

COLIN LANCELEY.
Inverted Personage.
1965. Albion College,
Albion, Michigan

Like David Hare, Lanceley creates a
metal metaphor—a comparison between
a person and a machine.

39

STUART DAVIS.
Report from Rockport. 1940.
Collection
Mr. and Mrs. Milton Lowenthal,
New York

The comic linear forms based on a gasoline pump and road signs in Stuart Davis's 1940 painting become sinister appendages of machine idols in the sculptures of Paolozzi and Voulkos in 1964 and 1965.

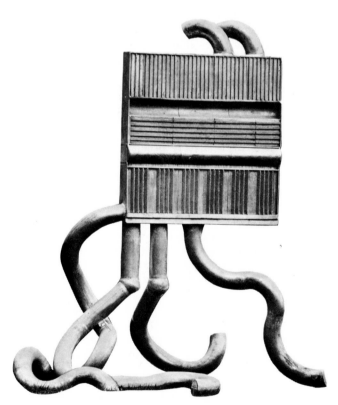

PETER VOULKOS. *Firestone.* 1965.
Los Angeles County Museum of Art.
Museum Purchase with Contemporary Art Council Funds

EDUARDO PAOLOZZI. *Medea.* 1964.
Kröller-Müller Museum, Otterlo,
The Netherlands

making a welded steel construction. Our aesthetic pleasure is based on the tension between our idea of a juggler and what has happened to that idea in the course of its embodiment in steel. This demonstrates how important the expectations of the viewer are in the total experience of art. *Your* idea of a juggler interacts with the *artist's* idea, which is physically, palpably, there to assert its validity.

Calder's mobiles show how a new sculptural type was developed to express an artist's interest in a certain kind of motion. Hare's sculpture is, very seriously, a "thing" which resembles itself as much as a juggler. Neither of these performs any of the world's work. But they do something for us as viewers: they afford pleasure based on our ability to follow the artist as he makes curious comparisons or metaphors relating ideas, objects, memories, and sensations. Since such works of art answer no practical need, we must approach them with a different mental set, a different logic from the one with which we confront the everyday world. We are not trying to prove we can recognize a juggler when we see one; we are interested in finding out what special entertainment is to be had in the *difference between* the sculpture and a juggler.

One of the most charming and personal developments of Cubism was created by the American painter Stuart Davis (1894–1964). In *Report from Rockport,* he used flat, geometric, spastic forms to designate the qualities of the places he enjoyed: street signs, billboards, gas pumps, the architecture of Main Street, noise, jazz, automobiles. The features of urban life that worry traffic engineers pleased Davis—the profusion and confusion of signs and lights that bedevil motorists; the gasoline gulches that spring up along every new highway; the speed of souped-up automobiles; the general lack of overall design and planning. Davis was an early and devoted follower of the jazz played in the saloons of Hoboken and Newark; this affinity is echoed in the dynamism and staccato rhythms of his painting. Out of the pictorial devices of Cubism, Davis developed a personal style which conveyed the impact of our distinctively American chaos. But he was neither an illustrator nor a social critic: his paintings accept the disorganization and commercial blatancy of our environment. He adds to our fund of aesthetic values because he teaches us to see the vulgarity of our highways and shopping districts as gloriously funny—confused, disordered, cacophonous, yet healthy.

The varieties of expression in contemporary art are too many to discuss with any completeness. There are works which appeal to all the senses through the visual; there are whimsical machines which contain motion and act as modulators of light; there are visual puns and metaphors, objects which impersonate and ridicule their models in life; there are works which celebrate the excitement and energy of places we normally regard as ecological disasters. Beauty, defined as ideality of form—especially when based on the human figure—is not a common trait of our aesthetic expression. When the figure does appear, it usually is revealed in unideal or ugly manifestations. We see it in the work of Bacon, Dubuffet, Paolozzi, and De Kooning, but it is lonely, awkward, repellent.

The reasons for this approach to so potent a symbol are complex and beyond the scope of this chapter. It is fair to say, however, that the initiatives of artists and the aesthetic needs of viewers *do* meet in a variety of contemporary works. Never before have the personal functions of art been so variously expressed. Perhaps we should not deplore the fact but rejoice in the array of choices art affords for our every mood and impulse.

2

THE SOCIAL FUNCTIONS OF ART

IN A SENSE, ALL WORKS OF ART PERFORM A SOCIAL function, since they are created for an audience. Artists may claim they work only for themselves, but by this they mean that they set their own standards. The artist always hopes, secretly perhaps, that there is a discriminating public which will admire his work.

SAMUEL LAROYE. Bicycle mask of the Gelede Secret Society, Yoruba tribe. 1958.
Art as an index of social change. By combining the traditional forms of Yoruba sculpture with contemporary imagery, a Western Nigerian sculptor participates in the transformation of African society and culture.

Consequently, works of art which have been created in response to private and personal impulses nevertheless function in a context which calls for a social response.

There are, however, narrower and more specific meanings for the social function of art. These meanings have to do with the *social intention and character of response* which works of art evoke. Thus art performs a social function when (1) it influences the collective behavior of people; (2) it is created to be seen or used primarily in public situations; (3) it expresses or describes collective aspects of life as opposed to personal kinds of experience. In all three cases, the individual responds with the awareness that he is a member of a group.

Many works are deliberately designed to influence group thinking. Artists may try to make us laugh at the same things; to accept economic, religious, or social ideologies; to identify with a class or ethnic interest; or to see our social situation in ways not previously apparent. The visual arts can function as languages of praise and celebration, anger and protest, satire and ridicule. In other words, art can influence attitudes, affecting the way people think or feel and, ultimately, the way they act. Advertising art is a common illustration: its purpose is to influence purchasing behavior. During a war, through posters, governments attempt to arouse hatred of the enemy, to stimulate enlistments, or to increase production levels. In peacetime, art is used to affect almost every conceivable kind of social goal.

Some persons regard works which influence social behavior as impure, as "mere" propaganda, as applied sociology, as debased art. And, given certain assumptions about the "appropriate" functions of

ISAMU NOGUCHI.
Monument to Heroes. 1943.
Collection the artist

LUCIANO MINGUZZI. *The Unknown Political Prisoner:
Figure Enmeshed.* 1953. The Tate Gallery, London

The public monument is an art form through which
a collective abstraction—society—acquires a memory and a conscience.

art, they may be right. But we could not present art's
complete role in contemporary culture if we ignored
its sociological functions. Furthermore, art history
shows that aesthetic excellence is unrelated to the
social functions art performs: excellence is not a
simple matter of serving noble or base purposes.

Political and Ideological Expression

Some artists are interested in the freedom to solve
special problems of style or technique. Others want
to use style and technique to express views about
society and political processes. Those in the latter
group often speak of "artistic responsibility." For

them, art does not exist merely to entertain and
gratify; it must edify. It must improve our collective
existence. So long as there are wrongs to be righted,
social conditions requiring change, art must participate in the shaping of attitudes which can lead to a
better society. This view of artistic responsibility is
opposed by those who feel they serve society best
when they concentrate on the discovery of new form
and the expression of their personal experience.

Although Cézanne, for example, could generate
aesthetic emotion through paintings of apples, other
artists have required themes of more obvious human
and social relevance. For example, Eugène Delacroix
(1798–1863) painted a great political spectacle in
Liberty Leading the People, one of the early monu-

EUGÈNE DELACROIX. *Liberty
Leading the People.* 1830. The
Louvre, Paris. Much blood, gore,
and commotion: all classes are
involved in a highly "partici-
patory" uprising. Still, in 1830
French revolutionaries required
an allegorical figure to inspire and
guide them.

Hans Erni. *Atomkrieg Nein (Atom War No)*.
1954. The Museum of Modern Art,
New York. Gift of the designer

ments of revolutionary art. Still, when a society is wealthy and free enough to indulge artists in the expression of their private and even capricious impulses, we nevertheless have others who freely choose to employ ideological themes.

REVOLUTIONARY ART: LATIN AMERICA

In this century, Mexico has produced three outstanding artists whose work has been frankly revolutionary: Diego Rivera (1886–1957), José Clemente Orozco (1883–1949), and David Alfaro Siqueiros (1896–1974). Their paintings, frequently in mural form, deal with themes like the poverty-stricken condition of the Mexican masses, the brutal conquest of Mexico by the Spanish invaders, and the exploitation of peasants by avaricious landowners. The paintings range from works of obvious ideological content to those in which an intense concern with human suffering is the dominant motive. *Echo of a Scream* by Siqueiros (compare this socially oriented work with a psychologically oriented work, *The Scream*, by Munch) employs the emotional force of a fantastic, almost hallucinatory pictorial device to express the idea of poverty. The word "echo" in the title and the repetition of the image of the screaming child, together with the deserted industrial wasteland which is the setting, tend to generalize and extend the theme of the work to the entire body of humanity. The pain of all abandoned children is symbolized here. The emotional strategy of such works is to arouse our feelings of

David Low. *Very Well, Alone*. c. 1940.
Cartoon by permission of the David Low
Trustees and the *London Evening Standard*

The cult of personality built around Mao Tse-tung in China does not obscure powerful impulses toward Westernization, as in this patriotic poster which borrows heavily from the greatest political cartoonist of the West, David Low.

Maoist poster.
Library, University of Georgia, Athens

44

With this denunciation of the university in 1932, Orozco anticipated many of today's bitter attacks on the "relevance" of academic study. Similarly, Siqueiros created in 1937 a hallucinatory image of poverty which might well apply today.

DAVID ALFARO SIQUEIROS.
Echo of a Scream. 1937.
The Museum of Modern Art, New York.
Gift of Edward M. M. Warburg

JOSÉ CLEMENTE OROZCO.
Gods of the Modern World. 1932–34.
Trustees of Dartmouth College,
Hanover, New Hampshire

sympathy. We are forced to confront an unpleasant social reality.

A particularly mordant social comment is seen in Orozco's *Gods of the Modern World*, a portion of the fresco mural in the Baker Library at Dartmouth College. A dissected corpse is shown stretched on a pile of books, where it is attended by a deathly figure in academic costume. Presumably, the corpse has given birth to an infant skeleton, also in academic cap, with the figure acting as midwife. In the background stands a collection of academics wearing their regalia, which survives in universities today from the costumes worn by medieval professors. The work is an example of gruesome humor, especially since it is in the library of a distinguished American university. Its function as preserver and mediator of ancient knowledge is presented as a necrophilic ritual. The mural expresses that revolutionary impatience and disgust with established convention which are traits of the satirist when he genuinely detests the subject he ridicules.

Diego Rivera's art has the same revolutionary commitment as Orozco's, but its formal organization is less violent. He is perhaps the best designer and ar-

tistically the most sophisticated of the Mexican artistic "troika." Nevertheless, he drives home his *political* message with an oversimple, unsubtle force. In *Night of the Rich* and *Night of the Poor* we have a morality play: the overindulgence of the rich, engrossed in the pursuit of profit, is contrasted with the innocent sleep of the poor, some of whom study at night to escape illiteracy, while middle-class types in the background evince their disapproval. In these works, we have the stereotyped portrayal of classes and racial groups according to Marxist dogma. The ideas are tremendously simplified because they are intended for the instruction of the uneducated. The principal objective of the mural is to endow the masses with the consciousness of belonging to an oppressed class. Just as early Christian artists confronted the problem of explaining the fundamental concepts of sin and expiation, so revolutionary artists endeavor to explain wealth and poverty, oppressors and victims, heroes and traitors. It is not surprising that Latin American artists, growing out of a tradition in which the influence of religion on culture was very potent, should employ the arts in a manner similar to that of the

DIEGO RIVERA.
Night of the Rich
and *Night of the Poor*. 1927–28.
Whereabouts unknown.
Mural art as an instrument
for developing class
consciousness.

Church, although, ironically, the doctrines of Rivera and his associates are violently hostile to organized religion.

ARTISTIC EXPRESSIONS OF HUMANITARIAN CONCERN

A modern industrial state contends with social problems radically different from those of a feudal, agrarian society. Problems associated with the modern administration of justice, the operation of democratic politics, and the regulation of a complex economy would seem unreal to people living in a state of peon-

age. For Americans, the impersonality of government has been well expressed by George Tooker (born 1920) in *Government Bureau*. Using repetition of figure and space, like the receding images in parallel mirrors, the artist endows a government building with a quality of Surrealist terror—the quality of an orderly, methodical, perfectly credible nightmare. Is this the image of government by federal bureaucracies which lies behind attacks on "overcentralization" of power? What Tooker has done is to dramatize the loneliness and alienation felt by ordinary people when taken out of their living, organic setting and placed into the

GEORGE TOOKER. *Government Bureau*. 1956.
The Metropolitan Museum of Art,
New York.
George A. Hearn Fund, 1956

46

ISAAC SOYER. *Employment Agency*. 1937.
Whitney Museum of American Art,
New York

sterile, nightmarish interior of a typical administrative labyrinth.

Isaac Soyer (born 1907) in *Employment Agency* presents an aspect of the operation of our economy in human terms. When economists speak of different kinds of unemployment—of transitional unemployment, of the absorption of new workers by the labor market, of workers with obsolete skills, of displacement due to automation—we may not understand what these phrases mean in terms of the individuals affected and of their efforts to cope with an economy which seems to work against them. Soyer views the waiting room of an employment agency as a theater for the enactment of a psychological drama. Unemployment translates itself into the feeling of being unwanted by the world, and it is one of the profoundest spiritual experiences of the modern era. As an artist, Soyer can offer no economic solution; he presents the qualities of the experience itself.

A sculpture which deals with industrial phenomena in social terms is *Mine Disaster* by Berta Margoulies (born 1907). It is a kind of memorial to the wives of men who are periodically trapped, even today, in mines far below the earth's surface. The social and psychological implications of the event are stressed here. These women cling to hope mingled with the expectation of disaster; perhaps they know that proper safety precautions have not been taken. As in many works of social protest, the device of huddling the figures is employed together with psychological analysis of the mixed emotions of hope, suspense, and despair in the faces.

In *McSorley's Bar* (1912), the American painter John Sloan carries on the tradition of vivid reporting and accurate social description which characterized the work of the so-called Ash Can School, a group of artists who organized themselves as "The Eight" in 1908. They were experienced as reporters and illustrators, their services being essential for the illustrated dailies and monthlies which flourished before the de-

BERTA MARGOULIES. *Mine Disaster*. 1942.
Whitney Museum of American Art, New York

JOHN SLOAN. *McSorley's Bar*. 1912.
The Detroit Institute of Arts.
Purchase, General Membership Funds

ALFRED STIEGLITZ. *The Steerage.* 1907.
Philadelphia Museum of Art. Stieglitz Collection

Film still from *America, America.* Directed by ELIA KAZAN. Copyright © 1963 by Warner Bros.-Seven Arts, Inc. A young Greek living in Turkey in 1896 determines to seek liberty in America. Crammed into steerage with hundreds of others he sails to this country.

ERNST BARLACH. *Veiled Beggar Woman.* 1919.
Private collection

DOROTHEA LANGE. *White Angel Breadline, San Francisco.* 1933.
The Oakland Museum, Oakland, California

Compare the photographic and sculptural versions of the same theme. Notice how the individuality of the person is suppressed in order to emphasize a generalized social symbol.

velopment of photojournalism. In rebellion against the salon art of Europe, they portrayed working-class themes without any hint of condescension or of discovering "picturesque" subjects in hitherto ignored environments. Emphasis was on truthful representation, dramatic lighting, spontaneous brushwork, and the capture of transient movement. Social themes, such as a workmen's bar, were not recorded from a particularly ideological or class-conscious point of view. In fact, Sloan was as concerned with paint and light as with class or economic issues. Still, his choice of a proletarian subject represented an act of rebellion against the official art of the period.

A great work of humanitarian concern—also an important historical document—is the photograph by Alfred Stieglitz (1864–1946), *The Steerage*. The picture was taken in 1907 at the height of a massive migration of people from all parts of Europe to the United States. The steerage was the most uncomfortable part of the ship—the cheapest way to cross the ocean for the desperately poor who came to America seeking a new life. The film, *America, America*, written and directed by Elia Kazan, vividly describes the voyage of a Greek immigrant who so idealized life in America that he endured incredible hardships to get passage on one of these ships. The steerage photograph resembles a medieval cosmological painting in which condemned people come out of some hellish place where they have been confined, as if in an ocean-going grave, to greet light and life.

The German sculptor Ernst Barlach (1870–1938) typifies the artist whose work expresses a universal, humanitarian concern although it grows out of particular, national stylistic roots. His sculpture derives in part from the medieval Gothic tradition of wood carving and has an affinity with the socially conscious themes of twentieth-century German Expressionism, although it is not agitated but quietly self-contained. In *Veiled Beggar Woman*, the theme is organized around one emotion—compassion. The identity of the woman is concealed by the cloak over her head, so that the main idea of the work is concentrated in the supplication of the hands. The anonymity of the subject helps us to see the sculpture as the expression of a collective idea of silent protest against conditions which lead any person to beg.

Perhaps the most monumental work of social expression in our time is Picasso's *Guernica*. The painting, of mural size, was executed in 1937 to memorialize the frightful bombing of the Basque town of Guernica by German planes (flying for Franco) during the Spanish Civil War. In it Picasso created the imagery which has influenced an entire generation of artists, when their theme is violence, suffering, war, and chaos. Using black, white, and gray only, the artist tried to create a work which would simultaneously express multiple perceptions of a single catastrophic event: newspaper accounts of the bombing, the terror of victims, civic disaster, the laceration of human flesh, and the meanings of modern war from the standpoint of history. Images such as the fallen statue, the mother and dead child, the burning building, the shrieking horse, and the spectator bull, function as actual descriptions of a civilian bombing at the same time that they symbolize a new concept of war compared to the traditional confrontation of armies. Picasso often makes reference to an antique conception of serenity and order. Here the classical

PABLO PICASSO. *Guernica*. 1937. On extended loan to The Museum of Modern Art, New York, from the artist's estate

FRANCISCO GOYA. *"Nothing more to do."*
From the series *The Disasters of War*. Issued 1810–63.
The Hispanic Society of America, New York

GEORGE SEGAL. *The Execution.* 1967.
The Vancouver Art Gallery, British Columbia

Despite the mechanization and depersonalization of war, the cruelty of individual executions has not greatly changed—from Goya's nineteenth-century etching to Segal's twentieth-century *tableau vivant*.

image operates as a symbolic reference *against which* modern violence is portrayed. The drawing style of children is employed to express their presence and victimization. Adult perception and pictorial logic would have inhibited the artistic objective, which was the representation of the inner and outer meanings of a disaster. The opened mouth is a recurrent symbol in this work, standing for fear and pain. Only the dead child to the left has a closed mouth. The work is a terrifying document of the devastation of human values.

While this work of Picasso is relevant to the contemporary problems of humanity, it exists within the same frame of reference as Goya's *The Disasters of War*, created in the nineteenth century. Is it equal to the conceptual challenge implied by calculations of the fifty or eighty million casualties a society might sustain, according to some thinkers, in a first assault by modern weapons of destruction? The *Guernica* of 1937, therefore, may be the last important work to deal with war as an enterprise carried on by semi-industrial but not automated methods. It was still possible for Picasso to think of war as a catastrophe which has *individual* consequences. Now its scale has been so enlarged and its methods so transformed that artists are compelled to use an abstract and dehumanized form language to cope with modern modes of obliteration (see Adolph Gottlieb, *Blast II,* 1957, p. 230).

Social Description

One of the social functions of art is performed by simply describing life without implying there is a problem to be considered. The act of selecting portions of ordinary existence for artistic treatment helps focus attention on the quality of daily life. Only when a "frame" is placed around events do we begin to discover their distinctive flavor.

If some works attempt to govern the viewer's attitude, others are governed by the viewer's already formed attitudes. The *Pool Parlor* by Jacob Lawrence (born 1917) can be seen as a seriocomic portrayal of pool-hall drama. The artist has exploited the attitudes commonly associated with life in the ghetto by creating mock-sinister silhouettes of black men's bodies, viewing them through the glaring lights hovering over a group of "pool sharks" going about their business. If we think pool halls are sordid places where criminal plots are hatched, then we react in humorless, moralistic terms and miss the comedic point, the parody of the folklore about pool parlors—a parody that succeeds because the sinister action is exaggerated. In contrast to this version of pool-hall emotion is the dramatic film *The Hustler*, in which Paul Newman and Jackie Gleason portray rival pool "artists." In both works we see how urban patterns of male gregariousness, idleness, and leisure are given aesthetic significance.

The cultural patterns of ethnic groups, particularly of the first and second generations in America, have been the subject of systematic study by sociologists. One of their findings is that the first American-born generation is anxious to forget its inherited ethnic practices. The next generation, feeling more secure, is often proud of its heritage and even endeavors to revive the customs of its immigrant forebears. Louis Bosa (born 1905) has drawn primarily on the customs of immigrant and first-generation Italian-American families as they try to maintain their traditions, to transplant them somehow, in their new country. *My Family Reunion* shows one of those old-country "tribal" feasts set in Italy but seen through American eyes. Bosa's art relies on his appreciation of the incongruity of Mediterranean customs viewed against the predominantly Anglo-Saxon background of American culture. His people are painted to reveal their feelings of awkwardness and also their determination to conserve and perpetuate the ancient festivals and family rituals which make life meaningful for them.

Images of the landscape or cityscape have their social connotations whether people are visible or not. We see the signs of human use: care or neglect, affection or abandonment. The environments that people build influence their builders; at the same time they reflect human choices and limitations of imagination. In *Landscape near Chicago*, Aaron Bohrod (born 1907) offers an ironic comment on that halfway region—neither urban, suburban, nor rural—one sees on the outskirts of large American cities, with its homemade, cinder-block architecture, accumulation

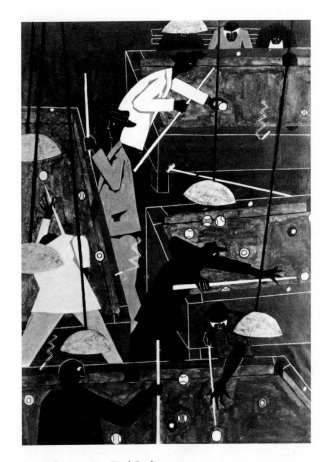

JACOB LAWRENCE. *Pool Parlor*. 1942.
The Metropolitan Museum of Art, New York.
Arthur H. Hearn Fund, 1942

Film still from *The Hustler*.
Directed by ROBERT ROSSEN.
© 1961 Rossen Enterprises, Inc.,
and Twentieth Century-Fox Film Corp.

LOUIS BOSA.
My Family Reunion. 1950.
Whitney Museum of American Art,
New York.
Gift of Mr. and Mrs.
Alfred Jaretski, Jr.

JESSE TARBOX BEALS.
Photograph of Italian children.
1900

LOUIS GUGLIELMI. *Terror in Brooklyn*. 1941. Whitney Museum of American Art, New York.
A Surrealist version of the sense of loneliness and menace which the city's streets can evoke.
Compare the terror of these Italian women with the mysteriousness of Louis Bosa's family
scene in "the old country."

AARON BOHROD. *Landscape near Chicago*. 1934.
Whitney Museum of American Art, New York

EDWARD HOPPER. *House by the Railroad*. 1925.
The Museum of Modern Art, New York

of rusting equipment, and signs of repairs begun but never completed. Bohrod's detailed naturalism is ideally suited to painting the portrait of a house—and, by implication, of its inhabitants, people who occupy the lonely, undefined space between country and city, who cannot quite mold their environment into a convincing imitation of a human community. Edward Hopper (1882–1967) painted a similar building portrait in *House by the Railroad*, although here it is the faded glory of a Victorian mansion, as opposed to the impoverished style of building and living shown in the Bohrod painting. Hopper's house may now be a relic: perhaps it has become a rooming house whereas once it represented elegance; still it has its own wilted dignity, conferred by the artist's presentation of the forms as a unified, coherent, sculptural mass, isolated but wearing its dated architectural adornments with a certain forlorn pride.

Two versions of New York City's "El," the extinct elevated railway, are seen in a watercolor by Dong Kingman (born 1911), *The "El" and Snow*, and in *Third Avenue* by Franz Kline (1910–1962). Kingman's facility with watercolor is challenged by the enormous variety of surface and material in the city. The artist

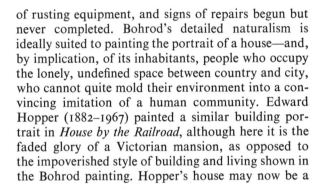

DONG KINGMAN. *The "El" and Snow*. 1946.
Whitney Museum of American Art, New York

FRANZ KLINE. *Third Avenue*. 1954.
Collection Mr. and Mrs. B. H. Friedman,
New York

GEORGE TOOKER. *The Subway*. 1950. Whitney Museum of American Art, New York. Juliana Force Purchase.
The subway felt as urban man's experience of the physical and psychological underground.

revels in structural complexity: he has selected an intricately built-up location, with its tangle of street signs, traffic signals, utility poles, overhead wires, and store-window displays. In an overwhelmingly man-made situation, nature is modestly represented in the form of snow. Kingman's approach to social description is through representing the complex layers and levels of the dense environment in which urban man makes his home. Kline, on the other hand, is more selective; he describes less of what is seen and more of what is felt. For him, the structural steel of the elevated constitutes an opportunity to paint black mechanical forms advancing toward the viewer, almost filling up the canvas. The effect on the viewer is of shapes about to occupy the entire optical field: they seem capable of blotting out all light. Kline's image is sufficiently abstract to suggest any large-scale structural element. His execution is purposeful and decisive, carrying all the authority of engineering—its formidable, masculine power and aura of menace.

The theme of urban struggle is explicitly treated in *Battle of Light, Coney Island* by Joseph Stella (1880–1946). The fascination with movement, which Stella imported from Italian Futurism, is given full scope by the distractions and attention-getting devices of a famous amusement park. For Stella, flickering neon signs, the amplified voices of barkers, the on-and-off patterns of colored light bulbs, and an authentically honky-tonk atmosphere epitomized a new American harmony of sensuous and dynamic forces.

Stella transmuted the blaring sound and flashy illumination of Coney Island into a brassy spectacle in 1913; in 1936 Mark Tobey (1890–1976) undertook a similar theme in *Broadway*. Tobey was equally fascinated by the light from a thousand signs—its ability to express the search for fun by millions drawn like moths to the synthetic jubilee in the center of Manhattan. Later, in 1942, Piet Mondrian (1872–1944), the Dutch abstractionist, succumbed to Broadway's glitter with a sparkling canvas, *Broadway Boogie-Woogie*. Tobey's tempera painting is "written" in light, a sort of neon script blurring into an incandescent haze in the center of the picture. But Mondrian views the Great White Way as a musical composition. The restrictions imposed by his rectangular mode of composition do not allow the freedom of description we see in Tobey, or the radial devices Stella employs to suggest explosiveness. However, with dozens of little squares and abrupt changes of primary color, Mondrian could convey the flickering, dancelike quality of light and movement, the scurry and halt of the Broadway "mell-o-dee."

Satire

The social function of satire is to ridicule people and institutions so that they will change. As a type of humor, satire is not merely aimed at the feelings of relief and superiority we get from laughter; satire is also aggressive in intent. It makes fun of its object—sometimes bitter, derisive fun. Although laughter is involved, satire is a *serious* art form, serving to cut the mighty down to size, to dramatize the gap between official promises and actual performance.

Societies often go through solemn phases when

JOSEPH STELLA. *Battle of Light, Coney Island*. 1913. Yale University
Art Gallery, New Haven, Connecticut. Gift of the Société Anonyme

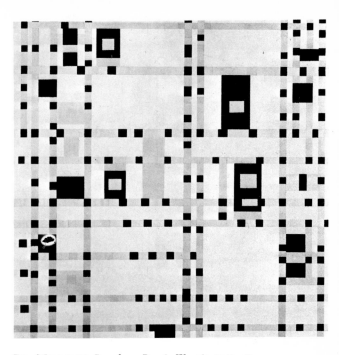

PIET MONDRIAN. *Broadway Boogie-Woogie*. 1942–43.
The Museum of Modern Art, New York

The neon spectacle of Broadway can be expressed as white writing, or
as little squares of alternating color, or by shaping the neon tubes
themselves into an abstract simulation of the glittering scene.

MARK TOBEY. *Broadway*. 1936.
The Metropolitan Museum of Art, New York.
Arthur H. Hearn Fund, 1942

CHRYSSA. *Fragments for the Gates to Times Square*.
1966. Whitney Museum of American Art,
New York. Gift of the Howard and Jean Lipman
Foundation, Inc.

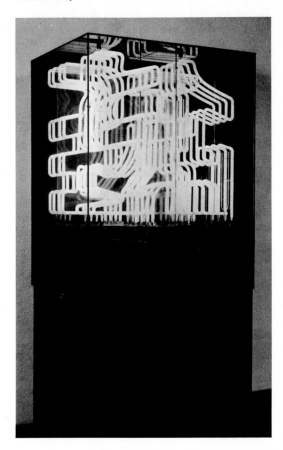

AL CAPP. Panels from *Li'l Abner* Ugly Woman Contest. 1946. Copyright News Syndicate, Inc. Capp's professional interest in comic repulsiveness or ugliness was fully echoed by his readers, who generously contributed drawings of their candidates in a contest for the supreme ugliness accolade.

Caricature from the ceiling of Horyu-ji, Nara, Japan.
8th century A.D.

LEONARDO DA VINCI.
Caricature of an Ugly Old Woman.
Biblioteca Ambrosiana, Milan

When satire dwells on the ugly, it has a timeless and universal character; very little separates Al Capp's twentieth-century version of ugliness from the repulsive countenance drawn by a Japanese artist twelve hundred years ago.

satire is regarded as negative and divisive, if not subversive. A government's humorless image of itself may be caused by the personal traits of its high officials, variations in their ability to "take it." Yet is there any special trait of satire which makes its victims more uncomfortable than does conventional criticism?

First, to be ridiculed is probably more difficult to bear than to be scolded. To be laughed at by a community is very much like being ostracized. It is a severe humiliation. Second, laughter is both physiological and psychological; it involves the total organism and implicates us completely in an act of ridicule. We are likely to remember a satirical reference to a public figure long after we have forgotten his policies. Finally, visual satire often uses caricature to exaggerate the physical shortcomings of its targets. Needless to say, we are usually aware of our imperfections; to have them magnified is very painful, especially if our psychic defenses are not strong.

Fashioning grotesque images of real or imagined people is a universal practice. Children are especially intrigued by fantastic or incredibly ugly faces. Leonardo da Vinci made many such grotesque heads, his investigations of departures from the beautiful; but they were, from a psychological standpoint, similar to the images children and others create—explorations of the frontiers of the human. Such graphic images are comparable to the rich body of spoken and written insult most of us know. Adolescents are especially adept at creating derisive physical descriptions and comparisons. Comedians can convulse audiences for hours with detailed descriptions of the ugliness of their relatives. In short, fascination with ugliness is widespread; it is perhaps as pervasive as the interest in beauty. The interest may appear to be malicious, but more likely it grows out of anthropological or psychological curiosity which has little connection with malice.

Perhaps the greatest political satirist of World War II was the Briton David Low (1891–1963). His cartoons were in many respects visual counterparts to the speeches of Winston Churchill: he could ridicule the Fascist dictators, summon the courage of his countrymen when they were taking a terrible beating, express fierce defiance when Britain faced invasion, appeal for help from America, and grieve over the valorous dead. Low was especially successful in his personality formulations, his characterizations of Der Führer and Il Duce. At a time when their military and racial insanity, matched with total political power, had succeeded in terrifying the civilized world, David Low shrewdly managed to identify Hitler and Mussolini as asses—dangerous, to be sure, but asses nevertheless, and thus hardly supermen. Low's assessment was not complete or entirely accurate, but it encouraged the hard-pressed Britons; he used satire to reduce the dictators to less than invincible size.

The political satirist at his best is shown in Low's cartoon *Rendezvous*, which deals with one of the strange consequences of political expediency—the

DAVID LOW. *Rendezvous*. 1939.
"The scum of the earth, I believe?"
"The bloody assassin of the workers, I presume?"
Cartoon by permission of the David Low
Trustees and the *London Evening Standard*

Russo-German nonaggression pact of 1939. The Russians hoped by the treaty to avert an invasion by Germany. And Germany hoped to secure the neutrality of Russia during its planned attack on Poland, France, and the remainder of the West. Hence, the mortal enemies, soon to be locked in the bitterest struggle of the war, greet each other with feigned and exaggerated gestures of courtesy while addressing each other with their customary rhetoric of insult.

We expect satire in the graphic arts, especially in news media, but it also occurs in "serious" painting. Most of the work of the American painter Jack Levine (born 1915) is satiric in intent, *The Feast of Pure Reason* constituting a typical example. The ironic point here lies in the contrast between the title, which celebrates a rational approach to human affairs, and the actualities of decision-making in some places—the secret meetings of corrupt officials, politicians, and businessmen. Levine identifies moral and civic corruption with physical grossness. His people are meant to be detested rather than laughed at.

Woman, I by Willem de Kooning (born 1904) possesses satirical values, although the violent execution of the painting may prevent our seeing its element of burlesque. The artist presents an older woman, heavyset, wearing a flimsy shoe, overexposing her body, and grimacing although she wishes to appear bewitching. The oversized eyes are probably the result of grossly overdone makeup; the mouth tries to smile through ill-fitting dentures. The tiny ankle and the swollen foot attempt to support a massive superstructure. We see the fierce and pathetic exertions of a "mom" gone berserk. The artist presents an authentic portrayal of the inner and outer condition of a sizable body of women in our culture. He is enraged to the point where he wants to make a horrible contrast between

JACK LEVINE.
The Feast of Pure Reason. 1937.
On extended loan to The
Museum of Modern Art, New York,
from the United States WPA Art Program

WILLEM DE KOONING.
Woman, I. 1950–52.
The Museum of Modern Art, New York

PEGGY BACON. *The Patroness*. 1927.
The Museum of Modern Art,
New York.
Gift of Abby Aldrich Rockefeller

H. C. WESTERMANN. *Nouveau Rat Trap*. 1965.
Collection Mr. and Mrs. Robert Delford Brown, New York.
Art satirizing art: a semiabstract sculpture
which pokes fun at the Art Nouveau style.

the woman's pretensions and the results we see. De
Kooning barely establishes his forms before tearing
into them with angry, slashing painterly attacks.

A work of similar satiric anger is the etching *The
Patroness* by Peggy Bacon (born 1895). Here, too,
the subject is fat and ham-handed. Her face is twisted
and pinched in contrast to her bulk—a symbol of small-
mindedness combined with excessive wealth. The work
is an expression of the attitude of the artist toward a
patron, a compensatory act of derision toward the
person the artist depends on, a malicious bite of the
hand that feeds the artist.

Satire thrives whenever there is freedom from political or social repression. As the visual arts have em-
braced abstraction, however, there has been a lessen-
ing of artistic ridicule. Art seemingly withdrew from
the social and political arena after 1946 and devoted
itself more to the analysis and refinement of visual
language. Pop art had satiric potential, although it
lacked the deadly aim of genuine satire. Its target was
very broad: all of modern culture. However, it was
difficult to say whether it derided or celebrated the

MEL RAMOS. *Chiquita Banana*. 1964.
Collection Ian W. Beck, New York.
An example of the appropriation by a Pop artist
of an ancient "advertising" device for selling anything.

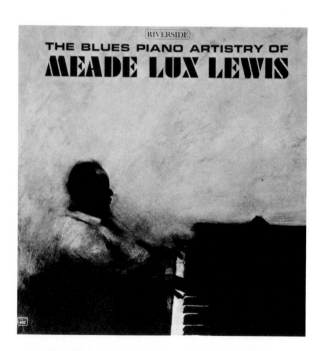

The Blues Piano Artistry of Meade Lux Lewis.
1962. Riverside Records, New York. This record
album cover, which presents a relatively simple
image of high artistic quality, nevertheless entails
the collaboration of several persons: the client,
artist Peter Max, art director and designer Ken
Deardoff, and a number of graphics specialists.

banalities of popular culture. Still, Pop seemed to be aware of the visual noise and commotion around us and it developed some powerful weapons to cope with their noxious effects.

Graphic Communication

We are accustomed to think of art in terms of precious objects. But visual art also constitutes an inexpensive public language. Its forms and images can be organized to communicate with extraordinary persuasiveness, and, in conjunction with verbal language, their precision of meaning is maximized. Understandably, our civilization, which has perfected mass production and distribution, employs the language of visual art extensively in its marketing operations. And graphic design, particularly of posters, packages, books, and other printed matter, is an indispensable tool of the communications industries. What is known as advertising design, or graphic communication, used to be called commercial art. Although such labels are not very important, they call attention to the crucial function of art in conveying information from government, business, and industry to the social groups they wish to influence.

THE PROBLEMS OF COMMUNICATION

What problems of information design must the artist solve? First is the matter of arresting the attention of the public. This is a problem for all effective communication. Its challenge varies from the five-second viewing of an outdoor poster to the fifteen- or twenty-minute perusal of a magazine page. Second is the problem of sociological and psychological strategy: identifying the group to be reached and knowing its interests and motivations. Third is the problem of characterizing the product, idea, or service. How can a new idea or product be presented quickly and memorably to a vast public which is under almost continuous visual assault from competing products? Finally, there is the problem of the verbal material, which may appear as a caption for a poster, as copy for an advertisement, or as dialogue on television. The design of letter forms constitutes a graphics problem which is often more significant than the verbal-literary problems of communication design. Increasingly, our learning takes place through nonverbal media. Accordingly, new problems are faced by graphic designers for films and television who must relate imagery to unseen words or music—material which occupies aural but not optical "space."

Visual logic and simplicity are the dominant traits which emerge from the solution of problems in information design. Visual simplicity implies a bias in favor of open space and bold, clean forms—forms which are easily seen, quickly identifiable, and capable of controlling a desired set of symbolic meanings. By logic I mean a sense of connectedness among the ele-

GEORGE APTECKER.
Photograph of a wall at Coney Island. 1968.
Communications design practiced as a folk art.

BRUNO MUNARI. *Campari*. 1965.
The Museum of Modern Art, New York.
Gift of the designer

Advertisement for film *The Two of Us*. Designed
by SAUL BASS and ART GOODMAN. 1968. A word-
image combination in which a maximum of characterization is achieved within very narrow formal
constraints.

SEGUNDO FREIRE. Carnival poster. 1957

PABLO PICASSO. *Pierrot and Harlequin.*
The Metropolitan Museum of Art, New
York. Gift of Paul J. Sachs, 1922

ments of a total design: the product or idea, the pictorial or visual material, and the copy or verbal
material. Often graphic designers have drawn on
contemporary painting to solve problems of formal
innovation and stimulation of interest. The following
illustrations demonstrate this dependence on the allegedly useless fine arts.

SOLUTIONS

A Mexican carnival poster by Segundo Freire shows
the unmistakable influence of Picasso's treatment of
harlequins and musicians. The poster designer, however, retains only the flat patterning of Cubism and
does not go so far as to slice the figure and recompose
its elements to the point where his work would require
too much intellectual effort of the viewer. A certain
amount of simplification of the figure is an aid to recognition in advertising; hence Cubist abstraction has
been a fertile source of ideas for graphic designers.

PINO TOVAGLIA. Railway poster. 1957.
Courtesy the artist and Ferrovie Nord Milano

FERNAND LÉGER. *Three Women*
(Le Grand Déjeuner). 1921.
The Museum of Modern Art, New York.
Mrs. Simon Guggenheim Fund

ALVIN LUSTIG. Cover design
for *Fortune* magazine. 1952.
Courtesy Time, Inc.

PABLO PICASSO.
Bottle of Suze. 1912–13.
Washington University, St. Louis

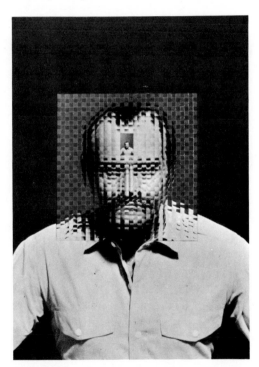

Photographic collage for cover of
Crybaby of the Western World, a novel by
John Leonard. Designed by ALEX GOTFRYD.
Collage by CHARLES ALMON.
Photo by FRANK STORK. 1969

PABLO PICASSO. *Daniel-Henry Kahnweiler.* 1910.
The Art Institute of Chicago

The jacket designer has created a mysterious personality symbol through the photographic adaptation of geometric forms originally developed in Analytic Cubism.

TSUNEJI FUJIWARA. Cosmetics poster. 1957

The Italian designer Pino Tovaglia has created a striking railroad poster based largely on the style of Fernand Léger. *Three Women* by Fernand Léger does not, of course, contain machinery, but it does attempt to convert all visual forms into efficient mechanical equivalents. It is possible to think of this crisp, powerful poster design as a kind of artistic triple play—from Picasso and Braque, to Léger, to Tovaglia.

A cover design for *Fortune* magazine by Alvin Lustig (1915–1955) reveals the influence of another facet of Cubism—collage. Picasso and Braque combined pasted material with drawn or painted forms, as in the Picasso collage *Bottle of Suze*, which contains papers, newsprint, wallpaper, and the label from a liquor bottle. Lustig has employed the words and type faces of the collage material to reinforce his theme—"the language of advertising." Furthermore, his shapes are those of television masts and billboards. The designer tries for increased effectiveness by stating the message two or three times, and with different formal devices. The Picasso collage, on the contrary, has no explicit message; it communicates an aesthetic effect. The print is not there to be read but to be experienced as texture and color.

An especially interesting example of cultural diffusion is visible in a Japanese cosmetics poster by Tsuneji Fujiwara. The faces are remarkably similar

AMEDEO MODIGLIANI.
Detail of *Anna de Zborowska*. 1917.
The Museum of Modern Art, New York.
Lillie P. Bliss Collection

Mask, from Ivory Coast.
Collection Peter Moeschlin, Basel

to those painted by Amedeo Modigliani, an Italian-born artist who spent most of his working life in France. Modigliani began his career as a sculptor and was especially influenced by African wood carving as in the example illustrated, translating African forms into the small mouth, elongated ovoid head, and delicate stylized arches over the eyes of the women in his paintings. Apparently, the Japanese designer found in Modigliani an ideal of female beauty which would appeal to the audience he was trying to reach.

Information Design

WALTER ALLNER. Cover design for *Fortune* magazine, February, 1965. Courtesy Time, Inc. Here a graphic designer assumes the role of sculptor. For an audience of industrial executives, he creates a dazzling organization of old and new metallic objects. The design transcends its vehicle, a magazine cover, because photographic imagery is now capable of eliciting tactile, as well as visual, responses.

PAUL RAND. Poster for Advertising Typographers'
Association of America. Courtesy the artist. The
picture of an idea in parallel with Whitehead, no
less. It succeeds through an extraordinary graphic
invention: the arrow penetrates the apple, causing
it to share its red with the letter.

GIOVANNI PINTORI. Poster for Olivetti 82 Diaspron.
Courtesy the artist. Purely visual communication.
This work represents a brilliant wedding of the
qualities of the machine—accuracy of engineering,
measured shape, controlled motion—and the traits
of its product: the scrutable mark, the precise
word, the significant symbol.

SAUL BASS. Poster for Pabco Paint Company. 1957.
Courtesy Napko Corporation, Houston

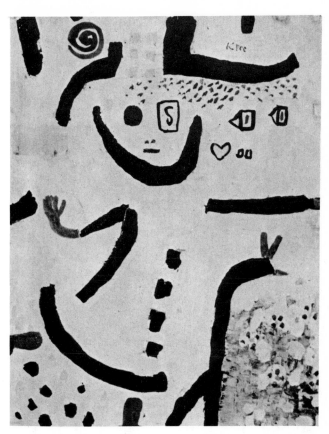

PAUL KLEE. *A Child's Game*. 1939.
Collection Felix Klee, Bern.
Permission Cosmopress Geneva, 1971

JOAN MIRÓ. *Nursery Decoration*. 1938. Collection Mr. and Mrs. Richard K. Weil, St. Louis

The origin of the forms in the poster by Saul Bass (born 1921) for Pabco Paint Company would not be difficult to trace to Paul Klee or Joan Miró. What is interesting is the adaptation of Surrealist imagery to advertise house paint. The strategy of the imagery makes marketing sense: the manufacturer has to interest housewives in his product, and a key problem lies in convincing them that house painting is not a dirty job. Klee did considerable research into child-like imagery, while Miró added his whimsical conception of a world perceived through the eyes of children. Both artists succeeded in invading a carefree world where adult fears and responsibilities had not yet penetrated. Bass's forms tend to express the idea of freedom from inhibition, a neurosis-free approach to adventure and chance-taking. The housewife is encouraged to view the operation as a romp, easy enough for a child to accomplish. This design also

VICTOR VASARELY. *Vega*. 1957. Collection the artist

Since many viewers are disoriented by Op art, it seems logical to exploit Op-art effects in the jacket design for a murder mystery dealing with hallucinatory drugs.

Advertisement for *Murder on a Bad Trip* by June Drummond. Holt, Rinehart and Winston, Inc., 1968. Courtesy Denhard & Stewart, Inc., New York

tells us a great deal about the advertiser's perception of women and their purchasing behavior. Thus, although the image is simple and easily perceived, it makes sophisticated use of modern art and unconscious suggestion to reach its objectives.

The foregoing examples have tended to emphasize the dependence of information design on the seemingly autonomous fine arts; yet there is no reason why originality and excellence of a high order cannot occur in graphics. Apparently, relationships among artists, designers, and patrons in our society are very complex. As yet, most fine artists live and function in

the time-honored tradition of economic malnutrition. Some are employed as designers; but few seem to flourish in both areas at a high level of performance, although the education of artists and designers is very similar. Happily, we are beginning to witness an increase in the professionalism of designers for industry and commerce. We may eventually arrive at a condition like that of the Renaissance, when no line could be drawn between artists and designers since, with few exceptions, they were the same persons.

3

THE PHYSICAL FUNCTIONS

OF ART

BOTH PAINTINGS AND BUILDINGS CAN SERVE AS SYMBOLS, but only buildings perform a physical function. By the physical function of art I mean the creation of objects which operate as containers and tools. By "container" we designate a range of objects from a carton of milk to an office building. Both need to be shaped and constructed according to the requirements of their contents (if people can be thought of as "contents"). Both are used as well as looked at. A tool can be a tablespoon or a locomotive. One is a simple, the other a complex, machine. Both need to be designed to operate efficiently. And one aspect of their operation is their appearance. Any tool or machine looks like something. The artistic problem is to make it look like what it does, while making it look "good" to the persons who use it.

The difference between a painting and a building or a machine is that a painting is used *only* by looking at it; a building or tool is used by doing something *in* it or *with* it, as well as by looking *at* it. It was formerly thought that art affected useful objects by adorning them or by creating skins which concealed their working parts. To some extent, this view survives in debased conceptions of industrial design. Presumably, the important problems of function are handled by engineers, while artists look after superficial beauty. But we are beginning to recognize that appearance and function are linked. Many useful objects today are totally created by artist-designers. The profession of industrial design constitutes a fruitful synthesis of art, engineering, and marketing.

During the Renaissance, artists often served as architects and engineers simultaneously. The Industrial Revolution of the eighteenth century was mainly responsible for the separation of art from the structural aspects of building and manufacture. Civil, industrial, and mechanical engineering developed as professions separate from art and architecture. As a result, society has experienced a proliferation of ugliness in our large- and small-scale environment. Often engineers have been excellent designers, but increasing technical specialization often led to trashy design early in the history of mass production.

Between the eighteenth and the twentieth century, the handicrafts survived mainly as obsolescent vestiges of pre-industrial modes of making, as status symbols for the few who could resist engineer design, or as focal points of idealism for craftsmen like William Morris, who hoped to reverse the development of industrialization and capitalism through a revival of medieval artisanship.

In addition to the design of tools and machines, private dwellings and public structures, art is concerned with the design of the man-made environment. Many of the problems of urbanism have their origin in failure to plan *comprehensively* and in advance of need. Here, as in the case of industrial design, art consists of more than the embellishment of outdoor spaces with parks, plazas, and monuments. Unlike product design, however, the process of community planning entails complex relationships with sociology, law, and politics. The design of a community has to be undertaken in the light of a total philosophy of social and personal interaction.

The physical functions of art, therefore, affect us in our intimate lives as well as in our public role as citizens—as people who use and are used by the man-made organisms called communities.

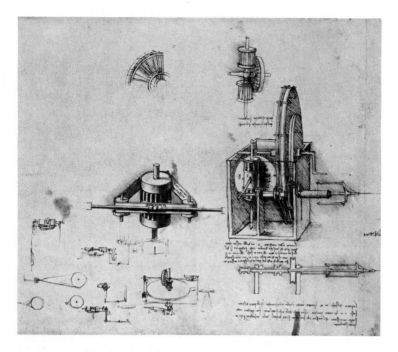

LEONARDO DA VINCI.
Plans for a Spinning Wheel. c. 1490.
Biblioteca Ambrosiana, Milan

The careers of Michelangelo and Leonardo show that the design of anything—from fortifications to industrial machinery—was within the artist's province in the fifteenth and sixteenth centuries. But this work was done in their capacities as artists; the radical separation of the aesthetically meaningful from the physically useful had not yet taken place.

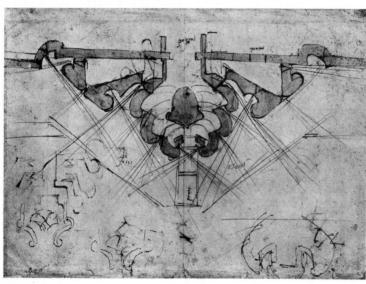

MICHELANGELO. *Drawing for the Fortification of Florence.* c. 1529. Casa Buonarroti, Florence

Architecture: The Dwelling

Of all the building types the dwelling is the earliest, the closest to our daily lives, and perhaps the best illustration of the technological innovations and design philosophies which affect and afflict architecture. Architecture is a social art, and in the dwelling we see its effect upon that prime social institution, the family. It is worthwhile, therefore, to look at some of the effects of families on homes and of architecture on families.

The home today is intended almost exclusively for the child-rearing family. It does not usually have room for the permanent residence of grandparents, maiden aunts, bachelor uncles, or other relatives. Nor does it any longer have a parlor, library, pantry, or front porch. Instead, there may be new rooms or spaces—the game room, patio, family room, carport, recreation room, and bar. Compared with the homes of a generation ago, there is less privacy, more open planning, and fewer single-purpose spaces. Partitions are eliminated, or do not go from floor to ceiling, or do not really separate and insulate spaces and sounds from one another. Also, homes are increasingly built on one level or on split levels, but they seldom have three or four distinct layers, one on top of the other. The one-level, or ranch-type, dwelling promotes mobility and the loss of privacy mentioned above. Multipurpose rooms reduce the overall size of the house and intensify use of space and wear of equipment. Labor-saving devices built into the home have absorbed a larger proportion of its total cost, and these have become for most people a principal index of its value—economic and aesthetic. That is, we probably love our dishwashers, air conditioners, automatic ovens, tile bathrooms, and built-in stereo equipment more than the spatial qualities which architectural design can bring to the home.

If these observations are correct, it would appear that Le Corbusier's old dictum—"The house is a machine to be lived in"—is accepted in practice if not in theory. However, what factors have made it possible for the modern dwelling to operate as an efficient machine while retaining some of the warmth of the old idea of home? Obviously, technology is an indispensable factor since it cuts down the space and time needed for food preparation and storage, laundering and house cleaning, heating and cooling, decoration and maintenance. Modern building techniques have enlarged the possibilities open to the designer: light; strong structural elements, some of them metal and plastic instead of wood; plate glass; new insulation materials, adhesives, and fasteners; strong new surface materials—paints, plastics, metals; prefabricated units, especially for kitchens and bathrooms; and almost universal availability of low-cost electricity (until the 1930s many rural homes had no electric power).

Plate glass may be the single most influential ma-

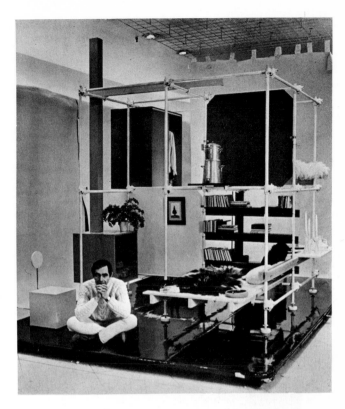

KENNETH ISAACS.
Ultimate Living Structure. 1968

All of an individual's physical needs for domestic living are packaged in a single double-decker unit. Can this represent Le Corbusier's "machine for living"?

BRUCE DAVIDSON. Photograph of people on East 100th Street. 1967. When thinking about buildings, we must think about the people who live in them. Architecture is above all a social art.

PLASTIC AS PLASTIC exhibition at the American Crafts Council's Museum of Contemporary Crafts, New York. 1968. By using plastic art objects, furniture, and appliances, combined with light from naked fixtures, designers achieve an environment of multiple reflection, highly regular smoothness, and transparency of objects. Such spaces and their contents seem designed to simulate trancelike and hallucinatory states: they act like the visual equivalents of drugs.

BUCKMINSTER FULLER. Proposed geodesic dome over New York City. 1961

terial affecting the design of the dwelling. Ideal for warm climates, it is also used extensively in temperate and cold climates because we have enthusiastically accepted one of the main tenets of modern domestic architecture: the interpenetration of indoor and outdoor space. The contemporary house is designed so that its outer shell constitutes a screen rather than a barrier. The one-level dwelling has many openings: its floor is close to ground level; it usually has a patio; it tries to locate a "lamp and picture window" opposite a vista more inspiring than the neighbor's back yard. These are so essential to our way of life that even apartment dwellers have them, with a balcony substituting for the patio, although that balcony high above the traffic is rarely used; it is usually an architect's device for breaking up a monotonous exterior facade or a realtor's device for renting apartments. There are, however, technical and structural reasons for the widespread use of glass. (1) The walls of modern buildings can be penetrated at almost any point because they do not bear weight; they act as curtains. (2) The loss of heat through glass has been greatly reduced by double paning, while the framing and walls around glass are tight and well-insulated (older homes had no insulation except air space or, sometimes, layers of brick). (3) Modern plate glass is strong and durable, even over relatively large areas.

(4) Intelligent orientation of the house on its site and proper location of windows admits the sun at the time of day when it is most desired. The architect who chooses to cooperate with nature can design eaves, overhangs, or sunbreaks so that the heat of the summer sun is blocked out while the warming winter sun is invited in.

Air conditioning is not only a form of technology but also a symbol of philosophic disagreement in modern architecture. We possess the technology (but not the energy) to air-condition all interior living space. (If Buckminster Fuller succeeds in throwing domes over our cities, we shall be able to air-condition or weather-condition the urban out-of-doors too. Victor Gruen, an architect and city planner, has already constructed shopping centers whose outdoor areas are thoroughly air-conditioned.) Much of modern domestic architecture, especially under the influence of Frank Lloyd Wright, is based on the goal of continuity with nature—using technology to build structures which seem to grow out of their surroundings. But the philosophy of the International Style architects, exemplified best by Walter Gropius, Ludwig Mies van der Rohe, and Marcel Breuer, urges the conception of the dwelling—or any building—as an interior environment which can be completely controlled by technology. Architects have designed buildings without windows, with no modification of their exterior form in response to climate and view. Since engineering can manage these problems, the architect devotes his energies to designing beautiful interior spaces. And where the focus of activity is almost wholly internal—as in a museum, factory, department store, church, gymnasium, or laboratory—such buildings have been very successful. The high-speed elevator, the steel-frame skeleton, and light curtain-wall construction have enabled us to build almost as high as we wish, and to create a uniform atmosphere throughout the structure. But there are some disturbing rumbles: the costs of climate control are getting out of hand, and when the technology is not working well, uncomfortable temperature variations develop; where there are no windows, the inhabitants want to look out; when the air-conditioning does work, the dwellers wish to sense the advent of spring, the odor of gasoline fumes and damp city streets, the sound of automobile horns, and the scuttle of pedestrians racing for cover. Such noises and waftings serve the urban office worker as the sound of a neighbor's gasoline lawn mower and the fragrance of burned barbecue serve the suburbanite. At any rate, they are among the goals of an art which, according to Vitruvius, the Roman architect and theoretician, must provide firmness, commodity, and *delight* (strength, utility, and beauty).

FRANK LLOYD WRIGHT

The great artist-poet of the dwelling was Frank Lloyd Wright (1869–1959). In a long and controversial career he brought to the art of creating human shelter an original, pioneering, and distinctively American genius. He was independently ahead of European architects in many ways: in his understanding and exploitation of modern technology, in his revolt against the stultifying architectural baggage of the past, and in his aesthetic innovations—that is, his ability to deal with the dwelling as an art object, as something beautiful to look at and a delight to live in. Wright's forays into social philosophy and community planning have not been as universally praised. His houses—especially his Prairie Houses—are his chief monuments; indeed it is difficult, when we look at a building so sculpturally vital as the Robie House, to realize that it was built as early as 1909.

Perhaps the most widely reproduced house by Wright is Fallingwater, built in 1936 at Bear Run, Pennsylvania. It is at once a triumph of architectural romanticism and an example of the brilliant exploitation of technology. Only steel-and-concrete cantilever construction would permit such graceful but massive overhanging slabs, which complement the rugged natural setting with rectangular precision. There is an echo of International Style devotion to the unadorned cubical mass, but the overall conception is romantic. The heavily-textured masonry of the vertical masses associates the building with the materials of the site, an association which is an axiom of the Wright philosophy of building.

Wright's ideas about the internal organization of the house still provoke controversy, although many have been widely accepted. He held that a massive fireplace and hearth should be the physical and psychological center of the house. He disapproved of

FRANK LLOYD WRIGHT. Robie House, Chicago. 1909

FRANK LLOYD WRIGHT.
Fallingwater, Bear Run,
Pennsylvania. 1936

FRANK LLOYD WRIGHT. Interior, Taliesin East,
Spring Green, Wisconsin. 1925

FRANK LLOYD WRIGHT. Interior, Hanna House,
Palo Alto, California. 1937

basements and attics. Materials like paint, plaster, varnish, and wood trim were to be avoided. Ornament was not to be *applied* but would result from the natural patterns *inherent* in building materials or grow logically out of the processes of forming and fabrication. Cooking and dining facilities should be adjacent to the living room, located in the center of the house, away from the exterior walls. The kitchen or "work area" should be a tall space behind the fireplace so that cooking odors flow up through it rather than into the house. The rooms radiate from the fireplace core, so that Wright's houses tend to have a cross-shaped plan. The arms of the cross are thus open to the outdoors on three sides, with horizontal bands of windows around them and very wide eaves which create porchlike spaces underneath.

The interior of Mr. Wright's house, Taliesin East, in Spring Green, Wisconsin, shows the inviting warmth and variety of surface, space, and light that he built into his Prairie Houses. Oriental rugs are used to break up the floor space and to define functional areas, while Japanese screens and Chinese figurines are located on ledges set at various heights so that the eye is encouraged to linger and refresh itself. Wright's interiors were sometimes criticized for being too dark. But it would appear that he took care to calculate the modulation of light more than designers who simply flood a room with light, obliging the occupants to install acres of drapery to gain privacy and control over outside illumination. A corner meant for conversation needs a modulated light rather than the inhibiting glare of flood illumination. Of course, this room suggests the cave more than the tent or the metal cage. Perhaps we are drawn inward by our atavistic desires—deep, unconscious feelings of safety and comfort derived from the Paleolithic memories of the race.

The living room of the Paul Hanna House (1937) in Palo Alto, California, has a less cavelike quality than Taliesin and shows how important the pattern of light and cast shadow is in Wright's total conception. There are very few right angles in the room itself, with its gently sloping ceilings and the powerful fireplace projections. Into this complex space sunlight is admitted, but it must pass through tree branches first, then through the small windowpanes and past the chairs until it reaches the fireplace wall and the sunken, stepped-down hearth, which makes its own shadow pattern. Thus, we have a marvelously rich orchestration of the textures and colors of materials, with moving, patterned light working on them.

LUDWIG MIES VAN DER ROHE

The austere style of Mies van der Rohe (1886–1969) can best be understood against the background of Art Nouveau, a manner of design and decoration which affected all the arts at the turn of the century. The subway, or Métro, station, one of several designed for the city of Paris by Hector Guimard (1867–1942), exhibits most of the features of an Art Nouveau struc-

HECTOR GUIMARD. Métropolitain station,
Place de L'Etoile, Paris. 1900
(demolished)

DER SCUTT. Conversation pit. 1967. Through a circular, multilevel conversation pit, a contemporary architect endeavors to elicit the feeling of warmth and protection which man first enjoyed when he sat near a fire in the mouth of a cave.

VICTOR HORTA. Stair hall, Tassel House,
Brussels. 1892–93

LUDWIG MIES VAN DER ROHE.
Floor plan of Farnsworth House

LUDWIG MIES VAN DER ROHE.
Farnsworth House, Plano, Illinois. 1950

LUDWIG MIES VAN DER ROHE.
Crown Hall, Illinois Institute of Technology,
Chicago. 1952

LUDWIG MIES VAN DER ROHE. Interior,
Tugendhat House

ture: the use of ornamental and structural elements of
cast iron, the avoidance of right angles, heavy reliance
on a serpentine line, and the location of curves at every
joint and change of direction. This style had a revival
which started slowly after World War II and reached
its peak in the early 1960s. Perhaps affluence encourages baroque impulses in fashion and design. In prosperous times, the doctrine of Mies van der Rohe that
"less is more" begins to seem too ascetic; we grow interested in a kind of frivolous elegance. But Art Nouveau was not really elegant in the classical manner;
rather it sought to unite art and nature—nature conceived as a forest grove—through imitating organic
forms, especially plant life. The International Style
architects, strongly under the influence of the Bau-

PHILIP JOHNSON. Glass House, New Canaan, Connecticut. 1949

haus, seemed as devoted to the right angle as Art Nouveau adherents to the S-curve. Hence, from the 1920s until about 1942, with the exception of Wright and his followers, avant-garde houses were austere white cubes, devoid of ornament, with extensive glass facades and no-nonsense flat roofs minus eaves. Small wonder that the popular reaction to these buildings was chilly and that the style became known irreverently as "gas-station moderne."

Of course, in the hands of a master like Mies the International Style had authentic elegance, as in his Tugendhat House in Czechoslovakia, designed in 1930. Floor-to-ceiling windows, black marble partitions, polished metal columns, silk curtains, and Oriental rugs created an atmosphere of refinement and sensuous appeal within a controlling intellectual framework. Mies appears to have been the most craftsman-like of the International Style designers; he never abandoned an ideal of *beauty* achieved through well-made and well-proportioned parts, never became addicted to design as multiplication of standardized parts: he showed how to achieve a quiet, controlled splendor by attention to detail without architectural histrionics.

In the Farnsworth House (1950) built in Plano, Illinois, Mies employed a vocabulary similar to one he would use again in his School of Architecture for the Illinois Institute of Technology in 1952. Both structures are approached from a raised platform, and both make elegant use of a series of slablike steps as a transition from the ground level to the plane of the floor. In the Farnsworth House, Mies used large expanses of glass, whose reflected images establish continuity with nature. Extreme simplification of form and function is seen in the use of white posts to support the roof, to separate the large glass panes, and to

act as stilts, raising the house off the ground. In the Illinois Tech building, Mies hung the ceiling from imposing steel girders stretching across the roof to black exterior steel columns; they also function visually as satisfying vertical accents. The building is not raised off the ground as is the Farnsworth House, but the platform and two sets of gently ascending steps create that impression. The repeated horizontals of the steps help to balance the vertical rhythm of the columns and thus endow the structure with a classic dignity and repose.

A Miesian house is essentially *one* large cube in which functional space divisions are achieved by non-structural partitions. For Mies, the real work of architecture lay in the creation of unencumbered interior space which the occupants could subdivide and use as they wished. Perhaps Philip Johnson's glass house in New Canaan, Connecticut (1949), expresses this point of view best, although it represents an obviously limited solution to the problem of shelter for a family. By refusing to be concerned about *who* used his buildings, or *how* they employed the interior vistas he created, Mies was able to concentrate on the design of that rarest, most unobtainable commodity in the modern world—pure, undemanding space.

LE CORBUSIER

Le Corbusier (Charles Edouard Jeanneret-Gris, 1887–1965) began with assumptions similar to those of Mies but moved in a more sculptural direction as his career progressed; increasingly he employed poured-concrete forms and left the steel-glass vocabulary to others. In 1929, Le Corbusier's Villa Savoye exhibited the influence of Cubist painting (he was himself an active abstract artist). The house also shows an early use of

FRANK LLOYD WRIGHT. Interior, Johnson Wax Administration Building and Research Center, Racine, Wisconsin. 1938

his stilts, a brilliant structural device which has been widely adopted. These reinforced columns of concrete, which the architect called *pilotis*, exploit the fact that our steel-and-concrete technology has freed architecture from earthbound construction. A structure can be lifted into the air, freeing the space at ground level. This open area creates an appealing visual organization, with a strong shadow pattern at the building's base defining the concrete forms above it.

Wright developed "mushroom" pillars (something like pilotis) in the Johnson Wax Building interior (1938), as a structural and also as a decorative device. Since his houses generally rose from a concrete pad, he used cantilevers to open up ground space and to provide an interesting light-and-shade pattern. But Wright was temperamentally attached to the earth. Le Corbusier and the Bauhaus designers had a better appreciation of the possibilities of suspension engineering; indeed, they developed several classic chairs based on suspension and tension principles.

LE CORBUSIER. Villa Savoye, Poissy-sur-Seine, France. 1929–30

LE CORBUSIER. Interior, Villa Shodan. In the interior of the villa, Le Corbusier virtually paints with light through the design of the window perforations, much as in his chapel at Ronchamp.

In the Villa Shodan, built for an Indian businessman
in 1952, Le Corbusier shows the development of his
style along the directions of the Villa Savoye of 1929.
The mastery of poured concrete is now well established, with textures imprinted by rough wooden formwork serving to overcome any mechanical slickness
of surface. We also see the full development of Le
Corbusier's invention, the *brise-soleil*, or sunbreak, a
device which is especially useful in tropical countries.
The occupants can see out, yet the exterior rooms are
shaded against the steady sun; visually, a delightful

LE CORBUSIER. High Court Building,
Chandigarh, India. 1955–56

articulation of surface, of light and shadow, is achieved. The Brazilian Oscar Niemeyer (born 1907) has been much influenced by Le Corbusier, and throughout South America there are magnificent public and private buildings of poured concrete in which Niemeyer, and others, employ sunbreaks and pilotis.

The complicated wooden formwork required to build these virtually sculptured concrete structures is more feasible economically in countries which have

OSCAR NIEMEYER. President's residence, Brasilia. 1960

PAUL RUDOLPH. Art and Architecture Building, Yale University, New Haven, Connecticut. 1963

inexpensive sources of hand labor. Le Corbusier could employ his structural vocabulary on a vast scale to create an entire capital city, as at Chandigarh, India. And Niemeyer was engaged on a project of similar size—the building of a new capital, Brasilia, in the interior of Brazil. However, when reinforced concrete is employed in industrially advanced countries, construction time must be held to a minimum, and therefore variations in shape and space tend to be eliminated. A building vocabulary of steel frame, glass wall, and metal panels with some minor masonry trim, is more suitable to our economy. An expensive exception is the Yale art school, designed by Paul Rudolph (born 1918). Here we see the lavish use of poured concrete which contains a special aggregate to give the building's surface a rich, coarse texture. After the concrete was poured, its surface was hand-hammered by workmen, adding to its cost but enhancing the grainy effect.

THE APARTMENT HOUSE

If Wright was poet of the house, Le Corbusier was poet of the apartment and the multiple dwelling. His Unités d'Habitation (apartment houses) have been widely imitated, especially his building at Marseille (1947–52). Le Corbusier conceived of an apartment as a drawer sliding into a building skeleton; the whole might be compared to a chest of drawers. In the Marseille building, each apartment is a self-contained unit of two levels which can slide into a standardized cavity in the building skeleton. If mass-production methods were fully extended to housing, these drawers could be completely fabricated in factories, hoisted into place in the building skeleton, and plugged in. At Marseille, the apartments are sound-insulated by lead sheets between the common walls, something we would appreciate, as there has been virtually no acoustical privacy in many of our costly new multiple dwellings. The kitchens are air-conditioned; living rooms are two stories high and face a balcony with sunbreak and view. On every third floor there is a corridor, called an "interior road," which runs the length of the building. The interior roads on floors seven and eight contain an indoor shopping center. The Unité has many of the features of a resort hotel but is intended for *permanent* residents. It can accommodate large families or unmarried individuals. The seventeenth floor has a kindergarten and nursery; on the roof is a roof garden, children's swimming pool, gymnasium, running track, solarium, and snack bar. The various roof structures for elevators, ventilation, and other utilities have been designed as playful sculptures, while the machinery for elevators, generators, and air-conditioning is tucked under the first floor above the stilts.

It is clear that Le Corbusier intended to make urban living a satisfying experience, not merely a compromise for people who would rather live elsewhere. In this country, our population has become increasingly

LE CORBUSIER. Unité d'Habitation,
Marseille. 1947–52

urbanized but, it seems, increasingly unhappy with
urban living. We have built immense multiple dwellings for persons of all economic levels, but however
"modern" these structures may appear from the outside, we do not seem to be able to develop satisfying
patterns of life within. At least, those who can escape
continue to do so. What can the reason be for these
costly failures? Is it that Le Corbusier's pattern does
not work? Or is it inapplicable to the circumstances
of American life? Do we design and build badly? Do
our huge apartment houses constitute a *new conception* of social living responding to new conditions of
urban life? Or do these structures represent the same
old ideas of urban life in multiple dwellings which have
been given a spurious novelty by application of the
latest steel-and-glass technology?

THE MODERN DWELLING

Wright, Mies, and Le Corbusier, then, are the three
acknowledged geniuses of modern architecture. Their
contributions to design have been among the most
influential features of our civilization. Many have
understood, adapted, and refined the language of
form inherited from these masters. But the genius of
the "form-givers" consisted of their ability to create
new conceptions of dwelling space based on stubbornly held convictions about the nature of living
together under one roof, the requirements of modern
life, and the array of forms, processes, and tools
created by technology. That is why these architects
are honored above others.

What are some of the principles or guiding ideas
about domestic architecture that can be used by the
well-intentioned citizen who feels liberated by contemporary design but perplexed by its infinite variety?

1. A house does not exist in a physical or social
vacuum. It is not primarily a form of self-expression. It is oriented on a specific site to which it
should seem to belong and from which it should
derive advantages. Increasingly, it does not shut
out the environment but chooses to include parts
of the environment within itself.

2. The real substance of a dwelling is the shape of
its space, not its kitchen and bathroom fixtures.
Utilities change and can be replaced, but the spaces
through which we move remain fairly constant, and
they are the chief determinants of our psychic satisfaction in the dwelling. Space should be shaped
around the requirements of a particular family
rather than the requirements of fashion. This calls
for self-knowledge, a realistic assessment of one's
needs and habits. Since it is difficult to predict
needs with accuracy, flexible space arrangement is
best for most people.

3. The outside of the dwelling is a membrane which
selectively transmits light and heat and reflects the
shape of the interior space. Traditional features of
building—cornices, gables, cupolas, and so on—
tend to be survivals of obsolete building technologies. They are often less dramatic than the forms
which can be created with modern materials and

RICHARD NEUTRA. Kaufmann House, Palm Springs,
California. 1947

FRANK LLOYD WRIGHT. Living room,
David Wright House, Phoenix, Arizona. 1952

CHARLES EAMES. Living room, Eames House,
Santa Monica, California. 1949

PIERRE PAULIN. Undulating furniture. 1970. Designed for Artifort Holland. Distributed by Turner Ltd., New York.
Furniture trying to revive prenatal memories. The repetition of undulating forms in a soft, billowy material aspires to the security of the womb.

structural devices. Unfortunately, some builders combine brickwork, stonework, wood, concrete, stucco, glass, marble, mosaic, asbestos, plastic, and metal in the same structure. Simplicity of material is a virtue in building.

4. Interior decoration should mean more than the application of ornament, the collection and display of objects, or the selection of furniture. But since interiors are experienced visually as well as used, their arrangement needs to be considered from an aesthetic as well as a practical standpoint. Resourceful interior design is most needed in apartments, where architectural qualities are generally limited and where emphasis must be placed on furniture, color schemes, and lighting. For *any* dwelling, the problems of unity, focus, coherence, and expressiveness must be solved, regardless of furnishings and no matter how well the space was originally designed.

CONCLUSION

Since the days when people lived in caves or tents, domestic dwellings have gone through immense transformations accompanied by equally great changes in human personality. Now space exploration and scientific fantasy contemplate residence on distant planets in strange or nonexistent atmospheres. In the present era of innovation and experiment, the very idea of a shelter which assumes a hostile environment—a safe inside and an unfriendly outside—may become obsolete. If climate is controlled, our only shelter might be our clothing, and that for privacy, not protection. Perhaps houses will be only storage places for certain private possessions while life is carried on in structures designed for particular activities. There may even be special structures for the enjoyment of privacy, just as there are buildings where we go for collective dreams —motion picture theaters. The line between the home and the community may disappear. Perhaps families will live in disposable dwellings like the nests which birds build and discard each year. Designers can accomplish such wonderful (or dreadful) things now, if we wish. But do we wish? We should look around and see what it is that gives form to the social and architectural fabric of the community.

Large-Scale Design: The Community

Everyone seems to be aware of our problems of crowding, air pollution, traffic snarls, noise, visual chaos, and ugliness. We also know that communities are not always afflicted by these problems. Communities are built by people, hence people are responsible for the predicament we are in. Only people will get us out of our difficulties. What are the remedies which have been proposed to make human communities truly livable? If communities are thought of as works of art—either well or badly executed—what are the elements of that art?

We know how to design and construct excellent buildings and roads, but we do not seem to be able to put them together so that the results are anything short of lethal. If the automobile is a deadly weapon, can we minimize its destructiveness? Can we build cities and towns which are not completely at the mercy of noxious exhausts and murderous fenders? Is peaceful coexistence possible? Since man is a social being, can we create the physical arrangements that will allow him to enjoy social life?

Architects and planners, engineers and philosophers have thought about these problems and have made proposals ranging from extreme utopianism to cautious reform. We shall examine a few of their ideas.

Traffic on Los Angeles Freeway

EBENEZER HOWARD: THE GARDEN CITY

In the nineteenth century, as today, people left farms in droves and added to the congestion of cities. The countryside was depopulated and the cities teemed. In 1898, Ebenezer Howard, an Englishman without architectural training, realized that the problem was not merely to reverse the flow of migration: it was necessary to create communities that combined urban and rural features. His solution: "Town and country *must be married*, and out of this union will spring a new hope, a new life, a new civilization."[1] He wrote a book which advanced the concept of the "garden

CONKLIN AND WITTLESEY. Town center, Reston, Virginia. 1961.
Ebenezer Howard's Garden City concept is given contemporary expression in the town of Reston.

FRANK LLOYD WRIGHT. Broadacre City plan. 1933–40.
Reprinted from *The Living City*
by Frank Lloyd Wright, copyright 1958,
by permission of the publisher,
Horizon Press, New York

city," a community of concentric belts of land alternately used for commerce or manufacturing and "green" belts or park land. The greenbelts would insulate functional areas from each other while providing recreation space and that balance of rural and urban qualities needed for a healthy and satisfying

DAVIS, BRODY AND ASSOCIATES. Riverbend Houses, New York. 1966–68. Good design in middle-income housing: private entrance to each duplex, floor-through living space, walled terrace, continuous outside gallery, spectacular views; a creative adaptation of Le Corbusier's *ville radieuse* philosophy on behalf of the black residents of Harlem's tenements.

existence. He planned to locate administrative and recreational buildings at the core of these communities—something like the squares and village greens which give emotional and visual focus to small towns and some city neighborhoods.

Land would not be individually owned but would be held and developed by a common body which would limit growth to about 30,000, thus preventing speculation and high density. Beyond this population, it would be necessary to start a new garden city. The outermost belt of each community might be used to grow food for local consumption or be left uncultivated so it could be used for recreation space.

Howard hoped his plan would lead to the decentralization of London, an event which never took place. But it *was* translated into reality in several English and American suburbs. The *word* "greenbelt" has been widely adopted, but rarely have all of Howard's principles been applied in a single community: controlled growth; ownership of land by a common authority; and the separation rather than the mixing of residential, industrial, recreational, and administrative functions.

It should be stressed that Howard's garden city was to be a balanced community, with work, recreation, residence, and government carried on within it. Today's suburbs or satellite towns are mainly one-function communities: they have been called "dormitory suburbs." Without an industrial base, home-owners are hard pressed to finance and maintain good

Photograph of a slum scene in Harlem

school systems, not to mention other essential services. But as industries move or are lured into such communities, as the highways to the central city grow more crowded, as commercial and industrial facilities sprawl outside their corporate limits, the suburbs lose the advantages of decentralization which their residents left the city to gain. Aside from the moral aspects of suburban parasitism—using urban services without contributing to their maintenance and support—there are practical disadvantages in an arrangement which grows increasingly insupportable from an economic standpoint and is architecturally monotonous. One begins to learn painfully that no community is an island.

FRANK LLOYD WRIGHT: BROADACRE CITY

Of course, one way to deal with the problems of urbanism is to eliminate cities, to start all over again, in a sense, by reorganizing society into small, almost self-sufficient communities. Or, if cities cannot be abandoned and their problems are too deep-seated to be solved, we can reform *part* of society by creating ideal communities outside the megalopolitan monsters. This might be called the Noah's Ark approach to urban redesign. If the ugliness as well as the social disorganization of the city is due to overcrowding, then decentralization—spreading out the population —overcomes the spatial and social problems of urbanism. Also, it enables people to establish a better relationship to the land and to nature. In his Broadacre City plan of the 1930s, Frank Lloyd Wright proposed a decentralized solution: an acre of land for each person. Farmers would have ten acres, but all would raise some of their own food, supplementing what full-time farmers could grow. This procedure might be less efficient from the standpoint of agricultural yield per acre, but Wright believed, as did Jefferson, that moral benefits accrue to people who till the soil at least part of the time. Today, some young people have taken to living in communes, as much concerned with the moral advantages of group living as with escaping the evils of urbanism.

In a land area of four square miles, fourteen hundred families or six thousand people could live, produce some food, provide each other with a variety of personal services, and engage in some light manufacturing. Wright believed, quite correctly, that the automobile and helicopter liberate men residentially. Unlike nineteenth- and early-twentieth-century workers, we need not live next to where we work. The telephone enables us to communicate easily with cities, if we need to; radio and television broadcast news and entertainment; motion picture theaters are everywhere. Thus, we do not have to live *in* the city to use the goods and services created there. (Some of us can live parasitically *off of* the city, however.)

But can communities of six thousand create the necessities of modern civilization? How many people are associated with a modern university? Thirty-five thousand? Fifty thousand? How many are needed to support a first-class museum, hospital, theater, department store, school system, steel plant?

Wright did not plan to dispense with cities at once, however. Eventually they would wither away. The existence of the city was part of his plan (albeit grudgingly), since some of the residents of Broadacre would commute there to work. (Today commuters wonder whether two or three hours of daily travel are sufficiently rewarded by character-building activities in the suburbs like raising tomatoes and mowing the lawn.) Still, contemporary suburban life is a caricature of the Wright idea. He really wanted people to raise their own food, to improve the land, to be free of money and its evils. Their houses would be designed by architects like Wright, who would relate their dwellings to the shape of the land. People would not own land in Broadacre City but would hold it so long as they could make productive use of it. Land would not be a commodity which is traded for profit but a source of sustenance and delight.

The principles on which Broadacre City would be organized are best summarized in the following list prepared by Wright himself:[2]

> No private ownership.
> No landlord and tenant.
> No "housing." No subsistence homesteads.
> No traffic problems. No back-and-forth haul.
> No railroads. No streetcars.
> No grade crossings.
> No poles. No wires in sight.
> No ditches alongside the roads.
> No headlights. No light fixtures.
> No glaring cement roads or walks.
> No tall buildings except as isolated in parks.
> No slum. No scum.
> No public ownership of private needs.

LE CORBUSIER: LA VILLE RADIEUSE

The garden city is a suburb; the suburb is a tentacle of the city. According to Le Corbusier, it creates more problems than it solves: commuting, expensive installation of utilities from the central city, too many

LE CORBUSIER. Ville Radieuse: Voisin Plan for Paris. 1925

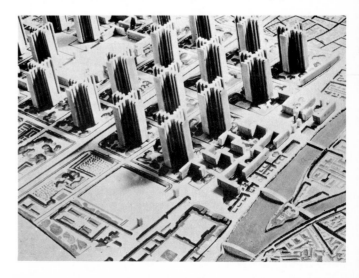

New town in Cumbernauld, Scotland. 1965

vehicles, costly maintenance. And eventually the garden city is absorbed by the spreading central city. Instead, Le Corbusier proposed the Ville Radieuse, a plan for as many as three million people. Unlike Wright the American, who generally detested skyscrapers, an American invention, Le Corbusier the Frenchman found them absolutely essential. He would create *vertical* garden cities. The Ville Radieuse would have a higher population density than present cities and yet *more* open space. The explanation lies in its huge but widely separated office buildings and apartment houses. Instead of being clustered to form the canyons of Manhattan, they would be open to light and air, surrounded by park areas, and approached by unimpeded highways on several levels. Highways and subways would radiate outward from the center of the city, like the streets in Washington, D.C. At the outer rings of the city would be large apartment houses of the type at Marseille, fifteen or twenty stories in height, with some individual dwellings among them. Industry would be located farther out from the city, but not very far from the apartments where its workers would live.

The space opened up in the city by high-density skyscrapers could be safely used by pedestrians since different kinds of transportation would have their own levels. This is an ideal of today's city planners which we cannot seem to reach: many of our modern urban redevelopment schemes locate parking garages in the core of the city, drawing vehicles into the center city and forcing pedestrians to compete with them for space.

Le Corbusier was reconciled to the existence of the city and its unique culture. He did not seek to escape but to change the city. And the world seems to have accepted his commitment to high-rise structures but, until recently, has been unwilling to carry out radical surgery in the central city necessary to rationalize its transport systems and admit light, sun, and air to downtown areas by opening up the space around skyscrapers.

A tremendously productive person as writer, painter, sculptor, architect, and planner, Le Corbusier feared boredom. According to him, the detached family dwelling in the suburbs is efficient for about twenty years, while a family is being raised. Then the children leave, and parents, alone in a house larger than their needs require or their strength can maintain, are vulnerable to attacks of boredom. This would not happen in the Ville Radieuse. Instead of social isolation, there is the companionship of people in one's Unité d'Habitation. The residents are of all ages and family conditions, unlike the single-age-group environment of American retirement communities. Apartments are not primarily for lifetime residence; one occupies them so long as they meet one's needs.

Le Corbusier admired the skyline of Manhattan, but only at a distance. He deplored the living and working arrangements which it implied: "Our American friends have erected skyscrapers and made them work. They are constructions of an astonishing technique, tangible proofs of present possibilities. But, from the planning point of view, their skyscrapers are tiresome and their towns wretched to live in (though vibrant and meriting the closest attention)." And he went on about single dwellings: "Instead of multiplying innumerable suburban houses let us equip ourselves with impeccable dwelling-units [that is, apartment houses] of an appropriate stature."[3]

Le Corbusier insisted that, since urbanism is an inescapable fact of modern life, rational ordering of space can make urban life satisfying, even exciting. Great architecture is possible without return to the building techniques and living patterns of the past. Reinforced-concrete construction ("reconstituted stone," as he called it) can be spiritually satisfying, functionally adequate, and reasonable in cost. Good design results from artistic sensitivity wedded to a conception of man: his work, recreation, visual needs, feelings about space, and desire to move freely on his own feet. Indeed, if any architect can devise ways for people to move on foot freely, safely, and with delight, in communities numbering in the millions, then individualism will have a chance to survive.

Following are the principles of town planning advocated by Le Corbusier:

The *keys* to town planning lie in designing for the four functions: Living, Working, Recreation, Circulation.
The *materials* of town planning are sunlight, space, greenery, and steel-reinforced concrete.
Enough dwellings should be concentrated in one building to liberate the space around it.

Pedestrian routes and mechanized-transportation routes should be separated.

Distance between home and work must be minimized.

Living quarters should have the best urban sites.

Pedestrian paths should not be obstructed by buildings, which should be elevated on stilts.

Autos, buses, and other vehicles should travel on elevated roadways, beneath which are housed pipes and other utilities now buried below ground; easier repair and maintenance would result.

Industrial areas must be separated from residential areas by greenery.

Architectural monuments should be safeguarded.

ELEMENTS OF PLANNING: RESIDENTIAL GROUPING

Almost all community plans call for special areas set aside for residential purposes. These areas are occupied chiefly by detached, single-family dwellings. They vary greatly in cost, quality of design, and orientation on their sites. They are built speculatively, in huge developments, or they are built on an individual, custom-made basis. Yet some developments contain costly dwellings, while some individually built houses are inexpensive. Cost and organization of construction do not always govern the patterning of home sites, roads, and open space in a residential area, although the builder of a large development has the best opportunity to provide for comprehensive design.

What personal and social objectives are sought in the grouping of houses, the design and location of roads, and the shaping of open space? The chief reason most persons choose to buy separate dwellings is to live in a quasi-rural setting, to capture, if possible, the charm of village life while enjoying the amenities of modern suburbanism. They hope their houses will blend gracefully with the landscape; afford convenient and safe access to neighbors; provide roads nearby for reaching shops, schools, churches, recreation; and present a varied but unified appearance.

Curving roads are best for providing visual interest and variety; they also tend to slow down motorists. Of course, a main thoroughfare should never pass through a residential area. Where straight roads are necessary, houses need not be set parallel to the road; all can be given a slight, consistent tilt to create more varied space intervals and to take advantage of the best orientation to sun and view. But if every house in a group is independently tilted on its lot, the result can be chaotic. Some zoning ordinances attempt to prevent this through rules for uniform setbacks and minimum distances between houses. So far as intersections are concerned, the four-corner intersection should be avoided. The simple T intersection is best. A variety of road types can be employed to connect with larger arteries: the cul-de-sac, dead end, loop street, the collector road, plus their modifications and combinations. Hopefully, the bulldozer will be used as

SVEN MARKELIUS. Vällingby, Sweden. Begun 1953

sparingly as possible; natural contours will be respected; good trees and interesting stone outcroppings will be permitted to stand.

Flat terrain lends itself to any pattern, but good design tries to avoid the obvious, especially the rectangular grid; an effort should be made to introduce variety where nature has not been generous with trees or rolling landscape. It has been found in highway design that a good view is improved if it is approached by a curved route. By this principle, even a commonplace row of houses can be made more attractive if we do not see them all at once—as if lined up along a railroad track. In addition to horizontal curves, the vertical curve, the rise and dip of the road, can add interest to individual dwellings and to a group. Houses should be designed to take advantage of changing levels of vision. And it is best if dominant roof lines follow the slope of the land. When close together, houses harmonize well if there is some continuity among their roof lines: they should seem to flow together, and this effect can be enhanced through landscaping.

Unfortunately, one of the motives for living in detached houses is a laudable but misunderstood individualism. To avoid the monotony of some mass-produced developments, homeowners indulge in orgies of spurious originality in their fencing, lampposts, mailboxes, garden sculpture, and so on. Horrors are perpetrated in an effort to deny that the houses carry approximately the same price and contain about the same number of door knobs. But outrageous aesthetic efforts work against the homeowners who

ALFRED NEUMANN and ZVI HECKER. Apartment house, Ramat Gan, Israel. 1960–63. The sculptural excitement in this apartment building (above) proves that modern technology can generate the same feeling of community that we sense in the adobe pueblo, America's oldest highrise dwelling (below).

sought the suburban development to avoid the visual discontinuities of the city in the first place.

Richard Neutra has written candidly about the problems and illusions of homeownership. The freedom and independence that homeownership seems to imply is rarely exercised in any real sense by the time land developers, zoning boards, lending institutions, contractors, building trade unions, and public utilities have organized their skills, assets, energies, and interests to produce the dwelling the citizen buys. Indeed, that citizen is not likely ever to *own* his house.

But it is his to use and pay for. And the detached dwelling, with its design atrocities and illusions of individualism, may yet constitute a better solution to the problems of shelter than the alternative—undistinguished boxes in larger urban boxes increasingly reserved for the very rich or the very poor. Unfortunately, the poetic promise of the domestic dwelling inherited from Frank Lloyd Wright has not been realized in housing for the millions. Perhaps it never can be. But it would seem that here architecture and planning are ahead of society. We know how to design better communities than we are permitted to build, better indeed than most citizens realize are possible.

ELEMENTS OF PLANNING: THE HIGHWAY

Trains and buses are more efficient vehicles of transportation than automobiles. Nevertheless, if we have a choice, we prefer to drive an automobile to the same

Indian village, Taos, New Mexico

place we could reach by bus. Why? There is the sense of freedom and personal control in a car. An auto trip has elements of the unexpected. If modern existence is increasingly mechanized and automated, driving provides the opportunity to exercise skill and judgment. Also, the automobile is felt as an extension of the driver's body: he wants to test it against the rigors of distance, the cars of other drivers, the demands of the road. The auto voyage along with the shopping trip is one of the fundamental experiences of twentieth-century mankind. Despite transportation alternatives and casualty statistics, motorists surge toward our concrete strips like lemmings drawn to the sea.

What draws the motorist in addition to the need to get somewhere is the opportunity to feel the land moving under his vehicle, to view the changing sky and countryside at 75 mph, and to sense the response of the car to the shifting shape of the road. We have to acknowledge the fact that highways, parkways, bridges, and viaducts constitute art objects, sources of aesthetic experience for the millions.

Safety is a principal goal of the highway designer. But aesthetic considerations are intimately related to safety. The designer can shape a motorist's visual experience because he knows how far ahead a driver can see at given speeds, his degree of peripheral vision and ability to discriminate objects. He knows how the banking and grading of the road and the transition to and from curves affect comfort and pleasure as well as safety. We have a deep-seated desire for precision—for smoothness and regularity of surface and contour.

For the motorist, the need for precision is satisfied in the pleasurable feelings experienced in smooth car maneuvers assisted by the shape of the highway and its access roads. The well-designed highway *leads* the eye of the driver, preparing him for certain operations while affording sufficient variation to avoid monotony. Variety is desirable because monotonous highway design becomes dangerously hypnotic.

The design of viaducts, bridges, multilevel interchanges, side slopes, retaining walls, safety rails, and embankments presents difficult aesthetic problems as well as challenges to engineering ingenuity. For example, we are rarely able to bring a highway through a city harmoniously. How can major arteries be visually integrated with the structures and facilities which surround them? What are the best shape and scale relationships for the areas created by the crossing, paralleling, descending, or rising of freeway ramps as they meet local traffic patterns?

And there are other questions: What can be done to minimize the number of signs posted by well-meaning highway departments? Can visual information be

Expressway through Lefrak City in Queens, New York. An automotive conveyor belt surrounded by an anonymous collection of boxes for middle-income apartment dwellers. The result of this architectural relationship of mutual indifference and disregard is ugliness.

Complex freeway interchange in Los Angeles

Terracing along Highway 70 outside Denver, Colorado. Sound highway engineering here creates an impressive geologic display as well as an aesthetic effect appropriate to the grandeur of the Rocky Mountain setting.

given more concisely, and sufficiently in advance of need? Can the right-of-way be extended so that billboards will not invade the motorist's privacy or exploit citizens traveling on thoroughfares built with public funds? Vision is essential to driving; hence billboards cannot be "turned off." Obviously, the best efforts of architects, engineers, and planners will be frustrated if there is no legislation to protect the visual, structural, and topographic relationships they are learning to create.

Although the automobile is the cause of much civic and social mischief, it is also the parent of the highway and parkway. These, in turn, have been carried to the point where they constitute complex and monumental art forms. Given its most expensive expression in America, the modern highway illustrates our resemblance to the ancient Romans—solid builders and administrators but not especially sensitive to human or aesthetic relationships. Since 1946, Germany and Switzerland have demonstrated more advanced ideas of the highway as a form of architecture. But the world's greatest democracy has yet to accept the legitimacy of spending public funds for sculpture to enliven dull stretches of road. The pathos of Edward Hopper's *Gas* tells the story well. But we are learning that with our frontier gone and natural resources limited, the spoliation of the landscape must cease. The highway may be our most effective instrument for educating the millions to enjoy the countryside and to preserve it unravaged.

ELEMENTS OF PLANNING: PLAZAS, MALLS, CIVIC CENTERS

Television has made our public life a living-room experience. Momentous events are witnessed from the same sofa which used to serve for courtship before

automobiles overtook us. The deaths of presidents and popes are experienced over television with all the immediacy and sense of distress that are felt by members of a family. For a long time, it has been apparent that we cannot gather in a single square to hear issues debated and see the people's business settled. Our communications media have recently become vivid enough to provide an alternative sense of community. However, television, radio, and the news magazines create only a community of opinion, entertainment, and information. We need physical symbols of community too—places in the open where we can come together out of the darkness of TV dens to experience the exhilaration of *being with*, as opposed to *looking at* or *reading about*, people.

What are the places that bring large numbers of people together? They are shopping centers, parks, sports arenas, schools and universities, theaters, civic centers, airports, train terminals, hotels, and museums. As individual structures, such buildings may work fairly well—as technical if not aesthetic entities. But the space *around* them does *not* work very well because it has rarely been planned: it is merely leftover space, occupied largely by the avenues and streets required to carry people. The noise, jostling, auto fumes, and confusion of even distinguished thoroughfares are so disturbing to the pedestrian that he must flee indoors to hear himself think.

Yet we want to stroll, windowshop, sit on benches, and watch the passing parade. These are the deeply rooted desires of people who congregate in market places, church plazas, and parks. Americans visit Europe for these reasons—so that they can browse in outdoor book stalls, shop in open markets, explore crooked little streets opening into enclosed squares where there might be a church, some statuary, a fountain, some children playing, or older people chatting in groups. Imagine that—people carrying on a conversation out of doors!

Happily, shopping space has been made congenial for pedestrians in centers created by Victor Gruen in Minneapolis, Minnesota (the Southdale Shopping Center); Cherry Hill, New Jersey; Rochester, New York (Midtown Plaza); and elsewhere. These shopping malls may be enclosed structures with natural light admitted at the top, generous and often exotic plantings, and air-conditioning throughout. A mall may be created by closing off downtown streets, as in Rochester. Converting some of the streets of "center city" to pedestrian use can accomplish a great deal toward reclaiming the city for people: this does not necessarily require that buildings be torn down; auto traffic can be rerouted and underground garages built. Such measures are sometimes taken to counter the flow of retail business to outlying shopping areas. But they must be accompanied by large-scale redesign of the slums and obsolete structures which usually surround downtown areas.

Rockefeller Center in New York City, begun in 1931, provided a giant impetus for the design of public plazas and buildings in the high-density core of a modern metropolis. It consists of sixteen buildings occupying fourteen acres of choice real estate in Manhattan; the complex surrounds a pedestrian mall and a sunken plaza which is an ice-skating rink in the

DONALD RAY CARTER. Photograph of Galleria Vittorio Emanuele, Milan.
A city is not great unless it creates places where citizens can enjoy the variegated delights of a rich street life.

winter and an outdoor restaurant in the summer. The buildings are massive slabs representing the first significant departure from the idea of the skyscraper as a tower, a sort of oversized church steeple. The group embodies a frank if unspectacular solution to the problem of getting a maximum of light into the interior of very tall structures. No office is more than twenty-seven feet from an exterior wall; all have light, fresh air, and a view. The clean plane of the walls of the RCA Building is given a pleasing surface texture by the vertical strips of light-colored stone facing; its profile departs only slightly from a perfect rectangle in staggered setbacks located where the elevator shafts end. But the main advantage of the unbroken curtain-wall surfaces lies in the sense of enclosure and protection they give to the plaza and mall on the ground. The popularity of this site grows out of the feeling it gives the pedestrian of being at the focal point of an energetic and exciting city. With its Gothic stonework, St. Patrick's Cathedral, across the avenue from the complex, provides a satisfying complementary architectural note and appears to be enhanced by contrast with the scale of its neighbors.

A great city is large and frustrating, at once exhilarating and depressing. The individual privately lost in its often depersonalized routine needs to be publicly reminded of his participation in humanity— that is, of his capacity to experience emotions arising from large-scale, collective effort. Knowing that

JACQUES MOESCHAL'S 1968 sculpture for Mexico City's Route of Friendship

Victor Gruen Associates. Midtown Plaza,
Rochester, New York. 1961–62

Parly II, an American-style shopping center between Paris and Versailles. The American cultural
invasion of Europe continues. Here our design and
technology enhance the traditional Continental
marketing experience: the pleasure of visiting
dozens of little shops and vendors' stalls in comfort
and on foot.

Rockefeller Center, New York. 1931–37

Lincoln Center for the Performing Arts, New York

Piazza San Marco, Venice. Begun 1063

powerful persons and institutions have assembled vast resources to please him (as well as justify their power) has comforted the ordinary citizen from ancient times to the present. We realize that vast projects are endowed by men anxious to show they are worthy stewards of the world's wealth; still, the satisfaction we experience in the presence of great public architecture is undeniable. We honor the Medici of Florence and the doges of Venice for the monuments which they caused to be built. These stand after their builders have been forgotten.

ELEMENTS OF PLANNING: INDUSTRIAL AND COMMERCIAL STRUCTURES

Not long ago, a factory or warehouse was an ugly place—grimy, surrounded by refuse, clutter, and foul smells. Viewing the industrial sprawl from the train window as one crossed the New Jersey meadows, one wondered how workers ever became accustomed to the sights and sounds once they had overcome reactions to the stench. The same wonder arose in connection with steel-mill towns along the Ohio River, wood-pulp mills in the South, the slaughterhouses of Chicago and Kansas City, and the scarred mining towns of Pennsylvania and West Virginia. Their active and obsolete remains still mark the places where we live and work. From the standpoint of aesthetic detachment, they are often romantically picturesque or symbolically impressive: the open-hearth steel mills of Gary, Indiana, at night; the oil refineries of Galveston and Bayonne; the railroad marshaling yards of Chicago; the almost deserted textile factories of New England; the "gas-house" area of any large city hard by its abattoirs and fish markets. But these romantic and/or malodorous places are disappearing, mainly

Steel mills, Pittsburgh

The romantic and picturesque imagery associated with artfully photographed industrial structures is not always compatible with an aesthetically satisfying way of life for nearby residents.

FRANK LLOYD WRIGHT.
Johnson Wax Administration and
Research Center, Racine, Wisconsin.
1936–39, 1946–49.
Views by day and by night

SKIDMORE, OWINGS AND MERRILL.
Lever House, New York. 1952

SKIDMORE, OWINGS AND MERRILL.
Chase Manhattan Plaza, New York. 1961

EPSTEIN & SONS. Kitchens of Sara Lee Administration Building, Deerfield, Illinois. 1964

because their operation has become uneconomic. They were in the wrong location; they were too costly to maintain; some of them could be automated; or their managements became concerned with public image. The Victorian notion that industrial manufacture was an inherently ugly process, even though its products were necessary, has given way to the idea that the rationality, order, precision, and planning which are essential for any successful industrial enterprise can also be visible in the places where that enterprise is carried on.

A pioneering industrial statement was made, once again, by Frank Lloyd Wright in his administration building (1936–39) and research tower (1946–49) for the Johnson Wax Company. Some of its features appear dated now, and the structural vocabulary (with the exception of the tower) seems more related to the domestic dwelling than to business activity. But is that bad? Should we criticize factories because they look like college buildings? Worker morale is improved and management is enabled to attract the personnel essential for survival in a modern economy. The Johnson buildings are located in the center city, where architectural quality and sculptural accents are a valued asset. A globe of the world, given a prominent location in a formal setting, is rather trite, somewhat reminiscent of exposition planning. In the Johnson complex at Racine, the genuinely interesting forms belong to the structures themselves and to the research tower, which rises dramatically from a hovering plat-form. Its horizontal bands repeat the emphasis of the administration buildings, and its circular roof turrets give variety to the tower while restating similar forms which appear elsewhere. The floors, or layers, of the tower are cantilevered from a central core which passes through the building and is visible as the turret on the roof. Night illumination reveals the structure clearly and shows the Wrightian concept of a tall

building as opposed to the Chicago and New York skyscraper conception. A high-rise structure resting on a platform is a device increasingly used today, and with conspicuous success, as in Lever House (1952) and the Chase Manhattan building (1961), both de-signed by Skidmore, Owings and Merrill. It unifies the site while creating a useful protected space beneath the platform.

The extent to which industrial buildings have de-parted from factory stereotypes can be seen in Paul Rudolph's Endo Pharmaceutical Center. The build-ing vocabulary employed in Rudolph's Yale School of Art and Architecture is repeated here. Similarly, the Sara Lee bakery plant appears to have been influenced by the architecture building at Illinois Tech designed by Mies van der Rohe.

Dramatic industrial and commercial structures can also be seen in Ely Kahn's (1884–1972) Municipal

E. J. KAHN. Municipal Asphalt Plant, New York. 1944

Asphalt Plant in New York City, the St. Louis airport terminal by Minoru Yamasaki (born 1912), and the North Carolina State Fair Arena by Matthew Nowicki (1910–1949) and W. H. Deitrick (born 1905). The late Eero Saarinen, who collaborated with his father in the design of the somewhat reserved General Motors Center, displayed more theatrical gifts in the TWA terminal at Kennedy International Airport. However, before congratulating ourselves on the drama and grandeur of contemporary architecture, we might look at the main concourse of Pennsylvania Station, designed in 1906 by McKim, Mead and White, the classicizing old firm which based the waiting room of the terminal on the Roman baths of Caracalla. Here we could see drama in unadorned steel equal to the best modern work. But we can see it no longer: the venerable landmark was torn down to make way for a sports arena.

MINORU YAMASAKI. St. Louis Airport Terminal. 1954

MATTHEW NOWICKI and
WILLIAM H. DEITRICK.
J. S. Dorton Arena,
Raleigh, North Carolina. 1953

EERO SAARINEN.
TWA Terminal,
Kennedy International Airport,
New York. 1962

McKim, Mead and White.
Main concourse,
Pennsylvania Station,
New York. 1906

John Andrews. Scarborough College, University of Toronto. 1966

The "megastructure" approach to the architecture of great institutions and even of whole cities. Such continuous structures are open to social and technological change because they are designed to receive "add-on" or "clip-on" units which are mass produced by industrial methods instead of being custom-made on the site.

Safdie, David, Barott, and Boulva. Habitat, EXPO 67, Montreal. 1967

The present is a time of frantic urban and regional transformation. The convergence of several forces has brought this about: (1) we realize that many social problems, now at the stage of crisis, originate in the physical design of the community; (2) we realize that our society is rich enough to undertake the massive architectural measures needed to rebuild the environment; (3) we realize that problems of health, transportation, work, and recreation often transcend traditional political units—they embrace regions; (4) modern technology has provided the tools which make it practical to think in terms of large-scale, comprehensive design; (5) various specialists—architects, engineers, ecologists, lawyers, administrators, land-use experts—are developing patterns of unified action for community and regional design; (6) architectural education has evolved to the point where designers can deal with the problems involving regional environments.

The Crafts and Industrial Design

We have already observed that art performs a physical function through the design of tools and containers. The important principle is that art is not only decorative or symbolic: it is also utilitarian. There are significant differences between handmade and machine-made objects. But we should not forget that while methods, materials, and processes vary, the business of organizing them to satisfy human needs is an artistic problem.

At different times the individual responsible for creating eating and cooking utensils has been called an artisan, a craftsman, an engineer, or a designer. The family itself has produced its own food, clothing, shelter, and most of its tools and utensils. The hardworking housewife of colonial days may not have regarded herself as a craftsman or designer, but she made her own cloth, cut and sewed clothes for her family, made blankets and rugs, painted and embroidered textiles, and worked at other crafts we would normally assign to specialists. But here our interest in the method of making an article or in the occupation of its maker is based mainly on curiosity about the form of the object itself and our effort to understand its functions.

The water jug made by a potter and the aluminum pitcher produced by machine are similar in shape and function. The fingers and art of the potter formed the clay jug. Forming the aluminum pitcher was different. But the pitcher—resulting from the collaboration of man and machine—has its own distinctive excellence: it too is an "art" object. Here we shall examine some of the historical, technical, and psychological factors involved in the transition from clay pot to metal pitcher. In effect, we ask the question, "Can people teach machines to create art?"

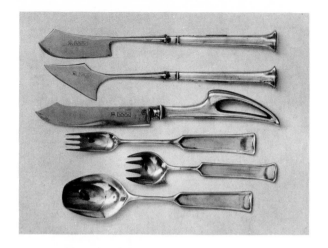

RICHARD RIEMERSCHMID. Table flatware. 1900. Württembergisches Landesmuseum, Stuttgart. As early as 1900, Richard Riemerschmid combined the rational analysis of function in useful objects with a sensitive and restrained adaptation of Art Nouveau forms.

CHARACTERISTICS OF HANDCRAFT

Usually, a handmade object has been planned and executed by the same person. This is always true if the maker is what we call an artist-craftsman. In the cottage and village crafts of pre-industrial economies, some division of labor occurs, so that artisans may execute the designs created by others and employ members of the family to carry out minor operations. Nevertheless, there is a certain unity of control and execution in the handmade object. The excellent craftsman not only does all the work himself but also adjusts his design according to the requirements of a customer. A tailor or shoemaker undertakes to satisfy the individual in terms of his personal measurements. Hence, the characteristics of handcraft include unified responsibility for making the object and adjustment of design to the customer's individual needs or caprice. The result of this process inevitably exhibits variation. We can speak of the craft object as "one of a kind," no matter how similar it is to other objects of its type. The uniqueness of the object may be based on idiosyncrasies of the craftsman's technique or the special desires of a patron. In any event, that uniqueness is identified by many as the essence of art. It pleases us to know that we own or are looking at an object which is absolutely singular, which cannot be found elsewhere.

Another feature of handcraft is, paradoxically, its relative sameness. Variations in detail occur because absolute duplication is not possible in handmade articles. But the people and the craftsmen working in a folk tradition do not regard change for its own sake as a value. They change their modes of making, thinking, and behaving very slowly. Peasants and artisans are inclined to resist novelty. Consequently, craftsmen in peasant or folk cultures are content to use formulas and patterns inherited over the generations. For them,

Violin made by Antonio Stradivari. 1721. The Metropolitan Museum of Art, New York. Bequest of Annie Bolton Matthews Bryant, 1933. The crafts tend to perpetuate tradition: we do not expect "originality" in the design of a violin.

inherited practices constitute an honored tradition which they must pass on as closely as possible. Persian rug-making is a good example. Traditions in the crafts promote a high degree of technical skill, since the folk craftsman concentrates on mastery of skill more than originality of expression. The problems of design and meaning have been solved for him. It does not occur to him to change his designs, especially as life itself does not change very much. This timeless quality fascinates and charms the visitor, even if the peasant may not think of his work as "charming."

Although the older craft tradition places no premium on novelty, it *does* stress the proper use of tools and materials and the importance of durability. "Proper" means employing the "correct"—that is, inherited—technique, respecting the working properties of leather, fiber, wood, metal, or stone. Furthermore, it means producing long-wearing, durable objects. Since the craftsman-customer relationship is a close one, the craftsman cannot easily escape responsibility for what he has made. Thus, we derive one of the fundamental meanings of craftsmanship: the patron values the handmade object because he knows and trusts the craftsman who made it. Modern manufacturers attempt to develop a similar trust, but as a rule consumers can depend only on independent testing and evaluation.

One other trait of handcraft may account for the survival of artist-craftsmen today, notwithstanding their struggle with the economic facts of life: it is difficult to produce a great many ugly products by hand. There are inferior craftsmen, of course, but they are usually discouraged, weeded out by a poor reception of their work. Second, it is difficult for any human being to make something badly over and over again. He inevitably improves a little bit. But the machine can produce badly designed objects at a fantastic rate. The result improves only if the designer improves. In the meantime, a vast amount of trash can be manufactured. In an industrial civilization, excellence is often defined in terms of mass acceptance, an

ROY LICHTENSTEIN.
Ceramic Sculpture I. 1965.
Private collection

MERET OPPENHEIM. *Object.* 1936.
The Museum of Modern Art, New York

These works rely for their Surrealist impact on the deliberate violation of the craftsman's aesthetic: appropriateness of material, decoration, and mode of making to the form and function of the object.

acceptance which may only reflect the absence of superior alternatives.

During most of our history, objects of daily use have been made with the aid of small hand tools which are virtually extensions of our fingers and senses. We have been thoroughly habituated to the visual and tactile characteristics of handcraft. It is doubtful that we shall ever escape our emotional attachment to the properties of material worked by hand. But civilization as we know it depends on mechanical and automated forms of making. Since 1750, the world has been going through a conflict between our emotional attachment to the crafts and the mechanical, automated basis of civilization. Now the conflict is almost over. That is, machine methods of making and machine-made products have been successfully absorbed by almost all societies. Those newly emerging nations which still subsist on the basis of a handcraft economy are rushing eagerly toward machine-based industrialism. Some states, on gaining independence, almost immediately begin to build skyscrapers and steel plants although they do not have the supporting facilities for high-rise buildings and could buy steel more cheaply than they can manufacture it. Mechanical-industrial production has become a symbol of national prestige; handcraft is regarded as a survival of colonial dependence. More experience with self-government and the operation of an industrial economy is needed to find the right mixture of handcrafts and mechanical production.

THE ORIGIN AND PRINCIPLES OF MASS PRODUCTION

To understand how industrial design functions and to see the role of the machine as an artistic tool, it is necessary to describe the changes brought about by mechanization and mass production.

The principles of mass production are *duplication, accuracy, interchangeability*, and *specialization*. Casting, the oldest method of duplication, goes back to Neolithic man. From this art, the enormous metal foundries of the present evolved. Today, there are few manufactured products which do not contain cast-metal or -plastic parts. A second Neolithic invention, the potter's wheel, led to the wood lathe and the metal lathe, which is the basic machine tool of metalworking. Die stamping, another method of duplication, was used by Darius in the fifth century B.C. to manufacture coins. Gutenberg's invention of movable type is the method of duplication most familiar to all of us, and one of the most far-reaching in its effects. His movable type involved a kind of interchangeability, since letters could be used over again in different combinations. But tolerances of accuracy were wide, and the interchangeable principle was applied only on a two-dimensional surface without moving parts. Eventually a degree of accuracy was developed which not only improved efficiency but also permitted interchangeability of parts: the stock of spare parts we now take for granted, and the possibility of manufacturing in one

place and assembling in another. These developments depended on uniform standards of measure—agreement about the meaning of dimensions—something handcraftsmen did not have because they did not need it.

Specialization in mass production refers not only to workers but also to machine tools. The ideal machine is designed to carry out a single operation or set of operations on a particular product. And the ideal factory consists of a series of such machines connected to each other, all electronically guided by instructions from a computer which has been programmed by human beings.

The assembly line is the manufacturing device which fully employs duplication, accuracy, interchangeability, and specialization in machines and, to some extent, workers. It is associated with Henry Ford, although Eli Whitney set up an assembly-line system to manufacture guns in the eighteenth century. In the early twentieth century, Ford and other manufacturers realized they could tolerate no hand-fitting because it caused inaccuracy and waste of time. Quality and numbers were sought by eliminating the possibility of human error. Human error could be reduced by making man's contribution as remote as possible from the process of making.

So the germ of the idea embodied in mass production might be summarized as follows: the quality of a product can be improved, its price lowered, and greater numbers produced if component parts are made accurately with specialized tools operated by workers who could not make the whole product alone.

Modern manufacturing operations fall into three distinct phases: plant layout and tooling, duplication of parts, and assembly of duplicated units. These phases follow decisions to manufacture a new product or model—decisions that are guided by capitalization, research, engineering, marketing, and design. It is difficult to generalize about the role of design in research, engineering, and marketing since it varies with the type of industry and the size of an enterprise. But obviously, redesign involves costly retooling operations in the automobile industry, and evidently is a crucial factor in any company's prosperity. The practice of building models following marketing and engineering specifications might more accurately be called "styling" than designing. Styling is a type of design which changes the superficial appearance of a product, often in response to marketing pressures. Its role in product design and some of the ethical and aesthetic questions it raises will be discussed below.

THE EMERGENCE OF INDUSTRIAL DESIGN

One of the consequences of the Industrial Revolution might be called "the replacement of the human hand." Until that time, no basic changes in manufacture had taken place since the Bronze Age; tools were more refined, but principles of operation remained the same.

WOODEN DOOR WITH CARVING IN RE-
LIEF, from Baule, Ivory Coast. Rietberg
Museum, Zurich. Von der Heydt Collection. There is no difference between
the fine and the applied in African
art: utilitarian purpose and expressive
form coexist harmoniously.

TUTANKHAMEN'S THRONE. C. 1350 B.C. Egyptian Museum, Cairo. Sheathed in gold, inlaid with precious stones, and adorned with lions, pictures of the sun, and an attentive queen, the Pharaonic chair had to function as a symbol of the king's divine origins.

CARVED SPOON, from Luzon, The Philippines. 19th century. Bernice P. Bishop Museum, Honolulu. The practical function of a spoon and the commemorative function of an ancestral figure can be successfully combined if the sculptor knows how to adjust their basically abstract forms.

HAND-BLOWN GLASS BOTTLES. Designed
for Blenco Glass Company, Inc., Milton,
West Virginia. Mass production and
quality of craftsmanship need not be
incompatible: it is a matter of identifying the most appropriate roles for designers, craftsmen, and engineers.

BENVENUTO CELLINI. *Saltcellar of Francis
I.* c. 1540. Kunsthistorisches Museum,
Vienna. Craft or fine art? This object
served to pique the taste of an aristocra-
cy accustomed to prodigal displays of the
goldsmith's art and the extravagant alle-
gories of Late Renaissance humanists.

CHARLES EAMES. *Solar Toy (Do Nothing Machine)*. 1957 (destroyed). Designers like Eames have carried us across the threshold separating handcraft from machine technology; they create aesthetic delight out of the typical shapes, materials, and processes associated with mechanization.

Micronesian stool for grating coconuts, from the Mariana Islands. In the folk tradition of handcraft, the analysis of function and the fitting of form to material and mode of making occurs very slowly, often resulting in a unique sense of rightness.

LAWRENCE VAIL.
Bottle with Stopper. 1945.
Collection Mr. and Mrs. Bernard Reis,
New York

UMBERTO BOCCIONI.
Development of a Bottle in Space. 1912.
The Museum of Modern Art, New York.
Aristide Maillol Fund

Two approaches to the bottle: in
neither case is it a container, since
neither artist is concerned with utility. Boccioni dissects the bottle in a
search for its hidden geometry. Vail
projects his fantasies, so that the
bottle becomes a fetish object.

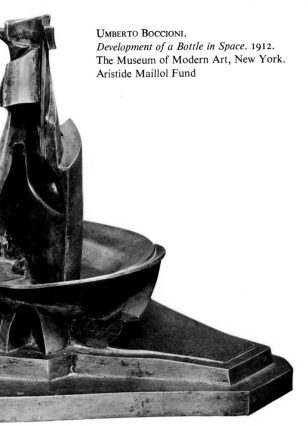

Ford Motor Company assembly line. Early 1900s

used. Craft revivals were attempted, notably by William Morris, who was influenced by John Ruskin; but the artistic problems raised by mass production were not effectively faced until Walter Gropius (1883–1969) established the Bauhaus in the twentieth century.

Gropius realized that the essential difference between craft and machine production was due to a basic difference in the *control* of the process of making: one person in the crafts; a division of labor in industry. He had written a paper, "Industrial Prefabrication of Homes on a Unified Artistic Basis," which recommended mass-production techniques for building and the possibility of achieving high quality through industrial methods. The net result of these ideas was the opening of the Bauhaus at Weimar in 1919, with Gropius as its director. It was formed by the combination of a trade school with a school of fine arts.

At first, each Bauhaus student had two teachers, one an artist and the other a master craftsman, because no instructors could be found who combined the qualities of both. It was necessary to give art students experience with machine production to provide

Pre-industrial manufacture assumes that the craftsman applies skill and imagination to raw materials which, when formed into a finished product, have added value. After the Industrial Revolution, the workman's contribution ceased to be skill and imagination. He offered only labor, which became a commodity like wool, leather, metal, or wood. Machines accomplished the changes from raw material to finished product with results that were uniform and predictable. The craftsman ceased to be an important variable in production; he became an anonymous, constant factor.

The social consequences of the Industrial Revolution were, from a human standpoint, disastrous. Human skill having lost its unique value, work was turned into labor, a commodity. Women and children competed to sell their labor with steadily diminishing bargaining power; workers' wages and living conditions were wretched. The machines which created more real wealth, and also more jobs, paradoxically brought poverty and lowered standards of living for those who tended them.

The sordidness of cities, the wretchedness of the working classes, and the monotony of labor led to a romantic escapism in the arts. Sensitive people could not conceive of art in a context which was so ruinous of human resources. And the early products of mechanization gave little contrary evidence. Machine tools were used to imitate handmade ornament, with results totally unsuited to the materials and processes

German Rose Engine. c. 1750. British Crown Copyright, Science Museum, London. How could the machine tool be humanized? By converting it into "art"—by covering all its surfaces with irrelevant ornament.

MARIANNE BRANDT. Teapot. 1924.
The Museum of Modern Art, New York.
Phyllis B. Lambert Fund

JOHN PRIP. Silver teapot. 1953.
Museum of Contemporary Crafts, New York.
Permanent Collection

An ideological commitment to geometry and the machine is evident in the
Bauhaus-inspired design of 1924. The contemporary craftsman feels free to
express his feelings in organic terms as well.

industry with the integrated control it lacked. Accordingly, the Bauhaus taught science, economics, and craftsmanship as well as the fine-arts curriculum of drawing, composition, painting, sculpture, and art history. In this manner, industrial designers as we know them were first trained.

In 1925 the Bauhaus left the hostile atmosphere of Weimar and reestablished itself at Dessau, where a new faculty, now composed of Bauhaus graduates, combined technician and artist in the same instructor. The school became an experimental workshop in which models for mass production were continually developed and improved. A mechanical idiom or style was created, one which was distinctly different from handcraft styles. Of particular importance, invidious distinctions among painters, sculptors, craftsmen, and architects were substantially abandoned.

In 1933, when the Nazis came to power, the Bauhaus was driven out of Germany and subsequently one of its younger instructors, László Moholy-Nagy, established an American branch in Chicago, where it was absorbed into the Illinois Institute of Technology. By the time of World War II, it was plain that the Bauhaus had created a new profession, industrial design, and permanently influenced the education of artists throughout the world.

FORM AND FUNCTION

It was Louis Sullivan (1856–1924), the teacher of Wright, who originated the phrase "Form follows function." Applied to architecture or manufactured objects, the phrase became an axiom for all modern design. It means that the outer shape and appearance of any object results from its inner operation. The object should look like what it is and does; that is, there should be no deceptive appearance—metal should not imitate wood, plastic should not imitate marble. The design of buildings and useful objects often began with the outer shell or the facade, and then proceeded to divide and arrange interior space. Where the form of an object was functionally determined, ornament was applied to cover its nakedness, so to speak. Thus, architecture and design had become increasingly decorative. Form did *not* follow function: it followed prevailing taste in period styles and decoration.

Industrial design was able to bring common sense to machine-made objects. However, as the practice of design evolved, it became subject to aesthetically irrelevant pressures. Sophisticated and even misleading interpretations of form and function were invoked. Does "function" mean only physical and utilitarian operation? Is only one "form" possible in the solution to a design problem? Doesn't the appearance of an object function by appealing to consumers? If so, the form of an object must enable it to compete commercially with similar products.

Thus, we come to a child of industrial design—styling. Manufacturers discovered in the 1930s that the clean, functional lines of Bauhaus design stimulated sales. Hence, they employed industrial designers to redesign their merchandise. It was a simple step, then, to conclude that periodic redesign would increase saleability *whether or not* changes in physical functioning had taken place. Novelty became as important in saleability as operational factors. A newly styled product had the effect of making older designs seem less valuable. This cycle of design, redesign, and new styling, leading to an apparent loss of

Automobile grilles. Courtesy *Design Quarterly* magazine. During the 1950s, American automobile designers embarked on a monumental "front-end" binge, which they followed with a tailfin orgy. A true example of American Baroque, the phenomenon had an industrial father and a psychological mother: the manufacturer's need for salable packages mated with the stylist's need to express his sculptural impulses.

WILHELM VON DEBSCHITZ. Inkstand. 1906. Württembergisches Landesmuseum, Stuttgart. An impressive but pretentious solution to the design of a useful object: Von Debschitz tried to transcend utility by disguising the function of the object beneath sculptural gestures.

value in older models, has been called *planned obsolescence.*

The quick obsolescence of useful objects has important economic implications. Industries need to use their productive capacity to keep their workers employed. Obviously, workers cannot buy automobiles, refrigerators, and other appliances if they are not earning wages. Hence, persuading the public to use and discard goods rapidly is vital to an expanding economy. Without doubt, planned obsolescence has contributed to the raising of the American standard of living in the course of the effort to use more of the productive capacity of industry.

However, our standard of living may be defined too exclusively in terms of the *number* of useful objects we own and the *frequency* with which we replace them. A country as rich in resources as the United States could afford, until recently, to employ its design skills in the creation of disposable packages and containers, while other societies stressed reusable containers, durable products, and continuity of style (see the Volkswagen, for example). Today, planned obsolescence and disposability haunt us in the form of pollution and ruination of natural resources.

The industrial designer has been inescapably drawn into the world of economics and marketing. His training equips him to analyze a product and to find the best combination of form and materials to suit its function. His knowledge of production methods enables him to keep manufacturing costs to a minimum consistent with quality. He is trained to consider packaging, shipment, and display. Unfortunately, he is often obliged to fabricate a new "skin" for a product—to arrive at a result which is spuriously "different." Perhaps, as commerce and industry grow more complex, the people who serve them will become more strongly professionalized. The competitive forces which gave prominence to industrial design have created the opportunity for ethical designers to prosper. As design professionalism grows, we can expect designers to offer the quality and integrity of service one expects from the best lawyers and surgeons.

INDUSTRIAL DESIGN: THE CHAIR

Until we sit on it, a chair is a work of abstract sculpture. It is also a complex engineering problem. The habit of sitting in chairs, which we take for granted in the Western world, is carried on in many positions, for different purposes, and with a wide variety of apparatus. We expect comfort, support, and stability from our seating equipment. And we like to get into and out of a chair with a certain amount of dignity: some chairs make acrobatic demands of the middle-aged. We want some chairs to be light and portable, others to be sturdy and resist abuse; some will be outdoors and must be weather-resistant. Generally, chairs should not be too bulky; the contemporary home or apartment cannot afford to invest a great deal of space

Constantin Brancusi. *Sculpture for the Blind.* 1924.
Philadelphia Museum of Art.
The Louise and Walter Arensberg Collection

The biomorphic perfection of the egg can be exploited at several design levels: it can yield practical dividends (the Aarnie chair); or it can be enlisted in the service of tactility (the Brancusi sculpture).

Eero Aarnie. Gyro Chair. c. 1965–66.
Distributed by Stendig, Inc., New York

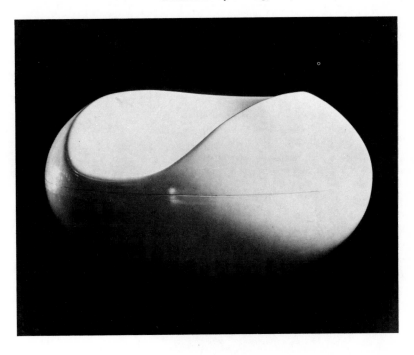

in a chair which approaches comfort by assembling mattresses. As sculpture, chairs possess symbolic value: they can designate the seat of a ruler, the throne of a king or bishop, the inviolable perch on which the master of the house dines, reads his paper, or watches television. Chairs are feminine or masculine, juvenile or adult, shy or assertive. To a crawling child or a kitten, chairs constitute a forest of legs. To a mother of small children, chairs may represent nonwashable surfaces in which margarine and jam become too easily embedded.

A total design philosophy can be revealed in a chair. The attitude of the designer toward comfort, toward the chair as architecture or decoration, toward exposure or concealment of the structural elements is clearly expressed. For example, the famous Barcelona lounge chair by Mies van der Rohe is an eloquent demonstration of his architectural philosophy: less is more; simplicity of materials and form; careful attention to details ("God is in the details"), especially at intersections; absence of ornament; and elegance of proportion. Technological innovation is also evident. The cantilever principle is used in conjunction with the elasticity of metal. The same continuous metal bar serves as curved leg and back support while functioning visually in counterpoint to the metal element it crosses. Finally, the tufted leather cushions offer bulk, warmth, and color in contrast to the thin metal members. The chair is a masterpiece, likely to endure as a classic for many years to come. It is

WENDELL CASTLE. Oak-and-leather chair. 1963. Castle is a contemporary craftsman who chooses to develop the sculptural possibilities of the Thonet furniture of the 1860s, the Art Nouveau swirls of the early 1900s, and the tubular-metal constructions of the 1920s.

GEBRÜDER THONET. Rocking chair. 1860. The Museum of Modern Art, New York. Gift of Café Nicholson

LUDWIG MIES VAN DER ROHE. Barcelona Chair. 1929. The Museum of Modern Art, New York. Gift of Knoll Associates, Inc.

CHARLES EAMES. Lounge chair. 1958. The Museum of Modern Art, New York. Gift of Herman Miller Furniture Company

GUNNAR AAGAARD ANDERSON. Armchair. 1964. The Museum of Modern Art, New York. Gift of the designer. Ostensibly, this chair of poured urethane plastic represents the creative marriage of art and technology. But the object makes no real contribution to chair design: it functions chiefly as a fascinating demonstration of liquid tactility.

LE CORBUSIER. Chaise longue. 1927. The Museum of Modern Art, New York. Gift of Thonet Industries, Inc.

CHARLES EAMES. Chaise longue. 1970. Designed for Herman Miller, Inc., New York

The 1970 chaise by Charles Eames builds on Le Corbusier's architectural solution to the reclining chair (1927). But Eames has new materials to work with: foam-rubber cushions, zippered pillows, and a cast-aluminum frame covered with dark nylon.

all the more remarkable when we consider its date, 1929, and the fact that designers today still specify the Barcelona lounge chair.

Where sturdy, inexpensive, easily stacked and transported seating has been required, especially for public uses, designers have been drawn to molded- and stamped-plastic forms with tubular- or rod-metal legs and supporting elements. Naturally, when cost is a factor, comfort is pursued with molded plastics rather than with more expensive and destructible leather or fabric coverings. A mass market and lowered unit cost are ideas built into the philosophy of modern design. Expensive new models are eventually "adapted" and brought to a large public at low cost. Charles Eames, George Nelson, Henry Dreyfuss, Russel Wright, and Raymond Loewy, among others, brought design of good quality to American consumers at reasonable prices. Ironically, American manufacturers were better able to apply the design

philosophy of the Bauhaus than the manufacturers of Europe, where capitalism, in general, was less creative, more tradition-bound, and, until the Common Market, adjusted mainly to the requirements of national markets.

Today an enormous world market for good design has emerged. Production facilities are widely dispersed. Population increases imply that products do not need to be transported long distances to reach a good market. People in what were remote places have acquired appetites for quality in design. We are entering an era in which the tools of production will be radically transformed, many of them miniaturized, computerized, and electronically linked. Already, good design is crucial for the capture and retention of markets, the conservation of raw materials, the discovery of new human needs, and the employment of human energies to make beauty and utility synonymous.

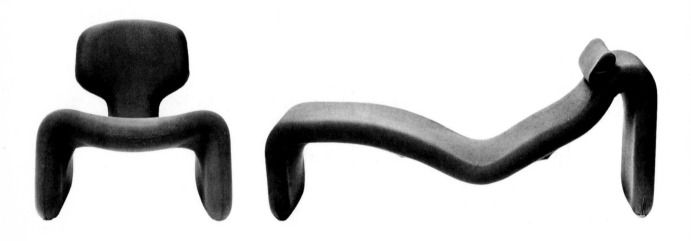

OLIVIER MOURGUE. Chairs. 1965.
The influence of painters Arp and Miró on
contemporary French furniture design.

4

THE IMAGE OF WOMAN IN

MODERN PAINTING

THIS BOOK DEALS INDIRECTLY WITH THE SUBJECT OF women in its picture essays: *Modern Figurative Modes, The Human Image in Modern Painting, The Ancestral Couple* and *Couples in Modern Sculpture*. We also examine various images of women from the standpoint of their social and sexual roles as implied by the work of art itself. In these observations I have tried to confine myself to what could be inferred from the visual image rather than what is known from written documents. Now we shall focus on images specifically devoted to woman and her situation in the world, keeping in mind the fact that style may affect content as much as subject matter.

The representation of woman would be a fascinating subject in the art of this or any period. Today, however, that subject is especially important because of the attention concentrated on the worldwide women's movement for equality of rights and status. In Western societies especially, a considerable literature has grown up on the subject of feminism in general and the struggles of individual women to exercise their economic, legal, and sexual prerogatives. But while we can read about women's wages, occupational opportunities, property rights, control over their children, and so on, this literature does not tell us how women are perceived visually. Written sources inevitably offer us an incomplete picture of women, either as individuals or as representatives of a general type. Painting, however, provides us with an array of images that is rich enough to show us how women are seen from various, often divergent, points of view. Certainly visual representations help complete the picture we get from other sources. So it should be enlightening to look at ideas of woman as expressed through modern painting, if only to compare them with impressions we receive elsewhere.

Quite obviously, the number of images we might discuss is staggering. To narrow the field we shall deal mainly with "modern" images of woman, that is, with works of the last two centuries or so. And we shall look primarily at pictures painted by well-known artists. Thus museums, critics and collectors help us decide which works of art—and by implication, which images of women—have been found significant. The artists represented are male and female, but the artist's sex is not the reason for the selection of a work: we have chosen images that make an important statement and important statements do not care who makes them. Picasso's *Girl Before a Mirror* is a good example. It may be one of the few major representations of womankind which does not declare that it was made to be seen primarily by men. Neither is it addressed exclusively to women. A major point of this work from the standpoint of aesthetics is that artists of either sex are capable of identifying with the other. There are good biological and psychological reasons why this is so.[4] Hence, when we encounter pictures painted by men that deal inauthentically with the realities of women's inner lives, or works by women that deal inauthentically with the inner lives of men, it is not because the artist is of the wrong sex; it is because the work of art is somehow faulty.

One further point: our emphasis on modern images should not be taken as indifference to historical prototypes. Contemporary art often gives us access to ideas about womankind that we mistakenly thought were buried. This is because few modern artists work in ignorance of artistic traditions that are very old. Second, the human imagination seems to carry the memory of exceedingly ancient specimens—archetypes perhaps—of humanity. Third, the living men and women that artists see are by no means cut off from their historical ancestors. That is, while our costumes change along with our occupations and lifestyles, the chemical, biological and social codes that shape our humanity are remarkably stable. For that reason, we can still recognize the womanness of the *Venus of Willendorf* or the *Venus of Lespugue*, remote as these women are in time and condition from their modern counterparts.

Woman's Face and Sexual Dimorphism

The differences between those prehistoric Venuses and modern women give us some idea of how extraordinarily flexible the human body is. Woman's figure, especially, has been molded by numerous forces: religious, economic, geographic, industrial, sartorial—even dietary. At the same time, male-female physical differences have to concern us even though we shall be dealing mainly with women. Such differences testify to the sexually variable effects of history and culture; in addition they obviously affect what the artist sees and represents.

Physical anthropology throws an interesting light on certain contrasts between male and female, especially because of what is called sexual dimorphism, the differences between men and women in body size and shape. These differences or variations probably emerged during the pre-human stage of primate evolution, perhaps after the last Ice Age, when our ancestors took up big game hunting. With males hunting in packs and females remaining behind in camps to gather food and look after infants, a division and specialization of labor developed which resulted in a marked difference in the appearances of the sexes. For our purposes this difference is visible in the form of the figure and especially in the form of the face. Clothing may conceal, minimize or exaggerate bodily differences. But most peoples do not hide the face; so even the subtlest facial differences—between the sexes as well as within the sexes—carry important cultural weight. Artists, of course, are aware of these differences, although they may train themselves to ignore them. The question is: How does physical variation bear on the subject of women's image, which is a matter of anatomy and physiology as well as cultural convention and artistic style?

Without going into the full range of somatic differences between the sexes, we ought to mention those that are visible in the face. Among all the races of mankind there is always some contrast between men and women, although it is more marked among Europeans than Asians, for example. In general, the female face is more regular in form, smoother and more symmetrical: its protuberances and depressions are not as great as in the male. The male face is characterized by a more pronounced chin, brow ridges and nasal and cheekbones. Also, a man's pores are larger than a woman's, giving the skin a rougher surface.[5] And the male beard, if permitted to grow,

Venus of Willendorf. c. 15,000–10,000 B.C. Museum of Natural History, Vienna

changes the shape of the head and its visual proportions as a whole. When the beard is shaved, of course, there are visible differences in facial color and texture.

Now the qualities of smoothness, regularity and symmetry make the female face conform to an egg-shape more than is the case with the male. Indeed, sculptors like Brancusi, Epstein and Arp have been quick to exploit the feminine qualities of the oval—not just its symbolic associations with the egg but also its physical resemblance to the female face. However, that ovoid shape, while it is generally felt to be beautiful, also works against the expression of individuality in female character. After all, eggs look alike, even to a chicken. So it might be said that nature has conspired with culture to homogenize or de-individualize women's faces. Certainly there is abundant evidence that portrait painters and sculptors find it difficult to represent the distinctiveness of female personality. Perhaps that is why one hears so much about the mysteriousness and inscrutability of the female face.[6]

It would seem that female individuality constitutes a special problem for the artist. This difficulty may date back to the Old Stone Age when women were shown as faceless. Even when women's faces *were* represented, a rather standardized formula was used—more so than in the case of men. As late as the Renaissance, a period of marked individualism *among men*, we detect a decided sameness in the faces of the women painted by Leonardo, Botticelli, and Raphael. The problem of expressing female individuality became acute during the Enlightenment of the eighteenth century in France, a period during which women of remarkable social and intellectual gifts presided over salons, grand gatherings of brilliant guests featuring scintillating conversation and exchanges of ideas. If nothing else, the salon revealed very active brains at work behind the oval faces of certain Parisian women, at least—brains whose presence one might not suspect from the rather insipid portraits of aristocratic females painted by Reynolds and Gainsborough in England, or by Boucher and Nattier in France.

Of course painters could not help but notice the great differences among women; and they knew, too, that women could be intelligent or stupid, agile or clumsy, happy or morose. But the conventions of art as well as of society militated against the portrayal of their mental gifts, their psychological moods, their physical variations. In general, women who were rich or important enough to have their portraits painted had to be presented as specimens of an approved type, a type embodying the mainly decorative values of the

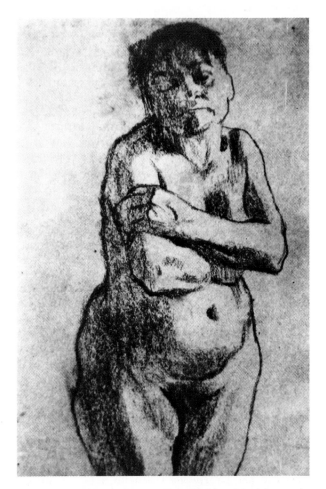

KÄTHE KOLLWITZ. *Nude.* 1905. Zentralinstitut, Munich

female, that is, her freedom from physical defect and her usefulness in displaying costly fabrics and fashionable garments. The essentially aesthetic and economic values of her person were reinforced by poses and outward signs of those womanly traits considered desirable: fragility, piety, bodily restraint, sentimentality toward animals (in England, horses and dogs), lack of curiosity and usually a certain emotional emptiness. As Geraldine Pelles says of the ladies painted by Chassériau and by the Pre-Raphaelites, "they appear . . . actually immobilized by the discrepancy between their bodies and their indifferent heads which seem too weak to will to move the heavy limbs."[7]

Happily, the art of the nineteenth and early twentieth centuries expresses a much wider range of traits and qualities in its representations of women. Perhaps that is because modern artists have an important asset when it comes to the delineation of human personality: the freedom to depart substantially from its physical foundation. In portraying women the modern artist is not necessarily bound to respect the visible evidence of sexual dimorphism—the small size, subtle changes of plane, and generally regular contours of women's features. The legacy of nineteenth-century Romanticism and Symbolism, with their emphasis on the crucial importance of the individual's inner life, gave the twentieth-century artist a license to suppress, distort or exaggerate physical facts in the interest of expressing what were felt to be underlying psychological truths.

Ironically, the perfection of photography in 1839, which was seen as a threat to painting, contributed to the artist's liberation from visual appearances; it freed the painter to explore those psychological realities which are hidden to the eye—or the lens. When depicting a woman's face, therefore, painters often engaged in a kind of artistic over-compensation. Perhaps the smooth quality and even spacing of her features encouraged painters to project their personal or stylistic biases into the representation of woman; increasingly, distortion seemed essential if a woman's individuality were to be visible in her face instead of her clothes. This is not to say that her natural face was seen as an empty slate on which artists could write what they wished. It is rather that woman's face—the object of so many fantasies and desires—was inevitably converted into a mirror expressing the values (and fears) of the artists, predominantly male, who painted it.

The Emergent Person

When does the modern idea of woman arise? Must her real-life type appear before her artistic image? Or is her type a creation of professional image-makers? That whole question—of the priority of images in the shaping of social or psychological reality—needs serious study. Here we can point out that glimmers of modernism appear as early as the seventeenth century in Holland. While Rembrandt is certainly not a modern painter, his depictions of woman seem wholly modern in their freedom from Baroque excitability and the histrionic conventions of seventeenth-century figurative art. Not only does his *Bathsheba* (1654) look like a real person, but he also pays woman the unusual compliment of showing her in the act of thinking, that is, weighing the conflicting claims of marital loyalty and an attractive offer from a powerful man. Perhaps it is an offer she "can't refuse," to use a modern expression. Bathsheba is confronted with a genuine dilemma and Rembrandt handles it as an artist who can read between the lines of the Biblical narrative and see into a woman's mind.

The lithograph, *Nude* (1905), by Käthe Kollwitz offers us a more recent example of the unideal female nude stemming from the tradition established by Rembrandt. Because of her socialist convictions we would expect Kollwitz to portray nakedness in terms of economic deprivation or social injustice. But here the idea of woman has the same roots as the woman by Rembrandt: the Protestant practice of regular, moral self-examination. Superficially, she appears to be shivering; perhaps she is cold. Or maybe she is ashamed of her nakedness: that would place her in the Biblical tradition which shows Eve expelled from Eden and suddenly aware of her guilt. But if we examine the face we can see that Kollwitz has chosen to deal with a profoundly modern dilemma: this woman clasps herself in a deeply moving act of self-acceptance. It is neither an act of surrender, as in Albright's *Ida*, nor a declaration of erotic satisfaction, as in Modigliani's sad young bohemians. Kollwitz chooses to make a radical statement about an older woman's body, a statement that DeKooning misses in his rage. She discusses a subject that modern culture passes over as uninteresting, namely, that the human possibilities of woman's body and person are not exhausted in her forties.

It would appear that Isabel Bishop's *Nude* (1934) is also the beneficiary of Rembrandt's portrayal of woman as capable of serious moral reflection. As a twentieth-century painter Ms. Bishop tends to see her subject in a psychological rather than a religious light; nevertheless, in common with Rembrandt she investigates the interaction between a woman's body and mind. To be sure, Bishop's woman seems especially wrapped up in examining her toes; she carries the personal grooming situation to a physically awkward, indeed an acrobatic, extreme: this is the sort of pose that would have pleased the misogynist Degas. But Isabel Bishop, like Rembrandt, uses the awkward pose to tell us something else: she shows us an obviously thoughtful person who is real to herself and therefore to us; her figure is not set up for exhibit. The work implies that a healthy, serviceable body in a female is not inconsistent with a complete mental life.

Francisco Goya (1746–1828), so modern in visual approach and intellectual outlook, was an admirer of women in the *macho* tradition. That is, while his *majas* were in reality tough, streetwise, independent and sexually self-assured women, he tended to see them through Rococo eyes: so they are presented as coquettes with a Spanish intensity substituting for French chic. His *Maja Nude* (1800), with her small hands and feet, narrow waist, wide-spaced breasts and sidelong glance at the viewer, is displayed so as to inflame a man. When Manet took up the same theme in his *Olympia* (1863) the Rococo element of flirtatiousness had completely disappeared. Her hands and feet are actual size and her waist is a bit thick; her breasts are correctly formed rather than artificially lifted and turned outward. But compare the faces! The *maja's* smoldering look has been replaced by an appraising stare. In a psychological sense it is the viewer who is undressed.

Notwithstanding the candor of *Olympia*—her shamelessness, as French viewers felt—she remains to some extent an object held up for inspection. And she is aware of being seen. Degas, on the other hand, may have been the first major painter to represent women as they actually looked when not on display. More than that, he deliberately chose to show them in ungainly poses, carrying out prosaic tasks, and, if possible, unaware of being watched. His objective was twofold: to break down the classical conventions of female beauty and grace, conventions that could be traced back to the dawn of Mediterranean art. Secondly, Degas wanted to crack certain myths about the essential loveliness of woman as a creature.[8] No lady looks good scratching her back or rubbing an aching ankle, yet these were the activities Degas chose when representing ballet dancers and bathers—not so when he painted men, however. Degas' strategy had twin motivations: on the one hand he had a low opinion of women; on the other he had a fanatical dedication to visual truth. For a nineteenth-century painter to express himself truthfully it was first necessary to destroy the old pictorial conventions. Those conventions placed women on a pedestal, literally and figuratively. In knocking down that pedestal Degas caused a certain amount of distress to the ladies who were accustomed to plant themselves on it. And he disappointed the men who rather enjoyed seeing them there. However, whether for the right or wrong reasons, Degas may have done everyone a service in the long run.

The women of Mary Cassatt (1845–1926), Degas' student and friend, are modern only in that they are natural; she portrays them without much attention to the artificialities of makeup, clothes, or pose. As for status, one quickly senses they belong to Henry James' and Edith Wharton's American patrician class. Possibly because of her association with Degas, she employed a technique and a palette that was very similar to his; but she lacked his mordant bite. If we compare her *La Toilette* (1886) to a Degas woman stepping out of a bath it is clear that almost identical kinds of drawing, color and brushwork are being directed to opposite ends. For Degas, intimate situations provide the opportunity to show that women, if you see them truly, are very like cats: they scratch their backs, scrub their bodies, towel their wet skin, and brush their hair like felines licking their coats or stretching their limbs after a nap. Cassatt, a proper daughter of Philadelphia's upper crust, uses the informal toilette situation to celebrate the healthy pink complexions and fresh wetness of babies and young girls after a bath; but she is far from seeing any qualities of animal grace in their bodies. The skin she paints is kissable, like a baby's bottom, and delightful to hold, like the infant in Raphael's *Sistine Madonna*. But Cassatt makes no connection between the sensuous and the erotic. Her achievement is similar to that of the medieval painters of the Blessed Virgin: they painted a delectable creature who was both mother and maiden at the same time—immensely appealing but without a hint of carnality. It was not until Nabokov's invention of the nymphet Lolita,[9] that certain dimensions of this great mystery were revealed to the literary mind. In visual art it is apparent in *The Golden Days* how Balthus created, indeed anticipated, the Lolita type. It is interesting that in both cases it was necessary for such girlish "wickedness" to be recognized by European eyes.

The Identity Dilemma

Woman may always have been a mystery to men. The modern woman, however, is seen as a problem, not only for men but for other women and for herself. But there is no mystery about the source of what seems so problematic: it is the changing function and status of woman today. We realize she is no longer a chattel, permanent domestic worker, perpetual child-bearer, lifetime partner of one man, adored child-wife, or pampered creature of leisure; still, she has not quite arrived as a full-time and wholly integrated member of the "outside" world of work. Her role is ambiguous: it has been shifting continuously since the eighteenth-century Industrial Revolution. In the United States especially, the changes in woman's status following World War I have been swift and profound. Understandably, these changes have fostered a certain amount of anxiety. Much of what appears to be male hostility in the face of these changes is due to plain frustration, the product of his inability to solve the feminine enigma, to see what is permanent and predictable about the various women in his life. A peculiar sort of restlessness affects every female he has known: mother, sister, wife, daughter, mistress. Furthermore, her dilemmas are his, too. And with woman joining the work force, he can no longer escape to the office, factory or shop.

In trying to deal with the confusion about women's changing social roles, men have been tempted to offer global explanations of what is happening. It is nat-ural, when living within a problem, to fashion theories and deliver opinions as if they were ultimate truths. But obviously, none of us—husbands, wives, lovers, artists or critics—has perfect knowledge in these matters. Still, it is interesting to notice how the force of our convictions varies directly with the degree of our perplexity. So it may not be surprising that one of the most troubled of modern artists, Edvard Munch (1863–1944), laid down what seemed to him, at the turn of the century, a kind of *law* of woman's psychosexual development.

In *The Dance of Life* (1899–1900) Munch advances a rather schematic version of the three stages in the evolution of woman's psyche: first there is the dreamy, idealistic girl, virginal and reaching out toward life as symbolized by a blossoming flower; then comes physical passion, total involvement with man, who is both lover and victim; finally there is woman as widow—bitter, disapproving, asexual. In the background of the painting Munch paints the moon or midnight sun presiding over a group of gyrating dancers like a stern God who has ordained that woman's innocent hopes will be followed by sexual rapture; this state to be followed by guilty knowledge, remorse, shriveling of the flesh, and finally, coldness and death.

Now it would not be difficult to dissect Munch clinically, to explain the morbidity induced by his work in terms of Norway's short summers, the brief appearance of the sun followed by those long, gloomy winter nights. But that would reduce his painting to a local, purely Nordic version of the opposition between nature and culture. Or his picture may be interpreted as an eccentric notion of the Biblical creation myth. For our purposes, however, it presents a view of woman that transcends its personal and national origins. To be sure, Munch delved deeply into his own unconscious and courageously examined his fears, some of which may seem to us exaggerated, as in a delirium. Still, he returns from his bad dream with a set of female images that occupies a place in the consciousness of people who live as far away from Norway as India.

A major theme of Munch's painting, expressed especially in the rigid posture and cadaverous face of the male dancer in the center,[10] is that woman's sexuality is destructive: she slays man in the act of love. We know this is true of certain insects. But here we see that idea employed to explain the complexity of male-female relationships in human culture: woman's embrace is a kind of smothering; her love leads to asphyxiation. According to this view, man tries to withhold himself from woman even in their sexual encounters; he fails, however, because of her irresistible power as temptress. So the male tries to escape her entrapment by spiritual withdrawal. In this way he thinks he can save his soul as well as achieve psychological dominion over her. It is a psychosexual strategy based on the metaphor of woman as a kind of vampire: she drains men biologically,

PAUL CÉZANNE. *Woman with a Coffee Pot*. 1890–94.
The Louvre, Paris

leaving them half dead. So the war between the sexes is more than an angry exchange of words, or a disagreement about petty domestic problems. At first it seems to be a battle over whose priorities will govern family life; but ultimately it is a struggle to determine who will live and who will die.

CÉZANNE, PICASSO AND MATISSE

Cézanne's awkwardness, or anxiety,[11] with respect to the unclothed female figure will be discussed below. Here we should mention the effect of his formal legacy upon the contemporary image of woman. It is understandable that an intelligent nineteenth-century painter would react against the barely concealed prurience of Cabanel, Gérôme, or Bouguereau, a master of what Pelles calls "slickly contrived, pseudo-chaste, photographically explicit nudes...."[12] Gérôme's *Roman Slave Market* (1884) is typical of the genre. On the other hand, Cézanne's *Woman with a Coffee Pot* (1890–94) constitutes a different kind of dehumanization. To be sure, his proto-Cubist style can be seen as an attempt to rationalize form, to drain it of sentimentality and make it suit-

able for the architectonic construction of pictures. But it can also be argued that this treatment of figurative forms does more violence to woman's image than man's. That is, an art dedicated to overlapping and intersecting planes may produce images that mutilate or harden the forms we associate with life and love.

Still, it is interesting that Picasso, who often constructed female figures with straight lines and flat planes, managed to express a feminine idea even within the austerities of a fully Cubist vocabulary. Why does his *Woman Weeping* (1937) succeed where Cézanne's does not? It will not do to say that Cézanne was indifferent to the womanly qualities of Madame Cézanne, or his housekeeper, or the other female models he saw. For one thing, when he painted men—as in his *Card Players*—the masculine qualities came through loud and clear. In addition, Cézanne was a better orchestrator of color and plastic volumes than Picasso; his control of paint as a sensuous substance reached a level far above anything we see in Picasso. We have to conclude that the significant difference revolves around the outlook and psychology of each artist: Picasso was capable of identifying with the inner life of his subject; that is, he could feel, hence see, the process of releasing a wet flow of tears. Cézanne could not. It would appear that he feared moisture, wetness, the female element.

The case of Matisse is entirely different. Ardently devoted to woman's person, and determined to record his visual sensations with the full force of their initial impact, he reconciled these two interests—woman and color—by integrating them in elegant ornamental motifs. Where Cézanne converted woman into an assemblage of neutered planes, Matisse changed her into a gorgeous arabesque.

Matisse was our most sophisticated painter of woman as decorative object. His art quite deliberately reduced her to a kind of lay figure, covered with brightly printed fabrics, glimpsed through a pattern of wrought iron on a balcony window, and posed in a manner emphasizing her belonging to a room and its furnishings. Now his men may be painted the same way, except that he paints them very rarely. Which is to say that he likes women, provided they are seen in a special way. The choice of woman as motif, and her essentially ornamental function—the erotic element is suggested obliquely—points to a remarkable achievement of high European art: woman is almost completely divested of her traditional attributes and functions; the residue of warm and sensuous meaning that people associate with her person is transferred first to the room or space in which we see her, and ultimately to the plane of the picture itself. The viewer is encouraged to assign his feelings about woman to a specialized kind of commodity—an oil painting that is more valuable than anyone or anything it represents. Its value depends on the soothing effect it creates, its ability to convert human reality into areas of pleasing color that make optical rather than emotional demands.

PABLO PICASSO. *Woman Weeping.* 1937.
Penrose Collection, London

WOMAN AND WORK

We cannot deal at any length with the vexing problems of woman's work, woman as worker, and woman as artist.[13] Obviously, they are closely connected. So far as any discussion of woman-as-artist is concerned, it should begin, I believe, with a thorough exploration of her various careers: from food gatherer to temple prostitute, from midwife to hospital nurse, from potter and spinner to garment worker and shipyard riveter. I stress woman's many jobs because art appears as a type of making and doing before it turns into a specialized way of seeing or thinking. Better stated, specialized ways of seeing and thinking emerge from long, well-established kinds of workmanship. Although any distinctively sexual features in the outlook of woman-as-artist would have to be attributed to unique features of her consciousness, that consciousness has certainly been influenced by the tasks that women have traditionally performed.[14] And they bring that experience to the work they do today. What I am saying is that we have to look at images of women working, at women as themselves shaped by work, in order to understand them as creative persons.

The contemporary image of woman as a worker has nineteenth-century roots in the art of such painters

as Millet, *The Bleaching Tub* (1861), Daumier, *The Laundress* (1863), and Degas, *Two Laundresses* (1884). Picasso took up the theme early in the twentieth century with his *Woman Ironing* (1904). The differences in approach are instructive: Millet never sentimentalized working people—male or female—despite *The Angelus* (1858) and saccharine imitators, such as Jules Breton. He had the same background as the young peasant, and physical labor for him, whether in the household or in the fields, was hardly a curse. Digging and shoveling, lifting and carrying, was as normal for women as for men on a French farm. So Millet's laundress goes about her task energetically; and if she is not overjoyed about her job neither is she miserable. What Millet's workers convey is competence. Daumier, too, shows a working woman and her child without grieving for her. But he paints her concern more than her actual labor. The life of a laundress may be difficult but it is not demeaning; in fact, it yields a certain dignity since work enables her to take care of her youngster. Degas' ironers are the most realistically represented of all—at least from an optical standpoint. Typically, he has caught one of them with her elbow awkwardly raised and a hand on her sprinkling bottle, as if she were reaching for a drink; she might as well be yawning and belching in a local bistro. The monotonous work of the nineteenth-century drudge had no ideological significance for Degas; this scene is simply another occasion to exercise his extraordinary powers of observation. With Picasso's ironer, however, a different note is struck: the woman is obviously worn out; her gaunt face and bony frame express fatigue, perhaps hunger, and a kind of poetic melancholy at the same time. We also have in this painting a fairly early anticipation of the view, sometimes held in feminist circles, that household work is the lowest form of drudgery—at least for a sensitive person. Picasso's painting asks us to think of domestic toil as incompatible with the noblest activities of the human spirit. The idea is as old as Plato: Athenian aristocrats of his day were convinced that menial labor denies one the opportunity for leisurely contemplation, thus preventing the development of the higher faculties. So that sort of work was reserved for slaves. Wellborn women, of course, had servants to perform dirty, repetitive, time-consuming household tasks. Even so, it was not really believed that females—whether slaves or free—could benefit mentally from leisure. Hence woman's freedom from toil in classical cultures was a sign of social status rather than intellectual opportunity. But there is also in Picasso's painting the suggestion of a new idea about woman's work, namely that poverty, fatigue and desperation produce a distinctive personal and visual quality: a kind of starved elegance. In fact, this woman's emaciation is not without a certain erotic appeal; it reminds us of the cadaverous glamour of the models in *Vogue* and *Harper's Bazaar*. Perhaps it was from Picasso's Blue Period that Cecil Beaton, Richard Avedon and slick magazine photographers

JEAN FRANÇOIS MILLET. *The Bleaching Tub*. 1861.
The Louvre, Paris

HONORÉ DAUMIER. *The Laundress*. c. 1863.
The Louvre, Paris

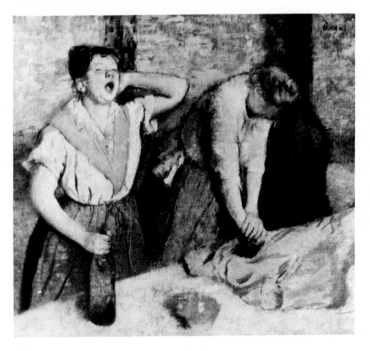

EDGAR DEGAS. *Two Laundresses*. c. 1884.
The Louvre, Paris

PABLO PICASSO. *Woman Ironing*. 1904.
The Solomon R. Guggenheim Museum, New York.
The Thannhauser Foundation

REMBRANDT VAN RIJN. *Bathsheba*. 1654.
The Louvre, Paris

ISABEL BISHOP. *Nude*. 1934.
Whitney Museum of
American Art, New York

Woman's flesh: many painters
can render its voluptuous
possibilities; only a few see it
as an arena of conflicting needs
and desires.

FRANCISCO GOYA. *Maja Nude.* 1800. The Prado, Madrid

EDOUARD MANET. *Olympia.* 1863. The Louvre, Paris

Sexual emancipation probably began with courtesans. These women are anything but toys.

EDGAR DEGAS. *Two Laundresses.* c. 1884.
The Louvre, Paris

HENRI DE TOULOUSE-LAUTREC.
Deux Amies. 1894. The Tate Gallery,
London

Working women: Degas shows them as
bored and boring; Lautrec has discovered their refuge in each other.

PAUL CÉZANNE. *Woman with a Coffee Pot.* 1890–94. The Louvre, Paris

Unable to deal with a woman's human qualities, Cézanne converts her into a magnificent monument. Is it possible that the triumphs of modern painting are founded on his fear of tenderness?

EDVARD MUNCH. *The Dance of Life.* 1899–1900. National Gallery, Oslo

EMIL NOLDE. *Dancing Around the Golden Calf.* 1910. Stiftung Seebüll Ada und Emil Nolde, Neukirchen über Niebüll

The Teutonic version of an exceedingly ancient prejudice: when man and society are lost in sin, it is woman's fault.

MARC CHAGALL. *Her World.* 1945.
Musée National d'Art Moderne,
Centre Pompidou, Paris

From the romantic reverie of the bride
to the grim reality of everyday mother-
hood. But these are stereotypes: brides
are not that naive and mothers *do* have
fun.

MARISOL. *The Family.* 1962.
The Museum of Modern Art, New York.
Advisory Committee Fund, 1962

AUDREY FLACK. *Golden Girl.* 1979. Collection Mr. and Mrs. Walner, Illinois

WAYNE THIEBAUD. *Girl with Ice Cream Cone.* 1963.
Collection Mr. and Mrs. E. A. Bergman, Chicago

ROY LICHTENSTEIN. *Blonde Waiting.* 1964.
Collection Mr. and Mrs. Richard L. Weisman, New York

Essays on the myth of the dumb blonde (or brunette). At a deeper level these works are engaged in
a continuing symbolic struggle: to topple woman, or to restore her to a pedestal . . . of sorts.

PAULA MODERSOHN-BECKER. *Self-Portrait*. 1906. Kunstmuseum, Basel

The autonomous woman. A female intellectual makes a sexual advance . . . tentatively. This is a courageous move; hence we see boldness and hesitation in the same image.

ISAAC SOYER. *Employment Agency.* 1937. Whitney Museum of American Art, New York

by the score discovered the wan, ethereal type of female. Of course one could cite the somewhat tubercular heroines of Dante Gabriel Rossetti, or of Aubrey Beardsley and the Decadents at the turn of the century. Perhaps it is because of these images that our high-fashion models fast until they are reduced to little more than skin and bones. Oscar Wilde was right: nature *does* imitate art.

In our discussion of Ivan Albright's *Ida* we will emphasize his technique, his accumulation of detail to suggest the passage of time and the aging of the flesh. But *Ida* can be seen as a victim of work as well as the passing years. The breakdown of her body leads to the failure of hope; it may be the result of what engineers call "materials fatigue." Of course, Albright portrays the fatigue of the spirit as well as the flesh: *Ida* is a working-class woman who has been used up in every way. Her legs and thighs tell a sad story: poor circulation, varicose veins, a sickly skin. She is caught in the woman's predicament of the 1930s: how to put long hours into a job—a job that keeps her on her feet all day—and yet look as fresh as a woman of leisure. We must remember that between

the two World Wars women who worked, whether in office, shop or factory, were regarded as unfortunate. The fact that many housewives worked harder made no difference: work for wages outside the home (except for school teachers and, perhaps, nurses) represented a loss of status from a middle-class standpoint. Besides, the woman who took outside work still had her own housework to do. It was an almost impossible situation: that is what *Ida* realizes. Albright painted her realization of this dilemma as much as the collapse of her tissues.

The black woman in Isaac Soyer's *Employment Agency* was painted in 1937 but there is no reason to believe that her plight has changed much today. The theme here is work for women, not woman's work. Still, what kind of job can she get? In agrarian or handcraft economies woman's work was arduous and repetitive, but there was always enough of it to go around. However, the need for labor in industrial and commercial economies fluctuates widely; and female workers are especially vulnerable during the downward phase of a business cycle. According to psychologists, men identify with their occupations more-than women. So it was believed that women were less damaged psychologically by being out of work. But that may be changing. At any rate, Soyer's painting seems to regard the trauma of unemployment as the same for men *and* women. Perhaps there is a racial factor at work: Black women have had to work because their men are more frequently unemployed. But whatever its social or economic implications, Soyer's image of a woman out of work—wholly unencumbered by ideology—is an exceptionally moving tribute to her human dignity. It is significant, I believe, that he shows her primarily as a person, not as a statistic, a sociological token, or a standardized racial type.

THE CHILD-WOMAN

When Ibsen wrote *A Doll's House* (1879) he recognized the tragic potential in a very old notion about the incompleteness of woman's mental and emotional development. The notion is false, but it persists in art because we are reluctant to see little girls grow up. In addition, certain kinds of men require it. We have to mention Renoir in this connection even though he could be an excellent painter of mature women, as in *The Box at the Theater* (1874). Still, this

PIERRE AUGUSTE RENOIR. *The Box at the Theater.* 1874.
The Courtauld Institute of Art, London. Courtesy of the Home House Trustees

was a fashionable portrait made to advance his career more than to express his convictions. When he wanted to paint woman for the ages, woman as man sees her in his fondest dreams, she turns out to be a mindless creature with a fleshy Titianesque torso supporting the head and face of a twelve-year-old. Two centuries earlier, Rubens had shown his devotion to the same juvenile type, although the faces of his women look slightly older—seventeen perhaps. It is this female type, incidentally, which the Pop artists, Wayne Thiebaud and Mel Ramos, lifted from advertising art and exploited so cleverly as a symbol of desirable young womanhood.

Child-women actually exist, to be sure, in the drum majorette, the beauty contest winner, and in the squads of cheerleaders who exhort professional football teams on to victory. They greet us from most magazine covers (including the porno magazines) and they constitute the basic type on which Hollywood builds its indistinguishable variations. What we see, in the amazing continuity from Titian to Rubens, Renoir, Thiebaud and Ramos, is the progressive transformation of an ancient type: the hunting and fertility goddess, the great mother of the Stone and Metal Ages, now divested of her fearsome aspect and turned into a sexy little girl. Men still worship this creature because she inspires them to great exertions. Such girls hold out to men the hope of remaining ever young and virile; they promise sexual bliss to those who try the hardest.

Any discussion of the childlike image of woman would be incomplete without mentioning Chagall. He is our supreme poet of woman as perpetually naive. She grows up, but only on the outside. The main purpose of growing up is to recall the sweet fantasies of young girlhood. At first glance, *Her World* (1945) seems to fit the pattern of masculine patronizing, of describing woman's inner life as completely wrapped up in nostalgia and sentimental fictions. But Chagall also shows that her world is his world; both of them live in the same enchanted reverie. Both hearts are warmed by the same red-haired angel, the same candle-bearing dove, the same scene of a moonlit village and the same memory of standing together under a bridal bower. The secret of Chagall's unique appeal is that he was able to gain access to the imagination of little girls. Furthermore, he managed to persuade grown women that the little girl's world—the world that exists before the intrusion of coarse men and insistent sex—could remain alive well into middle age.

The modern child-woman—the one who sells the most merchandise, who appears most frequently in print media, films and television—is portrayed with almost painful candor in Wayne Thiebaud's *Girl with Ice Cream Cone* (1963). He shows us a grown-up "baby doll," a woman who has literally become a child-adult, no small feat when we consider the social forces that try to make people grow up. Physically mature, she knows how to look girlishly petulant; someone has given her an ice cream cone to stop her from crying. Significantly, the girl-and-ice cream-cone image serves here as a symbol not unlike the girl and double ice cream cone in Picasso's *Fishing at Night off Antibes*. In both cases we see a well-endowed child-woman who does not know (or pretends not to know) what is going on.

The fact that Chagall shares his wife's girlish fantasies testifies to an exceptional love and devotion. Perhaps it is the sincerest kind of love a man can give to a woman. Still, it is predicated on the assumption that her happiness would be destroyed if she were allowed to emerge from the chrysalis of childhood. Picasso's bike-rider at Antibes approaches the same idea from another angle: while men are engaged in real action, women are spectators—and uncomprehending spectators at that. But Thiebaud's child-woman gives the game away: the purpose of modern culture is to breed a new type of earth mother—sexy but not crafty, always desirable but not really capable of thinking things through.

SOLITARY WOMAN

Woman's aloneness—because she chooses to live alone, because she is not surrounded by children, because many of her social ties have been broken—is an essentially modern theme. We do not sufficiently appreciate the fact that until recently women were rarely alone unless they were sick, abandoned, or praying. Even a saint undergoing her martyrdom was likely to be shown surrounded by humanity. Real physical separateness for any length of time was, for a woman, exceptional—the privilege of a few well-born ladies. If an artist painted a woman by herself, he was sure to include the accessories and possessions that would indicate her social situation. Normally, she would have only limited opportunities to enjoy solitude, if only because a truly private existence assumed free time and personal space that few women had. Moreover, the contemplative life presupposed mental gifts that most women were not believed to possess.

The inner life of woman is more commonly treated in literature than art. Perhaps that is because her thoughts and feelings can more conveniently be written down in private. The logistics and physical facilities for practicing an art—say, painting, sculpture or printmaking—are not easily arranged in the typical household.[15] But literary space is readily used as a substitute for personal space. And as far as the public is concerned, it is easier to read what a woman thinks when she is alone than to see what she looks like in her solitude. A few painters, however, have taken up the theme of woman in isolation. It is not a simple task: the conventions of art favor the presentation of individuals in social contexts. Even the persons represented in portraits are meant to be seen and judged in public situations; so it is the external self that is displayed. But there are exceptions.

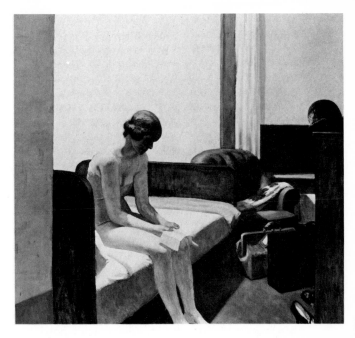

EDWARD HOPPER. *Hotel Room.* 1931. Whereabouts unknown

Among American painters, Edward Hopper is perhaps our best poet of loneliness—not only of people, but of streets, rooms, furniture, houses, gas stations. We have already mentioned his unusual capacity to render the isolation and forlornness of a building, as in *House by the Railroad*. He transfers these qualities to couples, too, and they are especially visible in his women, as in *Hotel Room* (1931). Here we see a woman in a cheerless room in a cheap hotel, a room she shares with her husband (notice the masculine luggage); but we have the strong impression that she is tragically alone, psychologically abandoned. She looks as if she has been deposited like the shoes, clothes, suitcases and other articles in the room. Sitting on the side of the bed, with an open book she is not especially interested in reading, this woman is just waiting, killing time. We can tell from her posture— the drooping shoulders and the rather submissive position of her head—that she has nothing important or exciting to wait for. Hopper's version of female loneliness goes beyond physical isolation: what he really paints is spiritual resignation, a woman's acceptance of days, weeks, years of sheer, drear, boredom.

Following the rise of abstract and nonobjective painting in the United States, especially after World War II, it became fashionable to deride pictures with social or psychological themes; artistic studies of anguish and anxiety seemed more appropriate to the Depression years. And it is true that the nervous, pensive or brooding young women painted by Raphael Soyer—*Woman Biting Her Nails* (1972), for example— made no contribution to post-Cubist analyses of space; they offered nothing new in the realm of pictorial organization. But why were we indifferent to Soyer's human message? Perhaps because Americans had become exceedingly prosperous, and while their emotional lives were sufficiently troubled to keep battalions of psychiatrists busy, they were not especially interested in looking at pictures of unhappy working-class girls. The sophisticated viewer already knew what these girls were thinking about: their worries and concerns bored the knowledgeable art lover. Who cares, really, if the girl in *The Brown Sweater* (1952) wishes she had a few dollars to buy a new dress?

Nevertheless, Soyer continued to paint these shy creatures. Instead of the drama of intersecting planes, or of brushwork moving at sixty miles an hour, he concentrated on the drama of a woman's indecision, of her solitude, of her wanting what she cannot have. Of course, such paintings—and the women they represent—make emotional demands simply by the way they look. And that is what some viewers resented. It must be admitted, too, that certain kinds of men want to be released from womanly appeals. Soyer's girls enlist our sympathies in a way that Cézanne's women (or trees or apples) do not. It takes a certain maturity, however, to realize that it is emotionally possible to appreciate Cézanne's apples without feeling obliged to deride Soyer's depictions of female loneliness.

In moving from the worlds of Soyer and Hopper to the world of Alexander Colville (born 1920) we encounter a totally different emotional climate. To be

RAPHAEL SOYER. *The Brown Sweater.* 1952.
Whitney Museum of American Art, New York. Purchase

sure, in *The River Thames* (1974), Colville deals with a solitary woman, but it is apparent from her stance that aloneness for her is not an affliction. Clear-eyed and alert, she calmly contemplates the mirror of the river, her weight evenly distributed on both feet; she stands as straight as a regimental guard. We sense that the body inside the coat (fashionable but not too chic) is erect without being rigid. The comprehensive image is one of perfect mental control. Colville has set her amid essentially male structures: the powerfully thrusting bridge and the businesslike buildings on the river bank. The implication is that she can cope. Indeed, she surveys the situation as if to command it—her hand might be an emperor's, resting on an orb of the world. Even her umbrella is superbly poised.

What can the river, the bridge and London's ancient buildings mean to a solitary young woman? In this case, it means they are hers. She owns the city in the sense that confident seeing confers a peculiar sort of property right. She takes it in as a place and an image. And that image includes her single self, standing up to the place.

BAD WOMEN

The history of art is replete with idealized portraits of women—superb specimens without physical flaws

RAPHAEL SOYER. *Woman Biting Her Nails.* 1972.
Collection the artist

and untainted from a moral point of view. Many art museums specialize in images of saintly females, ideal as wives and mothers and perfect as vessels of goodness and love. Of course, these images are difficult for real women to live with. But they serve a purpose: on the one hand, they represent models women can strive to emulate; on the other, they represent a kind of reproach, a permanent visual reminder of what actual women have failed to become. Men may enjoy such images; as for women, they are expected to try harder.

Apart from their pictures of goddesses and saints, museums usually conserve the proud tradition of the idealized nude. This pictorial type serves at least two functions: first she reminds men of their sexual mastery; second, she testifies to the value—the commodity value—of what men have been able to master and possess. But there is also a counter-tradition: as women become individualized, as they are seen to have an existence over and above the sexual and reproductive, the tradition of the female nude changes: it is associated with "bad" women, prostitutes mainly. Or it is academicized, that is, drained of human individuality and reproduced monotonously according to a standard formula. Today that formularized nude, or semi-nude, performs a specialized role in attracting male attention: it serves as a stimulus for merchandis-ing goods. From that commercial use it is but a short step for the nude to go underground to become the central motif of pornographic art.[16]

The counter-tradition of female imagery, the tradition that emphasizes woman's intimate association with corruption and vice, is especially strong in German Expressionism, although we can see it in a Frenchman—Rouault; a Belgian—Ensor; and a Russian Jew—Soutine. Among the Germans, Emile Nolde (1867–1956) is especially important because his art, like that of Rouault, grows out of strongly held religious convictions (now Protestant rather than Catholic) and an impassioned search for the primitive roots of human nature. The result, as in *Dancing Round the Golden Calf* (1910), is a consistent portrayal of woman in terms of Biblical disgust. Her body may be shown in wild, contorted positions but it is her smiling face that reveals Nolde's fundamental position: woman's smile is a terrible trap. It is precisely when she is most endearing that she is most dangerous[17]— dangerous, that is, to man's spiritual health.

If we move from Nolde's frenzied, hysterically painted females to those of Toulouse-Lautrec, we witness a change that is positively benign. To be sure, he depicts "fallen" women candidly, but without Munch's fear or Nolde's hatred. Lautrec's *Deux Amies*

ALEXANDER COLVILLE.
The River Thames. 1974.
Collection J. H. Clark,
North Bay, Canada

GEORGES ROUAULT. *Prostitute*. c. 1924–27.
The Museum of Modern Art, New York.
Gift of Abby Aldrich Rockefeller

HENRI DE TOULOUSE-LAUTREC. *Deux Amies*. 1894.
The Tate Gallery, London

(1894) has a clearly ironical title: the girls are indeed friends; they are also prostitutes and quite possibly, lesbians. At any rate, we can take it that their friendship is somehow special. Lautrec shared with Degas a fascination with brothel scenes and a determination to represent sordidness exactly as he saw it; both artists were superb draftsmen who made it a point of honor never to flinch at facts. But unlike Degas, Lautrec found something strangely endearing in these pathetic creatures: their complexions are pasty white; rouge fails to conceal the pouches in their skin; lamplight is unfriendly and daylight is a disaster. These women are expected to give love without receiving it; they are obviously much used. So what is left for them? They have a few friends.

Compared to Lautrec's "Friends," Rouault's prostitutes are utterly without redeeming qualities. There probably were and are such women in the brothels of Paris, but that is not the point. These women have been denuded of their humanity. Or, better stated, their grossness and obesity are signs of what humanity can become when it is wholly dedicated to sin. Rouault uses the physical condition of such women to make a moral statement: this is what the Godless soul actually looks like; they are so far gone that only Christ can save them. Now it is interesting that Degas

and Rouault (again Lautrec is an exception) portray depraved women, but not their depraved patrons. Is this another case of nineteenth-century male chauvinism? Only in part. Rowlandson and Hogarth—men of the eighteenth century, to be sure—represented male depravity with considerable candor, although they employed more humor and less righteousness than Rouault. But why do artists in general choose women instead of men to illustrate the unredeemed condition of humanity? The underlying reason can be traced back to the roots of our religions: the Western imagination has been nourished for almost three thousand years on accounts of the vilest human behavior, loathsome practices originating in late Neolithic fertility rites over which women presided. Subconsciously, men retain the memory of those old cult goddesses. It is a mixed memory in which high excitement is combined with guilt and fear. The artist, it would seem, cannot help reminding us of those glamorous temple prostitutes: their images stimulate him enormously. The rest of us are drawn to them, almost involuntarily. And we hate them, too.

Willem de Kooning's *Woman* series may be the ultimate expression of our female-hatred. Certainly it is more than a demonstration of what happens when a slashing abstract style encounters the conventions of

European academic figure painting. In important respects De Kooning builds on the European tradition of figurative art, from Rubens to Courbet to Picasso. But what is significant from our standpoint is his consistent use of the image of a somewhat matronly woman to embody everything that is repellent about Americans and their culture as a whole. De Kooning expresses his social criticism through quintessentially female forms—the breasts, bellies and thighs of those Paleolithic mothers first revealed to us in the *Venus of Willendorf*. We realize, of course, that ancient fertility associations can be used by modern advertising to sell anything from bicycles to chewing gum. And some may resent this exploitation of the goddess that mankind has always worshiped. But in expressing that resentment, De Kooning does not denounce our merchandising culture as such: instead he heaps abuse on a maternal creature who is its victim as much as anyone else.

Is it a matter of having missed the target? Of blaming the victim instead of the criminal? No. The image of a fierce mother is too deliberately used to be an accident. Her type is unmistakable. These images bearing the marks of accurately aimed salvos of paint need to be recognized for what they are: frenzied assaults on the one person we hold responsible for everything that went wrong.

THE BOHEMIAN WOMAN

The bohemianism of the nineteenth and early twentieth centuries grew at first out of negative impulses— the typical rebellion of middle-class youth against the comfort and predictability of their parents' bourgeois lives. But to the extent that these bohemians were talented as well as rebellious, they made the era prior to World War I an unparalleled period of artistic innovation. The careers of most of the masters of modern art were incubated in the Paris of that time. And it was not only in painting, poetry and music that they were original. They also created a lifestyle in which poets and painters shared the existence of clowns, acrobats, tramps, thieves and street-walkers. It was in this milieu that Picasso found the subjects for his Blue Period paintings. Young artists and students were at first attracted by the exoticism of the Parisian demimonde, but in time their own poverty and pariah status made bohemianism a necessity, not a device. The problems of personal and artistic survival were inextricably mixed, and out of that fusion came the impetus that projected woman to the forefront of the stage of modernism. Perhaps it was only in an atmosphere of outcasts and nonconformists that women could be accepted as social and artistic equals. At any rate, the bohemian woman became the pioneer of a new female type. It was a type in which freedom, poverty, love, and misery were combined in a bittersweet blend. That blend is still appealing, and the bohemian type is very much alive.

WILLEM DE KOONING. *Woman, II.* 1952.
The Museum of Modern Art, New York.
Gift of Mrs. John D. Rockefeller

Modigliani was hardly a founder of bohemianism as a lifestyle, but he was certainly one of its most vivid exemplars. And it is no accident that many of his best pictures are of female nudes—paintings of his friends or mistresses, the only people he did not need to pay for posing. Stylistically, he descended from Cubism via Brancusi, and ultimately from Cézanne. But he was an important exception among the followers of Cézanne: while conscious of the geometric solids at the foundation of Cubist form, Modigliani could not suppress a deep appreciation of the sensuous qualities of the contour lines describing women's bodies. Contour line had eluded Cézanne, so he concentrated on the movement of colored planes. But while Modigliani wanted to paint the architectonic succession of planes he could not do so without compromising the sexuality of his subjects. Hence his paintings, while solid enough, did not exhibit the sheer monumentality of Cézanne's landscapes and still lifes.

Modigliani was one of the great voluptuaries in the history of modern art. Of the many artists who lovingly painted female flesh, he seemed to know best what made it lovable. Moreover, he was able to combine admiration for woman's body with genuine affection for her person. That affection was based on

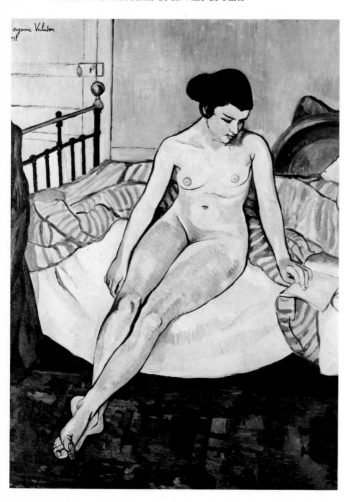

SUZANNE VALADON. *Nude Seated on a Bed.* 1922.
Musée d'Art Moderne de la Ville de Paris

JULES PASCIN. *Nude with Green Hat.* c. 1925.
Cincinnati Art Museum. Virginia Helm Irwin Bequest

an unusual ability to identify with her feelings of sensual fulfillment. Modigliani's achievement, not unlike Titian's, was to show woman as a willing participant in the rites of sex: she enjoys her body as much as any man she shares it with. Titian had created his goddesses on the model of the well-respected Venetian courtesan, a woman of business as well as pleasure: she could associate with men on the basis of equality so far as intelligence, conversational gifts, and the management of money were concerned. Modigliani's models, painted around World War I, were taken from a different class. These bohemian girls had chosen to defy both the standards of Victorian respectability and Edwardian wickedness. They were not fallen women, compromised by their emotions and bad luck. Neither were they coquettes trying to ensnare wealthy businessmen. They thought of themselves rather as collaborators with the artists they posed for and lived with: it was not money but art and sexual self-expression that explained their lives. Long-term love and a life of comfortable domesticity was reserved for their bourgeois sisters; it was beneath their contempt.

In some ways the bohemian woman was very innocent: her existence could be explained in terms of an inability or reluctance to cast her sexuality in a commercial mold. Suzanne Valadon (1867–1938) epitomized the type. She was, like Modigliani, a famous figure in the world of Montparnasse. A circus acrobat, an artist's model, and a painter herself, she also became the mother (out of wedlock) of Maurice Utrillo (1883–1955), a well-known painter of Montmartre scenes. There is a certain irony in the fact that Utrillo enjoys the larger reputation, although Suzanne Valadon was by far the stronger painter. One can see in her *Nude Seated on a Bed* (1922) a mastery of drawing (probably acquired from Degas and Lautrec, for whom she posed) and modeling with pigment, that gives her a well-deserved place in the grand tradition of European figure painting. But her alcoholic son, Maurice, whom she encouraged to paint so that he would drink less (again the romantic bohemian idea of art as a means of personal salvation) is widely reproduced in anthologies of art while his mother's work is barely mentioned.

Valadon's woman is rather severely delineated. As a person she seems not unlike Manet's *Olympia*, someone who makes few concessions to sentiment. As for Modigliani, he employs an even sharper drawing line but it serves to heighten the model's gentle qualities of lyric melancholy. All of these traits properly belong to the bohemian type; still, there is another important version painted by Jules

Pascin (1885–1930). To be sure, he specializes in prostitutes, but he endows them with a romantic sort of wickedness that is not without bohemian overtones. A superb draftsman, Pascin likes to lose his contour lines in soft atmospheric tones that flicker across his girls' small bodies and tiny features like firelight. These models appear to be very young and in their half-undressed poses they have the distinct quality of adolescent girls trying to look depraved. Pascin's *Nude with Green Hat* (1925) cannot be taken seriously as a representation of a woman abandoned to lust. She may be a bit loose but the overwhelming impression she makes is of a precocious young woman who has already learned that sex is a game—or an art.

Three Women by Three Women

Are women alone capable of painting women authentically? I have already pointed out that many artists have the capacity to cross the barriers of gender to identify with the feelings of the so-called opposite sex. Still, we know there are *experiences* unique to each sex.[18] Following are three nudes painted by women. Could they have been painted by men? In other words, is the sex of the artist a crucial factor in the expressiveness of the work? In my opinion, no categorical answer can be given. The Modersohn-Becker seems to exhibit a distinctively feminine point of view. I am less certain in the case of Valadon. As for Tamara de Lempicka's woman, I suggest she could have been painted by Richard Lindner.

SUZANNE VALADON. *Nude Reclining on a Couch.* 1928. The Metropolitan Museum of Art, New York. Robert Lehman Collection, 1975

In Paula Modersohn-Becker's *Self-Portrait* we have an exceptionally candid self-revelation by a woman, especially if we consider the date, 1906. The artist presents herself in the nude—a bold action then—and would seem by the motion of her right hand to be making a gesture of invitation. The left hand, more stylized and shy, is directed back to her body. Still, both hands hold flowers, as if to offer them as gifts—one to us and the other to herself. The head is inclined

TAMARA DE LEMPICKA. *Reclining Woman in Pink.* 1927. Whereabouts unknown. Photo: FAR Gallery

toward the viewer and the mouth is about to speak or smile. Lush vegetation in the background plus flowers in her hair make unmistakable reference to the subject of fertility, as does her body. But notice that the face is modeled in some depth whereas the figure is rather two-dimensional, notwithstanding the well-rounded breasts and shoulders. Thus we are given to understand that the person who addresses us rather quizzically and diffidently lives in her mind as well as her flesh. Indeed, the fact that she has a mind is the primary fact behind her somewhat tentative gesture of sexual invitation. If we compare the stylized, classicistic treatment of her figure with the firmly stated planes of the face it is clear that she has painted her head with more conviction: this is where she really lives; her life and person are organized according to a hierarchy in which intelligence dominates passion.

One year after painting this self-portrait, Paula Modersohn-Becker died following the birth of her daughter.

In Suzanne Valadon's *Nude Reclining on a Couch* (1928) we see again her powerful and assured style of drawing and modeling. However, if we look into the model's face we realize that her strong, healthy body belongs to a woman who is psychologically vulnerable. She holds herself protectively with one hand while the other nervously clutches a piece of drapery. We are no longer confronted with Olympia's brazen stare, or the sexy insinuations of Goya's *Maja*. This woman is tense: look at her feet! Next to one of Modigliani's relaxed hedonists she is a bundle of nerves and apprehensions. Is it Valadon's expressionistic technique that accounts for the tensions we feel in this image? Or is it a woman's act of empathy? Before attempting to answer, we should look at *The Spirit of the Dead Watching* by Paul Gauguin.

Compared to Valadon's soft, insecure person, the *Reclining Woman in Pink* (1927) by Tamara de Lempicka confronts us with an amazonian creature of monumental hardness: she could have been carved out of stone, or hammered out of sheet metal, like one of Léger's intrepid, industrial females. The architectural quality of this figure derives, of course, from Cézanne. But de Lempicka has tried, through a provocative pose, to combine the strength of the figure with her model's voluptuous and feminine qualities, her potential for erotic pleasure. In addition, if we look at the face, we can see an uncanny resemblance to the face of Richard Lindner's fiercely impersonal females (see *Hello*). There is the same shiny, almost plastic hairdo; the same sharp nose and small eyes; the same expressionless lips; the same full body revealed by tight-fitting clothes.

Because Lindner painted his picture almost forty years after de Lempicka he was perhaps in a better position to speculate about the mechanization of woman's body and soul. Hence his creature is at once more fantastic and frighteningly real. But it is significant that as early as 1927 Tamara de Lempicka sensed the transformation that was about to engulf her sex:

woman's sensuality was in the process of being packaged. First, however, her arms, breasts and thighs had to be measured, weighed and standardized. Then they could be served up by the media in the millions, like so many hamburgers or fried chicken parts. Once organic form was converted into stereometric parts, it could be sold by the piece or by the bucket.

"Pop" Women

The Pop art movement was characterized by a distinctive subject matter rather than a single artistic technique or way of seeing. Yet we see a common idea of woman in the work of its chief representatives. Tom Wesselmann's *Bathtub Collage* (1963), Roy Lichtenstein's *Blonde Waiting* (1964), Mel Ramos' *Nude and Coke Bottle* (1966), and Andy Warhol's *Marilyn Monroe* (1962) all testify to woman as essentially witless. The stress varies: Wesselmann places her in an insipid, plastic environment and implies that her body and mind were manufactured out of the same stuff as a bathtub curtain, towel rack, or the phony wall tiles. Lichtenstein gives us the supreme irony of a comic-strip blonde trying to look thoughtful. Like certain fashion models we see in television dramas she tries desperately but with little success to project deep emotion. Ramos offers us the consummation of a love affair that we have long suspected: the union of Miss America and the Coke Bottle. Their marriage is long overdue; after all, the courtship has lasted about eighty years and the public is now mature enough to accept their strange relationship.

The monotonously duplicated image of *Marilyn Monroe* by Andy Warhol makes an accurate statement about the role of repetition in our culture as well as the commercial use of woman's face. At one level the picture refers to the phenomenon of cheaply reproduced images. He even uses the silkscreen printing technique which is so widely employed in outdoor posters. Although the technology of printing was originally developed to publish sacred texts inexpensively, it has evolved into a virtually architectural force; through large-scale photography and color lithography it is now possible to transform the appearance of the physical environment. At another level Warhol's picture describes the rows and rows of almost identical female images we see on our drugstore and newsstand magazine racks. We cannot tell whether he is fascinated or repelled by the spectacle of woman's face converted into our supreme symbol of boredom. But it is clear that the replication and homogenization of her facial type has had enormous consequences for our culture. For one thing, it devalues the faces and figures of non-European racial types. And even within the European category it devalues all the interesting departures from the standardized features of a rather standardized person. The successful promulgation of the same face with the same expression has an insidious effect on women.

TOM WESSELMANN. *Bathtub Collage*. 1963.
Hessiches Landesmuseum, Darmstadt

MEL RAMOS. *Nude and Coke
Bottle ("Coca-Cola Banner")*.
1966. Collection the artist

ANDY WARHOL. *Marilyn Monroe.* 1962. Collection Vernon Nikkel, Clovis, New Mexico

KÄTHE KOLLWITZ. *Self-Portrait*. 1934.
Los Angeles County Museum of Art.
Los Angeles County Funds

JOSÉ CLEMENTE OROZCO. *Portrait of Mother*. 1923.
Whereabouts unknown

Two images of women widely separated by geography and culture:
one German, the other Mexican. It is interesting that as women grow
older they also look like older men; sexual dimorphism seems to disappear. All that is left is individual character.

Some can manage, with the help of cosmetics and hairdressers, to achieve a look that approximates the look on the magazine cover. Others cannot, and consequently they are alienated from much that seems desirable in American life. But to the extent that millions of women *do* succeed in resembling magazine covers they succeed in reducing themselves to a banal commodity—humanoid in form but interchangeable so far as person and personality are concerned.

Unlike Andy Warhol, whose art treats women as part of a tedious commercial spectacle, Marisol has a decidedly caustic point of view. She is fond of creating family group sculptures, or tableaux, in which rather talkative suburban wives are shown with their empty-headed husbands and neatly dressed, plastic-looking children. Is it possible that these fashionable and loquacious matrons evolved from the silent, stolid sort of mother we see in *The Family* (1962)? Here mother's image would seem to be based on one of those snapshots, taken early in the century, in which a hard-working hausfrau takes a moment to pose with her brood on the front porch. Presumably, the father is at work; or maybe the woman is a widow. Much is made of the likeness of the kids to the mother—almost as if they had been cloned. Mother and chil-

dren have the same squinty eyes; they all need glasses; their postures are rigid. Marisol's woman is a kind of sociological stereotype—accurate enough and cleverly presented: she and her family can readily be classified in terms of income, education, and class origin; it is not especially difficult to score points against them. But is it right to hold this woman up to ridicule? Obviously, she is not a swinger: she knows nothing about contraception; she doesn't smoke Virginia Slims. She represents everything modern women do not want to be, and Marisol is ingenious in using truthful detail—carefully selected—to make a feminist case against her. Still, there are truths about that mother which another sort of investigation might reveal. One such truth is that she is a very tough old bird. When it comes to dealing with an energy shortage, pill-popping adolescents, or the impact of inflation on a small family budget, she may well be able to cope when others cannot.

Conclusion

Is there any single idea which underlies the various images of women we have examined? There is, if we realize that a fundamental concept can take different visual forms, depending on shifting economic, social and technological factors. The common idea that seems to shape almost all images of woman is fertility, the ability to cause something in the inner or outer environment to increase, to flower, to proliferate. Women have been seen not only as procreative machines in themselves, but as promoters of the fertility of others—of wild animals in hunting societies; of domesticated animals in pastoral societies; of grain and fruit in agrarian societies; of minerals and gems in extractive societies; of machines and goods in industrial societies; of fashions and manners in courtly societies; of ideas and information in scientific and intellectual societies; and of money and profit in capitalist societies. The original, essentially biological image of woman tends to be enlisted in the service of new needs as the focus of human activity shifts from the problems of physical survival to the problems of increasing production, distributing goods, maximizing wealth.

It would seem, from the diversity of the works we have examined, that the image of woman can sometimes be an artistic afterthought. That is, questions of technique and style are often foremost in the imagination of the artist, and images—whether of women or men, people or things—are only incidental. Certainly that is an impression one may get from those contemporary works in which no human image appears. But our analysis should have shown that no matter how remote an artistic image may be from the demonstrably human, human considerations in gen-eral, and sexual considerations in particular, are not easily forgotten. Technical or stylistic problem-solving always presupposes some underlying conviction about the way our minds and bodies are related to the rest of reality, if only by analogy. Human sexuality is a very potent force in all forms of art: the painter who believes he attends to pure line, form, color or space cannot escape the influence of our sexual differences and similarities.

What have we learned from this consideration of the images of women in modern painting? Well, it should be obvious that such images tell us a great deal about men. They tell us mainly what men have liked (or resented) and how women were expected to look and behave. They show us the models that women in fact tried to emulate—if they saw these images. We cannot always be certain. Today, fortunately, there is no sexual segregation in looking at pictures. Even in the case of pictures painted by men for men to see,[19] we can be reasonably sure that women will see them, too. As for images of women painted by women, we can expect to see more of them; they should enlarge and elaborate everyone's ideas about the female sex. And they will not necessarily be sentimental, benign or decorative. They *should be* less physically cruel. In any case, the history of art henceforth will be created by both sexes.

So a certain kind of game is over: each sex will have a better idea of what the other sees and thinks about. If nothing else, then, we will be able to conduct our lives together on the basis of shared information; and that, in turn, should make us rather more honest with each other than we have been.

PART TWO

THE STYLES OF ART

Introduction

THE STYLES OF ART

THE CONCEPT OF STYLE IS INDISPENSABLE FOR THE study of art, and yet it can be a source of confusion because the word has so many meanings. Sometimes, style refers to the work of a particular historical period. It may refer to the art of a nation or a region within a country. The growth of a single artist's way of working is often called "the evolution of his style." In addition, style can be a certain technical approach to the creation of art. The word is also used as a term of approval. In connection with clothing or the changing appearance of appliances, "style" is equivalent to the latest fad or fashion. All the uses of the concept, however, seem to have one purpose—the classification of a variety of works into categories which will make them easier to talk about and understand. At the most general level, therefore, an art style is a grouping or classification of works of art (by time, region, appearance, technique, or subject matter) that makes further study and analysis possible.

As with all scientific classification, the sorting of phenomena into categories is based on the observation of common traits or qualities. Styles of art, therefore, can be thought of as families. Just as members of a family have certain features which give them what is called a "family resemblance," works of art can also resemble each other. They may have differences, too, but they have at least *some* common traits which are discernible and hence make classification possible. That uniting element may be visible in a particular use of line, color, shape or space; or it may be detected in a qualitative relationship. In other words, style may be discerned not only in what is visible on the surface but also in the overall feeling or quality a work seems to express. This overall, or *pervasive*, quality of a work frequently constitutes the basis for its classification. But it is not very helpful if style qualities are merely identified and classified. We need to know what traits of a work help to "place" it. In other words, we must try to *explain* the connection between the work and the style quality it seems to possess.

The reasons for studying the styles of art might be summarized as follows:

(1) To acquire useful categories for thinking and talking about the common traits of works produced during various periods.
(2) To understand artists, historical periods, countries, or regions in whose art a certain style appears frequently.
(3) To compare intelligently (perhaps to judge) works of art which are stylistically related.
(4) To see the connection between an artist's way of working, his visible results, and our reactions to his work as a whole.

With an understanding of art styles, we are in a position to read the so-called "hidden language" of art. Style leads us to look for meanings beneath the subject matter and apparent purpose of a work of art. Just as handwriting conveys meanings which are not in the words alone, style reveals much about an artist's way of thinking, about his environment, and about the society and culture in which his work is rooted. Archaeologists use style to reconstruct past cultures. They put pieces of stylistic evidence together like a mosaic, to form an idea of a culture or civilization as a whole. Similarly, we study the styles of art—to assemble in our minds an idea of the changing condition of man. We are, in a sense, archaeologists of the artistic image of humanity.

At the present time, art is being created in many styles at once throughout the world. Therefore, instead of searching for a single common denominator for the art of our time, it might be better to describe the principal stylistic tendencies which appear to be operating today. Some of these tendencies may be seen as modern versions of styles which have persisted throughout the history of art.

STYLISTIC CHANGE

Although several styles may coexist, especially in modern cultures, there are periods when a single style predominates. But every style is succeeded by another, and in recent years, styles have succeeded each other rapidly. Of all the styles described by art history, only the folk or peasant styles seem to persist regardless of cultural change—a phenomenon which is probably due to the isolation of folk culture. Today, however, it is difficult for any group to be completely detached from the main currents of world culture; consequently folk and peasant art is disappearing. This disappearance calls attention to the dynamic and transient character of style in the mainstream cultures. What accounts for stylistic change? Is it caused by artistic responses to the world? Or do artists themselves create innovations which catch fire, so to speak, and grow into conflagrations that eventually burn themselves out?

Scholarly answers to these questions differ according to the discipline of the observer. Critics and art historians tend to attribute stylistic change to the creative inventions of artists working in certain times and places. The artist generates new ways of seeing— ways that subsequently enter the worlds of work, pleasure, and power. Behavioral scientists, on the other hand, attribute stylistic change to shifts in political, economic, religious, or ideological factors. They see the artist as one who reacts more than he innovates, who, when he thinks he is innovating, is in fact reacting to forces that are so subtle, or so powerful, that he is unaware of their existence as influences on his work.

Can the morbid qualities in Munch's painting be attributed to the long Scandinavian winters; or to the character of Protestantism in Norway; or to Munch's neurotic spells and bouts of alcoholism? In other words, should we seek a geographic, religious, psychological, or even a medical explanation of his style?

But why try to account for stylistic change? Because we suspect that large-scale changes in art may portend changes in life. Perhaps a style that many artists adopt represents a type of adaptation to change by the total culture. In other words, artists may serve as society's antennae. Artists may even *generate* changes in the way people feel and see the world. Perhaps artists are the ship's rudder rather than its radar.

No matter how we account for stylistic change, we feel we can recognize the emergence of new styles and the decline of old ones. Styles seem to possess living, organic traits; we speak of them in terms analogous to life cycles—the budding, blooming, and wilting of flowers; the childhood, maturity, and death of persons. To be sure, these analogies are inexact if not misleading. Still, they call attention to something we are aware of in all human affairs, not only art; they seem to hold a secret about fundamental human mysteries. When styles change, whole societies react like early men witnessing the advance or retreat of a polar glacier. Clearly, style is an enormously potent symbol for civilized people. It replaces weather, the migrations of game, and the condition of animal entrails as a sign of change. Hence, we study style a little in the spirit of those ancient Roman augurs who counted the flights of birds or examined the organs of animals to guess what might happen in the world and in the lives of people.

5

THE STYLE OF OBJECTIVE

ACCURACY

THE STYLE OF OBJECTIVE ACCURACY IS FAMILIAR TO most people whether they have studied art or not. It is the style many feel confident in judging, since they can compare a painting or sculpture with what they believe is its original in life. For many persons, accuracy, or closeness of resemblance to life, is the principal way of judging the excellence of a work of art.

Since most of us have good vision, we feel we can judge an artist's fidelity to his model, or his skill in creating the *illusion* of reality. To create the *illusion* of reality, some artists reproduce every visual detail of a model on the assumption that a convincingly real work is the sum of carefully observed and executed parts. Sometimes this kind of artistic approach is called "photographic realism." Of course, the invention of photography has made photographic realism almost obsolete. The masters of the past knew how to create the *illusion* of reality without reproducing everything the eye can see. And most artists today see little reason to compete with the camera in the pursuit of realism. Hence, the problem of many contemporary artists is to create an impression of reality through a selective use of visual facts. Clearly, this approach requires more than good eyesight to be successful.

In this chapter we shall discuss the varieties of expression which are possible within the style of objective accuracy. We shall mention some of the ways artists represent reality without reproducing all the details of an object or place. Also, we shall speculate about why some artists prefer accuracy of representation, or the illusion of nature, instead of abstraction or distortion of what the eye sees. Although the style of objective accuracy rises and falls in popularity, it is nevertheless a permanent way of expressing ideas and feelings. We need to distinguish between works which

SIDNEY GOODMAN. *The Walk*. 1963. Collection Dr. and Mrs. Abraham Melamed, Milwaukee. A truthful visual account can generate its own peculiar mystery. The strange angle of vision may unnerve the viewer and leave him open to a number of dark suggestions.

slavishly imitate visual details and those which use accuracy to imply more than is seen. To investigate this problem, we shall examine the work of traditional and contemporary artists who create images that are recognizable while using visual facts to convey meanings beyond the visible.

The Imitation of Appearances

Why does a painting or sculpture which looks like its model fascinate us? Why do artists imitate what the eye can see or what the camera might record? These questions are fundamental, since almost everyone assumes that accurate representation is the basis of art. Also, it is true that the earliest known art, the cave painting of Paleolithic man, is highly representational, beautifully accurate. Children, too, endeavor to represent objects accurately, although they do not succeed from an adult standpoint. But when they are young, children are not bothered by adult visual logic; as they grow older, however, they *do* try to imitate appearances as accurately as possible. Imitation for them is part of coming to terms with the world.

It is likely that imitating reality represents an effort to control reality. At deep levels of awareness, our desire to paint a head so that it seems alive is part of an effort to develop mastery over life. Drawing an object over and over again creates confidence in our ability to control it. We think we are less likely to be victims of capricious events in a world we do not understand if we can create images which are accurate enough to replace pieces of the world we must deal with.

For the viewer, a naturalistic work may be fascinating because he admires the artist's skill. At another level, the viewer is attracted by successful imitation because he knows he is really looking at artistic ef-

fects—not at flesh, leaves, sky, cloth, and so on. Many of us enjoy fool-the-eye paintings for this reason. There are stories as far back as the Greeks about artists who could paint grapes so faithfully that birds were tempted to pick at them. But basically the appeal of a work executed in a style of objective accuracy relies on tension between appearance and reality.

Another kind of accuracy grows out of a concern with narration—telling the viewer as clearly as possible what happened. From its beginning, art has played a role in the transmission of information. Although photojournalism has largely supplanted the artist as a recorder of events, artists continue to create works which inform the viewer through naturalistic description and representation. Andrew Wyeth (born 1917) uses this style to convey moving dramas about the lives of plain people, objects, and places. In *Christina's World*, we become aware of the struggle and loneliness in the inner life of a physically handicapped woman. Wyeth's attention to detail helps establish the moods of harsh reality and pathos which are conveyed by the scene. The tempera medium gives the work a dry, matter-of-fact quality which heightens our awareness of Christina's difficult existence. Location and selection of details are crucially important. Notice the high horizon and the low position of the figure. This connects her more closely to the ground; we see more of the earth than of the sky. Distances must be tremendous in her groping world; this impression is created by the skilled use of perspective— the small, distant house, the large expanse of field between the figure and the house. It is difficult to paint so large an area of unimportant material—grass— and keep it interesting to the viewer. Yet Wyeth succeeds in giving the field a powerful psychological charge because of the tension created between the girl and the house: we view the grass as space which must be painfully traversed. The design of the picture com-

ANDREW WYETH. *Christina's World.* 1948. The Museum of Modern Art, New York

GRANT WOOD. *American Gothic*. 1930.
The Art Institute of Chicago.
Friends of American Art Collection

OTTO DIX. *My Parents*. 1921.
Kunstmuseum, Basel

bines with the artist's representational skill to create psychological impact.

There is a tendency in American art and thought to favor accurate, matter-of-fact representations of life. This may grow out of the suspicions of a frontier society toward the culture of the Old World: older civilizations are associated, perhaps wrongly, with corruption caused by the pursuit of luxury. *American Gothic* by Grant Wood (1892–1942), by contrast, celebrates the homely, unadorned virtues of rural life. The picture and its title constitute an ironic comparison with the soaring complexity of Gothic architecture. The wood-frame dwelling in the background exemplifies the so-called Carpenter Gothic style, the American version of the illustrious European style ornately carved in stone. The sardonic force of the work is based on the convincing likeness of a farm couple who are as plain as Gothic is fancy. Their simplicity is severe and pathetic, but authentic too.

An interesting comparison can be made between Wood's solemn couple and the double portrait *My Parents* (1921) by the German artist Otto Dix (1891–1969). Here are similar human types, but Dix departs further from naturalism, while creating an overwhelming impression of realism. The enlarged hands and emphasis on wrinkles, echoed in the clothing, convey the awkwardness Europeans associate with peasants. Wood distorted his heads imperceptibly to stress their oval shape and to repeat the shape of the pitchfork.

Otto Dix has employed somewhat more distortion and exaggeration. Does his work belong to the category of objective accuracy? Probably it does, because the narrative element, the purely reportorial, dominates the painting. The work is responsive to what must have been the visual facts.

The similarity in the paintings by Otto Dix and Grant Wood reflects a similarity of outlook in two artists separated by nationality but united by a common interest in fidelity to optical evidence. It appears that the style of objective accuracy is based on a human trait which is more fundamental than nationality. A type of magical behavior is involved in artistic representation. This accounts for the fascination which the imitation of appearances holds for artist and viewer alike.

The Artist as Detached Observer

Another characteristic of objective accuracy is the concealment of technique by the artist. It is as if he were trying to deny that pictures are made of paint or sculptures modeled in clay. The marks of his tools must not be visible in the final product. The artist wishes to focus attention on the subject, not on the way the picture was put together. There is a certain modesty implied by this approach, a self-effacement in the interest of heightening the illusion created by

CHARLES SHEELER. *City Interior*. 1936.
Worcester Art Museum,
Worcester, Massachusetts

the image. Where Soutine was anxious to reveal his brushstrokes, an artist like Charles Sheeler used a smooth, impersonal technique which seems highly appropriate to his machine-made industrial theme.

The attitude of the objective artist is one of detachment. He presents himself to his audience as a person who selects, arranges, and represents reality but suppresses his personality in the process. If we learn anything about the artist as a person, it is through choice of themes and organization of subject matter, not because of his manner of execution. There is something scientific in such an attitude. A scientist takes precautions to be sure private feelings will not affect his observations. He hopes other investigators will come to the same conclusions if they examine the same data. The artist interested in accuracy also wishes his results to have a validity independent of personality: the work should appear to be almost anonymous; only the signature reveals the author.

The suppression of the personal is due to the artist's desire to make vision, the act of seeing, the most important part of experiencing his work. In a sense, the Impressionists fit this description: they used scien-

CLAUDE MONET. *Cathedral in Sunshine*. 1894.
The Louvre, Paris

CLAUDE MONET. *Cathedral in Fog*. 1894.
The Louvre, Paris

150

tific theories of color and optics; they exchanged technical "secrets"; they painted as accurately as possible the object seen quickly in a particular light. For example, in the Rouen Cathedral series of Claude Monet (1840–1926) we have a very single-minded effort to represent the same building under varying light conditions according to a theory of color which was considered more "realistic"—that is, based on a firmer scientific foundation—than conventional ideas of color. It is quite correct to think of Impressionism as a style of objective accuracy, since it constituted a disciplined endeavor to use scientific discoveries about color and visual perception to present the object in its atmospheric setting with full fidelity. The genius of the Impressionists lay in their realization that objects could not be represented accurately without considering the atmosphere around them and the kind of illumination which enables us to see them in the first place.

So long as an artist can deal with reality optically—through his eyes alone—he adheres to the style of objective reality. But when he becomes emotionally involved with his subject, or with some feature of technique, he loses his detachment and his status as a "disinterested observer." Of course, this change of style may be logical and desirable. It is caused by a different attitude toward vision and the world on the part of the artist. He has placed a higher priority on the personal act of seeing than on the objective character of what is seen.

In the work of Edgar Degas (1834–1917), we see a style of supreme fidelity to optical reality while an Impressionist palette is employed. In *The Glass of Absinthe*, the artist plays the role of reporter, of detached observer of humanity. We can read for ourselves the dull, weary state of the woman and the sodden look of the man. Degas seems to be a disinterested eye: he catches the couple casually, toward the side of the picture, as if he were using a candid camera. As a matter of fact, Degas was interested in the seemingly accidental compositions of photography and designed his pictures to look as if their subjects had been suddenly discovered. As a result, his pictures of ballet dancers, women bathing, jockeys, and so on are convincing because we sense an element of candid observation as opposed to theatrical staging. Later, Henri de Toulouse-Lautrec (1864–1901) would benefit from the compositional audacity and psychological honesty of Degas. His portrait *M. Boileau at the Café* (1893) employs the same diagonal treatment as the Degas, together with figures spilling out of the upper right-hand edge of the canvas. However, the central figure is more conventionally located. Also, M. Boileau is hardly a derelict; he is the very solid embodiment of bourgeois self-satisfaction.

The art of Degas and Lautrec shows how Impressionist color, space representation borrowed from Japanese prints, and pictorial composition influenced by photography cannot obscure the fundamental psychological stance of the artist toward the

EDGAR DEGAS. *The Glass of Absinthe.* 1876. The Louvre, Paris

HENRI DE TOULOUSE-LAUTREC. *M. Boileau at the Café.* 1893. The Cleveland Museum of Art. Hinman B. Hurlbut Collection

151

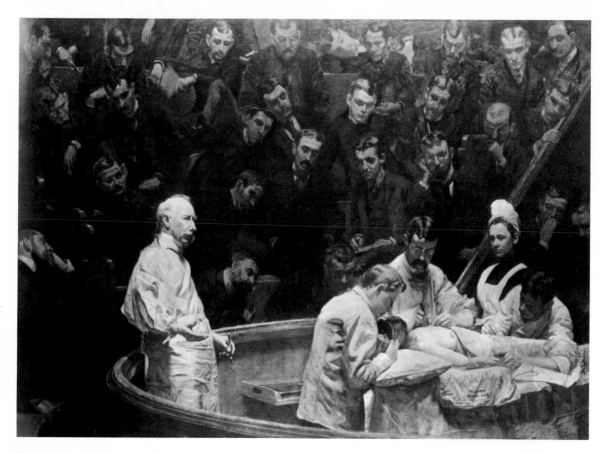

THOMAS EAKINS. *The Agnew Clinic.* 1889.
School of Medicine,
The University of Pennsylvania,
Philadelphia

REMBRANDT VAN RIJN.
The Anatomy Lesson of Dr. Tulp. 1632.
Mauritshuis, The Hague,
The Netherlands

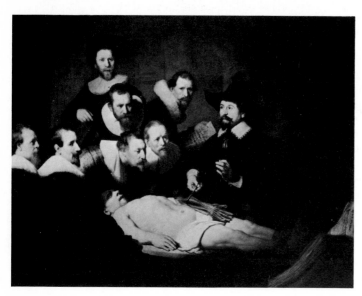

THOMAS EAKINS. *The Gross Clinic.* 1875.
The Jefferson Medical College
of Philadelphia

world. Both men were passionate observers of behavior; but they refrained from insinuating their own moral judgments. They were *detached observers*. This much we can conclude from their work, without looking into their biographies. They were the radical empiricists of painting: ideas and knowledge are based on observation of the real world; everything must give way to the necessity of seeing clearly what is out there and reporting it without distorting the visual facts.

For the detached observer, distortion is a type of artistic and moral vice. The Philadelphia painter Thomas Eakins (1844–1916) felt that distortion was ugliness; his entire career as artist and teacher seemed to be an almost fanatical pursuit of the methods which would ensure the sort of accuracy which results from scientific knowledge of what the artist sees. He taught artists anatomy by dissecting cadavers and took an almost perverse delight in portraying the unvarnished facts of operating technique, as in *The Agnew Clinic* (1889). Dr. Agnew was not pleased to be shown with blood on his hands as he lectured, but Eakins was too stubborn to compromise the facts. He had been similarly candid in 1875 when portraying a blood-spattered Dr. Gross and assistants in *The Gross Clinic*. By contrast, Rembrandt's *The Anatomy Lesson of Dr. Tulp* (1632) is a restrained and dignified tribute to the dedicated pursuit of learning.

The Artist as Selective Eye

The artistic concern with accuracy does not always result in photographic realism. Often the illusion of reality is created by elimination of details the eye might see. At other times there is a deliberate piling up of detail to create an impression of the complexity of the object. For some artists an obsession with the subject makes it difficult to leave a work: such an artist will embellish and enrich its surface. The result may show the months or years of labor put into its execution. Ivan Albright's painting is the result of years devoted to the amassing of detail. Appropriately enough, Albright was chosen to paint the portrait for the film of Oscar Wilde's *The Picture of Dorian Grey*. As in Wilde's story, Albright's paintings appear to have aged along with their subjects. The viewer feels obliged to examine with great seriousness a work so arduously produced. The evidence of long and sustained effort by the artist induces a type of empathy in the viewer: the respect for work is converted into respect for the painstakingly produced art object. Hence, by choosing to show a multitude of visual facts—more than would be casually noted—the artist governs the attitude of the viewer.

Among artists who simplify while maintaining the feeling of objective reality is Edward Hopper. *Nighthawks,* for example, is divided into quiet, uncompli-

EDWARD HOPPER. *Nighthawks.* 1942. The Art Institute of Chicago. Friends of American Art Collection

153

IVAN ALBRIGHT. *Into the World There Came a Soul Called Ida*. 1929–30. The Art Institute of Chicago. On permanent loan from the Collection of Mr. and Mrs. Ivan Albright

RENÉ BOUCHÉ. *Elsa Maxwell*. 1958–59. Collection Mrs. René Bouché, New York

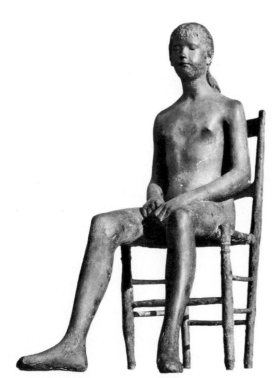

GIACOMO MANZÙ. *Girl in Chair*. 1955. The Hirshhorn Museum and Sculpture Garden, Smithsonian Institution, Washington, D.C.

WILHELM LEHMBRUCK. *Young Man Seated*. 1918. Wilhelm Lehmbruck Museum, Duisberg, Germany

cated areas. The brushwork is hardly evident; we sense the materials of the place instead. The mood of silence, of a great city asleep, is accentuated by the small inactive figures, the emptiness of the street, the crisp shadows thrown by artificial light, the dominance of vertical and horizontal lines. Hopper shows just enough of a building or a person to permit identification; he is not a "tricky" painter: each area of his picture seems to have been carefully pruned of non-essentials, reduced to the minimum needed for recognition. Like Wyeth, Hopper relies on placement for psychological emphasis. Undramatic execution creates a cumulative effect which has a quiet drama of its own. The areas of light and shadow tend to be flat; he uses perspective and strong contrasts of light and dark to suggest the solidity and heaviness of a place.

Into the World There Came a Soul Called Ida relies on accumulation of detail to suggest the process of human aging and deterioration. An almost pitiless observer, Albright brings out the evidence of sagging flesh while revealing the woman's pathetic effort to reverse the aging process. Still, we are aware of the artist's compassion for Ida: her face, which is plain, is shown in a tragic light, as if she knows that cosmetics, clothes, and even hope will not restore the appearance of youth. The details, which reveal so much, combine to create a living organism—Ida, who is both painted surface and human document. She is trapped by unwanted flesh.

In the portrait of Elsa Maxwell by René Bouché (1896–1963), we see another use of accuracy to convey the drama of aging. Bouché chose to view his subject from below her eye level, which, in an elderly and stout person, is unflattering. Indeed, there is a nervous, comic, but oddly *dignified* quality about this portrait. Whenever a sitter is presented honestly, without attempts at beautification, a certain measure of respect is earned by the subject. So the lady retains a measure of human dignity despite the artist's presentation of her in a hard, uncompromising light, from a bad view, in a slightly uncomfortable pose.

Among sculptors, the Italian artist Giacomo Manzù (born 1908) exhibits a refined sort of realism. It has roots in Renaissance classicism yet appeals to modern tastes nourished on distortion and abstraction. *Girl in Chair* is an example of careful observation combined with an elimination of detail so subtle that it is difficult to say where the simplification has taken place. The serenity of the figure results partly from the sculptor's ability to convince the viewer that a particular person has been represented at the same time that the basic forms have been stripped of all but their most essential qualities of shape and surface. The figure has extraordinary psychological presence. Even the chair has a curious perfection: it falls just short of a sculptor's abstraction (after all, a chair *is* an abstract object). Its spare, open form accents the solidity of the girl's slender body. In choosing a subject who is neither child nor woman, Manzù has undertaken a difficult challenge: he must manage to

DIEGO VELÁZQUEZ. *Sebastian de Morra.* 1643–44. The Prado, Madrid. The tradition of visual candor reveals its capacity for moral sensitivity in Velázquez's dignified and compassionate portrayal of the dwarfs kept as living toys by the Spanish court.

imply her uncertainly defined form and personality within a format of correct observation. Yet he must not fall into the trap of reproducing dimensions as if for a dressmaker's dummy. His solution stresses accuracy in the overall dimensions of the figure combined with simplification in the modeling of subordinate forms: thus he approaches but does not quite touch abstraction.

Manzù's girl could be compared with *Young Man Seated* by Wilhelm Lehmbruck (1881–1919). Although the figure conveys despondency or fatigue in contrast to the more confident attitude of the girl, it also exhibits careful observation of the adolescent body together with simplification of surfaces. Lehmbruck, however, goes beyond objective accuracy in his elongation of forms. This "stretching" of the normal dimensions expresses the idea of rapid growth in youth and the kinds of physical unease and psychological tension which accompany such growth. Lehmbruck's forms also reflect the Gothic tradition, a tradition of building and carving which stresses tall, narrow solids and voids.

The suppression of detail without the loss of essential traits cannot succeed unless the artist has observed his subject very carefully. He must *know* the subject as well as *see* its surface characteristics; otherwise his work of simplification will fail: the result will be simple and empty rather than simple and significant. Every work represents the end result of a process of observation and simplification. Even the work of Albright, with its elaboration of detail, represents a synthesis of many perceptions. Manzù and Lehmbruck convey what they "know" by eliminating inessentials. But Lehmbruck created new visual facts through distortion. Clearly, his departure from "the facts" represented a decision about the priorities to be placed on visual fidelity relative to emotional evocation. Art becomes a game played according to rules the artist recognizes. One of the satisfactions of our subject is finding out the rules which the artist appears to recognize and then deciding how well he has played the game.

Variations of the Style

Although many artists faithfully render what is seen, they nevertheless reveal their individual viewpoints. For example, Ben Shahn in his painting *Handball* gives us an accurate and matter-of-fact image of city boys caught in somewhat awkward athletic and spectator poses, an image which is quite different in mood and feeling from the equally accurate Wyeth, *Christina's World*. Both pictures employ isolated figures. In the wall of the handball court, Shahn, like Wyeth, shows a large expanse of relatively uncluttered space. He uses some urban detail around the edges of his canvas to establish his setting, just as Wyeth silhouettes his small houses at the top of his canvas, against the horizon. Shahn freezes the action of his characters, like Wyeth. But note that Shahn deliberately draws his figures so that their clothes seem lumpy and rumpled, their bodies stubby and ungraceful.

BEN SHAHN. *Handball*. 1939.
The Museum of Modern Art, New York.
Abby Aldrich Rockefeller Fund

JOHN KANE. *Self-Portrait*. 1929.
The Museum of Modern Art, New York.
Abby Aldrich Rockefeller Fund

Their surroundings are drab; they are trying to find excitement in a place which appears indifferent. If the painting of a group of awkward boys has elements of pathos, it is an impersonal, collective pathos. Christina's tragedy is individual and personal because Wyeth has painted her, not as an example of a type, but as a unique personality. It is easy to conclude that Shahn is mainly interested here in the problems of people in the aggregate, whereas Wyeth concentrates on the dramas of the individual.

John Kane (1860–1934) shows in his *Self-Portrait* how an untrained artist approaches objective accuracy. Stripped to the waist, he paints his hard, aging body, showing muscles and flesh as honestly as his command of technique and anatomy will allow. He reveals a combination of pride in his strength and pugnacity, along with honesty about the kind of man he is. Notice that the edges are hard and sharp and that the modeling is achieved with difficulty. The primitive artist usually tries for accuracy by the use of line and multiplication of detail. He can rarely use masses of pigment or intense color skillfully since these call for art-school training as a rule. Even if he is interested in evasion of truth, he does not possess the technique to heighten one area and suppress another. Furthermore, it is often a matter of principle to be scrupulously candid. Viewers admire this art precisely for its sometimes brutal or naive candor. In a sense, we can only learn the truth about people and places through seeing them portrayed by an

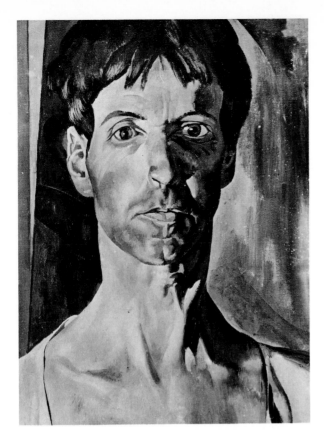

STANLEY SPENCER. *Self-Portrait.* 1936.
Stedelijk Museum, Amsterdam

Although his painterly technique is more accomplished, Spencer exhibits the same attitude toward the self—the same asceticism and absence of posturing—that we see in Kane's self-portrait.

artist who has not been trained in the tradition of representing reality in a prescribed way.

Charles Sheeler (1883–1965) is an artist whose work seems closely related to photography, and he was, indeed, a distinguished photographer. However, his paintings of industrial subjects or of machinery, as in *Upper Deck,* reveal an interest in geometric purity of form rather than the real surfaces and objects which an industrial world creates. His pictures are characterized by immaculate whiteness, regularity of shape, and absence of blemish. Although he seems to be a realist, he actually portrays a world in which noise, dirt, and confusion have been eliminated. Sheeler shows how accuracy of representation, if combined with an almost photographic technique and the suppression of chaotic detail, can create a convincing result which is nevertheless much idealized. His is an art which helps us to see the possibilities of formal beauty where it normally is not thought to exist.

There is another type of realism, "magic realism," which falls within the style of objective accuracy. An example is *Old Models* by William M. Harnett (1848–1892). Such works rely on a sort of photographic accuracy. That is, they re-create on canvas the retinal image of arranged objects. Also, the juxtaposition of still-life materials provides a com-

fortable set of literary or practical associations. After the viewer has finished comparing the painting to reality, he can enjoy a moment of philosophic contemplation as he recognizes the relatedness of the objects, the beauty of commonplace things, the inevitable failure of art to capture reality, the visual thrills in seeing painted nails driven into painted wood, painted letters written on painted paper, and so on. Needless to say, comparable effect can be achieved by skilled color photography. The "magical" element consists of the viewer's awareness of looking at artificial images whose skillfully created illusions *almost* convince him of their reality. Perhaps Harnett, John Peto, and the "little masters" of seventeenth-century Holland, who were also magic realists, served as precursors of Surrealism, which also relied on illusionistic painting. The Surrealists endeavored to excite emotion by unusual juxtapositions of objects. But illusionists like Harnett do not appear to have had a strategy of psychological shock. At most, they sought to undermine the viewer's reliance on the absolute validity of sense experience. Thus they challenged the occasionally naive empiricism of nineteenth-century American culture. It has not been easy to understand the difference between art as the creation of illusions and art as the visual presentation of

CHARLES SHEELER. *Upper Deck.* 1929.
Fogg Art Museum,
Harvard University, Cambridge, Massachusetts.
Purchase, Louise E. Bettens Fund

WILLIAM M. HARNETT. *Old Models*. 1892.
Museum of Fine Arts, Boston.
Charles Henry Hayden Fund

what someone knows about the world. Once the difference is learned, however, art becomes a highroad to knowledge that is not easily gained through other studies.

Devices of Objective Accuracy

We have already discussed some of the ways artists arrive at convincing representations of reality. Obviously, accuracy of size and shape relationships— "correct" drawing and modeling—are the most common devices. This sort of mastery is not easily acquired, although the impression of accuracy can be achieved with assistance from photographs, tracing,

slide projection, calipers, and other measuring and reproducing devices. Commercial artists and illustrators, of course, use whatever mechanical devices they can, because they frequently work under the pressure of time. Besides, individuality of vision or style may not be their primary objective. Normally, the attempt to draw an object accurately produces numerous variations from what a photograph would show. It is the drawing "error" due to the artist's age, sex, characteristic touch, and attitude which creates interest in the style of objective accuracy.

In addition to true size and shape relationships, the artist's control and handling of illumination help in creating realistic images. The amount of light an object receives, the shapes of its shadows, the transition from light to shadow, the source of light—these the artist learns to observe and control in the media he uses. Through mastery of represented light alone, he can model objects and spaces illusionistically. In sculpture, although the artist creates the actual forms the viewer sees, control of light as it falls over forms is very carefully considered.

Another device of the artist is focus: sharpness or softness, distinctness or vagueness of form and contour. The rather elementary fact about optics—that objects lose distinctness at the periphery of our field of vision—becomes a device for controlling the spectator's visual experience. The eye is drawn, of course, to the most distinctly represented form, other things being equal. As a painted form or object has its edge softened or blurred, we tend to view it as further away from the center of our field of vision. In drawing, forms in the same plane can be made to advance or recede depending on the "lose-and-find," "hard-and-soft," "light-and-dark" characteristics of the contour line. Hence an artist like Léger deliberately uses a line of uniform weight, thickness, and color to prevent forms from shifting in space. Masters of drawing from Holbein to Picasso, on the other hand, have varied the focal properties of line to move forms in and out of pictorial space.

In sculpture, forms may be sharply raised or softly melted, thus controlling the attention of the viewer. For the sculptor, the degree to which a form emerges into "full round" becomes a tool of artistic expressiveness. Thus, in *L'Età d'Oro* by Medardo Rosso (1858–1928) we see soft focus used to create a poetic and romantic impression, as of forms perceived through a haze. Aristide Maillol (1861–1944) also avoided sharply undercut forms so the unity of the entire work, rather than the realism of any single part, is achieved. Yet Maillol's sculptures seem to possess the weight and warmth of flesh and bone, much as Rodin's do, while using a different surface entirely. Epstein's portraits, executed in clay and cast in bronze, are sharply focused to heighten the sense of aliveness of his subjects. The modeling is exaggerated —that is, the hollows of the eyes, cheeks, and lips are deeper than would be the case in life. Rough projections of clay catch the light and bring forms

MEDARDO ROSSO. *L'Età d'Oro*. 1886.
Collection Mr. and Mrs. William E. Loving, Jr.,
Columbus, Ohio

AUGUSTE RODIN.
Head of Eustache de St. Pierre
(detail of *The Burghers of Calais*).
1886. Rodin Museum, Paris

JACOB EPSTEIN.
Head of Joseph Conrad. 1924–25.
The Hirshhorn Museum and Sculpture Garden,
Smithsonian Institution, Washington, D.C.

ERNST BARLACH. *Man Drawing Sword*. 1911.
The Galleries, Cranbrook Academy of Art,
Bloomfield Hills, Michigan

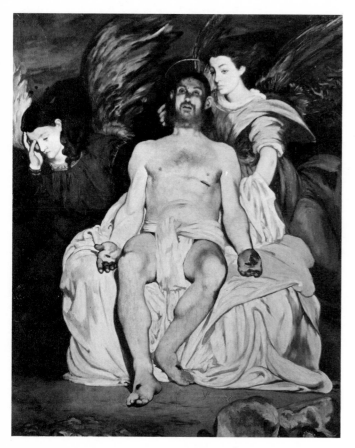

EDOUARD MANET.
The Dead Christ with Angels. 1864.
The Metropolitan Museum of Art, New York.
The H. O. Havemeyer Collection.
Bequest of Mrs. H. O. Havemeyer, 1929

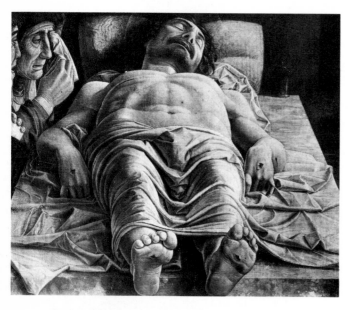

ANDREA MANTEGNA.
The Lamentation. c. 1490–1500.
Pinacoteca di Brera, Milan

sharply before our eyes. It is interesting to compare the agitated surface of the head of Conrad by Epstein with the more melting forms on the equally agitated head of Eustache de St. Pierre by Rodin. Ernst Barlach (1870–1938), working mainly in wood, defines his forms less sharply than Epstein but nevertheless gives wood the soft and hard properties of flesh, cloth, or bone as the subject requires. He maintains our awareness of the material, the process of carving, and the identity of his subject at the same time.

Color, of course, is a powerful instrument. Many painters try to create form by color alone, and if line or illumination is present in their work, it is managed solely through chromatic manipulation. For the artist intent on accuracy, color is mainly connected with the description of objects. The color of these objects varies, of course, depending on the amount and source of light they receive and on their location in space. Just as we know that focus grows less distinct as objects recede in space, we also know—at least since Leonardo—that color becomes less intense as objects recede. Conversely, brightly colored forms appear to be closer to our eyes. Brilliance of color combined with sharpness of focus is a powerful means of attracting attention and defining forms so that they appear to be truthful.

Sometimes an artist uses color arbitrarily but combines it with precise drawing. Even the most "naturalistic" artists may exaggerate color while remaining faithful to the contours of objects. It is as if the artistic conscience permits a certain amount of playfulness with color but no deviations from reality so far as drawing is concerned.

Perspective is the pictorial device (really a body of knowledge and devices) most laymen know about. It is related to an artist's ability to create the illusion of deep space within the picture frame. The technical features of linear and aerial perspective—the perspective of shadows and reflections, of receding measured forms, of advancing or foreshortened forms, of single- and two-point systems, of the interaction of perspective with color and illumination—are exceedingly complex. Suffice it to say that an understanding of at least the fundamentals of perspective enables the artist to simulate many optical experiences. Here again, the modern movement has first questioned and then largely abandoned the simulation of deep space in painting. The Surrealists have been the principal modern users of perspective, mainly to create fantastic illusions of infinitely receding space. In the Cubism of Picasso, Braque, and Gris, we see amusing combinations of conventional perspective and modeling with arbitrary anti-illusionistic devices. Having learned, since the Renaissance, to "read" pictures in terms of deep space, we have been taught by twentieth-century art to see pictures phenomenologically—as they actually are: flat surfaces with colored lines and shapes resting on them.

It seems likely that artists will always endeavor to master the devices which create illusions. As they

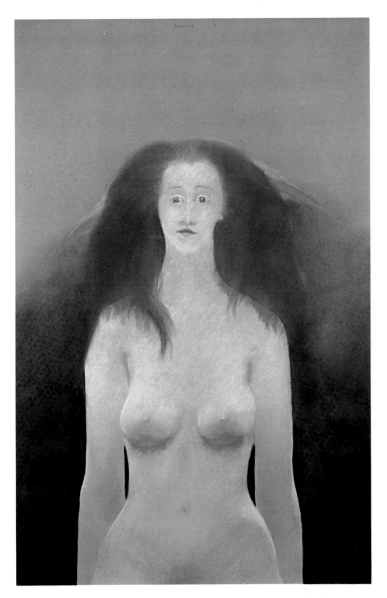

MORRIS BRODERSON. *Good Morning, Starshine.* 1969. Collection
Naomi Hirshhorn, Hollywood. By combining a soft, pastel
technique with lush color and accurate representation, the artist
achieves an eerie sensuality—a hint of terror beneath the nubile
forms.

WILLEM DE KOONING. *Two Women.* 1952. The Art Institute of Chicago. Pastel again, but the intense color is more aggressively applied. The signs of artistic outrage are everywhere, especially in the treatment of the heads, hands, and feet.

PHILIP PEARLSTEIN. *Two Seated Models.*
1968. Collection Mr. and Mrs. Gilbert
Carpenter, Greensboro, North Carolina.
Because the figures have been arbitrarily
cut off and almost photographically
rendered, the viewer perceives them as
anonymous flesh. There is a strange tension between the realism of the forms
and their human emptiness.

CHAIM SOUTINE. *The Madwoman.* 1920.
The National Museum of Western Art,
Tokyo. Presented by Mr. Tai Hayashi,
1960. Loaded-brush technique often expresses agitated or pathological states;
here it enlists our sympathy for the
subject.

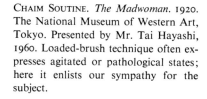

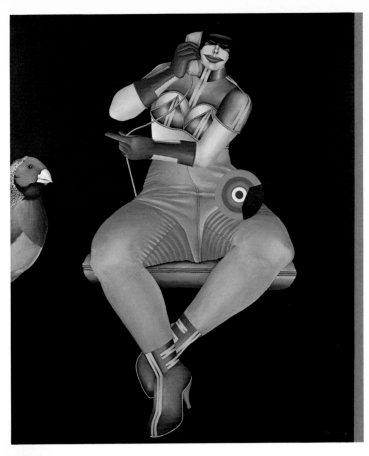

RICHARD LINDNER. *Hello.* 1966. The Harry N. Abrams Family Collection, New York. The pose, the clothing, the low angle of vision, the space-age rendering—all combine to create a fearful Amazonian creature.

MAX BECKMANN. *Columbine.* 1950. Collection Morton D. May, St. Louis. Another antifeminine version of woman, this time in a circus setting. Both Beckmann and Lindner revert to a Neolithic fertility image—the "displayed" or "shameless woman" motif—which originated long before Western conceptions of love or tenderness had developed.

grow beyond the student stage, they may abandon some of these devices, or they may discover new uses of the tools they have acquired. Certainly our principal masters have undergone the discipline of reporting their visual experience accurately, and it has served them well when they have sought "to render the invisible visible." But mastery of the techniques of representation is not undertaken merely to discard them later, or to possess the confidence which is based on having endured a difficult discipline. Learning to draw accurately teaches the artist to see, that is, to *understand* what he is looking at. He must learn to distinguish between imitation of surfaces and informed representation. Laymen can benefit from the artist's struggle to see, if they compare his rendering of reality with the world as they know it. In the difference between the two lies an important body of meaning which the study of art endeavors to uncover.

RICHARD ESTES. *Store Front*. 1967. Allan Stone Gallery, New York. Converging lines deny the planarity of the picture surface, and painted reflections deny they are pigment resting on canvas. The result convinces: an art of magical illusionism is created.

6

THE STYLE OF FORMAL ORDER

POLYCLITUS. *Doryphorus (Spear Bearer)*. Roman copy after an original of c. 450–440 B.C. National Museum, Naples. Although Polyclitus designed his figures in conformity to a geometrical formula, he was the first of the Greek sculptors who could also convince the viewer of the naturalness of his figures.

THE STYLE OF FORMAL ORDER EXPRESSES AN ARTIST'S preference for stability in his creative work and, by implication, in the world. To the extent that Western civilization bears the imprint of classical Greek thought, order has been its constant ideal. The Greeks sought order through measure and proportion—through the expression of mathematical relationships. *Formal order* is balance, harmony, or stability in art created through rules of measure. It is another term for classicism—a classicism found in all periods.

The immediate source of proportions for order and hence of beauty was, for the Greeks, the nude human figure. They discovered that what we call "beautiful" is the result of a harmonious relationship among the parts of any whole. The human body is beautiful, they believed, because it is an expression of the order in the universe. The problem of the artist is to apply that universal order to the design of buildings, the writing of music, and the fashioning of images. Human images were rarely drawn from specific personalities; they were "idealized"—that is, they embodied a mathematical average of the best proportions the Greeks knew. Zeuxis is supposed to have studied many beautiful women before he painted Helen of Troy. Always, in classical art, there is a rule of number or measure applied to the problems of artistic creation. Art is a search for "right" proportions.

But Western man has not been unswerving in his devotion to classical ideals of measure, order, and moderation. Periodically, he has been caught up in violent convulsions. Even the classical Greek passion for formal order gave way to Hellenistic ideals of dynamic movement and unstable form. Similarly, today's art has been characterized by violent style features as well as by rationality and order. Often, in the career of a single artist—Picasso, for instance—both formal order and violent expression may be seen. Apparently, Nietzsche was correct in his analysis of Greek culture into Apollonian and Dionysiac strains: the Apollonian strain expresses a *dream* of order and serenity; the Dionysiac strain expresses *frenzy,* an explosion of energy. In the past, one strain or the other may have dominated; today, both exist side by side.

The openness of modern culture (at least in the West) permits artists the almost totally unhampered expression of their Apollonian *or* Dionysiac impulses. The style of formal order, therefore, need not be the only artistic expression of a people. Nor does it necessarily represent the official taste of the establishment. Rather, it expresses the choice of artists who prefer stable forms and balanced composition—those who possess a serene vision of the world. In other words, the style results from *personality* factors in the artist rather than *power* factors in the culture. We have to understand classicism as a wish that the world were governed by reason and logic. Through the evidence of art, we see how deliberation and measure, calculation and the weighing of alternatives, have overcome the spontaneous expression of feeling. We see Maillol instead of Rodin, Mondrian instead of De Kooning. We see the artist *measuring, anticipating,* the visual consequences of forming and building.

The Transient and the Permanent

If there is one attitude that characterizes an artist who works in a style of formal order, it is an interest in dealing with what is fixed and permanent. When he works with a dynamic subject, he finds some way to stress its quiet qualities. He selects positions where the figure tends to be stable, avoiding the suggestion that it is about to change location. One of the reasons Rodin's *St. John the Baptist Preaching* (1878) was criticized was because it gave the impression of a figure walking off its pedestal. Sculpture, it was felt,

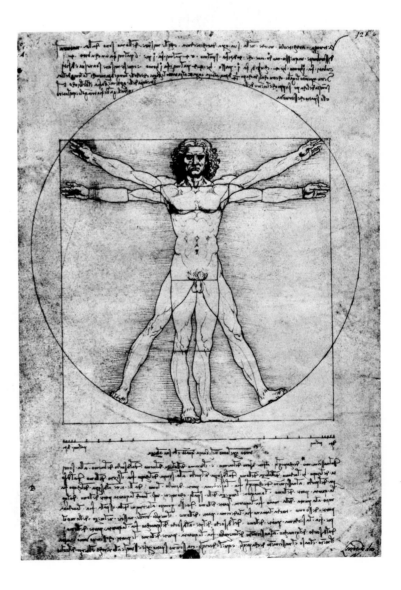

LEONARDO DA VINCI. *Studio del Corpo Humano.* c. 1492. Geometry at work—Leonardo tried to solve a problem of incredible difficulty: the determination of correct proportions in the human figure when it is at rest or in action.

should stand still. Furthermore, the French have always identified their culture very strongly with the classical Greek tradition; a statue which seems to move would violate that tradition. The suggestion of movement, which carries the viewer's eye beyond the art object, negates the idea of permanence. All monuments created to express the durability of a person or idea stress the motionless character of their forms; viewers need to feel that the monument has arrested the flow of time.

Academic art instruction was largely biased in favor of formal order. It taught the student to recognize shapes which are relatively fixed or to give changing shapes a permanent, classical quality. (Of course, the very act of drawing from a rigidly posed model has the effect of freezing movement.) The purpose of such instruction was to create works of art which would seem resistant to the forces of atrophy and change. The artist was asked to discover what it is that can survive amid all the things, including ourselves, which must die.

Students of philosophy will recognize this approach to art as Platonic, for it relates to Plato's interest in knowing the permanent forms of thought which lie behind the transient examples of being we commonly see. The beautiful is the imitation, not of appearances, but of ideal and unchanging essences. Such essences must be known intellectually and mathematically before they can be imitated; hence, the artist must

AUGUSTE RODIN.
St. John the Baptist Preaching. 1878.
The Museum of Modern Art, New York.
Mrs. Simon Guggenheim Fund

Jockey. c. 150 B.C.
National Archaeological Museum, Athens

study the ideal dimensions and proportions of a subject before he attempts to imitate its form. But artists working in this manner do so because of inner necessity rather than a deliberate philosophic choice.

The *Church of the Minorites (II)* (1926) by Lyonel Feininger is an example of the style of formal order by an artist who was much influenced by Cubism. There is a quality in Feininger's work which suggests an effort to impose the geometric order of crystals upon the visible world. Architecture lends itself to this treatment, but Feininger used a sharp-edged form language to represent *growing* things, even people. Cubism had created the breakthrough Feininger exploited to express the clear and restful qualities of the chapel. The subject and its world are treated like facets of a remarkable gem. Feininger's work implies that our universe has an underlying structure which is also fixed, ordered, and, perhaps, divinely decreed.

It is not difficult to see that formal order, in the hands of certain artists, has religious implications. This is understandable, since the Greeks had an almost mystical view of mathematics: it possessed divine beauty for them; art could share the divinity of mathematics. Hence, the implication in Feininger's work that the universe is permanent and orderly is very much like saying that God exists, has created the order reflected in art, and wishes it to continue. At any rate, Feininger's painting shows how an artist might make such a statement.

Kinds of Formal Order

Although the style of formal order is associated with stability and permanence, there are also variations within the style—different ways of exhibiting its qualities. These variations I call *intellectual order, biomorphic order,* and *aesthetic order*. Of course, these categories are not absolutely distinct, but one or the other tends to dominate a given work or an artist's entire output.

LUDWIG MIES VAN DER ROHE.
Seagram Building, New York. 1957

The crystalline tower has been built or imagined by men of every time and place. At first a solid megalith, it dematerializes as it grows higher, a case of the convergence of optical law and spiritual striving.

LYONEL FEININGER. *Church of the Minorites (II).*
1926. Walker Art Center, Minneapolis

PIET MONDRIAN. *Composition with Red, Yellow, and Blue.* 1921.
Gemeente Museum, The Hague,
The Netherlands

INTELLECTUAL ORDER

Perhaps the best-known contemporary examples of *intellectual* order are found in the work of Piet Mondrian. In his *Composition with Red, Yellow, and Blue,* we see a picture which has been created entirely with vertical and horizontal lines, areas of unvarying color, with no representational elements whatever. The elimination of curves, modeling, and subject matter obliges us to examine the work solely in terms of its restricted formal vocabulary. Yet within this narrow range of pictorial language the artist can produce considerable variety—in the shape of the rectangles (their ratios of height to width), in the length of lines, in the apparent "weight" and location of the colored areas, and in their spatial relationships. Indeed, it is the interaction among the forms which suggests its wholly intellectual order. The work reveals multiple balances of horizontal and vertical movements, of light and heavy shapes. By thus reducing his vocabulary, Mondrian tried to employ the pure activity of the viewer's eye to create impressions of motion, weight,

and balance. The elements of the design are *intellectually* interpreted as weight and space. The balance we perceive is a type of order based on operations performed by the mind more than the senses.

An early twentieth-century type of intellectual order appeared in Cubism, especially in the stage called Analytic Cubism (1910–12). Braque and Picasso worked together at this time, and their work is so similar that it appears either one of them could have painted any given picture. This similarity suggests that the same *intellectual method* of analyzing form was employed by both painters; individuality was subordinated to the requirements of an agreement about artistic representation. In Braque's *Man with a Guitar* (1911), we see straight lines, a narrow range of color, and a slicing of the figure into geometric shapes. We learn nothing about the age, appearance, or personality of the subject. The artist presents a quiet arrangement of geometric forms which seem to be floating gently in a shallow space. The figure's outline is indistinct; the forms are denser toward the center and more loosely distributed around the edges. It appears that we are dealing with an artistic approach to the nature of matter—the expression of the idea that, fundamentally, all substances have a com-

GEORGES BRAQUE. *Man with a Guitar.* 1911.
The Museum of Modern Art,
New York. Lillie P. Bliss Bequest

mon structure. The artist seems to be saying that all the variations in the visible world are superficial; underneath there is an order like that of mathematics. Here again, the influence of Platonic thought is evident.

Cubism offered an analysis of form that artists could use in many media for many expressive purposes. In sculpture, *The Horse* (1914) by Raymond Duchamp-Villon (1876–1918) appears to be an attempt to translate an animal into mechanical equivalents, using the geometric format of Cubism. The painterly language of Cubism was enlarged by the incorporation of forms taken from machines or the working drawings of mechanical engineers. Although the artist attempts to visualize motion, the stability of classical order predominates. It is the intellectual element, the process of taking apart the animal and reconstructing it along rational-mechanical lines, which characterizes this work.

Engineering and mechanization have been enormously fascinating to artists, whose reactions range from approval to revulsion. Classical artists, in general, tend to see their ideals of rationality, efficient organization, and mathematical order realized in the machine. Accordingly, they borrow the forms of mechanical engineering and incorporate them in their work. But as soon as machine forms are taken out of their original contexts and exploited in art, they begin to function as symbols. As symbols, geometric-me-

RAYMOND DUCHAMP-VILLON. *The Horse*. 1914. The Museum of Modern Art, New York. Van Gogh Purchase Fund

chanical forms need not necessarily operate within the style of formal order. In the crisp, Euclidian shapes of *My Egypt* by Charles Demuth (1883–1935), formal order is clearly the goal. But in the *Eiffel Tower* (1914) by Robert Delaunay (1885–1941), the forms are seen

CHARLES DEMUTH. *My Egypt*. 1927. Whitney Museum of American Art, New York

ROBERT DELAUNAY. *Eiffel Tower*. 1914. The Solomon R. Guggenheim Museum, New York

Geometrical forms can be used to express a restless, surging dynamism, as in the Delaunay, or, conversely, the order of forces that have been balanced and stabilized, as in the Demuth.

in partial disintegration; instead of resting, they appear to be exploding upward before coming down in a final collapse. While the choice of geometric or biomorphic forms may offer a clue to an artist's interests, it is their *organization* which establishes his style.

In architecture, the buildings of Mies van der Rohe are classically simple and severely intellectual. This may be due to the crucial importance he attached to purity of space and surface (as in the Seagram Building). There is no hint of handcraft or the skilled contribution of workers. The result is a product of design—that is, of thought applied to using industrial materials fastidiously. Mies, like Mondrian, restricted himself to a narrow vocabulary; he gave up the associations of natural materials as Mondrian gave up the associations of curving lines and representational forms.

The style has been widely imitated because it fits so logically into a world of technology and industry. It has been equally well used for apartment houses, libraries, and college buildings; it reflects man's search for permanent and unvarying forms. Indeed, Mies stated his interest in creating structures and spaces which could be universally used. His buildings do not reflect changes in function, client, or symbolic meaning. But this should not be regarded as a fault from the standpoint of classical order. Rather, it illustrates

the victory of architecture over the limitations of climate, handcraft, and literary association. It is the visible evidence of man's effort to create something more durable than the reflection of personality.

BIOMORPHIC ORDER

The term "biomorphic" designates artistic forms which *look as if* they had developed in the way living organisms develop: through the division of cells. An example is seen in Jean Arp's *Human Concretion*. Where some artists regard nature as fundamentally chaotic, this artist sees formal perfection even in organic life. The material of the sculpture is stone, and yet Arp gives it a soft, fleshlike quality. The connection with the human is remote, but the identification with the living and the organic is strong. In *Torso of a Young Man* by Constantin Brancusi (1876–1957), biological and geometric forms meet in the same work. There is no question of Brancusi's devotion to mathematical regularity and clear articulation. However, he is also determined not to let classicism sever the connection with organic life. The truncated cylinders stimulate memories of ancient sculpture—the armless or headless figures unearthed in Hellenistic ruins. At the same time, the trunk and thighs recall the African sculpture which so obviously influenced Pi-

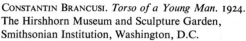

Constantin Brancusi. *Torso of a Young Man.* 1924.
The Hirshhorn Museum and Sculpture Garden,
Smithsonian Institution, Washington, D.C.

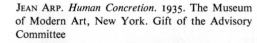

Jean Arp. *Human Concretion.* 1935. The Museum
of Modern Art, New York. Gift of the Advisory
Committee

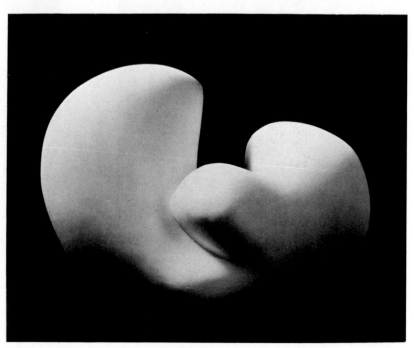

ALEXEJ VON JAWLENSKY. *Still Life with Lamp.* 1913. Private collection, Hofheim/ Taunus, Germany. The objects are barely identified—color striving to break loose. However, a stern linear structure holds everything together.

MAURICE ESTÈVE. *Rebecca.* 1952. Musée National d'Art Moderne, Paris. After establishing the huddled relationships typical among objects in a still life and thus generating a conviction of real things in real space, the painter leaps boldly into pure color and texture. Still, the reality of the picture keeps in touch with the reality of the object.

RICHARD DIEBENKORN. *Ocean Park, No. 22.* 1969. Poindexter Gallery, New York. This is the sort of controlled abstraction in which the light, color, or shape of a place is lifted out of context, so that its qualities are felt while its identity is obscured.

JULES OLITSKI. *Magic Number.* 1967. Massachusetts Institute of Technology, Cambridge. The painter maintains his governance over the dynamics of a vast pictorial field through subtle hints at the corners and along the edges of the canvas.

ROBERT DELAUNAY. *Homage to Blériot.* 1914. Kunstsammlung, Basel. Color theory began as a scientific idea and turned into an object—a wheel. Here the wheel becomes a bicycle, a spinning propeller, an airplane, a solar disk. Ultimately it is joined by man as bird, cosmic flyer, and finally Superbird.

STANTON MacDONALD-WRIGHT. *Abstraction on Spectrum (Organization, 5).* 1914. Des Moines Art Center, Des Moines, Iowa. Nathan Emory Coffin Memorial Collection. The solar disk of the Eastern sun-worshiping religions transformed into a gorgeous color symphony—or Synchromy, as Wright and Morgan Russell called it.

FRANK STELLA. *Sinjerli Variation I.* 1968. The Harry N. Abrams
Family Collection, New York. The color wheel in a new guise—
a set of intersecting protractors. There is no symbolic or expressive
intent here; still, the image cannot escape its destiny: three rising
suns whose radiation is intermixed.

ANDRÉ DERAIN. *London Bridge*. 1906. The Museum of Modern Art, New York. Gift of Mr. and Mrs. Charles Zadok. There is an attempt here to separate color as a sensation from particular colored objects; color must convey the emotional truth of an experience, not merely its appearance.

PIERRE BONNARD. *Le Compotier blanc*. 1921. Private collection, New York. If the viewer salivates, it is mainly because of the juicy colors, not the juicy fruit.

WASSILY KANDINSKY. *Landscape with Houses.* 1909. Kunstmuseum der Stadt Düsseldorf. Like Derain, Kandinsky was trying to attend to his sensations rather than the structures of these buildings and trees.

WASSILY KANDINSKY. *Study for Composition No. 2.* 1910. The Solomon R. Guggenheim Museum, New York. Despite visual analogies to Russian folklore and Slavic music, the purely sensuous force of colors and forms asserts itself here. To Kandinsky, with his interest in the spiritual and the occult, the power of visual sensations is a mystical phenomenon.

SAM FRANCIS. *Abstraction.* 1959. Whitney Museum of American Art, New York. Bequest of Udo M. Reinach. We see color and space, but we feel emotions largely associated with tactility. Francis is a master of the semitransparent mark, the wet stain, the moving spot, the orchestrated splash and trickle.

JEAN-PAUL RIOPELLE. *Vesperal No. 3.* 1958. The Art Institute of Chicago. Mary and Leigh B. Block Fund for Acquisitions. Aside from its structural qualities, this paint surface seems edible: the palette-knife technique reminds us of thick slabs of butter and globs of strawberry jam spread on bread.

MORRIS LOUIS. *Kaf.* 1959–60. Collection Kimiko and John G. Powers, New York. Through the management of fluid, overlapping stains on unprimed canvas, the characteristic mark of the brush—hence of the hand—is bypassed. We respond to a moist, multichrome mist, seemingly created by nature, not man.

PAUL JENKINS. *Phenomena in Heavenly Way.* 1967. Collection Mr. and Mrs. Jack Stupp, Don Mills, Ontario. Wetter than the Louis work, this has more puddle and flow. As the hand and brush become more remote, we enter a world of hydrodynamic engineering made gorgeously visible.

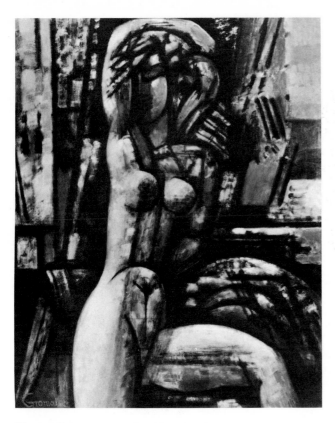

MARCEL GROMAIRE.
Nu, bras levé, sur fond gris et or. 1957.
Galerie Leandro, Geneva

OSKAR SCHLEMMER. *Abstract Figure.* 1962.
Bronze copy after plaster original, 1921.
Collection Frau Tut Schlemmer, Stuttgart

Often the classical artist feels the need to reach an accord with the machine. His work expresses the effort to reconcile the qualities of growing things with precisely measured shapes.

casso, Marcel Gromaire (1892–1971), Modigliani, and others. Brancusi and Arp demonstrate the compatibility of a style of formal order with rounded shapes and regular curves.

Henry Moore is also a classical artist, but his work is less abstract than that of Arp or Brancusi, closer to the identifiably human. His reclining figures and family groups are monuments to vital repose, as in the bronze *Family Group* (1948–49). Although Moore stresses the roundedness of forms, his figures are strong, not soft. This is because underneath Moore's smooth and rounded surfaces there is a virile understanding of structure, of a system which supports and controls massive weights. Because Moore successfully solved the artistic problems of the human and the abstract—of monumentality and control, of rounded form and structural power—we see his work as one of the most affirmative statements made about humanity in the twentieth century.

HENRY MOORE. *Family Group.* 1948–49.
The Museum of Modern Art, New York.
A. Conger Goodyear Fund

181

VICTOR LUNDY. St. Paul's Lutheran Church,
Sarasota, Florida. 1959

EDWARD WESTON.
Photograph of halved artichoke. 1930

The visual analogy between Weston's artichoke
and Lundy's church reveals the biomorphic
source of the feelings generated by the man-made
structure.

In architecture, biomorphic order has received fresh impetus from new materials and devices: collapsible domes whose skins are curved metal hemispheres; shells made of concrete sprayed over inflated balloons; ribbed ceilings possessing an almost botanical delicacy; paraboloid roof structures combined with daring suspension systems. The dome, which has always expressed biomorphic impulses, is a device going back to the early tumulus, or burial mound. It is a shape associated with our wish to live inside a womblike enclosure: either the artificial grave mound uniting us with Mother Earth or the curved ceiling of a church, the dome of the heavens, symbolizing the benevolent, maternal universe. These structures combine formal order with symbolic meanings which are ultimately biologic and religious.

Frank Lloyd Wright practiced what he called an "organic" philosophy of architecture—one in which buildings assert kinship with nature through rugged materials and cavelike spaces. But only in the Guggenheim Museum did he base his design on the structure of a natural object: an enormous nautilus shell. His biomorphism was followed in other contexts. Just as the gently descending ramps of the Guggenheim manage the aesthetic transformation of the modern museum-goer, the modern parking garage changes him from motorist to pedestrian. The garage is a sort of automotive Guggenheim whose outer skin has been stripped away. The engineer has created a gigantic, concrete sea shell, holding in its recesses thousands of nests for gasoline engines, temporarily still.

FRANK LLOYD WRIGHT. Interior,
The Solomon R. Guggenheim Museum,
New York. 1959

Aesthetic order is visible in works which appeal to us mainly through their sensuous organization. Thus an artist adjusts the various surface appeals of a work so we can experience its "beauty." Aesthetic order does not rely on visual resemblance or truth; it depends on our capacity to admire what is immediately satisfying. The simplest analogy is to our satisfaction in the taste of food. Such satisfactions do not occur because they mean something, look like something, or because they are useful. They make an appeal to something within us which responds with the emotion of delight. Perhaps there is some ideal organization of energies which works of aesthetic order encourage, leading to an experience that leaves us gratified without knowing why.

The Breakfast Room by Pierre Bonnard (1867–1947), for example, relies on coloristic invention to orchestrate a symphony of chromatic delight. Bonnard weaves a tapestry suggested only in part by the objects before him. The table, the window, the fragmented figure, and the scene through the window are just nominally established. They constitute an opportunity for the artist to create variations on yellow, yellow-green, yellow-orange, violet, blue-violet, and so on. Deep space is casually represented; the drawing is perfunctory. Most of the color does not "move" in or out of the picture space; rather it shimmers on the surface of the canvas. Painters like Bonnard do not try to remind us of the appearance of sky, fruit, and tableware: the material we are chiefly aware of here is paint. Bonnard and his predecessors Monet and Seurat convey a delight in pigment and color quite apart from what they represent.

Georges Braque, the early collaborator of Picasso,

PIERRE BONNARD.
The Breakfast Room. c. 1930–31.
The Museum of Modern Art, New York

GEORGE A. APPLEGARTH.
Downtown Center Garage,
San Francisco. 1955

moved their common intellectual style in the direction of aesthetic order. *Woman with a Mandolin* places the classical qualities of Cubism at the disposal of aesthetic pleasure. Compared with Bonnard, Braque is the better designer: his organization of space is more varied and inventive. He also has a deeper interest in different textures. Bonnard suppresses all textures in the interest of one—paint. Braque, using additives like sand and egg shells, manipulates pigment to increase tactile appeal. He exaggerates the wallpaper pattern, bringing it into the same plane as the figure, indicating that the sensuous qualities of the wall are more important than its "correct" location in space. He extracts the maximum decorative effect from each object or shape. As in Bonnard, we learn very little about subject matter: the subject is an opportunity for the artist to manipulate pattern, texture, and color.

Perhaps the most elegant modern master of aesthetic order was Henri Matisse (1869–1954). His style was enriched by the study of Persian art, which, as with much of Near Eastern art, emphasized opulence of color and elaborate decorative detail. In the painting of Matisse, there is an almost oriental emphasis on splendor, on subordination of expressive meaning in

GEORGES BRAQUE.
Woman with a Mandolin. 1937.
The Museum of Modern Art, New York.
Mrs. Simon Guggenheim Fund

HENRI MATISSE. *Lady in Blue.* 1937.
Collection Mrs. John Wintersteen,
Villanova, Pennsylvania

the interest of aesthetic surface. The *Lady in Blue* reveals the painter as a sophisticated European designer of decorative forms building on a Persian tradition. He can find precisely what he needs in what is set before him: the ornamented furniture, the rich gown, the room interior, a lady casually sitting, a bouquet of flowers to frame her head, and the pictures with somewhat classical evocations. This material is highly simplified; only shape has been taken from their total reality and then reassembled to create a new reality. Matisse subordinates drawing and color to a single pictorial effect which is meant to be pleasurable as a whole. In viewing his work, it is important not to let the eye linger on any part by itself; one must see the entire canvas at once, let it *fill the eye;* then the effect of the quantities and intensities of color will be felt.

An American sculptor, Harry Bertoia (born 1915), created a metal screen which richly exploits the aesthetic qualities of brass, copper, and nickel. It serves, of course, as a partition and also as a plane against which one sees the normal activity of the bank. Because this screen wall functions architecturally, the sculptor wisely decided to let the properties of the materials dominate rather than create symbolic forms to com-

pete for the viewer's attention. As a result, there is a mutually enhancing relationship involving the room, its people, and the wall itself.

In the work of an artist like Bradley Walker Tomlin (1899–1953), a type of order has been achieved which is in the classical tradition of the Parthenon and J. S. Bach. His *No. 10* is almost totally abstract; it is a product of calculation, simplification, and measurement, departing from Mediterranean conceptions of order only in the absence of a set of proportions based on the human figure. Unlike the Greeks, modern followers of classicism tend to put the human image aside. They rely on our highly developed capacity to perceive the order of ideas, or intellectual order; the order of living forms, or biomorphic order; and the order of sense data, or aesthetic order.

Conclusion

Classical styles of art have been closely associated with measurement, mathematics, and geometry. But the use of geometrical shapes is not necessarily a sign of formal order. The essence of formal order lies in its attitude toward motion and stability. If forms seem to be at rest, they suggest orderliness; if they appear to be moving, their motion must look measured and predictable. These assertions could be made about life as well as art. Parents often judge their children by the way they are moving: certain patterns mean trouble; others are reassuring. Of course, there are some parents for whom *any* movement signals danger; but they may be neurotic and are likely to raise neurotic children.

Extending this observation to art history, we find that in certain social and political climates there is a preference for absolute stability in the visual arts. The art of Egypt and Byzantium, for example, placed a premium on immobility. Should we conclude that it also reflected a neurotic obsession with order? It is true that both civilizations resisted change and also managed to last as empires for at least a thousand years. On the other hand, the sheer durability of a state may not signify that its people are living what we, or they, would regard as a good life. Conceivably, the style of formal order—especially when it is a prescribed style—is an instrument of social control. Modern authoritarians have shown a preference for a trite sort of classicism, possibly because they base absolute rule on society's need for discipline—a discipline imposed from above.

There are times in our lives when stability seems more desirable than anything else. On other occasions, formal order may strike us as painfully dull. From the standpoint of the health of society, the opportunity for nonformal styles to flourish *along with* classical styles seems essential. But today it is not possible to decree the creation of art in *any* style, much less to expect that the result will satisfy desires for something different. The underground hunger of Eastern Europeans for American and Western European cultural products is a sign of the boredom a style of dated classicism creates in a population which is hopeful of change. Sooner or later a stylistic reaction emerges—a reaction all the more extreme because it has been so long repressed. The coexistence of diverse styles in free societies, then, appears to be one of the best signs, not only of a healthy culture but of properly functioning social and political institutions.

HARRY BERTOIA. Screen for Manufacturers Hanover Trust Company, New York. 1954

BRADLEY WALKER TOMLIN.
No. 10. 1952–53.
Munson-Williams-Proctor Institute,
Utica, New York

7

THE STYLE OF EMOTION

IN THE VISUAL ARTS, TRAITS WHICH STRESS THE EX-pression of feeling occur so often that we can refer to a "style of emotion." Often, an artist cannot "speak" in any other language. Van Gogh and Soutine were such men: their pictures of people, flowers, trees, or even chairs, burst with intensity. For such artists, what matters is not accuracy or the measured expression of order; rather, the communication of anxiety, pity, or rage—an emotion—takes precedence over everything else.

If we say that emotion is important to a certain kind of artist, do we mean the emotion he feels or his arousal of emotion in others? It can be both. As viewers, however, we have only a secondary interest in the artist's feelings; we are mainly concerned with the way art *objects* are responsible for our responses. Sometimes the language used by critics to describe the emotional impact of a work gives the impression that the artist experienced the same feelings in advance of creating it. That may or may not be true. And it is not our purpose to find out. Certain theories of art criticism assume that artistic excellence depends on whether the viewer is convinced the artist truly experienced the emotions we see in his work. The study of style, however, focuses more sharply on the art object than on the artist's behavior. When examining a work of art, the viewers ought to be more interested in *their own* biographies and *their own* emotions than in those of the artist. We should ask, "Does the *work* convince me of the reality of the world it attempts to create?" rather than, "Did the artist really feel the emotions portrayed here?"

There are differences of opinion about what constitutes the "expression of emotion" in art. The view taken here is that emotions are the names we give to neuromuscular reactions—feelings—which have been triggered by the organization of elements in an art object. The *energy* for such feelings comes from the viewer, but the feelings are *organized* by the work of art. Consequently, emotions are *caused* and *shaped* by the art object; they are *portrayed* in it.

There are differences *within* the style of emotion. That is, works of art have the capacity to arouse a *range* of feelings and dispositions—all of which are emotional but differing in their content. Obviously, we can be elated by one work and depressed by another. Emotional responses may be caused by the subject matter or theme of the work; or they may be due to the type of aesthetic "signal" the work transmits. For example, abstract art often has no apparent subject matter, yet it can cause complex emotional responses. Something in the visual organization of abstract works must be responsible for these reactions. Consequently, we shall be dealing in this chapter with *two* sources of artistic emotion: thematic or subject-matter sources, and organizational or design sources.

The style of emotion designates *any* means of arousing feelings in a viewer. Its most stirring examples reveal the mutual influence of theme *and* design. Examples might be seen in the *Side of Beef* by Chaim Soutine and *The Bat* by Germaine Richier (1904–1959). Both subjects are distasteful, and the organization of forms in each case reinforces our normal feelings of revulsion—feelings clustered around the idea of slaughter, or attack by a hideous creature. On the other hand, Henry Moore's *Falling Warrior* deals with killing, too, but the simplification of forms and freezing of movement divest the sculpture of any gory qualities the theme would be expected to have. In other words, what we know about Moore's subject does not interfere with the formal order of his sculpture. But the carcass by Soutine dramatizes the mu-

GERMAINE RICHIER. *The Bat*. 1952.
Whereabouts unknown

CHAIM SOUTINE. *Side of Beef*. c. 1925.
Albright-Knox Art Gallery, Buffalo, New York

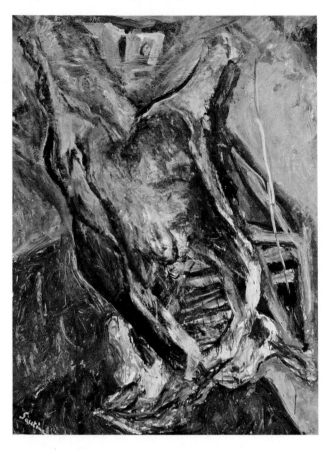

HENRY MOORE. *Falling Warrior*. 1955–56.
The Hirshhorn Museum and Sculpture Garden, Smithsonian Institution, Washington, D.C.

HENRY E. MATTSON. *Wings of the Morning.* 1936.
The Metropolitan Museum of Art, New York.
Arthur H. Hearn Fund, 1937

WINSLOW HOMER. *Northeaster.* 1895.
The Metropolitan Museum of Art, New York.
Gift of George A. Hearn, 1910

tilated character of eviscerated forms which once housed organic life. The carcass records the slaughter of a beast, not the slaying of a hero.

Richier's bat, with its webbed limbs radiating from a mammalian trunk, strikes a note of primeval terror because of some instinctive fear it arouses in us. Its resemblance to the human is stressed by the artist to arouse mixed emotions—emotions of recognition and dread. In this case, design is assisted by the *manipulation of symbolic meanings* to mount an assault on the viewer's feelings.

Themes of violence and an interest in mutilated forms are not uncommon features of the style of emotion today. However, we are not concerned with discovering whether we like or dislike these style features. We examine this art to gain insight into our world. If art reflects the times, it is worth attention whether we enjoy it or not. The style of emotion should help us to see what it is about life in the twentieth century that leads to the expression of terror and despair—or of joy.

Romanticism and Emotion

A prominent feature of the style of emotion is the apparent desire of the artist to *disclose* personal feelings. This attitude of emotional candor, of giving primacy to one's reactions, is also called Romanticism. The Romantic tends to believe that the important aspect of any person, place or event is *his* feeling about it. The claims of fact seem less urgent since his *feelings* are facts. Sometimes we speak of individuals as "losing themselves" in some idea, and this ability to "lose" oneself is characteristic of the Romantic. He may even lose his "sense of proportion." Looking at Romantic art, it is not difficult to feel *lost* in the work, to lose our common-sense idea of the rightness of things. Henry Mattson (born 1887)

in *Wings of the Morning* encourages us to feel *drawn into* the sea. He exhibits the typical Romantic reluctance to distinguish between subject and object, between the observer and observed. The ocean is not merely a body of water but a mysterious world in which we could somehow live. By contrast, Winslow Homer (1836–1910), who also painted the ocean with great power, conveyed the idea of the sea as an exciting but separate place.

Another feature of Romanticism is its interest in the exotic and the dangerous. Romantic artists have often been attracted to far-off lands, as Paul Gauguin (1848–1903) was to Tahiti. Unfamiliar places and customs allow us to forget our present lives and environments: we can *lose* ourselves, at least imaginatively. Gauguin's *The Spirit of the Dead Watching* (1892) perfectly fits the requirements of Romanticism: Tahiti is an exotic place; its people are unsophisticated—certainly to a Parisian; fantastic flowers and a mysterious inscription, "Manao tupapau" ("The spirit of the dead remembers her"), appear in the background. Most important, an atmosphere of supernaturalism hovers over the picture.

In contrast to the exoticism of Gauguin, there is the dreamlike and somewhat threatening world of the American painter Darrel Austin (born 1907). It illustrates the fascination violence has for the Romantic imagination. *The Black Beast* shows a fierce jungle cat resting with a dead bird under her paws, both set in an eerie, marshy landscape. The animal seems to glow because the painter has illuminated her from below or within, creating an almost phosphorescent effect. Also, the surface is exceedingly active, in contrast to the serenity of the animal. The Romantic emotion in this picture comes from the juxtaposition of the jungle cat with the mangled bird. Thus the artist suggests the duality of nature: killing exists side by side with majestic repose.

In sculpture, a complex Romantic work is seen in

JEAN DUBUFFET. *Leader in a Parade Uniform.* 1945. Collection Mr. and Mrs. Morton Neumann, Chicago. Dubuffet's imagery stands at the border where childhood, insanity, and hilarious burlesque meet.

ADOLPH GOTTLIEB. *Dialogue No. 1*. 1960. Albright-Knox Art Gallery, Buffalo, New York. Gift of Seymour H. Knox. A painting that tries to epitomize the world in two symbolic images: a pair of immaculate disks floats above an implied horizon while an uncouth pictograph explodes below.

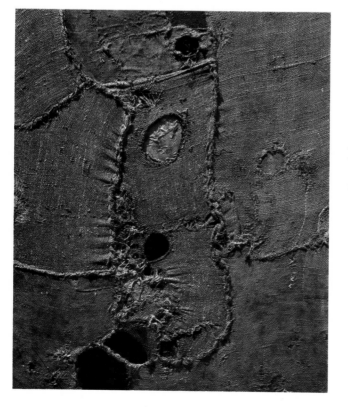

ALBERTO BURRI. *Sacco B.* 1953. Collection the artist. An open wound is visible through a tear in a rotting and patched sackcloth cover; other holes are burned out, dead. Does biological survival, or civilized life, depend on a fabric so worn and makeshift?

ROBERT MOTHERWELL. *Elegy to the Spanish Republic, No. XXXIV.* 1953–54. Albright-Knox Art Gallery, Buffalo, New York. Gift of Seymour H. Knox. One senses the desire to express a profound melancholy about the fate of the Spanish Republic. But a purely unconscious or automatic strategy of generating visual symbols can result in vaguely dismal forms of uncertain significance.

ARSHILE GORKY. *The Liver Is the Cock's Comb.* 1944. Albright-Knox Art Gallery, Buffalo, New York. Gift of Seymour H. Knox. For Gorky, the panorama of nature is fundamentally an erotic spectacle: any pleasure we feel in Nature's presence results from her prodigious expenditure of sexual energy.

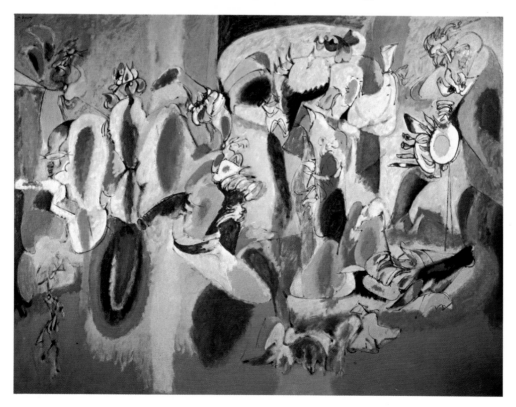

PABLO PICASSO. *Fishing at Night off Antibes*. 1939. The Museum of Modern Art, New York. Mrs. Simon Guggenheim Fund. Two women casually watch the spear-killing of fish attracted to a boat by the light of the fishermen's lantern. It is a scene of rich color and dark irony: men are predators at work or play. The ladies—one executing a pirouette, the other holding her bike and eating a double ice cream cone—enjoy the spectacle.

GRAHAM SUTHERLAND. *Thorn Trees*. 1945. Albright-Knox Art Gallery, Buffalo, New York. Sutherland has found in nature's thorns, prickles, and roots the metaphoric equivalents of what he sees as man's fundamental character: his capacity for inflicting pain and his possession of a convoluted underground existence.

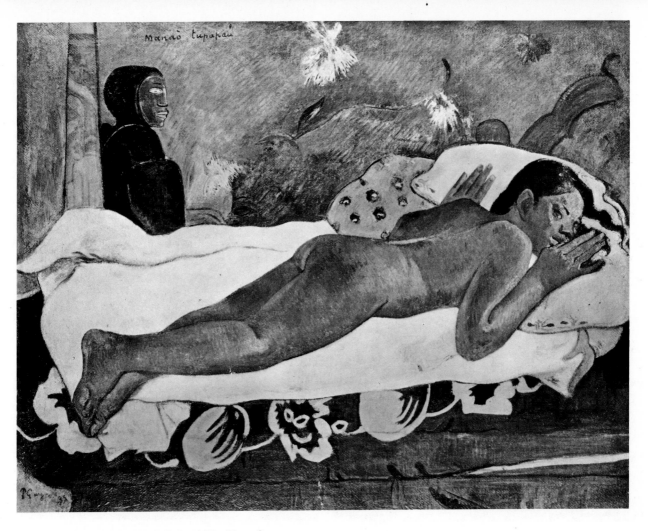

PAUL GAUGUIN. *The Spirit of the Dead Watching.* 1892.
Albright-Knox Art Gallery, Buffalo, New York.
A. Conger Goodyear Collection

DARREL AUSTIN. *The Black Beast.* 1941. Smith College Museum of Art,
Northampton, Massachusetts

THEODORE J. ROSZAK.
Spectre of Kitty Hawk. 1946–47.
The Museum of Modern Art, New York

THÉODORE GÉRICAULT. *The Raft of the Medusa.* 1818–19. The Louvre, Paris

Spectre of Kitty Hawk by Theodore Roszak (born 1907). The artist has invented a frightening creature based on the pterodactyl, an extinct flying reptile. Using steel, bronze, and brass, Roszak built a monster which suggests the mixed consequences of the invention of flight. Without the title and its reference to the Wright brothers at Kitty Hawk, would this work be effective? Probably. We would experience the same emotions; the idea of a predatory creature is communicated through the head and claws; the wings, body, tail, and other features hint at the airplane—perhaps after a crash. And the hard, hammered material suggests the metallic glint of a bird-machine.

Because the Romantic artist deals with pure forms as well as associations and symbols, he undertakes large risks: he has to control a complex vehicle of communication. The dangers of an easily dated sentimentality are very great. Some works of the Romantic masters Géricault and Delacroix may seem to us excessively melodramatic. Still, *The Raft of the Medusa* survives as an important work because of its formal organization and powerful execution. The forms carry conviction long after the theme ceases to to be interesting.

The Role of Distortion

Emotion relies on distortion because a viewer's feelings are readily aroused by any departure from the "normal." This is especially true of the human body. Also, distortion of objects in the natural or man-made world arouses the viewer because of a tension between what we "know" to be the case and what we see. Distortion means stretching, twisting, or otherwise deforming the shapes of things. But it also refers to exaggerating size, color and illumination, increasing the contrast between light and dark, or overstating textural and surface qualities. Generally, the choice of one of these types of distortion is not so much a calculation as a spontaneous result of the artist's attitude toward a subject.

Because of personality or training, an artist may enlarge or suppress certain features; or he may prefer to view subjects when they *seem* deformed. Even a photograph can exhibit distortion if the subject is seen at an odd moment or from an unusual angle of vision. Michelangelo often portrayed figures in writhing attitudes, employing his famous *contrapposto*—an extreme twisting action through the shoulders, trunk, and pelvis. Some of the apocalyptic feeling of his *Last Judgment* in the Sistine Chapel is due to the representation of muscles in tension. The viewer feels such tensions physically and emotionally.

Distortion serves many purposes: it may be sardonic observation and pity in Lautrec, anxiety in Munch and Soutine, isolation and despair in Giacometti. Van Gogh seems to have distorted because of an almost mystical projection of himself into his work. Francis Bacon achieves his macabre effect by suggesting that beneath man's civilized surface the mentality of a savage is in command. Some distortion is pleasant: the attenuated figures of Lehmbruck endow adolescence with harmony and grace. Modigliani's stretching

Distorted photograph of a man.
The high-speed camera reveals distortions we do not normally see, or it can be manipulated to create a distorted image. In either case, the viewer feels an impulse to imitate what he sees with his body. Thus, emotions are generated within him.

MICHELANGELO. Detail of *The Last Judgment*. 1534–41. Sistine Chapel, The Vatican, Rome. The flayed skin of St. Bartholomew provided Michelangelo with an opportunity to show his own contorted face and what he felt to be his miserable and unworthy soul.

Photograph of Pete Maravich, January, 1970

JACK LEVINE. *Welcome Home*. 1946.
The Brooklyn Museum. J. B. Woodward Memorial Fund.
To create satire, indignation is not enough: acute observation and hostile analysis are also required.

and simplification of contours results in a heightening of sensual qualities. But both these artists would be described as classicists; their distortion is mainly attenuation for the sake of refining form.

In Jack Levine's *Welcome Home* (1946), distortion is employed in an artistically complex and thematically developed work. The persons in the painting are held up to ridicule and contempt: we are encouraged to see their bodies as the physical containers of the vices of pride and gluttony. At the same time, the artist makes sure that moral deformity is joined with social prominence. He lavishes attention on the details of the table service; the obsequiousness of the waiter; the elegant dress of the diners; the woman, upper left, who embodies wealth and emaciated glamour. Noteworthy also is Levine's use of a distorting perspective to enlarge the heads; the view from above lets us "look down" on the celebrities; we feel superior to them as they gorge themselves—middle-aged heroes celebrating a victory won with the lives of boys. The kind of satire that Levine practices calls for a tremendous capacity for indignation. Hypocrisy fascinates the satirical artist; he seems to love the signs of grossness and corruption.

Anxiety and Despair

Because we have known several wars in this century and live with the knowledge of possible extermination in another, it is not surprising that art expresses symptoms of fear and hopelessness. The style of emotion also describes our periodic lapses into depression, our feelings of doubt that the world can ever right itself. Artists, like philosophers and theologians, try to explain what is happening to the human species. Some condemn the social or economic conditions which cause wars; others look within man himself. Some artists may not try to explain their anxiety: they express its consequences. They create images of sickness; they stress the ugliness of human nature; they dwell on the failures of civilization.

There is an eloquent tradition of artistic protest against war's inhumanity, from Goya's *Disasters of War* etchings to Picasso's *Guernica*. Beyond that, the side effects of war are felt in many ways, and these are inevitably present in visual art. There is also a despairing art related mainly to personal suffering without any apparent social connection. An example of this is *The Scream* (1893) by Edvard Munch. It shows a person on a bridge, hands held to the ears, with his mouth open in what seems to be a drawn-out howl. We are uncertain of the person's age or sex, and we do not know the reason for the grief. There is something deathly about the face, as in most of the pictures by Munch. Two anonymous figures on the bridge symbolize the indifference of the world to the private tragedy of the subject. The drawing is very generalized; the lines of sky and harbor seem to be echoes of the cry. Munch used very simple means to describe

EDVARD MUNCH. *The Scream*. 1893.
National Gallery, Oslo

LU DUBLE. *Cain*. 1953.
Whitney Museum of American Art, New York

196

HIRAM WILLIAMS. *Guilty Men.* 1958.
Collection Mr. and Mrs. Dalton Trumbo, Los Angeles

FRANCIS BACON. *Study for a Head.* 1952.
Private collection

what seemed to him the essential suffering of life. He invented visual symbols to express the *invisible* anguish of existence.

The sculpture *Cain* by Lu Duble (1896–1970) constitutes an *external* image of torment in its agonized portrayal of the Biblical personality who murdered his brother. A powerful diagonal line expresses the agitation of Cain, distorting the head and out-thrust jaw to keep the diagonal force. This is a good example of the way a dancer might use his body to express guilt and remorse. The figure becomes a vehicle for externalizing the spiritual condition of its owner. Biblical narrative is rarely subtle: a tense, dramatic image seems appropriate to the moral scale of the Biblical account.

In *Study for a Head,* Francis Bacon (born 1910) presents the image of a person who is either mad or turning into a beast. Whereas the cry in the work by Munch suggests loneliness and suffering, this scream is related to the savagery of civilized life. The figure is presented as a reasonably well-dressed man sitting in a chair. But instead of a study of character, the connection between man and brute is emphasized. Of course, this version of man is very disturbing. Does it tell the *whole* truth about the human condition? Still, Bacon has influenced many artists, even in the United States, where bitterness has not been a notable

theme of artistic expression. Hiram Williams (born 1917) appears to have been attracted by the Baconian image of man. The blurring of features and the combination of formal dress with a suggestion of the monstrous is characteristic of Bacon's work and the work of artists he has influenced. Bacon is not a facile painter; he concentrates on the ungraceful creation of images which disturb any comfortable notions we may have about human dignity.

Rico Lebrun (1900–1964) in *Migration to Nowhere* deals with war by making a macabre dance out of the flight of its crippled victims. Through distorted perspective he has enlarged the feet and hence the idea of flight. The vacant horizon symbolizes the hopelessness of escape for these figures, which lose their corporeality as they recede into the picture space. Yet there is a curious grace in their movement, in their billowing garments, in their use of crutches with the skill of players in a horrible game. Lebrun's imagination ironically makes a desperate situation bearable by invoking the agility of the maimed; Bacon finds nothing redeeming in the image of man: he wants to terrify us to the marrow of our bones.

A subject similar to Lebrun's is treated by Ben Shahn in *Liberation.* Here the figures are deliberately awkward; they seem maimed although they are not. Lebrun's figures, on the other hand, are graceful al-

RICO LEBRUN.
Migration to Nowhere. 1941.
Whereabouts unknown

OSKAR KOKOSCHKA. *Self-Portrait.* 1913.
The Museum of Modern Art, New York

BEN SHAHN. *Liberation.* 1945.
Collection James Thrall Soby,
New Canaan, Connecticut

though crippled. Irony is a major quality in Shahn's work; the children play in a bombed-out setting; they pursue the normal pleasures of childhood under desperate circumstances. Just as Lebrun looked for a type of grace in deformity, Shahn gratified an aesthetic interest in design and texture with his slanting treatment of the sky, the leaning building, and the carefully rendered rubble. In his drawing of the children he has dwelt on hunger and pathos. By examining their silhouettes, noticing especially the foreshortening of the legs, we sense the horror of the scene, its images of broken cities and human dismemberment.

Europe's recurrent agonies have contributed to a characteristic central European type of artistic anxiety, so well depicted by Oskar Kokoschka (1886–1980).

His *Self-Portrait* (1913) reveals the typical distortions of Expressionist art: the large eyes and hand; gaunt, bony head; agitated paint application; flickering light; and a facial expression hovering between profound sadness and guilt. The hand seems to accuse the artist while his mouth cannot say what it is that condemns him. The restless contours of the face heighten the central idea of this work—that a man feels himself to be under a terrible judgment.

Perhaps Kokoschka best expresses the theme of modern anxiety without venturing as far as Bacon. His subject remains capable of feeling guilty about the world; but we would find it difficult to attribute such feelings to Bacon's man. However, the Bacon painting was created in the 1950s and Kokoschka's portrait dates from one year before World War I. So, on the evidence of these two works, there has been a considerable moral deterioration in our civilization; of course, this evidence is incomplete and may reflect only the opinions of two atypical observers. It remains to be seen whether joy can be expressed with as much conviction.

Joy and Celebration

It should not be surprising that the style characteristics which express anxiety can also be employed to celebrate human experience. There are comedians who can act as tragedians. Indeed, students of drama believe that a comedian like Chaplin is a genius because he closely approaches pathos while seeming to work for laughs. Celebration in art, however, is not *directly* related to the comic spirit; it deals with life's festive and exultant moments: victories over fear, consummations of love or ambition, affirmations of the goodness of being alive.

The indirect connection between celebration and the comic is visible in *Hassidic Dance* by Max Weber (1881–1961), where the members of a mystical Jewish sect dance and sing to express their feelings of elation in the created universe. The dance is ecstatic, joyous, and reverent at the same time. And because the men wear high hats and long, almost funereal garments while dancing in a spirit of what is, for them, complete abandon, they create a somewhat comic effect. Much of the appeal of this work derives from the contrast between the awkwardness of the men, the somberness of their dress, and the passion with which they throw themselves into the dance.

Using another technique, John Marin (1870–1953) displays his typically vigorous, uncomplicated approach to the expression of joy. Marin worked mainly in watercolor, painting scenes alive with movement and energy. *Maine Islands* typifies his use of a few slashing, wet watercolor strokes to suggest the whole panorama of nature: sky, sun, air, water, and mountains. Although his style was highly individual, Marin's principal influence was Cubism. He used an abbreviated, notational, straight-line style which derives ultimately from the carefully hatched planes of Cézanne. Vigorously executed though carefully composed, his pictures create a slapdash impression. The generous use of white paper and a fast wet brush gives his work sparkle and freshness. Marin's world is happy: he painted a few sun rays almost as children do. His universe is untroubled, full of radiant energy; its motion and noise are friendly to man.

Marc Chagall's paintings may seem naive because they exhibit a childlike belief in love's power to remove anyone beyond "the here and the now." In *Flying over the Town* a couple floats above a village as if in a dream. Chagall illustrates the beliefs of childhood: that love transcends physical facts and mystic-

MAX WEBER. *Hassidic Dance.* 1940.
Collection Mr. and Mrs. Milton Lowenthal, New York

JOHN MARIN. *Maine Islands.* 1922.
The Phillips Collection, Washington, D.C.

Marc Chagall. *Flying over the Town.* 1914. Collection Mrs. Mark C. Steinberg, St. Louis

ally overcomes the laws of gravity and aerody-namics. He is a joyous artist because of his complete devotion to romantic love: its erotic aspects are very minor. Even his portrayal of the female nude avoids suggestions of physical desire. Rather, his models appear to be women as conceived by the minds of children. Chagall's view of love is that it is a joy so intense that it liberates people from their earthly roots.

Can architecture deal with joy and celebration? It is difficult, since a building must, before anything else, solve the problem of stability. Yet Ordoñez's and Candela's Los Manantiales Restaurant in Xochimilco, Mexico is joyously festive. Here the principal engineer-ing device, thin-shell concrete shaped in the form of dramatic hyperbolic curves on a circular plan, solves the problem of structure and expression brilliantly. The thin-shell structure acts as roof, side wall, and window opening at the same time. While the shell is strong, its visual effect suggests the delicacy of curved paper. In contrast to the mathematical beauty of these curving shapes, the designers used a rugged masonry foundation and wide, gentle steps to create a horizon-tal base for the soaring forms above. The large open-ings are inviting from the outside, while, for those inside, they create a maximum opportunity for un-obstructed vision. For Candela it was not a matter of finding a stereotyped building type and imposing it on the requirements of a situation. Instead, he exploited modern materials to create architecture which is uniquely fitted to a particular place. Without the use of the human figure or the employment of trite sym-bols, the inert materials of building, skillfully orga-nized, can support a wide range of human feelings. We get buildings that express elegance, lightness, and gaiety without becoming frivolous or sensational.

JOAQUÍN ALVARES ORDONEZ (architect) and FÉLIX CANDELA (structural designer).
Los Manantiales Restaurant, Xochimilco, Mexico. 1958

VICTOR BISHARAT/JAMES A. EVANS AND ASSOCIATES. General Time Building (now
occupied by States Marine Line, Inc.), Stamford, Connecticut. 1968. With a
circular plan on a masonry base, repeated inverted arches, and a reflecting pool,
the General Time Building employs several of the devices used by Candela to
arrive at a fresh structural solution.

8

THE STYLE OF FANTASY

As artists manipulate their materials, they often discover that they can invent forms that were never seen before. Some will not permit their work to stray from the logical or probable, but others enjoy creating new worlds. And most artists have the skill to make such worlds seem real. These fantastic creations reflect the artist's perception of his role as one who obeys the rules of reality or as one whose mission is to *change* the rules. Either he creates strange new forms or he *lets fantastic forms happen*, regarding himself as an instrument that cooperates with the processes of creation in the universe.

Every reality in the man-made world almost surely had its origin in someone's fantastic imagination. It is very likely that architects imagine spaces and shapes before they think of any practical purpose for them. Even engineers, as Arthur Drexler says, "have subjective, if not actually arbitrary, preferences for certain kinds of shapes."[20] Painters and sculptors, more liberated from practical necessity, can pursue inner vision wherever it leads. The important point is that fantasy—the imagination of unreal forms, places, and events—is a universal human trait, and art is the principal means of expressing it.

All man-made realities were once fantasies, but all fantasies do not necessarily become realities. Chagall's people flying through the air are fantastic, but they do not anticipate general diffusion of the gift of levitation. Some artistic fantasies have utopian implications: the architect who conjures up an ideal but fantastic city may be instrumental in converting dreams into reality. In fact, most of the major architects of this century have proposed utopian structures or communities which constitute fantastic solutions to human problems. City planning, which is largely practiced by architects, might be regarded as the professionaliza-

tion of the tendency to propose utopias. Certainly many of the architectural fantasies of the 1920s and '30s are facts today. Private dreams *can* become public realities.

Some utopian fantasies deal with personal and social relationships. The *Peaceable Kingdom* by Edward Hicks (1790–1849) is based on the Biblical description of a world in which natural enemies live together without conflict, and men (exemplified by William Penn and the Indians in the background) negotiate their affairs harmoniously. The work is fantastic because the world it portrays is not the one we live in. Such works may not overcome our doubts, but they persuade us that the ideal they embody is real.

Because fantastic art originates in both logical and irrational mental processes, it presents no common set of visual qualities. Fantastic works may be objectively accurate or subjectively distorted. We can speak of a fantastic *style*, then, only because certain works exhibit a logic based on dreams, hallucinations, utopian hopes, and speculative vision. That is why we discuss fantastic art in relation to science as well as myth. So far as art is concerned, science and superstition are equally useful sources of imagery. The cognitive claims of science afford material for the creation of art as much as the magical practices of shamans, the prophecies of wise men, or the hopes of religion.

Myth

As children we were told fabulous stories and we usually accepted them without question: they seemed to explain the world in a way that satisfied our curiosity. With increasing sophistication, myths or

Edward Hicks. *Peaceable Kingdom.* c. 1848.
Philadelphia Museum of Art.
Bequest of Lisa Norris Elkins

Film still from *Beauty and the Beast.*
Directed by Jean Cocteau. 1945.
Courtesy Janus Films, Inc.

fairy tales were revealed as neither scientifically nor historically true. They remained entertaining as fiction but not as reliable accounts of real events or as accurate explanations of the way the world really "works." But mythology was not entirely abandoned: it was converted into folk wisdom, ultimately enshrined in our mental lives in the form of unexamined beliefs and convictions. Officially, we think of myths, fairy tales, and nursery rhymes as the fantastic entertainments of a stage we have left behind.

But when an artist like Jean Cocteau (1891–1964) represents a myth in a film—for example, *Beauty and the Beast*—our adult sophistication receives a shock: we never completely lose our faith in the validity of myth. Folk tales have the capacity to stir our deepest selves long after we imagine that we are immune to superstition. The Swedish film director Ingmar Bergman (born 1918) likes to create conflicts between characters representing the scientific, rational mind and the mythic, poetic, or religious mind. Often, he

Film still from *The Magician*.
Directed by INGMAR BERGMAN. 1958.
Courtesy Janus Films, Inc.

Film still from *The Cabinet of Dr. Caligari*.
Directed by ROBERT WIENE. 1919

shows how both tendencies exist in the same person, as in *The Magician,* where a physician succumbs to fantastic fears—fears to which he believed himself immune because of his scientific training.

Why does myth have the power to compel our belief? It is not that myths are true as science defines truth. Rather, myths establish connections with the way our minds grasp reality. People are not wholly rational, not completely evolved from their earlier psychological selves. Myths are truthful accounts of the way we have seen ourselves and the world for most of our life on earth. They accurately explain a great deal about the way we think, feel, and behave.

In visual art, as in life, mythmaking goes on continually. The visual arts use plastic fantasy—the invention of strange forms, or strange associations of known forms. These may be initially suggested by accidental technical effects, as in the "planned accidents" of Max Ernst. Or the artist relies on hidden, mysterious sources of form. Some believe that relatively uncontrolled creation will connect their work with the mythic roots of personality. Thus, surrendering to fantasy is not abandoning truth; it is a way of gaining access to *a special type of truth*—a type civilization does not value highly but which nevertheless explains a great deal about our behavior.

One of the best-known fantastic paintings showing the mythic imagination at work is *Hide-and-Seek* by Pavel Tchelitchew (1898–1957). It seems to be the picture of a tree, then of a hand, a foot, a system of nerves and blood vessels, then of embryos, babies, and children. Everywhere we look, passages of wet, flowing color merge with forms of biological life. The blood vessels appear to be illustrations for a medical anatomy; tiny lights seem to illuminate beautifully the

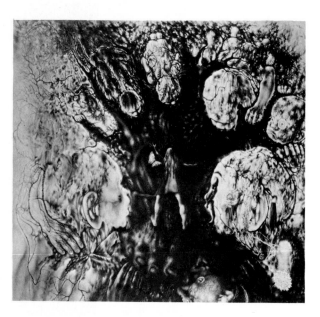

PAVEL TCHELITCHEW. *Hide-and-Seek*. 1940–42.
The Museum of Modern Art, New York.
Mrs. Simon Guggenheim Fund

rendering of an ear or the place where the veins of a leaf merge with fine capillaries feeding a human fetus.

Of course, children do not grow on trees, and the similarity between a hand and a tree is only superficial. But for the mythic imagination, things that look alike are aspects of the same reality: men once worshiped trees; children are the "fruit" of our bodies. Our arteries and nervous systems branch out like the limbs of a tree, the fingers of a hand, the tendons of a foot. But the painting by Tchelitchew is not a treatise on physiology; it shows how the primitive portion of our personality confronts such themes as the life of the unborn, the drama of nourishment, the connection between plants and human beings, the tension between consciousness and unconsciousness, the teeming activity beneath the shell of a living thing.

Dreams and Hallucinations

Our dreams are further examples of the connection between fantasy and the real world. They appear to lack logical organization after we are awake, but while we sleep, they seem very real, sometimes frighteningly so. An artist employing dream material can exploit its irrational qualities to jar people out of their usual ways of seeing. Such an art, using a realistic mode of representation, can employ images as they appear to us in hallucinations, images similar to those caused, for example, by a high fever. Such an art was Surrealism. As a formally organized movement embracing the visual arts and literature, Surrealism is largely spent; but its influence remains part of the creative approach of all artists.

It is easy to see how an artistic strategy relying on dreams and accidental technical effects would encounter resistance from those who think of art as a planned and reasoned approach to creation. However, even the most rational artistic approaches employ some kind of intuition, some reliance on sources of imagery hidden mysteriously in the self; otherwise, if artistic planning and execution were entirely a matter of applying known principles to known objectives, artists could be replaced by computers programmed by technicians.

For their interest in dreams, the Surrealists were, of course, indebted to Sigmund Freud. From Freud they learned that dreams are only *seemingly* illogical, that they have important meanings if certain principles of interpretation are known. Not that Surrealist paintings constitute a collection of symbols requiring a key for interpretation. But they do employ fantastic juxtapositions of images—combinations more like those seen in dreams than in waking life—to shock the viewer. Shock is believed to educate—causing the viewer to reorganize old habits of perception. Behind this interest in shock is the conviction that man and society are hopelessly enmeshed in wrong modes of thinking and acting.

In Salvador Dali's (born 1904) *Soft Construction with Boiled Beans: Premonition of Civil War* we see a naturalistic technique combined with mutilation and distortion of the figure. He employs strong contrasts

GIORGIO DE CHIRICO. *The Great Metaphysician.* 1917. The Museum of Modern Art, New York. The Philip L. Goodwin Collection. For De Chirico, a mythic world—what he called a metaphysical world—exists all around us, but it usually eludes our senses. His paintings give us a glimpse of captured moments when metaphysical space and time intersect.

MERET OPPENHEIM. *Object.* 1936. The Museum of Modern Art, New York. The idea of a fur-covered cup, saucer, and spoon is so fantastic that only a comic reaction can make the image bearable.

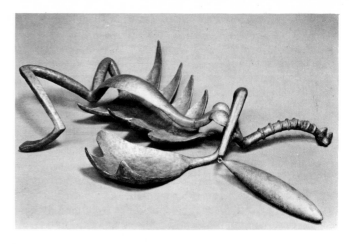

ALBERTO GIACOMETTI. *Woman with Her Throat Cut.* 1932. The Museum of Modern Art, New York. A gruesome fantasy made all the more lurid because it is rendered with exquisite clarity and loving attention to form.

Art Nouveau chair. c. 1910. Collection Mr. and Mrs. Leo Castelli, New York. A chair that wants to be something else. Wavy plant stems and female heads combine to create an object that seems to be having a terrible dream.

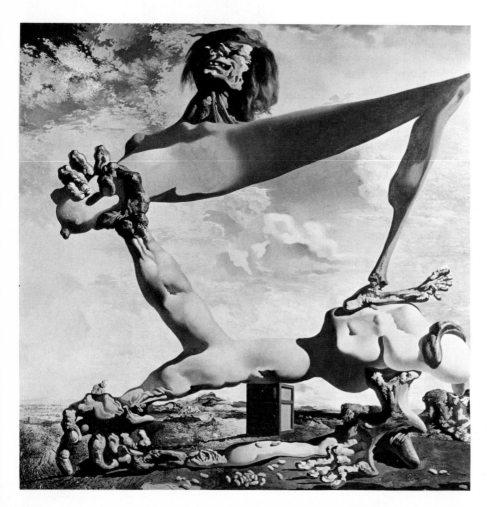

SALVADOR DALI.
Soft Construction with Boiled Beans: Premonition of Civil War. 1936.
Philadelphia Museum of Art.
The Louise and Walter Arensberg
Collection

of light and shadow plus careful modeling to add to the illusionism of his fantastic forms. The sky and landscape are presented in hues which might be seen in a Technicolor travelogue. This almost banal naturalism increases the shock value of the figurative elements. A small figure at the lower left establishes the monstrous scale of the central subject. We recognize portions of female anatomy, skeletal forms, and a grimacing head attached to a breast that is being squeezed by a clawlike hand. A supporting element seems to be a tree trunk which merges into a foot. The melting of objects—the man-made into the natural—is characteristic of Surrealist art. It is also a feature of dreams where persons and objects turn into something else. In mythology too, metamorphosis is common—persons and objects exchange identities readily.

We see a sculptural fantasy in *Secretary* by Richard Stankiewicz (born 1922), a work which contains an element of metamorphosis. The torso consists mainly of a cylinder with a typewriter embedded in its abdomen. Pipe-stem arms operate the typewriter, which is part of the secretary's body—an incongruous association of the mechanical and the human. A large part of contemporary art deals with the theme of the assimilation of people by machines: here we see an only slightly human figure as it absorbs a machine and then operates on its mechanical innards. Although welded sculpture is now a well-accepted contemporary medium, Stankiewicz was one of the first sculptors to use machine parts which have not completely lost their original identity.

A variation of the Stankiewicz fantasy in the service of advertising art appears in an illustration for the Royal typewriter. The idea of the typewriter emerging from a French horn is at once whimsical and absurd. We assume at first that the purpose of the illustration is mainly to demand attention. But the French horn is a beautiful instrument, the product of elaborate handcraftsmanship. So when we see it presenting the typewriter as if on a pedestal, or "giving birth" to the typewriter, we are encouraged to associate the craftsmanship of the horn with the industrially produced commercial machine.

One of the monuments of modern fantastic art is Picasso's etching *Minotauromachy* (1935). The work embodies almost all the elements of fantastic art: myth, dream, history, sexual hallucination, incongruous juxtaposition, the literal and the absurd, hybrid man-animal creatures. The artist deals with the Cretan myth of the Minotaur and with bullfighting today; he refers also to the Greek legend in which Zeus, in the guise of a bull, carried off Europa. The horse, which carries a sleeping or unconscious female matador, is badly wounded, losing its entrails through its torn belly. But the scene's violence is viewed calmly by faces of classical beauty. A flower girl holds a light against which the Minotaur, a symbol of violence and chaos, shields himself. Like a dream, the work does not lend itself to simple explanation; yet it makes us symbolically aware of many elements of modern

RICHARD STANKIEWICZ. *Secretary*. 1953. Whereabouts unknown

Advertisement, *A Christmas gift with keys so lively, they can go 115 words a minute.*
Courtesy Royal Typewriter Company, New York

PABLO PICASSO. *Minotauromachy.* 1935.
The Museum of Modern Art, New York

PABLO PICASSO. *Baboon and Young.* 1951. The
Museum of Modern Art, New York. Mrs. Simon
Guggenheim Fund. Picasso's use of a toy automobile for the baboon's head illustrates the Surrealist imagination at work. The visual resemblance is persuasive, but the logic of the sculpture
is so preposterous that we enjoy its absurdity.

European history. For a Spaniard like Picasso, the
tauromachy, the killing of a bull, is a reenactment not
only of a pre-Christian fertility rite but also of the
structure of life in the West. In other words, both the
myth and the modern spectacle are concentrated versions of what our history has been. Picasso explores
his Spanish heritage, his fascination with the ritual
murder of the bull, his sexual fantasies, and his feelings about contemporary civilization. Two years later,
in 1937, the artist painted *Guernica,* commemorating
one of the cruelest events of the Spanish Civil War. He
appears to have anticipated this work with the *Minotauromachy.*

In *The Dream* by Henri Rousseau (1844–1910), we
encounter a type of fantastic art that is based on the
imagination of a so-called primitive artist. In faithfully
reproducing his inner vision, he arrives at a curious
blend of heightened realism and pure dream. In this
gentle work, Rousseau lovingly portrayed his reverie
of a naked woman on a couch, mysteriously located in
the jungle with its wild birds and animals, exotic
natives, and lavish natural growth. Not only is this the
dream of the woman in the picture, but also it must be
the dream of the artist—naive and mildly erotic at
once—in which the wealth of nature is benevolently
arranged so man can find food on the trees, delight in
the natural forms, the friendship of animals and
natives, and the love of woman. The artist achieves a
magnificent decorative effect in the foliage and flowers,
and although his drawing of the nude is somewhat
stiff, he has been able to dramatize her figure through
careful modeling and intense illumination. In painting
this dream, Rousseau probably expressed the universal
fantasy of male adolescence, creating a timeless vision
in which each detail possesses an overwhelming
veracity.

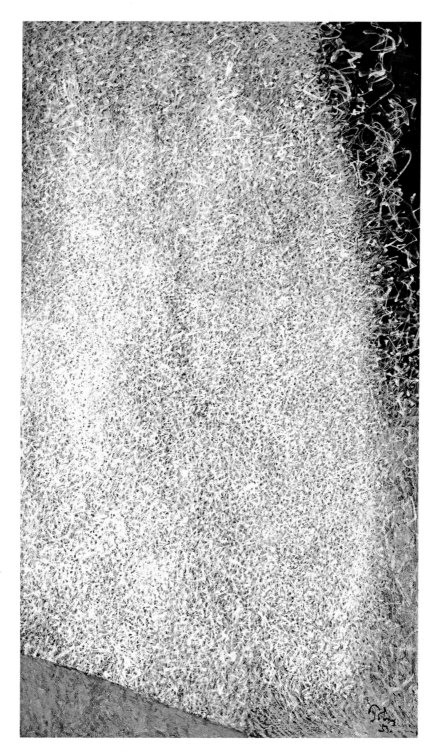

MARK TOBEY. *Edge of August.* 1953. The Museum of Modern Art, New York. Tobey's pursuit of mystical oneness through art—of a visual union between our inner and outer worlds—led to this synthesis of Western dynamism with the meditative scripts of Persia and China.

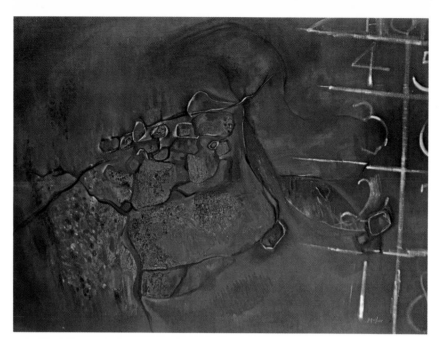

LOREN MACIVER. *Hopscotch*. 1940. The Museum of Modern Art, New York. Mysterious juxtapositions are so close that we overlook them. Here their placement seems to intimate a simple yet elusive truth.

MATTA. *Disasters of Mysticism*. 1942. Collection James Thrall Soby, New Canaan, Connecticut. While suggesting the sense of release that accompanies the exploration of boundless space, Matta also arouses our cosmic anxiety as he discloses the threat of conflagration in the new world of physics.

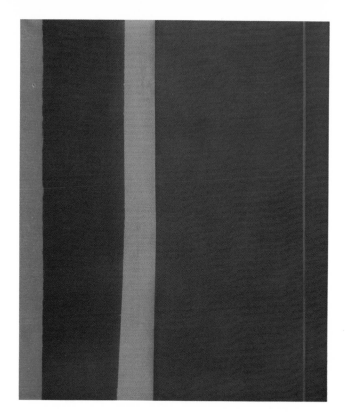

BARNETT NEWMAN. *Adam*. 1951–52. The Tate Gallery, London. Newman's vertical divisions represent a parting of the pictorial field, which then opens to the viewer a vast primordial space: the world at the beginning.

ARTHUR G. DOVE. *That Red One*. 1944. William H. Lane Foundation, Leominster, Massachusetts. Dove tried to work his way out of nature and then back again, cleansed by abstraction and armed with the radiant force of a powerful symbol: a black sun.

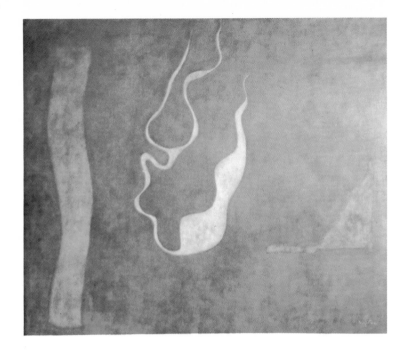

WILLIAM BAZIOTES. *The Sea.* 1959. Collection Mr. and Mrs. H. Grossman, New York. For a certain kind of artist, the miraculous emerges in the discovery that the act of painting can evoke a natural world nature does not know.

MARK ROTHKO. *Earth and Green.* 1955. Galerie Beyeler, Basel. Through color sensation alone, virtually without the agency of shape, we become absorbed into the experience of vision.

HENRI ROUSSEAU. *The Dream*. 1910. The Museum of Modern Art, New York.
Gift of Nelson A. Rockefeller

Nature, whose fecundity Rousseau perceived as generous and benign, is seen by
Ernst as an arena of cancerous growth. Plant and animal exchange identity, and
ceaseless reproduction spawns monsters that threaten to choke out the sky. As
the horizon disappears, the artist's hallucinations become more and more credible, until the real and the nightmare worlds become one.

MAX ERNST. *The Joy of Living*. 1936. Penrose Collection, London

Scientific Fantasy

Science and technology dominate our lives, so it is not surprising that art has absorbed many of their symbols. Science raises questions about outer space and submicrocosmic matter—questions that fascinate the popular imagination and stimulate many sorts of speculation. Speculation about technical questions by nonscientists is part of a natural process of *humanizing* radically new concepts which can modify our notions of space, time, matter, and energy. We deal with ideals which promise to alter our world by dreaming about them, incorporating them into jokes and tall stories, visualizing them in astonishing contexts.

But art does more than illustrate the consequences of science and technology. Artists play symbolically and sensuously with new principles. They try to discover whether novel ideas and materials can be expressively used in their private worlds of feeling and intuition. They wonder whether physical discoveries about the motion and energy of subatomic particles can change the way they think. And although such

ROGER DE LA FRESNAYE. *The Conquest of the Air.* 1913.
The Museum of Modern Art, New York.
Mrs. Simon Guggenheim Fund

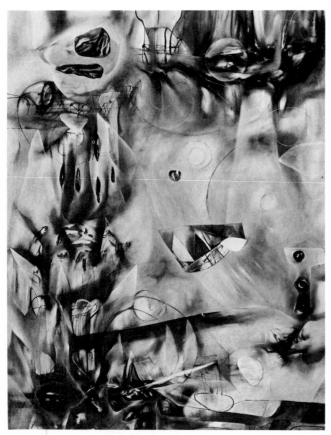

MATTA. *Here Sir Fire, Eat!* 1942.
Collection James Thrall Soby,
New Canaan, Connecticut

HIERONYMUS BOSCH. *Hell*
(detail of *The Garden of Delights*). c. 1500.
The Prado, Madrid

214

speculation does not add to the fund of knowledge regarded as scientific truth, it *does* add to our fund of humanistic knowledge—knowledge about the effects of science on our personal and social existence.

The Conquest of the Air by Roger de la Fresnaye, executed in 1913, seems a tame work of scientific fantasy when compared with space exploration today. It uses Cubist forms to cope with the intellectual aspects of extraterrestrial travel. A balloon is in the distance, a French flag is displayed, a sailboat floats at the right. Presumably, these symbolize the connections between sailing and flight and relate scientific achievements in space travel to French nationalism. The association between science and patriotism seems naive; however, we can regard this work, painted before World War I, as the reflection of an optimistic, essentially nineteenth-century attitude toward science, notwithstanding the use of a form language which belongs to the present century.

In the work of Matta (Echaurren), we have a frank effort to come to terms with the world revealed by modern physics. The foundation provided by Surrealism, particularly its invitation to the artist to surrender to his unconscious impulses, enables the painter to create an autonomous universe of visionary forms. These forms seem to grow out of an interest in the problems of electrical and magnetic energy, the motion of subatomic particles, their velocities, collisions, radiation, and brief life-spans. As the orbits of the particles overlap and combine with one another they seem to describe forms of almost architectural meaning. So, geometry enters Matta's paintings, but he never loses organic reference; a biological note, a humanistic idea, is always present. We can sense air, ocean, sunlight, moonlight, stars, and their romantic associations behind the movements of particles guided by the laws of physics.

Matta does not create models of the universe. He establishes a setting that suggests what might be seen by some superior eye which can understand the imagery of science and art at once. In short, we are dealing with art—that is, imagination—rather than with talented technical illustration. Perhaps the best analogy to Matta's work can be seen in Hieronymus Bosch's paintings of the fantastic creatures inhabiting Hell. Bosch presented in detailed, credible terms what no one had seen but what everyone speculated about— the tortures of the damned according to current notions of cosmology and theology. Sixteenth-century science and theology found visual expression in the art of Bosch just as modern science is dramatized in the fantastic world of Matta.

Fantasy and Illusionism

As with the style of objective accuracy, we shall examine some of the devices used to create fantastic illusions or to substitute real objects for the illusionistic treatment of reality.

YVES TANGUY. *Infinite Divisibility.* 1942. Albright-Knox Art Gallery, Buffalo, New York

Infinite Divisibility by the American Surrealist Yves Tanguy (1900–1955) employs the illumination and modeling we would expect in a conventional painting of still life. Light comes from a single source and causes the strange objects to cast sharp shadows which obey the laws of perspective as they move toward an infinitely receding horizon. In the distance are glowing light centers as if from strange suns. Their light comes through an atmosphere much as sunlight sometimes reaches us on earth—through a cloud (or pollution) haze. The objects themselves are arresting, appearing to come from a skeletal system—but whose? They seem to have both organic and mechanical origins. Some resemble stones or other geological forms. Yet a machine is suggested by the geometric arrangement at the left.

The infinite horizon helps create the mood of a dream and an atmosphere of silence. Deep space supports these feelings. In Tanguy's world, everything dissolves into a luminous haze in the distance after we have examined the highly detailed and carefully rendered forms in the foreground. Since the color is usually a silvery gray, this imagery can be seen as photographic realism.

The effect of the work is not to shock but rather to induce a calm acceptance of an environment which might be plausible to an astronaut. We can accept Tanguy's universe—so bare of the essentials needed to sustain existence as we know it—because of its all-pervading atmosphere of peace. There is no violence in Tanguy's "lunar" landscape; it seems to exist in a

MARCEL DUCHAMP. *The Bride*. 1912.
Philadelphia Museum of Art.
The Louise and Walter Arensberg Collection

JASON SELEY. *Masculine Presence*. 1961.
The Museum of Modern Art,
New York.
Gift of Dr. and Mrs. Leonard Kornblee

time *after* violence and passion have been spent. There
is a sense of stillness and freedom from human striving that we might associate with the fate of forms no
longer alive. In other words, we may be witnessing the
world as it would appear after we (and everything else)
are dead.

A different kind of illusionism is employed in *The
Bride* by Marcel Duchamp (1887–1963). We have the
convincing representation of geometric solids connected by a kind of mechanical-biological plumbing
system. The title adds to the effect of Surrealistic irony
as it contrasts the romantic-erotic meanings of "bride"
with a quasi-Cubist representation of her viscera. We
are shown what might be the interior of a complex
circulation system and are given visual hints of human
internal organs, arteries, and glands. The type of representation is the sort that would be used to illustrate
a catalogue for a manufacturer of laboratory equipment.

The illusionistic devices of Surrealist art relied on
discoveries made as early as the Renaissance. Many
contemporary artists, forsaking illusionism, pursue
realism by employing the real objects which formerly
would have been represented. An example is *Masculine Presence* (1961) by Jason Seley (born 1919). The
figure consists of welded automobile bumpers and a
grille. The result suggests the muscle and skeletal
system of a man, with the convex forms of machine
parts employed to achieve an organic effect. An interesting relationship between industrial design and
sculpture is implied here: the purpose of automobile
bumpers, as we know, was to provide a sturdy defense
for the easily damaged metal skin of the car. Over the
years, designers imposed a variety of curvilinear shapes
on the rugged old bumper: that is, they treated it like
sculpture, giving it the *qualities* of the human figure
but avoiding "museum-art" effects. In reassembling
these automobile parts, the artist returned their
organic qualities to the place from which they were
taken, and where, as sculpture, they appear perhaps
more appropriate.

Marisol (Escobar) (born 1930) has fashioned a

whimsical fantasy, *The Generals,* of painted wood and plaster. We recognize a barrel in the body of the horse and an ordinary table or bench in the legs. Her construction moves among several modes of meaning and representation at once: there is an overall hobbyhorse quality, particularly in the neck and head. In their stiffness and boxlike construction, the generals suggest children's soldiers; but their painted faces have the rigidity of Byzantine icons. Their boots—symbols of command—are painted on the barrel the way a uniform might be painted on a child's wooden soldier. So it is difficult to take their generalship seriously. For a heroic equestrian statue, the horse will not do. But why two on a horse?

The illusionism of these works lies in the employment of "real" materials we normally associate with other contexts. The artist exploits the conventional associations we make with these real objects. Her illusions are not of the fool-the-eye variety: no particular craftsmanship is required to mount boxes on a barrel; yet, with some visual hints, it is easy to imagine them as soldiers on horseback. The art consists in using the viewer's *knowledge* that boxes are being represented as generals or that an automobile grille is a man's abdomen. Our *knowledge* that table legs will not carry the generals into battle is also a part of the work. The traditional artist "persuaded" paint, clay, or stone to look like flesh or cloth; the contemporary artist employs real objects along with illusionistic fragments to create several levels of reality in one work. She "plays with" the viewer's frame of reference. The result might be disorientation or the discovery of new meanings in the reality of commonplace things. Fantastic art thus manipulates illusion and reality. It moves beyond dream and shock to create new perceptions of the real world.

MARISOL. *The Generals.* 1961–62.
Albright-Knox Art Gallery,
Buffalo, New York.
Gift of Seymour H. Knox

PART THREE

THE STRUCTURE OF ART

Introduction

THE STRUCTURE OF ART

WHEN AS CHILDREN WE LEARNED TO TALK, WE TRIED almost from the beginning to express ideas, desires, and feelings. Adults helped us to pronounce words, but they did not provide us with definitions of nouns, verbs, and adjectives, and then ask us to put them together. Somehow we learned to talk and to understand at the same time. Although humans possess innate language capacities, it was through trial and error and successful or meaningful reactions to our speech that we learned *to use* language. It was not until later that teachers dissected the language for us, broke it down into parts of speech and rules of usage. Before that, without consciously knowing the rules, we managed to understand what people were saying.

Now we are about to study the *structure* of art. Sometimes, art is thought of as a language which one learns to understand by studying how it is put to-gether. But, as observed above, we learned spoken language as a whole *and then* were taught parts of speech, rules of usage, and the rest. It would seem that studying the *construction* of language or of art is not absolutely necessary for understanding what it means. There must be some other reasons for learning the structure of artistic forms, or the effort might well be abandoned.

The view taken here is that the parts and organizational devices of a language have meanings of their own and are worth studying for their own sake. Listening to the way a soprano sings certain notes is a pleasure in itself; it adds to the enjoyment of her song as a whole. So this discussion of the visual elements and their organization is intended to draw your attention to additional sources of interest and meaning.

9

THE VISUAL ELEMENTS:

GRAMMAR

PEOPLE SEE IMAGES, NOT THINGS. LIGHT SENSATIONS falling on the retina are transmitted as energy impulses to the brain, where they are almost simultaneously translated into a meaningful entity called an image. Not that there is a picture, an optical projection, in the brain itself. The optical processes are in the eye, of course. But perception is a function of the mind. We cannot experience sensations without characterizing them. An image, therefore, can be defined for our purposes as *the result of endowing optical sensations with meaning.*

For practical purposes, the common images we see have labels like house, tree, sun, and sky. But we can learn to identify the elements of images. That is, we can learn to focus on the shape, color, texture, or light patterns which are parts of images. In fact, when we focus on *part* of an image—its shape, for example—that part *becomes* the image; it becomes the meaningful locus of our interest.

Here we are concerned with the visual elements as they are employed by artists. After we have learned to see them in art, we may discover the same constituents in nature. To see the visual elements of art in the natural world is to project upon nature certain acquired habits of perception which we find pleasurable or useful. Consequently, one of the indirect dividends of studying the structure of art is the added satisfaction we can get in perception of the real world.

The labels for the visual elements tend to vary according to the user, but what the labels refer to is fairly consistent. It does not matter greatly if one authority uses "form," another "contour," and a third "shape." What is important is that the viewer understand the properties of art which the words designate.

The discussion of the visual elements which follows does not constitute a set of rules which artists disobey at their peril. I offer it as a visual grammar based on artistic *usage*—a *functional* explanation of the visual elements.

Line

There is a difference between *a* line and *line-in-general*. *A* line is the path made by a pointed instrument: a pen, a pencil, a crayon, a stick. A line implies action because action was needed to create it. Line-in-general suggests direction or orientation. An effect of movement can be achieved by a series of shapes, none of which is thin, sharp, or linear but all of which imply a direction. In other words, *a* line is a mark made by a sharp, moving instrument, whereas line-in-general is a *conclusion* by the viewer that a set of forms has an orientation, a direction. For the most part, we shall be talking here about *a* line, the definite series of points.

Because we all have used lines to write, to make marks in the sand, in dirt, or on sidewalks, we know that making a line entails some exertion and that a choice must be made about where the line will go. In learning to write, we discovered that "wrong" lines resulted in letters or words which could not be understood. Since line forces an individual to commit himself, there are, from a certain standpoint, right and wrong lines. A "wrong" line is one we cannot control, or it is the result of incorrect knowledge. In writing, an agreement about what letter forms should look like and the muscular coordination of the writer produce linear structures that people can read. Thus, among our earliest personal experiences with line was the effort to use it "correctly." In trying to draw, we wanted to exercise a similar control over line so that others would see the resemblance between our lines

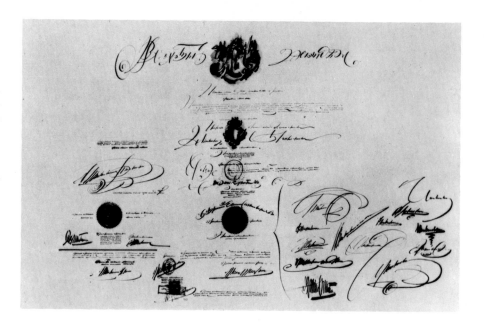

SAUL STEINBERG. *Diploma.* 1955. Addison Gallery of American Art, Phillips Academy, Andover, Massachusetts. Although the writing on this diploma looks authentic, it cannot be read: the artist has exploited all the linear and compositional conventions of diploma art except those concerning correct letter form.

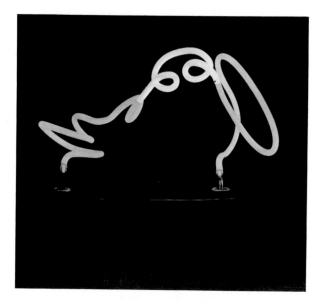

BILLY APPLE. *Untitled: Multiple Edition of 10.* 1967. Multiples, Inc., New York. The handwritten line has long been simulated by the neon sign. Now that same technology serves the linear impulses of abstract sculptors who wish to trace luminous paths in space.

NORBERT KRICKE. *Raumplastik Kugel.* 1955. Collection Hertha Kricke, Düsseldorf. The complex linear system that Kricke builds with white wire no longer refers to an organic act—the path of a person's hand as he writes; instead, it relates to subatomic-particle trajectories, or to celestial motion, as in the painting of Matta.

and visual reality. Therefore, the idea that there is a linear agreement about how lines communicate was established early in our lives.

Line combinations also acquired magical properties: a circle could be the sun, a face, the world. Line was alive with possibility, potent with meaning. Artists, however, may go *behind* the conventions of writing to the magical-symbolic origins of linear properties. Indeed, the artistic employment of line can become the basis of new linear conventions which people recognize and understand almost immediately. This would seem to be the case with Picasso's linear formulations of the crying woman in *Guernica*.

USES OF LINE IN WORKS OF ART

For a demonstration of line employed simply and accurately, we can study Picasso's drawing of the ballet impresarios Diaghilev and Selisburg. The artist who gave the world so many distorted images of the figure here shows his mastery of drawing as it was understood by the academic tradition. He goes beyond the display of representational skill and uses line accented by pencil pressure to describe the volume of the forms enclosed. The absence of shading imparts a classical elegance to these already elegant, well-fed gentlemen. The hands of M. Selisburg together with his fleshly face are executed with a line of dazzling precision and simplicity. Even in a naturalistic vein, Picasso knows how to use the power of geometric forms—underlying ovals, cones, and cylinders—to strengthen the work.

The idea of a linear journey is well demonstrated in the work of Paul Klee (1879–1940). Not only does line describe the shapes of things, it also calls attention to the act of making itself. He indulges in a type of metaphysical wit, creating linear illusions of reality and then employing them to tell the viewer he has been deceived about the reality of an image. Actually, Klee lets the viewer in on a private joke: the artist is not too sure whether the image he draws is "out there," somewhere inside him, or created by unseen hands. *Family Walk* perfectly illustrates a discussion of line. In his witty performance, a few geometric shapes and edges are sufficient to describe characters in a procession, evoke family associations, and carry off the artistic point that reality can be described with line combinations that embody the structure and movement, but not the *appearance*, of people. In *Flight from Oneself*, Klee attempts a more serious study: a visualization of split personality. The repeated gestures appear to be decorative until we realize that they represent the dual aspects of a single soul. The meandering line, apparently a disciplined scribble, turns out to be sufficiently controlled to repeat itself exactly in different scale. The figures are separate but joined, made of something like string, and attached to each other by the same "string" which accounts for their being. Klee portrays the reality of the psyche and the illusory character of the body at the same time.

We see line employed as in a map in *Drawing in Color* by the Belgian artist Corneille (Cornelis van Beverloo). It is not a real map; rather it imitates and exploits the linear *qualities* of maps. There are some black blots which might stand for bodies of water but function here like the knots in Jackson Pollock's paintings—as places where things get "tied up." Notice that the freer lines are ungraceful, their move-

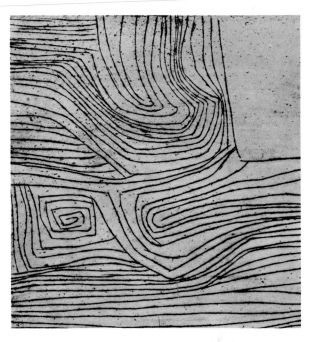

VICTOR PASMORE. *Linear Development No. 6: Spiral.* 1964. Collection Mrs. John Weeks, London. A system of drawn lines serves as a visual analogy for processes in nature: growth, flow, resistance, and mutual adaptation.

PABLO PICASSO. *Diaghilev and Selisburg.* 1919. Collection the artist's Estate

225

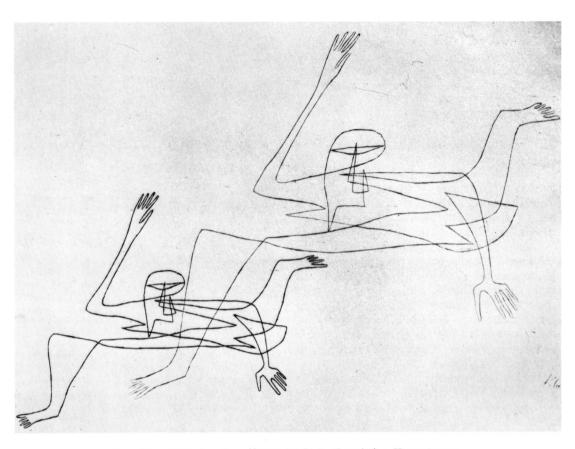

PAUL KLEE. *Flight from Oneself*. 1931. Paul Klee Foundation, Kunstmuseum,
Bern. Permission Cosmopress Geneva, 1966

PAUL KLEE. *Family Walk*. 1930. Paul Klee Foundation, Kunstmuseum, Bern.
Permission Cosmopress Geneva, 1966

CORNEILLE (CORNELIS VAN BEVERLOO). *Drawing in Color*. 1955. Collection the artist

ment hesitant and awkward. The open blocks do not have the rhythmic, undulating qualities of nature; they suggest lots that had buildings which have been torn down, the neighboring areas awaiting "clearance." The awkward, scratchy line is an expressive comparison between bad pen writing and the urban experience. To make the metaphor more specific, the work compares the act of writing with an old steel pen to moving—physically or visually—through the city.

Drawing lines occur in sculpture, too, except that they move in three dimensions. A good illustration is a humorous little work, *The Hostess*, by Alexander Calder. The penetration of formerly solid sculptural forms has encouraged linear tendencies in welded sculpture. One of the first modern sculptors to exploit the linear properties of iron was Julio Gonzalez (1872–1942), who, logically enough, grew out of the rich Spanish tradition of decorative ironwork. In *Grande Maternity* (1930–33) he employed welded iron rods to create a stately, monumentally dignified version of a woman. This sculpture eliminates a great deal, arriving at form by implication rather than addition. Squint your eyes in looking at the sculpture to gain some idea of the masses which are so sparingly suggested by the sweeping lines of the rods and the cagelike structure of the skirt.

In *Royal Bird,* David Smith employs a dominant horizontal line. Here, as in Theodore Roszak's *Spectre of Kitty Hawk*, visual metaphors based on the bird's skeleton are used as the primary sculptural forms. However, the calm horizontal is counteracted by the fierce beak-and-jaw construction, the spikes darting out of the head, and the aggressive stance of a fighting bird. The pattern of the rib cage, translated into metal, recalls the armor of medieval knights more than Thanksgiving leftovers. But if we

ALEXANDER CALDER. *The Hostess*. 1928. The Museum of Modern Art, New York. Gift of Edward M. Warburg

DAVID SMITH. *Royal Bird*. 1948. Walker Art Center, Minneapolis

JULIO GONZALEZ. *Grande Maternity*. 1930–33.
The Tate Gallery, London

FERNAND LÉGER. *La Grande Julie*. 1945.
The Museum of Modern Art, New York.
Lillie P. Bliss Bequest

HENRI MATISSE. *Nude with Face
Half-Hidden*. 1914.
The Museum of Modern Art, New York.
Frank Crowninshield Fund

PAUL KLEE. *And I Shall Say.* 1934.
Paul Klee Foundation,
Kunstmuseum, Bern

personality employed by contemporary "cartoonists" like William Steig and Robert Osborn. Beyond the cryptic title, Klee relies on linear invention to do the job. The figure's position, the eyes directed inward, the idea of the child in the adult—all combine to describe a person pathetically wrapped in fantasy. Her mouth is closed, her mind is speaking. She listens to herself making reply in an imaginary dialogue.

Line is perhaps the most crucial of the visual elements. Its importance might be summarized as follows: (1) Line is familiar to everyone because of our almost universal experience with writing and drawing. (2) Line is precise and unambiguous; it commits the artist to a specific statement. (3) Line leads the viewer's eye and involves him in its "destiny." When we handle objects we trace their out*lines,* in effect, with our fingers. In our development, the outlines of things became keys to their identity.

Outline suggests shape, which is sometimes considered an extension of line. Shape seems to take priority over line, color, and texture in our recognition of phenomena. Hence, we shall devote the next section to an examination of shape as a crucial element of art and visual perception.

WILLIAM STEIG.
Drawing for an advertisement for the French Line. 1970.
Courtesy N. W. Ayer & Son, Inc., New York

can suppress our associations with the bird and see the horizontal pattern as a script, we can almost read the construction as metal calligraphy.

Contrasting linear attitudes can be seen in the *Nude with Face Half-Hidden* (1914) by Matisse and *La Grande Julie* (1945) by Fernand Léger (1881–1955). The line Matisse uses is knowledgeable and confident: when representing the swelling curves of the figure, he does not lose sight of its independently abstract quality. It is both a drawing line and an ornamental arabesque. Léger employs a heavier, mechanical line of unvarying weight throughout. Julie is perhaps a symbol of mechanized young womanhood, a bicyclist who has created a new Christ out of sprockets, gears, and handlebars.

Another deployment of line by Klee appears in his drawing *And I Shall Say* (1934). The torso seems to have been executed with a slightly directed scribble. The hands and feet imitate the drawing of children. But the head could only have been done by a skillful draftsman. He has united three modes of drawing in a single, psychologically convincing characterization. Here we see the model of an approach to the visualization of

JEAN ARP. *Star.* 1939–60.
Collection Edouard Loeb, Paris

Shape

Our discussion of line touched on shape since closed lines become the boundaries of shapes. But shapes can be created without lines: when a painter establishes an area of color or a sculptor creates a three-dimensional volume. Drawn lines are unnecessary in either case. Shapes have *linear* quality if our attention is drawn to their boundaries; but contours usually make us aware of *shape*—that is, they point to the silhouette of the area they enclose.

The shapes that artists create have a variety of sources: some are directly drawn from nature or the man-made world; others reflect the mark of the tool used to create them; there also are shapes which are "invented" by the artist. However, a viewer cannot help seeing them—no matter how abstract—in terms of his experience with reality. That is, we cannot see a triangle without regarding its corners as sharp and hence related to something with a point, which can puncture, which is potentially dangerous. This does not mean that triangles are necessarily dangerous. A triangle resting on its base also suggests stability, like a football lineman crouched in a three-point stance.

The meaning of a triangular shape depends on the properties of a triangle the artist chooses to emphasize. If an artist uses a triangular shape to describe something which in life is curved, the departure provides a clue to the meaning of the total image. Why, for example, does the mother's tongue in Picasso's *Guernica* come to a sharp, dagger-like point?

In examining some of the shapes which occur in art or in reality, we shall find that the artist often endeavors to *redefine* the conventional properties of shape. This effort takes place, however, within the context of common experience with the properties of shapes as we encounter them in life.

Leonardo was said to have drawn perfect circles freehand. But whenever we encounter a perfect geometric shape, we do not believe it was made by hand. Perfect straightness and absolutely regular curvature imply a mechanical origin. The beauty of machine-made objects, as opposed to handcraft, lies in geometric precision. Irregularity and variation of shape characterize handmade forms. Machine forms, we realize, are the result of human planning and design, activities which are essentially intellectual. Consequently, geometric shapes possess cerebral qualities; they appear to be products of the intellect. Geometry can be found in nature, of course, in crystals and snowflakes, for example, and in certain geological formations; but nature confronts the unaided eye overwhelmingly in the form of irregular, uneven shapes.

Our bodies and the bodies of animals are a main source of the curvilinear shapes which seem to have biomorphic qualities. They are modeled ultimately on the patterns of organic growth through the division and integration of cells. Crustaceans defy this principle since they are living creatures which possess sharp, jagged, almost geometrically shaped armor. But their armor, which is so suggestive to sculptors, is like our fingernails—lacking the nerves, blood vessels, and capacity for sensation of flesh; hence it is not "organic."

Star by Jean Arp (1887–1966) exemplifies organic shape given to something usually conceived in geometric terms. A star is, after all, light from a distant body. We do not really see the source, just its light waves. But Arp has chosen to construct a biological model of the conventionally pointed diagram. The star has lost its geometry and its radiating points. It has gained skin and flesh, with bones implied underneath, and an opening in the center. The contradiction between the standard idea of a star and its organic embodiment invites us to think of the universe in essentially biological terms.

Architecture seems to be an unlikely source of organic shapes since its structural devices are usually geometric. However, the development of plastics and reinforced concrete has vastly enlarged the vocabulary of the architect. Indeed, one of the criticisms of some contemporary buildings is that they are too sculptural, seeking to create exciting shapes at the expense of

Spiny lobsters

The weapons and armor of crustaceans offer a form language which has a curious fascination for contemporary painters and sculptors.

THEODORE ROSZAK. *Sea Sentinel*. 1956.
Whitney Museum of American Art, New York

functional efficiency. Le Corbusier's chapel at Ronchamp, however, satisfies structural and functional requirements while using organic shape to enhance symbolic expressiveness. The roof, particularly, resembles in profile a sculpture by Brancusi, the *Fish*. Although it might be forcing the comparison to suggest that the roof is a literal image of the fish, a central symbol in Christian iconology, the biomorphic shapes in the building do increase its capacity to express the idea of the Church as a container, the body of Christ.

Another architectural use of organic shapes is seen in the Casa Milá apartment house in Barcelona. Antoni Gaudí (1852–1926) always avoided geometric shapes, and in the stone columns, particularly, gives the impression of great elephants' legs. In Gaudí's work and the Art Nouveau movement in general, organic shapes were employed consistently without regard to the function of the work, or the processes of forming and fabrication. Hence, the style often appears to be a triumph of the imagination over the character of materials, the submergence of architecture in organic sculpture.

Arp's *Madame Torso with Wavy Hat* is clearly comic in shape and purpose. We can readily identify

the basic hourglass figure, while the head, hat, and hair develop into an Ionic capital, ocean waves, or an inverted handlebar mustache. The convex, rounded forms are balanced by the negative, *concave* shapes located where the thighs would fit into the torso. And the raised relief of the figure casts shadows which strongly define these negative shapes. Why do these forms seem frivolous? Because organic shapes without structural firmness seem to wriggle. They describe a biological entity without bones, the movement of a gelatin dessert.

Adolph Gottlieb (1903–1974) presents in *Blast II* a laboratory demonstration of the properties of shape. The canvas is occupied by two forms of the same area and mass, but the upper one is smoothly rounded whereas the lower one is ragged and chaotic, smeared at the edges. The title suggests that the work is an abstract version of a nuclear explosion. The circular form appears to represent the familiar mushroom cloud, while the agitated shape below symbolizes destruction. The cloud has a serene, floating quality which contrasts with the "noisy" form underneath. Notice the blotched quality of the brushstrokes around its edge: the artist does not emphasize the destructive force of a nuclear blast so much as its

LE CORBUSIER. Notre-Dame-du-Haut, Ronchamp, France. 1950-55

CONSTANTIN BRANCUSI. *Fish*. 1930.
The Museum of Modern Art, New York.
Lillie P. Bliss Bequest

The fleshy facade Gaudí designed for the Casa Batlló acquires strength and firmness through thin, bony columns which seem to be supporting enormous Surrealistic eyelids.

ANTONI GAUDÍ. Casa Milá Apartment House, Barcelona. 1905-10

ANTONI GAUDÍ. Casa Batlló, Barcelona. 1905-7

JEAN ARP. *Madame Torso with Wavy Hat*. 1916.
Hermann and Margrit Rupf Foundation,
Kunstmuseum, Bern

ADOLPH GOTTLIEB. *Blast II*. 1957.
Joseph E. Seagram and Sons, Inc., New York

Billowing spinnakers. Shapes also possess volumetric meanings; we perceive them as the containers of dynamic forces. The beauty of a sailboat
(as well as its female associations) is based on the
container idea, here expressed in the spinnakers.

PAUL KLEE. *The Great Dome*. 1927.
Paul Klee Foundation, Kunstmuseum, Bern

"dirty" character. And, since scientists and military men speak of "clean" bombs, the idea is appropriate. An *unclean* bomb yields a large amount of radioactive fallout. Obviously, the artist has attempted to express this idea by using smudged, disorderly shapes against an immaculate background above which floats a bright, carefully brushed-out cloud form.

From the imagination of Paul Klee comes a striking illustration of the two major types of shape—the biomorphic and the geometric. In addition to its visual interest, *The Great Dome* constitutes a psychological statement in the guise of architectural description. The structure on the left represents the triumph of ancient Middle Eastern building—the heavenly dome. At the same time, it is the architectural expression of the female breast, the symbol of maternal nurture. In the right half of the picture, Klee portrays a tower, symbol of the male principle, which is essentially geometric, a system of triangles. These basic shapes are starkly presented, each occupying half of the picture space. They are somewhat connected along the base, but it is worth noting that Klee employs no device to harmonize the two shapes, to soften their opposition. Furthermore, in his title he ignores the tower. If we may permit ourselves some amateur psychologizing, Klee is here expressing (a) the eternal war between the sexes and (b) his admiration, as a man, for woman. As in *Flight from Oneself*, the artist shows his interest in the duality of all unities. Just as human personality struggles with itself and sometimes becomes alienated, the sexes, which must unite to be creative, are nevertheless seen as opposed or indifferent to each other.

An extreme example of the use of geometric shapes to represent human beings is seen in *Composition: The Cardplayers* (1917) by Theo van Doesburg (1883–1931). Did *The Card Players* by Cézanne of 1890–92

THEO VAN DOESBURG. *Composition: The Cardplayers*. 1917. Gemeente Museum, The Hague, The Netherlands

anticipate the complete dematerialization of the gamesters in Van Doesburg's work? We are aware of progressively smaller forms, densely packed at the center of the picture, where hands and cards meet. A few large, right-angle shapes suggest shoulders, knees, chairs maybe. Organization takes precedence over representation. The organic shapes of reality have been converted into the geometric shapes of a completely rationalized art. It is not surprising that a device now exists which can create patterns for electronic circuitry, patterns which bear a remarkable resemblance to Van Doesburg's painting. The patterns are made by a technician using an instrument called a "coordina-

PAUL CÉZANNE. *The Card Players*. 1890–92. The Louvre, Paris

Technician using coordinatograph to prepare
pattern for microelectric circuit

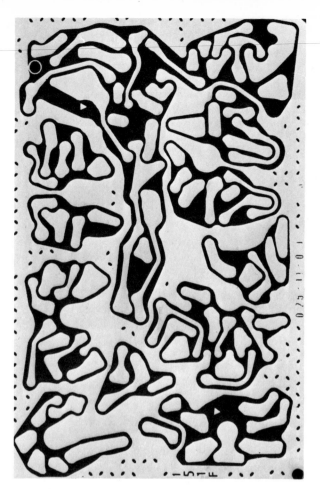

Printed circuit (used in television sets).
The Museum of Modern Art, New York.
Gift of Warwick Manufacturing Company, U.S.A.

Printed circuitry and a section
of fruit; their similarity shows
how advanced technology approaches
art and how both approach the
organic.

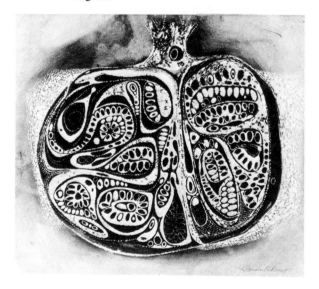

H. DOUGLAS PICKERING. *Pomegranate.* 1955.
Collection the artist

tograph." Did Van Doesburg unwittingly anticipate
printed electronic circuits? Will more sophisticated co-
ordinatographs supplant painters? Can electronic
engineers create art?

Light and Dark

On his deathbed Goethe is reported to have uttered
the phrase, "More light." Rationalist philosophers of
the En*light*enment spoke of "the light of reason." In
this context, light clarifies; it dispels darkness. In the
humanist tradition, light is a symbol of mind operating
to illuminate what is hidden and mysterious, to reveal
the shining face of truth. It is also a masculine symbol; all the ancient sun gods were male: Apollo,
Mithras, Mazda, and Horus. The earth and the moon,
which receive or reflect light, are female symbols;
without them light is invisible. Reality requires both—
yin and *yang*. Our eyes are light-sensitive organs,
equipped to receive energy which is absorbed or reflected from objects to form the sensory data of
images. Darkness is not positive, it is the absence of
light.

Art, however, is created by people, not by nature.
Artists use darkness as a positive tool: they work with
shadows to imply light. Symbolically speaking, they
work with both male *and* female elements. The light in
Klee's *Self-Portrait* is the absence of shadow; the
exposed paper is perceived as light because of its
contrast with the black areas painted by the artist.
Without *some* contrast, we would have the sensation
of light but would be unable to perceive line and
shape. The *Suprematist Composition: White on White*
painted by Kasimir Malevich (1878–1935) shows how
the virtual elimination of light-dark contrast almost
results in the inability to discriminate form. Actually,

PAUL KLEE. *Self-Portrait.*
Drawing for a Woodcut. 1909.
Collection Felix Klee, Bern

KASIMIR MALEVICH. *Suprematist Composition:*
White on White. c. 1918.
The Museum of Modern Art, New York

Malevich used two kinds of white—warm and cool—so that perception is possible on the basis of a "thermal" difference rather than light-dark contrast. But for the most part, artists employ distinct contrasts of light and dark or of hue to delineate form.

A drawn line is visible only because of contrast, whether a dark line on a light ground or a white line on a dark ground. Since colors differ in degree of lightness or darkness, they can be used to establish light-dark differences and thus visible form. Yellow is lighter than red, blue is darker than yellow. Sometimes, however, colors are mixed to the same degree of lightness or darkness, and then the eye is obliged to discriminate between them on the basis of their *chromatic* quality alone.

The simplest type of light-dark contrast is visible in the silhouette. Usually a solid black against a white ground, the silhouette provides a maximum of contrast and visibility. But it directs the viewer's eye to its shape as a source of information. Its interior is uniform and flat; it interests by virtue of its contour. Silhouettes occur in nature, as when we see an object against the light. But usually, objects are illuminated by one or several light sources. This play of light, when imitated by art, results in a naturalistic appearance. The manipulation of light and dark to create the illusion of volume on a two-dimensional surface is called "modeling"—a term borrowed from sculpture. An object can be "modeled" with only the stark contrast provided by two "values"—black and white. But a more convincing and subtle representation of reality can be created by imitating a wider range of light intensities. This type of modeling, which was perfected during the Renaissance, notably by Leonardo da Vinci, is called *chiaroscuro.*

By taking great pains, an artist can almost simu-

late photographic naturalism. However, the eye can discriminate more degrees of light intensity than the skill of the artist can reproduce. Consequently, artists do not usually attempt to compete with nature *or* the camera. Instead, they look for *patterns* of light and dark which they *can* imitate.

Much of the symbolism of light is mythic in character. Yet in the visual arts, the transitions from light to dark have meanings of their own—that is, distinctively aesthetic meanings. The gentleness or abruptness of halftones, or transitional areas, creates emotional responses. The source of illumination—from above or below—affects our perception. The distinctness or indistinctness of shapes is controlled by line and also by the manipulation of light and dark. Some shadows seem empty or opaque; others are luminous and mysterious. They invite closer inspection or they direct our attention back to the light areas they define. We have already noted that some architects design interiors which are bathed in strong light while others create forms which will cast shadows or break up the intensity of direct light.

As with the other visual elements, our perception of light and dark is guided by our experience in life. And in life we avoid too much of either: we can be as blinded by light as by its absence. Strong light-dark contrasts are equated with sharpness of focus, and since near objects come into sharp focus, degrees of contrast provide information about location in space. Because of the eye's preference for avoiding extremes of light or darkness, the late afternoon seems to afford the most interesting shadows and halftones compatible with the pleasing delineation of form. Consequently, it is a good time for social life. Ladies beyond the bloom of youth always seem to have known this. Only teenagers have the temerity to brave a Coke date

236

GEORGES DE LA TOUR. *Saint Mary Magdalen with a Candle*. 1625–33. The Louvre, Paris. La Tour's light represents the cleanliness of a spirit which has been washed and scrubbed by the effects of endless moral reflection.

CARAVAGGIO. *The Calling of St. Matthew*. c. 1597–98. Contarelli Chapel, S. Luigi dei Francesi, Rome. For the sixteenth-century mystic, darkness was a spiritual opportunity—not merely the absence of light. In the shadows of Baroque painting, the substance of the soul made itself felt.

REMBRANDT VAN RIJN. *Man with a Magnifying Glass.* 1665–69.
The Metropolitan Museum of Art, New York. Bequest of Benjamin Altman, 1913

Rembrandt was devoted to "the light that never was, on land or sea." He kept
trying to find it in the faces of the less than perfect citizens of Amsterdam.

REMBRANDT VAN RIJN. Detail of *Man with a Magnifying Glass.*

El Greco. *The Agony in the Garden of Gethsemane*. c. 1580. The National Gallery, London. El Greco's fundamental metaphor is of one flame beckoning to another. The visual image and the spiritual life complete themselves when all bodies are consumed in a single culminating blaze.

at noon or in the fluorescent glare of a modern soda-drug-and-pill emporium.

One consequence of the vigorous use of color in modern painting is the tendency to think of light in terms of color. Nevertheless, our perception of objects is primarily affected by the distribution of light on their surfaces. Form determined by shape and light, therefore, is a principal tendency of the history of art. In the following pages we discuss some examples of the dramatic use of illumination in traditional and modern art.

BAROQUE EXPERIMENTS WITH ILLUMINATION

After the masters of the Renaissance perfected chiaroscuro, the later Mannerist and Baroque painters went on to employ unusual illumination to dramatize their subjects. In Caravaggio's *The Calling of St. Matthew* (c. 1597–98), for example, the source of light from the extreme right—as indicated by the cast shadow on the wall and the direction of Christ's hand—endows the event with a highly theatrical quality. About eighty percent of the figures are in shadow; light creeps around their edges to perform a descriptive function and seize the eye of the viewer. Study of these areas reveals they carry the real burden of the work. Georges de La Tour (1593–1652) went a step further, using *artificial* light to construct solid forms of classic simplicity. His *Saint Mary Magdalen with a Candle* (1625–33) shows how the Baroque artist creates quiet pictorial drama through light-dark patterning within the boundaries of visual realism. Although most of the picture is in darkness, it is a comfortable darkness, made so by the reasoned shaping of the lights.

El Greco is known as a superb colorist, having carried the Venetian tradition of Titian and Tintoretto to Spain. Yet he was also the master of a so-called flickering light—a light more animated than that of La Tour. Both are Baroque painters, but La Tour exhibits a formal order which relates him to modern classicists like Seurat, while El Greco employs an agitated style which may be felt in modern Expressionists like Munch, Kokoschka, and Soutine. *The Agony in the Garden of Gethsemane* (c. 1580) appears to be artificially illuminated, especially in the Christ figure, in which the light-dark contrast is powerfully distinct. El Greco's technique of monochromatic underpainting followed by transparent overglazing permitted separation of two crucial phases of pictorial composition: light-dark modeling and color distribution. Contemporary painters tend to deal with color, light, and shape at once: what is gained in spontaneity, though, is lost in the opportunity to calculate the dramatic impact of the whole. El Greco also seems modern in the inconsistency in his light sources. The angel receives a different illumination from that of the Christ, a difference which seems appropriate for the treatment of a mystical-religious theme.

In Rembrandt we encounter perhaps the most moving synthesis of Baroque experiments with dramatic illumination. The richness of forms in the light, the cultivation of mystery in the darks, the buildup of pigment in areas of maximum illumination—these are readily at his disposal. Rembrandt underpaints and overglazes, but he also paints opaque passages into transparent areas. His transitional tones bear the closest study because it is there that he departs from abstract patterning of light and dark to reveal the distinctive insight into the human condition which raises his art above merely skillful modeling. In *Man with Magnifying Glass* the loss of light in the halftones and shadows seems to symbolize all that is human—that is, vulnerable—in his subject. The light areas consist of a vigorous, masculine impasto swimming among liquid glazes which begin the transition to the luminous shadows. The light might be regarded as the virile, affirmative element—meeting our eyes first, establishing the principal forms, struggling to expand and assert its dominance. The halftones represent modifications of light, the feminine element which seeks to find accommodations to the incursion of light by resistance, compromise, and yielding. Halftones operate in those areas which light cannot entirely occupy. In the shadows we see death and defeat, their luminosity being the visible record of invasions by light which failed. But if the darks allude to death, they do not symbolize despair. The light is dynamic; it has been where the shadow is; one feels it will return.

LIGHT AND DARK IN MODERN ART

The modern use of light and dark was spectacularly inaugurated by Edouard Manet, especially in his "scandalous" painting *Le Déjeuner sur l'herbe.* But his *Olympia* (1863) is an even more dramatic example of the impact of lighting. It must have been this merciless flat light as much as his subject which aroused the indignation of the French public. That is, they thought they were objecting to his candid treatment of a prostitute, but perhaps they were offended by his unsentimental application of paint and glaring treatment of light. Manet tended to eliminate halftones and subtle modeling effects. He painted directly, without glazes, and with a preference for bluish black in the shadows and transitions. The *Olympia* has some of the quality of a candid camera photograph in which the flash bulb has flattened out the forms. This flattening was to influence subsequent painting in bringing all forms up to the picture plane. By 1892, Paul Gauguin, in *The Spirit of the Dead Watching,* could benefit from the innovations initiated by Manet. Gauguin was able to concentrate on symbolism and psychological expression while exploiting the devices of light and composition pioneered in Manet's *Olympia.*

The woodcut *Prophet* (1912) by Emil Nolde (1867–1956) shows how expressive strong contrasts of black and white can be when all middle tones are eliminated. Of course, the woodcut medium is highly suited

HENRI DE TOULOUSE-LAUTREC.
Maxime Dethomas. 1896. National
Gallery of Art, Washington, D.C.
Chester Dale Collection. Silhouette
used to create pictorial space and to
direct the spectator's vision.

KÄTHE KOLLWITZ. *War Cycle: The
Parents.* 1923. National Gallery of
Art, Washington, D.C. Lessing J.
Rosenwald Collection. Silhouette
used to force the eye inward where it
can find details animating the
total form.

to this treatment of light. But we would not accept it if not for the example set by Manet. The bridge and wings of the nose in Nolde's *Prophet* are entirely black, though the logic of illumination would dictate otherwise. But by 1912, an artist could mix abstract and descriptive elements almost arbitrarily, in this case producing a harrowing impact through the pattern of darks connecting the brows, nose, and mustache. The tool used to cut the wood block imparts a characteristic shape to the forms; it does not change direction easily because it must contend with the resistance of the wood grain. The consequent harshness of shapes becomes an attribute of the subject: the prophet is ignored because he declares truths the multitude does not wish to hear.

Rouault's *Dura Lex sed Lex (Harsh Law, but Law)* (1926) is very much in the spirit of Nolde's earlier woodcut. Here, too, the pictorial structure is basically an extreme light-dark contrast, with the inclusion of a few halftones which modulate the light intensity somewhat. The texture Rouault achieves with the printing plate creates a painterly richness of surface, so that this work seems less obedient to the character of printmaking than the Nolde. The emotional expression of an idea is paramount in Rouault.

Color

Color *theory* can be discussed here in summary fashion because it is treated exhaustively in a number of specialized works. Besides, color theory often provides answers to questions which are not often asked when examining works of art. Some color systems are related to the physiology of perception rather than aesthetics. Others have evolved from industrial needs for the classification of dyes and pigments. At any rate, artists work with color on an intuitive more than

a scientific basis. Even so rational a colorist as Josef Albers paints his pictures by making intuitive adjustments to the requirements of his own vision rather than by applying the data of color physics. The French Impressionists, who were influenced by the color theories of Helmholtz and Chevruel cannot be accused of knowing as much about color theory as today's college physics student. Their opportunity to see the work of Turner and Constable in England in 1870 may have been a more potent influence on their painterly development. And teachers who have inflicted color wheels, color binaries, and triads on generations of students appear divided about the ultimate effectiveness of this material.

COLOR TERMINOLOGY

There is, nevertheless, a terminology of color which permits orderly reference to the properties which we believe generate aesthetic emotion. Following are brief definitions of the terms most commonly used, chiefly the effects attainable with artists' pigments.

Hue refers to the names of primary colors such as red, yellow, and blue. Note that these are different from the colors of the light spectrum as taught in physics. The primary hues are theoretically the basis for mixtures resulting in orange, green, and violet; presumably, the primaries are *not* the result of a mixture. But in practice, the most intense hues are achieved by mixture. The names given by manufacturers to colors are usually a form of labeling designed to distinguish a color from its almost identical cousins made by other manufacturers. Thus we have "Mediterranean Gold," "Colonial Yellow," "Roman Bronze," "Canary Yellow," And finally we have the artists' pigments: yellow ocher, gamboge yellow, chrome yellow, and so on.

Value refers to the lightness or darkness of a color.

From Boucher to Manet to Gauguin one travels through distinct modes of viewing woman. At first she is a delightful toy; then she becomes a more complete person—still used for pleasure, but humanized to the point where her stare is embarrassing; finally she reverts to fearful adolescence as the child-woman imprisoned by the superstitions of a witch.

FRANÇOIS BOUCHER.
Miss O'Murphy. 1752.
Alte Pinakothek, Munich

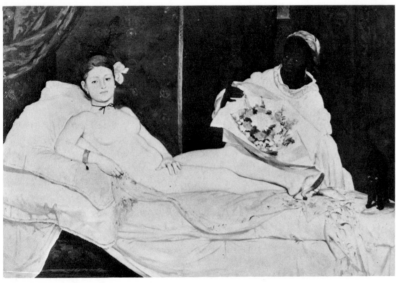

EDOUARD MANET.
Olympia. 1863.
The Louvre, Paris

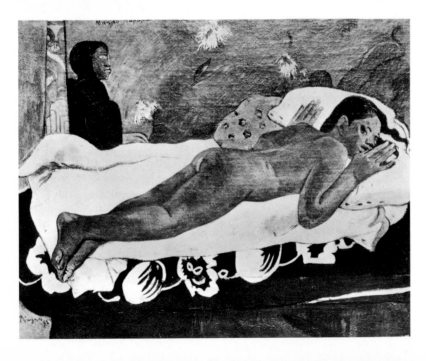

PAUL GAUGUIN.
The Spirit of the Dead Watching. 1892.
Albright-Knox Art Gallery, Buffalo, New York.
A. Conger Goodyear Collection

EMIL NOLDE. *The Prophet.* 1912.
National Gallery of Art, Washington, D.C.
Lessing J. Rosenwald Collection

"redness" of the fire engine. Similarly, distant mountains appear to be blue or violet although we know that their local color is green.

Complementary colors are opposites. They are opposite each other on a color wheel; more fundamentally, the presence of one denotes the absence of the other. In this sense, no other color is as different from red as green. To the human eye, the afterimage of red is green; the afterimage of green is red. If red and green are side by side, the red looks redder and the green looks greener; the afterimage of each enhances the actual image of the other. If complementaries are mixed, they cancel each other out—that is, they produce a gray or, more likely, what painters call mud; they neutralize each other. A small amount of red added to a large amount of green will gray the green; white added to the mixture will raise the value; and thus a variety of interesting grays can be mixed without using black.

Analogous colors are relatives, kinsmen, as opposed to strangers like complementaries. They are related because they share the same "blood lines"—red and orange, orange and yellow, green and blue, blue and violet, violet and red. Analogous colors are contiguous on the color wheel, so that families of color do not end distinctly at any point but seem to "intermarry" with their close neighbors. Being relatives, they "get along," if that is true of relatives. They are

As white is added, a color becomes "higher" in value until pure white is reached. Conversely, as black is added, or some other color which has a darkening effect, the value becomes "lower" until pure black is reached. As you approach pure white or pure black, you become less aware of the chromatic or color quality and more aware of its lightness or darkness, which is to say its *value.* Yellow is already high in value. It can be used to raise the value of colors darker than itself. Blue is already low in value. It can lower the value of lighter colors.

Intensity refers to the purity of a color, the absence of any visible admixture. As mentioned above, pigments seldom present a hue at its fullest intensity. For example, the pigment called alizarin crimson can be made into a very intense red by the addition of a small amount of yellow or cadmium orange. Ultramarine blue is very dark as a pigment and becomes an intense blue hue only with the addition of white. But too much white will kill its intensity and give it a faded appearance.

Local color is the color we "know" an object to be as opposed to the colors we actually see. We know a fire engine is red, but depending on light conditions, its distance, reflective quality, and so on, it will appear red, violet, orange, or even green in some places. Its highlights might be almost white. At least, a painter would use these colors in representing the

GEORGES ROUAULT. *Miserere: Dura Lex sed Lex.*
1926. Philadelphia Museum of Art.
Purchase, Temple Fund

245

harmonious next to each other; they mix with each other without becoming gray.

Colors are called *warm and cool* because of our psychological associations with blood, fire, sky, or ice. Reds, yellows, and oranges are warm; blues, greens, and some violets are cool. But these "thermal" properties are relative. Yellow-green would be cool next to orange but warm next to blue. Gainsborough introduced some purple into the shadows of his *Blue Boy* to warm up what would have been a chilly figure. Picasso did the same thing in his Blue Period paintings. Painters often create forms by contrasts of warm and cool rather than of light and dark. The warm colors seem to advance, the cool colors tend to recede. This illusion results not only because of association but also because the wave lengths at the warm end of the light spectrum are stronger—that is, more visible—than those at the blue-violet end. Ultraviolet, of course, cannot be seen at all.

Tonality refers to the overall color effect of a work of art when one color and variations of it seem to dominate the whole. Rousseau's *The Dream* has an essentially green tonality, for instance. At times we speak of warm or cool tones, which is a way of referring to variations of color built around a dominant warm or cool hue. A painting with a blue tonality may contain reds and yellows, but, because of the *quantity* and *distribution* of blue and its *tonal* variations, the comprehensive effect is of the prevailing blue. Tonality imposes at least a color unity upon a work, simplifying the problems of composition by reducing the number of color variables the artist must harmonize.

COLOR AS LANGUAGE

It should be plain that very little can be said about colors in isolation. They always occur in a context or relationship—in art and in life. The *quantity* of a color can change our ideas about advancing/receding, expanding/contracting, warm/cool relationships. And, of course, the *shape* of a color area affects its impact, as does its *application*. In addition to the optical properties of color, there are symbolic properties to consider. Needless to say, there is an enormous body of folklore about color as well as a psychology of color, both available to the artist.

One of the prominent goals of modern art has been the use of color as an independent language of meaning and emotion. Abstract and nonobjective art liberated painters to the extent that they could minimize the use of the other visual elements and endeavor to communicate by color exclusively. The intention of some painters was to imitate music, which presumably communicates through "nonobjective" sound. Wassily Kandinsky, who seemed to think of colors as analogous to musical notes, is credited with the first nonobjective paintings, works which set out to use color as a direct language of emotion. The Fauves ("Wild Beasts")—chief among them Matisse, Derain, Friesz, and Vlaminck—had carried the coloristic advances of Impressionist painting into the realm of arbitrary color. Several movements early in the century tried to extend color into new realms of symbolic expression. Among them were Synchromism, Orphism, Die Brücke (The Bridge), Der Blaue Reiter (The Blue Rider), and Expressionism as a whole. Here we might discuss the color contributions of a few of the leading personalities of contemporary art.

London Bridge by André Derain (1880–1954) might be taken as a transitional work from Impressionism to Fauvism. It has the crisp, bright touch characteristic of Impressionist paint application, but the blurring of edges and the pursuit of atmospheric effects is absent. Intense yellow marks on the bridge do not locate themselves properly in space but jump out of their places and begin to function independently. Local color is exaggerated. The sky is vividly orange without any optical "explanation." Yellow reflections in the water are theoretically possible, but not probable. The drawing is only adequate; it is clearly subordinate to the activity of the brushwork and the dynamism of the pigment. At a time when the innovations of Impressionism were still controversial, it is understandable that the color and drawings of the Fauves would arouse violent reactions from critics and the public.

Still Life with Lamp by Alexej von Jawlensky (1864–1941) (see also his *Self-Portrait*), dates from the same time as *London Bridge;* it has moved still further in the direction of independent color, retaining only a nominal connection with visual reality. Although the structural organization is strong, it offers no particular eloquence in shape or line. The design is simply a scaffold on which to hang the intense, vigorously applied color. Jawlensky's subsequent Expressionist development is foreshadowed here in a rather coarse manner of execution. But he is well on the way to a type of abstraction in which pictorial structure is based on color intensities. It should be remembered that at this time French developments in abstraction were mainly monochromatic; Cubism was concerned with the analysis of shape and space. Synthetic Cubism permitted itself the indulgence of arbitrary color and texture, but always within the framework of its own logic. It is as if the French would not permit any thoroughly irrational development in pictorial composition. Yet Matisse, the informal leader of the Fauves, was thoroughly Gallic. The "wildness" of his color was not inspired by a desire to escape rationality but by an urge to discover color which could directly express feeling. He was fairly well convinced that color imitation constituted an impediment to successful expression.

The *Landscape with Houses* of 1919 by Wassily Kandinsky (1866–1944), although later than the Derain, is closer to Impressionism in its gradations and traces of color-vibration technique. His edges are not as harsh as Derain's, and the drawing is not as rebellious. But the color spots on the rooftops also "jump out." The pictorial space is pressed forward, although Kandinsky has not reached the control of the picture plane which Cézanne achieved in the 1890s. He never became as interested in pictorial architectonics as Cézanne and the French Cubists. For Kandinsky, the metaphysical possibilities of color were central.

In Mark Rothko (1903–1970) we have a painter who endeavors to use color as a mystical light which surrounds the viewer. *Earth and Green* consists of two unequal rectangles superimposed on a blue field. The pigment is applied like a stain; hence we are not aware of it as a brushed-on substance. It seems to be an integral part of a canvas which radiates colored light. Within the rectangles there are subtle changes of tonality of the sort seen in the painting of William Baziotes. Rothko was seeking a way of changing the viewer's consciousness through color. He wanted painting to get behind one's thought and feeling. This would be comparable to affecting human experience in a manner which is possible only through drugs or a mystical discipline. Since color is very powerful in its capacity to affect the nervous system, it is quite possible that Rothko was on the right path. It is interesting that his ambitious goal was approached through colors which are serene, deceptively simple, and very pleasing to the eye. Unlike Op art, which also endeavors to "shake up" consciousness through the eye, the art of Rothko does not involve dizziness, or any threat to the viewer's equanimity.

Surrealism, too, sought the alteration of consciousness. Its principal instrument was shock arising from the hallucinatory juxtaposition of incongruous material. But Surrealism relied on the cognitive meanings of subject matter; its approach was literary. Hence, its capacity for surprise diminished as the public grew familiar with the strategy. However, painters like Rothko seem to have found a way to create pictures which temporarily change one's sensuous environment, inducing a pleasant, contemplative state of being. Matisse was also interested in an art which would afford an opportunity for contemplation. We are perhaps about to enter an era when paintings, largely through color and shape, will carry out transactions directly with the nervous system, offering occasions from which the individual can emerge calmed, invigorated, quietly renewed.

Texture

We speak of getting "the feel of things" as if touching were the best way to know something. The fact is that feeling things is our *earliest* way of dealing with objects. As we develop, however, tactile sensation gives way to visual sensation as the principal mode of knowing. Still, we regard touch as more authentic than vision. If you have had a bad fall, you are likely to *feel* your body—"looking" for breaks or bruises;

a surface that "looks" all right may conceal damage that has to be felt to be discovered. Babies, we know, examine objects by putting them in their mouths—feeling them with the lips, tongue, and inner surfaces of the mouth. To be sure, they have no teeth to get in the way. A time arrives, however, when learning to know the world by touching or tasting becomes dangerous; seeing is safer.

Adults learn to look before they touch, but their looking is often undertaken as a tactile inquiry. That is, we use vision to find out what something would feel like if we touched it. This connection between visual and tactile sensation is so well developed that we can fall in love just by looking at someone. Notice, however, that so far as physical love is concerned, looking contemplates tactility. In other words, we move back to our earliest sensory modes when seeking the total knowledge of a person implied by an act of love.

Unlike color and light, which can only be seen, a texture can be felt as well. Hence, "seeing" a texture really means having a good idea about its surface quality. Much visual representation consists of providing viewers with reliable cues about the surface qualities of things.

What, then, are some of the tactile properties of surfaces that can be rendered visually? Essentially, they are phenomena related to the light-absorbing and light-reflecting abilities of materials. These, in turn, are represented graphically in terms of light-and-dark patterning, light intensity (or value relationships), color relationships, and, to some extent, line and shape. In other words, texture must be represented in art like anything else—through manipulation of the other visual elements. In sculpture and architecture, of course, textures are created, not simulated.

If texture can be represented through combinations of light, dark, color, shape, line, and so on, why do we regard it as one of the fundamental visual elements? Probably because the sense of touch has priority over the other senses in our development. Hence, we are "programmed" to attend to the textural qualities of objects as crucial attributes of their being. We expect our eyes to tell us not only how an object is shaped and where it is located in space, but also how it feels. We want to learn from texture what an object is made of, how it was formed, and whether it is safe to handle.

The early dependence on touch in human sensory development is reflected in the prominence of tactile qualities in the art of tribal peoples. Their art exhibits a textural force and vividness which is especially attractive to contemporary artists—notably those who have exchanged representational objectives in favor of making direct sensory appeals. For the tribal artist, however, textural effects are not primary aesthetic goals; they emerge as concomitants of ritualistic purpose.

Today, there appears to be a powerful desire to return to tactility in art—to the primal foundations of sensory experience. It may be due to distrust of remote visual stimulation, as in reading and scanning. At any rate, the textural qualities we see in contemporary art reach back and down into the deepest strata of human personality and historical consciousness.

Conclusion

Because it is devoted to explaining the "parts of speech" in art, this chapter has been entitled "The Visual Elements: Grammar." Works in which one of the elements is crucial for the total meaning have been examined. But in attempting to concentrate on the role of line, light, shape, color, or texture, we found these elements are invariably affected by association with the other elements. In verbal language, the way parts of speech "associate" with each other is called syntax; art, too, has what might be called "visual syntax."

While *rules* of syntax do not operate in art as strictly as in speech or writing, there are principles of organization which seem to be employed consistently; they help to maximize the effectiveness of a work of art, no matter what its meaning or purpose. We turn in the next chapter to these principles, sometimes called principles of design.

Nail fetish, from the Lower Congo. 1909. Museum für Völkerkunde, Basel

EDUARDO PAOLOZZI. *Saint Sebastian No. 2.* 1957. The Solomon R. Guggenheim Museum, New York

Nail fetish of Clous Yombe tribe, the Congo. 1878. Royal Museum of Central Africa, Tervuren, Belgium

Heavily textured surfaces have symbolic as well as sensory meaning. Very little semantic space separates the Congolese fetish figures from Paolozzi's St. Sebastian: the African tribal artist depicts his enemy with nails driven into him, while the contemporary sculptor shows his victim, mechanized man, lacerated with springs, wires, bolts, and gears.

SEYMOUR AVIGDOR (designer). Interior with patterns. 1969. Material found at Vice Versa Fabrics, New York. The appeal of overall repetitive patterns is fundamentally tactile. The patterns become textures because we cannot deal visually with so many little images—they have to be perceived in the same way that we see grains of sand, beans in a pot, or bees in a hive.

JEAN DUBUFFET. *The Sea of Skin.* 1959. Collection Daniel Cordier, Paris. Dubuffet can organize the textures of century plants so that they make a statement about the aging of all organic materials.

10

ORGANIZATION OF THE
ELEMENTS: DESIGN

No matter what the function of a work of art, its parts or elements are organized to be seen. That is, the purpose of a chair is to support someone and *to be seen.* The purpose of a poster is to persuade someone and *to be seen.* Stated more accurately, a poster *must be seen first,* before it can be persuasive. Consequently, the organization of the elements of art has a common goal along with a variety of personal, social, and physical goals. That common goal might be called *organization for visual effectiveness.*

A painting, which functions by providing the opportunity for significant *seeing,* needs to be designed if it is to be effective. Now the term *design* has been substituted for *organization. Design* is a process which is common to the creation of all works of art. No essential distinction is made in this book between the design of paintings and the design of objects of daily use, such as chairs. According to some, the word *design* should be restricted to the creation of utilitarian objects, while the creation of "nonuseful" objects like paintings and sculpture should be called *art.* I do not make that distinction for the following reasons:

1. The useful objects of the past frequently become the "use*less*" objects, the *fine art,* of the present. Although their status changes, their visual organization, or design, remains the same.

2. So-called nonutilitarian objects *do* have a purpose, but not a physical one. They function by being seen, by arousing feelings, by "explaining" the world.

3. The functions of works of art affect the way their visual elements are designed, but the need for design—that is, for organizing the elements to be visually effective—remains constant.

By insisting that design is a process common to all works of art, and by refusing to set up a hierarchy among art objects—calling some *art* and others *applied* or *minor art*—we gain certain advantages. We avoid being embarrassed by history, as when a magical fertility sculpture becomes a "fine-art" object in a culture which does not practice certain kinds of ritual. We are not caught in classification dilemmas by having to make arbitrary distinctions about the physical utility, aesthetic value, or psychological expressiveness of stained glass in Gothic cathedrals, of medieval tapestries hanging on damp castle walls, or of Romanesque sculpture telling Bible stories to a populace that cannot read. Is the Brooklyn Bridge symbolically less potent because it was *designed* to carry people across a river?

As soon as materials are formed or assembled, they constitute a visual organization which operates effectively because its elements work together. Now, all works of art exhibit certain patterns of "working together" that are called *principles of design.* These principles are based on the way people see effectively and pleasurably and on the way materials can best be formed. In a sense, the so-called principles of design are the result of long-term experimentation. The history of art can be regarded as a history of the types of formal organization which have been found effective in various times and places.

ALEXANDER CALDER. *Acoustical Ceiling*. 1952. Aula Magna, University City, Caracas. Calder's floating forms constitute an immense floating sculpture designed to improve the acoustical and visual qualities of the architectural space. Aesthetic and practical values are thus united in the same construction. Should it be classified as art or as engineering?

It cannot be claimed that any single design precept—for instance, unity in variety—constitutes a "rule" for artistic and aesthetic effectiveness. Distinguished works can be found that defy the principles of design cited here or in other places. Furthermore, the capacity to experience unity in variety differs among cultures: the unity of a Hindu temple may be less apparent to Western than to Indian eyes; the unity of Gothic architecture was doubtless absent for persons habituated to classical Mediterranean forms of artistic order. Nevertheless, these variations aside, the principles of design are based on habits of visual perception, and these are greatly influenced by the common physiological equipment of the human race. The habit of reading from left to right, or top to bottom, or right to left does affect perception. But everyone has to measure size relationships, the speed of moving objects, the distance of objects from the viewer. Binocular vision and perceptions of size, brightness, color, shape, texture, speed, and depth probably confer more uniformity than diversity

on mankind's vision. It is because of similarities in vision and perception that we dare to speak of design elements and principles as if they applied to everyone. In fact, as languages go, the language of vision may be best for communicating the unity of man. As Kepes says: "The visual language is capable of disseminating knowledge more effectively than almost any other vehicle of communication. With it, man can express and relay his experiences in object form. Visual communication is universal and international: it knows no limits of tongue, vocabulary, or grammar, and it can be perceived by the illiterate as well as by the literate. Visual language can convey facts and ideas in a wider and deeper range than almost any other means of communication."[21]

Unity

Perhaps unity is the only principle of visual organization, and the others merely different ways of achieving it. For unity ultimately represents the desire of the individual to relate all visual facts to one person— himself. No matter how well or badly an artist organizes the visual elements, *they will be seen as a whole*. That is because, as viewers, we have to close or end our visual experience in order to move on to other things. But if the viewer requires unity and is capable of supplying it himself, what is the purpose of trying to achieve unity through design? Our answer must be that the artist is engaged in an effort to *communicate his unity*. Ineffective design will result in the termination of the viewer's experience; the viewer will stop looking. The act of "not looking" is a type of completion; it represents unity, but not communication. Usually, all the visual elements are present in a single work: many kinds of line, shape, color, texture, and patterns of light and dark. A variety of visual events occurs within the type of organization we call a work of art. One of the objectives of design, then, is to create some kind of unity among them, *before* they are seen by a viewer. What are the principal ways of doing this?

One is *dominance and subordination*. Here the artist attempts to control the *sequence* in which visual events are observed and the *amount of attention* they are paid. The dominant element of a work is the one the others depend on for their meaning, or visual value. It is achieved most easily by *size*, the largest form being seen first. Secondly, it is achieved by *color intensity*. Other things being equal, an intense area of warm color (which tends to advance) will dominate an intense cool area of the same size. A third way of achieving dominance is through *location:* the viewer's eye is usually drawn toward the center of any visual field: objects located there are more likely to receive attention. That is why the head in most portraits is centered between left and right and above the midpoint of the canvas; it thus corresponds to the viewer's idea of the location of his own head.

Tovi's light fixture builds on the abstract sculptural tradition practiced by Brancusi. Maurer's Pop-art lamp is, of course, a representational form: it looks like a light bulb. However, both fixtures reflect design decisions related to sculptural surface and volume, physical utility, and aesthetic expressiveness.

MURRAY TOVI. Tovibulb. 1969. Designed for Tovi & Perkins, Inc., New York

INGO MAURER. Giant bulb. 1967

DESIGN IN USEFUL AND "FINE" ART

The *convergence* of lines and principal directions on a point can give dominance to that point without the aid of size and color. The eye finds it difficult to resist the point from which lines or strong light radiate. For instance, we are tempted to look at the bright sun although we know it will hurt our eyes. Hence, a very light area will dominate its darker surroundings by analogy to the sun in the sky. Finally, dominance can be achieved by *difference* or *exception*. We know that nonconformity stands out. If an ovoid shape appears among a number of squares, it will be seen as the exception; it will stick out like the proverbial sore thumb. Subordination results from using the opposite devices: small size, peripheral location, dull or grayed color, remoteness from converging or radiating lines, and similarity to surrounding shapes, colors, and textures.

Coherence refers to the sense of *belonging together* in the parts of a work of art. If any visual organization is so carefully adjusted and harmonized that change in one of its parts ruins its effectiveness, we respond as if in the presence of a living organism. Its unity depends on the viewer's feeling that the organization as it stands is inevitable: it could not be otherwise and still exist.

Visual coherence can be pursued through analogous color and color tonality—the prevalence of a single color or admixtures of it throughout a work. *Similarity* of any kind—of shape, color, size, illumination, or texture—will promote the impression of

253

DOMENICO GHIRLANDAIO.
The Virgin and Child with Four Saints.
Undated. Alte Pinakothek,
Munich

Unity can be achieved by a hierarchical design—dominance and subordination—or by the manipulation of light. In the Ghirlandaio, each person is delineated with equal clarity, but rank and importance are determined by location on a pyramid of ascending majesty. In the Rembrandt etching, Christ occupies the central position and is only slightly higher than the others. His figure dominates by virtue of frontality, gesture, and painterly modeling of form.

REMBRANDT VAN RIJN. *Christ Healing the Sick (The Hundred Guilder Print).* c. 1648–50

RICHARD LIPPOLD. *Variation Number 7: Full Moon.* 1949–50.
The Museum of Modern Art, New York.
Mrs. Simon Guggenheim Fund

HERBERT FERBER. *"and the bush was not consumed."* 1951–52.
B'nai Israel Synagogue,
Millburn, New Jersey

coherence and unity. But this device has its perils, since sameness also leads to monotony. Our tolerance for sameness is limited; we require variety to satisfy our visual appetites and yet not so much variety that the sense of wholeness is sacrificed.

Forms which are *dis*similar can be unified by the device of clustering. If they are unlike in shape, color, or texture, their *closeness* suggests coherence. If they are surrounded by open space, dissimilar forms located near each other tend to be seen as a unit. This principle of unity is illustrated in Braque's *The Round Table.* It contains a variety of objects and shapes, no two of which are alike. But they are held together by the encircling form of the table top and the open space around them.

Unity based on converging or radiating lines is fairly common and easily employed. The design problem is to avoid the obvious. We see this type of unity in an almost pure manifestation in the wire constructions of Richard Lippold (born 1915). But Lippold creates subsidiary centers of interest; also, the color and shimmer of his fine metal lines appeal

directly to the eye, thus mitigating what might be a too insistent stress on the radiant center. In *"and the bush was not consumed,"* Herbert Ferber (born 1906) has created a radiating composition based on the V form; but although the lines converge at the point of the V, a number of minor variations in shape and direction serve to avoid a too obvious, hence tedious, reliance on the basic device.

An instance of unity by central location occurs in *Nachi Waterfall,* a silk-scroll painting of the Kamakura period of Japanese art (1185–1333). Although paintings of this type had a mystical-religious function, they can be perceived by modern eyes in terms of their mastery of pictorial structure. The dead-center location of the water could lead to monotony if not for the sensitive adjustment of dark weights left and right, top and bottom. A rocky profile is dramatized at the point where the eye is led by the falling water; there the artist introduces several diagonals to counteract the dominant verticals. He also reserves his strongest light-dark contrasts for the spot where the water crashes against the rocks, after which it trickles away to a

Nachi Waterfall. c. 1300. Nezu Museum, Tokyo

different tune. Although an almost mechanical unifying device has been chosen, the artist sustains the viewer's interest by ingenious use of subordinate measures for creating variety without detracting from the principal event.

Balance

Aside from the legend that Galileo dropped weights from it, the Leaning Tower of Pisa is renowned because it is out of balance but manages to stand. The building is a worldwide curiosity. Our expectation is that the forces at work in the structure must be resolved—one way or the other: the building will either balance or it will fall. That it does neither is visually disturbing. Balance is the resolution of all forces in a structure leading to equilibrium. It is visible in nature, in the human figure, and in the man-made world. We expect it everywhere.

Balance in structures is largely a matter of reconciling weights and stresses. In the biological world it may be a chemical process. In art, balance is an optical condition, and terms like weight, stress, tension, and stability, which are borrowed from physics and engineering, take on perceptual meanings. It would not be surprising if the problems that students of physics solve are intuitively solved by artists and viewers as they calculate whether certain visual forms are pleasing. One thing is certain: having gone through a period of instability during infancy, we are very sensitive to all signs of imbalance.

Symmetry is the simplest and least interesting type of balance. This form of balance has a spontaneous appeal due to the bilateral symmetry of the human body. Also, it requires a minimum of perceptual effort to understand. The elements in each half may be very complex and in themselves difficult to fathom, but as soon as they are recognized as echoes or mirror images of each other, they acquire an interest which is curiously satisfying. Perhaps this pleasure is related to the manner in which electrical charges are distributed over the hemispheres of the brain during perception. The other main type of balance, *asymmetrical balance,* is more complex and interesting, although it may, by a more devious route, provide the viewer with the same pleasurable reactions.

Balance by weight (usually asymmetrical) suggests a lever and fulcrum, or a seesaw. It is assumed that the center of a picture, or of the visual field in the case of sculpture and architecture, corresponds to the fulcrum on which a lever or seesaw is poised. A heavy weight can be counterbalanced by a lighter weight which is located at a greater distance from the center. Of course, we are dealing with visual weight rather than physical weight. However, although gravity does not *actually* operate on the objects in paintings, we perceive them *as if* it does. What are the properties of the visual elements with respect to weight? Clearly, size is the first consideration. Other things being equal,

The centrally located figure, presented in a frontal pose, creates a problem in pictorial architecture which only the best designers can solve. This solution is formal but also achieves a visual balance or reconciliation of all pictorial issues and appeals—sensory, thematic, spatial, psychological, and intellectual.

HENRI MATISSE. *Carmelina*. 1903.
Museum of Fine Arts, Boston.
John T. Spaulding Fund

SYMMETRICAL AND ASYMMETRICAL BALANCE

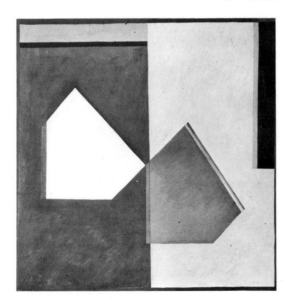

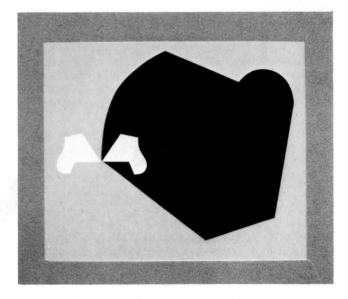

PIERO DORAZIO. *Janus*. 1949.
Marlborough Galleria d'Arte, Rome

JEAN ARP. *Olympia*. 1955.
Private collection, Switzerland

Balance exemplified by Janus, the two-headed Roman deity, and Olympia, the reclining lady made famous by Manet. Dorazio's composition is almost symmetrical, but color and value differences seem to require small adjustments in the placement and direction of subordinate forms. Arp balances his work by exploiting the viewer's interest in the pair of small forms at the left; they manage to counteract the massive torso form occupying most of the picture space.

BEN NICHOLSON. *Painted Relief*. 1939.
The Museum of Modern Art, New York.
Gift of H. S. Ede and the artist

JEAN GORIN. *Composition No. 9*. 1934.
Private collection

ASYMMETRICAL BALANCE ASSOCIATED WITH MECHANICALLY PRECISE FORMS

the larger shape seems to be heavier. Color, too, is important. In general, warm colors are heavier than cool colors, those of strong intensity heavier than those of weak or faded intensity. Coarsely textured surfaces appear to be heavier than smooth surfaces, perhaps because the tactile feeling excited by coarseness alerts the organism to the possibility of cutting or abrasion.

Balance by interest is another asymmetrical device. It is based on the excitation of the viewer's *curiosity,* usually to counteract impressions of weight. The idea that psychological interest adds weight may be open to question. Still, it is clear that artists have long employed interest to balance shapes of obviously greater mass. Psychological interest is generated by formal or symbolic complexity. Therefore, a large, brightly colored form can be balanced by a small, neutrally colored form if its shape or texture is complex. Interest can upset the logical operation of structural-mechanical forces in visual art. Symbols and signs arouse complex emotions and associations; they can influence perception in ways that are irrelevant to formal structure. For example, it is difficult to perceive Surrealist works apart from their symbolic meanings. Many viewers say they enjoy the color of Chagall's paintings, but it is likely that they are attracted by his romantic imagery. At any rate, the pictorial structures of Chagall owe their appeal to the *interest* he creates through symbolic and narrative modes. They do not possess *formal* balance.

There is also a *balance by contrast,* or opposition. It is a type of asymmetry—difficult to achieve because it involves calculating the visual demands of unlike elements. It includes not only oppositions between colors (as in warm vs. cool) or between shapes (as in geometric vs. organic) or between light intensities

(as in gray vs. dark) but also opposition between color and shape, size and texture, or shape and illumination.

Balance of weight by interest is cleverly illustrated in Miró's *Maternity*; the artist virtually sets up a laboratory experiment for us. Two straight lines cross in the center of the picture, forming an X. The point where they cross acts as a fulcrum. A large form at one end shaped like a wedge of pie is balanced by a small, insect-like form at the other end. A wormy shape also joins the insect, although it does not seem attached to the lever arm. The heavy shape stands for the male, the hole in the wedge serving to characterize it as a sort of eye, while the wormlike shape symbolizes the spermatozoon seeking the ovum. The other arm of the X is, of course, the female, divided by the fulcrum point into two equal segments, one presumably internal, where the ovum is located, and the other external, where we see a hemispherical shape suggesting a breast. The feathered little creatures at both ends, which suggest the female biological symbol, ♀, seem to be engaged in a seeesaw game: the ovum swings closer to, or farther from, the sperm. The position of the egg and the title of the picture imply that they will meet. Miró has created a playful enactment of the drama of human conception, divesting the process of its dark, clinical mystery. He presents fertilization as a slightly comic natural event in which delicate timing and physical engineering play crucial roles.

Rhythm

The term "rhythm" applies basically to poetry and music; it relates to measures of time. But seeing also takes time: from the standpoint of the viewer, it is

EDVARD MUNCH. *The Dance of Life.* 1899–1900. National Gallery, Oslo. This almost completely symmetrical composition employs balancing figures at both extremes to symbolize the opposed notions of joy and sorrow, vitality and death.

BALANCE BY INTEREST

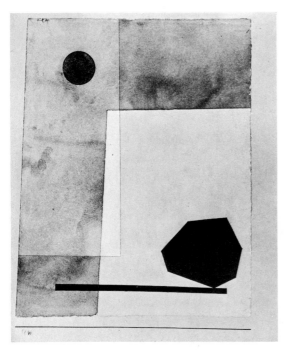

PAUL KLEE. *Daringly Poised.* 1930. Paul Klee Foundation, Kunstmuseum, Bern. The irregular dark shape (lower right) far outweighs the smaller, lighter circle (upper left) until we realize that the circle may be an eye. In that case, the rectangles at the left form a head, acquiring increments of psychological value and optical weight in the process.

JOAN MIRÓ. *Maternity.* 1924. Penrose Collection, London. Balance of weight by interest.

most pleasurably done in a rhythmic way. In the visual arts, rhythm is the *ordered or regular recurrence of an element or elements*. The main types of rhythm can be labeled *repetitive, alternative, progressive,* and *flowing*. The repetition of the same or almost the same shape, color, line, or direction sets up a rhythm which can hold our interest apart from considerations of function, structure, or expression.

We know that men march, lift, or pull together with more effectiveness if their effort is regulated by a rhythmic stress or beat. They tire less easily, too. In performing repetitive tasks, people try to find a comfortable rhythm. Up to a certain point, *repetitive* rhythm helps to reduce weariness and maximize efficiency. But experimenters in industrial psychology have discovered that operators performing repetitive tasks on dangerous machinery—such as stamping and sawing machinery—tend to suffer injuries. Injuries can be reduced by rotating operators after a certain length of time. Apparently, the human organism finds repetitive action boring and resists by breaking the rhythm.

The usual objective of artists and designers is to exploit the comfortable qualities of repetitive rhythm without incurring tedium. Hence, they employ repetition with variation, comparable to theme and variation in music. Simple *alternations* between black and white, solid and void, warm and cool, for instance, can be varied by the introduction of an unexpected element, a slight change in emphasis that does not destroy the rhythmic pattern of the whole. Rhythm,

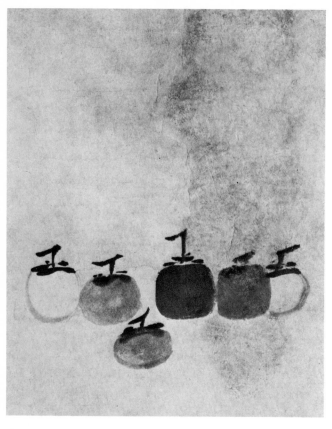

Mu Ch'i. *Six Persimmons*. c. 1270. Daitoku-ji, Kyoto, Japan

The rhythm of Mu Ch'i is accomplished through repetition of shape, with variations in tonal value and spacing subtly introduced. Thiebaud forces the viewer to seek variations in a deliberately repetitious series.

Wayne Thiebaud. *Seven Jellied Apples*. 1963. Allan Stone Gallery, New York

JOERN UTZON.
Sydney Opera House.
Bennelong Point,
Sydney Harbor, Australia.
Completed in 1973

therefore, exploits the viewer's expectation of regularity. It can achieve variety within unity by frustrating expectation temporarily—in other words, by an occasional surprise. But it must ultimately satisfy the expectations it originally aroused.

The establishment of a rhythmic sequence rarely occurs as the result of accident: it has to be calculated. Such calculations can easily become mechanical patterns requiring only the capacity to follow directions. But when the viewer senses the noncreative

REPETITIVE RHYTHM

ANDY WARHOL. *Brillo Boxes.* 1964.
Leo Castelli Gallery, New York.

PROGRESSIVE RHYTHM

KASIMIR MALEVICH. *Eight Red Rectangles.* 1915.
Stedelijk Museum, Amsterdam.

character of such rhythms, his experience tends to be wearisome. Some Pop-art works by Andy Warhol seem to fit this category. But we can think of other examples—from architecture and industrial design—which exhibit a deadly sameness. Art seems to consist of the saving variation which enlivens the rhythmic whole.

Progressive rhythm involves repetition with the addition of a consistently repeated change. The expectation of the viewer is aroused in terms of a goal, a culmination. It is exploited in architecture very often by the order of the steps or setbacks of tall buildings. Or, when moving through a building's interior, one may experience a sequence of progressively enlarged or diminished volumes, arousing the expectation of a certain kind of space, volume, or light at the conclusion. The architect may satisfy this expectation, or he may work for a dramatic effect through surprise. But a surprise totally unrelated to what precedes it sacrifices the unity of the whole. Some qualities of the introductory sequence must be present in the dramatic climax. In other words, there are good surprises and bad surprises.

Rhythm as continuous flow is suggested by the motion of waves: the regular recurrence of curvilinear shapes; emphasis at the crests and pause in the troughs; and smooth transitions from one wave form to the next. The crucial feature of this type of rhythm is the transition between forms: how is the movement of the eye from one nodal point to the next accomplished? We feel that when the eye is encouraged to move along a curvilinear path with no sudden changes of direction, it describes rhythmic or continuous flow. There are also staccato rhythms. We see them in the paintings of Stuart Davis, Bradley Walker Tomlin, and John Marin. Flowing rhythm is associated with the work of sculptors like Jean Arp, Aristide Maillol, and Henry Moore. In architecture, fluid rhythms are more difficult to achieve, although, as we know, the Art Nouveau designers carried curvilinear forms to an exuberant extreme. Aalto's bentwood experiment seeks a practical application in chair design, but it is also a good abstract image of flowing rhythm based on human contours.

The photograph of a pole vaulter by Thomas Eakins illustrates repetitive rhythm. Eakins, a serious student of anatomy, shared with the photographer Eadweard Muybridge a scientific interest in motion, and the results of his investigations happily exemplify the design principle of rhythm. In painting, *Nude Descending a Staircase, No. 2* by Marcel Duchamp makes the same point, as do such Futurist works as the *Dynamic Hieroglyphic of the Bal Tabarin* of Gino Severini (1883–1966). It exemplifies rhythm in its repetitive, alternating, progressive, and flowing varieties: there are color, line, and shape repetitions and progressions which can occupy the eye endlessly. The painting also has the quality of an organized explosion—similar to, but less raucous than, Joseph Stella's *Battle of Light, Coney Island.* The Futurists,

ALVAR AALTO. Experiment with bentwood. 1929. Courtesy Artek, Helsinki

HANS HOKANSON. *Helixikos No. 1.* 1968. Borgenicht Gallery, New York

fascinated by mechanization and motion, clearly made rhythmic capital out of the austere Cubist analysis of form.

Proportion

Proportion refers to the *size* relationships of parts to each other and to the whole. The size of a shape in itself has no proportional meaning: it must enter into

262

MARCEL DUCHAMP.
Nude Descending a Staircase, No. 2. 1912.
Philadelphia Museum of Art.
The Louise and Walter Arensberg Collection

THOMAS EAKINS. *Multiple Exposure Photograph
of George Reynolds, Pole Vaulting.* 1884–85.
The Metropolitan Museum of Art, New York.
Gift of Charles Bregler, 1941

GINO SEVERINI. *Dynamic Hieroglyphic
of the Bal Tabarin.* 1912.
The Museum of Modern Art, New York.
Lillie P. Bliss Bequest

a relationship with other shapes before we can be aware of its proportion. It should also be understood that there seem to be no permanently valid *rules* fixing "correct" or harmonious proportions.

There have been attempts to set up rules of perfect proportion—rules that would automatically confer pleasing intervals on all artistic structures. The most enduring has been the so-called Golden Section. It divides a line into two segments so that the smaller has the same ratio to the larger as the larger has to the whole. (Expressed algebraically as: $a/b = b/(a + b)$.)

The Golden Section has long been used, but there seems to be nothing remarkable about it as a formula beyond its recognition that a line divided in half makes a dull pair of intervals. Nor are segments of thirds much better than halves. Efforts to discover a magical geometric ratio that underlies all beautiful proportions will no doubt persist. But history will most likely continue to show examples of pleasing works that do not conform to the rule.

If eternally valid rules for perfect proportion do not exist we nevertheless make judgments about proportion. People have strong ideas about what constitutes good proportion in pictures, sculpture, useful objects, and in other people. We are taller and larger today than the men who wore medieval armor, so it is likely that our conceptions of pleasing height, if not width, in men and women have changed. But if there has been a change in preference since the Middle Ages, it has been caused not by a rule of geometrical ratio but by better nutrition.

The figures in contemporary fashion illustrations are some ten or twelve heads high, although this ratio changes. Yet art students used to be taught that seven and a half heads was the correct measure for men, and six and a half for women. If a model did not conform, the head was drawn larger or smaller as needed. Aside from the ratio of head to height, it is probable that the size of the human figure, and the relationships among its parts, constitute the model for *thinking about proportion* for almost all visual phenomena. In other words, we see a doorway or ceiling height as providing so much open space above the *height of a person*. Drivers may see in terms of car lengths and widths. But when we see for the sake of seeing—when vision is self-conscious, so to speak—the referent is the human figure.

Accordingly people are continuously if unconsciously engaged in making visual calculations and comparisons. They may use a scale of feet and inches, as when they say, "That man is six foot two." They may also say, "She is about my height, but a little stouter." Here there would be a hint of proportional judgment. We may visit friends in a new apartment and feel uncomfortable during the visit without knowing why. Did the builder skimp on the ceiling height, so that we felt squeezed? We walk along the downtown canyons of a large city and feel depressed for no apparent reason. Are the buildings so high that we cannot perceive them as multiples of the

ALBRECHT DÜRER. *Study for Adam.* c. 1507. The Albertina, Vienna. Dürer kept searching for the geometrical secret of classical figurative proportions.

human figure? It appears to be difficult for contemporary tall buildings to have what is called "human scale." Does the fault lie in their proportions or in the lack of optical space around them?

One function of architectural design is to manage proportion so that the disadvantages of the *spatial envelope* can be minimized. Manipulation of the visual elements can create "adjustments" in the ratio of width to height. Isolating a large shape makes it appear smaller. Horizontal patterning and segmentation of a tall shape reduce its apparent height. Just as the size of repeat designs in a fabric affects its advancing/receding qualities: a large motif brings the pattern closer. Coarseness and fineness of texture can also be regarded as a dimension of proportion, coarseness tending to approximate the large motif, which thus advances relative to the small figure or the fine texture.

A final point needs to be made about the designer's use of proportion: since we tend to perceive variation

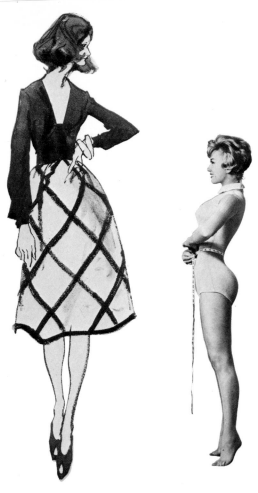

Fashion drawing   Female figure. Photograph of
Debbie Drake from the jacket
of her *Easy Way to a Perfect
Figure and Glowing Health,*
Prentice-Hall, Inc., 1961

able to do so. The severe flat roof of International Style architecture in the 1930s seemed dreadfully stark, naked, and arbitrarily cut off. Viewers wanted psychological interest at the top of a building as well as at its entrance—whether overhanging eaves, entablatures, and triangular pediments were functional or not. Apparently, the earliest skyscrapers were seen as structures requiring a capital, a "head." A building had to be "topped off" with something that would give it "good" proportion, that is, a complete *body.* The designer's "block" was his inability to free himself from the idea of the building as a symbol of the human figure. We see this idea expressed quite literally in the buttresses of the Nebraska State Capitol in Lincoln. The structure is dated 1922, only nine years before the Radio City complex was begun. The proportions of the complex express the technology of modern construction and the solution of contemporary functional problems. The vocabulary of form and proportion was now based on the abstract creations of the machine rather than figurative symbols and analogies retained from the past. This does not mean architecture and sculpture are permanently divorced, but the means of reconciling them is still in the process of being discovered.

from a norm as distortion, proportion can be used for expressive effect. We are familiar with the effect of attenuation in the sculpture of Lehmbruck and Giacometti; Modigliani and Picasso have placed small heads on large bodies to convey qualities of stability and calm. Viewers see not only the head size but also, more importantly, the proportional *relationship* between the head size and the bulk of the body: it is the *proportion* which carries the expressive burden. Monumentality is a matter of proportion and generous spacing rather than mere height, breadth, and mass.

In architecture, viewers have been accustomed for centuries to the intervals found in classical Greek and Roman buildings. Modern buildings, even skyscrapers, have been adorned with miniature Greek temples at ground level or on their roofs. Aside from paying homage to tradition, this practice recognized the fact that the classical civilizations solved the problem of proportion while we have rarely been

Buttress of the State Capitol, Lincoln, Nebraska

Conclusion

Although unity, balance, rhythm, and proportion are objectives of the designer, we found it necessary to discuss the contribution of the viewer too. That is, in addition to knowing some of the designer's devices, we need to know why viewers are interested in them. To some extent, an artist's effectiveness depends on understanding the way people respond to his organization of the visual elements. Usually, he is guided by his own responses in estimating its visual effectiveness for others. The principles of design we have discussed need not be the *conscious* aims of artistic creation: from the artist's standpoint they are labels we give to an often intuitive effort to discover form, express meaning, organize materials, and solve practical problems.

Such "labels" help us to understand the principles of visual organization which make works of art effective. There may be a temptation to set them up as standards against which specific works can be measured. But that would be a mistake. Their use should be limited to *explaining* the visual organization in a work of art. The problems of art criticism, discussed in Chapters Sixteen and Seventeen, are more complex because they involve philosophic as well as design considerations. However, we have been acquiring the tools which should help in performing our critical tasks.

PART FOUR

THE INTERACTION OF MEDIUM AND MEANING

THE INTERACTION OF
MEDIUM AND MEANING

HOW DO THE TERMS MATERIAL, MEDIUM, AND TECHNIQUE differ? We should have a clear idea about them before investigating the interactions between artistic expression and the various media. *Material* causes no difficulty: it designates the *physical elements* of art, such as paint, stone, clay, and metal. They are available to the artist in a variety of natural or manufactured forms, and he works with them directly or supervises workers who shape and assemble them according to his intent.

Medium is a more difficult term. In the dictionary definition it is the "substance through which a force acts or an effect is transmitted." In other words, it is a vehicle for converting materials into artistic form. In painting, there is also a technical meaning of medium: it is the liquid in which pigment is suspended—linseed oil, casein glue, egg yolk, varnish, synthetic resin, and so on. But that definition would not apply to architecture, sculpture, and film. A definition of *medium* that can apply to all the arts follows: a medium is a characteristic way of using materials for an artistic purpose. Architecture is not a medium, it is an art. Cast concrete, however, is a medium used in architecture. Sculpture is an art, not a medium. But welded metal is a sculptural medium.

Technique and medium tend to overlap in ordinary usage, but we can define *technique* with more precision here: *technique is an individual or personal way of using a medium.* For example, many artists employ the medium of oil paint in their work. But Jackson Pollock developed a *personal technique* in dripping his paint. Ibram Lassaw has a different technique from that of Richard Stankiewicz, although both employ the medium of welded metal. Le Corbusier, Nervi, and Candela developed personal techniques in the cast-concrete medium.

Our problem in the following chapters is to show how the nature of a medium influences what is done *with* it and what is expressed *through* it. Each medium has inherent possibilities and limitations. Some artists submit to the limitations and achieve excellence through their awareness of what can or cannot be accomplished within them. Other artists ignore the known limitations and either fail or succeed in extending the range of the medium. *Craftsmanship* can be understood as the *knowledge* of what can be done in a medium and the *ability* to do it. But all the possibilities of a medium cannot be known in advance. Hence, any artistic medium holds out a challenge to the skill and judgment of the person who uses it.

Art, however, is not identical with technology. Although technical skill is necessary in art, it is a *means* to an end. In art criticism, we often find ourselves judging the suitability of ends and means, that is, the *quality of interaction between medium and meaning.* We try to discover, in our examination of a work, how the medium has influenced what appears to be expressed. At the same time, we are interested in how the expressive content has affected the employment of the medium. It goes without saying that critical viewers ought to have experience with many works in various media; otherwise, they will not be able to tell how the medium and its meaning have interacted. Some believe that personal artistic experience is necessary if these relationships are to be understood. The purpose of the following chapters, therefore, is to provide information about medium-meaning interactions in the principal art forms. This is a difficult objective because we are attempting to communicate in verbal form the sort of knowledge which is normally gained by direct observation or practical experience. Furthermore, new technology or exceptional artistic ingenuity can make generalizations about media obsolete. However, if we make observations about specific works of art, they, at least, will stay put. You may extend them to other artistic phenomena at your own risk.

ROBERT CREMEAN. *Swinging Woman.* 1960. University of Nebraska Art Galleries, Lincoln. Gift of Mrs. A. B. Sheldon

EDGAR DEGAS. *Developpé en avant.* 1920. Bronze copy after wax original, 1880. The Metropolitan Museum of Art, New York. The H. O. Havemeyer Collection. Bequest of Mrs. H. O. Havemeyer, 1929

Two representations of woman in motion. Notice how material and technique influence the resultant form and meaning.

11

PAINTING

OF ALL THE VISUAL ARTS, PAINTING IS THE MOST WIDELY practiced. Children and grandparents, professionals and amateurs, physicians and prizefighters—all paint, with considerable satisfaction to themselves if not always to others. Is there any reason why this art should have attracted so many devotees? There are, of course, several reasons, but one of them concerns us especially: the flexibility and versatility of painting, particularly in oil, tempera, and acrylics.

The discovery of oil painting in the fifteenth century opened up a pictorial realm with immense possibilities. It was the type of technological innovation that exemplifies our theme: the interaction of medium and meaning. Oil paint has blending and modeling qualities unobtainable with tempera paint. The slow-drying oil vehicle permits the artist to modify a still wet paint film by adding paint, wiping it out, introducing darker or lighter tones, scratching in lines, and even manipulating the paint with the fingers. Yet the paint film will dry as a single "skin" in which all of these applications and afterthoughts are physically united. Since oil paint dries to a fairly elastic film it should not seriously crack when the canvas buckles a bit. Large canvas areas can be painted as opposed to the small wooden panels required for tempera. Before the perfection of painting in oil, mural-size works had to be executed in fresco—which is to say, fresh plaster—and on the site of the wall itself. Only later did artists take advantage of the possibility of executing huge canvases in their studios, afterward transferring the canvas to the building for which it was intended. So Michelangelo had to paint the Sistine Ceiling on his back, supported by scaffolding under the ceiling. Fresco did not afford the sharpness of delineation he wanted, so he also used

fresco secco (which is really a type of egg tempera), applying it over the plaster to bring out the forms.

Painting is attractive to persons varying greatly in skill and sophistication, while sculpture appears to be an art for the hardy few: sculpture is more limited in subject matter than painting. To be sure, Bernini could execute lace in stone and fashion sculptural shafts of light behind St. Theresa, but these are painterly effects, an observation which brings us to another of the distinctive qualities of painting—its capacity to create *veritable illusions*. Sculptors seeking naturalistic effects had to *paint* their figures in order to close the gap between reality and its representation. But key inventions in painting—linear perspective, chiaroscuro, oil painting, foreshortening, glazing, and color complementarity—opened up opportunities for illusionism that sculpture could not match. Finally, in comparing painting to sculpture or architecture, we should observe that poorly executed sculpture cannot easily conceal its lack of craftsmanship, and poorly designed buildings are at least inconvenient and at most dangerous. Bad paintings, however, endure physically in spite of their craftsmanship. Painting possesses no "built-in" characteristics which might discourage ineptness in technique. Everything survives.

Because the media of painting are flexible, durable, and inexpensive, because it attracts many temperaments, because almost any theme can be treated, and because works of modest imagination and indifferent technique survive physically as well as masterpieces, painting is one of the most popular of the visual arts. Now, having noted these factors, we can discuss the technical and expressive qualities of the art itself. But no matter how revolutionary the invention of oil painting appears to be, remember that it is the fundamental human need to create images which causes technical advances in the medium.

The Fugitive and the Permanent

In a well-designed building we can see that a truss, an arch, or a dome is *doing the work* of supporting weight and enclosing space. The forms are felt as a physical system which is or is not likely to hold together as we use it. No such consideration, however, enters into the perception of painting. Nevertheless, the art of painting has a physical basis which, like that of architecture, is concerned with durability.

The stone vaults of Gothic churches were developed because fires were so common in the medieval world that wooden-roofed churches burned down repeatedly. We can be sure that the physical survival of man-made structures was very important in medieval communities. This interest in durability was reflected in all the arts. For painting, durability meant permanence—resistance to fading, peeling, cracking, warping, and splitting. Since a picture was a valuable material commodity, painters had to master "correct"—that is, permanent—technique. So-called fugitive colors could fade, especially the blues and violets. Others might turn black or "bleed through." Colors applied to a ground that was too absorbent would "sink in." A thousand perils hovered over every painter's brush.

Artists were members of the goldsmiths' guild during the Renaissance, and although masters like Leonardo, Titian, and Michelangelo had risen above the artisan class, they were deeply immersed in problems of craftsmanship. Their training and professional roots were in artisanship and the guild system. Leonardo and Cennino Cennini wrote treatises on the art of painting which contain lengthy discussions of technical methods. Cennino's, however, is more like a cookbook, while Leonardo's penetrates beyond cookery into psychology, anatomy, composition, and philosophy.

But if painting technique begins as an interest in physical durability, it ends as an aesthetic requirement. Artists' contracts stipulated the amount of lapis lazuli (the semiprecious source of blue pigment), gold leaf, and other costly materials, much as architectural specifications today require materials with certain performance ratings. When the social and professional status of the painter became more firmly established, the intangible qualities of his art were stressed, and although sound technique was assumed, it was realized that genius consisted of more than costly materials. As the architect Filarete wrote in the fifteenth century, "The knowledge of painting is a fine and worthy thing, and really an art for a gentleman."

One can find many contemporary paintings which observe ancient traditions because they seem to yield aesthetic gratification even though they have no foun-

MICHELANGELO. *Isaiah* (detail from the ceiling of the Sistine Chapel). 1508–12. The Vatican, Rome. The good physical condition of Michelangelo's Sistine Ceiling paintings makes us wish that Leonardo had used the same fresco technique in his *Last Supper*. The color in a fresco does not *rest* on the surface; it sinks into, and becomes part of, the wall. Thus a fresco can withstand a great deal of punishment.

dation in the requirements of permanence. The resemblance of Jack Levine's technique to Rembrandt's has been mentioned. The same can be said of Soutine. His *The Madwoman*, however, exhibits more direct brushwork in the darks than Rembrandt would have used. The brilliant cadmium reds, alizarins, and madders used by Soutine were not available to Rembrandt or El Greco, for example. Perhaps we should say they were not available in such stable, light-proof pigments. Hence, the masters used a reddish glaze over a greenish tempera underpainting which itself rested on a luminous white ground. Soutine used opaque reds and alizarins applied directly to a primed canvas. The colors retain their brilliance because they are almost chemically inert. Soutine could paint his twisting shadows with loaded brush quite spontaneously; the agitation of the result owes a great deal to this direct execution. El Greco's flickering effects had to be

LEONARDO DA VINCI. Detail of *The Last Supper*. c. 1495–98. Sta. Maria delle Grazie, Milan. Instead of the time-honored fresco technique, Leonardo used tempera on a masonry wall dubiously sealed with a varnish of pitch and resin. (He may also have applied an oil glaze over the tempera painting.) Soon after completion, *The Last Supper's* paint film must have begun to peel off the wall, thus leaving Leonardo's most magnificent conception to the ministrations of a succession of more-or-less inept restorers.

planned in advance. In the sixteenth century laying opaque paint into a wet glaze called for sureness of hand and a clear idea of the desired effect. Today Willem de Kooning, more influenced by Rubens than El Greco, is especially prominent among painters who practice loaded-brush, wet-in-wet technique.

Inevitably, the durability of goods has a different meaning today than it had in the scarcity economies of the past. Although some of us may have experienced scarcity, an enormous number of citizens are unaware of any obligation to make things last or to buy only those which seem durable. Instead of fixing a broken part, we replace it. This even makes economic sense, since the labor cost of repairs is often greater than the purchase cost of a replacement. (Of course, we rarely calculate the ecological costs of discarding usable goods, collecting and relocating trash, of polluting water, land, and air with the wastes created by ac-

celerated consumption.) In this context, an artistic concern with permanent technique seems to be an anachronism. Consequently, the physical durability of art objects ceases to be a crucial concern.

Since we are reasonably assured of the physical survival of a painting, our concern shifts to its durability as a significant statement. We want to know whether it will live as a vehicle of sustained *aesthetic interest*. Our interest in this kind of survival is not rooted in an artist's technique so much as in his capacity to make original statements in a medium. As George Moore said, "It does not matter how badly you paint, so long as you don't paint badly like other people."

The *time* required to execute a work by traditional methods worked against a casual approach toward theme and technique. As the oil-painting medium was perfected, however, technical skills were often devoted

CHAIM SOUTINE. *The Madwoman.* 1920.
The National Museum of Western Art, Tokyo.
Presented by Mr. Tai Hayashi, 1960

SCHOOL OF REMBRANDT VAN RIJN. *Old Woman Cutting Her Nails.*
1648. The Metropolitan Museum of Art, New York.
Bequest of Benjamin Altman, 1913

to apparently insignificant themes. For example, courts of love by Jean-Honoré Fragonard (1732–1806) seem trivial and saccharine for modern, democratic taste. However, the fluid execution of *The Meeting* is a triumph of painterly virtuosity. Beyond the theatrics of the situation, drawing and composition are managed with a high degree of artistry. Some contemporary painters, on the other hand, undertake themes of large importance while using a technical approach which seems rather casual and offhand. *La Mort d'Attila* by Georges Mathieu (born 1921) is such a work. The value of painting has been relocated: it now lies in the act of execution. Modern man does not look at a painting as medieval or Renaissance man did, inquiring into its craftsmanship, its likelihood of surviving as an idea. The contemporary collector is aware of the work as a possession he may sell if it ceases to interest him or if its market value increases. Modern men and women have a *different sense of time.* Under the impact of rapid social change, and particularly of cultural relativism, confidence in fixed values has broken down. The idea that man-made structures can or should survive forever seems slightly absurd, just as it would have seemed absurd to medieval men that anything be made *not* to last.

If the decline of older ideas of permanence has cost

us certain artistic values, there have also been compensations. Experimentation with design, materials, and themes has generated dividends in visual variety. Painting is perhaps more entertaining than it was. At the same time, it has not ceased to be concerned with serious issues. Although the perfection of photography and motion pictures poses a threat to the survival of picture-making as a handcraft, painting appears to be responding to the challenge vigorously. Indeed, the art is more widely practiced and exhibited than ever before; it has extended its range of social and personal functions; and, as will be seen, painting has acquired some of the traits of sculpture, architecture, and even drama.

Direct and Indirect Techniques

Simply stated, direct painting seeks the final effect immediately. Indirect painting calls for a stage-by-stage approach. These two approaches represent fundamental contrasts in technique and in artistic psychology. In general, traditional methods are indirect, systematically planned in advance. Modern approaches tend to be direct and spontaneous.

As long as painting is regarded as an elaboration

of drawing, the indirect method prevails. If painting is the application of color to a scheme already worked out, it makes sense to employ the indirect method. It amounts to a problem in the division of labor. First comes the conception of the work, its theme, its specific content, its overall setting, and so on. Next, drawings are made to explore spatial representation, the arrangement of landscape and architectural features, and the figures. For the Renaissance artist, drawing was a means of *studying* the things he would later paint.

Studies of drapery, hands, facial expressions, and figure anatomy were undertaken so the artist could be assured of an intellectual and visual grasp of the subject. Then he felt ready to transfer his drawings to a prepared surface. Following enlargement to the scale of the final work, the artist could begin painterly execution. The preliminary painting in tempera would usually be monochromatic. This underpainting served as a guide for translating the drawing into paint, establishing the compositional scheme, placing lights and darks, and modeling large forms. Because tempera paint dries quickly and is very opaque, corrections which cover mistakes can be made easily. Oil paint dries slowly and becomes transparent as it grows older; hence passages which have been painted out tend to show through eventually. However, tempera does not blend easily; so it is difficult to conceal uncertainty by a wide, blended passage. Egg tempera, especially, is difficult to spread on in large areas. Large forms have to be built up by "hatching" (creating a small *area* of color or tone by a series of lines painted close together); it is a linear technique.

When the indirect method is employed, underpainted shadows can be executed in cool tones if warm-tone glazes will be applied over them at the end. Then, by glaze manipulation, the painter will be able to achieve a warm-cool balance. The light areas are usually painted "higher" or "chalkier" than they will finally appear because overpainting and glazing will

JEAN-HONORÉ FRAGONARD. *The Meeting.* 1773. Copyright The Frick Collection, New York

lower their value. In traditional painting techniques, it was assumed that white pigment (usually white lead), together with final varnishing, would tend to yellow the painting. That constituted another reason for favoring a cool tonality in the underpainting.

Before the discovery and wide use of oil painting—in the form of oil glazes over tempera or in direct application to a primed canvas—most paintings were

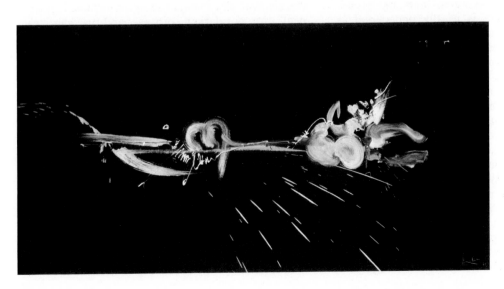

GEORGES MATHIEU. *La Mort d'Attila.* 1961. Collection Jean Larcade, Paris

MICHELANGELO. Studies for *The Libyan Sibyl.*
The Metropolitan Museum of Art, New York.
Joseph Pulitzer Bequest, 1924

MICHELANGELO. *The Libyan Sibyl*
(detail from the ceiling of the Sistine Chapel).
1511. The Vatican, Rome

The drawing is more detailed than the final fresco painting because it truly is a "study"—a device for *knowing* a phenomenon
visually and intellectually.

completely executed in tempera (the other principal
forms were encaustic, which is a wax-based medium,
and fresco, which employs water, lime, and plaster
as its vehicle). Tempera is usually understood as
any painting medium based on a glue. Older glues
came from cooked animal skins—rabbit skin, for
instance. As you may know from scraping breakfast
frying pans, eggs are a powerful adhesive. Casein,
a milk derivative, is a modern glue that makes an
excellent tempera. Polymer tempera comes close to
being an ideal medium since it possesses all the assets
and none of the liabilities of the traditional tempera
and oil media. However, tempera paintings until the
1940s were mostly executed with the traditional egg-
yolk medium. Today, Wyeth, for example, employs
the classic egg-tempera medium.

Many contemporary painters were taught Cennino's
recipes for preparing a gesso ground (thin, white
plaster-of-Paris layers applied over a coating of size)
on a wood panel (today Masonite hardboard is usually
employed), and learned how to puncture the egg-yolk

sac, "cook up" an egg-and-water or egg-and-oil
emulsion, and then mix the emulsion with powdered
dry pigment. The pure egg-tempera medium is permanent, does not darken with age, and provides clean,
bright color. But it usually calls for a rigid support
and, as mentioned above, is not well suited for covering large areas. Furthermore, it dictates a slowly
built-up, step-by-step mode of execution. And it tends
to force a linear design upon the artist.

Direct painting begins when the artist starts to increase the pigment in his oil glazes. The Venetians are
credited with introducing loaded-brush technique (the
brush is "loaded" with paint of a pasty, viscous con-
sistency which is then applied in short "touches"
rather than evenly brushed out). This technique is accompanied by freer departures from the controlling
tempera underpainting. We see a line of development
in the use of the oil medium from Titian to Rubens to
Delacroix. Delacroix, perhaps, represents the critical
departure from reliance on the underpainting; with
him, spontaneous execution begins to assert itself very

EUGÈNE DELACROIX.
Sketch for *The Lion Hunt*. 1860–61.
Private collection

EUGÈNE DELACROIX.
The Lion Hunt. 1861.
The Art Institute of Chicago.
Potter Palmer Collection

forcefully. His contemporary, the classicizing Jean-Auguste-Dominique Ingres, practiced an impeccable technique with nowhere a brushstroke seen. But Eugène Delacroix consciously and effectively exploited the emotive possibilities of brushwork. His oil sketch for *The Lion Hunt*, executed about 1860–61, shows forms created directly with the brush. Drawing is felt or understood, but it is subordinate to the painterly establishment of form. The dynamism of this composition derives basically from its underlying pattern of whirling forms which appear to radiate from the center

and then rotate in a counterclockwise direction. Delacroix is not content to rely on the dynamics of the composition: he supports its movement with brushstrokes that have a life of their own. It is interesting to compare this oil sketch with the final work, which is modified in composition and is, of course, more "finished" in execution. From the standpoint of contemporary taste, the sketch is more abstract, less finicky, and fresher in its use of paint. The contemporary quality of the Delacroix oil sketch is brought home when we examine a painting by the American artist

Richard Lytle (born 1935), *The Possessed*. Lytle is clearly the beneficiary of Delacroix's form language. The antecedent of these works, both in subject matter and painterly execution, is Peter Paul Rubens's *Lion Hunt* (1616–21). Although Rubens employed a preliminary underpainting, he clearly relied on a direct type of overpainting executed very spontaneously. Hence, notwithstanding many innovations, there is considerable continuity of outlook and of method—from Rubens in 1616 to Delacroix in 1861 to Richard Lytle in 1959.

The question arises as to *how* brushwork performs emotionally. Fundamentally, a viewer's perception of the artist's brushwork involves an internal "acting out" of the process of wielding the brush applying paint. Most viewers have had experience with brushes, either in art classes or in some other, more prosaic connection. Hence, it is easy for them to identify with and to simulate inwardly the motions implied by the brushwork they see. This does not mean that viewers perform gymnastic maneuvers before a painting which has an active surface. It *does* mean that a variety of physiological reactions are set in motion within the viewer by such a work, and these reactions produce feelings.

Indirect technique does not rely on brushwork to express emotion. Because indirect paintings are executed in separate layers, distinct marks of the brush tend to be lost. Pronounced ridges of paint would show through as textures; hence they must be eliminated or the final effect may be spoiled. The element of planning tends to reduce the appearance of spontaneous execution, which is an important means of arousing empathy. Masters of indirect technique such as Ingres or David brushed out their paint, leaving no

surface sign of the process of execution; the response of the viewer had to be based on subject matter and design. For artists who favored historical themes and allegorical composition, such a response was intended: indirect technique draws attention to the subject mat-

RICHARD LYTLE.
The Possessed. 1959.
Collection the artist

PETER PAUL RUBENS.
Lion Hunt. 1616–21.
Alte Pinakothek,
Munich

JEAN-AUGUSTE-DOMINIQUE INGRES.
Madame Moitessier Seated. 1851.
The National Gallery, London

ter of a picture whereas direct technique emphasizes the way it was painted.

Direct technique combines almost all crucial decisions in the single act of applying paint. The artist may make preliminary sketches but the final effect is not built up: drawing, color, value, shape, weight of pigment, and paint quality are determined as the paint is laid on. A spontaneous appearance is sought even if the painter works slowly and deliberately. If he does not achieve the desired effect at once, he scrapes the paint off until he succeeds. Oil paint, of course, is ideal for this sort of trial-and-error execution. But when an artist continues to paint over his earlier efforts rather than scrape them off, a labored, rather tortured paint surface often results. Direct technique, therefore, is not well suited to frequent "overpaints." The color tends to become muddy; it begins to look tormented; clarity of color and crispness of brushwork are lost.

Since direct technique usually emphasizes the *performing* aspect of painting, attention is drawn to the evidence of paint mixing and application. Cézanne and Van Gogh are instructive performers to watch. There is more building up of planes in Cézanne, but his "touch," while careful, is rarely hesitant. He does not push the paint around indecisively. He seems to know the color and value of each stroke before he commits himself. Frequently, Cézanne's canvas shows through as the white paper does in some watercolor paintings. Consequently, his surfaces have a freshness and sparkle which a more labored technique would not yield. Van Gogh's *The Ravine* might be regarded as a demonstration of the emotional power of short, distinct brushstrokes. They set up staccato rhythms which reinforce the impact of the vibrating color. Thus, the colors of the paint, as well as its application, contribute to the gushing motion one "feels" in the

The impression of swiftness and spontaneity calls for considerable assurance on the part of the artist—assurance based on solid knowledge, power of observation, and shrewd grasp of character.

FRANS HALS. Detail of *Governors of the Old Men's Almshouse, Haarlem*. 1664. Frans Hals Museum, Haarlem, The Netherlands

water. A brushed-out technique or a luminous glaze would surely ruin this effect. The flickering light of El Greco's *The Agony in the Garden of Gethsemane* is a different phenomenon entirely; it was achieved by the *shape* of the light-and-dark patterns. El Greco came as close as one could to conveying an agitated movement of light and form while using indirect painting technique.

If we trace direct painting technique from its beginnings among the Venetians during the fifteenth century to its full development in our own time, it seems that the method has paralleled the growth of individualism in society and of autonomy among artists. Since direct technique emphasizes the uniqueness of the painter's execution, it is best suited to artists who set a premium on the expression of their personalities regardless of theme. Indirect technique has suited artists who did not wish to display their "handwriting." In recent work, these contrasting attitudes remain visible although almost all artists paint directly. The so-called "hard-edge" and geometric painters employ an anonymous technique, relying on design and the optical effects of color to carry the burden of the work. For "action" painters, the path of the painter as he travels across the canvas with loaded brush is often the theme of the work. Such paintings express the extraordinary personal freedom of the artist today. Indeed, this emphasis has aroused the hostility of some observers. Perhaps they are offended by forceful assertions of freedom; or perhaps they cherish classical ideals of moderation more. But Aristotelian counsels are rarely heeded in contemporary art: media and techniques celebrate the individual—his freedom or his anxiety, his indifference to the themes and methods of yesterday's masters. What matters is the search for new structures of meaning.

PAUL CÉZANNE. *Aix: Rocky Landscape*. 1885–87. The National Gallery, London

VINCENT VAN GOGH. *The Ravine*. 1889. Museum of Fine Arts, Boston. Bequest of Keith McLeod

ALBRECHT DÜRER. Detail of
The Painter's Father. 1497.
The National Gallery, London

These are stubborn men. So were
the artists who painted them—
stubborn, that is, about telling
the whole truth.

JAN VAN EYCK. Detail of
The Virgin and the Canon Van der Paele.
1436. Groeningemuseum, Bruges

LEONARDO DA VINCI.
Detail of *Portrait of a Musician.*
1490. Biblioteca Ambrosiana,
Milan

What generous expressions! How
intelligent the eyes! The noses and
chins are constructed as nobly as
Greek temples. Even if they are
idealized, such men *should* have
existed.

MICHELANGELO. Detail of
The Prophet Joel. 1509.
Ceiling of the Sistine Chapel,
The Vatican, Rome

above left: EL GRECO. Detail of *Fray Felix Hortensio Paravicino.* c. 1605. Museum of Fine Arts, Boston. Behind those penetrating eyes, which seem to take one's full measure, the viewer senses the controlled intensity of a totally dedicated man, a "true believer."

above right: PETER PAUL RUBENS. Detail of *Self-Portrait.* 1638–40. Kunsthistorisches Museum, Vienna. The self-assurance of an older man who has been very successful. An intellectual as well as a highly physical person, Rubens was never assailed by doubts about the ultimate unity of spirit and flesh.

left: REMBRANDT VAN RIJN. Detail of *Head of Christ.* c. 1650. The Metropolitan Museum of Art, New York. The Mr. and Mrs. Isaac D. Fletcher Collection. Bequest of Isaac D. Fletcher, 1917. For Rembrandt, the image of Jesus posed a special problem: the dominant Catholic tradition of the Baroque called for an idealized, somewhat mannered personification, but Rembrandt's painterly style and religious commitment had their roots in Protestant realism. His solution: a Jewish model in whose countenance we see a remarkably credible embodiment of manliness and compassion.

JACQUES-LOUIS DAVID. Detail of *Man with a Hat*. After 1816. Royal Museum of Fine Arts, Antwerp. Even in the work of a classicist like David, the force of a private personality asserts itself—especially in this candid portrait. A new cult of individualism is emerging—casual, studied, self-assured. The manner of aristocrats is now enjoyed by a confident bourgeoisie.

THÉODORE GÉRICAULT. Detail of *The Homicidal Maniac*. 1821–24. Musée des Beaux Arts, Ghent. Pursuing the varieties and extremes of individualism, the Romantic inevitably examines one of the most tragic forms of human suffering and alienation: madness.

DIEGO VELÁZQUEZ. Detail of *Pope Innocent X*. 1650. Doria-Pamphili Gallery, Rome. A work of the seventeenth century, but thoroughly modern in its approach to painting and personality. Its optical realism anticipates Impressionism and photography. The only barrier between the viewer and a complete disclosure of Innocent's character is the aristocratic reserve of the artist.

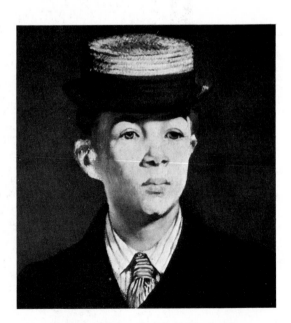

EDOUARD MANET. Detail of *The Luncheon in the Studio*. 1869. Neue Pinakothek, Munich. The self-assurance of this young man corresponds to certain arrogant qualities in Manet's style: a frontality based on exceedingly flat lighting, a refusal to tamper with or idealize visual facts, a determination to set the painterly act above pictorial convention.

EUGÈNE DELACROIX. Detail of *Portrait of Chopin*. 1838. The
Louvre, Paris. The painter grows interested in the correspondence between heightened emotion, form, and brushwork; he
believes turbulent feelings generate a corresponding visual
resonance.

PAUL CÉZANNE. Detail of *Victor Chocquet Assis.*
c. 1877. Columbus Museum of Art, Ohio.
Howald Fund Purchase

Cézanne sought a prismatic mode of perceiving form and personality; his art would bypass subjective impressions, destroying natural objects in order to reconstruct them along rational, architectonic lines. Picasso carried the dematerialization of form further—toward a thorough interpenetration of solids and voids. But his sense of the dramatic would not allow him to abandon the representation of human motifs. With Gris we have a new ambition: to create a geometry of form so fundamental that it could be used to designate real objects, people, and places. Cézanne would have approved.

PABLO PICASSO. Detail of *Portrait of Ambroise Vollard*. 1909–10.
Pushkin Museum, Moscow

JUAN GRIS. Detail of *Portrait of Picasso*. 1912.
The Art Institute of Chicago

The common trait of Expressionist works of art is their capacity to make us spectators of the moment when a person confronts his own particular dread. The soul, if not the body, is invariably shown naked and shivering. We see more than a person's fear of responsibility, guilt, physical deterioration, or a life of emptiness; we witness a sense of awe when these abstractions become final meanings in personal existence.

GEORGES ROUAULT. Detail of *The Tragedian*. 1910. Collection Professor Hahnloser, Bern

EDVARD MUNCH. Detail of *Puberty*. 1894. National Gallery, Oslo

Oskar Kokoschka. Detail of *Self-Portrait*. 1913.
The Museum of Modern Art, New York

Ivan Albright. Detail of *And God Created Man
in His Own Image*. 1930–31. On permanent
loan to The Art Institute of Chicago
from the Collection of Ivan Albright

In a sense, Matisse, during his Fauvist period, was responsible for the development of all these artists—even the Germans and Slavs. While pursuing his serene pictorial objectives through a system of arbitrary color, he opened up a new set of emotional options for figural representation—options that were eagerly seized by men of restless disposition. Although Matisse was concerned with man's image only as a motif in a grand scheme of light, movement, and pleasure, these Expressionists followed a different path—a path of agonizing self-examination and private anguish.

HENRI MATISSE. *Green Stripe (Madame Matisse)*. 1905.
Statens Museum for Kunst, Copenhagen. Rump Collection

ALEXEJ VON JAWLENSKY. *Self-Portrait*. 1912.
Collection Andreas Jawlensky, Locarno, Switzerland

Max Beckmann. Detail of *Self-Portrait in a Tuxedo*.
1927. Busch-Reisinger Museum, Harvard University,
Cambridge, Massachusetts

Ludwig Kirchner. Detail of *Portrait of Gräf*.
1924. Kunstmuseum der Stadt Düsseldorf

KAREL APPEL. Detail of *Crying Nude*. 1956. Collection
Mr. and Mrs. Alan Fidler, Willowdale, Ontario

ANTONIO SAURA. *Imaginary Portrait of Goya*. 1963.
Museum of Art, Carnegie Institute, Pittsburgh

LARRY RIVERS. Detail of *Celebrating Shakespeare's 400th Birthday
(Titus Andronicus)*. 1963. Collection Clarice Rivers, New York

RICHARD HAMILTON. *Fashion-plate study (a) self-portrait.*
1969. Collection Rita Donagh, London

To the extent that the human image survives in recent painting, it is either mutilated or derided. Appel
and Saura carry the Expressionist idiom to the limits of abuse, trying to find mythic power through
intoxicated painterly tirades. Rivers and Hamilton are cooler: they play allusive Pop-art games with
drawn, pasted, and painted human images. But they refuse to take these images seriously as symbols
of human beings; the idea of man is a source of embarrassment to many contemporary painters.

Frottage, Grattage, and Decalcomania

The spontaneous application of paint with a loaded brush is one type of liberation from the traditional approach to painting. In this technique, the artist exploits the fact that the *marks of the tool*—the brush marks—are expressive in themselves. Once this was discovered, it was a simple step to the realization that changing tools results in new possibilities of meaning. Some artists devised new techniques for manipulating paint, which *itself* became the subject of their imagery. Among the most inventive has been Max Ernst (1891–1976), a prolific creator of new pictorial devices.

For most of his career, Ernst was associated with the Dada and Surrealist movements; irrational impulse played a major role in his art. *Chance arrangement* is a principle of Dadaist composition, while the juxtaposition of unrelated images is a principle of Surrealism: clearly, the movements are linked. Ernst's technical discoveries result from a search for imagery which is not known in advance, which cannot be calculated consciously. It must be developed in response to "accidents" caused by interactions between paint and process. But although the results appear to be unplanned, the artist works hard to create his accidental situations.

Frottage is the best known of Ernst's techniques. You may be familiar with it as the popular art of rubbings: pencil or crayon rubbed over paper placed on a textured surface transfers a negative image of the texture underneath. Archaeologists use rubbings to make copies of stone or metal reliefs. Purely abstract patterns such as wood grains can be transferred and then worked up into recognizable images. Frottage, then, is a technique which has a practical, record-keeping value; it also can be used to stimulate the creation of fantastic forms. For Ernst, it was a means of suggesting unplanned images of natural or accidental origin like those in clouds, wall stains, rock fissures, and so on. He found a way to use frottage in oil painting by placing a freshly painted canvas over a relief texture and then scraping away the paint. The unscraped paint left in the valleys and crevices of the canvas creates a pattern corresponding to the texture below. The process does not involve rubbing, but it results in a transfer of the pattern underneath by a technique similar to frottage. As with *decalcomania* (see below), the key concept is *transfer*—in other words, *informal printing*. Another informal printing process involves the dipping of leaves, kitchen utensils, toy parts—anything that can be held in the hand—into wet paint; then the object is used like a hand stamp to transfer the pattern to canvas. However, we should distinguish between printmaking, the intentional forming of images to make many reproductions, and frottage, the transfer of "found" textures and patterns in the context of a single painting.

Grattage, another Ernst technique, is the grating or scratching of wet paint with any of a number of tools: a comb, a fork, a pen, a razor, a needle, an irregularly

WILLEM DE KOONING. *Woman, II.* 1952. The Museum of Modern Art, New York. Gift of Mrs. John D. Rockefeller. Employing direct technique, contemporary painters use pigment as a vehicle of angry self-expression.

shaped piece of glass. Grattage takes advantage of the plastic character of wet oil paint just as the paintbrush does. But the brush is designed to *apply* paint and blend it—only secondarily to leave its mark. These new tools manipulate paint which is already there. Grattage involves an almost sculptural or architectural working of paint, the pigment being seen as a type of building material like concrete. (In this connection, it should be mentioned that Le Corbusier liked to "scratch" images into his poured-concrete wall surfaces.) The conception of paint as a material which can be scratched, abraded, or otherwise tortured represents a departure from the idea of paint as a descriptive substance. In traditional painting, the pigment was not really "there." It was "transparent," that is, it designated something else.

In *decalcomania* as used by Ernst, wet blobs of paint are squeezed between two surfaces which are then separated. Variations in pressure force the paint into random patterns, forming crevices and rivulets which can be exploited for their formal and thematic suggestions: fantastic geological structures, landscapes of unknown planets, prenatal memories, feverish projections of the imagination. Still it is the artist's

The painter builds a surface through carving, scratching, and abrading; his picture is something "real" rather than a system of illusions.

imagination which acts as creative instrument. Decalcomania, frottage, and the rest are strategies of imaginative stimulation.

Another Ernstian technique, *éclaboussage*, is widely practiced by painters. It involves dropping paint or turpentine from a height to a prepared canvas. Ernst dropped paint from a perforated tin can swung from a string suspended above the canvas. The paint splashes were manipulated like the squeezed pigment in decalcomania. Turpentine dropped on a freshly painted canvas was also used to create splash patterns to expose the bare canvas or dilute the wet paint partially. The turpentine was blotted up or permitted to stand, puddle, or run in random paths. There was only a short step from dropping paint to throwing it from a brush or dripping it from a stick like Jackson Pollock.

For centuries, the brush was an extension of the artist's hand, but when used to spatter paint it is a different tool. Among the more bizarre methods of distributing paint is the technique of Niki de Saint-Phalle (born 1930), who fired a rifle at bags of paint suspended before a wall covered with relief sculptures. The explosion of the gun and the bag of paint created two dramatic events—the performance itself and the record of its violence on the paint-spattered wall. Compared with Ernstian techniques of stimulating the imagination, this method shifts attention from the *result* of the creative process to the act of execution.

Once the brush lost its central position in painting— once, indeed, that pigment was abandoned altogether—then the tools and materials of image-making became capable of almost infinite extension. A bulldozer might logically be employed as a sculptor's tool. César Baldaccini (born 1921) has created objects with the powerful hydraulic press used to squeeze junked automobiles into compact cubes of anonymous metal. He calls the method "governed compression." One cannot escape the impression,

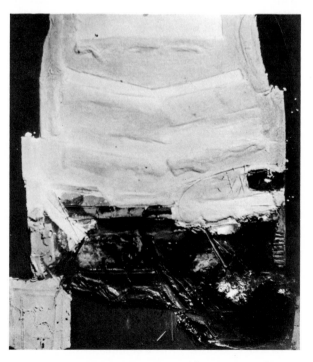

Photograph of Niki de Saint-Phalle about to paint with a rifle

once again, that so theatrical a gesture represents a shift of focus from the object to the symbolic meaning of the act of creating it. In such "sculpture" and in the "paintings" of Ms. de Saint-Phalle, we see the crossing of the line from plastic art to dramatic art: the object reminds the viewer of an earlier *dramatic enactment*.

The tendency of painting to seek assimilation by the dramatic arts will be discussed in further detail. But with reference to painters like Klee, Ernst, Duchamp, and Dubuffet, I want to stress their work in devising

new creative strategies. These strategies were tools for the creation of art objects. But another generation of artists has been impressed by painterly strategy for its own sake. The *process* of throwing, dripping, or exploding paint has opened up possibilities which are felt to have aesthetic value apart from their results. In a subsequent section of this chapter, "Beyond Collage: Assemblage, Environments, Happenings," we shall analyze these more recent developments in painting and/or drama.

The Picture and the Wall

Abstract Expressionist painting, which dominated the art scene from 1946 until approximately 1960, reintroduced the huge canvas of Baroque and Neoclassic vintage. Canvases with dimensions of up to sixteen feet were not unusual. However, this new scale of painting signified a fundamental change in the way painting was intended to operate in its setting and for its public.

"Action painting" was dependent for its effectiveness upon the communication of the artist's brushing gestures—gestures accomplished mainly through the movements of the large muscle groups of the body. This point is obvious in a work such as De Kooning's *Black and White, Rome D*. The viewer's reaction must be kinesthetic as well as optical if he is to appreciate the painting. Its reproduction in a book does not stimulate the appropriate bodily responses.

Large pictures have been created, of course, during almost all periods of art history. However, their size was based on the need to accommodate many figures, buildings, landscape details, and so on. Scale and

GOVERNED COMPRESSION

CÉSAR. *Portrait of Patrick Waldberg*. 1961.
Collection the artist

CLAUDE MONET. *Water Lilies.* c. 1920. The Museum of Modern Art, New York. Mrs. Simon Guggenheim Fund

format were keyed to the actual size of real objects. Pictorial perception was related to a close or distant view of reality. Then with Impressionist painting, the distance of the viewer from the *picture* became crucial for understanding the work. At one distance, perception would be of fragments, of color patches and color vibrations. At a greater distance, the color areas and fragments would come into *focus*, yielding a relatively stable image of the whole.

WILLEM DE KOONING.
Black and White, Rome D. 1959.
Collection Taya Thurman,
New York

Paintings executed by direct technique also exhibited some indistinctness when seen up close. But the vital discovery of Impressionist painting was that unfocused color areas sustained interest as images in themselves. And as mentioned earlier, the expressive potential of color could be exploited only after it was substantially detached from a descriptive function. Such a development appeared in the combination of free color, active brushwork, and large-scale abstract design in a huge canvas mural, *Water Lilies,* painted by Monet about 1920. The work is over eighteen feet wide and is executed in large, loosely brushed color areas. Although the overall design is somewhat governed by the natural setting, it is difficult to see the entire canvas at once because of its size. One views a succession of parts, and these are abstract, the color and paint quality taking precedence over description. Now the *scale* of the painting became as significant as the brushwork. This work constitutes an important monument of large-scale abstract art.

The large scale of modern works has several implications for contemporary painting. The first is that passages of color and texture are frequently larger than the viewer, making it difficult to maintain an attitude of detachment during perception. Areas and shapes become not so much the objects of perception as *part of the environment.* A color area *surrounds* the viewer. Mark Rothko made especially effective use of this factor. There is an analogy here to the relation of the motion-picture image to the television image. Empathy is easier with the motion-picture screen than with the home tube. The motion-picture image communicates meaning visually, while the television image seems more like an extension of radio, of sound, of the spoken word. In other words, the small image in television or painting bears a closer relation to literature than the cinematic or large painted image.

A second implication of large-scale painting lies in the tendency of the picture to merge with the wall and to become an architectural element rather than a work *attached to* a wall. Thus painting returns to its mosaic and stained-glass antecedents. The modern development began with the flattening of space by Cézanne and the Cubists. Illusionistic effects—the

The painting in this office affords independent aesthetic values; nevertheless, its abstract forms harmonize in terms of size, shape, and texture with the furniture, walls, and floor covering of the room.

Office of David Rockefeller,
Chase Manhattan Bank,
New York. 1961

The storage and display of paintings in the seventeenth century emphasized their separate character: each picture represents a self-contained world independent of the architectural setting in which it is encountered.

DAVID TENIERS.
*The Picture Gallery
of Archduke Leopold
Wilhelm.* c. 1650.
The Prado, Madrid

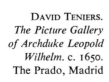

creation of pictorial space through perspective and chiaroscuro devices—were violations of the integrity of the wall and the reality of architectural space. Now the imagery of painting rests on the surface; it makes no claim to occupy deep space. Because it does not conflict with the spatial identity of the wall, the large painting—in visual terms, at least—*is* the wall.

The return of painting to architecture is part of a drive to create environments. In this tendency, painters have been encouraged by modern architectural practice. Some architects see their role as extending beyond the creation of space: they also endeavor to control the character of surfaces. To the extent that they design these *surfaces*, architects perform a painterly function. Buildings by Wright and Le Corbusier often seem satisfactory without painting and sculpture. And some painters feel that Wright's Guggenheim Museum dominates the pictures in it: the interior design satisfies all the visual and plastic requirements of viewers; hence paintings are superfluous. Buildings by Mies van der Rohe, on the contrary, seem to welcome painting and sculpture. Perhaps that is why his colleague, Philip Johnson, has become one of the leading designers of museums in the United States.

There is an abundance of anonymous space and plain wall surfaces in modern American building. Perhaps this creates a vacuum which painters instinctively endeavor to fill. Besides, the large scale of modern painting has effectively removed it from the domestic dwelling; public buildings are becoming its natural habitat. Increasingly, painting is intended for the spacious walls of galleries and museums or for the corridors and executive suites of banks.

Small works are still created for homes and apartments, but few major works by "important" painters can fit into the homes of even the affluent middle class. Collectors are obliged to design special facilities for their collections. Clearly, paintings have escaped the category of Victorian knickknacks. They are too large, too bright, too disturbing to rest quietly against the wallpaper, ornately framed, sharing soft light from a table lamp with collections of china, family photographs, and travel souvenirs. Painting has become an art of public statement and public performance. It is difficult to believe that large-scale paintings are created today without any awareness that they are destined ultimately for public ownership and display. The small picture, the easel painting, is diminishing in importance. Happenings and Environments have become possible as the dimensions of the canvas approximate the dimensions of the wall or room. Pictures as ornaments, traded like furniture or household items, may continue to be created; but they are unlikely to occupy a position close to the heart of painting as an art form.

Beyond Collage: Assemblage, Environments, Happenings

In every generation, painters feel that their elders have carried the medium as far as it can go and that they must strike out in radically new directions—in theme, materials, technique, and creative approach. One powerful reason for their dissatisfaction has been the attraction of the film—an attraction which is understandable, since motion pictures are a major extension of the art of creating images practiced since Paleolithic times. Spurred by the need to compete with new media of communication, painters have tried to cross the line separating their art from sculpture and architec-

ROMARE BEARDEN. *Family Group*. 1969. Private collection, New Jersey. Here the collagist employs fragments of reproduced photographic imagery for their cognitive meanings as well as their colors, shapes, and textural possibilities; he operates simultaneously from narrative and painterly sensibilities.

ture. They have abandoned representation, creating works which are "real." They have fashioned works which destroy themselves as we view them and works which spectators enter physically, like actors in a drama. Such innovations may be understood as the endeavor of image makers to compete with new materials and new visual technologies.

Assemblage is an example. As the word implies, it is the creation of art objects by putting things together—usually by combining them in new contexts. Painters often think of the debris and the found objects they incorporate into their works in terms of the usual visual elements: line, shape, texture, color, and light. But instead of simulating the qualities of objects with brush and paint, the artist employs the object itself. This procedure relieves the painter of the obligation to employ skills in the *re*-presentation of reality, skills which have grown progressively less vital to painting as photography and the film have advanced.

In addition to the cultural conditions which led to assemblage, the technical ground was prepared by *collage*. The media are similar except that collage calls for the *gluing* of materials to a surface. Assemblage employs *any* method of joining or fastening. Some of these methods carry it into sculpture. Although many painters practice sculpture, they restrict their three-dimensional explorations, *as painters,* to textural elaboration and the creation of *illusions* of depth. But fastidiousness about categories began to break down under the assaults of Dada artists such as Schwitters, Arp, Ernst, and Duchamp. Today, painting studios display almost as much three-dimensional work as sculpture studios.

Among practitioners of collage and assemblage today, Jean Dubuffet (born 1904) can be compared to Ernst in imaginative and technical fertility. Although he too has abandoned the paintbrush, Dubuffet has a more authoritative command of pigment and color than Ernst. His work grows out of an authentic "feeling for paint." Dubuffet's mixtures of pigment, asphalt, tar, cement, varnish, glue, sand, and so on seem to be efforts to convert the artist's canvas into a *wall* which can be scratched, modeled, and then painted. He appears to be creating a contemporary kind of fresco or wall painting, inspired by *graffiti,* the wall and sidewalk markings found in most human communities. Dubuffet has been powerfully attracted to debris as a source of materials. He has created works out of butterfly wings, tobacco leaves, papier-mâché, metal foil, driftwood, banana peels, fruit rinds, coal clinkers, and dirt. In his art we see a special case of the general interest among artists in discarded and worthless materials.

The refuse of an industrial civilization is, of course, enormous in amount and variety. Moreover, it possesses a built-in visual history. For an artist like Dubuffet, there seems to be an obsessive delight in employing garbage of one sort or another *in place of* conventional oil paint or in conjunction with it. Like many artists, he seems anxious to demonstrate that

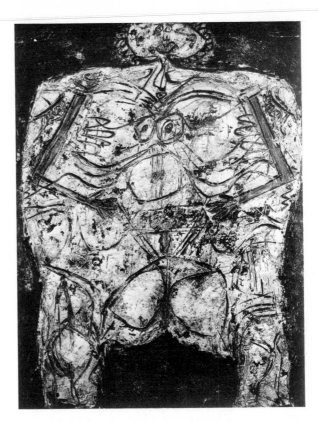

JEAN DUBUFFET. *Corps de Dame.* 1950. Collection Alfonso A. Ossorio, East Hampton, New York

JEAN DUBUFFET. *My Cart, My Garden.* 1955. Collection James Thrall Soby, New Canaan, Connecticut

the excellence of a civilization is not measured by its rate of consumption; values can be created with insignificant materials; the human contribution is the most important ingredient of all.

Industrial debris, garbage, and earth itself—stones, minerals, dirt—provide the materials of "painting" now that pigment is being displaced. Inventing prob-

Tom Wesselmann. *Still Life No. 15*. 1962. On permanent loan to the University of Nebraska Art Galleries, Lincoln, from Mrs. Adams Bromley Sheldon

Andy Warhol. *Marilyn Monroe*. 1962. Collection Vernon Nikkel, Clovis, New Mexico

lems with materials becomes an unconscious expression of the burdens of painterly freedom. The constraints of indirect technique are gone. There is no hierarchy of subject matter: any theme is as good as any other. The hostility of the public toward experimental art has all but evaporated. Moving from a position of alienation, painters are often celebrated as culture heroes, supported by foundations, employed as "stars" by universities, and encouraged to exhibit in new museums and cultural centers. This combination of social acceptance and absence of technical restraint seems "unnatural" to many artists. Their uneasiness stems from the nature of artistic effort, which requires some kind of resistance—the recalcitrance of materials; the limitations of "sound" technique; the Philistinism of the public. When these elements are absent, the artist contrives somehow to reintroduce them. This would help explain the extraordinary variety of materials in assemblage and the pronounced interest in themes which might shock the apparently unshockable middle class.

POP ART AND COMBINE PAINTINGS

We know that everything in the built environment has been designed: design is commonly used to communicate, persuade, entertain, sell, or decorate. An enormous amount of visual material is reproduced to carry out these functions. Hamburgers and hot dogs, soft drinks and bathing suits, automobiles and rocking chairs—all are designed; and their images saturate our surroundings, greeting us on television, jumping out from road signs, enveloping the reading matter in newspapers and periodicals, and mounted on groceries in supermarkets. When we do not see this imagery, we hear it described through other media. To carry on our normal lives, we have *adjusted* to the world of public images; we do not really see them, or we learn to see them selectively. Pop (for popular) artists have chosen this world as the source of their *own imagery*; they are determined to make us see what our nervous systems have mercifully managed to suppress.

Large scale is an important part of the strategy of Pop. Another feature of Pop is repetition, mechanical repetition, as in *Marilyn Monroe* by Andy Warhol (born 1931). A major technique of radio and television commercials is repetition—a device which eventually overcomes indifference or resistance. So Warhol uses visual repetition in his painting and in three-dimensional "sculptures"—reproductions of containers for soap, soup, breakfast foods, and so on. Obviously, he is not selling the product, he is pointing out an important feature of the visual environment.

Anonymity is another feature of Pop. Robert Indiana's paintings of stenciled signs betray nothing of the personality of the artist except his lettering skills and determination to paint the sign. Warhol's Campbell's Soup labels—hundreds of them—might have been painted by some other, equally meticulous, designer. Some thought, skill, and effort are visible, but they do not seem to belong to any particular artist. Pop echoes the homogenized character of the designed environment as contrasted with the highly individualized creations of fine art.

Other Pop artists—Robert Rauschenberg, Wayne Thiebaud, and James Rosenquist—have a more personal approach to painting while still drawing on popular imagery with varying degrees of literalness. Rauschenberg (born 1925) appears to control his material more as a conventional painter of "pictures." His work grows organically out of Abstract Expressionism. However, he is more inclined to paste up or silk-screen an image than to paint one. He applies paint and attaches objects to images already manufactured by the world of commerce, his vision being essentially that of the collagist. Perhaps the work of Rauschenberg and the other, less painterly Pop artists signifies that the "hand-painted" image is dead.

Rauschenberg's "combine" paintings freely associate many of the stylistic and technical developments

of twentieth-century painting. In such a work as *Canyon* (1959), the principal ingredient is collage together with attached objects—a stuffed eagle and a suspended pillow—plus painted areas, paint drippings, and a stick nailed to the wooden picture support. The work does not easily lend itself to interpretation in terms of any single idea which the materials and their organization seem to embody. As in Pop and Dada before it, the prevailing theme is nonmeaning, the absurd. But the choice of materials provides some indication of the picture's realm: it is a world of simultaneous fascination and disgust with the visual environment, particularly as it is manifested in hard-sell advertising, packaging, labels, and trademarks. The early use of printed matter by collagists like Picasso, Braque, and Gris was based on the color, texture, and "reality level" of these materials. Pop artists, however, seem interested in the *semantic content* of the material they assemble. Rauschenberg has gone so far as to use paint smears and drippings which simulate mud or

CHARLES McGOWEN. Photograph of raindrop reflections in a screen door. 1970. We can see a marvelous repetitive order in the chance interaction of natural and man-made structures. But nature is less resolute than man: given the slightest opportunity by the shape of the wire mesh, nature affords variety, or, at least, relief.

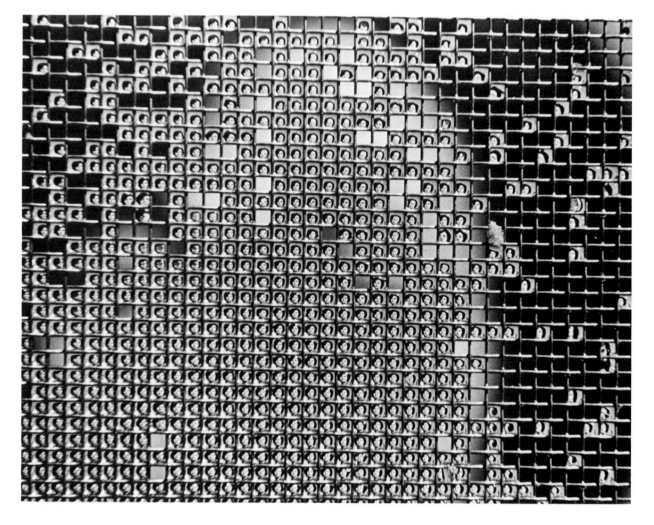

ROBERT INDIANA. *The Beware-Danger
American Dream #4.* 1963.
The Hirshhorn Museum and
Sculpture Garden, Smithsonian
Institution, Washington, D.C.

ROBERT RAUSCHENBERG.
Canyon. 1959. Collection Mr. and
Mrs. Sonnabend, Paris

other substances thrown at a wall. The "splatter" idea is pervasive in modern painting—from Ernst, to Hofmann, to Pollock, to Niki de Saint-Phalle. It may be the most graphic symbol of defiance and contempt that can be used on a flat surface.

A dilemma for some Pop artists is their inability to decide what stance to take toward the visual environment. It is difficult when viewing works of Andy Warhol, Robert Indiana or Roy Lichtenstein to discover whether they are repelled by the commercialism of our culture or whether they are endeavoring to *embrace* the environment, trying to merge with it. We look for signs of a point of view, but we receive only an exclamation point.

HAPPENINGS

Architecture is the art of creating a physical environment in which people can live or work. For long, painting and sculpture were *part* of architecture—focal points of the architectural environment. Now some painters are trying to create living environments which change as they exist in space and time. Instead of being a statement *about* life, art becomes an activity which is coextensive *with* life, *which is lived as it is created*. Unlike ordinary pictures, such images are not perceived from the outside, but are created from within by spectators who move through them. They have been described by their inventor, Allan Kaprow, as "surrounding[s] to be entered into" or "Happenings" and "Environments."

The Happening grows out of collage and the type of Environment created by the Dadaist Kurt Schwit-

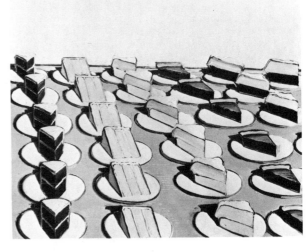

WAYNE THIEBAUD. *Pie Counter.* 1963.
Whitney Museum of American Art, New York.
Gift of the Larry Aldrich Foundation Fund

ters (1887–1948) in his famous Merzbau constructions of the 1920s and '30s. Built in Schwitters's home in Hanover, the earliest Merzbau might be described as an architectural collage, a modulation of interior space using refuse and found objects as structural and decorative elements. Schwitters worked on it for several years, bringing it to completion around 1924 and giving it the title *Cathedral of Erotic Misery*. A subsequent Merzbau, dated about 1933, is more architectonic, less reminiscent of collage techniques. Schwitters built little grottoes into his constructions, dedicated

ROY LICHTENSTEIN. *The Kiss.* 1962. Private collection. Does this enlargement of the comic-strip version of romance constitute a critique of our mores, or is it a search for significance in the meticulous rendering of the banal?

KURT SCHWITTERS. *Merzbau*, Hanover.
1924–37 (destroyed)

personality, his creativity flourished in the generally disillusioned environment of Central Europe after World War I—an environment characterized by a disastrous economic decline and the rise of Fascism. These conditions combined to create a watershed in history for many artists and intellectuals who felt trapped by the war and betrayed by their civilization. For them, the forms, values, and institutions that had existed up to and through World War I were associated with disaster. It is against this background that Dadaism and its products must be seen.

The Happenings and Environments of the contemporary scene may be regarded as more ritualized versions of the Dadaist events and antiart of the 1920s. In one reported incident, Schwitters took the discarded socks of a friend, cast them in plaster, and incorporated the casting into one of his Merzbau grottoes. Such gestures exhibit features common to expressions of revolt in the art of the twentieth century: (1) discarded materials and debris are preferred to traditional media; (2) there is a deliberate avoidance of "beauty," especially Mediterranean conventions of form; (3) the gesture of creation is more important than its outcome; (4) humor is based on defiance of authority and established values; (5) only absurdity is meaningful; (6) the gap between art and life is reduced as much as possible; (7) caves and grottoes proliferate—both Happenings and Merzbau constructions explore and decorate interior, womblike spaces.

A relatively little-known American primitive, Clarence Schmidt, created a series of grottoes within his winding, cavelike house on a hill in Woodstock, New York. Schmidt, who had general carpentry and building skills, had no formal artistic training and was almost certainly unaware of the Dada art of the 1920s, much less of Schwitters. Yet his fantastic house can be compared in important respects with Merzbau constructions. Like Schwitters, he recited poems of his own composition; he probably thought of himself as following in the tradition of Walt Whitman. Apparently primitive and sophisticated artists are equally stirred

them to friends, and incorporated in them discarded clothing and similar "nonart" items, much as Robert Rauschenberg includes old socks in his paintings. It is significant that Schwitters was quoted as having said, "Anything the artist spits is art."

Schwitters was attempting through his constructions to arrive at a synthesis of the arts of poetry, architecture, painting, and drama. A versatile and spectacular

EDWARD KIENHOLZ. *The Beanery.* 1965. Stedelijk Museum, Amsterdam. This Environment is the replica of a time and place, an "event" whose cozy squalor has aroused the artist's obsessive affection.

KURT SCHWITTERS. *Cherry Picture.* 1921. The Museum of Modern Art, New
York. Mr. and Mrs. A. Atwater Kent, Jr., Fund. Collage and assemblage constitute an unconscious return to tribal modes of artistry, particularly in the equation of the tactile with the visual. But instead of using seeds, shells, stones, and
fiber as raw material for his imagery, the modern artist employs commercial
garbage—especially the abundant rubbish of the textile and print industries.

JOAN MIRÓ. *Poetic Object*. 1936.
The Museum of Modern Art, New York.
Gift of Mr. and Mrs. Pierre Matisse

From a certain standpoint, both works can be
seen as elaborate displays of the taxidermist's
art: stuffed pedestals for stuffed birds. However, the purposes they serve are internal to
art: to get away from abstraction, calculation,
deliberate design, and cerebral form—to
reestablish the status of things as things.

ROBERT RAUSCHENBERG. *Odalisk*. 1955–58.
Collection Mr. and Mrs. Victor W. Ganz, New York

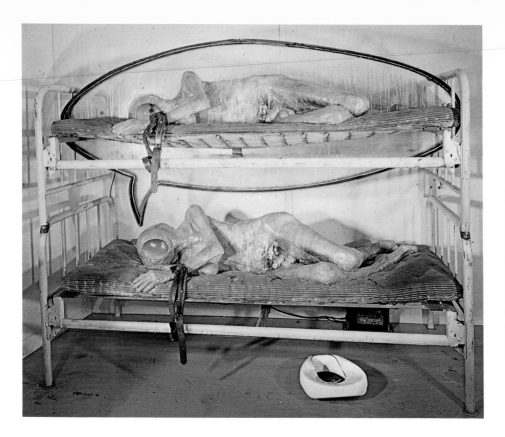

EDWARD KIENHOLZ. *The State Hospital*. 1964–66. Moderna Museet, Stockholm. As an impresario of mixed media, Kienholz bears a curious resemblance to the Baroque sculptor Bernini: the theatrical requirements of the spectacle take precedence over rules about the separation of painting, sculpture, and architecture. But this spectacle celebrates misery, not mystical transcendence.

MIRROR FETISH, from the Lower Congo. c. late 19th–early 20th century. Ethnographical Museum, Antwerp

The fetish figure has to be a "mixed-media" construction since it functions as a container for magical substances in its abdominal cavity. In the Congolese fetish, a mirror serves to frighten off demons. In the contemporary "fetish" by Arman, tubes of paint embedded in a female torso pour ribbons of color into her polyester belly and womb.

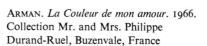

ARMAN. *La Couleur de mon amour*. 1966. Collection Mr. and Mrs. Philippe Durand-Ruel, Buzenvale, France

Gaudí and Rodia both conceived of architecture as the creation of expressive forms that appear to have grown by natural accretion. This view demanded labyrinthine passages, surfaces like tribal sculptures, and coloristic effects of Byzantine brilliance. A mixed-media approach is almost inevitable when the designer feels that every part of a structure is magically alive.

ANTONI GAUDÍ. Detail of spire, Church of the Sagrada Familia, Barcelona. 1883–1926

SIMON RODIA. Detail of Watts Towers, Los Angeles. 1921–1954

to recite, perform, and *live* in their constructions. Schwitters's Merzbau was begun in the basement of his house and grew until an attic tenant had to be evicted. Schmidt lived in his "house" and added to it continuously, so that it resembles a "many chambered nautilus," with new rooms and grottoes appearing as the construction winds down the hill and burrows into the earth.

The Happenings of Allan Kaprow are more formally staged. They call for a script or scenario to articulate the time element, while people, as spectators or actors, move through the garage or gallery where the event takes place. Kaprow says that these events grew out of his work in collage and assemblage, and he lists the typical materials used: "painted paper, cloth and photos, as well as mirrors, electric lights, plastic film, aluminum foil, ropes, straw; objects that could be attached to, or hung in front of, the canvas along with various sounds and odors. These materials multiplied in number and density, extending away from the flat canvas surface, until that pictorial point of departure was eliminated entirely and the whole gallery was filled. I termed this an environment." As the two-dimensional confines of the canvas were left behind, real environments were simulated: "a subway station, penny-arcade, forest, kitchen, etc." The gallery gave

Photograph of Clarence Schmidt in residence, 1964

ALLAN KAPROW. From *Orange*. Happening. 1964. A form of expression that wants to escape framing, geometric positioning, specific location in time or space. Art without limits cannot be exclusive; everyone gets into the act.

BRIDGET RILEY. *Blaze I.* 1962.
Collection Louise Riley, London

way as a place for staging Happenings to a "a craggy canyon, an old abandoned factory, a railroad yard, or the oceanside."[22]

Unlike conventional theater, Happenings do not have a developed dramatic structure—that is, a beginning, a middle, and an end; plot and character development; conflict, climax and denouement. They retain connections with assemblage and add elements of other art forms—movement, sound, and speech. Kaprow defines his Environments as "slowed-down, quieter, happening[s]"—large-scale dioramas which can last for several weeks, while the Happenings compress time and last for only a few hours. Of course, motion pictures have better technical devices for the compression or expansion of time and the further advantage of being reproducible. The Happening contains so many spontaneous elements that it is confined to a single enactment and viewing.

What is the meaning of the Happening for painting? It bears a superficial resemblance to theater, but is dramaturgically clumsy because complex spatial-temporal events cannot be structured with sufficient precision to maintain control of its form. Only in the film, with its montage techniques, can one manipulate the time dimension without losing pictorial control. As sculpture or as painting, the Happening surrenders the monumental and durable character of these art forms, their capacity to linger before our vision. Yet the collage and assemblage antecedents of Happenings and Environments suggest different objectives. Happenings by Kaprow and Environments-plus-Sculpture, like those George Segal creates, appear to be efforts to discover the hidden ritual which lies beneath the surface of ordinary events in everyday life. Like Schwitters and Dubuffet, these artists are trying to find the meaningful in what is apparently worthless and meaningless.

The Happening, however, does not seem to be a vehicle of major aesthetic value. It serves better as a creative discipline for the artist, as a means of stimulating and focusing perceptual energies on realms of experience which may find their way into painting and sculpture. Some arts perform a preparatory function for the creation of other works of art. Painters are often stimulated by literature, music, dance, and film. Drawing and collage collect shapes and sensations on two-dimensional surfaces where they can be exploited by the painter. But the kinds of experience which drawing and collage compress into manageable form appear to be too limited for many contemporary artists. They require an instrument which does more than reflect in concise form what is seen. Like scientists, artists need a device which *interferes with* reality, which can take events apart and reveal new or unsuspected meanings. It would appear that Happenings constitute a new artistic strategy—a strategy foreshadowed in techniques like Merzbau constructions, Surrealist automatic writing, and the nihilistic stunts and gestures of the troubled generations that lived between and after great world wars.

OP ART

In Op, or optical, art, which followed the premature decline of Pop art in 1964, painters attempted to construct works that would rely solely on the physiology of vision. In a sense, the color divisionism of Seurat (with its dependence on afterimages to create colors that were not present as pigment), and Josef Albers's chromatic venerations of the square, were precursors of Op art. Its practitioners employed mechanical motion, artificial light filtered through prisms, images which shift depending on the viewer's angle of vision, and mechanical devices to produce optical sensations beyond the reach of conventional painting. The optical knowledge of physics was brought into the realm of aesthetics by Op; the sociological comments of Pop gave way to an art which bypassed the mind and imagination of the viewer. And the effectiveness of Op on its own terms is undeniable; it produces feelings of disorientation or exhilaration purely by visual means.

The desire to transform the physical basis of consciousness has always been latent in painting, and in Mark Rothko's work (as mentioned earlier) it has become an explicit objective. Op art appears to be a systematic attempt to take hold of the organism and change its psychic condition.

The similarity of Op's objectives to those of modern biochemistry may be only coincidental. Nevertheless, Op has brought about the discovery of new powers in painting; and painting, as a result, has found a new *raison d'être,* a new claim on human attention. Art now competes with tranquilizers and mood-altering

JOSEF ALBERS. *Homage to the Square: Red Series—Untitled III.* 1968. Pasadena Art Museum, Pasadena, California. Albers established an important precedent for minimalist painters by showing that pictorial values can be generated almost solely through the color interactions of simple geometric forms.

drugs as a depressant or a stimulant. Even Matisse said he dreamed of an art "which might be for every mental worker. . . like an appeasing influence, like a mental soother, something like a good armchair in which to rest from physical fatigue." For the present, Op seems more effective as a stimulant than as a pacifier or soporific. Psychoanalyst Anton Ehrenzweig has compared it to a plunge into a cold shower. But surely an art capable of producing such physical effects will also be able to induce the soothing feelings Matisse longed for.

As objects of aesthetic value, Op works are not easy to judge. They cause the difficulty which the psychologist Theodor Lipps saw as an obstacle to aesthetic response—awareness of one's bodily feelings precluding any sort of psychic experience. Also, the pursuit of purely optical responses results in an uninteresting experience for those who expect more emotional, intellectual, or formal nourishment from art. West Coast painter Jesse Reichek comments: "The question seems to be whether optical tricks that massage the eyeball, and result, in some cases, in physiological effects, provide a sufficient task for painting. I don't believe such tricks are sufficient."[23]

Compared to the Neo-Plastic art of Mondrian and the De Stijl group, Op art arouses reactions which are quicker, easier, more physical, and less intellectual. The movement has not articulated a philosophic rationale, which would be needed to guide its further evolution. It appears to be arrested at a stage more re-

lated to physics than aesthetics—a stage where its discoveries are not convincingly integrated into the humanistic mainstream of art.

Minimal and Color-Field Painting

Reductionism is a persistent tendency in recent art. If painting can cast off some of its inherited baggage, some artists feel it will have a better chance of being itself. Of course, painters differ about what is essential and what is expendable. They need to redefine their art periodically, to breathe in an aesthetic environment unconstrained by the aims of their predecessors. For minimal and color-field painters, these inherited aims are emotional expression, symbol making, social comment, and deliberate disclosure of the self. Minimalists react against styles allied to history, literature, politics, psychology, and religion. What is left? Perhaps beauty.

The seeds of this art may have been sown by Malevich, Kandinsky, Mondrian, and, more recently, Albers. A forceful polemicist was the late Ad Reinhardt (1913–1967), who said: "Art-as-art is a concentration on Art's essential nature. The nature of art has not to do with the nature of perception or with the nature of light or with the nature of space or with the nature of time or with the nature of mankind or with the nature of society."[24] Minimalists want to create forms meaningful in themselves, perfect to behold and

AD REINHARDT. *Abstract Painting Black*. 1960. Whereabouts unknown. Reinhardt's goal was to create paintings which would be something while closely approaching nothing.

unsullied by contact with the world. This is to say that minimal art aspires to the status of ultimate form, behind which there is nothing more, less, better, worse, or the same as.

In appearance, minimalist canvases are large, abstract, bright, often hard-edged, and highly simplified or flat in color. They tend to suppress figure-ground relationships created through overlapping, color-value differentials, and perspectival devices, especially they avoid the "handwriting" of the painter, as in Abstract Expressionism. Hence, there is a certain anonymity about their forms and painted surfaces which leads the viewer to feel he is in the presence of a mass-produced industrial object. We shall see the same result in minimal sculpture, which can be manufactured industrially according to specifications written or telephoned by the artist.

Color-field painting is flexible enough to permit variation—from floating mists to hard-edge geometry. It employs techniques such as staining unprimed canvas; applying pigment with a squeegee, spatter device, paint roller, or airbrush; or flowing diluted paint onto a canvas which is turned and tipped to create form through controlled puddles and spills. Although these techniques afford much variety of edge and a wide range of depth, transparency, melting, and interpenetrative illusion, they consistently avoid the brushed look, the drawn line, and the painterly marks of wrist, fingers, and thumb. We are given to understand that it is the medium itself which does the job, combined with human intelligence, to be sure, but without those manipulative skills originated and nurtured by the tradition of handmade imagery.

The Shaped Canvas

The rectangular canvas is one of many possible shapes. But it dominates all others mainly because of the Renaissance convention that a picture is a window opened on the world and then painted by an artist. The convention has been so thoroughly absorbed by our culture that we are hardly aware of it; it crops up in popular architecture as the "picture window." The design of a wall around a scenic or pictorial opening is a strange reversal of history, because pictorial imagery has usually been *subordinated* to architecture—in mosaics, stained glass, murals, and large-scale tapestries. Painting tends to "obey" externally determined formats.

CHARLES HINMAN. *Red/Black*. 1964. Krannert Art Museum, University of Illinois, Champaign. New visual problems are raised for the painter who applies color to a surface of bent and curved planes: the irregular contour of the canvas sets up tensions that threaten to run away with the image.

FRANK STELLA. *Sangre de Cristo*. 1967. Collection Dr. and Mrs. Charles Hendrickson, Newport Beach, California. A purely retinal "theology" is, of course, inconsistent with the theology of a man-god sacrifice. The title of this work functions as a device for deflating the viewer's conventional humanistic expectations about the blood of Christ.

Obviously, the modern painter does not function within a tradition of obedience to architectural surfaces, of simulating the world seen through an elaborately framed window. As the painted image ceases to decorate or symbolize something else, the shape of its container tends to be determined by necessities internal to the visual images or the processes of visual perception. The *shape* of the canvas can be one of the expressive elements of the total work; it need not act as a container; it is not part of the wall. The optical image has become more important than formerly. The real picture has shifted from the wall to the viewer's eye. So the shaped canvas is a device for announcing the freedom of painting from the constraints of walls —of architecture. It endeavors to organize the forces within the viewer's perceptual field by manipulating the outer edges of the image and introducing projections from its internal surface. Literally, of course, the shaped canvas hangs on a wall and has to be perceived within a two-dimensional field. But we seriously underestimate its ambition if we think it is a type of painted sculpture. The strategy and tactics of this sort of painting are pictorial without being illusionistic. One cannot, as with sculpture, walk around a shaped canvas. So, if the painting has been liberated from architecture and yet falls short of free-standing sculpture, the only space it can effectively occupy is within the eye—retinal space. That is where this new kind of pictorial experience is designed to begin and end.

The older painting traditions endeavored to enlist the total apparatus of vision, not the optical organ alone. Humanists, especially, were concerned about the career of the image *after* it ceased to be a retinal projection. Artists know that the retina is an arena where complex, dynamic forces interact. This knowledge has created the possibility of an art whose ambition is almost exclusively retinal—an art which defies interpretation along symbolic, cognitive, and affective lines. As Frank Stella comments: "I always get into arguments with people who want to retain the old values in painting, the humanistic values that they always find on the canvas. My painting is based on the fact that only what can be seen there is there. It really is an object."[25]

Erotic and Obscene Art

One of the earliest functions of visual art was the stimulation of sexual feeling, if only to encourage human reproduction. But erotic art continues to be created in societies that have passed beyond the tribal stages of culture. Today, when human overpopulation is an urgent concern, there has nevertheless been an increase in the creation of works devoted to erotic themes. Some persons react with a sense of being liberated from what they feel are unjustified inhibitions on the expression of healthy sexual feeling. Others are offended: they perceive erotic art as pornographic or obscene and fear that necessary restraints on the expression of sexuality are breaking down in our civilization.

The public celebration of the human body, especially the female nude, constitutes a well-established tradition in Western art and culture. However, it has always been accompanied by a more or less clandestine art in which the human figure is shown in explicit sexual practices. Now, in the permissive climate of contemporary culture, that clandestine art is created and exhibited openly. The change we witness is not so much in the fact that erotic art exists but that it is abundantly visible.

Without doubt, some erotic art is created as a mode of protest. As such, it is part of the intergenerational conflict which has grown so intense in the industrial nations of the world. Viewed as a tactic in a generational struggle, its unlovely or obscene content becomes explainable: it endeavors to wound and offend by celebrating what an older society felt to be wrong and ugly.

However, there are also art-historical reasons for the flourishing of erotic and obscene art. For at least a half century, the artistic imagination has been fired by abstract and nonobjective art. Even in its figurative manifestations, abstraction tends to divert the impulses we associate with sexual expression. Much of modernist painting, for example, stems from Cézanne, an artist whose genius was inhibited in the presence of the unclothed human figure—male or female. Cézanne did execute nudes, expecially during his early career when he pursued an erotic vision of the female figure. But it appears to have been a vision uncongenial to his inclination as a painter and, perhaps, as a man. It is more a structural legacy that Cézanne left us. Understandably, his artistic descendants have excelled where the master excelled. To the extent that the example of a single personality can dominate the evolution of several artistic generations, Cézanne has done so. His work stands in relation to modern art almost as the Epistles of Paul do to the development of Christianity.

The emergence of obscene art, then, may be ascribed in part to the difficulty artists experienced for close to a century in perceiving the human figure affectionately. They shied away from the voyeurism of a Gérôme or a Bouguereau, on the one hand, and away from the hothouse eroticism of a Modigliani, Pascin, or Balthus on the other. As a result many artists prefer to explore the fascinating problems of space and object organization opened up by the Post-Impressionists in the late nineteenth century. But space is a medium in which human beings move and encounter each other. A need is asserted, ultimately, to examine *every* kind of human encounter. This assertion seems exaggerated and perverse when it appears in the form of erotic art, but it must be remembered that it contends with the expression of anonymity on an enormous scale, as in minimal and serial art. To be sure, it often substitutes lasciviousness and scatological shock for erotic

JOAN MIRÓ. *Persons Haunted by a Bird.* 1938. The Art Institute of Chicago. Peter B. Bensinger Charitable Trust. In 1938, Miró's phallic fantasies could be assimilated by the Surrealist format of dream symbolism and sexual horseplay. But before he was a Surrealist, Miró was a humorist.

PAUL CÉZANNE. *The Bathers.* 1899. The Museum of Modern Art, New York. Lillie P. Bliss Bequest. The human figure presented mainly pictorial and "architectural" problems for Cézanne; he could not see its spiritual dimension—its role as the subject and object of love.

JEAN-LÉON GÉRÔME. *Roman Slave Market.* c. 1884. The Walters Art Gallery, Baltimore. The official art of the nineteenth century was often an exercise in disguised voyeurism. Under the pretext of teaching history, some painters catered to the prurient interests of the public.

BALTHUS. *The Golden Days.* 1944–46. The Hirshhorn Museum and Sculpture Garden, Smithsonian Institution, Washington, D.C. The awakening sexuality of the girl adolescent has absorbed much of the career of Balthus. His art thrives on the conflict between bourgeois respectability, as represented by comfortable, well-appointed interiors, and the less-than-innocent reveries of good little girls.

JEAN-AUGUSTE-DOMINIQUE INGRES. *Odalisque with a Slave.* 1840. Fogg Art Museum, Harvard University, Cambridge, Massachusetts. Bequest of Grenville L. Winthrop

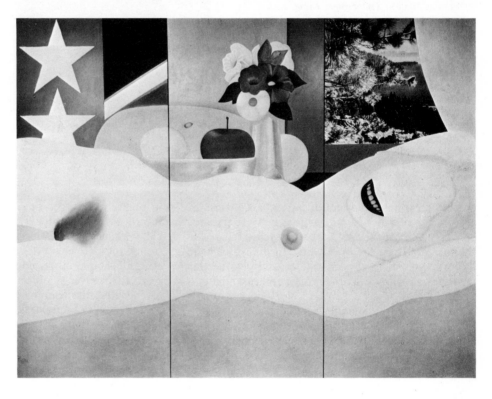

TOM WESSELMANN. *Great American Nude No. 51.* 1963. Collection the artist. The reclining nude has a venerable history as a theme of Western painting. Thus Wesselmann presents the same subject but uses deliberate vulgarization, breaking with conventionalized treatment. As a result, the viewer is confronted with a type of nakedness to which he has not been habituated.

feeling; at times it associates sexuality with pathological behavior, as in Rivers' *Titus Andronicus*. These are the excesses that accompany the easing of a long repression. But they will be moderated when the classical conventions for dealing with eroticism in art are rediscovered or reinvented.

Conclusion

The employment of trash-can contents in collage by Schwitters; the use of botanical materials, fruit rinds, and butterfly wings by Dubuffet; the incorporation of "real" objects in paintings by Pop artists; and Hap-

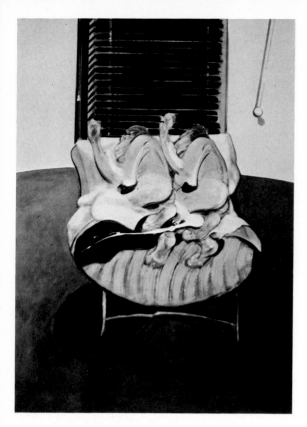

FRANCIS BACON. *Two Figures Lying on a Bed with Attendants* (panel of a triptych, *Three Studies for a Crucifixion*). 1968. Marlborough Gallery, New York. Today all the arts feel free to deal with the theme of homosexuality. In Bacon's work, this motif is overshadowed by a consistently animalistic view of man—even in his efforts at love, which come to resemble the copulation of beasts.

LARRY RIVERS. *Celebrating Shakespeare's 400th Birthday (Titus Andronicus)*. 1963. Collection Clarice Rivers, New York. A mutilated female nude, symbol of Venus and maternity; a "cool" diagram of dismembered human parts; the portrait of a solemn black man; and a reference to one of Shakespeare's plays. Here are all the areas of contemporary social concern: art, race, sex, and violence.

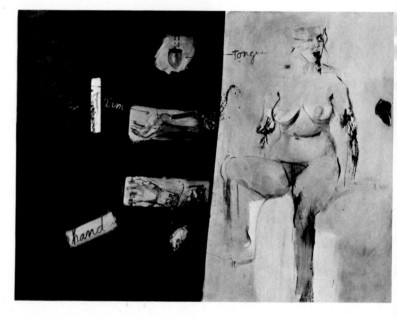

penings creating a transient, theatrical art—these developments suggest new connections between painting and gastronomy, spectator sports, psychodrama, and the theater. There are even works of art which echo the processes of food preparation, eating, collecting the leftovers, discarding the refuse, and assembling it again.

For many years, a popular act of the comedian Jimmy Durante was the tearing apart of a piano before a nightclub audience. The process of decomposition possesses its own aesthetic fascination, as might be confirmed by anyone who has watched the wrecking of

a building, a staged auto crash, or a child knocking down a house of blocks he has laboriously built up. The "controlled-compression" sculpture of César represents an effort to convert the destruction of an automobile into a constructive act. These are efforts to discover an affirmative meaning in all the acts of needless destruction and senseless consumption which mark contemporary civilization.

Artists are not always aware of the meaning of their work; but civilization operates through them nevertheless, exploiting their fascination with materials and processes for what are, hopefully, humanizing ends.

12

SCULPTURE

LIKE PAINTING, SCULPTURE HAD ITS ORIGIN IN THE forming of figures for primitive magic and, later, for religious ritual. In viewing subsequent developments, one should remember this early association of sculpture with magic. The ancient Greek myth of Pygmalion and Galatea symbolically expresses a number of insights into sculpture. Pygmalion, a sculptor, fell in love with Aphrodite and, because she would not have him, made an ivory figure of the goddess and prayed to her. Eventually she took pity on the man and entered into his sculpture, giving it life as Galatea. Pygmalion then married Galatea, who bore him two sons.

The essential ingredients of sculptural creation are present in the myth. The artist's motive for creating the work arises from an emotional crisis—personal yearning and cosmic anguish. He tries to control reality by fashioning an object that portrays the outcome he desires. The pity of the goddess gives life to the artist's effort. Then he falls in love with an image he has created. Thus art acquires a life of its own. Out of the union of creator and creature comes the continuation of life. That is, the strange longing of a man for a goddess is converted into a living reality by his compelling skill with the materials of art.

Painting, too, has magical associations but it requires the capacity to create illusions, whereas sculpture can give corporeal reality to our hopes and fantasies. Consequently, sculptures have served more prominently than painted images as vessels for the souls of departed chiefs and kings—as totems and cult objects among primitive peoples.

The capacity of sculpture, no matter what its materials, to occupy real space and to compel belief in its aliveness distinguishes it from painting and graphic art in general. Consequently, sculpture has remained, throughout its history of changing form, material, and function, the same art which Pygmalion practiced—the art of making three-dimensional materials come alive to objectify fantasies, memorialize personalities, and satisfy human longings for perfection.

Modeling, Carving, and Casting

The sculptural processes are simply the most suitable ways of working available materials. Obviously, stone can only be carved, drilled, abraded, and polished. It appeals to artists who are comfortable with highly resistant materials. Wood lends itself to the same processes more easily; but modern technology permits it to be permanently bent and molded, as in Thonet and Eames chairs. Metals can be cast, cut, drilled, filed, extruded, bent, forged, and stamped. More recently, powdered metals have been combined with plastic binders so that they can be modeled, almost like clay. They can be assembled by welding, soldering, and riveting, and with adhesives also. Plastics were brought into sculpture by the Constructivists, although tasteless employment of plastics has created unfortunate associations which are only now being overcome. But there is ready acceptance of metal sculpture no matter how it is fashioned. Metal is, after all, a plastic material which has had thousands of years of artistic use and visual familiarity.

For traditional sculptors, mastery of the basic processes—modeling, carving, and casting—constituted the principal artistic challenges. It remains important, but is not indispensable today because, as in painting, technology permits the forming and assembling of materials by other means. However, the modern sculptor confronts new problems of aesthetic choice due to the variety and flexibility of processes and materials available to him.

Monumental statuary has in the past been cast in

bronze or carved in marble. Today, welded metal is growing more common in public sculpture, especially as figures recede in importance. Naturalistic statuary, of course, must be modeled, then cast in bronze; or it must be carved in stone. Public buildings and parks still abound with statuary of this kind, and it continues to be commissioned by conservative groups. But sculptors who can or will create such works are a diminishing minority. Contemporary buildings seem to be more friendly to sculpture which is, in general, more open, less monolithic in form than older works.

It is difficult, however, to conceive of a sculptural group like Rodin's *Burghers of Calais* being created through any process other than bronze casting. The psychological characterization of several figures; the naturalistic treatment of flesh, bone, and sinew; the range of surface subtlety in Rodin's group—these would be hard to achieve with welding or assemblage processes. Yet monumental work has been attempted by contemporary sculptors. If the subtleties of modeling with clay or marble are sacrificed, still, a marvelous freedom of extension into space together with generous scale is now possible. Also, many of the techniques of industrial production and fabrication are used by sculptors today. The mallet and chisel have been joined by the acetylene torch, the hydraulic press, and the electronic welder.

The Greeks knew the art of bronze casting, and they also had an abundance of good white marble. They must have prized marble more for its durability than for its appearance, since their marble statuary was painted. It was not the stone's whiteness or texture

they admired so much as its capacity to reveal their love of clear and stable forms, their understanding of the body in action or repose, and their conception of the ideal embodied in the form of a human figure. The Greeks chose marble to fix the "now" forever. Sculpture was a means of demonstrating that perfection and reality meet in human forms which can endure eternally.

Michelangelo believed his art was mainly one of releasing the forms hidden (or imprisoned) within marble. This idea is not surprising in an artist influenced by Neoplatonic thought; it also typifies the carver—one who begins with the stone block or the wood log and cuts away until the form in his mind's eye is revealed. Carving, a *subtractive* process, has always been considered the most difficult of sculptural processes because it calls for a conception of the result before the work is begun. The carver subtracts nonessential material to liberate an image which already exists. Yet the grain of wood, ivory, or stone significantly determines what forms will emerge. For example, diorite and basalt, used by the sculptors of ancient Egypt, are extremely hard granitic stones which resist detailed carving; consequently, Egyptian sculpture is characterized by large, simplified forms which adhere closely to the shape of the stone block as it was quarried.

Casting accurately reproduces the forms and tool marks of an original clay or wax model. Its advantage lies in the translation of clay or wax into a material which is more durable than the original; it can be transported without breaking and can also be duplicated. But durability and surface quality rather than

duplication are the chief motives for the use of casting techniques. Bronze, the most common casting material, has beautiful surface and color characteristics. The surface of a bronze casting develops a rich patina with age; it can also be burnished or treated with chemicals to produce a wide range of color from gold to deep brown or greenish black. Its surface can be dull or glossy, depending on the sculptor's intent. Similar surface possibilities are available with other metals. It should be remembered that the earliest sculpture—whether of wood, stone, metal, or clay— was painted, glazed, or inlaid with gems and other materials, in an effort to create convincing and vivid effigies. Terra-cotta sculpture was frequently polychromed to achieve a high degree of naturalism. Today, a similar naturalism might be achieved with the use of plastics. For example, Frank Gallo's *Swimmer,* executed in polyester reinforced with Fiberglas and wood, offers a conventional range of form in an unconventional material. The work is deliberately "pretty" in the Pop style. This sculptor often seats his figures in real chairs, thus juxtaposing an effigy with a "real" object made by industry. Gallo (born 1933) is here similar to George Segal, although his figures are more sculpturally modeled and "prettified" than Segal's. Perhaps the closest modern counterparts to ancient painted sculptures are found in store-window figures made of painted papier-mâché or plastic. Synthetic hair and eyelashes are attached and the figures are then decorated. The mannequins' parts appear to be interchangeable and, like their ancient predecessors, they have a certain cultic significance.

Unlike Michelangelo, Rodin defined sculpture as "the art of the hole and the lump." Although he produced many carved marble works, Rodin's statement is characteristic of the sculptor who is a modeler; he builds a surface *additively.* Clay is more responsive than wood or stone. The sculptor's hand creates the forms and leaves the marks of his thumbs and fingers in the material. Nothing is so personal and direct as clay; painters need a brush, and even those who abandon the brush must substitute some other tool or process. Yet clay has distinct limitations when compared to wood or stone. It possesses little strength in tension or compression and hence requires an armature for support. Clay is not itself a permanent material. If fired, it is subject to the size limitations of a kiln and a variety of engineering considerations. Hence, clay is generally used to make preparatory "sketches" for sculpture to be executed in other materials. As ceramic sculpture, however, it is cheap, durable, and reproducible. It can be given a wide range of glossy or matte color, has many textural possibilities, and honestly reflects the marks of the tool used to shape it.

One of the satisfactions of viewing bronze sculpture, by Epstein or Giacometti, for example, arises from knowing that a soft, plastic material has been "frozen" into a hard, resistant material. Bronze castings are hollow but they *look* solid and massive; they retain the earthy quality of clay or rock. Hence, clay seems to call for bronze casting. For a master like Rodin, clay's capacity to yield a surface of great tactile variety—one which modulates light at the same time that it describes shape—was perhaps its principal attraction.

That bronze casting is a difficult and expensive process has not diminished the virtue of clay as a cheap and versatile material; it remains one of the most satisfying ways of "thinking" in three dimensions.

Wood appeals for its grain, its color, and its origin in a living tree. It has greater tensile strength than stone, and hence can be given projecting forms with less fear of breaking. Also, wood is warm and pleasant, even sensuous to the touch. It is not cold like metal or abrasive like stone. The disadvantages of wood lie in its dimensional instability—its tendency to warp or crack. Wood can be worked more easily than stone, yet it offers enough resistance to cutting to require carving tools which leave their marks. A great advantage of the material, much exploited in contemporary work, is its versatility in techniques of con-

LUCA DELLA ROBBIA. Detail of
Madonna and Angels. c. 1460.
National Museum, Florence.
Polychromed terra-cotta

MICHELANGELO. *Unfinished Slave.* 1513–16.
Tomb of Pope Julius II, Rome

Carving: the figure seems to emerge from the marble.

structed or assembled sculpture. There is a special expressiveness in wooden joints, whether those of the skilled cabinetmaker or of the sculptor employing improvised methods of joinery. In today's climate of indifference to permanence, the fact that wood may warp or crack counts little as a liability. Also, the new adhesives form joints which are often stronger than the materials they join. Finally, there is a long tradition of painting wood, covering it with fabrics, and embedding foreign materials in it. Hence, it fits well into the creative strategies of sculptors influenced by collage and assemblage.

We see a contemporary use of wood in *Wall Piece* by John Anderson (born 1928). It combines carving and construction techniques in a work that pretends to have some mechanical action. Forms projecting from a slot appear to be levers, doorknobs, or faucet handles, suggesting that the viewer should pull, lift, twist, or turn them, depending on their shapes and his mechanical experience. That these operations cannot be performed does not prevent the sculpture from arousing our expectations of performance anyway. *It looks as if it could work.* Magic sculpture *looks as if* it could throw a switch, turn on a motor, put an engine into neutral. The connections between form and meaning are logical enough, since levers and knobs are meant to be grasped, and wood is inviting to the touch. This work functions at several imaginative levels: it suggests a curious mechanical device and it makes connections with tribal animistic sculpture through its carved figurative forms and limb fragments.

The sensuous potential of plywood, a construction material which is usually covered or hidden, is beautifully revealed in the laminated wood sculptures of H. C. Westermann (born 1922). *The Big Change*, a huge wooden knot, constitutes the sort of contradiction between shape and material, form and function, which appeals to the Surrealist interests of Westermann. Aside from its meticulous rendering of the absurd and

its use of a material without ancient credentials, the work possesses the unity of form, consummate craftsmanship, and monolithic stability of classic sculpture.

Few final sculptures are done in wax. It is not very permanent; it can too easily be changed or damaged in handling. Wax, however, was congenial for the nineteenth-century sculptor Medardo Rosso (1858–1928). In *The Bookmaker*, which was made of wax over plaster, we see a painterly interest in light similar to that of Rodin and Degas, both of whom executed sculptures in wax. The figure by Rosso, dated 1894, is extraordinary for its delicate treatment of a heavy body reminiscent of Rodin's monumental *Balzac* figure. The transitions from form to form are so gently accomplished that they appear to be blended with a soft brush. Although the work is small, it suggests a

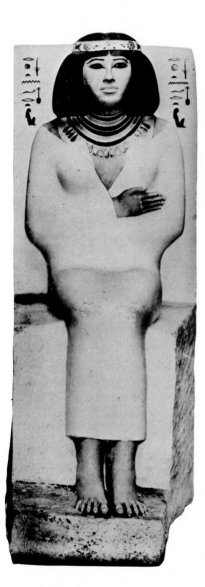

The Lady Nofret. c. 2650 B.C. Egyptian Museum, Cairo. Painted stone

JŌKEI. *Shō-Kannon.* Kamakura period (1185–1333). The Kurama Temple, Kyoto, Japan. Painted wood

FRANK GALLO. *Swimmer.* 1964. Whitney Museum of American Art, New York. Gift of the Friends of the Whitney. Colored polyester, Fiberglas, and wood

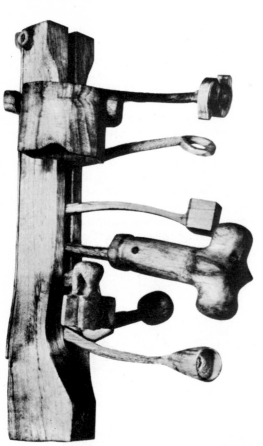

JOHN ANDERSON. *Wall Piece*. 1963.
Allan Stone Gallery, New York

Portrait jar, from the Chicama Valley, Peru.
400–600 A.D. The Art Institute of Chicago. Painted
clay. Utilitarian function united with realistic
portraiture seemed entirely plausible to ancient
sculptors. Commemorative or effigy vessels evolved
from an early belief in the soul as a liquid substance, hence the combined pottery-portrait form.

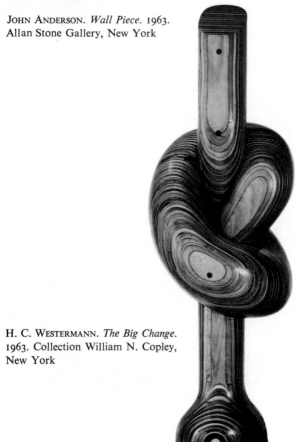

H. C. WESTERMANN. *The Big Change.*
1963. Collection William N. Copley,
New York

large scale because wax has no grain, no texture visible
to the eye: it is capable of almost infinitely detailed
modeling.

A tremendous change in sculptural attitude has
taken place since Rosso modeled his delicate figures in
the 1890s. An excellent summary of it is given by the
critic Clement Greenberg: "Space is there to be
shaped, divided, enclosed, but not to be filled. The new
sculpture tends to abandon stone, bronze, and clay for
industrial materials like iron, steel, alloys, glass,
plastics, celluloid, etc., etc., which are worked with the
blacksmith's, the welder's and even the carpenter's
tools. Unity of material and color is no longer required, and applied color is irrelevant: a work or its
parts can be cast, wrought, cut or simply put together;
it is not so much sculptured as constructed, built, assembled, arranged."[26]

ANCESTOR FIGURES OF THE DOGON TRIBE, Mali. Reitberg Museum, Zurich. Von der Heydt Collection. As long as the original parents are perceived as the source of an awesome generative power—a power still active in tribal life—their effigies must be rigidly frontal, solemn, unmoved. The slightest deviation from verticality is felt as the weakening of a force that must endure through eternity. What is remarkable is the variety of shaped forms and spaces that can be achieved within these constraints.

UMA-MAHESVARA MURTI (SIVA WITH PARVATI AND HOST), from Rajasthan or Kajuraho region, India. 10th–11th century A.D. Seattle Art Museum. In India the affection of the ancestral pair assumes an explicitly sexual character. Innocent of Western prudery, medieval Hindu temples were densely populated with "loving couples" in exuberant settings much like their teeming earthly communities.

KING MYCERINUS AND HIS QUEEN KHA-MERER-NEBTY, from Giza. 2599–2571 B.C. Museum of Fine Arts, Boston. Unswervingly pointed toward eternity, the royal pair also evidences an interest in the pleasures of marital intimacy. This interest is based on the discovery of the body as aesthetically pleasing and erotically exciting—ideas visible in the figures' contrasted forms: his—athletic and virile; hers—rounded and soft.

DETAIL OF SARCOPHAGUS, from Cerveteri. C. 520 B.C. Museo Nazionale di Villa Giulia, Rome. To preserve the alive quality of this couple, the Etruscan sculptor shows them with their hands arrested, as if caught in a moment of animated conversation. Also, vividly painted eyes, hair, and skin must have compensated somewhat for the archaic stiffness of the heads.

CRUSADER AND HIS WIFE. c. 1163. Chapel of the Grey Friars Monastery, Nancy, France. A touching wifely loyalty and devotion struggle to emerge from this rude Romanesque carving; nevertheless, the stone image more truly discloses a barbarian couple whose human awareness of each other has not yet been quickened by a Christianity they profess but do not understand.

EKKEHARD AND UTA. Naumburg Cathedral, Germany. 1250–60. Conjectural portraits of the founders of the Cathedral. One hardly doubts they are a contemporary, that is, a Gothic, couple. Their relationship—more realistic than romantic—seems based on a "sensible" arrangement: the alliance of an influential, somewhat cynical German margrave with a stylish and elegant Polish princess.

MEDARDO ROSSO. *The Book-maker.*
1894. The Museum of Modern Art,
New York. Lillie P. Bliss Bequest

AUGUSTE RODIN. *Balzac.* 1892–97

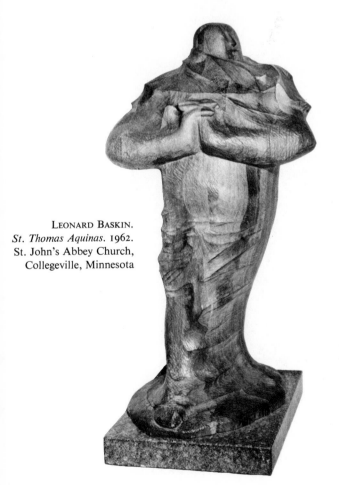

LEONARD BASKIN.
St. Thomas Aquinas. 1962.
St. John's Abbey Church,
Collegeville, Minnesota

Clearly, we are in the midst of a revolution in sculptural materials and technique, a revolution which responds to the unprecedented social, technical, and spiritual changes of modern life. But changes in tools and materials generate new artistic ideas and aesthetic effects. In the following sections we shall examine some of the more prominent among them.

From Monolith to Open Form

The sculpture of antiquity reflected the tree log, stone block, or marble slab from which it was carved. Even where the material permitted major extensions, hammer and chisel could break or split it. That is why totemic sculpture, for example, so closely resembles the tree trunk and why Egyptian Old Kingdom figures closely follow the granite block. Only the casting process could reproduce complex open shapes. Even so, metal casting was used largely to fashion weapons, amulets, harness decorations, and the like, rather than the monumental figures we associate with the settled peoples of the old Mediterranean world. Sculpture in general, and carved sculpture in particular, aspired to the monolithic (similar in form to a single stone). Whether it was hewn out of a single stone or not, it tended toward the shape of the stone unit. A notable exception, the Hellenistic sculpture *Laocoön*, was carved from several blocks of marble, and although it represents a remarkable technical achievement, it is not considered aesthetically successful because its parts seem disunited; the feeling of a single, embracing shape, the *monolithic feeling*, has been lost.

In addition to considerations of material and process, monolithic form dominated early sculpture for religious and psychological reasons. Stability, permanence, and resistance to change are qualities associated with uncomplicated shapes. Perforations and extensions suggest motion, the enemy of the timeless and eternal. As we know, Rodin's *St. John the Baptist Preaching* was criticized because the figure seems to be walking off its pedestal. The pyramids of Egypt and the temples of Greece stress the triangle resting on its base, or the triangle supported by re-

peated massive verticals. Religious sculpture tries to *arrest* change, to create monuments which can resist the ravages of time. So the sacred sculpture of the ancient Mediterranean world (excepting the later Greek, or Hellenistic, development) was largely solid, frontal, and monolithic.

A major source of open form in sculpture was the barbarian peoples whose incursions through Europe from the steppes of Asia eventually destroyed Greco-Roman civilization. Their nomadic existence and their skill in metalworking predisposed them to an art of linear dynamism. Heated metal lends itself to curved, serpentine, and spiral shapes. And since nomadic means continuous movement, early Celtic, Scandinavian, and Germanic art, created by the European descendants of the Eurasian nomads, reflected a fascination with complex abstract movement. The barbarian consciousness was nourished on incessant travel, hunting, and battle. For peoples free to move indefinitely in any direction along the seemingly end-

SEYMOUR LIPTON. *Archangel*. 1963–64. Lincoln Center for the Performing Arts, New York. Working directly with bronze over Monel Metal, Lipton has elaborated the forms of cymbals to create a sculpture which seems to declare a resounding optimism and faith.

Figure of a dancer.
Gallo-Roman, 3rd or 4th century A.D.
Musée
Historique, Orléans

HENRI MATISSE.
Serpentine. 1909.
The Hirshhorn Museum and
Sculpture Garden,
Smithsonian Institution,
Washington, D.C.

AGESANDER, ATHENODORUS,
AND POLYDORUS OF RHODES.
Laocoön. Late
2nd century B.C.
Vatican Museum, Rome

Maori prow ornament, from New Zealand. Museum für Völkerkunde, Munich

Vikings and Polynesians—both warlike, seafaring peoples—created a complex linear art in which spirals, interlaces, and elaborate perforations almost obliterate their much-loved animal motifs.

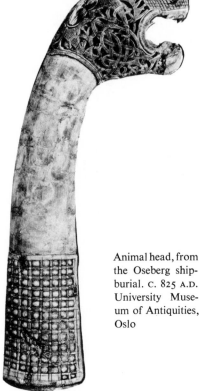

Animal head, from the Oseberg ship-burial. C. 825 A.D. University Museum of Antiquities, Oslo

HENRY MOORE. *Reclining Mother and Child.* 1937. Walker Art Center, Minneapolis. In Moore's penetrated forms we see the culmination of a long process of accommodation between the nomadic obsession with open, serpentine shapes and the classical Mediterranean concern for balance and stability.

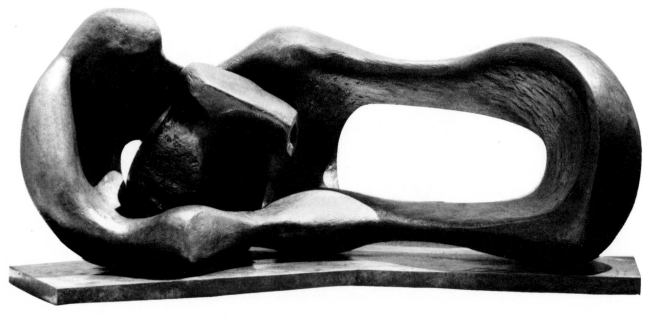

Pharaoh Khafre. C. 2600 B.C. Cairo Museum

less Asian plains, the concepts of visual stability and enclosed space were not easily discovered. Consequently, the art of the wanderers who settled Europe from Russia to Ireland was one of endless convolutions on a flat plane. Their three-dimensional expression consisted mainly of the *assembly* of two-dimensional, linear structures.

The development of Western art reflects the struggle between Mediterranean closed-form or monolithic ideas and nomadic, serpentine, open-form ideas. On the one hand, sculptors from Michelangelo to Maillol endeavored to preserve classical order; on the other, Romanesque and Gothic sculpture express the barbarian obsession with convulsive movement. If the Gothic cathedral is the culmination of Christian art, then the nomadic conception of form and space prevailed. The revival of classical order during the Renaissance never succeeded in displacing entirely the taste for complex motion which had been whetted by barbarian art. With this background, contemporary sculpture in the West would be expected to reveal

anticlassic tendencies—that is, resistance to distinct, naturalistic forms and balanced relationships. Furthermore, it should display shapes created by puncture; twisting, ropelike knots and coils; and a great deal of linear detail.

Such expectations are, in fact, borne out in recent sculpture. As in painting, antiacademic tendencies predominate. The feeling of the monolith, which derives so much from the carving tradition, has been substantially abandoned. It survives conspicuously in the work of a master like Henry Moore, although his penetrations of solid forms betray a distinctly modern consciousness.

A rare monolithic work is seen in Leonard Baskin's *Seated Man with Owl.* Baskin's sculpture is a version of a theme which appears frequently in Egyptian art, as in the *Pharaoh Khafre,* behind whose head is the hawk-god, Horus. But in the modern work, the bird—now an owl—is much inflated and stands forward on the man's arm, almost obscuring him from view. Baskin's sculpture shares the frontality and immobile

NAUM GABO. *Linear Construction #1.* 1942–43.
The Hirshhorn Museum and Sculpture Garden,
Smithsonian Institution, Washington, D.C.

expression of the pharaoh but is otherwise a modern personality. Where Khafre is slim, athletic, and youthful, the modern man is overweight, stolid, and middle-aged. The Egyptian sculpture conveys a powerful sense of enduring mass, because it is without a trace of motion. Baskin's figure has the ponderous bulk of a flabby person whose sitting down is an act of collapse. The pharaoh looks confidently toward a future which he expects to dominate eternally, while Baskin's man is somewhat bored. Thus, the monolithic quality of Egyptian sculpture, present in a modern work, can express different qualities. It becomes a tool of psychological analysis, a portrayal of man's resignation in the face of life's everlasting sameness.

Further illustrations—from the work of Maillol, Brancusi, and Arp—would show that monolithic form still survives. However, these sculptors are among the "old masters" of modernism. As we approach the present, artists seem to choose media and techniques which yield dynamic, perforated, abstract forms. The nonfigurative bias of modern sculpture also indicates the collapse of the classical, monolithic tradition. But it is conceivable that the taste for dynamic, broken

forms will be oversatisfied and that a desire for its opposite will emerge. Then the stylistic pendulum may swing back to monolithic form.

Constructivism

Constructivism was an early-twentieth-century movement which formally abandoned the monolith and the central axis as the foundations of sculpture. It introduced new materials like plastics, Plexiglas, and metal wire, and it made a complete break with the figurative tradition. Its leading personalities were Vladimir Tatlin (1885–1956) and two Russian brothers who used different names, Naum Gabo (1890–1977) and Antoine Pevsner (1886–1962). They advocated an approach which would bring sculpture into harmony with physics and mathematics, and, via engineering, with industrial design. But although the Communist government of Russia supported them following the revolution of 1917, it became unsympathetic to abstract and experimental art by 1921, even though Constructivists hoped to revolutionize architecture

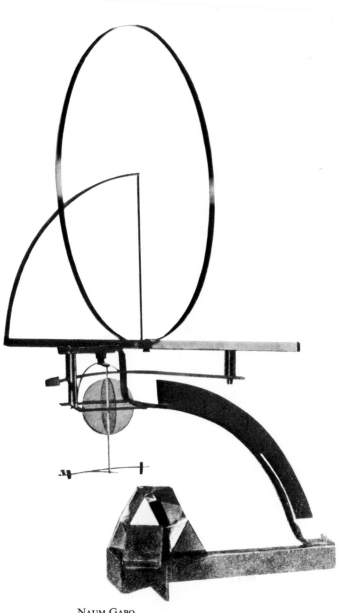

NAUM GABO.
Monument for a Physics Observatory.
1922. Collection the artist

ANTOINE PEVSNER. *Torso.*
1924–26. The Museum of
Modern Art, New York. Katherine S. Dreier Bequest

and industrial design as well as painting and sculpture.

Leaving Russia in 1922, the Constructivists spread their ideas through associates at the Bauhaus. Gabo settled in the United States in 1946 and made his home in Connecticut. By 1965 the influence of Constructivist conceptions of form and space had taken firm hold in America and throughout the world.

What bearing does Constructivism have on sculpture today? Its main traits are abstraction, transparency, interpenetration of sculptural form, overlapping of planes, and the employment of lines in tension to describe direction and movement. Gabo's *Linear Construction # I* (1942–43) exhibits many of the qualities of a mechanical drawing executed in three

dimensions. Its curves do not betray any irregularity because they are divorced from the effort to record organic shapes. *Torso*, executed by Pevsner in 1924–26, is, by contrast, a figurative abstraction very close to Cubist painting. Like the sculpture of another Russian, Archipenko, it stresses negative—that is, concave—volumes, in the presentation of forms which in life are convex. The materials are translucent brownish plastic sheets, and copper. In this work, the Constructivist determination to avoid volume or solid forms is especially evident. The translucency of plastic enables Pevsner to stress the negation of mass. Hence, two traits of the monolith are undermined: (1) solidity or volume: the occupation of space by three-dimensional forms; (2) mass or weight: the determination of forms by gravity requirements. As with Cubism, the influence of physics is apparent.

Gabo's *Monument for a Physics Observatory* (1922) eliminates the distinctions between sculpture and architecture. Although the model is made of plastic, metal, and wood, as sculptural form it bears an interesting resemblance to a wrought-iron sculpture, *Woman Combing Her Hair*, by Julio Gonzalez (born 1908). The work of both artists demonstrates the new openness of sculptural space. From its agelong rootedness in the earth, from its resemblance to masonry-wall construction, sculpture had moved confidently into a kind of interstellar space.

Although modern physics has permanently altered our ideas about the concreteness of matter and the nature of space, sculptors would not entirely abandon the use of massive, opaque, volumetric materials in favor of plastics, wire, and glass. Pevsner, who was trained as a painter, tended to use solid metals, particularly bronze rods bonded into curved planes, in his later work, like *Developable Column*. Apparently, the sensuous appeal of metals counteracts extreme tendencies toward dematerialization.

JULIO GONZÀLEZ. *Woman Combing Her Hair.* 1936. The Museum of Modern Art, New York. Mrs. Simon Guggenheim Fund

ANTOINE PEVSNER. *Developable Column.* 1942. The Museum of Modern Art, New York

CONSTANTIN BRANCUSI. *Adam and Eve.* 1921.
The Solomon R. Guggenheim Museum, New York

In the Brancusi, a scarred Adam supports a
smoother and rounder Eve. By presenting the
figures in a vertical plane Brancusi creates
a type of hierarchy. Giacometti places man and
woman on the same horizontal plane; there the
man becomes a sexual aggressor.

ALBERTO GIACOMETTI. *Man and Woman.*
1928–29. Collection Henriette Gomès, Paris

MAX ERNST. *Le Capricorne.* 1964. Musée National d'Art Moderne, Paris.
Ernst compromises the dignity of royalty by presenting this couple as a
pair of hybrid creatures compounded of geometric elements and anatom-
ical portions of man, fish, goat, steer, and giraffe.

ETIENNE-MARTIN. *Le Grand Couple*. 1946. Collection Michel Couturier & Cie., Paris. The united couple is compared to a powerful, earthy generative force by heightening their resemblance to a huge convoluted tree root.

BARBARA HEPWORTH. *Two Figures*. 1954–55. Collection Mr. and Mrs. Solomon Byron Smith, Lake Forest, Illinois. These figures constitute pairs so abstract that they relate to each other mainly through shared affiliation with the oval or with cubical geometry. We see hardly any male-female differentiation because the concern with form has transcended the polarities of sexual role and appearance.

HENRY MOORE. *King and Queen*. 1952–53. The Hirshhorn Museum and Sculpture Garden, Smithsonian Institution, Washington, D.C. In this royal couple, Moore tries to gain access to those mythic feelings which connect the destiny of a land and its people with the strength and harmony of its rulers.

KENNETH ARMITAGE. *Diarchy*. 1957. Private collection, Chicago. The slablike device makes a literal unit of the couple, forces us to view the unit frontally, and magnifies the impression of obstinate regal power.

JOAN MIRÓ. *Man and Woman*. 1962. Pierre Matisse Gallery, New York. Miró shows that it is possible to be light-hearted about sculptural forms while holding serious convictions about the necessity of using them to make a statement.

MARISOL. *The Bicycle Race.* 1962–63. The Harry N. Abrams Family Collection, New York. An almost Egyptian solemnity pervades this work. Still, there is something more than a satirical comment about a couple of earnest bicycle riders: he is No. 1, and she is No. 2—and they hate each other.

GEORGE SEGAL. *Lovers on a Bed II.* 1970. Sidney Janis Gallery, New York. A couple that *succumbs* to love; the tawdriness of the setting and their own plainness make their embrace a compromise between Eros and fatigue.

EVE RENÉE NELE. *The Couple*. 1961. Bayerische Staatsgemäldesammlungen, Munich.
This is the fetish pair of a civilization consecrated to engineering: in their abdominal
cavities nuts and bolts are renewed; armatures are magically rewound.

BENVENUTO CELLINI. *Saltcellar of Francis I.*
1539–43. Kunsthistorisches Museum, Vienna

Sculptural Assemblage

Assemblage is significant for the history of sculpture in that it abandons carving, modeling, and casting. It begins with materials and objects which already have a rich accretion of meaning. It parallels the flight of painting from the creation of illusions. The sculptor apparently does not wish to participate in a process which pretends that stone is flesh or that metal is hair. Seley's automobile bumpers are very sculptural in the spatial sense, but they do not cease to be bumpers. In other words, assemblage does not involve total *transmutation of materials*. Rather it involves composition with the meaning as well as the substance of existing materials.

The reluctance of sculptors to engage in transmutation of materials represents a profound change in art and in sculpture. As we know, medieval alchemists labored to transmute ordinary materials into gold. There was, for them, a hierarchy of substances. Modern artists are less willing to accept such a hierarchy. Certainly, science and technology have encouraged this attitude, since so many things we value are derived from abundant substances like coal, petroleum, nitrogen, soy beans, and so on. Secondly, the entire process of creating illusions has acquired some of the associations of deceit. "Honesty of materials" was a goal of the pioneers of modern industrial design—a reaction against practices like marbleizing wood or painting wood grains on metal. The "honesty-of-materials" idea has created a climate in which transformation of the inherent properties of a material seems faintly unethical.

Another reason for the importance of sculptural assemblage lies in the sense of inadequacy a sculptor may feel when confronting the forming and fabrication achievements of industry. When Cellini made his

Ultrasmall electronic circuit, a high-speed binary electronic counter for use in a spacecraft

famous saltcellar, he could rightly feel that it represented the highest degree of technical mastery of his age. But the modern artist is daily exposed to miracles of miniaturization which make hand carving and casting seem to be puny achievements. Space flight represents a social organization of technology so remarkable that meticulously carved stone and marble appear, from a technical standpoint, to be medieval survivals. Consequently, there is a certain practical wisdom on the part of the sculptor who incorporates the products of industry into his work. His creative strategy shifts from an emphasis on forming skills to an emphasis on ideas and composition, which is to say, on *design*.

Some of the richness and variety of sculptural effect possible through assemblage is suggested in the following works. They seem virtually a new art form. Even so, the viewer with a good memory will not find it difficult to discover echoes of historical forms and ideas.

Lee Bontecou (born 1931) capitalizes on a personal and craftsmanlike assemblage technique in her relief made of canvas stretched over bent steel wire mounted on a metal frame. The forms of this sculpture bear a strong resemblance to the tribal masks of the Northwest American Indians. The technique is similar to one employed in early aircraft manufacture—stretching and gluing fabric over a wire-frame skeleton; its alternating light and dark canvas areas suggest the painted-wood effects in masks carved by Nigerian sculptors. The most prominent elements in her work are the ovoid apertures which can be experienced as eyes or as openings in a curiously abstract mask.

The fundamental sculptural metaphors here are the mask and the membrane. The light, sturdy construction of the sculpture suggests the Indian practice of building a canoe by stretching hides over a wooden frame. The membrane arouses primitive, animistic feelings; air trapped inside the work seems to be exerting a force outward, a living, invisible force of the sort that holds up airplane wings in flight. The ability of the sculptor to encourage such illusions creates feelings which are further supported by the visible stretching of the canvas over the wire frame.

In *Europa on a Cycle*, Richard Stankiewicz (born 1922) draws and constructs with old chains and rods; he builds with parts as they are found, or cuts metal

A fire-damaged telephone echoes Oldenburg's soft telephone. Using nonrigid materials like canvas, vinyl, kapok, and foam rubber, Oldenburg has elevated limpness to high status among the expressive qualities of sculpture.

Burned phone, from advertisement for Western Electric Phone Company. 1968. Courtesy Cunningham & Walsh, Inc., New York

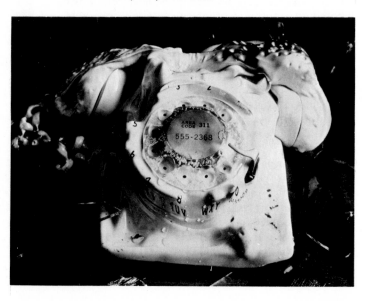

CLAES OLDENBURG. *Soft Pay-Telephone.* 1963. Collection William Zierler, New York

LEE BONTECOU. *Untitled*. 1962. Collection
Mr. and Mrs. Seymour Schweber, King's Point, New York

Painted leather shirt.
Tlingit Indians of Alaska.
Collected in 1918.
University Museum, Philadelphia

The magical motifs of tribal artists are often taken up, either unconsciously
or intentionally, by the creators of "museum" art. But little has changed except the labels assigned by critics and historians.

shapes with his torch. The several forms of metal—
wire, pipe, sheet, rod, spring, tube, bar, and plate—are
united by a single method of attachment—welding—
and a single color and surface texture—rust. The
sculptor is thus free to deal with problems of volume
and contour, movement and balance, illusion and
reality. The silhouette of the *Europa* has graphic
interest, as in a print by Gabor Peterdi (born 1915).
The notion of a beautiful woman carried off by a rusty
wheel would surely appeal to Picasso, who made good
use of bicycle handlebars in his *Goat Skull and Bottle*.

The Juggler by Robert Mallary (born 1917) is executed in particularly exotic materials for sculpture—
plastic-impregnated fabric and wood. Using a man's
shirt and trousers, which are soaked in plastic and
attached to a burnt-wood support, Mallary arrives at
the figure through suggestions of the clothes meant to
cover it. The hollow arms and legs, now given a certain
rigidity, exist as real limbs and heavy rags at the same
time. The plastic freezes the action of the fabric
stretched by its own weight and suspended from a
wooden frame like a crucifix. Burnt wood is, of course,
one of the primal materials of religious sacrifice;
hence, Mallary has brought together some of the basic
symbols of suffering and transfiguration. As he "puts
on his act," the juggler falls into the position of the
Christ on the Cross, thus expressing dying-in-living
and failure-in-success—the tragic ideas at the heart of
existence.

The Stove by Claes Oldenburg, a Pop version of
assemblage sculpture, consists of painted plaster
"food" displayed on a real but very antiquated cooking range. The range is reminiscent of the "ready-
mades" of Marcel Duchamp. But the luridly colored

provisions are the contribution of Oldenburg alone.
Sculpture as the logical or pleasing organization of
forms and volumes is irrelevant here. The design
principles of unity, rhythm, balance, and so on are
ignored. Instead, the viewer is encouraged to perceive
food and food preparation as disgusting. The artist
seems to be directing a program of sabotage against
what the housekeeping magazines, with their delicious
colorplates, attempt to encourage. We see the nakedness of groceries and cooking. A familiar event thus
becomes hideously ugly. Such an antiart objective tries
to create its own kind of legitimacy.

John Chamberlain's assemblage of crumpled automobile parts seems to be an earlier stage in the process
of machine destruction seen in the "compression"
sculptures of César Baldaccini. Although these parts
are "found" in junkyards, Chamberlain (born 1927)
bends, welds, and paints them himself, constructing
works which do not rely on their automotive origins.
In other words, the dead automobile is a source of
cheap raw material. The *Essex* acknowledges a venerable vehicle as ancestor but is more closely influenced
by action painting than by speculation about the
destiny of machines in our civilization. The scale of the
work (nine feet high by seven and a half feet wide)
creates some difficulty for the viewer if he attempts to
see it as a large, colored metal painting. But that is
clearly its objective. The work adheres to the rectangle; its holes, valleys, and crevices occur in the consistently shallow space of Abstract Expressionist painting. However, unity of form and expression seems to
elude the sculptor. Why? Because signs of age in the
metal conflict with the new and shiny paint film given
to the old surfaces. A "logic of materials" is not

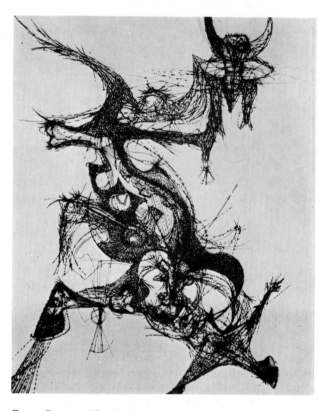

Eau de Vroom. Advertisement for Crêpe
de Chine perfume. 1967. Courtesy Berta,
Grant & Winkler, Inc., New York. The
sculptural strategy of assemblage is
brilliantly illustrated in a perfume advertisement that combines masculine machinery (the Honda), a soft saddlebag (can it
symbolize Europa?), and a precious
fragrance.

ROBERT MALLARY.
The Juggler. 1962. Allan Stone Gallery,
New York

CLAES OLDENBURG. *The Stove.* 1962.
Private collection

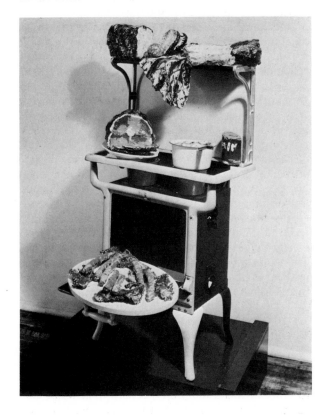

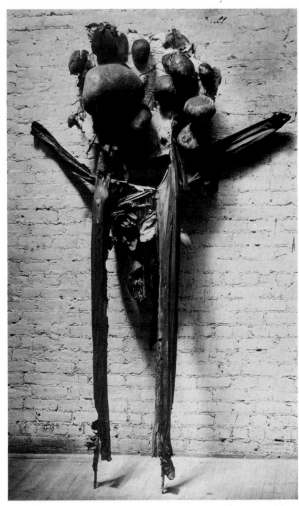

permitted to assert itself. César's *Sculpture Picture* may be a more successful integration of sculpture in a painterly format.

Edward Kienholz works in the Pop-art vein but is more explicit in his social criticism than other members of this group. His *John Doe* is an assemblage consisting of a mannequin, a perambulator, paint, wood, metal, and plaster. A lettered placard at the bottom reads:

RIDDLE:
Why is John Doe like a piano?
ANSWER:
Because he is square, upright and grand.
—OLD SOOTHE SAYING

The "square-ness" of some Americans has been well developed in literature by H. L. Mencken, Sinclair Lewis, and others. Kienholz approaches the square viciously. The regular features of the mannequin's head (which includes, perhaps unintentionally, an archaic Greek smile) have been "abused" with painted stripes and spills; the eyes have been crudely outlined in paint; the usually inoffensive store-window dummy

has become gruesome. John Doe wears an outsized badge—a cross—over his heart. The paint runs and spatters degrade him. And, of course, placing an adult in a child's perambulator is another insult. It is a bitter statement; it reveals little inclination to indulge the square. He is offered as a monument fit for oblivion.

The employment of *wrappings* has enlarged the artistic vocabulary of terror. Using methods we associate with mortuaries or shipping rooms, two sculptors, Bruce Conner (born 1933) and Christo (born 1935), have independently developed a gruesome and mysterious sculptural rhetoric. Both create an imagery in which shrouded figures or objects seem to be struggling to escape their wrappings. The situation has clinical as well as sculptural overtones, relying on the viewer's fear of confinement. That is its funereal side. But the convention of the chained or bound figure has a history as old as Prometheus. For example, Michelangelo's *Rebellious Slave* describes a drama of imprisoned form which, under various disguises, appears in almost all his figures.

Conner's *Child* shows a wax figure on a high-chair enmeshed in a gauzelike material made of torn nylon stockings. The device suggests the flimsy bonds of

349

cobwebs. It also functions like Francis Bacon's blurred contours to create the illusion of movement and the quality of an agonized, silent scream.

Package on Wheelbarrow by Christo describes the ghoulish struggle of an unknown thing against a random system of knots and bindings. Its wrapping, a sheet, maintains its anonymity, and the wheelbarrow keeps the secret, adding only the possibility that the writhing form will be carried away. As a result, the viewer experiences the tensions usually sustained by "abstract" sculptural form. But an imagination nourished on horror films may discover a taste for the macabre rather than abstract art at the root of this work.

Little Hands by Arman (born 1928) continues the macabre note struck by Conner and Christo. Consisting of dolls' hands (some of them broken) glued into a wooden drawer, it initiates a series of grisly perceptions, beginning with a collection of mutilated toys and ending with the uncovered mass graves that turn up in wartime. The drawer functions first as a frame, then as a container, and finally as a tomb (see section below, "Niches, Boxes, and Grottoes"). To equal its content of horror, one would have to go back to Hieronymus Bosch. Even then, the images wrought by hand lack the clinical detachment possible for the artist who assembles limbs originally meant to function normally.

Arman created *Chopin's Waterloo* (1962) in a humorous vein. Many citizens, it seems, harbor a secret desire to tear a piano apart. Arman has done it for them (as Jimmy Durante or the Marx brothers used to do), and has given the dismemberment permanent form in a type of piano collage. The idea may be trivial, but the visual effect is one of splendid destruction—splinters, ivories, and piano wire in gorgeous disarray. Perhaps a piano sustains more visual interest when disintegrated than when healthy and whole. By tearing a piano open, the sculptor reveals it as a type of machine; and then, to gratify our desire to see machines break down, he kills it. For these or similar reasons, Jean Tinguely (born 1925), a Swiss sculptor celebrated for machines which destroy themselves, included a "flayed" piano in his kinetic sculpture performance at the Museum of Modern Art, *Homage to New York*. Arman's piano collage might represent the aesthetic vindication of small boys who take clocks apart but cannot put them together again.

The interest in violent and gruesome phenomena is visible in all forms of art and popular culture. There has been, for example, a vigorous market for the horror films of Vincent Price; and revivals of the early (1933) film *King Kong* have been enthusiastically received. Sculptural assemblage, too, has been technically congenial to the expression of violent emotions. The sculptor *begins* at a well-developed level of meaning and is able to devote his effort to exploring the forces which hold things together or tear them apart.

Niches, Boxes, and Grottoes

The niche is a recessed place in a wall where a sculptured figure or bust can be located. So it is important to think of niche sculptures as *born from* walls, conceived out of the necessity to endow plane surfaces with dramatic meaning. The niche encloses forms

CÉSAR. *Sculpture Picture.* 1956.
The Museum of Modern Art, New York.
Gift of G. David Thompson

JOHN CHAMBERLAIN. *Essex.* 1960.
The Museum of Modern Art, New York.
Gift of Mr. and Mrs. Robert C. Scull
and Purchase

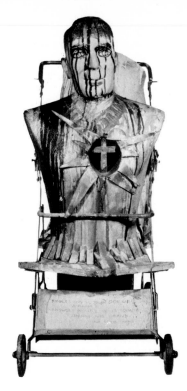

EDWARD KIENHOLZ. *John Doe.* 1959. Collection Sterling Holloway, South Laguna Beach, California

MICHELANGELO. *The Rebellious Slave.* 1513–16. The Louvre, Paris

BRUCE CONNER. *Child.* 1959. The Museum of Modern Art, New York. Gift of Philip Johnson

physically. It governs the angle of vision from which a sculpture can be seen. Psychologically, the sculpture is *protected* by its enclosure; it is removed from full exposure to the elements and can thus be perceived as something which requires shelter, possibly because it holds a valuable secret.

These psychological meanings of niche sculpture also adhere to the box sculptures and constructions which figure prominently in twentieth-century art. The box sculpture can be regarded as a detached niche, a secular shrine which has been lifted from an architectural setting that never existed. When we look at the box sculptures of industrial civilization, it is difficult not to project on them all our associations of the tem-

CHRISTO. *Package on Wheelbarrow.* 1963. The Museum of Modern Art, New York

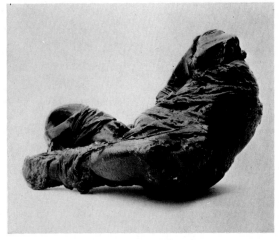

RICO LEBRUN. *Bound Figure.* 1963. Collection Constance Lebrun Crown, Malibu, California

ARMAN. *Little Hands*. 1960. Collection the artist

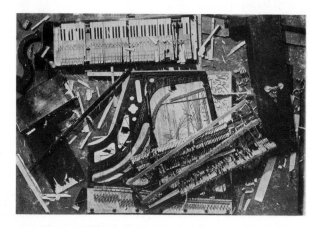

ARMAN. *Chopin's Waterloo*. 1962. Collection the artist

JEAN TINGUELY. Piano before its incorporation into *Homage to New York*. Self-destroyed March 17, 1960, in the garden of The Museum of Modern Art, New York

ple recess or cathedral niche, the mysterious little place which is seen as a shrine and addressed with awe.

The grotto, like the niche, is a man-made recess or excavation. But it is not associated with the wall. It relates instead to the vault or the convoluted inner spaces of natural caverns. The shaping of interior space is, of course, architecture, but the work of Frederick Kiesler (1896–1965) resembles a hybrid form of sculpture *and* architecture. But as a modern sculptural type the grotto has little concern with shelter. It is better understood as interior sculpture. Certainly Schwitters's Merzbau was a quasi-Cubist grotto, employing geometric solids instead of the organic forms used by Kiesler. And in the grotesque—that is, grotto-like—passageways and roof structures of Antoni Gaudí, we see the creation of truly sculptural concavities. Interior sculpture by architects like Gaudí and Kiesler reflects the modern survival of our eternal attraction to the cave.

The *Room* by Lucas Samaras (born 1936) is a twentieth-century grotto, a three-dimensional interior assemblage. It consists of possessions collected and attached to the walls of a teen-age cave. Its claim to style lies in a total lack of style, and its vividness is reinforced by the viewer's knowledge that the room is utterly real and typical. If its visual disorganization seems to constitute a scandal, a poor reflection on adolescents growing up in America, then we should remember that it accurately mirrors the space organization of the large-scale environment created by generations of adults in our society. There is also the possibility that modern conceptions of order—influenced by the austerities of Mondrian and Mies—fail to perceive a logic in the apparent illogic of the Samaras room.

Boxes differ from grottoes and niches in that they close and become packages. The niche is part of a stationary wall; the box is a portable container for something worth keeping. It has many of the ancient associations of a reliquary—a container which holds the bones of a saint, sacred texts, or precious remnants. These religious uses of boxlike containers suggest the ancestry of boxes in modern sculpture.

The authority of the niche is powerfully demonstrated in the sculptures of Louise Nevelson (born 1904), which usually are collections of boxes or cells—little rooms. Painted in monochrome—black, white, or gold—they convey an impression of compulsive neatness and order, of well-arranged, frequently cleaned drawers. Without knowing what the contents are, one senses they have been carefully classified, reviewed from time to time, and periodically dusted. They consist, in fact, of pieces of wood molding, bowling pins, newel posts, chair legs, and lumberyard odds and ends. What distinguishes *Royal Tide I* is not so much the origin of the fragments as the control one senses in their location. Since no significant meaning can be attributed to the wooden shapes themselves, how can we explain their power?

far right:
Santo Jesús Nazarino.
El Santuario de Chimayo,
Chimayo, New Mexico.
1813–16

right:
BENEDETTO ANTELAMI.
King David. c. 1180–90.
West facade,
Fidenza Cathedral,
Emilia, Italy

FREDERICK KIESLER. *Endless House.* 1949–60

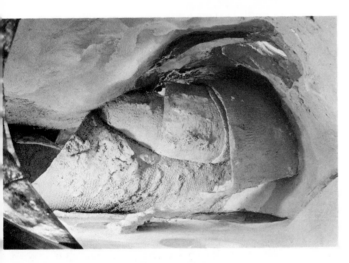

LUCAS SAMARAS. Detail of *Room.* 1964.
Pace Gallery, New York

ANTONI GAUDÍ. Original attic (garret), Casa Milá
Apartment House, Barcelona. 1905–10

ANDRÉ BLOC. *Sculpture Habitacle No. 2.* 1965

A sculpture in which one could live,
or a dwelling which invites the plastic
responses appropriate to sculpture.

ANDRÉ BLOC. Detail of *Sculpture Habitacle No. 2*

LOUISE NEVELSON. *Royal Tide I.* 1960.
Collection Howard and Jean Lipman,
New York

Just as the monolith is a basic sculptural type which
expresses order, so is the box a type which commands
belief; it is convincing on sight. The box form in
general, and Nevelson's work in particular, constitute
a latter-day magical art. The artist who uses this form
is a sorcerer; the box sculpture becomes a container
for fetish objects. It is not necessary to know what the
wooden shapes mean so long as we believe they will

LOUISE NEVELSON. *Totality Dark*.
1962. Pace Gallery, New York

within a box which resembles an attaché case. Its carefully dimensioned spaces make room for small reproductions of each of the sixty-eight principal works Duchamp created before abandoning art for chess. In all, three hundred editions of the "museum" and its contents were built. But the box is more than a handy container for his artistic output; it is an ironic device. By miniaturizing works of art which were originally scandalous and giving them locations according to the impartial logic of the valise, the objects become a businessman's inventory—merchandise which can be displayed as in a salesman's sample-case.

MARCEL DUCHAMP. *Boîte-en-valise* (*The Box in a Valise*). 1938–42. Dwan Gallery, New York

ward off evil—that is, the anxieties we normally treat with pills. Indeed, the anonymity of the boxes sustains faith in their magical influence. It is a case of the *form of presentation* taking possession of the material presented.

Marcel Duchamp's *Boîte-en-valise* (*The Box in a Valise*) is a craftily compartmented little museum

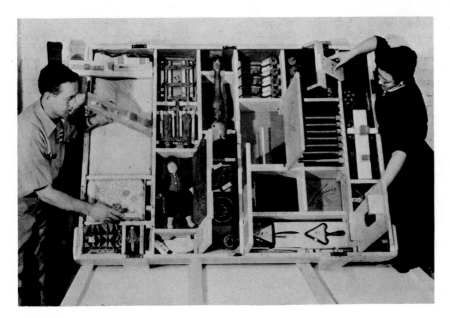

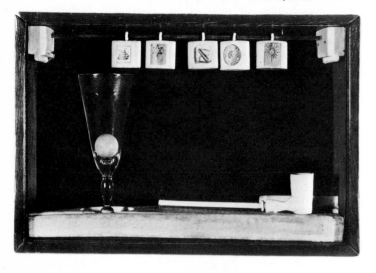

JOSEPH CORNELL. *Soap Bubble Set.* 1950.
Collection Mr. and Mrs. Daniel Varenne, Paris

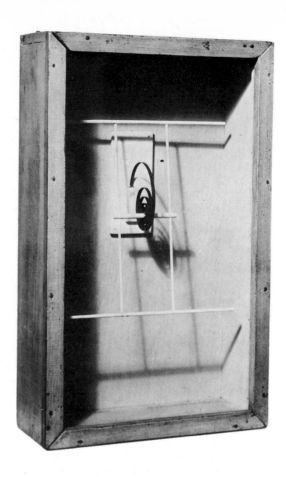

JOSEPH CORNELL. *Blériot.* 1956. Collection
Mr. and Mrs. E. A. Bergman, Chicago

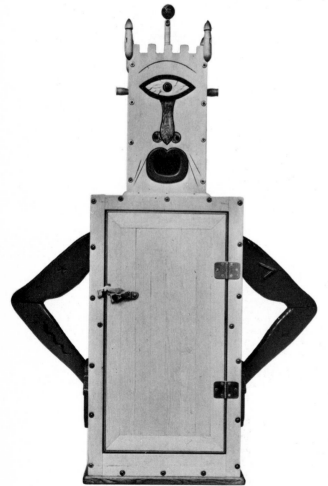

H. C. WESTERMANN. *Memorial to
the Idea of Man, If He Was an Idea.* 1958.
Collection Lewis Manilow, Chicago

The boxes of Joseph Cornell (1903–1972) are also surreal containers—collections of objects which seem related until the viewer realizes that the logic of common sense leads to questions one cannot answer. For example, *Soap Bubble Set* (1950) has all the serenity and simplicity of a Chardin still life. The objects are not anonymous, like Louise Nevelson's wood fragments; they have real identities. They also have the capacity to induce dreams of old possessions and places, recollections of lost things. Somehow, Cornell manages to scramble one's time sense, which is fitting and proper for Surrealist art. The experience is entirely pleasant; it leaves no scars. The collections awaken places or times we never knew and then return us to the present.

Cornell began creating his enigmatic constructions in the 1930s, apparently uninfluenced by other developments in art. In his work the connection with sculpture is very tenuous; he is really an Imagist poet who uses objects in space to create opportunities for reverie or ironic comment. *Blériot* (1956) has the spare, open structure of Constructivist sculpture. It is also a prime exemplar of quietly stated visual wit. The rusted spring mounted on a kind of trapeze or parrot's perch symbolizes the first Frenchman to fly across the English Channel. Ever economical with his means while seeking to encompass the widest range of ideas, Cornell extends the metaphor to bird and machine flight, to planetary orbits in space, and back to a bird in its cage.

H. C. Westermann's boxes are distinguished by

their careful craftsmanship and their grotesque connection with the human figure. *Memorial to the Idea of Man, If He Was an Idea* is a large (fifty-five inches high), well-made cabinet-and-Cyclops who has crenellations for a crown, like the battlements on a castle tower. The door of his torso, when opened, reveals an interior lined with bottle caps. It also contains a headless baseball player and an armless acrobat, plus a black ship sinking in a sea of bottle caps.

It is not unusual for primitive sculpture to include magical substances in the abdominal cavity. In *African Art* Werner Schmalenbach says: "A [fetish] figure can be used as one only when it is charged with some magic content. . . . Every conceivable thing is used as a magic content: bits of bone, teeth, animal claws. . . . They are often placed in a cavity hollowed out in the head or belly, or, too, in a little horn on top of the head."[27] Westermann, responding to a similar impulse, lavishes considerable effort on the interior finish of his boxes. His approach to sculpture is totally different in concept from previous examples; he does not rely entirely on the outward aspect to make his statement; he fabricates the visceral contents too, although they will not necessarily be seen. Together with the evidence of superior joinery and the obvious durability of the box, this completeness of construction suggests that Westermann is fashioning real beings who exist by virtue of their built-in equipment and according to their own laws. The fact that their insides are lined with the debris of an afternoon at a baseball stadium is no more remarkable than the fact that our insides may contain partly digested hamburger and Coke.

Beyond Constructivism: Primary Structures

Under the influence of Constructivism, sculpture has tended to divest itself of figurative, gestural, and symbolic meanings. Not only did Constructivism emphasize the analysis of matter and motion as if sculpture were an extension of physics, it also encouraged the dissolution of monolithic forms and thus contributed to the breakdown of classic conceptions of sculpture. It was perhaps inevitable, then, that sculpture would reconstitute itself as a new process of visual inquiry—the exploration of architectural space.

Primary structures are not intended to be precious objects—to be worshiped, owned, institutionalized, isolated in special places, or employed as architectural adornments. They are instead the monumental by-products of spatial investigations—rational, intuitive, geometrical, or technical—undertaken to discover the impact of large-scale forms on human awareness. The role of the primary structuralists involves building real forms in real space. Hence, no matter how cerebral their works may appear, we are aware of their corporeal existence as occupiers of the same world we all live in.

If the figure of man is not present in primary structures, human responses to spatial openings and enclosures must nevertheless be assumed. This presence is what abstractionists invoke when they insist that a

RONALD BLADEN. *Cathedral Evening.* 1969. South Albany Mall Project, Albany, New York. An important change in perception occurs when sculpture (or painting) assumes the scale of architecture: we no longer feel ourselves in the presence of represented forms; we tend to regard the object as a primary rather than a derived phenomenon.

GEORGES VANTONGERLOO. *Construction $y-2x^3-13.5x^2-21x$*. 1935. Kunstmuseum, Basel. An early and austere example of sculpture created according to a mathematical equation. But notice the uncontrolled reflections, shimmers, and diffractions in the nickel-silver surfaces. Were they also planned?

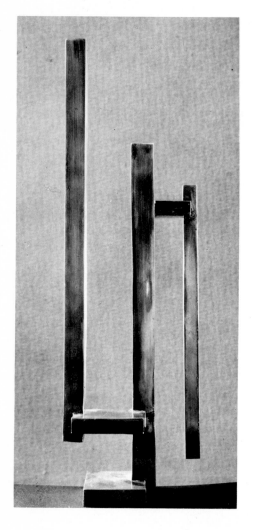

SOL LEWITT.
47 Three-Part Variations on 3 Different Kinds of Cubes. 1967.
Dwan Gallery, New York

DONALD JUDD. *Untitled.* 1968.
Collection Mr. and Mrs. Frederick B. Mayer, Denver

Through the absolute predictability of serial imagery, the sculptor tries to empty his forms of emotional and historical "debris." But then a conflict arises: these constructions occupy real space on a real planet whose gravity, atmosphere, and motion (night and day, light and dark) inevitably affect man-made or natural structures and our perceptions of them.

humanistic art need not include *representation* of the figure: they design with the perceptual and physiological behavior of human beings in mind.

Primary structuralists vary, however, in the degree to which they are committed to intuition or calculation in design. Some are willing to surrender the control of sculptural form to prepared number systems, equations, and formulas. Some would use computers for design. Of course, artists have sought a "science of proportion" since the ancient Greeks. A mathematically precise series of voids and solids is pursued because it seems to obey laws outside the chaos of human thought and desire.

Today, labels like "serial sculpture," "system sculpture," and "ABC art" are used to describe works which rely heavily on simplicity of basic volumes and voids, mechanically produced surfaces, depersonalization of shape, and the algebraic playing out of permutations and combinations of form. Impact on the viewer, however, is anything but simple and precise; architectural emotions are involved because of the scale of what the viewer sees, the engineered character of the forms, and the implied invitation to move under, around, and through the sculpture. In the end there is no way for artists or spectators to escape their humanity.

Isamu Noguchi. *Floor Frame.* 1962.
Collection Mr. and Mrs. Robert A. Bernhard,
Portchester, New York

> Sculpture becomes the art of engineering
> a stately geometric twist, or of subjecting
> post-and-beam forms to diagonal
> stresses, seeming to bury and then
> resurrect them. Despite their monu-
> mental scale, these are humorous works.

Tony Smith. *Cigarette.* 1967.
Albright-Knox Art Gallery,
Buffalo, New York.
Gift of the Seymour H. Knox Foundation, Inc.

Kinetic Sculpture

Sculpture-in-motion has a history as old as the Trojan
horse and as recent as the figures which strike the hour
in front of Macy's department store. It is demonstrated in the widely owned but aesthetically unmen-
tionable Swiss clock, as well as in millions of spring-
driven, motor-driven, and rocket-actuated toys. The
combination of sculpture with mechanical motion
occupied some of the great minds of the Renaissance,
including that of Leonardo da Vinci, who designed
sculptural-mechanical devices for princely entertainments and city festivals.

As we know, Leonardo also designed an early flying
machine, repeating the exploit of the Greek sculptor
Daedalus, who, according to the myth, achieved
successful flight but with disastrous results for his son
Icarus. Flying too close to the sun, which melted his
wax wings, the boy fell into the sea and was drowned.
Thus did the ancients describe the fate of men who
usurp the prerogatives of gods. Daedalus may also
have been the mythical ancestor of all kinetic sculptors, since he devised dolls with movable limbs for
the daughters of the king of Sicily. At any rate, the
ability to make objects which can move by themselves
has always seemed to be one of the great mysteries.

Richard Hunt. *Icarus.* 1956.
Albright-Knox Art Gallery,
Buffalo, New York.
Gift of Seymour H. Knox

ALEXANDER CALDER. *Red Gongs*. 1955.
The Metropolitan Museum of Art, New York.
Fletcher Fund, 1955

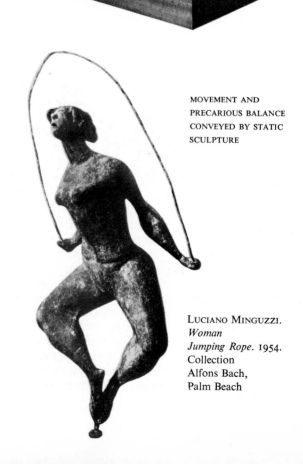

BRUNO LUCCHESI.
Seated Woman #2. 1963.
Whereabouts unknown

The mystery surrounding motion as an idea fascinates artists. In kinetic sculpture, motion becomes one
of the visual elements, like shape or color. Futurist art,
as we know, was officially dedicated to the expression
of movement, especially mechanical movement, which
was considered "more beautiful than the *Victory of
Samothrace*." But the Futurists stayed within the static
conventions of painting and sculpture; their work
represented motion and mechanization; it did not
absorb them into the art form itself.

In 1920, Naum Gabo created the first modern
kinetic sculpture and exhibited it in Berlin. The
statement which he and his brother then made in their
Realist Manifesto served as a foundation for kinetic
sculpture as well as Constructivist aesthetics: "We free
ourselves from the thousand-year-old error of art,
originating in Egypt, that only static rhythms can be
its elements. We proclaim that for present-day perceptions the most important elements of art are the kinetic
rhythms."

But Gabo concentrated on constructions which
penetrate volume and minimize mass. He executed few
works which actually employ movement as an element. It remained for the American sculptor Alexander Calder to create in the 1930s an art form—
mobiles—which successfully integrated motion into
art.

Calder's mobiles are sensitively balanced systems
which are set into motion by the gentlest of air currents. Thus, while they receive their motive force from
the invisible environment, the parts and subsystems of
mobiles move in orbits designed by the sculptor. The
energy which actuates the mobile may be random, but
the character of its movement is anticipated, that is,
formed.

It is possible to discuss Calder's sculpture as if it

MOVEMENT AND
PRECARIOUS BALANCE
CONVEYED BY STATIC
SCULPTURE

LUCIANO MINGUZZI.
*Woman
Jumping Rope*. 1954.
Collection
Alfons Bach,
Palm Beach

were static sculpture. The original contribution of mobiles, however, is to raise the possibility of responding to *qualities* of movement. Calder's shapes appear to be biomorphic forms similar to those used by Arp and Miró. For the most part, they are playful, reminiscent of fish, animals, leaves, and flowers. But his sculptural *movement* interests us here. Some works suggest the stately motion of great tree branches; others are as comic as Charlie Chaplin strolling and hopping his way down a street. The fact that mobiles are widely imitated—they have become virtually an American folk art—suggests that it is their organized motion which has caught the popular imagination, since abstract forms do not usually receive such broad acceptance.

EXAMPLES OF KINETIC SCULPTURE

Mechanical motion is understandably attractive to kinetic sculptors. Besides, the machine as an idea and as a feature of the visual environment is inevitably part of our time. The problem of the kinetic sculptor lies in going beyond the mere incorporation of machine forms in his work. Some kinetic sculptures consist of machines designed for no purpose other than to exhibit their own operation. They are distinguished from "real" machines in that they perform no practical work. In his fantastic designs for machines, the cartoonist Rube Goldberg humorously exploited a single idea—the absurdity of a complex apparatus performing a really unnecessary job. Our fascination

Whistle in the form of a swinging girl,
from Remojadas region,
Veracruz, Mexico. 300–900 A.D.
The Museum of Primitive Art, New York

Noguchi's little person, though static, aims at the same dynamism as the swinging-girl whistle.

JOSÉ DE RIVERA.
Homage to the World of Minkowski. 1955.
The Metropolitan Museum of Art, New York.
Fletcher Fund, 1955

ISAMU NOGUCHI. *Big Boy.* 1952.
The Museum of Modern Art, New York.
A. Conger Goodyear Fund

LEN LYE. *Fountain.* 1963.
Collection Mr. and Mrs. Howard Wise, New York

LEN LYE. *Fountain* (in motion)

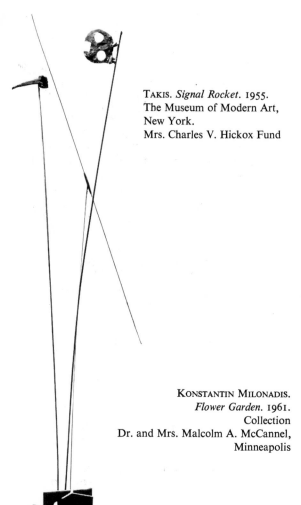

TAKIS. *Signal Rocket.* 1955.
The Museum of Modern Art,
New York.
Mrs. Charles V. Hickox Fund

KONSTANTIN MILONADIS.
Flower Garden. 1961.
Collection
Dr. and Mrs. Malcolm A. McCannel,
Minneapolis

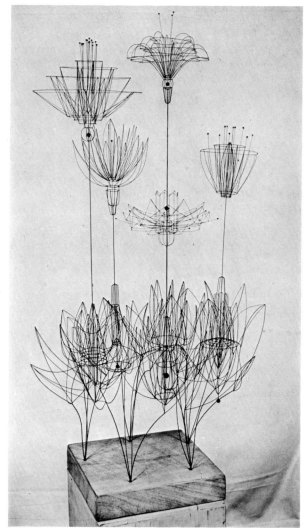

ARTHUR SECUNDA. *Music Machine*. 1964–65.
Whereabouts unknown

LIN EMERY. *Homage to Amercreo*. 1964.
American Creosote Works, Inc., New Orleans

with the precision and reliability of machines is mixed with resentment and hostility: they seem perfect and absurd at the same time.

Music Machine by Arthur Secunda exhibits Goldbergian absurdity in a craftsmanlike, operational sculpture. It consists of a gilded construction of wood, metal, and machine parts built around a music box. Its associations with the mechanics of sound are abetted by radio antennae, a built-in xylophone, a guitar handle, and other noise-making and electronic odds and ends. Externalizing gears, sprockets, springs, and so on is part of an effort to derive visual poetry from mechanized innards. And it is consistent with the general tendency in contemporary art to expose working parts.

A practical application of kinetic sculpture is seen in Lin Emery's *Homage to Amercreo*, a mobile fountain whose forms fill with water until they tilt over, empty themselves, and then return to be filled again. Although the work functions as a machine, its mechanical operation is subordinate to its visual performance. Perhaps this idea could be applied to other machines in our civilization with immense visual benefits. Of course, the purpose of a fountain is to create visual entertainment by the display of water in motion. The viewer may be grateful that Emery's forms are not nymphs and sea creatures acting out an allegorical charade.

Study: Falling Man (Figure on a Bed) by Ernst Trova presents an aluminum figure strapped to an

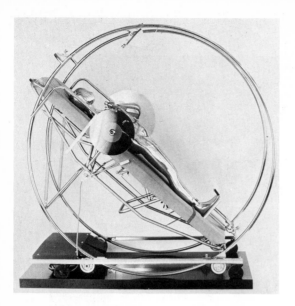

ERNEST TROVA.
Study: Falling Man (Figure on Bed). 1964.
Pace Gallery, New York

Man-size mannequin, from advertisement
for Ford Motor Company. 1966

apparatus with clinical-experimental overtones. The work is terrifying because the apparatus is so obviously clean, efficient, and well calculated to carry out a job of scientific dehumanization. The figure is a model of urban, middle-aged man—slightly paunchy, sway-backed, faceless, and curiously without arms. In some respects he resembles the mannequins used in autocrash experiments. Trova has created an image of man as ideal subject for clinical experimentation. But we do not know the purpose of the experiment. Perhaps the figure will be rocked, whirled, and rotated like an astronaut undergoing a simulated experience in weightlessness. Another of Trova's works, *Study:*

Falling Man (Landscape #1), offers three versions of the same man, beset with mechanical equipment to regulate his movement. His nakedness, the Buck Rogers accessories strapped to his body, and the shiny aluminum surface he has for skin convey eerie evocations of that depersonalized humanity described by George Orwell in his not very fantastic novel *1984*. A harmless creature is about to go through some sophisticated maneuvers. Precautions have been taken so that he will emerge whole, but will his manhood survive?

Jean Tinguely's kinetic sculptures are mechanical poems about the absurdity of machines and of a

ERNEST TROVA. *Study: Falling Man (Landscape #1)*. 1964. Pace Gallery, New York

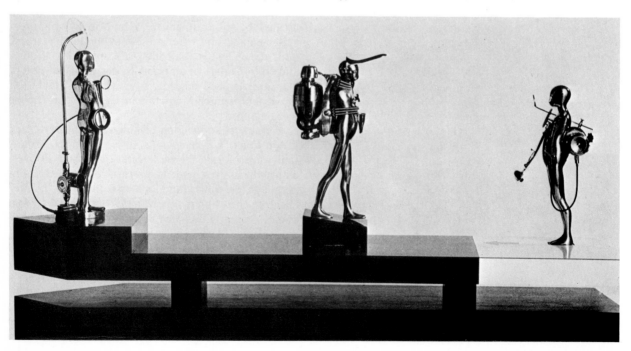

Photograph of Jean Tinguely at work

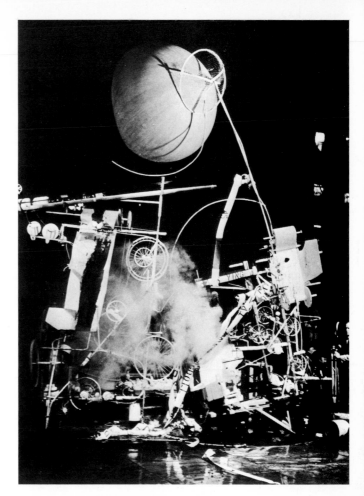

JEAN TINGUELY. *Homage to New York*. 1960.
Self-destroyed March 17, 1960,
in the garden of
The Museum of Modern Art, New York

civilization which permits itself to be governed by them. His *Homage to New York* was a type of mechanized Happening. In addition to the battered piano mentioned earlier, drums, bicycle wheels, Coke bottles, a typewriter, a drawing machine, and a weather balloon figured as performers. Fifteen rickety motors powered the shabbily constructed affair. The entire assembly was designed to make music, create drawings, issue reports, give birth to machine offspring, set itself on fire, and finally destroy itself. The noise, the drawings, the typed reports, and the bursting activity in general were aimless in true Dada fashion. At the same time, the suicidal machine constituted a junkyard parody of contemporary civilization.

The short career of *Homage* was witnessed by a distinguished audience on March 17, 1960, in the garden of the Museum of Modern Art. But, contrary to expectation, the machine did not destroy itself completely, and Tinguely's intervention was required to set it finally on the path to self-immolation. With the aid of its maker, the whole whirring, flapping spectacle began to smoke, and at last exploded into flame, its "useful" life ended with the assistance of a fire extinguisher.

Homage to New York, like the Happenings of Kaprow and associates, may belong to theater more than sculpture because its existence was so brief. However, Tinguely has created other works which resemble *Homage* but do not attempt to explode. *Méta-Mécanique* exhibits the sculptor's fascination with mechanical movement and his addiction to bicycle wheels, discarded metal, and belt-driven systems for transmitting motion. Tinguely's kinetic sculptures move and sound something like a one-man band, with motors substituting for the embattled musician. They

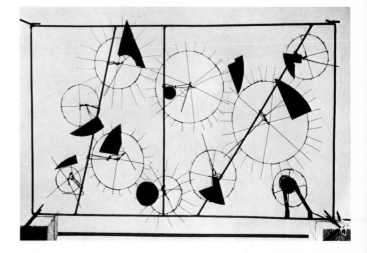

JEAN TINGUELY. *Méta-Mécanique*. 1954.
Museum of Fine Arts, Houston.
Purchased with funds donated by D. and J. de Menil

thump and pound, vibrate and oscillate, producing to-and-fro alternations or ongoing cycles, as in *Homage*, where the machine endlessly dispatched soft-drink bottles down an inclined plane to a crashing finale.

From the water clocks of Greece to Leonardo's mechanized entertainments for the Duke of Milan, to the Swiss cuckoo clock, to Calder's mobiles, to the parodies of Rube Goldberg, to the automated protest sculpture of Jean Tinguely is a long kinetic voyage. But Tinguely's machines have not come abreast of modern, electronically guided tools; they more nearly resemble the equipment which must have adorned the bicycle shop of Orville and Wilbur Wright. That comfortable old noise and clangor has today been supplanted by new, quiet, and more insidious processes of mechanization and automation. Perhaps that is why *Méta-Mécanique* is not frightening, but quaint, in the manner of antique coffee mills and sculpture that stands still.

The Crafts and Sculpture

The crafts have been involved in a maneuver of disengagement from useful manufacture, steadily fortifying their claims to fine-art status. Even though they

PETER VOULKOS. *Gallas Rock.* 1959–60. Dr. and Mrs. Digby Gallas, Los Angeles

BRUCE KOKKO. *Paint Can with Brush.* 1965. Whereabouts unknown

are defended as useful art forms, the crafts are increasingly prized for their sculptural values. Handmade ceramic pots, for example, cannot compete economically with mass-produced containers made of metal, plastics, or clay. Nevertheless, they continue to be made by potters, exhibited by museums, and purchased by collectors. Clearly, they satisfy aesthetic as well as utilitarian needs. Pottery forms are often assembled with no claim to function as containers. The potter's wheel is now a tool of sculpture.

Peter Voulkos (born 1924) has been in the vanguard of artists who explore the expressive possibilities of forms developed by potters. There are overtones of assemblage in his *Gallas Rock*, which was created by combining hand-built pottery forms. The act of putting them together, of crushing the forms against each other, results in some of the violence and excitement associated with action painting. Indeed, Voulkos might be regarded as an "action potter." He has taken the crucial step away from the pot as container and into the realm of sculpture as assembled, nonfunctional container.

Similarly, jewelry and metalwork, silversmithing and enameling, may be regarded as small-scale sculpture practiced with special materials. Woodworking in combination with metal, fabric, or leather, as in furniture, falls into the same sculptural category. The point is that the crafts seem to be emerging from their "previous condition of servitude." While they continue to serve practical ends, they also perform the functions of sculpture; the crafts must be seen as expressive form.

Beyond the Museum: Earth Sculpture

We know that almost all objects *in* the environment have been designed by man. Now, a number of artists want to work on an environmental scale. But their "environment" is not the designed local space of human communities; it is the entire terrestrial environment—mostly the land, air, and water outside heavily populated places. Like civil and mining engineers, or farmers, they would change the shape of the earth. Natural space, which has hitherto been the *container* of art, would become the object—or the victim—of the artist's designing impulses.

The results of sculpture's new ambition are called earthworks, skyworks, or waterworks. They yield a cliff wrapped in canvas, a small hole in a park or a great trench in the desert, captured stones and contained dirt, redirected streams of water, immense shafts of light or luminescent gas-filled bags of plastic sent into the sky. Like Happenings, these constitute objects or events that are frequently too vast, fragile, temporary, or distant to be experienced for long by many people; often they can only be heard or read

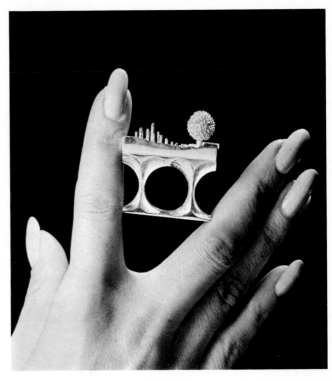

ROGER LUCAS. Three-finger ring. 1969.
Without a visual cue to its scale,
this ring might easily be mistaken
for monumental sculpture.

OTTO PIENE. Stage of *Manned Helium Sculpture,* one of three days of "Citything Sky Ballet," Pittsburgh. 1970

These gestures have little to do with the ecological ethic presently emerging. They are meaningful mainly with reference to what they reject in the history of art and in the implied revision of our ideas about artistic materials and forming processes.

MICHAEL HEIZER.
Isolated Mass/Circumflex. 1968.
Massacre Dry Lake, Nevada

DENNIS OPPENHEIM. *Annual Rings.*
Aerial photograph of the frozen
St. John River at Ft. Kent, Maine,
the time zone and international boundary
between the U.S. and Canada. 1968.
Courtesy Mr. and Mrs. Kelly Anderson

WALTER DE MARIA.
Mile Long Drawing. 1968.
Mohave Desert, California.
Eroded by wind within one month

ALAN SARET. *Untitled.* 1969–70.
Art Gallery of Ontario, Toronto

Dirt, assorted trash, and industrial waste have been dumped where they are not supposed to be. We are invited to examine them sympathetically—not as something to get rid of.

about. They can be commissioned, but they are difficult to purchase, sometimes impossible to see, and meaningless to own. Surely they cannot be exhibited in museums. In a parody of commodity ownership, the artist may issue a certificate to a patron, testifying to the ownership of an earthwork, just as a broker conveys certificates for shares he has sold in cotton and grain futures or pork bellies.

No doubt the terrible but effective depredations of technology have contributed to a conception of sculpture as an exercise in megalomania—a tendency further encouraged by the formation of organizations uniting artists and technologists. In addition, the upsurge of ecological concern has stimulated thinking in terms of planet-wide ecosystems; human imagination now ranges over the biosphere, the noosphere, and the atmosphere. Such developments open up extraordinary creative vistas for sculpture, and there is in earth sculpture the promise of prolific aesthetic offspring—the fruit of a marvelous synthesis between human forming capacities and the earth and life sciences. But thus far, earth sculpture constitutes mainly a change in the materials, scale, and ambition of art; it appears to be, moreover, a type of antiart—a gesture by artists that expresses disgust with civilization, resentment toward art institutions, and contempt for the artistic traditions of usefulness, object-ness, and meaning.

ROBERT MORRIS. *Earthwork.* Installed in the Dwan Gallery, 1968. Courtesy Leo Castelli Gallery, New York

ROBERT SMITHSON. *Nonsite.* 1968. Collection Virginia Dwan, New York. Through the progressive design of the containers for these rocks, Smithson betrays a forming and not merely a collecting intention. Presumably the rocks seemed too anonymous without their shaped enclosures.

Pratt & Whitney RL10 rocket engine, from advertisement for United Aircraft Corporation. 1969. Courtesy Cunningham & Walsh, Inc., New York

A fortuitous resemblance, of course. But consider how Henry Adams regretted the replacement of the twelfth-century Virgin by the twentieth-century dynamo. For us, the RL10 inspires faith—just in the seeing. Without doubt it is the sculpture of our time.

Snake Goddess. C. 1600 B.C. Heraklion Museum, Crete

LÁSZLÓ MOHOLY-NAGY. *Light-Space Modulator.* 1923–30. Busch-Reisinger Museum, Harvard University, Cambridge, Massachusetts. Sixty years ago, Moholy-Nagy anticipated many of today's experiments with light-and-motion sculpture. His machine is not only a working device, it is also a kinetic sculpture.

ANGELO LELII. Cobra Lamp. 1970.
Distributed by George Kovacs, Inc.,
New York

FRANCESCO BOCOLA.
Quasar Lamp. 1970

Further evidence of the powerful attraction that
contemporary sculpture has, not only for craftsmen
but also for industrial designers.

Conclusion

Of sculpture it can truly be said that in the midst of
change there is abiding sameness. Magic and sorcery
survive in an art whose materials and techniques have
undergone radical transformations. But through all
the innovations of form and concept, sculpture has
retained its identity as an art of physical material
occupying real space, persuading us to believe its
forms are alive. The history of sculpture is a history of
innovation in material and technique, changes in form
concept, and shifts in the interrelations of the various
media. But the pursuit of vitality remains constant.

Sculpture's loss of volume and mass—from the
monolith to the metal filament—and its gain in
motion—from the static statuary of Old Kingdom
Egypt to the kinetic sculpture of the twentieth
century—find art knocking at the door of physics.
But it is interesting that artists like Gabo, Pevsner, and
Moholy-Nagy—men with strong scientific interests—
grew increasingly attracted to the sensuous qualities
of matter as their artistic careers unfolded. To the
extent that they were sculptors, the medium continued to make tactile claims which could not be
denied. Sculpture is an art which involves us in physical reality. It obliges us to celebrate the world in
concrete form; the substance must precede the idea.

13

ARCHITECTURE

A BUILDING RESULTS FROM THE INTERACTION OF MANY factors: site, climate, function, materials, client, building codes, workmanship. For any given structure, one or more of these factors can assume crucial importance. But *all* of them must be considered in the solution of an architectural problem. We see the physical result, but rarely know the priorities which affected the architectural solution. It would be almost impossible to know every fact about a building's design and construction. It *is* possible, however, to know the materials and devices available to architects and to understand how they work.

Architecture relies on structural devices like arches, domes, trusses, and cantilevers, which can be made of materials like wood, stone, or steel. These devices are fundamental because they govern the space enclosed

Aerial view of Stonehenge

Model of Hypostyle Hall,
Temple of Karnak,
Egypt. 1350–1205 B.C.
The Metropolitan Museum
of Art, New York.
Levi Hale Willard
Bequest, 1890

in a building. Materials are important because they determine how structural devices operate. A truss can be made of wood or metal, a post can be made of stone or steel. Different materials require different dimensions to do the same job; hence, visual results depend on the architect's choice and design of particular structural devices *and* materials.

Now, in these choices the art of architecture emerges. There are usually several ways to enclose space, support weight, admit light, or finish a surface. The architect makes choices and solves problems in the light of *an idea*—usually an idea about the impact of shaped space on people. (Churchill once said, "We shape our houses and then they shape us.") If designers had no choices—if they could not *design*—their services could be performed by a computer, and architecture would not be an art. Indeed, some buildings appear to have been designed by computers, which means that the same architectural solution has been used over and over again. Similarity of needs plus standardization of building components have led to a certain amount of monotony in modern architectural practice. But the distinguished buildings which *are* constructed show that architectural problems are *not* alike, that design alternatives *do* exist, that architecture *is* an art.

The Classic Materials

The earliest builders used materials which were close at hand and in good supply. Then as now, building devices and techniques resulted from a combination of ingenuity and the inherent possibilities of available material. The African villager today builds his hut with sticks and grass because vegetable fiber is the most profuse material in his environment. For the same reason, the Eskimo builds an igloo of ice when he settles down for the winter. On the move, he fashions shelter from reindeer skins and bone, much as the American Indian constructed a tepee of wooden poles and animal hides. The humble igloo is a domical structure resting over an excavation in the ice, solving in its modest way the same problem as Michelangelo's dome of St. Peter's; and the Indian's conical tepee may be comparable as portable housing and superior as architectural form to the modern auto trailer. The African hut of grass and twigs often consists of a cone-shaped roof resting on a cylindrical base. Its materials may be simple, but their geometric form is, from an architectural standpoint, quite sophisticated.

During the great periods of Egyptian and Greek architecture, stone grew to be the favored material as the tools for quarrying, transporting, and erecting it were developed. But the Mesopotamians, having little stone, used brick and glazed tile for building. In most places, however, wood probably preceded stone as a structural material, or at least it was used as the supporting framework for "curtain-wall" surfaces of vegetable fiber and mud. Early men used stone for religious and commemorative purposes, as in their mighty *menhir* statues (upright stones serving as homes for departed souls) and *dolmens* ("table" slabs set on upright supporting stones and used as altars or open tombs). Such stone arrangements, which raised enormous engineering difficulties for prehistoric men, found more complex expression in the *cromlechs* at Carnac and Stonehenge. Cromlechs were circular arrangements of menhirs around a dolmen. They probably served astrological and religious purposes. The total plan of this organization of stones, with its orientation toward the sun, prefigured later architectural developments in the temple, the amphitheater, and the cathedral.

It is important to recognize ecological influences on

the beginnings of architecture. Egypt had not only an abundance of stone but also a great river, the Nile, along which heavy stone could be carried to construction sites. The wood of native palm trees was not very strong and the importation of better woods was too expensive. Hence, the Egyptians used stone roof lintels rather than timbered ceilings. As a result, their interior spaces look like forests of massive columns, since stone cannot span a very wide space. The Egyptian builder, who worked with little more than the lever, the pulley, and the inclined plane, had, in his slaves, thousands of efficient human engines. For the pharaohs, it was economical to raise grain in the fertile Nile valley, feed it to peasants, and exploit their labor for a lifetime greater than that of a modern machine. *Our* civilization would rather convert grain to alcohol and use it as fuel to operate machines, thus releasing men from animal toil.

Following is a brief survey of the classic materials —wood, stone, and brick—with observations about their working properties, their advantages, and their liabilities.

WOOD

Wood appears in nature as a working, structural material rather than as an inert, mass material like

Church of Lazarus, Kizhi Island, U.S.S.R. 14th century

SMITH & WILLIAMS. Detail of plywood supports, Congregational Church, California City. 1964.

Wood is warm in color, flexible in form, but alas, combustible.

stone. Its wide distribution in all but the most arid regions, and its strength, ease of handling, and adaptability to tooling enable it to compete successfully with many specialized materials. It can serve as a covering surface as well as a structural member. But the variety of its grain, the principal source of wood's beauty, also accounts for its structural unreliability. In the natural state, wood varies in strength; consequently, wood construction requires inefficient safety factors: larger dimensions than would seem necessary, and frequent reinforcement to defend against failure due to hidden defects.

American building has always been lavish in its use of wood, but design considerations, the disappearance of the frontier, and the development of competing materials will probably reduce at least the excessive and ill-considered uses of wood. Furthermore, wood has distinct disadvantages. (1) It is combustible: what must have been magnificent Scandinavian and Russian churches are lost to us because of fire. (2) Wood is highly responsive to temperature and moisture changes; its dimensions are not stable. Nails shift and slip as wood dries out and shrinks; joints loosen. (3) As an organic material, wood is subject to attack by rot, fungus, and insects.

Some of these liabilities have been overcome by technology. Plywood, for example, made of veneers of wood glued together at right angles, cancels out the tendency to warp. These veneers, made by a rotary shaving of the log, constitute a very economical use of the raw material. Also, plywood is more consistently uniform in strength than natural wood. It can be employed in skeletal structures or in stressed skin and shell structures. Wood in general is remarkably light for its strength. In the construction of small and medium buildings, boats, and aircraft, plywood is very useful. Laminated wooden beams create a vast array of architectural possibilities. Indeed, plywood, molded wood, and pressed wood, or fiberboard, constitute wholly new building materials.

STONE

Men originally found shelter under stone ledges and in the mouths of caves. They used stone for their earliest tools and weapons and kindled their first fires within stone enclosures. The stone fireplace is still a symbol of warmth and safety in dwellings otherwise bearing no resemblance to a cave. Heavy and virtually indestructible, stone was probably the first material used to commemorate the dead. But piling up stones was not, strictly speaking, building. *Construction* with stone began with the building of so-called Cyclopean walls—made by placing rough stones on top of each other (as in dry-wall masonry today), a type of masonry in which sheer weight and bulk produce a crude form of stability. When satisfactory cutting tools were developed, it became possible to shape and fit stones to create true masonry. It was then feasible to build stone shelters—not only for the dead, but for the living.

The earliest construction employed no mortar. Instead, stone and marble blocks were carefully fitted together. A knife blade could not be inserted into the joints of the masonry used to face the pyramids. The same can be said of stone walls built by the Incas of

MASAYUKI NAGARE. Wall of the Japan Pavilion, New York World's Fair. 1964. Stone-masonry wall given a contemporary treatment.

Peru. Since the Greeks did not develop mortar until the Hellenistic period, they used metal dowels and clamps to prevent shifting of the marble. Stone masonry employing mortar offers new assets: it does not require the precision of dry masonry, and it offers greater resistance to shifting. The weight and bulk of stones joined by mortar create a structural fabric of tremendous durability.

But stone is heavy, costly to transport, and expensive to erect. Like brick, it is rarely used in modern building as a structural material. Stone and marble veneers are laid over structures of steel, concrete, or cinder block. Thus stone masonry becomes a cosmetic operation—a far cry from the pure stone engineering of the pyramids, the Parthenon, or the Romanesque and Gothic cathedrals. The Romans may have been the first large-scale builders to veneer brick or rubble masonry with stone or marble slabs. The Babylonians used what little stone they had for statuary but followed a practice similar to veneering by facing brick walls at key locations with glazed tiles.

The prestige of stone today is such that great cities and important buildings must exhibit large expanses of it, even if some commoner material lies beneath. The Sam Rayburn House Office Building for the House of Representatives in Washington, D.C., cost between 80 and 100 million dollars, much of that expense due to the mountains of marble and limestone required to clothe it. Almost universally regarded as an architectural disaster (Wolf von Eckardt comments that it is "not only the most expensive building of its kind in the world but probably also its ugliest"[28]), the building is, hopefully, the last structure which will endeavor to overcome the defects of poor design with simulated classical masonry. The United Nations

Stone wall built by the Incas in Cuzco, Peru

Building, on the other hand, employs marble veneers on its end walls very successfully. Authentic stone masonry could never reach that high in a single plane: the marble frankly serves to accent the severe planarity of a tall, slablike structure.

BRICK

Lacking fuel to fire brick, and living in an arid land where wood was scarce, the Sumerians made sundried bricks much like the adobe bricks of the Southwestern American Indians. Even in a dry climate, however, the so-called mud-brick wall is subject to erosion and needs to be repaired regularly. Fired brick, however, is very durable and maintenance-free. It is really a type of artificial stone which has several advantages over natural stone: standardized dimensions, uniform quality, strength and lightness, wide range of color and texture, and adaptability to mass-production manufacture from inexpensive raw materials.

Since brick is a ceramic material, it tends to resemble a ceramic mosaic when laid up in a wall. But a mosaic is a type of wall "painting," whereas brick is a structural material. Today it is most commonly used as a brick veneer—it really *is* a mosaic. For modern usage, then, brickwork is valued for its textural and coloristic properties—its painterly qualities—as well as for its remembered association with the hand-fabricated wall. Because it is such an ancient material, brick confers familiarity on architectural forms which might otherwise seem unconventional. Its warm colors and its weather-resistant qualities inspire confidence. The viewer also knows that a brick wall has been laboriously built.

HARBESON, HOUGH, LIVINGSTON & LARSON.
The Sam Rayburn House Office Building,
Washington, D.C. 1965

The mortar joints of brick masonry are a growing disadvantage of the material: brick masonry is expensive. A large proportion of a brick wall consists of mortar joints which require careful hand labor; mortar joints are also subject to more shrinkage than the brick itself. Finally, a brick wall is fabricated slowly; for tall buildings, an elaborate scaffolding is required. That is why metal panels are used increasingly for the exterior walls of large structures. Brick offers good sound insulation but tends to transmit dampness, as does stone, unless combined with additional insulating material.

In the stone and brick architecture of Egypt and Babylonia, the amount of interior space compared to the amount of exterior volume was exceedingly low. Such construction seems to us not only inefficient but also appalling in its social implications. Perhaps the ratio of interior space to exterior volume in the architecture of any civilization is an index of the freedom of its people. Slave labor inhibits architec-

WALLACE K. HARRISON and others.
United Nations Building, New York, 1949

Spiral minaret of Samarra, Iraq. 9th century

The Mission of St. Francis of Assisi, Taos, New Mexico. 1772–1816. Basic building materials influence architectural form regardless of time, place, or building tradition. Sun-dried adobe brick requires the construction of walls of enormous thickness, tapering as they go up, thus creating inclined planes of magnificent abstract power and simplicity.

tural imagination. Today's light and thin-walled buildings create interior space almost equal to the volume of the whole—a triumph of engineering. Aside from aesthetic considerations, such structures reveal the valuation a civilization places on human labor, since economy of materials and maximization of usable space reflect, in part, the wages paid to artisans.

To say that wood, stone, and brick are classic materials does not imply that they have been totally displaced in contemporary architecture. They continue to be used, but less frequently for structural reasons. Now their contribution is aesthetic and symbolic, since they have been divested, in most cases, of weight-bearing and space-enclosing functions. The classic materials may linger awhile in the intimacy of the domestic dwelling. But even there, glass, steel, aluminum, and plastics supplant them in their structural roles.

Modern Materials

Steel, concrete, and glass are, of course, old materials, but their structural use in architecture is comparatively new. The Romans mixed stone rubble with mortar in the construction of walls, a practice which was really an extension of masonry. But the use of *poured* or *cast* concrete, reinforced with steel rods, is

entirely different. Similarly, the tempered-steel weaponry of medieval warriors has little in common with the rolled-steel I-beams in modern steel-frame construction. And the lovely opalescent glass bottles of ancient Egypt are only distantly related to the sheets of plate glass which fill rectangular openings in cage structures today.

Architecture has been hugely transformed by these "new" materials because the specialized techniques of mass manufacture produce a superior product on a large scale and at reasonable cost. Factory manufacture and prefabrication reduce costs and improve quality, while the handcraft operations which still survive in building are associated with waste, uneven quality, frequent delays, and confusion. Reinforced-concrete structures are usually fashioned at the building site, although some concrete beams and slabs are factory-produced like steel beams. But ferroconcrete fabrication is not a handcraft process in the classical sense; it is better described as a collective manufacturing operation at the site.

Laminated wooden beams have to be manufactured in a factory and carried to the site. Here again, the techniques of bending and gluing wood were known to tradition. But the older, animal-skin glues cannot compare with today's powerful adhesives. As a result, we possess the technology to exploit the lightness, strength, and resilience of wood in continuously

PIAZZA SAN MARCO, Venice. Begun 1063. Underlying the visual pleasure of the piazza is a governing proportion which can be felt only by people on foot—citizens standing, walking, or talking with each other. A marvelously exhilarating arrangement of space and structure, it depends on a scale that encourages human modes of watching, moving, and meeting.

ROCKEFELLER CENTER, New York. 1931–37. It was natural for
Americans, inventors of the skyscraper and managers of the world's
most commercial economy, to create megalopolitan spaces by enclosing a shopping area with offices stacked in monumental steel
and concrete slabs, rationally aligned and having a certain impassive
grandeur.

MARINA CITY, Chicago. 1964. Here is Chicago's pragmatic solution to the storage of automobiles (in the first eighteen stories of each Marina City tower), the storage of people (in the rest of the tower), the control of traffic, and even the flow of the Chicago River. These towers generate a feeling of masculine vigor that commands admiration.

CONSTITUTION PLAZA, Hartford, Connecticut. Hartford's urban redevelopment square was built by first eradicating an "antiquated" neighborhood—a solution that leaves a number of social questions unanswered. Still, the plan has succeeded in diverting automobile traffic, concealing parking underground, creating visual variety in the multilevel ground space, and organizing the enclosing groups of buildings on a human scale.

Safdie, David, Barott, and Boulva. Habitat, EXPO 67, Montreal. 1967. Safdie's Montreal mega-structure, like Rudolph's project for a Manhattan Graphic Arts Center, aims at fulfilling one of the great dreams of twentieth-century architecture: the industrial fabrication and construction of staggered, add-on units that afford versatile visual and spatial combinations.

Le Corbusier. Secretariat Building, Chandigarh, India. 1958. Le Corbusier wanted to separate the excitement of life on the ground from its inconveniences. At Chandigarh he created a vertical city of high-rise apartments, government offices, shops, schools, gardens, and theaters. This was his contribution to architecture and urban planning: to liberate ground space for the circulation of people, to segregate them from dangerous machines, and to shape overhead space for human beings to live and work in.

Prefabricated stack houses in housing project in Israel. 1965. Reinforced-concrete rooms, cast on the site, are lifted into place.

Interior, the shrine chapel of Our Lady of Orchard Lake, Oakland, Michigan. 1963. Laminated wood beams.

curved, load-bearing members of considerable grace. They permit the spanning of good-sized spaces without interior supports, creating some of the dramatic structural excitement of Gothic stone arches. Laminated beams and arches are monolithic members and hence can be erected by cranes, thus avoiding the complex scaffolding of stone masonry. The warmth of wood, the pattern of its grain, and the rhythmic effect created by repeated laminations make such beams attractive and practical devices for homes, churches, and auditoriums.

CAST IRON

Cast iron, the first metal substitute for wooden posts and stone columns, has characteristics similar to stone: great strength and weight, brittleness, and internal flaws or strains which develop as the molten iron cools in its mold. But cast iron permits the erection of tall buildings without prohibitively thick walls. Hence, the second half of the nineteenth century witnessed the construction of huge and often exceedingly delicate structures built with prefabricated cast-iron columns and beams. They tended to imitate the stone masonry of Italian Renaissance buildings, hence the magnificence of the facades for factories, shops, and warehouses built in lower Manhattan in the 1850s and now, alas, threatened with extinction. The Haughwout Building, designed by J. P. Gaynor and erected in 1857, is a cast-iron version of a Venetian palazzo. The Bradbury Building in Los Angeles is chronically in danger of destruction; yet it should be preserved, to show the delicacy of wrought iron in the hands of a gifted designer.

Cast iron set the stage for steel-skeleton construction in railroad sheds, exhibition halls, libraries,

market halls, and so on. Bridge engineers appreciated iron and steel better than architects, who had used iron structurally (as in the dome of the Capitol in Washington) but made sure to conceal it. Even today, few designers are willing to expose steel structural members if it can be avoided. When cast iron was brought out of hiding in the nineteenth century, it was often given a form based on stone or wood. Unlike steel, cast iron lends itself to a variety of derivative and uncongenial shapes. Since it is a plastic material like concrete, though capable of being modeled in greater detail, it has been fair game for some questionable sculptural impulses. The Paris Métro stations by Hector Guimard and the ornamental cast-iron columns, banisters, and canopies of other Art Nouveau designers show the material imitating terracotta panels or High Gothic stone filigree. Engineers like Joseph Paxton, John Roebling, and Gustave Eiffel, on the other hand, were the most authentic designers with metal in the nineteenth century.

John Roebling's Brooklyn Bridge (1869–83) used the compressive strength of stone masonry for massive piers but demonstrated a dramatic new combination of delicacy and strength in its steel suspension cables. Roebling (1806–1869) pioneered the development of engineering data for suspension bridges, but his aesthetic contribution lay in the design of a metal structure which could stir the emotions while it superbly performed a practical function.

Although suspension bridges made of wood and rope were used in Asia thousands of years ago, the nineteenth-century development of suspension engineering, so dramatically advanced by Roebling, revealed the structural and aesthetic possibilities latent in metal under tension. In the twentieth century, designers like Pier Luigi Nervi (1891–1979) and Eero

GEORGE HERBERT WYMAN. Interior,
Bradbury Building, Los Angeles. 1893

JOHN A. ROEBLING and WASHINGTON A. ROEBLING.
Brooklyn Bridge, New York. 1869–83

Saarinen (1910–1961) would employ suspension engineering to create superb interior spaces.

The Crystal Palace (1851) owed its originality to the fact that its designer was not trained as an architect and hence did not have to overcome the Beaux-Arts addiction to classical construction methods based on timber and stone engineering. The design experience of

Joseph Paxton (1801–1865) was gained in building huge greenhouses. His structure for the London Exposition in 1851 consisted almost exclusively of prefabricated wrought- and cast-iron units and glass panes, manufactured throughout England, and bolted together on the site, one story at a time. The Crystal Palace was then the largest building in the world, enclosing seventeen acres under one roof. Yet it was constructed in six months, easily dismantled when the Exposition was over, and erected again at another site, where it stood until 1935. The construction method and the use of an iron skeleton anticipated the present-day bolting, riveting, and welding of prefabricated steel components into a cagelike structure. Manufacture of standardized parts for on-site assembly was shown to be practical and economical. Masonry vaults and domes whose strength depended

SUSPENSION BRIDGE ENGINEERING APPLIED TO ARCHITECTURAL DESIGN

EERO SAARINEN. Dulles Airport, Chantilly, Virginia. 1962

GUSTAVE EIFFEL. Eiffel Tower, Paris. 1889

A COMBINATION OF BUILDING
AND BRIDGE IN A SINGLE
STRUCTURE

PIER LUIGI NERVI. Detail of Burgo Pape
Mill, Mantua, Italy. 1964

on mass and, as in St. Peter's, on iron chains embedded in their mortar, could be supplanted by thin mem-
branes of concrete or glass. Strength could be achieved
by substituting lightness and precision for heaviness
and bulk.

The Eiffel Tower in Paris, like Paxton's Crystal
Palace built for a large industrial exposition (1889),
was also made of wrought iron. Even though steel
produced by the Bessemer process was available,
Gustave Eiffel (1832–1923) built with iron since he
lacked performance data on steel in high-rise structures. In his specifications, however, he anticipated
steel-girder and ferroconcrete construction. His originality lay in erecting an open structure without the
expected masonry facade—a boldness for which he was
severely castigated. Nevertheless, the thousand-foot

tower went up, despite objections from leading architects and artists, and became *the* symbol of Paris. The
entire structure was prefabricated; it was assembled by
only 150 men using scaffolds, winches, and rigging
designed by Eiffel. The project was completed without
accident in seventeen months and established a
crucial precedent for skyscraper architecture.

STRUCTURAL STEEL

The principles of skeleton construction, known in the
1890s as "Chicago construction," were developed
with iron. Much of the distinguished work of the
"Chicago School" of architecture, leading to the
development of the skyscraper, was carried out with
wrought-iron or rolled-iron framework. Rolled-iron

I-beams were a vast improvement over the cast-iron columns used in American commercial architecture earlier in the century. But iron is not as strong as steel (particularly under tension); hence its members cannot be as slender as steel girders. High-rise structures (above twelve or fifteen stories) could be built with iron, but not economically. Consequently, steel has almost completely replaced iron in modern construction.

The cost of steel per pound, however, is higher than that of any other structural material. And, since steel has high tensile strength, rolled-steel-plate beams are designed in shapes which exploit that strength while keeping weight and cost to a minimum. The I-shaped beam is most common because the vertical section can be quite thin while resisting any force which seeks to bend it, and the horizontal flanges defend the beam against lateral bending. But large structural members, such as trusses and built-up girders, cannot be manufactured in the form of a single rolled-steel beam. They must be assembled, usually in the form of latticework, to reduce weight and to take advantage of the tensile properties of the material. The visual result is of complex geometric openings and weblike patterns of metal. Viewed from a distance, the poetry of steel construction is often very striking, as in the Golden Gate Bridge, for example. When seen up close, however, steel construction often appears harsh. Steel construction often exhibits an almost deliberate indifference to aesthetic effect. Indeed, when we think of engineering as inhospitable to art, we probably refer to some defiantly ugly steel structure.

But the technology of steel manufacture and fabrication advances in response both to the competition of other structural metals—notably aluminum—and to the requirements of designers. Welded connections may yield cleaner joints and better continuity within a structural system. Tubular, extruded, and corrugated-steel products open up new formal possibilities. Still, covering steel with other materials will probably continue because it is so difficult to achieve appealing surfaces with this material.

A few architects have successfully exposed steel members, thus converting a practical necessity into an aesthetic asset. In Maryville College, Maryville, Tennessee, the designer, Paul Schweikher (born 1903), shows how exposed steel I-beams can be exploited to give linear emphasis to large planes of brick masonry. And Crown Hall at the Illinois Institute of Technology, by Mies van der Rohe, is a brilliant demon-

A joint of the Eiffel Tower

EDUARDO TORROJA. A joint of the Tordera Bridge

SIR JOSEPH PAXTON. The Crystal Palace, London. 1851

PAUL SCHWEIKHER. Fine Arts Center, Maryville College, Maryville, Tennessee. 1950

LUDWIG MIES VAN DER ROHE. Project for circular
glass skyscraper. 1920–21

stration not only of exposed steel but also of structural function in the suspended roof.

The technical and aesthetically indifferent character of steel is often responsible for the anonymous quality of modern buildings. In general, the versatility of the steel frame places designers in a quandary. So far as the skyscraper is concerned, they do not know what to emphasize. Should it be a slab, a honeycomb, or a crystal? Is it an obelisk or a layer cake? As a young man, Mies proposed a circular steel-and-glass skyscraper. More recently, Gropius collaborated in the design of the Pan Am Building, a huge slab with tapered ends. But the building is less than successful. The glass skyscraper of Mies was not accepted, although other circular towers have since been built. The most spectacular is Lake Point Tower in Chicago, a modern version of Mies's 1921 proposal. Today, major construction in steel proceeds furiously in a variety of directions, with the Miesian idiom dominating high-rise architecture. But when horizontal space is desired, when the problem is an arena, a great hall, a chapel, or an airport, the most exciting buildings seem to be made of reinforced concrete.

REINFORCED CONCRETE

Although the Romans developed a mortar based on volcanic ash, it was not until 1824 that the first Portland cement was produced by Joseph Aspdin in Leeds, England. In 1868, a French gardener, Jacques Monier, hit on the idea of reinforcing concrete flower pots with a web of wire, thus creating a small-scale reinforced structure. However, reinforced concrete, or ferroconcrete, was not widely employed as a building material until the 1890s.

The continuously curved and warped ferroconcrete slab results in a structural member which does not imitate masonry, wood, or metal. Since complex stress patterns are distributed throughout the slab, there is *no distinct break between the functions of supporting*

ANDRÉ MORISSEAU. Marketplace, Royan, France. 1958

SCHIPPOREIT-HEINRICH, INC.
Lake Point Tower, Chicago. 1968

and being supported. Thus, the curved ferroconcrete slab is the logical and organic fulfillment of older structural types. It is also vastly more efficient than stonemasonry piers and arches.

Although curved slabs and shells enclose space in a pleasing manner, their curves must be correct from an engineering standpoint. But it is worth noting that as engineering criteria are perfected, their visual results tend to resemble natural forms. The eggshell, for example, is one of the strongest and most beautiful of natural containers because its curvature constitutes the most efficient and accurate relationship between its contents, the shell material, and the environment. Some of the most dramatic ferroconcrete structures exhibit curves which resemble the organic forms we see in seashells, honeycombs, mushrooms, soap bubbles, corals, and so on.

It is generally conceded that the joints are the weakest points in classical structures: they are the places where loads change direction and where a multitude of complex stresses occur. One of the assets of the curved ferroconcrete member lies in its virtual elimination of such joints. As with the eggshell, loads are distributed over the entire fabric rather than concentrated at particular points. This feat is accomplished by locating the steel rods at the points of greatest tensile stress, that is, the points where the concrete particles would tend to tear or pull apart. The concrete is thickest at points of greatest compression, that is, places where the particles would tend to be crushed. The steel rods are covered with enough concrete to prevent rusting, and they are given slight surface irregularities to prevent slippage after the concrete hardens and is subjected to a live load. As a result, ferroconcrete has the virtues of steel *and* stone without their disadvantages. Stresses are transferred back and forth between the two materials. A slab of ferroconcrete can span a much greater space than a stone slab. The ferroconcrete slab can also support more weight at less cost than rolled steel.

Elysian Viaduct over
Arroyo Seco Flood-Control Channel
near Los Angeles. 1964

Elevated highway,
Berlin. 1963

PERRY NEUSCHATZ AND GARY CALL. Convention hall, Phoenix, Arizona. 1964.

Aside from its practical advantages, ferroconcrete appeals to the designer because he can choose among several structural solutions and can express his forming and shaping impulses. Of course, his sculptural aspirations are limited by the wooden forms which can be built, the setting of the steel rods, and the process of placing the concrete. As the technology of ferroconcrete advances, more and more is known about the interactions between steel and concrete, the size of stone aggregates and the amounts of mortar needed to bind them together, and the usefulness of additives to lower weight, speed drying, add color, or transmit light. Such knowledge enlarges the range of potential aesthetic effects.

One of the supposed disadvantages of concrete is its unsuitability as a surface material. Many architects use it for structural purposes only, covering it with veneers of brick, stone, marble, opaque glass, metal, plastic, and so on. Others cover it with stucco and concrete paints. Quite possibly, cosmetics are unnecessary. Le Corbusier has shown what vitality and textural interest can be obtained by exposing the concrete and the marks of the formwork. Furthermore, rough concrete surfaces function effectively as a foil for smooth, machine-made materials like glass and metal.

Along with the steel-frame skeleton, ferroconcrete has revolutionized architecture by eliminating the weight-bearing masonry wall. Skeleton construction combined with recessed columns permits a skin almost totally composed of glass. Buildings such as Lever House show how appealing the tinted-glass curtain wall has become. The structural revolution brought about by ferroconcrete and steel has changed many of our deep-rooted attitudes about inside and outside, privacy and exposure, skeleton and membrane.

The Structural Devices

One of the aims of architecture is to enclose space. To carry out this aim, materials must be organized. Architectural structure, therefore, is the science and art of shaping, arranging, and fastening materials to resist the opposition of gravity, the attacks of weather, the wear caused by human use, and the processes of fatigue and decomposition within the materials themselves.

The emphasis on structure and building in this chapter does not mean we are indifferent to the role of architecture as a vehicle of ideas and emotions. On the contrary, an understanding of structures enhances the capacity to experience architectural forms intelligently. An argument for understanding structure is given by Eduardo Torroja: "This matter of the unseen thickness of dimensions is fundamental in construction. It might be said that it constitutes a fourth dimension in the interplay of volumes enclosed by the apparent enveloping surfaces. 'It is this quality of depth that alone can give life to architecture,' says Frank Lloyd Wright; the designer must be continually reminded of the necessity to make it easy for the view-

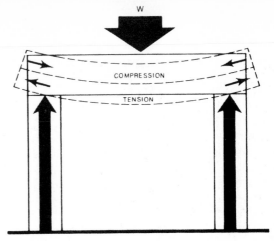

POST-AND-LINTEL

er to sense and feel these thicknesses. The work cannot be appreciated without that 'fourth dimension' essential to the nature and beauty of the whole."[29] In another place, Torroja gives advice to designers which might be useful for anyone seeking a genuine understanding of architecture: "One should become so familiar with the structure as to have the feeling of being, in full vitality and sentiment, part of it and of all its elements." The discussion which follows constitutes only a beginning of that endeavor to "feel" structure.

THE POST-AND-LINTEL

The post-and-lintel is the most ancient of construction devices and it enjoys wide use today. It consists of two vertical supports bridged over by a horizontal beam. The dolmen of prehistoric man was an approximation of the post-and-lintel, the upright stones serving as posts and the horizontal table rock acting as a lintel. In this system there is a distinct demarcation between the supporting and the supported members. Certainly its clarity of function appealed to the Greeks, admirers of precision in all things. It was also used exclusively by the Egyptians, since the post-and-lintel is very secure and capable of supporting great weights.

Stone, as we know, was the chief material employed in ancient post-and-lintel construction; in modern times wood-frame construction involves post-and-lintel as well as truss features. But ferroconcrete and steel are mainly used in modern post-and-lintel construction, especially in large buildings. The contemporary architect, however, may have different motives for using this system: the resolution of the principal resistant forces into vertical and horizontal components permits a high degree of rationality in the planning of space and considerable efficiency and precision in the use of materials. Further, since each structural member is very specialized, performing the function for which it is best suited, a high degree of standardization becomes possible, leading to prefabrication, mass production, and lowered costs.

WALTER GROPIUS. Workshop wing,
The Bauhaus, Dessau, Germany. 1925–26

FRANK LLOYD WRIGHT.
The Kalita Humphreys Theater,
Dallas, Texas. 1959

The post-and-lintel system is also responsible for the strong emphasis on window walls in modern building. Large openings permit wide windows, wide vision, good interior ventilation, and generous display possibilities. With supporting posts set back from the curtain wall, no structural interruption of windows is necessary; window design is restricted only by the optimum size of glass panes and the framework needed to hold the glass in place. The Bauhaus building, designed by Walter Gropius (1883–1969) in Dessau, was an early instance of the use of continuous horizontal bands of glass uninterrupted by exterior posts. This type of design became common in all kinds of buildings—but especially those in which a great deal of daylight was required. In the 1930s, factories were the main beneficiaries of the recessed posts and continuous window walls made possible by steel-cage construction. Today, designers rely far more on artificial illumination for industrial plants, office buildings, department stores, and so on, but the glass wall is retained if only because, viewed from the outside, reflections in the glass enable the frequently austere forms of contemporary architecture to harmonize with the environment.

In addition to its role in glass-wall design, the post-and-lintel system as used in steel- or ferroconcrete-cage construction affords regular spacing of posts and thus of partitions, creating interchangeable cubical spaces. Such spaces lend themselves to the methods required by modern commercial enterprises: efficient sale and rental of space; standardized design of fixtures and furnishings; orderly circulation of people; and maximum return on investment. It is easy to see how space created by arches, vaults, and domes is wasteful from a commercial standpoint. What is lofty and inspiring in a church or the reading room of a library represents an uneconomic expenditure of funds in a commercial structure.

WELTON BECKET AND ASSOCIATES. First State Bank of Clear Lake City, Texas. 1965

THE CANTILEVER

A cantilever is basically the horizontal extension of a beam or slab into space beyond its supporting post. Its free end is unsupported, and the point where it rests on its post acts like the fulcrum of a lever. If the internal end of the beam were not bolted down or counterweighted, the cantilever would rotate around its fulcrum. But since the inside end is fixed, the free end is rigid. The cantilever relies simply on the resistance to breaking of its material and the secure fastening of its internal end.

The cantilever principle has been known at least from the time of the first overhanging stone lintel. A tree branch resembles a cantilever; the strength-to-weight ratio of wood makes it suitable for light cantilever construction. But steel and ferroconcrete are the ideal materials.

As an architectural device in major construction, the cantilever has become increasingly feasible with the availability of strong materials at reasonable cost. For domestic dwellings, wooden cantilever beams can be used, but they cannot be extended as dramatically as steel. Multiple dwellings often employ narrow cantilevered balconies as sunbreaks. But the dramatic impact of cantilever construction is not felt unless an extension approaching the limits of the material is created. As with the suspension bridge and the lightweight truss, the defiance of gravity by strength of material and ingenuity of design accounts for the beauty and excitement of the device.

The portion of the floor projecting beyond the columns in buildings exhibiting a continuous window band is, of course, cantilevered. Its supporting columns may be concealed within wall partitions so that no interior posts are seen. Thus, instead of being extended freely in space, the edge of the cantilevered floor becomes an attachment for a curtain wall of glass or metal panels. Hence, the cantilever is not visible, although its operation is essential for curtain-wall treatment.

Exciting uses of the cantilever are seen in ferroconcrete canopies, roofs, pavilions, grandstands, aircraft hangars, and theater balconies. Here the imagination of the architect and the ingenuity of the structural designer combine to create some of the most striking structures in contemporary architecture.

THE TRUSS

The truss is an application of the geometric fact that no angle of a triangle can be changed without altering the dimensions of the sides. It is a system of triangles (with the exception of the rectangular Vierendeel truss) arranged to work like a beam or lintel. Such systems can be made very rigid, and thus capable of bridging exceedingly wide spans. Truss construction is used where great spaces must be spanned with few or no interior supports. Wood and metal are the principal materials used because these materials possess high

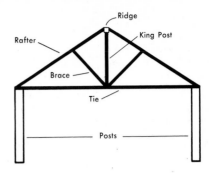

WOODEN ROOF TRUSS

Ridge
Rafter
King Post
Brace
Tie
Posts

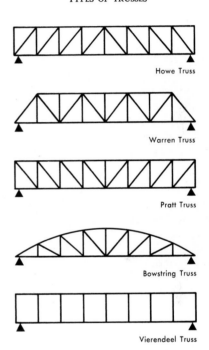

TYPES OF TRUSSES

Howe Truss

Warren Truss

Pratt Truss

Bowstring Truss

Vierendeel Truss

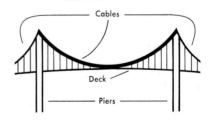

SUSPENSION BRIDGE

Cables
Deck
Piers

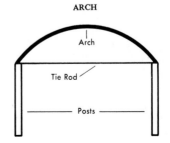

ARCH

Arch
Tie Rod
Posts

Roof truss, Old Ship Meetinghouse,
Hingham, Massachusetts. 1681

tensile strength for their weight, and most of the members of a truss are in tension. In bridges, theaters, convention halls, gymnasiums, assembly plants, and in most dwellings featuring gable roofs, the truss is indispensable.

The pediment of the Greek temple constitutes the most beautiful application of the truss in the shape of a triangle itself. This triangle has so firmly established itself in our consciousness that it is difficult to imagine a traditional house, barn, or church which does not have a triangular gable. Even though the short distances between the walls of domestic dwellings can be spanned by other means, the triangular-gable roof "feels" safe because of our long conditioning to its use. A flat roof is accepted very reluctantly, if at all, in low structures. Of course, the space *within* the gable roof has been useful in the form of a sleeping loft, grain storeroom, attic (appropriately a Greek word), or merely as insulating space. In the sturdy Cape Cod cottage, Yankee ingenuity found space for extra bedrooms, which accounts for the wide popularity of the New England saltbox dwelling even today. In contemporary homes, the flat ceiling can be eliminated, converting the gable space into the prestigious "cathedral ceiling." Furthermore, the gable roof also sheds snow and rain conveniently and offers a profile of low resistance to wind.

Although trusses are systems of triangles, their overall shape need not be triangular: most trusses are long rectangles in the shape of a beam. As mentioned above, they are a type of beam which substitutes stiffening struts, braces, or bars in place of the solid wood, metal, or stone of a beam. Other trusses may be straight along the lower edge and arched or paraboloid

along the top—the so-called bowstring truss. Usually the upper chord of a truss and its vertical members are in compression while the lower chord and the diagonals are in tension.

Anyone who has traveled over a bridge supported by a truss or stood under a roof supported by trusses has wondered how vast spaces can be spanned by such slender members. The insecurity we feel is usually based on our willingness to believe only in the strength of material under compression; we underestimate the strength of materials—especially steel—in tension. Most of the members in an overhead truss have been designed so that the weight of the roof works to *pull apart* rather than *bend* the steel braces. But because of the crystalline structure of steel, it is almost impossible to pull it apart, and the designer has usually given each brace a cross-sectional shape which will stubbornly resist bending. So, those fears based on age-old memories can be set aside.

THE ARCH

The post-and-lintel represents the simplest means of using gravity to enclose space; the arch is considerably more sophisticated. In both cases, vertical supports or columns are used. But the means of bridging over space—always the central problem of architecture—is vastly different. The arch originally relied on the compressive strength of bricks or cut stone. The separate units of an arch, called *voussoirs,* are in effect "welded" into a single curved member as they are squeezed together by the weight above and around them. The arch does not begin to function until the voussoir in its center, called the *keystone,* is set into place. As the keystone is the last stone to be placed, the arch has to be supported, during construction, by a structure of wooden forms, called *centering.* The curve of the arch carries weight to its columns along a path which is not only graceful but which also corresponds to the pressure lines over the opening which the arch protects. In other words, if a square-shaped opening were cut in a solid wall, and if we could see the distribution of the stresses in the wall over the opening, they would meet over the door to form a shape similar to an arch.

The arch was probably developed by the Mesopotamians some four thousand years ago. They found that wedge-shaped bricks could be fitted into a semicircle to hold each other in place and to support weight above them. However, the load which the arch carries to its supporting posts develops almost horizontal reactions, called thrusts, which tend to force the posts outward, bringing about collapse. That is why arches appear in series or in walls but rarely alone. The outward thrust of the arch must be resisted by some type of buttressing or by a heavy masonry wall. The area of masonry which surrounds an arch is called a *spandrel.* It prevents bulging or deformation of the arch under pressure. It was the principal mode of reinforcement used by ancient builders. A *free* arch, on the other hand, requires some buttressing, but it relies

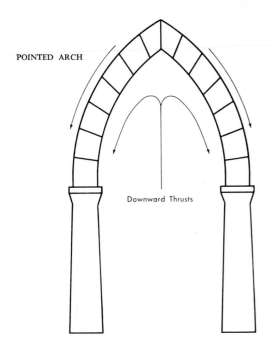

POINTED ARCH

Downward Thrusts

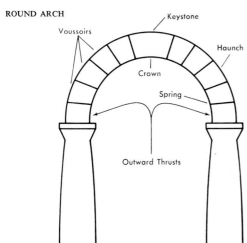

ROUND ARCH

Keystone

Voussoirs

Haunch

Crown

Spring

Outward Thrusts

Crypt, Speyer Cathedral, Germany. 1040

Pont du Gard, Nîmes, France. 1st century A.D.

EERO SAARINEN. Interior, Ingalls Hockey Rink,
Yale University, New Haven, Connecticut. 1958

mainly on the correctness of its design and the strength
of its own materials for security. It is the principal type
used in modern construction. The systems of abutments
and buttresses used in place of solid masonry to counteract the outward thrusts of the free arch grew out of
engineering necessity, yet they are responsible for
much of the aesthetic effect of late medieval and
Gothic architecture.

EERO SAARINEN. Kresge Auditorium, Massachusetts Institute of Technology, Cambridge. 1954

The arch was much used in Renaissance construction, in combination with the post-and-lintel, but usually as part of a wall and without external buttresses. The triangular pediment shape, based on the roof truss, was commonly alternated with the arch over windows and portals, frequently *as a decorative rather than a structural element*. Although builders of this period possessed the engineering capacity of their Gothic predecessors, their architectural tastes differed: structural functions were frequently concealed, while pilasters, blind arcades, arches, pediments, columns, architraves—the whole range of classical building— were exploited for visual purposes. Still, the arch tempts builders to become great engineers.

The arch permits high and large openings, and the successive positions of its frames help to establish a

rhythmic pattern of forward or upward visual movement. It is also a versatile device, lending itself to the rugged honesty of early church architecture, in which coarse masonry walls and piers were used for abutment, or to the delicate, soaring effects of Gothic structures in which weight-bearing walls were virtually eliminated. In both cases, tall, vertically shaped space was the objective. The early Romanesque basilica, however, emphasized a darkly mysterious interior, lit mainly from within; those chapels, like early Christians themselves, were indifferent to their outer garments. By contrast, Gothic interiors were illuminated by outside light passing through colored glass.

The pointed Gothic arch had the effect of directing its thrusts more nearly downward than in the almost horizontal direction of the round arch. As a result, its buttresses could be quite slender and its stained-glass windows could be relatively unobstructed by thick masonry abutments and cast shadows. In addition, the pointed arch raised the interior space. Eventually, Gothic ribbed vaults became, in effect, segmented domes, the area between the ribs being filled with a masonry fabric which functioned much as the membrane materials in contemporary thin-shell domes.

Today the free arch is used mainly to support bridges and viaducts and in association with large domical and vaulted structures. Made of reinforced concrete, steel, or laminated wood, the modern arch is a monolithic member—much stronger than its brick or stone ancestors. In wide-spanning concrete arches, such as in the Ingalls Hockey Rink at Yale by Eero Saarinen, the supporting posts are omitted; the arch springs (begins its curve) from the ground. Consequently, the action of the arch resembles the action of a huge bowstring truss, or a beam employing a single, curved brace. Nevertheless, true arch action is in-

EUGÈNE FREYSSINET.
Airport hangar, Orly, France. 1921

Chapel, King's College, Cambridge, England. 1446

aqueducts were arcades, successions of arches in rank order—side by side. Interior space of any size was spanned by arches in the form of a semicylinder—the so-called barrel vault. (Even the dome can be thought of as a shape which results from the rotation of an arch around its vertical axis.) The groined vault of Romanesque and Gothic building resulted originally from the intersection at right angles of two barrel vaults.

The disadvantage of the barrel vault, going as far back as the Chaldeans and Romans, was that it could not be pierced by windows without being substantially weakened. That is one of the reasons why early Romanesque naves were so dark. The replacement of barrel vaults by a succession of groined vaults enabled the nave to go higher; the vaulting had become lighter and did not require such heavy walls and abutments for support. By the twelfth century, however, pointed arches and rib vaulting began to replace the round arches, heavy groins, and square bays of Romanesque construction. The ribs were lighter than the groins they replaced and could be built wherever they were needed—not just at the points where the old barrels would have intersected. By multiplying ribs, the stone panels between them could be narrowed, and lighter-weight stone could be used, greatly reducing the total weight of the vault. As the ribs multiplied, for both decorative and structural reasons, the panels between

volved, since the entire member is in compression while the ground level serves as a tie rod or as the lower chord of a truss.

Because of strength of materials and precision of engineering, the modern free arch is capable of spanning enormous spaces while yielding considerable variation in shape. Its shape is not unlike the opening of a curved shell as in Saarinen's Kresge Auditorium at M.I.T. or in Freyssinet's airport hangar at Orly. Today's assimilation of the arch into stressed-skin shells and vaults recapitulates the evolution of the classical arch and the Romanesque cross-vault into late Gothic vaulting, as in the cathedral at Exeter and the chapel of King's College, Cambridge. Mastery of structural devices and building materials reaches the point where an almost organic unity is achieved; there is hardly any separation between skin and bone, between support*ing* and support*ed* members; the designer disperses the weight-bearing function throughout the building fabric.

THE VAULT

The classical vault was a succession of identical arches in file order—one behind the other. The wall was a masonry plane punctuated by arches. Bridges and

Nave (vaulted c. 1095–1115), St.-Savin-sur-Gartempe, France. Barrel vault.

Nave (vaulted c. 1115–20), St.-Etienne,
Caen, France. Groined vault.

them grew lighter, and their weight-bearing function was distributed through the whole surface of the vault. The result, as mentioned earlier, was a dynamic pattern of stresses which resembles modern stressed-skin or shell construction. The ribs tended to prevent lateral slipping, a danger of groined vaults which discouraged their use over very wide spaces. The rib vault, the pointed arch, and the flying buttress—all variations of the same device—made possible the triumph of Gothic construction.

THE DOME

The vault evolved as a solution to the perennial problem of bridging great spaces without interior supports while avoiding wooden trusses—which might burn—or stone lintels—which would break of their own weight. The solution was based on arch combinations. The dome represents another solution. A dome is essentially a hemisphere, although it can bulge into the bulbous shape of an onion, as in the multiple domes of the Cathedral of St. Basil in Moscow (1555–60). Usually a circular opening or skylight, called an *oculus*—or a *lantern* if the opening has a tower—is left at the top. The weight of a tower, of course, increases the tendency of the dome to bulge. That is why chains or metal rings were embedded in the masonry of classic domes. The Pantheon in Rome, built in 120–24 A.D., although hemispherical when seen from inside, has a high, thick mass of masonry on the outside surrounding it up to the haunch (the area on the curve of

an arch or dome which is about halfway up to the top, or crown), so that the dramatic exterior form of the dome is almost lost. It appears to be a shallow mound resting on a high drum (the cylindrical ring of masonry upon which the dome rests).

The placement of a dome on a cylindrical drum over a circular foundation is logical from the standpoint of geometry and construction. But most domed structures rest on rectangular foundations. The dome emphasizes a vertical orientation of vision, while the rectangle, preferred in Western churches, stresses a forward-looking orientation. Aesthetically, it appears to be an extravagant device for focusing attention on a point directly beneath its center. In the Middle East, where the dome probably originated, its ceiling was regarded as an image of the cosmos and was frequently covered with stars. (Even the modern planetarium is dome-shaped.) It had religious and cosmological meaning. The cosmological function survives in Western churches in the semidomes of apses with their mosaic representations of Christ as Pantocrator (ruler of the universe). For the same cosmological reason, perhaps, the Pantheon, the Roman temple of all the gods, is not especially impressive from the outside. From within, however, it conveys the sense of a world apart, self-contained and secure. Doubtless these qualities of the dome appealed to the emperor Hadrian, its builder. It motivated Pope Julius II to rebuild the wooden basilican church of St. Peter in 1505 as a great stone structure under a central dome.

A number of devices have been used to manage the transfer of load from the circular edge of the dome to the rectangular foundation on which it ultimately rested. The most common were called *pendentives* and *squinches*. The pendentive system rests the drum of the dome on four arches springing from four powerful piers located at each corner of a square plan. The arches meet the rim of the drum at only four points, however. Between these points are four curved triangular sections—the pendentives—which connect the rim of the drum to the curves of the arch and carry its weight down to the piers. Hagia Sophia in Istanbul, built under Justinian in 532–37 A.D., is the supreme example of a dome on pendentives. The great outward thrusts developed in the arches and pendentives are carried down by a beautiful system of half domes and powerful exterior abutments. The dome itself has no oculus but is pierced instead by windows running continuously around its lower edge, a device which creates the impression that the dome is floating. The narrow spaces between the windows seem to define vertical ribs which transfer the dome's weight to the drum. In the interior of the Pantheon, a system of hollow rectangular shapes called *coffers* seems to define vertical and horizontal ribs, although the dome was in fact built of horizontal courses of brick laid to form two shells between which concrete was poured.

The system of squinches, used by Byzantine and Islamic builders, is not as rationally articulated as the pendentive solution. It too rests the dome on four arches sprung from four corner piers, creating a square support for a circular edge. But in place of pendentives in the corners, smaller arches called squinches are substituted, forming an octagonal support at eight points. The octagon approximates a circle better than a square, and so, with some adjustments in the masonry, the dome can rest on what is, in effect, a polygonal drum. Squinches have the visual advantage of creating niches in the corners between the main supporting arches, forming semidome shapes which rhythmically repeat the shape of the major dome they support, as is seen in the detail from the interior of the mosque at Isfahan. But otherwise, squinches represent an *approximate* solution as compared to the pendentives in the world's great domed buildings: Hagia Sophia and the Mosque of Ahmet I in Istanbul, St. Peter's in Rome, and St. Paul's in London.

Cathedral of St. Basil, Moscow. 1555–60

The Pantheon, Rome. 120–24 A.D.

G. B. Piranesi.
Interior of the Pantheon. c. 1760

John Nash. The Royal Pavilion,
Brighton, England. 1815–18

397

Corn Palace, Mitchell, South Dakota. 1921. Domes, turrets, and annually rotated mosaic panels made of corn illustrate the uninhibited expression of folk architecture.

MICHELANGELO. St. Peter's, Rome. 1546–64 (dome completed by Giacomo della Porta, 1590)

Mosque of Ahmed I (Blue Mosque), Istanbul. 1609–16

Interior, Hagia Sophia, Istanbul. 532–37 A.D.

Detail of Mosque
of Ahmed I

View into outer portal, Masjid-i-Shah, Isfahan, Iran. 1616

The Architecture of Interior Space

INTERIOR, ST. MARK'S, Venice. 1063–94. Christianity is an indoor religion; hence it has traditionally required large, unobstructed interior spaces. The Byzantine tradition created them magnificently, generating immense surface areas for the play of light, color, and imagery. These surfaces were used for Biblical depictions to explain the faith; thus the meaning and function of the church structure were chiefly visible on the inside.

FRANK LLOYD WRIGHT. Interior, The Solomon R. Guggenheim Museum, New York. 1959. Wright's museum is like a cathedral—much in the tradition of early Christian domed churches. But unlike the mosaics of St. Mark's or St. Sophia, the pictures in this "church" keep changing. The building and its art do not explain, they only tolerate, each other.

LE CORBUSIER. Interior, Notre-Dame-du-Haut, Ronchamp, France. 1950–55. Rectangular openings in a thick concrete wall visually dramatize the process of light entering an interior at many eye levels. It is as if a sculptor had reinvented the window.

EERO SAARINEN. Interior, TWA Terminal, Kennedy International Airport, New York. 1962. The sweeping structural shapes and curved edges are clearly meant to suggest the trajectories of flight. The interior spatial expression is of a great womblike cave, with light from a multitude of organic openings penetrating its earthly recesses.

SAFDIE, DAVID, BAROTT, AND
BOULVA. Detail of Habitat, EXPO
67, Montreal. 1967. Superb opportunities for light modulation and
a truly sculptural environment
present themselves in the sheltered
transitional spaces formed by interlocking units.

MARCEL BREUER. Interior, garden
level, Whitney Museum of American Art, New York. 1966. Breuer
achieves a miracle of spaciousness
on a shallow site by moving the
viewer's eye through a number of
interpenetrating indoor-outdoor
spaces at the basement and street
levels. He compensates for lack of
acreage with vertical variety and
a masterful articulation of surface
planes.

LOUIS I. KAHN. Interior, The Salk Institute for Biological Studies, La Jolla, California. 1962–66. Kahn's detailing—his clarity in design of surfaces, joints, and changes of plane—results in a revelation of the total structure at work. There is no sculptural or decorative excess, only the expression of the building's integrity in each of its spaces.

I. M. PEI. Interior, Everson Museum of Art, Syracuse, New York. 1965–68. A monumental room in a small museum achieved by attention to fundamentals: honest and uncomplicated enclosure of space, a practical device for washing the walls with light, and a modest amount of wall punctuation that allows the art objects to breathe.

E. H. Brenner. Women's Clinic, Lafayette, Indiana. 1965. A complex of seven interlocking domes built by spraying concrete over a wire mesh framework resting on a structure of curved polystyrene planks. A band of translucent glass admits light, maintains privacy, and creates a floating effect—much as in the ring of windows at the base of St. Sophia's dome.

BUCKMINSTER FULLER.
American Pavilion, EXPO 67,
Montreal. 1967

SHELL STRUCTURES

Modern shell structures are the beneficiaries of reinforced concrete and superior mathematical tools for
calculating stresses and the strength of materials. As
a result, the classical masonry dome has been supplanted by shell structures which are usually flatter
and wider than their predecessors. Concrete shells
are so thin that their dead weight is negligible; the
engineering problem lies in maintaining stability and
resistance to buckling because of stresses caused by
rain, snow, wind, or uneven heating by the sun. Since
shells enclose a great deal of space with a minimum of
material, they are very economical.

Shells can also be made of metals. Geodesic domes
designed by R. Buckminster Fuller (born 1895) have
been made of aluminum, steel, wood, concrete, plastics, and even paper. Plastic and Fiberglas sheets

stretched over cable systems or metal-mesh supports
may eventually compete with concrete for the construction of shells. These materials create forms
similar to those seen in tents, kites, and umbrellas.
Shell structures have already been constructed by
spraying cement over an inflated rubber balloon, then
deflating the balloon after reinforcing members have
been embedded and the concrete has set. Sprayed
plastics and impermeable fabrics have design poten-
tials which are now being seriously investigated.

Since fair and exposition architecture is temporary,
it is frequently the source of new material applications
and structural devices. The Berlin Pavilion at the New
York World's Fair of 1964–65 was a type of shell or
tent structure made of vinyl-coated canvas stretched
into a stressed skin and supported by tension cables
and steel masts. Buildings of this type are not only
visually pleasing, they are also inexpensive. If prob-

Umbrellas over trade section,
Swiss National Exposition,
Lausanne. 1964

Architects persistently seek the tent
experience—for religious or secular purposes—because of the sense of protection
it fosters while we feel bathed in a
wonderful overhead light.

JULIO MICHEL.
Sanlazaro Subway Station,
Mexico City. 1969

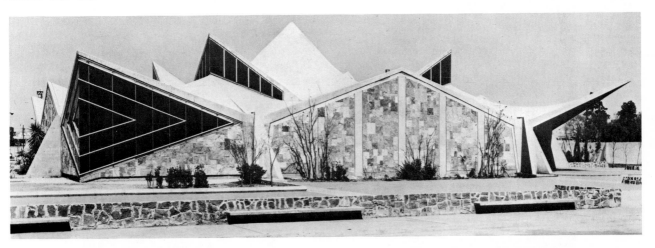

FRANK LLOYD WRIGHT. Interior, Wayfarer's
Chapel, Palos Verdes Estates, California. 1951

WALLACE K. HARRISON. Interior, First Presby-
terian Church, Stamford, Connecticut. 1958

PAUL RUDOLPH. Project for Graphic Arts Center, New York. 1967. For the center of Manhattan—a megastructure visually if not functionally—Paul Rudolph has proposed one immense, articulated building complex which would carry out rationally the unwitting logic of the island's architecture since the skyscraper mania began in the early twentieth century.

lems of long-term durability and weather resistance can be overcome, their use might spread to permanent buildings. Like the tents of nomads or the geodesic domes of Buckminster Fuller, these structures may cause a general revision of our attitudes toward temporary and permanent architecture. By radically lowering the costs of construction, new space-enclosing methods may alter total philosophies of design.

The ability to enclose enormous spaces may lead to the design of total communities in single structures—in so-called *megastructures*. Our capacity to do so has been apparent for some time—perhaps since Le Corbusier planned his Unités d'Habitation for large communal groups. Similar ideas are implied by huge hotels, ocean-going superliners, great shopping and entertainment centers, industrial parks, and resort centers. By locating all of their building

Two branch banks, both in warm climates. One expresses the engineer's intelligence and calculation while the other aspires to the picturesque, straining for sculptural significance and symbolic meaning.

REED, TORRES, BEAUCHAMP, MARVEL.
Chase Manhattan Bank,
San Juan, Puerto Rico. 1969

WIMBERLY, WHISENAND, ALLISON & TONG.
Model of Waikiki branch,
Bank of Hawaii. 1965

units on a single raised platform, for example, designers suggest the direction of the future: comprehensive design of communities through integration of their major solids, voids, and utilities in a single structure to which additional units can be added, clipped on, or removed as necessary. This idea does not represent a sharp break with the past, nor does it constitute a threat to individualism. Rather it confirms in architectural terms what is already a fact—namely, that communities are multicelled organisms increasingly interrelated by common systems of power, transport, communication, and government.

Constructors and Sculptors

Is any pattern discernible in contemporary architecture as a whole? Is there any common idea about building shapes or structural systems which pervades architectural practice now? The answer has to be that no single idea dominates architecture. In almost any given place, buildings are being erected which express divergent philosophies while using similar materials and structural devices. Yet, to the extent that contemporary architectural expression can be categorized, two camps can be described: constructors and sculptors. What is common to each camp is an attitude toward form, engineering, architectural emotion, and the purposes of design.

From the preceding discussions, we can see how structural and technological developments have liberated architecture from decorative, ornamental, and constructional systems which had existed for centuries. A revolution against applied ornament, the classical orders, facades false to their interiors, eclectic mixing of styles, and imitation of materials has been won. The turning point may have come with the great nineteenth-century engineers—Paxton, Roebling, Labrouste, and Eiffel; or it may have been the writing and example of the Americans—Sullivan and Wright; or the central Europeans—Gropius, Mies van der Rohe, and the Bauhaus designers; or the genius of Le Corbusier alone; or the great modern engineers—Perret, Maillart, Nervi, Morandi, Freyssinet, Candela, and Torroja. Today all designers enjoy a heritage of design freedom that has been used to generate architectural quality through an emphasis on (1) the revelation of structure, or (2) the subordination of structure to sculptural form.

The label "constructor" can be applied to designers who favor the dramatization of engineering devices to create exciting architecture. The word "constructor" is also used to designate the person who practices what Americans call structural engineering. In

409

both Europe and America, architecture and structural engineering are independent though cooperating professions. Today, while the professions are formally distinct, each shares many of the competencies of the other. That is why it is accurate to think of some architects as constructors—designers who try to exploit the emotional qualities of engineering. For them, the engineering solution is fundamental; architecture is, as Nervi has called it, "structural truth."

The label "sculptor" characterizes designers who are interested in pictorial and symbolic forms as sources of architectural emotion. They use engineering devices to build, but these are regarded as means rather than as ends. The sculptural architect is interested in the play of light among forms for the sake of visual excitement; he endeavors to create space-enclosing shapes that symbolize the purpose of a building or the attributes of its users. Such designers believe that architecture should be expressive of ideas and feelings.

Today, many buildings exhibit an elaboration of form which goes beyond the strict requirements of structure and utility. Philip Johnson's rich orchestration of domes for the museum at Dumbarton Oaks

PHILIP JOHNSON. Museum of Pre-Columbian Art, Dumbarton Oaks, Washington, D.C. 1963

HACKER and SHARON. City Hall, Bat Yam, Israel. 1964. An interesting wedding of art and engineering: the utilitarian structures on the roof—"cubactohedrons" —have been converted into powerful abstract sculpture.

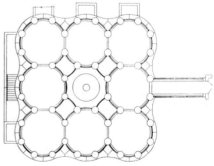

PHILIP JOHNSON. Plan of Museum of Pre-Columbian Art

involves the decorative rather than structural employment of a building device. The interior space divisions
indicate that the engineering advantage of the dome—
enclosure of large-scale interior space without internal
supports—is not the reason for its use. Instead, the
symbolic function of the dome—its creation of a
whole and separate world—has been exploited to
create a contemplative and mystical atmosphere for
the viewer's examination of small, exquisitely presented art objects.

From the standpoint of constructors—designers
like Gropius, Mies, Neutra, I. M. Pei, Marcel Breuer,
or Gordon Bunshaft—the work of the sculptor may
represent a turning away from the tenets of modernism. It may seem to be a revival of the old architectural traditions, except that modern materials and
structural devices have been substituted for classical
orders and systems of embellishment. In Yamasaki's
work, for example, Gothic arches of metal or pagoda-
like roof canopies in ferroconcrete are employed. His
buildings "borrow" the symbolic meaning of older
systems of construction without indulging in the obvious eclecticism of the nineteenth century. Edward
Stone, too, uses modern materials and devices to
create architectural reminiscences—particularly of the
lacy arabesques of Persian and Moorish structures of
the late Middle Ages. But while his arcades, columns,
and perforated metal or concrete walls may exhibit the
qualities of Islamic building, they also represent a

NARAMORE, BAIN, BRADY & JOHANSON
AND MINORU YAMASAKI & ASSOCIATES.
IBM Building, Seattle. 1961. Steel arches
at ground level covered with marble.

EDWARD DURELL STONE. Beckman Auditorium,
California Institute of Technology, Pasadena. 1960

Court of the Myrtles, The Alhambra,
Granada, Spain. 1368

HARRISON & ABRAMOVITZ.
Assembly hall,
University of Illinois,
Urbana. 1963

BAHARUDDIN BIN ABU KASSIM.
National Mosque, Kuala Lumpur,
Malaysia. 1965

FAIRFIELD AND DUBOIS
and F. C. ETHERINGTON.
Central Technical School,
Toronto. 1965

search for living symbols by a designer who is not too proud to base his style on the past. Stone endeavors to satisfy with modern devices the same appetites for patterned surfaces and stately shapes which were satisfied in the medieval architecture of India and Persia. Compare his Beckman Auditorium at the California Institute of Technology with the colonnade in the Court of the Myrtles of the Moorish-Spanish palace, the Alhambra. The forms are not identical, but the designer of the modern building has clearly drawn on the qualities of the older building.

Ironically, a Muslim mosque built in Malaysia breaks with the medieval tradition of Asian and African mosques. The new National Mosque in Kuala Lumpur, designed by Baharuddin bin Abu Kassim, features a huge prayer hall whose pleated roof of reinforced concrete indicates acceptance of the most modern structural idiom for large interior spans. Rather than revive memories of the Alhambra, a potent influence on Stone and Yamasaki, Abu Kassim has

PIER LUIGI NERVI. Little Sports Palace, Rome. 1957

built in the spirit of the Harrison & Abramovitz assembly hall for the University of Illinois.

Constructors take pride in an unsentimental approach to design. Indeed, the term "new brutalism" was used to describe the work of a British group of architects in the 1950s. An example, by no means harsh, of this philosophy of design is seen in a Canadian art school, the Central Technical School, Toronto, designed by Fairfield and Dubois. The building, framed in ferroconcrete, employs generous glass areas to light its studios, quarry-tile floors which are easy to maintain and almost indestructible, concrete-block walls, and movable plaster partitions. The rugged strength of the structure is not merely the result of a rough, poured-concrete exterior surface; it grows also out of a highly rational solution to the specific light and space requirements of an art school and the typical operations which must be performed in its studios.

Although Pier Luigi Nervi (1891–1979) was one of the great constructors, he probably used more columns than were structurally necessary in his Palazzo del Lavoro in Turin, Italy. The same is true of Wright's Administration Building for the Johnson Wax Company in Racine, Wisconsin. Nervi designed a modern equivalent of Gothic fan vaulting, and Wright's mushroom columns, like all man-made "trees," give scale, a structural reference to which man can relate himself and thus "feel" the dimensions of a great interior space. Anthropomorphic suggestions are not necessarily absent from the work of

PIER LUIGI NERVI. Palazzo del Lavoro Exhibition Hall, Turin, Italy. 1959

RICCARDO MORANDI.
Parco del Valentino Exhibition Hall,
Turin, Italy. 1958–60

EUGÈNE FREYSSINET.
Basilica of Pius X,
Lourdes, France. 1958

CURTIS & DAVIS. IBM Building, Pittsburgh.
1964. Here truss-wall construction serves as
the structural reason for a distinctive, diamond-
shaped facade and window treatment.

SKIDMORE, OWINGS AND MERRILL. Alcoa Building, San Francisco. 1968. The crisscross beams
designed to brace the structure against earth-
quakes convert the facade of this building into a
single, huge truss.

constructors: Morandi's Parco del Valentino Exhibition Hall in Turin and Freyssinet's Pius X Basilica in Lourdes express a sense of powerful supporting legs, arms, and ribs. Both structures are earth-covered and employ prestressed-concrete arches and braces. From within, one gains the impression of an enormous cavern or grotto.

Architectural emotion, therefore, arises from several sources: it can result from the careful adjustment of purely visual spaces and intervals, from the magic of geometry; it may rely on recollections of life under ledges, in front of caves, in the tops of trees, underneath woven boughs and bundles of straw, or in small

ERIC MENDELSOHN. Drawing for Einstein Tower. 1919. Mendelsohn's powerful ink drawing reveals his approach as a sculptural designer—one who initially *feels* a form and then creates a structure to match his emotion.

ERIC MENDELSOHN.
Einstein Tower, Potsdam, Germany.
1920–21 (destroyed)

MINORU YAMASAKI & ASSOCIATES.
North Shore Congregation Israel Synagogue,
Glencoe, Illinois. 1964

HUBERT BENNETT & ASSOCIATES.
Hayward Art Gallery,
London. 1968

Reinforced concrete is versatile enough to convey the slender grace of Yamasaki's synagogue or the formidable power of Bennett's art gallery.

PAUL RUDOLPH. Interior,
Southeastern Massachusetts
Technological Institute,
North Dartmouth. 1966

earthen craters; it may depend on the model of a tent in which a thin membrane barely separates a private world from the vastness of infinite space; it may recall huge stones modeled to resemble human bodily parts, the imagined dwelling places of procreative power and fertility. At different stages of his development man has sought to live in the bowels of the earth or on the summits of mountains. Depending on his luck and his mood, he reverts to one or the other. That is why architecture is so perplexing, so personal, and so diversified.

The moral and aesthetic superiority which constructors feel toward their sculptural brethren reflects the perennial conflict between abstraction and empathy, between the geometric and the pictorial. For one camp, architecture is structure, and structure is measure, and measure is geometry, and geometry is reality. For the other, architecture is sculpture, and sculpture is magic, and magic is illusion made real.

Design excellence in a distinguished private institution and in a newly established public institution. Here architecture practiced as an art results in shaped spaces that enhance human dignity.

LOUIS I. KAHN. Stairwell in residence hall, Bryn Mawr College, Bryn Mawr, Pennsylvania. 1964–65

416

14

PHOTOGRAPHY

IN AN ESSAY ON "PHOTOGRAPHY AND ELECTORAL AP-
peal"[30] Roland Barthes says that "photography has a
power to convert which must be analysed." He suspects
that photography misleads, that it is "an anti-intellec-
tual weapon." James Agee, a great friend of photography, also raises doubts about photographic veracity
when he says that "it is doubtful whether most people
realize how extraordinarily slippery a liar the camera
is."[31] Here, then, is an art form that requires close
analysis. And that is what we propose to do in this
chapter: analyze photography as a type of visual
speech and aesthetic power. We know that photography has an astonishing capacity to compel human
hearts and minds. If we could begin to understand
that power, the result of an intimate man-machine
collaboration, we might gain access to some of the
deepest secrets of visual art and human communication.

Today we are surrounded by photographs and photographic reproductions. Children encounter the photographic (or televised) representation of reality before they can speak. For the rest of us, pictures made
with light are seen so easily and often as to become
highly convincing substitutes—in fact, *preferred* substitutes—for the real world. But it is important to
emphasize that at the earliest stages of consciousness,
the stage where the attitudes and emotional habits of
a lifetime are established, we experience photographs
as real in the same sense that persons, places, and
things are real.

It should be remembered, too, that the wide influence of photography is closely connected to graphic
reproduction. This book would be impossible without both. Art as it is understood today could not
be taught or studied without photography and its
attendant technologies of duplication and reproduction. Photographs of works of art, and photographs
as works of art, give us access to more places and
objects than we could possibly visit in a lifetime. In
this sense, photographs are like books that permit us
to know the words and ideas of persons we cannot
meet directly because they live too far away, or because they are no longer among the living. To be sure,
the photographic reproduction of a building or a
sculpture is not identical to the original. But it resembles the original more closely than an English
translation of a Hebrew, Greek or Latin text.

All sorts of faults can be found with the photograph
as a facsimile. Certainly it is better to visit the Uffizi
Palace in Florence than to peruse its catalogue of
photographic reproductions. Ideally, one should do
both. But let us not forget the profound changes that
photographic facsimiles have wrought in our lives.
They have literally given us the capacity to see the
faces of humanity, the places where people live, the
work they do and the things they make. If these gains
have been won at the expense of demystifying original
works of art, divesting them of their remoteness,
uniqueness and preciousness, so be it. The fact is,
photographs transcend time and space and that is
why we find them continuously interesting.

In juxtaposing photographs with paintings or sculptures we invite the viewer to recognize their principal
similarities and differences. The main similarities have
to do with the fundamentally visual character of these
art forms, no matter how they were made. The differences have to do with the inherent superiority of the
photograph from the standpoint of fidelity to appearance. This superiority creates an illusion of objectivity and factual authenticity that establishes photography (and its cinema and television offspring) as
the most powerful instrument of information and

education the world has ever seen. So our comparison of photographs with older artistic forms is not undertaken merely to contrast their different aesthetic effects. In examining photographs as seriously as we study paintings and drawings, we are really engaged in probing the visual sources of human knowing, feeling, and valuing.

Photography and Reality

A close connection between the photographic print and objective reality was assumed almost from the nineteenth-century beginnings of the art. With the perfection of lens, camera, and plate it was the painter's eye and hand that came under suspicion as "true" recorders of reality. But if the photograph was more reliable from an optical standpoint, it was painting that gained ground as a vehicle of psychological expression, that is, of inner meaning. The dichotomy between photography and painting—between truth and poetry or science and art—persists into the present even though learned arguments can be given to show it is exaggerated if not false. The basis for

this dichotomy lies in the fact that the camera resembles in some respects the human eye; furthermore, it captures light rays and records them by a process that seems to exclude the intervention of the human hand. It was the painter's hand—not his eye—that raised doubts about his adequacy to deal with reality in all its detail. And it was the mass of neural tissue behind his eye—the brain—that raised doubts about his cognitive reliability. But the camera circumvented these imperfect human modalities. At least that was the impression created by its capacity to receive and record light rays simultaneously. As a result, nineteenth- and twentieth-century viewers attributed a special kind of credibility to the photograph, a credibility that they would not grant to any painterly style, no matter how objective or naturalistic. The photograph was seen as truthful in a scientific and historical sense; from that powerful combination of virtues came the idea of the photographic "document," the idea of a man-made image that is more reliable than words, less time-consuming, and more truthful than a human witness.

Critics and connoisseurs rightly insisted on the emancipation of the photographic print from painting

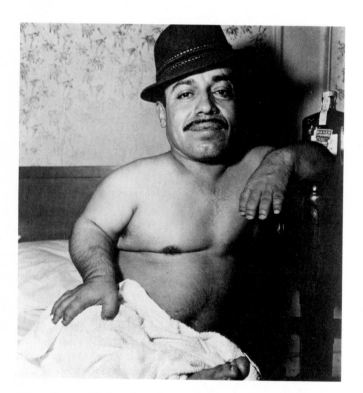

DIANE ARBUS. *Mexican Dwarf in His Hotel Room in New York City.* 1970. © 1971 The Estate of Diane Arbus

DIEGO VELÁZQUEZ. *Sebastian de Morra.* 1643–44. The Prado, Madrid

The secret of a photograph by Diane Arbus lives in her matter-of-fact approach to individuals who are condemned to be outsiders. Because she refuses to be shocked by their abnormality, Arbus forces us to look at them as persons when our instinctive reaction is to look away. The artist's victory lies in overcoming the impulse not to see, not to think, not to feel.

and drawing. But in this process, what is it that photography surrendered and what did it gain? First of all, it gave up pictorial quality and painterliness: it renounced the marks of the brush, the endeavor to simulate painterly blends, dissolved contours, heightened values, sharpened edges and exaggerated textures—effects that are relatively easy to achieve in the older medium. More important, photography surrendered the effort to represent what is known but not seen. That is, it gave up the effort to create symbols manually; it decided not to go down the metaphysical path. This latter concession was made very reluctantly by the earliest photographers because symbol-making had long been considered a vital function of visual art. But the emergence of the medium as a new art form came about precisely through this concession. By claiming to record only what is seen, the photograph offered the viewer a fundamentally new way of knowing; the photographic print assured the viewer that its imagery constituted a mode of cognition even more thorough and truthful from a physical and optical standpoint than the data delivered by human sensory equipment. No matter that the photographer chose his subject, selected "the decisive moment," and manipulated his print in a thousand ways. The technical character of the photographic impression was such that it participated in reality in a manner that could not be equaled by the most closely coordinated hand and eye. Some nineteenth-century viewers understood this instinctively; they believed that in seeing a photograph they came into actual, as opposed to symbolic, contact with reality. In the twentieth century that conviction became part of a general consensus. Thus photography became an art (as perspective had become an art in the fifteenth century) by entering the popular consciousness as a superior cognitive technology.

Photography and Painting

Historically, photography evolved out of painting. Its earliest practitioners were portrait and landscape painters. As the daguerreotype was perfected, life-size painted portraits went into decline and hand-painted miniatures virtually died out. As far as portraiture was concerned this was a simple case of technological obsolescence. The process was paralleled in the replacement of history painting by still photography and then newsreel photography which, in turn, gave way to television film and videotape. As always, however, technological obsolescence brings with it certain social and cultural effects.

Today, almost everyone owns dozens, hundreds, even thousands of photographs. And almost everyone possesses one or more cameras. And miniature cameras can be carried everywhere—concealed if necessary. So photography is now a folk art as well as a fine art. It is practiced—and practiced well—by far more persons than ever practiced the arts of drawing

EDWARD HOPPER. *Sunlight on Brownstones*. 1956. Wichita Art Museum, Kansas. Roland P. Murdock Collection

Both Hopper and Hofer are poets of urbanism. But Hopper is more strictly wedded to the city's rectangular relationships; notice how his couple looks at nature wistfully through a square opening in the canvas. Hofer, on the other hand, finds delight in a format of converging diagonals; she sees a speedier, more dynamic harmony in the repeated masonry forms. The result is a brownstone counterpoint that skips and sings. Hofer discovers melody where Hopper felt a pervasive silence.

EVELYN HOFER. *Brownstones on the West Side*. 1974. New York Times Pictures

DONG KINGMAN. *The "El" and Snow.* 1946.
Whitney Museum of American Art, New York

Both Dong Kingman and Berenice Abbott see the "El" as a
kind of carnival or bazaar. However, Mrs. Abbott stresses the
grittiness of the city scene while Kingman is impressed with its
melody. The watercolor medium seems ideally suited to Kingman's lyrical vision of steel girders and cast-iron lightposts
because it subtracts from their mass and presents them as a
collection of light, dancing surfaces. The photograph, on the
other hand, retains the weight of the steel: no danger of turning
the city's shadow patterns into tissue paper and lace.

BERENICE ABBOTT. *"El" at Battery.* C. 1933–37.
Courtesy The Witkin Gallery, New York

ARMAN. *Little Hands*. 1960. Collection the artist

Arman and Hartmann converge, not only in their choice of doll or mannequin parts to express the obscenity of Buchenwald, but also in their use of "real" objects to suggest the horror of a real event. Notice that Arman's hands do not touch; they are clearly dismembered and mutilated. Hartmann's hands and arms are intertwined and they reach toward the viewer rather gracefully. We have a more complex idea expressed in the photograph: it is a peculiar grace of writhing bodily parts. As viewers we are caught in a tension that is both moral and aesthetic—the contradictions between what we know and feel. Hartmann forces us to view the concentration-camp murders as a kind of high-fashion ballet. It is a deeply disturbing experience.

ERICH HARTMANN. *Mannequins*. © 1969 Magnum Photos

and painting. In addition, we have to remind ourselves that a century ago most persons saw themselves only in the mirror (which gives us a limited view as well as a reversed image). The middle classes and the rich might see themselves in more-or-less competently painted portraits, but the poor had no idea—no visual idea, that is—of themselves. Today, however, rich and poor see themselves in dozens of images— small and large, young and aged, formally posed or caught off guard. In other words, all of us have access to multiple images of ourselves, images recorded from a variety of visual angles. If we do not know who we are, at least we know what we look like to others.

Now the hand-painted image of a person is costly because the time of a well-trained artist is required to make it. The time spent by the painter is time spent seeing as well as making. Literally thousands of separate perceptions must be consolidated into a single image by the portrait painter. Even where the style is naturalistic and the technique meticulous, the necessary process of amalgamation entails synthesis, generalization, exaggeration, and simplification. Hence,

much as we admire the painter's craft, we know that it *changes* optical data. The invention and perfection of photography has taught us to see how painters change what they see. Oddly enough, we are less conscious of the fact that the camera also changes reality. Beyond that, most of us do not realize how much the photographer manipulates what the camera sees because we have been thoroughly conditioned to believe in the photographer's—as opposed to the painter's—mode of representing reality. For practical purposes this means that we regard photographic imagery as truthful while painterly imagery is viewed, at best, as poetic. Now the painted poetic image may be rich and eloquent, but photography introduces the idea that it is probably untrue. Untrue, that is, from a "scientific" standpoint. The photograph, on the other hand, cannot be false (we think) no matter who operates the camera. So photography has taken over the "truth" franchise formerly held by painting insofar as popular thinking is concerned. It alone can represent reality in a manner that still commands virtually universal acceptance.

The painter's use of photographs was often a fur-

IVAN ALBRIGHT. *Self-Portrait.* 1935.
Collection Earle Ludgin, Chicago

DOUGLAS H. JEFFERY. *John Gielgud as Shakespeare in Edward Bond's BINGO.* August 25, 1974. Royal Court Theatre, London. © Douglas H. Jeffery, 1974

Ivan Albright's *Self-Portrait* and Douglas Jeffery's photograph of John Gielgud portraying the aged Shakespeare offer an unusual opportunity to compare a painting and a photograph dealing with the same theme—the irony and disillusionment of old age. An interesting difference emerges: Albright's painting is hyper-realistic, more than photographic in its accumulation of detail. The photograph of Gielgud, on the other hand, is realistic by definition, so Jeffery does not feel constrained to drive home the surface evidence of physical deterioration. Albright builds a case against himself; the symbols of life's futility are patiently and lovingly assembled. Jeffery focuses our attention on a different sort of drama—the spectacle of a great Shakespearean actor, late in his career, playing the role of his aged master. The photograph functions simultaneously as a theatrical document and a work of visual art.

tive affair. Many regarded photographs as a crutch, a device employed only by artists who were weak in drawing, or lazy, or unwilling to take the trouble to work out their own compositions. The whole history of the relationship has been brilliantly related by Van Deren Coke[32] who shows with an abundance of evidence the full range of the painter's use of photographic "aids." It runs from pure and simple copying to highly sophisticated and oblique references to photographic ways of seeing.

It must be conceded that photography creates problems for the painter who prefers the record of the camera's glass eye to his own less "accurate" but nevertheless human mode of perception. In copying photographic imagery the painter may unwittingly copy its frozen or "stop-action" aspect. Or it is the characteristic camera distortions of form and space that he copies. When the painter does not realize that the camera inevitably distorts because of its monocular viewpoint, his copying results in an obviously inauthentic or "dead" look. Some artists are sufficiently experienced to conceal the photographic sources of their imagery: they can use the camera without being used. Others, however, deliberately simulate the frozen action of the camera image: here the painter chooses to represent a mode of representation. Some of the realist painters of the 1960s and

1970s were determined to remind the viewer of the necessarily artificial character of photographic seeing. But this effort, sophisticated in its intent, was fraught with peril: the photographic image is powerfully seductive; the artist may have begun with the hope of making a satirical statement about the monotonous character of mechanical seeing. But in the course of executing the copy (usually an oversized copy) it was the painter who ended up as the captive of the machine.

The Amateur with a Camera

The rudiments of taking a photograph are quickly and easily learned. And cameras are inexpensively available to almost everyone. This combination of factors has spawned a multitude of amateurs—persons who make photographs well or badly for their own enjoy-

Again the contrast between the photograph and the painting enhances our understanding of the distinctive excellence of each. For the sake of brevity let us say that their common theme is the impersonality of bureaucratic existence. Now how does each picture make its point? In Tooker's case it is through precise repetition of human and architectural forms within a fast-receding space. Duane Michals uses the same device: the central figure is much reduced in size compared to the foreground figure. His people are also destined to be swallowed up in a prisonlike office-tomb. But Tooker dwells on the paranoid atmosphere of the bureau, the sense of being spied upon; Michals emphasizes the utter alienation of man from man. His theme is Giacometti's theme—isolation. Here a photographic liability becomes an asset: the monocular lens of the camera produces an optical shrinking of the older, bald-headed man in the corridor. Thus we witness his tragic reduction in spiritual size.

ment. So we can describe photography as a folk art without denigrating its hard-won status as one of the so-called fine arts. Actually, a good photograph is good no matter what the experience, training, status or aspiration of the person who made it. A question that is more important has to do with the social, cultural and artistic consequences of the fact that millions of people—ordinary people—have the means of making fairly good pictures.

The most important consequence of the popularization of photography is the discovery that everything that can be seen can be photographed. (In addition, scientific investigators have shown that phenomena invisible to the naked eye can be made photographically visible; much research in physics, astronomy and biology, for example, relies on photographic evidence.) The idea that everything can be recorded by a camera creates an impact on the consciousness of the adult similar to the child's discovery that everything in the world can be named. It is a linguistic and ultimately a cognitive discovery. As millions of people made this discovery a fundamental change emerged in the philosophic outlook of our time. The technological developments that began in the eighteenth century were seen by the twentieth century as yielding benefits beyond the substitution of machines for human or animal effort; machines were now regarded as adequate—and more than adequate—substitutes for human mental and perceptual work. Who can doubt this in the age of the electronic calculator? The mechanization of seeing began with the perfection of the camera. And from this initial success there emerged a marvelous feeling of cultural confidence: not only seeing but perceiving and thinking could be mechanized. That is to say, machines would enable us to think faster and better—or more accurately, at any rate. Because millions of people were able to record the natural or man-made environment almost as spontaneously as they could see it, they developed a new sense of mastery over that environment—an environment that could be "captured" on film.

It is not generally realized that pictures—handmade images—were until recently the privileged possession of a small elite. The poor saw pictures in church. But the sacred place where they were seen, and the divine status of the persons they represented, reinforced an already well-established sense of powerlessness on the part of those who owned no images and certainly lacked the training, skill and equipment to make images. In a very real sense, therefore, the invention and popularization of photography in the nineteenth century had an effect as revolutionary as the invention of printing in the sixteenth century.

By endowing the masses with the means to take pictures of themselves and pieces of their environment, photography also raised the possibility that most people could understand what they were looking at. In other words, the amateur photographer became something of a critic—not only of photographic prints but also of photographic reality. Here we need make no claims about the amateur photographer's mastery of art or of his status as a connoisseur. For the most part, the amateur is more interested in the realism of his snapshot than the aesthetics of its visual organization. What we can assert about the fact that cameras are in the hands of millions is that the nineteenth and twentieth centuries witnessed a fundamentally new development in the history of art: (1) the privilege of owning images (a privilege traditionally confined to ruling elites) was now extended to the masses; (2) with the ownership of images went a quantum leap in the individual's capacity to see himself and his environment; (3) this privilege was perceived as evidence of enhanced capacity for self-government and participation in cultural affairs; (4) the collection of painting became, as a result, the increasingly specialized preoccupation of old elites whose status had already been secured, or new elites for whom the possession of one-of-a-kind art objects was a matter of pecuniary display. It is no accident that the invention and perfection of photography (as well as the technology of photographic reproduction) was accompanied by a substantial increase in popular political activity in those nations (France, England, the United States) which had gone through a democratic political revolution but had not completed a democratic social revolution. The widespread practice of amateur photography, therefore, was one of the prime ingredients in the generation of the cultural pressures that led ultimately to a desire among the masses to govern their own lives and to participate in cultural affairs on the same basis as aristocrats during pre-democratic eras.

Instantaneous Seeing

Because of the realism of the photographic image we tend to forget that its "stop-action" impression is artificial: we do not normally see the way the camera sees. In fact, a still frame taken from a roll of 35 millimeter motion-picture film gives us a somewhat better idea of what the human eye sees; it catches a generalized glimpse of things, a glimpse that turns into an image which is somewhat blurred and indistinct. The cinematic illusion of reality depends on motion more than sharpness and clarity of contours. In a sense, cinema proves that "there are no outlines in nature." So, aside from its small scale, its monocularity and flatness, and its more or less undifferentiated grasp of all details in a visual field, the photographic image is unique in a very special sense: it stops time.

When we say the photograph "stops" time, we mean that it condenses the flow of time into a single instant. That instant is indeed a moment in real time, but it succeeds in isolating a moment in the life of the object, lifting it out of its matrix in relation to what went before and what followed after. This visual isolation of a moment in time can be understood in terms of the physics of the camera. In addition, however, it has a psychological and aesthetic dimension: because human beings try to simulate what they see, the person who views a photograph tries unconsciously to "stop" his personal, or biological, time. As a result, the perception of photographic forms acquires a quality that is rarely experienced in the perception of painted, carved or constructed forms. To call that quality immediacy does not tell us much. What we see with the aid of the camera is something that is undoubtedly real and undoubtedly present when we are present. But somehow the naked eye does not catch this reality. Perhaps the eye sees but does not transmit what it sees. Or perhaps the brain does not register everything that the eye transmits. At any rate, the camera gives us access to a dimension of reality that normally eludes us. So the modern, high-speed camera exists as a magical instrument even before we introduce the controls and artistic outlook of the person who uses it. Like the microscope or the telescope, the camera "invades" a hitherto invisible realm and makes it visible.

Photojournalism

Art photography, scientific photography and portrait photography are older than photojournalism. However, the "success" of photography is more intimately connected to its association with print journalism and high quality, inexpensive print reproduction. By "success" I mean more than the popular acceptance or high commercial value of "sensational" news pictures;

Film still from *The Grapes of Wrath:* the Joad Family. Directed by JOHN FORD. 1940. © 1949. Twentieth Century-Fox Film Corp.

There is a continuous exchange of influence between photojournalists, documentary filmmakers, and directors of television and motion pictures. The Arthur Grace photograph here is very reminiscent of John Ford's film which, in turn, descended from the motion-picture documentaries of Pare Lorentz and the photographs of Walker Evans, Dorothea Lange, and Margaret Bourke-White. Their common theme is the timeless reality of rural poverty.

ARTHUR GRACE. *Nellie Hart and Sons.* 1974. New York Times Pictures

I mean that many if not most of the world's greatest photographs have been made by newspaper and magazine photographers. Although *Life* and *Look* ceased publication for several years, they were later revived. In their absence, their function was carried on by others. The tradition of photojournalism continues to operate vigorously in newspapers and newsmagazines and it is also felt as a strong influence on television news coverage and in motion-picture photography.

As the documentary photograph became our most trusted medium of information, its inexpensive reproduction by the printing press made it a prime contender with the printed word in a continuing struggle to occupy the minds of the public. If we reckon the progress of that struggle by the changed ratio of words to pictures in magazines, books and advertising matter, it seems clear that pictures (more often photographs than hand-painted illustrations) won the battle. When advertisers decided to shift most of their expenditures from magazines like *Life* and *Look* to television, they shifted to a medium that was almost wholly visual, with words spoken by a visible face or words merely heard in "voice-over" commentary. To

be sure the consequences for verbal literacy have been disastrous. Still, the public is not uninformed about national and international events. Indeed, it can be argued that functional illiterates are today better informed about world affairs than literate persons were two or three generations ago. It would appear that the technology of the cheaply reproduced image is superior to printed words from the standpoint of disseminating general information. Its superiority is such as to compensate substantially for educational or other inadequacies among persons who now get their information from reading pictures instead of reading words.

Photographs, inexpensively reproduced by the printing press, organized by skillful graphic designers, and supplemented by captions and text material, now give the masses an eyewitness account of contemporary history that seems to them more accurate than written history or print journalism. It becomes a pleasure to be informed. What are the sources of the immense appeal of photojournalism? Aside from low cost and ease of access, we can cite the following factors: (1) photogravure, and later, improved photo-

PAUL STRAND. *The Family.* 1953. © 1971
The Estate of Paul Strand

Paul Strand gives us a family of distinct individuals, mutually supportive but absolutely independent. Barbara Gluck Treaster's people are entirely dependent on each other. Where Strand emphasizes the spatial separation and parallelism of his figures, Treaster gives hers a common root in the old man's feet. All the forms in the photograph seem to converge on the little area where man and earth meet. Form and idea coincide. Each of these photographs is a masterpiece.

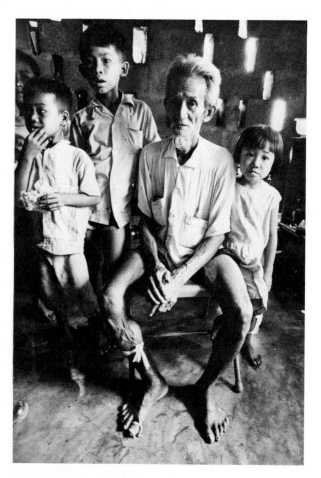

BARBARA GLUCK TREASTER. *Huyn Thanh and Descendants.* 1972. New York Times Pictures

offset printing, yield a very high quality reproduction of the original photograph; (2) the arrested or frozen action qualities of the photograph—its candid quality —make the viewer believe he is looking at an authentic, unposed slice of life; (3) the ostensible realism of the photograph gives it an inherent advantage over the more abstract language of print when it comes to reconstructing "the sense" of what actually happened; (4) photojournalism satisfies our voyeuristic impulses better than any other medium of visual or literary art.

Photojournalism has become the parent of the contemporary flood of books, magazines and posters devoted to visual gossip, sexual titillation, and hard and soft pornography. This potential was always latent in the nature of photography as a medium. The idea of the camera as a detachable eye, as an instrument capable of seeing quickly, from odd angles, and if necessary, surreptitiously, made photography the ideal medium of voyeurism. Here again, literature could not compete. The candid camera made it possible to see without being seen, to investigate reality without interfering in reality—a kind of triumph over Heisenberg's law. Photojournalism, as in the work of Dr. Erich Salomon, gave the world privileged access to the intimate meetings of international statesmen: one could catch Mussolini's facial acting—up close; a dead Confederate sniper by Mathew Brady—up close. The great war photographer, Robert Capa, said, "If your pictures aren't good, you're not close enough." Eventually he was killed. As were Werner Bischof and David Seymour ("Chim"). These photojournalists changed war photographs from pieces of history or literature or visual art into tactile experiences. The shocking qualities of battles and executions had always been somewhat softened by the abstraction and linearity of verbal accounts. Both literary journalism and historical painting had their built-in conventions for creating psychological distance. Photojournalism changed all this: it transformed the viewer from a spectator into a participant. Television might offer dramatic reconstructions of history entitled "You are there." But that was an understatement, especially when it came to photographing war scenes: the hand-held camera (still or video) placed the viewer's eye so close to the action that he felt totally involved—even in his living room. This was the "pornography" of war. In peacetime it became the "pornography" of violence. From there it was a short step to pornography in the usual sense of that word.

Principle of the Frame

The painter's picture frame had an architectural origin. This becomes clear when we realize that earlier pictorial types—mosaics and frescos—were a kind of "fill-in" art: they decorated surfaces created and defined by a building's structure. It was not until the

ERICH SALOMON. *Visit of German Statesmen to Rome.* 1931. International Museum of Photography, Eastman House, Rochester, New York

Erich Salomon pioneered the use of photography to show the world how statesmen actually operate. Visually, at least, his candid camera broke the barrier between the small circles of powerful men who negotiate the fate of mankind and the large body of humanity that looks on. His pictures are historical documents as much as they are works of art. In Teresa Zabala's picture the political photograph is carried beyond journalism: she gives us a psychological reading of these men that transcends the event itself. Whereas Salomon used the grouping of furniture and figures to generate an ominous, conspiratorial quality among his politicians, Zabala probes her people's faces, appraising them with a thoroughness we have not seen since the doctors in Rembrandt's *Anatomy Lesson*.

TERESA ZABALA. *Carter with Congressional Leaders.* 1977. New York Times Pictures

late Middle Ages that the pictorial image began to be seen as a window, a means of *seeing out* from an enclosed space, a room. Indeed, it was at this point that painting and photography merged in their fundamental outlook: the first *camera obscura* was in fact a darkened room that admitted light through a small opening on one wall, thus forming an inverted image on the opposite wall. Photography might not have been invented if Renaissance painters had not begun to think of art in optical, and, as they believed, scientific, terms. The whole development of perspective represented a radical reaction against the flat, conceptual approach to imagery that we see in Byzantine mosaics and paintings. Inspired by classical models of realism, and encouraged by a new scientific and religious spirit of openness to sense experience, the Renaissance artist undertook to see and represent the world truly.

Looking at a landscape through a window, or looking at a posed subject through an artificial, portable window—a rectangular opening cut into a piece of paper, for example—gives us the idea of framing as it was understood by the Quattrocento painter and as it is understood by the modern photographer. Moving the "window" closer or farther away from the eye enlarges or reduces the size of the visual field. And moving the "window" around in the same plane has the effect of composing the material presented by objective reality. This concept of composition relies ultimately on the idea of a portable window frame, a frame that can be moved about with almost as much freedom and spontaneity as the human eye itself. The camera, of course, is the photographer's movable window frame. Beyond that he has the device of cropping, a means of reframing the imagery he has caught in his print. Cropping has an almost metaphysical significance: it represents the photographer's "second chance" to arrange life. In cropping a print he treats photographic reality as if it were God's or nature's reality. Photography is not only a matter of selecting what the viewer will see; it is also a means of stating what there is to be seen. Thus, the photographer seems to create in a demiurgic or divine sense.

The ability to frame and crop reality lies at the heart of the photographer's art. These operations go by the names "composition" or "design" but they have a meaning in photography which does not obtain in painting. The photographic isolation or juxtaposition of objects occurs within the context of a convention that assumes the artist has "taken" or "shot" the picture all at once, in the presence of objects seen— not made. The order and location of the objects photographed may be chosen but they are not created. Even when subjects are posed, when the viewer witnesses a collaboration—a kind of conspiracy—between photographer and subject, there is an implicit assumption that the recorded image does not lie. Its arrangement may be designed but its details are real. So the photographer designs with reality. His manipulation of negatives and prints cannot destroy that principle.

Photography and Abstraction

In a sense, every photograph is an abstraction. Its flatness, small size, frozen motion and color (or lack of color) represent simplifications, reductions and generalizations of reality. Still, for a variety of reasons we accept these simplifications and generalizations as cultural and aesthetic conventions. That is, we agree to see the part for the whole, black-and-white for color, flatness for depth, and stillness for continuous action. Photographic abstraction operates in a realm where these conventions have not been established. Indeed, we may say that abstract photography deliberately "scrambles" our habits of seeing photographs. Its purpose is to gain new insights into visual form by surrendering the representational or mimetic function of photography. Technically and aesthetically, abstraction is the polar opposite of "straight" photography. The straight photographer feels obliged to let the print record everything—no more and no less than he saw with his camera. To the abstractionist, this procedure seems uncreative or excessively mechanistic. The straight photographer wants to "take" pictures; the abstractionist wants to "make" them.

There are essentially two kinds of photographic abstraction. The first might be called "straight abstraction" because it involves no alteration of the camera's optics and very little manipulation of the print during development. Instead, the straight abstractionist uses unusual angles of vision or he chooses to photograph unfamiliar fragments of familiar wholes to draw our attention to patterns and structures which, although they are real, cannot be easily recognized. This sort of abstraction exploits the convention of photographic objectivity to persuade the viewer that the real world holds infinite resources of undiscovered beauty. Underlying the practice of the straight abstractionist is the well-known formalist aesthetic, the conviction that the universe has been harmoniously designed and assembled: the artist's role is to direct the viewer's attention to that design. It must be admitted, however, that modern photography finds it almost ridiculously easy to offer the public hundreds and thousands of these formal revelations. While they may be admired by aesthetes, the public frequently finds them boring. Why? Because the discovery of the world's microscopic and macroscopic dimensions need only be made once. After that the public seems to lose interest. The formal dimensions of reality keep our attention only to the extent that they can be perceived as connected to the pattern of human concerns.

A second form of photographic abstraction can be called "synthetic" abstraction because the image it produces is almost artificially created and is virtually independent of objective reality. The connection with photography and the camera itself is somewhat tenuous; synthetic abstraction relies on the fact that, at a certain point in the creative process, visual forms have been recorded on a light-sensitive surface. Man Ray's *rayographs*, Moholy-Nagy's *photograms*, and Bruce Nauman's *holograms* testify by their different terminology to the awareness of these artists that their work constitutes an essentially new art form, a type of light construction. For the art historian new labels or classifications must reflect basic artistic changes; in synthetic photographic abstraction it is clear that a fundamentally different conception of artistic imagery is at work. The idea of the lens as a surrogate eye, or witness, or advocate, is substantially abandoned. The abstractionist photographer makes an image much as the abstractionist painter, lithographer or serigrapher does. So, from the standpoint of the history of man-made images, this type of photography represents a retrogressive development, a return to the manual fabrication of forms. However, it can be seen as progressive and creative if the art of photography is redefined as drawing or painting (by hand) with light.

The Photographic Slide

Many contemporary photographers prefer to make slides rather than prints. Indeed, more film is sold for slide transparencies than for any other purpose. Unlike the film negative which needs to be printed to produce a positive, the slide carries a positive image as soon as it is processed. The photographer projects the image on a screen to see or show his picture. Although paper-backed prints can be made from slide positives, the process is complicated and not as faithful to the original as when a print is made from a negative. So the practice of making slides rather than prints has grown in popularity among serious photographers and amateurs. The advantage of making slides lies in their low cost and the ease with which a large number of them can be stored and labelled for easy retrieval. In addition, color slides kept in a dark file box are less subject to fading than color prints. For this reason alone slides are especially useful in scientific and educational work. Nevertheless, viewers may have some lingering reservations about the slide as an art object: they do not normally see the slide, they see the projected image of it.

It is one of the truisms of our time that weddings, birthday parties and family reunions are staged for the purpose of taking pictures. As for the old-fashioned touristic pilgrimage, numerous jokes are told about people who do not really see the monuments they visit because they are too busy taking pictures. For the most part, these pictures are processed as slides that will be shown at home on occasions specially arranged for this viewing. So the somewhat ridiculous spectacle of the photographer thrusting himself into the most solemn moment of a wedding, for example, has a serious significance. In effect, the confirmation of the ritual—the authentic witnessing to the event—does not take place until a few close friends and relatives meet together in a dark room to look at and comment on a slide presentation. The wedding or Bar Mitzvah was not a charade—not exactly. It was a piece of folk theater meant to be solemnized under the auspices of the slide projector.

The aesthetics of the slide comes into play as we consider the image created when it is projected on a screen. What the viewer sees is light reflected back from a screen, or, in the case of rear projection (where the projector is *behind* the screen), light transmitted through a screen. The image can be quite large—cinema size, if desired; hence it can be seen by many persons at once. (Indeed, it can be projected into the night sky as at Las Vegas where, for five dollars, any ordinary citizen can have his image spread out across the heavens.) And, because the image consists of transmitted light, it is capable of carrying a much wider range of color and tonal values than an image printed on paper. The slide projection, then, possesses all the qualities of cinema imagery with the exception of motion.

As mentioned above, the photographic print produces its image by a process of darkening a surface—usually paper—covered with a photographic emulsion. We might say its forms are created by *subtracting* light from a surface that is white or off-white but surely not as bright as a source that appears to generate its own light. Hence, the slide projection seems to glow (special screen coatings enhance that effect) and thus the projected image is endowed with a heightened element of realism. For this reason, perhaps, students accustomed to seeing projected images in slide lectures may be somewhat disappointed when they encounter the original works of art.

The projected image is, of course, temporary. Although the slide can be retrieved and thrown on a screen for as long as anyone would wish, it does not have the permanent quality of a physical object, like a print which remains the same whether it is framed and displayed on a wall or stored away in a wallet. Because the slide gives us an essentially transient image, the photographer's work becomes part of a temporal experience much like theater, cinema, or life itself. But one cannot own pieces of theater or cinema; one can only own the right to see them. Similarly, one does not own a library book, only the right to use it. So it is not difficult to predict a time when people will borrow or rent photographic slides, much as they now borrow books, phonograph records and film reels or cassettes. From an economic standpoint this means that a fee will be paid—as with cinema—for viewing time, for an experience rather than the possession of a commodity.

If the slide represents one line of photographic evolution—the line that connects it to cinema and television—there are nevertheless other forces that connect photography to graphic art. Certainly the frame format is very important and it is directly inherited from painting. For many photographers and viewers it is difficult to conceive of the aesthetics of photography apart from a picture matted and framed in a size close to that of a drawing, etching or easel painting. But the size constraints of the graphic arts are also social constraints. They can only be overcome by inexpensive print reproduction. The slide projection, on the other hand, is tailor-made for collective beholding. Furthermore, the slide image (or the image created by projecting several slides simultaneously) is more or less unaffected by the idea of an enclosing edge created by a carved molding. As its edges dissolve, the slide image tends to destroy the idea of a photograph as a graspable object. The slide seems to enter experience in a dematerialized fashion, like light or air. It would appear that the size and shape of the slide projection are limited only by the physiological and cognitive capabilities of the human organism. So it is easy to foresee a time when the slide will evolve into something beyond photography while the photographic print consolidates and perfects the aesthetics of pictorial design. Like the older art forms, photography will continue to spawn new offspring while itself remaining essentially the same.

The Photographer as Artist

Oddly enough, photographic amateurism introduces distinctively new social and aesthetic considerations to the practice of photography as a "fine art." The factors that account for the spread of amateurism have an important influence on the work of the serious photographer: his inexpensive and easily used technology make it possible for the photographic artist to function far more independently than the painter, sculptor or filmmaker. Photographic prints can be cheaply reproduced and they are not difficult to display. Indeed they can be passed from hand to hand. Unlike the writer, the photographer does not depend on the costly technology of the printing industry; he need not contend with editors and publishers (unless he is a photojournalist); and he can function without the presumption of a literate reading public. Unlike the filmmaker, he does not depend on a team of skilled technicians, trade union regulations, large capitalization, and powerful organizations of film distributors and exhibitors. Because his training and equipment are relatively inexpensive, the photographic artist need not be subsidized for a long time; unlike painters and sculptors who traditionally have had middle-class origins, the photographer can come out

CLAES OLDENBURG. *The Stove.* 1962.
Private collection

The bitter, derisory statement made by Oldenburg's stove relies, in a sense, on the homely old image of a stove in the Evans photograph. Before he could make it ridiculous, Oldenburg had to festoon the stove with large portions of specially constructed, inedible food. Evans, on the other hand, celebrates the beloved cast-iron monster as the only solid, durable object in a seedy environment. The photographer's manipulation of context—the frontal "pose" of the stove, the decision to "place" the pots and pans at eye-level—is less obvious than Oldenburg's manufacture of a sleazy meal. But it is no less an act of artistic selection and organization.

WALKER EVANS. *Frank's Stove, Cape Breton Island.* 1971.
Yale University Art Gallery, New Haven.
Director's Purchase Fund

The bound or wrapped figure has been used as a symbol of confined power from Michelangelo to Rodin (see the *Balzac*) to Christo. Carolyn Watson's photograph retains the form but changes its meaning; her figures are more nearly related to Henry Moore's sleepers in the London underground during World War II. Why is this a great photograph? Because Watson saw a universal image in these two sleepers. Her print transcends the fact that two Americans had to bed down on a bench in London because of a shortage of hotel rooms. It is the capacity to leap from the recording of a local event to the representation of a general idea that accounts for the extraordinary potency of *Crash Pad.*

of the poor or working classes. Hence photographers often operate outside the constraints of educational and institutional orthodoxies; they are not especially dependent on the patronage of wealthy collectors. In this respect, at least, the photographic artist resembles the printmaker or independent craftsman: if he does not control museum or gallery access to the public he can gain access without too much trouble, mainly because his work can be priced so that it is affordable by large numbers of low- or middle- income people.

Cheapness of equipment and supplies has artistic and aesthetic consequences. Because the same mechanical equipment is available to almost everyone, the photographer's *attitude* is thrown into sharp relief as the distinctive instrument of his art. The painter's eyes, fingers and wrist are unique, and they are integral parts of the act of painting; we cannot make the same claim for the photographer's finger on the shutter-release. So his visual, intellectual, and moral qualities become crucial. The camera is fast enough to catch anything; and having no built-in mechanism of selection it necessarily depends on the intelligence and integrity of the photographer as a person as well as an artist. Since the camera cannot reject, the photographer's decision-making turns out to be the most creatively significant aspect of his art. But choices instantaneously made depend on a lengthy period of incubation. Photography is more than a type of mechanical seeing; it presupposes a capacity to know what is interesting, what is significant as opposed to strange or peculiar, and what is humanly *worth* seeing.

In emphasizing mental preparation as being crucial for the photographer we also imply that knowing what not to see is an essential component of his creative act. This does not mean that sensuous, unpremeditated delight in seeing is necessarily relegated to a secondary place. It does mean that a photographer who consistently takes good pictures has more than luck on his side; he is obviously *looking for something,* and good pictures are proof of his skill as a discoverer. The photographer's capacity for discovery lends a distinctive artistic element to the viewer's experience since the viewer participates in a kind of discovery-by-proxy. The viewer expects the photograph to be the product of informed seeing; otherwise it will not be regarded as an aesthetically significant event. It is deliberate and knowledgeable seeing that establishes the photographer's dominance over his equipment. As with all visual art, the spectator wants to believe that his perceptions have been shaped and guided by an exceptional human intelligence; otherwise the cognitive and expressive values of the photograph turn into a matter of ordinary optical recording. Ultimately, therefore, the great photographers impart the sense of encountering the world through *the mind* of an artist, an artist whose personal and social biases are discernible. Even when we do not share those biases we need to be convinced they are there. In photography, point-of-view has both ideological and optical significance.

Photographic Criticism

The criticism of photography is largely undeveloped for three reasons. First, in its perfected form the medium is only about two-thirds of a century old—hardly long enough to have developed a sophisticated body of aesthetic theory. Second, most scholarly writing about photography deals either with technical questions or the history of photography, that is, the history of camera equipment and developing processes and the biographies of famous photographers. Third, in its struggle to emancipate itself from the parent art of painting, photographic criticism has tended to avoid the aesthetic theories developed in connection with the older fine arts. It should be added, too, that conventionally trained art historians and critics have not paid much attention to the evolution of photography as an art. Although they often mention the influence of photography on Courbet, or on Degas and the French Impressionists, they rarely discuss the role of photography in our visual culture as a whole; they ignore the changes photography has wrought on contemporary modes of seeing and thinking. Without addressing these questions, however, photographic criticism hardly rises above shop talk; the central problems of aesthetic value are encountered only if the critic deals with photography as it confronts the major questions of mankind and society.

The battle to recognize photography as a full-fledged art form was fought and won years ago—by Alfred Stieglitz, Edward Steichen, Beaumont Newhall, Minor White, Helmut Gernsheim, John Szarkowski, Aaron Scharf, Peter Pollack, Van Deren Coke, and numerous other distinguished photographers, historians and museum curators. The winning of this battle had important consequences for criticism: membership in the fine arts "club" meant that photographs could be judged, in general, like other works of visual art. The early status of photography as a bastard art form had exempted the medium from serious consideration according to the formalist, expressivist or instrumentalist grounds discussed, for example, in the chapters on art criticism in this book. Now it is clear that, as with painting or printmaking, differences of medium and technique do not create for photography a wholly new set of aesthetic expectations. And the reason is that while sources of artistic form may vary, human needs with respect to any visual presentation are remarkably similar and consistent. So the general factors that make a photograph good or important are similar to those that operate in the case of drawings, paintings and prints.

But if the criteria of greatness in the various forms of visual art are generally the same, there are nevertheless "local" factors that operate more or less uniquely in the case of photography. These grow out of the technical features of the camera, the physical character of the photographic print, and the economic factors that govern the reproduction, distribution and ownership of photographs. We should especially emphasize the small size of the photograph—its portability and accessibility as a hand-held object. Its size relates it to the medieval breviary as well as to the modern book or magazine. In any discussion of the photograph as a work of art, therefore, we should remember its graspable quality and hence its capacity to enter our experience as a tactile as well as an optical object. The photograph is a possession that can be carried everywhere because it fits into a wallet or purse. Indeed, photographs or photoreproductions have been exchanged like paper money. Like money, photographs can be counted and examined in absolute privacy. And, like books, they can be privately studied and savored. Yet the photograph can also be vastly enlarged. As large-scale images for the information and display industries, photographs are perhaps the most public of visual art forms. Among the modern media, neither cinema nor television has so wide a range of size and accessibility. Only the "stillness" of the photograph, its tendency to "freeze" rather than mimic motion, prevents it from entering the dimension of continuous time and thus playing as large a role in the shaping of popular consciousness as television and cinema.

We come, then, to the distinctively photographic criteria of excellence. What are the aesthetic qualities of a great photograph as opposed to the technical traits of a very fine photographic print? We must, of course, judge the merit of a photograph according to its ability to meet the opportunities of the medium and to overcome the limitations presented by its technology. But it is important not to forget the above-mentioned discussion of photography as a cognitive art, an art that affords us a unique mode of knowing through a man-made way of seeing. Ideally, therefore, a theory of photographic excellence should help us discern the connections between technique and cognitive quality; that is, it should enable us to recognize quality in the interactions between medium and meaning.

In my opinion, a theory of photographic criticism must begin with the classical Greek doctrine of *mimesis*. Accordingly, the goodness of a photograph would lie in the validity of its claim to be a truthful imitation of reality. That truthfulness must first be created in the person of the artist. Only then can it be carried out with the tools and in the medium of his art. Both Plato and Aristotle recognize the role of the artist as a creator rather than a mirror or recorder of reality: the artist acts intellectually upon nature and natural materials, bringing to completion what nature has not finished. This accords with our notion of the photographer as a person who interferes with reality by "taking" pictures, by stopping natural action, by isolating fragments of natural appearance, and by imposing his own vision upon reality in "framing" sets of objects and forms. While a specific image of reality does not preexist in the photographer's mind, an artistic order or form does preexist to the extent that the photographer is mentally prepared to recognize and imitate the authentic and morally effective operation of universal laws. He sees these laws in the appearance of natural processes and in the visible products of human work. In other words, the photographic image or icon does not come ready-made; it requires the agency of the artist (in this case, the photographer), a person who possesses the requisite skills and mental development to impose form on matter.

Given this definition of the photographer as artist, what can we say about good and bad photographs? I think we can identify certain qualities that photographs must possess uniquely to be judged excellent. These qualities can be designated as positions on six bipolar scales or *continua* in which the first pole stands for a deficiency or minimum of quality and the second pole represents its plenitude. Since a given photograph—even a masterpiece—is unlikely to fulfill all of our ideal expectations we have to make an estimate of its cumulative achievement on all the scales in order to form an overall judgment of the merit of a particular photographic work.

Following are the scales I propose for estimating or judging photographic excellence: (1) from surface to depth, (2) from optical to tactile, (3) from pattern to idea, (4) from part to whole, (5) from singular to typical, and (6) from copy to original. The first three scales are meant to consider technical qualities to the extent that they are seen as vehicles of formal, cognitive or expressive value. The last three scales are meant to suggest the larger, conceptual considerations which enter into the evaluation of a photograph that meets our technical requirements. A photograph that "scores high" on any one of these scales would have to be interesting; a high evaluation on several scales would testify to the possibility of a masterpiece. The discussion in Chapter Sixteen, dealing with *Kinds of Critical Judgment*, may be helpful to the reader in justifying and applying general criteria of excellence to the evaluation of outstanding work of photographic art.

FROM SURFACE TO DEPTH

Obviously, this does not refer to depth-of-field, a matter of the right aperture and focal length of the lens. Photographic depth can be defined as the volumetric quality of form, the lack of which is felt as thinness, flatness or lightness. Lightness should not be confused with airiness or luminosity. Here it means an unconvincing representation of the mass or specific gravity of forms—a persistent problem in all pictorial and planographic art and especially in photography. To some extent, lightness or thinness is a technical fault due to improper exposure and/or poor lighting. But it is more fundamentally the product of the photographer's failure to visualize the hidden forces, the invisible tensions and strains, that contribute to the weight and shape of an object; it results also from an inability to account photographically for the distribution of objects in space. The formal satisfactions that a good print can yield depend to a considerable extent on the capacity of the photographer to represent three-dimensional volumes with a monocular instrument. Our pleasure in the pictures of Edward Weston or Ansel Adams, for example, relies importantly on their masterful control of the gradations of light that seem to give us the physical substance and spatial location of forms.

FROM OPTICAL TO TACTILE

The reality of matter is most confidently recognized through the feel or tactility of forms. Yet photography is an art that must approach reality from a distance and from a wholly visual standpoint. Furthermore it employs a developing process that subtracts light. Painting has the decided advantage of being able to construct forms either by building up lights or adding shadows, or both. But the photographer is caught between a rock and a hard place: he has to rely almost exclusively on optical detail to suggest the weight and texture of reality; at the same time the chemistry of photography tends to darken his print and to eliminate detail. So the photographer is always engaged in seeking an optimal balance between chiaroscuro and the accumulation of visual facts. The connoisseur is obliged to judge his success. We know, of course, how the grain of photographic emulsions and papers is

WALKER EVANS. *Graveyard in Easton, Pennsylvania.* 1936. Library of Congress. Farm Security Administration Collection, Washington, D.C.

ANDREAS FEININGER. *Cemetery in New York City.* 1948. *Life* Magazine. © 1948, Time, Inc.

The convincing distribution of objects in deep space calls for skillful technical control of the photographic medium. But technical control, while indispensable, cannot of itself produce depth as we intend it here. The ability to capture surface changes has to be the servant of a poetic sensibility. That is, textural change and spatial differentiation must be subordinate to the cognitive and emotive requirements of the image. Evans does only an adequate job of rendering the textures of the limestone cross, the scrubby grass, the brickfront houses, and the smoke stacks. Edward Weston or Ansel Adams could have produced a better print. But Evans' point of view, and his choice of a flat light over his shoulder, has yielded a type of depth that no amount of textural detail could equal. It is his angle of vision— just next to the large cross—that gives the spacing to the other grave markers. This is what causes the rapid reduction in size relationships, especially between the cross and the brick dwellings. It even helps to compress the layers of rooftops, chimneys, and buildings near the horizon. Thus a squeezing down in the distance produces a pressure that seems to spread out the foreground objects, thrusting the graves toward us. This manipulation of depth, as much as the symbolism of the cross, creates photographic quality. The principal objects receive precisely the amount of space and light needed to define their forms and,

more importantly, to reach a significant level of human meaning. Feininger is a more "scientific" photographer; hence his approach to physical or three-dimensional depth is a model of technical control. Yet it is a poetic device that creates the aesthetic depth of the work. Feininger has to contend with the fact that his telephoto lens inevitably foreshortens space, pressing distant forms into the frontal plane. To some extent he can cope with this flattening effect by relying on an Oriental pictorial device: movement upward means movement inward. But how can Western viewers be persuaded to accept this way of seeing? Feininger eliminates the horizon as well as any enclosing or framing lines. As a result we are forced to see the photograph very much as if it were a tapestry of gravestones. Our perceptual energies are concentrated on the texture of the fabric, so to speak. Now we can see subtle changes of light and dark seeming to form an S-curve that leads the eye very gradually into the upper fifth of the picture. There the gravestones lose much of their detail; they retain only their rectangular shapes, like the crisp gray notes around the edges of a Cubist composition. This Cubist dissolution of mass, accomplished before our eyes in a gently ascending movement, suggests a lovely analogy. In the bottom of the photograph the dead have begun to exchange their identities; by the time we reach the top their souls are dancing.

PAUL STRAND. *Ranchos de Taos, New Mexico.* 1931. © 1977 The Estate of Paul Strand

EDWARD WESTON. *Cabbage Leaf.* 1931. Courtesy Cole Weston

LILO RAYMOND. *Bed in Attic.* 1972. Courtesy the photographer

Here are three strong photographs that rely heavily on the sense of touch. Which is not to say they are merely textural studies. They do, however, demonstrate the power of the medium to create monumental effects without pictorial trickery. What we see is optical rendering carried to a peak of tactile expressiveness. Notice that the subjects are all presented frontally; the problems of composition are quite uncomplicated; and there is little or no appeal to narrative values. To be sure, Strand's *Ranchos de Taos* inevitably touches on regional and historical ideas, but it is mainly the weight and volumetric quality of the architectural forms that accounts for the impact of his image. The Weston cabbage leaf is an even purer demonstration of the power of photography to generate plastic, i.e., sculptural, values with very commonplace materials. It is significant, I believe, that Weston achieves a lyricism here which one cannot imagine in any other visual medium. Raymond's photograph is a tactile triumph of another sort. To be sure, the soft chenille fabric receives much of its sculptural quality from the bed and pillow underneath. But Raymond has also been attentive to the active notes struck by the folds at the head and foot of the bed. Finally and most photographically, these are contrasted to the flat, quiet texture barely visible in the wallpaper pattern. We know that black-and-white photography operates within a very narrow visual range. Hence our criterion—from optical to tactile—emphasizes the control of volumes through the visual orchestration of textures. It shows that although still photography is capable of suggesting some of the qualities of the non-visual senses—sound, taste, kinesthesia, and even smell—it is through rendering tactility that photography's claim to represent reality is most powerfully supported.

435

employed to supplement or improve upon the visual "facts." Beyond a certain point this sort of manipulation is anti-photographic; it simulates painting or printmaking. The tactile values of a good photograph must be perceived as the product of an ocular process. A critic should know whether or not the tactile values of a print are photographic in origin.

FROM PATTERN TO IDEA

As mentioned above, the photograph devoted to pure pattern is a commonplace achievement for the camera; it usually represents a high level of technical mastery combined with a modest level of humanistic insight. The camera is better employed as a machine that sees in order to know, to express and to explain. So the mere recording of patterns becomes photographic

kitsch—a pretense to aesthetic profundity. To be sure, patterns can be truthful as visual reports, but they need to *signify* in order to sustain our interest. Accordingly, patterns that require labels to be understood must be judged unsuccessful as photographic art, however interesting they may be as science. For an abstract pattern to succeed aesthetically we have to *see* its name, not read it. In other words, visual or formal photographic values require a larger context— the context of mind—as an essential support. The discovery of patterns in nature or in man-made objects becomes exciting and aesthetically potent when the photographer *shows us* their connections to the unfolding processes of nature or reveals them as products of human transformative powers. Otherwise we feel we are looking at a kind of vacant ornament, easily seen and easily forgotten.

GEORGE GERSTER. *Sahara Pollution.* © 1976 Foto George Gerster. Courtesy Photo Researchers, Inc., New York

An exceptionally eloquent example of pattern employed in a cognitive, as opposed to a purely formal, context. It is the juxtaposition of beautifully patterned sand and seemingly casual deposits of trash that makes the forms work expressively. By themselves, the wave-like sand forms would look like a thousand other photographs of desert rhythms. As for the trash piles, they are curiously, almost perversely, satisfying. Perhaps that is because the endless regularity of the sand patterns makes us hunger for signs of visual randomness. Notice, too, how the human figures on the upper left horizon provide a sense of scale for the picture as a whole. At the same time they hint at the essential idea of the picture—the painful connection between pollution and human settlement.

436

The camera necessarily shows us fragments. But photographic art has to reveal universals in details. It is not a question of dealing with large, panoramic scenes; it is rather the need to select and organize what is partial or half-done so that the viewer believes he sees what is entire and finished. Bad photographers manipulate their prints to achieve the effect of wholeness, usually by simulating the painter's tonalities and hierarchical organization of detail. This might be called "forced" unity. The good photographer must rely instead on (a) the selection of an intrinsically interesting subject; and (b) the presentation of that subject according to a logic that discloses its nature as an integral part of a complete universe. The viewer should be able to sense the totality of a situation through a privileged look at one of its parts.

WERNER BISCHOF. *Boy Leaving His Sick Grandfather, Korea.* Undated. Courtesy Magnum Photos, New York

The purpose of photographic composition is to make fragments of reality enter into complete relationships. Here portions of two figures have been organized into a whole which augments the expressive power of each part. The square window does more than frame the boy and concentrate our attention on his anguish: its placement initiates all the visual events within the image; it explains the darkness of the room; it dramatizes the somber texture of the wall; it contrasts the glaring outdoor illumination with the soft light barely crossing the grandfather's body. Most important, the diagonal formed by the boy's arm movement connects the pieces of the image with its narrative: it gives the angle and destination of his gaze; it makes us attend to the direction of the old man's stare—over our right shoulder and into the distance. Finally, it opposes the weight of the boy's arm and shoulder to the weightlessness of the sick man's hands. In purely design terms it relates the window to the room; in symbolic terms it compares the vertical situation with the horizontal situation. Bischof believed, and here demonstrates, that the pictorial dynamics of a great photographic statement are inseparable from its human meaning.

Compared to the other visual arts, photography can easily capture the exotic, the peculiar and the freakish. Thus it readily gratifies the human interest in weird people and violent actions. Indeed, that is what photojournalism often does in the course of carrying out its responsibility of reportage. But photography as art must go beyond the recording of shocking events or grotesque phenomena. In satisfying our curiosity it has to discover typical truths in strange forms and exceptional events. Otherwise it degenerates into a search for perversity, abnormality and varieties of visual outrage. There is a tendency for some photographers to confuse moral or optical shock with aesthetic surprise. Here Velázquez is the right model: he knew how to show human deformity as part of the human condition. Diane Arbus is perhaps less compassionate if less squeamish as she brings us face-to-face with physical and psychological abnormalities. But her work is done objectively and without censoriousness; it helps us to realize that her people are fellow sufferers. To find universal human qualities in people who are outcast, ugly or horribly afflicted is a remarkable feat.

Henri Cartier-Bresson. *Children Playing in the Ruins, Spain.* 1933. Courtesy Magnum Photos, New York

In the introduction to his book, *The Decisive Moment*, Cartier-Bresson says: "Above all, I craved to seize the whole essence, in the confines of one single photograph, of some situation that was in the process of unrolling itself before my eyes." Our criterion—from singular to typical—stresses this same objective. Cartier-Bresson's famous photograph illustrates the concept perfectly; both incident and idea are captured in a single image. Notice how Ben Shahn's *Liberation* employs the same notion of a picture; it is essentially a photographic approach: the grotesque incident frozen and transmuted into an idea. To some extent we can explain the expressive force of Cartier-Bresson's photograph in compositional terms: the children in the rubble-strewn street distributed along an S-curve which comes to an abrupt halt with the boy on crutches; the jerky rhythm created by the repeated angles of the children's bodies. But there are psychological factors at work here, too: in the tension caused by our fear that the boy's crutches will be caught in the stones and he will fall down hard; in the cruelty of boys at play; and in the contrast between the laughing faces and the rough frame created by a shell hole. Most important is the rapid divergence of the lines forming the wall against which this drama unfolds; it propels the crippled youngster forward like a shot. These devices, and more, lie beneath the photographic surface of the work. It has taken me some time to see them and a paragraph to describe them even briefly; Cartier-Bresson caught them in an instant. Such mastery must be the product of a long apprenticeship, a quick mind, an intelligent eye. By "intelligent eye" I mean the photographer's ability to make an immediate, almost instinctive connection between what he sees in a scene, what it signifies at the moment, and what it means in depth—what it means as an idea that can occupy the mind permanently.

The copy as replica or record tells us what we would have seen if we were "there." This sort of photograph is a convenient mechanical substitute for personal witness: it enables us to travel without leaving home, to remember without going through the trouble of summoning up mental images. Such pictures are valuable to the extent that they are reliable, that is, unsurprising. But an "original" photograph represents a discovery. That "discovery" is related to the instantaneous character of the photographic act; the "taking" of a picture involves the artist in the reality of what he records. But it is not enough to be "there"; it is necessary to see and reject, and to distinguish the prototype from the stereotype. The artist must know how to discriminate among his feelings and ideas in the presence of objects and places and to discard those that are trite. When this is done well, the photograph represents a genuine birth—in the spectator as in the world of art. The photographic witness to life as it is born is illusory, of course; it depends on the artist's ability to encounter the world as scientist and philosopher, as historian and critic, as poet and midwife. Beyond that, the photographer must pretend to see innocently—like a child.

ROBERT WALKER. *Find Coffee House.* 1971. New York Times Pictures

Here is a work that epitomizes my distinction between a photograph that serves to copy or record an event and a photograph that makes a discovery which is aesthetically and humanly significant. Walker's photograph, in my judgment, bears comparison with the masterpieces of Pieter Bruegel, Adriaen Brouwer, and even of Rembrandt. Consider the Caravaggio-like lighting that bathes the figure upper left: it is a little masterpiece in itself. The hand and head of the woman lower right could have been taken from an interior by Vermeer. Now these comparisons are not made to establish the greatness of a photograph by demonstrating its genealogy in the history of painting. It is rather to say that the same factors which make a masterwork of a Brouwer or Vermeer operate in the present instance. Notice how the size and focal properties of the man advancing with his crutches creates a superb, tension-filled space between him and the figures in the background. It is a space modeled in the tradition of the great Baroque canvases. At the same time, the scale relationships and perspectival effects are purely photographic. The ground plane moves up and away from us about as fast as the central figure moves toward us. The result is a powerful and dramatic pair of opposed movements, each culminating in an episode that demands our compassion in a different way. An isolated figure, almost lost in shadow (right middleground), provides precisely the right amount of interest and space modulation needed in that quadrant of the composition. The photograph satisfies our surface-to-depth requirements; it nourishes our tactile feelings through optical representation; it transcends the unusual or special character of the place and its people. And it takes up several great themes: helplessness, courage, loneliness, and love.

15

IMAGES IN MOTION:
FILM AND TELEVISION

"Until there is a chapter on film in every textbook of art . . .
we shall not have firmly established in the consciousness of
our generation this most important artistic development of
our century."[33]

ALTHOUGH AN ELABORATE TECHNOLOGY STANDS BEHIND motion pictures and television, it is correct to think of these media as extensions of painting or picturemaking. The pioneers of still photography operated on the basis of a painterly sensibility. Even today a pictorial tradition supports the work of photographers, cinematographers, and film and TV directors. This must be the case, inevitably, as long as cinema and television remain visual media which present themselves in a two-dimensional format. The creation of a credible illusion of motion was the revolutionary element that opened up and transformed the ancient art of painting.

The illusions of reality fostered by the cinematic media are so convincing that we are rarely aware of their pictorial connections. We are, perhaps, in the

In developing his theme of avarice in San Francisco about the turn of the century (the film is based on an 1899 novel), the Austrian Von Stroheim drew on a well-established European artistic tradition devoted to the gluttony of peasants at the table.

PIETER BRUEGEL THE ELDER. Detail of *Peasant Wedding*.
c. 1565. Kunsthistorisches Museum, Vienna

KÄTHE KOLLWITZ. *Peasant War Cycle: Sharpening of the Scythe.* 1905. Museum of Fine Arts, Boston. L. Aaron Lebowick Fund

Film still from *The Cabinet of Dr. Caligari:* Dr. Caligari. Directed by ROBERT WIENE. 1919

After World War I, a great Central European film style emerged based on German Expressionist graphic art, which had generated a powerful message by demoniacal lighting of subjects from below and by allotting as much area to grotesque shadows as to the people and objects that cast them.

position of Renaissance viewers confronting the optical illusions created by the newly discovered science of perspective. The convincing representation of objects in depth constituted a liberation of the imagination for artist and viewer alike. A persistent goal of the pictorial tradition has been the achievement of a lifelike illusion so truthful that man could be, like God, a creator of reality. In a sense, painting has been

a succession of triumphs in the realm of optical illusionism: each triumph has encouraged the viewer to believe he is in the presence of new dimensions of reality. Motion pictures seem to have accomplished the ultimate suspension of the viewer's disbelief.

In trying to understand motion pictures, we must consider two separate but interdependent factors: the long pictorial tradition with its drive toward reality substitutes; and the social and aesthetic effects generated by new technical devices for representing visual reality: the camera, synchronous sound and imagery, stereophonic sound recording, color film, the iconoscope or videocamera, wide-screen projection, videotape, BetaMax, and so on. Out of these technical inventions grew aesthetic devices like montage, close-up, slow motion, split screen, slow dissolve, freeze-frame, and instant replay. It can be argued that artistic necessity motivated these technical innovations. But in my judgment, the human drive to master reality by simulating its visual appearance is the ultimate source of both technical and aesthetic change—in cinema and in the other visual arts. Hence, students of filmed and televised imagery must consider technical and aesthetic factors—media-meaning relationships—if they hope to understand motion pictures as art.

The Manipulation of Space-Time

Artists have always tried to represent motion visually. They blurred the edges of forms, introduced "speed" lines, or represented imagined positions of bodies in

Film still from *Greed:* the "wedding feast." Directed by ERICH VON STROHEIM. 1924

motion. Of course, dance and drama enabled them to suggest movement through bodily mimicry. But the dancer's range of bodily imitation is limited, and it has no durable physical existence.

Unlike prehistoric hunters, most of us are not willing to believe that a dancer wearing a reindeer's head and antlers is in fact a reindeer. But we are willing to believe in the reality of light-and-shadow patterns created by pieces of film passing across a beam of light at the rate of twenty-four frames per second. It is more than magic; a physiological effect is involved: each picture lingers as an afterimage; it is not instantly extinguished in the viewer's eye; the eye fails to see the empty intervals (lasting 1/48 of a second) between the separate still images. Neither can one see the swift motion of the tiny electronic beam that scans the TV tube to create an image with little points of light. The optical persistence of the still image (or the "running together" of the points of light) combined with our delayed perception of the tiny changes from image to image causes us to believe we are witnessing real movement. Movement, in turn, is one of the most reliable indicators of life. A chain of physiological and psychological events, therefore, identifies the viewing of motion pictures with the viewing of reality.

When technology succeeded in representing motion believably, a new artistic exploitation of space and time became possible. The artists of the cinema could manipulate time and space because of their control of machines that create the fundamental illusion and because viewers identify cinematic space-time with real space-time. They were no different from Renaissance draftsmen who could draw lines converging on a horizon line, and thus convince viewers that they were seeing deep space. The Renaissance perspectivist could speed up or slow down a viewer's optical journey along a drawn line moving toward the horizon. Similarly, the cinematographer can represent the crossing of great distances or the passage of long periods in a few hundred feet of film. Conversely, he can make a short distance long or a brief event last interminably. The cinematographer can effectively represent slow motion, reverse motion, or speeded-up motion: the time machine allows him to control pieces of reality "trapped" on film. Through editing or montage, which is the fundamental creative act of filmmaking, he can play with film footage, confident that he is playing with segments of the viewer's perception of life. He can make the viewer live in his (the cinematographer's) world. Paradoxically, the technology that creates these fantastic possibilities is primitive compared to other achievements of modern applied science. Still, it is revolutionary as far as human imaginative life is concerned—the wheel, too, was a simple machine.

MARCEL DUCHAMP. *Nude Descending a Staircase, No. 2.* 1912. Philadelphia Museum of Art. The Louise and Walter Arensberg Collection

PHOTOGRAPHIC AND PAINTERLY
REPRESENTATIONS OF MOTION

HAROLD E. EDGERTON. Stroboscopic study of motion: swirls and eddies of a tennis stroke. 1970

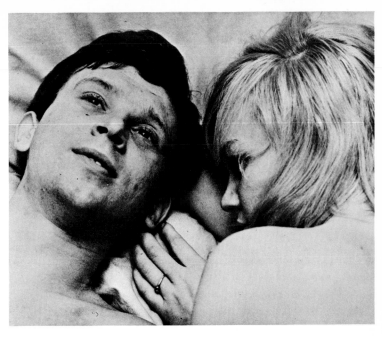

Film still from *The Sea*.
Directed by Patroni Griffi. 1962

Film still from *The Loves of a Blonde*. Directed by
Miloš Forman. 1967. Courtesy CCM Films, Inc.

Even though cinema is a public medium, it gives us access, through the motion-picture camera to
scenes of the utmost intimacy and tenderness.

FILM DEVICES

The artistic devices available to the filmmaker can
be divided into two categories: those that simulate
the natural activity of the eye and those that simulate
our mental activity in experiencing the duration and
quality of time.

The basic tool of cinematic space simulation is the
visual continuity sequence. This consists, very simply,
of the long shot, the medium or transitional shot, and
the close-up. The camera imitates the eye as it scans
a scene, establishing an overall situation for the
viewer; selects a subject within the situation by
moving closer to it; and concentrates on some
significant detail of the subject by moving close to it,
enlarging its size on the screen. David W. Griffith is
generally credited with the earliest use of the close-up,
a cinematic invention he employed sparingly and
eloquently. As an aesthetic device, the close-up is
tremendously powerful: it can exaggerate enormously
the most subtle and transient visual effects; it generates a unique sense of intimacy; and it has contributed
to a distinctive type of screen style—facial acting.
Limited facial movements acquire exaggerated expressive meanings through the close-up. In addition,
the enormous enlargement of persons and objects in
the close-up forces viewers to attend to the tactile
qualities of their visual experience. Not only can the
film director draw attention to significant details, but
he can also generate an intense awareness of the texture of these details. As a result, the viewer perceives
the sensuous qualities of images with a vividness
perhaps unequaled since infancy, when tactile examination of objects prevailed over visual observation.

Film close-ups break the normal cultural conventions
about the proper distance between a viewer and another person.[34] As conventions of distance are broken
down, the visual sense generates tactile feelings.

As visual continuity is established, objects and persons are located in space. However, the continuity
sequence is only a primitive unit, albeit a fundamental
one, of the motion-picture art; it corresponds to the
writer's words, phrases, and sentences. They have a
limited meaning by themselves, but they must be assembled and orchestrated in paragraphs and chapters
to support the range of meaning we encounter in a
story or a novel.

This assembling and orchestrating is an intellectual
as well as a visual activity. One of its chief purposes
is to govern the viewer's experience of time. In the
film, time is *abstracted* from things and felt increasingly for its own qualities. The other visual art forms—
painting, sculpture, and architecture—also endeavor
to manipulate time. But they do not enjoy the technical advantages of the motion-picture camera, which
converts time into linear-feet of film or tape. By
cutting and splicing film, the filmmaker can establish
temporal rhythms more convincing than those created
by the muralist, the comic-strip artist, or the easel
painter.

SOME MOTION PICTURE
TERMS, DEVICES, AND TECHNIQUES[35]

Frame	A single picture on a strip of film.
Shot	The fundamental compositional unit in a film sequence; a visual unit consisting of many frames. One element

	in a film scene, the shot corresponds to a sentence within a paragraph.
Sequence	A single filmic idea corresponding to a paragraph in prose. It consists of one or more shots or scenes, alone or in combination.
Montage	The editing of film through various sorts of cutting and dissolves.
Cut-in	Insertion of a detail, usually a close-up, drawn from the main action of a film sequence.
Cut-away	Insertion of a detail outside of, but related metaphorically to, the main action of a film sequence.
Overlap	Repetition of action from an immediately preceding sequence at the beginning of a new sequence.
Fade-in	The gradual emergence of the film image from darkness.
Fade-out	The gradual disappearance of the film image into darkness.
Dissolve	The fade-out of one image as another, over which it has been superimposed, takes its place.
Wipe	The displacement of a film image by another image or shape taking any direction across the screen as it erases its predecessor.
Dollying	Continuous motion of a platform-mounted camera toward or away from a subject, causing its image to grow larger or smaller on the screen.
Panning	Following the action of a subject with the camera, or moving the camera across relatively stationary objects.
Zooming	Rapid movement toward the subject by dollying or by use of a zoom lens which can achieve the same effect with a stationary camera.

Cinematic Types

Like all new media, films and television began by serving as new ways of presenting established art forms. Consequently, we see in films and television vestiges of older forms such as the novel, the stage play, the lecture, the sermon, the magazine, the short story, the outdoor poster, the medicine show, and the party joke. This variegated ancestry seems to justify Pauline Kael's irreverent description of the film as "a bastard, cross-fertilized super-art."[36]

The older forms have been translated into the new media, where they emerge as documentaries, animated cartoons, commercials, situation comedies, daytime serials, teaching films, feature-length dramas, news analyses, celebrity interviews, panel discussions, horror shows, and so on. To the extent that traditional forms have adapted themselves to the new media, they have acquired a new aesthetic identity. This is es-

pecially true of the documentary, the film drama, and the feature-length animated cartoon. But insofar as older art forms are reproduced unchanged, their aesthetic potential is diminished. A televised lecture can be as dull as its live original. At times it can be improved, if skillful camera work contributes new visual qualities. In general, however, the reproduction of older forms in new media results only in the wider dissemination of aesthetically inferior commodities.

There are, of course, information and entertainment values accessible through film even when it is used to transmit the content of another medium. Conceivably, one could enjoy a poem recited over the telephone. But viewers are disappointed by the visual reproduction of qualities typical of literature, the concert hall, or the lecture platform. The new media do not consist simply of words and music *added to* filmed imagery; these ingredients are changed by film or videotape because they occupy *visually represented* space instead of written space, printed space, or aural space. A documentary film, for example, is not identical to an encyclopedia article. The authority of print yields to the authority of cinematic representation, and this changes the meaning of literacy for our time.

Filmed Versus Televised Imagery

Too much can be made of the technical differences between filmed and televised imagery. Both media exploit fundamentally similar conventions: the realistic imitation of motion, and the identification of motion with reality. There are, of course, differences in the quality or resolution of their images, the faithfulness of their color, and the size of their pictures. Moreover, we view each medium under different circumstances. Still, most of these differences will be minimized by technical improvements in television, which, in any case, relies heavily on the broadcasting of film. In all likelihood, the media will converge because both are responsive to the central drive of all artistic representation—the mastery of reality through imitation or symbolic transformation.

A fundamental difference between filmed and televised imagery lies in their social effects, which, in turn, grow out of differences in their modes of production, distribution, and presentation to the public. These differences account for the distinctive qualities of television. When it is not showing feature films or material recorded on videotape, television has the ability to present living events with almost the same immediacy as personal witness. The TV viewer knows he is looking at a "live" telecast, and this knowledge becomes a factor in his aesthetic experience. Motion-picture film, however, must be processed; there is a time lapse between an event and its presentation to the public. This provides the opportunity to heighten or isolate qualities of the event—through editing—so that we may say that cinema is the more "artistic" of the two media. Television is more "historical," although,

Film still from *Potemkin:*
woman holding wounded child.
Directed by SERGEI EISENSTEIN.
1926. Courtesy Rosa Madell
Film Library.
Artkino Pictures, Inc.

Eisenstein's films are designed
visually. Their emotional and
ideological impact rely on more
than the accumulation of realistic
detail. They are composed like
the pictorial masterpieces of Goya
and Picasso.

PABLO PICASSO.
Detail of *Guernica.* 1937.
On extended loan to
The Museum of Modern Art,
New York, from the artist's estate

Photograph from a "Dick Cavett Show." From left: Noel Coward, Cavett, Lynn Fontanne, and Alfred Lunt. 1970. Courtesy Daphne Productions, Inc., New York. The collective TV interview has become an electronic version of an old, perhaps obsolete social form—conversation. Emphasis is on the glamour, opinions, and wit of famous guests. The popularity of the genre demonstrates the effectiveness of the medium in exploiting more-or-less spontaneous human interactions.

like written history, it, too, can shape the record of events.

Motion pictures are normally seen by a large audience, although it is possible to attend private screenings. Still, the medium is designed for an audience of the sort that attends a play, for example. Hence, films are planned with the expectation of group responses. Television shows are also intended for groups—indeed millions of viewers. But usually a closely related group—the family, or the family and friends—views television shows together. Consequently, television cannot depend on a large audience to influence an individual viewer. Unfortunately, television often tries to *simulate* large audience response by superimposing recorded noise and laughter over videotape or by televising performances before live audiences recruited to be seen and heard. In the latter case, television tries to approximate the experience of theater, usually with inferior results.

These inauthentic uses of television result from a failure to appreciate the distinctive advantages of the medium, which are based on its closeness to reality. In other words, television alone is capable of presenting the raw materials of history—events as they occur—before they have been processed.

The immediate relation of television to history is now best exploited in the reporting of sports events and news in general. Here TV demonstrates its superiority over the old filmed newsreel, which reached its audience after it had learned of events through radio and newspapers. The new element lies in the viewer's awareness of the simultaneity of the occurrence of an event, its representation in the TV medium, and its transmission to his living room. Indeed, the awareness of this simultaneity introduces a distorting element in the viewer's perception of history: he tends to believe implicitly in the truth of what he sees—by contrast with his reaction to verbal accounts—and may not realize that events can be staged, abbreviated, or isolated from context while appearing photographical-

Photograph of the hosts of the TV children's series "Sesame Street." From left: Bob McGrath, Matt Robinson, Will Lee, and Loretta Long. 1970. Courtesy Children's Television Workshop, New York. While it seems obvious that TV has enormous potential as a teaching medium, its educational values have nevertheless remained potential. Only "Sesame Street," the first noncommercial educational series to become a popular and critical success, combines visual excitement, fresh entertainment, and vivid teaching.

ly accurate. We have not yet built adequate defenses against the televised distortion of social reality; consequently, we encounter perils to our political life from the same source that deepens and extends our historical experience. Only with televised sports events—which are, after all, games—can we suspend historical judgment and surrender ourselves to the purely aesthetic pleasures available through instantaneous, visual participation in real events.

Films and Dreams

The darkened theater; a soft, comfortable seat; controlled temperature and humidity; and thousands of shadowy images moving across the screen—these strongly suggest the dream world each of us occupies while sleeping. It is possible to think of cinema as the deliberate manufacture of dreams. Psychological experiments reveal that individuals deprived of dreams—allowed to sleep but awakened when they begin to dream—move into a psychotic state. Clearly, dreaming is a biological and cultural necessity. In some way, our human psychobiological equipment is purged and regenerated while we sleep. Sanity is maintained, it seems, by the curious, illogical flow of images we call dreams. But why do we require dreams during the waking state?

It can be maintained that art has always served us as an alternative type of dream. That is, people have always manufactured visions to supplement their real dreams. But it is doubtful that this could be demonstrated scientifically—that dream-deprived individuals could be satisfied with artificial dreams such as pictures and films. Or perhaps such experiments have not been attempted. One need not, however, carry speculation that far. It is sufficient to observe, on the basis of the history of art, daydreaming, and the contemporary evidence of film and television viewing, that people have considerable need for a waking fantasy life.

It is the technical resemblance of films to dreams that arouses our interest. One of the earliest uses of motion-picture photography was in the study of animal movement. And films have considerable value as tools of scientific investigation. But that is not the use which has guided their technical development. Films have moved steadily in the direction of simulating the kind of perception associated with our imaginative life. Indeed, cinematic images are in many respects superior to the images human beings can construct with their biological equipment. It would seem that our civilization, which has created the most complex technology in history, is impelled to create dream-generating devices for the users of its technology. In other words, our need for synthetic dreams grows in direct proportion to the growth of complex machinery and technical systems in our work, play, and interpersonal relations. The dreams we create organically have to be supplemented by dream machines so we can

Film still from *The Silence:* boy in room of dying aunt. Directed by INGMAR BERGMAN. 1962. Courtesy Janus Films, Inc.

Two Scandinavian masters use similar devices to express the contrast between the pain of living and the finality of death. The tensions between silence and speech, past and future, resignation and hope are created by visual relationships of shape, direction, light, and space.

EDVARD MUNCH. *The Dead Mother.* 1899–1900. Kunsthalle, Bremen

447

Film still from *The Grapes of Wrath*: the Joad Family. Directed by JOHN FORD. 1940. © 1949. Twentieth Century-Fox Film Corp. Every generation and every group needs its own image—the mythic or historical account of its founding. For the displaced Southern and Midwestern farmers of the 1930s, that account was provided by John Ford's version of Steinbeck's novel. Using a realistic style based on the documentaries of Pare Lorentz, Ford fashioned a classic epic of migration and resettlement on a continental scale.

maintain some sort of human balance, or sanity, in our culture. In this way, perhaps, we can explain the development in the twentieth century of a major new art and its evolution toward a form that simulates our dream-life.

The Democracy of Film

Both film and television eliminate distinctions based on money and class, because access to them is inexpensive compared to attending live theater, the symphony, opera, or ballet. But they are democratic in a more fundamental sense in that every seat in a motion-picture theater is equal. That is, each viewer sees the same imagery; film actors cannot play to the boxes; seats in the balcony are as good as seats in the orchestra; sound is audible throughout the house. And, despite a certain amount of family scrambling, each television viewer has a prime location. Cinematic imagery tends to devour the space between the screen and the viewer; every member of the audience feels that the performance is being played for him alone. Furthermore, the moving camera has a compelling power to lead the viewer's eye into the spaces and places represented on the screen. The physical location of one's theater seat is forgotten as we begin to occupy cinema space. Happily, there is room in it for everyone.

Close-ups eliminate the distance between actors and audience—a distance that is social as well as spatial. This leads to the star system and the phenomenon of the fan who takes a deep personal interest in the lives of favorite film or TV actors. More important, cinema encourages very active processes of psychological identification; film and television audiences experience life-styles that are not necessarily available to them in reality. They "enjoy" products and services normally reserved for persons of wealth, acquiring a taste for these products and services that they want to satisfy in their real lives.

Although the democracy of film leads to commercial exploitation, it also plays other, more constructive roles. The first lies in its obvious educational influence on the lives of illiterate or impoverished people. Cinema gives them access to versions of behavior and social change that only educated persons enjoy. To be sure, motion-picture viewing does not solve the fundamental problems of poverty and ignorance, but it is perhaps the chief contributor to what has been called "the revolution of rising expectations" among the impoverished people of the world.

A second democratizing consequence of films and television applies mainly to advanced industrial cultures: the capacity of the media to generate a sense of community and social cohesion. Television, especially, can unite the often alienated citizens of a depersonalized mass society. As spectators of the same media events, millions share a common set of imaginative experiences. It is especially through televised events—whether tragic or triumphal—that the masses have an opportunity to identify with powerful symbols of communal anxiety, hope, or achievement. One thinks of the funerals of presidents and martyrs, the triumphant return of space explorers, or the great festivals staged for celebrities of the media: athletes, beauty queens, visiting statesmen, and uncommon common men. Without these media events, it would be difficult for the individual citizen to satisfy his need for identification with a community larger than his family or neighborhood—social units that appear to be increasingly fragmented and temporary. Thus, quite apart from their merits as vehicles of art, the motion-picture media perform a vital civic function: they help create a community out of millions of separate, more or less isolated, viewers.

The Critical Appreciation of Cinema

Despite a vast literature devoted to the film—historical, technical, and sociological—very little material instructs viewers in how to *attend to* films for the sake of increased pleasure and understanding. Critics write opinions and plot synopses; they offer interpretations of films; they publish anthologies of critical writing and discourse on the theory of filmmaking. Still, this literature does not directly instruct the viewer, who is rarely privileged to know how critics do, or should, function.

To begin to deal with this problem, I offer a typology, a set of concepts to direct the viewer's attention to the principal elements in the cinema experience. As a typology, it makes no claim to theoretical originality. Its purpose is to suggest the range of qualities within each element of the film.

A TYPOLOGY OF CINEMATIC FORMS

Image (medium)

I VISUAL COMPONENT	Texture: Shape: Size: Focus: Light: Color: Space:	rough-smooth, hard-soft, wet-dry round-pointed, organic-geometric large-small, exaggerated-reduced blurred-distinct, near-distant natural-artificial, strong-weak pale-intense, warm-cool, earth-sky shallow-deep, defined-unlimited
II DRAMATIC COMPONENT	Sound/Music: Language/Diction: Performance/Representation: Montage/Editing: Movement/Composition: Time:	emotive-descriptive, faster-slower spoken-recited, lyrical-literal naturalistic-stylized, accurate-distorted rhythmic-staccato, dominant-subordinate continuous-interrupted, parallel-diagonal swift-slow, cinematic-chronological
III LITERARY COMPONENT	Object: Place: Event: Sequence: Plot: Symbol:	whole-fragment, quality-thing open-closed, now-then, familiar-exotic many-few, probable-unlikely, verbal-visual linear-simultaneous, logical-irrational simple-complex, narrative-poetic personal-collective, realistic-abstract, spectacular-didactic

Idea (meaning)

Deployment of this typology accords with the critical method recommended in Chapter Seventeen. It should assist the viewer in describing and analyzing a film experience before proceeding to interpret and judge it. This device should enable viewers to attend to all sources of imagery in the cinema—visual, aural, kinetic, and verbal—while endeavoring to fathom their interaction and overall meaning.

The typology mentions nineteen elements of cinematic form (no doubt others can be thought of), each of which is followed by some typical qualitative pairs. Some effort is involved in learning the elements of cinematic form listed here. Once learned, however, they are easily utilized, with a genuine reward in breadth and depth of experience.

For simplicity, the visual, dramatic, and literary components of cinematic form can be described through the perception of the elements: Space, Time, and Symbol. The viewer is asked to examine a quality of Focus, for example, and relate it to Time or Symbol. Or he may notice a quality of Light and relate it to Object or Place. He must try to consider as many of the possible interfaces among these elements as he can, all the while being guided by the design of the film, that is, the organization of the entire work, and its influence on his own outlook.

As with the experience of all art, the richest reward accompanies the ability to attend to the largest number of elements. This implies that aesthetic intensity is a quantitative phenomenon. We may have believed

Film still from *La Dolce Vita:*
party scene. Directed by
FEDERICO FELLINI. 1960

The combined man-and-woman forms
are skillfully used here to suggest
animality—the loss of human dignity in
Fellini's image, and a crude parody of
physical love in the Antonioni image.

Film still from *Blow-Up*:
photographer and model.
Directed by MICHELANGELO ANTONIONI. 1966.
© Metro-Goldwyn-Mayer, Inc., 1966

that possessing *information* about a work of art was
the highroad to pleasure and understanding; but it is
the quantity of *fused perceptions* that accounts for the
intensity of aesthetic experience. To be sure, the capacity to fuse perceptions remains a personal art for
whose mastery only some general advice can be given.
This typology, then, is only a map showing where
those perceptions can be found.

Conclusion

In a recent article on film, television, and literature,
Michael Arlen wrote: "The audience for the serious
music of language seems to be drifting away, as if
mesmerized by paintings, photographs, moving pictures, videotape—by the new power of visual imagery." He went on to speak of a "childish battle . . .
between the print and visual interests . . . in which
the visual team now appears to have the upper hand."
Then he concluded that "the real issue remains in
doubt: respect for man and his art."[37] Arlen is clearly
unhappy about the closing of the cultural gap, the
growing equalization of the visual with the verbal in
our media of communication and expression. He sees
literary forms subordinated to visual spectacles and
hence he is not very optimistic about the prospects for
art *or* humanity. However, a major premise of this
book is that the visual arts, strongly assisted by the
newer media of photography, cinema and television,
have been engaged for over a century in restoring

balance to a cultural situation that has grown badly out of kilter. The overemphasis on printed words in our arts of expression and communication has caused, over the centuries, a pronounced underdevelopment of humanity's visual sense and a consequent distortion of consciousness itself. Now the rise of the visual media to unaccustomed prominence and power does not mean that civilization will revert to communication by mime and pictograph. It is plain that new and potentially very useful visual-verbal modalities are being developed. But it is highly unlikely that the power of visual expression, once learned and widely enjoyed, can ever be so thoroughly repressed again.

Film still from *La Dolce Vita:* Christ figure suspended from a helicopter. Directed by FEDERICO FELLINI. 1960. In one of the great symbolic images of modern film art, Fellini defines decadence for modern culture: just as cynical promoters exploit popular religious feeling by staging a fake miracle, so does Fellini's art, the film, contribute to the general corruption by encouraging people to believe in its shoddy spectacles.

PART FIVE

THE PROBLEMS
OF ART CRITICISM

Introduction

THE PROBLEMS OF
ART CRITICISM

EXPOSITION DES OUVRAGES DE PEINTURE ET DE SCULPTURE PAR M.RS DE L'ACADEMIE DANS LA GALERIE DU LOUVRE

Etching depicting exhibition of painters and sculptors at the Louvre. Bibliothèque
Nationale, Paris. Today, as in the seventeenth century, the display and criticism
of art is a social phenomenon, conducted with various degrees of knowledge,
seriousness, and intellectual probity.

ALMOST EVERYONE FANCIES HIMSELF AN ART CRITIC. AT
least, most people deliver critical opinions, no matter
how unfamiliar they may be with art or theories of art
criticism. This may be so because a democracy encourages its citizens to feel that their views on any
subject have equal weight, just as their votes count
equally in politics. As a result, a great deal of heat is
generated in critical discussions of art, and this heat
brings contemporary art forcibly to everyone's attention. Hence, it is regrettable that education devotes
so little time to the development of a systematic
foundation for practicing criticism. Even well-edu-
cated persons—when they look at art—find themselves
delivering the opinions of others, or offering their own

views without knowing how they arrived at them. To deal with the problem, this section is devoted to critical theory and method as applied to contemporary art. No attempt is made to deal with aesthetics or philosophy of art. Rather, my goal is to assist in the development of an intelligent *approach* to the business of forming interpretations and making critical judgments about art. Although there are no permanently correct interpretations and evaluations of particular works, I believe there are systematic procedures for making interpretations and evaluations which are fairly defensible. Hence this discussion of art criticism as a practical activity in which one can gain proficiency as one's critical grounds and procedures are subjected to logical scrutiny.

16

THE THEORY OF

ART CRITICISM

THE CHIEF GOAL OF ART CRITICISM IS UNDERSTANDING. We want to find a way of looking at art objects which will yield the maximum of knowledge about their meanings and merits. Works of art yield information to the trained viewer, but we are not interested in information for its own sake. For the purposes of criticism, we want to know how information about a work is related to its excellence. For this reason, archaeological, historical, or literary data about works of art may be fascinating but not necessarily useful in art criticism. In short, we want to understand the causes *in* the work of the effect it has upon us.

Another goal of art criticism, perhaps as important as the first, is delight or pleasure. To be sure, we derive pleasure from understanding, from knowing what it is in art that accounts for our gratifications. But the critical process enables us to carry on the search for meaning or pleasure systematically. The trained viewer can augment and intensify the satisfactions a work is capable of yielding. The value we derive from an aesthetic situation depends on the art object, to be sure, but also on how well a viewer can bring his experience to bear on its examination. So the practice of art criticism should increase the satisfaction derivable from any particular work.

Some persons believe that systematic scrutiny of art kills the pleasures that art can yield. Perhaps they assume that careful study is aimed only at gaining information. And that may be the case with the scholar who sees the art object as evidence for the reconstruction of a remote culture. But the information sought by the art critic is mainly about the sources of his satisfaction or about the bearing of the work on one's world and one's existence in it. Moreover, as we look, we discover that we are pleased or displeased.

Then, because we are human, hence curious, we want to know why.

The purposes of art criticism are not entirely centered on the search for causes. There is a real interest in sharing what we have discovered. It is very difficult to experience any satisfaction without a thought for the reactions of someone else. That is why we talk about art, music, films, and literature. We want to know whether others share our feelings. We may want to persuade them that a work is worth their attention. There is, then, a social motive in art criticism—assuming that, whatever else it may be, *art criticism is talk about art*.

Why do all of us, experienced critics or not, enjoy talking about art? Because talk about art is probably one of the ways we share our inner lives without embarrassment. Very few can resist the impulse to deliver opinions about a work of art, whether or not they can go into the details of the experience itself. Great art critics have an unusually rich and varied capacity for aesthetic pleasure, so when they disclose their discoveries, they enlarge our capacities for understanding and delight. In this sense, art criticism is like teaching; it is the sharing of discoveries about art or, in some cases, about life, where art has its beginnings.

One of the commonly accepted purposes of criticism is to make some statement of the worth or rank of an art object. Indeed, the purposes mentioned above are often held to be preliminary to the ultimate judgment of "how good" a work is. Here we face a persistent human tendency—the need to say that something is "better than" or "worth more than" something else. Obviously, this derives from our wish to possess what is valuable, a motive that is plainly very human. And

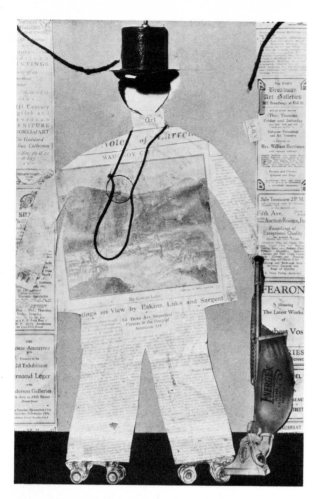

ARTHUR G. DOVE. *The Critic.* 1925. Terry Dinten-
fass Gallery, New York. Arthur G. Dove Estate.
The artist's mischievous image of the critic—a
ridiculous, top-hatted figure who rides around the
galleries on roller skates wielding a vacuum
cleaner.

Even when no financial transaction is involved, critical evaluations are important in the determination of
prestige among artists. And, of course, prestige is
sought for its own sake as well as for its connection to
wealth.

Collecting art, too, is related to art criticism, since
the collector, by his purchase, confirms his own or
someone else's critical judgment. And, since money is
a potent symbol in our culture, all the activities leading to the purchase of art have enormous cultural
significance. Clearly, art criticism as carried on in
newspapers, magazines, and universities, and by implication in galleries and museums, influences what
artists create. Thus we encounter an interesting
phenomenon: criticism of art—that is, more or less
informed talk about art—affects the production of
what it talks about. Therefore, our conception of the
relation of artist to the public needs to be enlarged.
Among the materials an artist works with, there is a
large amount of *critical commentary* coming from a
variety of sources. Of course, some artists deny that
critical opinions influence them. Nevertheless, others,
in their pursuit of recognition, endeavor to discern the
critical standards which seem to be prominent in the
places where they wish to be admired.

If the purposes of criticism begin with the need to
understand.art and to seek out its satisfactions, they
end with the formulation of a body of opinions and
responses which serve as *standards* for the creation of
art. As individuals, we may not have intended to
influence what artists create. But in the course of discovering what art means, searching for what we like,
and talking about it, we have indirectly brought critical standards into being. Such standards shift, of
course, and are difficult to formulate with precision.
Nevertheless, a process of social interaction and critical communication seems to be constantly at work,
involving popular discussion of the meanings and
values of art, together with artistic efforts to discern
the direction of this discussion and its implication for
their work.

The Tools of Art Criticism

What kind of equipment must a critic possess to function adequately? What knowledge must one have, or
what skills need one have mastered, to be qualified
beyond the layman?

Obviously, wide acquaintance with art, especially
the kind one proposes to judge, is fundamental.
Usually, this is acquired through formal study, particularly of art history. It is most important that knowledge of art be gained through original works as well
as reproductions. Many artists acquire this knowledge
from examination of works in museums as well as
from studio experience. But it is difficult, if not impossible, to gain an authentic understanding of art from
reproductions alone. They usually serve to *remind* us
of qualities we have found in originals.

it may account for the development of art criticism as
a serious discipline. Clearly, many persons want to
have a sound foundation for their judgments about
what is good, better, or best. Large sums of money
may be related to those judgments. To some extent,
even a scholarly discipline like art history is based on
the need to establish firmly that an art object is what
someone says it is. In the course of answering questions of authorship, provenance, and so on, the
historian discovers information which is humanistical-
ly valuable, apart from the data required to secure a
transaction. In connection with modern works of art,
there is usually little question about authenticity.
Hence, critical evaluations seem more related to
establishing monetary values for contemporary works.
(Of late, the existence of clever forgers and dealers in
faked works by modern masters has come to light.
Complex questions of aesthetics and art criticism are
raised when an apparently significant work suddenly
loses its value after it is discovered to be a forgery.)

Acquaintance with art implies more than visual recognition of the monuments of art history. It also calls for understanding the styles and functions of art, the social and cultural contexts in which artists have worked, and the technical factors which affect artistic execution in various media. However, the chief benefit of a wide acquaintance with art is breadth of taste. Critics should appreciate a wide range of artistic creativity. This is a defense against critical narrowness, the tendency to use standards based on scant knowledge of styles and limited experience with technical methods. Art historians, for example, do not usually gain much technical knowledge through their training. However, this lack can be somewhat overcome by study of works in various stages of execution. If nothing else, such experience gives the critic some understanding of the gap between artistic intent and achievement.

Many artists would hold critics in greater esteem if they knew their judgments were based on experience with artistic execution. Still, is it fair to require that a critic lay an egg before he can comment on an omelet? Of course, a number of critics have had artistic experience, and some are artists themselves. But usually we read criticism by persons with only avocational artistic experience or with purely literary and theoretical preparation. On the other hand, scholars can readily see emotional distortion and partisanship in the critical opinions of artists. Indeed, some feel that artists are constitutionally incapable of making critical judgments objectively. The question will doubtless continue to be argued as long as there are artists and critics. For a long time, universities employed only theoreticians to give art instruction. Now there is a growing tendency to employ theoreticians *and* practitioners, or individuals who have both kinds of training.

Critics with only theoretical preparation may be ill-equipped to assess the elements of technical intention and quality of execution in works of art. They have a tendency to denigrate technical facility, to regard it as evidence of superficiality. In addition, such critics often do not recognize poor craftsmanship when they see it. The art world is annually embarrassed when the work of amateurs, practical jokers, or animals is given serious attention, and occasionally prizes, in art exhibitions. These stunts, which are probably intended to indict modern art, have little to do with the achievement of serious artists. Nevertheless, they *do* constitute a scandal in the practice of art criticism and cannot be ignored when regarded as a comment on the quality of criticism often encountered in newspapers and art journals. Conscientious critics are eager to be fair, to be open to artistic expression no matter how shocking or experimental. Hence, it is possible for them to be occasionally deceived by a fraudulent work, unless they have sufficient technical experience and connoisseurship to *recapitulate imaginatively the technical execution of the work*. In short, if the critic is to be more than an essayist on art, he must know in general terms how the work was made. This knowledge is essential for critical expertise; without it, critical judgments may be interesting but hardly defensible except as literature.

"Critical sensibility" designates the ability of a viewer to respond to the variety of meanings in an art object. We know that people vary in the range of emotions they feel in connection with events in life. Likewise, individuals vary in capacity for feeling in connection with art. A critic, however, must have access to a wide range of aesthetic emotions, else his usefulness is limited. Many controversies about contemporary art may be based on restricted sensibility or range of aesthetic perception in critics.

Some of us may be limited in our emotional range and reluctant to extend that range further. Much of education, particularly in the humanities, should be directed toward enlarging our responses in the presence of art. Needless to say, the extension of our aesthetic range is a humanly enriching enterprise, a desirable goal of liberal education. That is why emphasis on critical capacity is as important as accumulating information in the study of the fine arts.

Not that a critic has no preferences. Like everyone, he carries a host of biases and constitutional affinities. Hence, another item of critical equipment might be called judicious temperament. By this I mean the ability to withhold judgment until all the evidence is in. Many persons make judgments too quickly; they state conclusions first and then look for reasons to justify their conclusions. A judicious temperament allows time for impressions, associations, sensations, and half-formed judgments to interact; it permits intelligence to operate in the task of sifting, sorting, and organizing. We need time to exercise logic and rationality when our feelings are being skillfully assaulted.

Types of Art Criticism

Although I have referred to a type of person called an art critic, there are in fact several kinds of critic, differing according to the social or professional role each performs. We are most familiar with the journalistic critic, the person who writes reviews of exhibitions, plays, books, and concerts. There are several varieties within this category, since a newspaper may employ one reporter to "do" art, music, and drama criticism, while an art journal may employ several critics with considerable specialized training. (Perhaps such journalists should be called "art writers.") Another kind of criticism occurs in schools, colleges, universities—wherever art is taught. Such criticism, conducted by teachers, might be called pedagogical criticism. In addition, scholars, usually associated with universities, also write criticism. Finally, there is popular criticism conducted by laymen; they are clearly the majority and they vary greatly in the degree of their expertise. The artist, too, is a critic.

Every decision he makes as he works has a critical dimension. He usually learns criticism from his teachers and fellow artists.

JOURNALISTIC CRITICISM

The main point about journalistic criticism is that it is a category of news. It is written to inform readers about events in the art world and to retain their interest as readers of a particular newspaper or journal. Hence, we speak of the "review," which is a brief summary of an exhibition; it is rarely long enough to constitute a systematic analysis of the works in a show. Indeed, a style of review writing has emerged which endeavors to create verbal equivalents of the works or the general atmosphere of the exhibition. Obviously, criticism which endeavors to be news and to substitute words for visual and aesthetic experience, while also passing critical judgment, labors under an impossible burden. The brevity of journalistic criticism obliges the writer to eliminate analysis and to rely on critical conclusions to create exciting copy. Unfortunately, this style of writing also appears in some longer magazine articles where there is less excuse for offering page after page of opinions as if these constituted reasoned critical analysis.

Notwithstanding the obligation of a journalist to satisfy the curiosity of many readers, to entertain them, to describe works they may not have seen, to avoid writing "over their heads," some excellent critical writing is found in newspapers and newsmagazines. The specialized monthly journals differ considerably among themselves as they become engaged in promulgating a "party line" or in castigating museums and foundations for failing to support their favorite artists. In general, the magazines serve to stoke the fires of critical controversy and, by expressing their biases forcefully, are largely responsible for the atmosphere of vitality and rivalry which surrounds the contemporary artistic scene.

Because journalistic critics write so often, and under pressure of deadlines, their output suffers from the perils of much newswriting: inaccuracy, hasty conclusions, the substitution of opinion for analysis, and a tendency to exercise wit at the expense of the unseen artist. But the discriminating reader learns to discount the biases of a critic in advance, to compensate by reading several writers, and to check for accuracy by viewing the work himself. Without such safeguards, the individual may find that his critical understanding consists of received opinions about the principal current reputations. Coteries and intrigues abound in the art world; one's judgment can easily become a by-product of the incessant jockeying for position which characterizes a realm where talented persons struggle for recognition.

PEDAGOGICAL CRITICISM

Pedagogical criticism is meant to advance the artistic and aesthetic maturity of students. It should not so much render judgments upon student work as enable them to make judgments themselves. The teacher of art should be capable of functioning as a critic of mature work; but for the pedagogic critic, professional work represents possibilities for stimulation and discussion; it should not represent absolute goals for achievement.

An important task of the teacher of art, one which involves his critical capacities, is the sensitive analysis and interpretation of a student's work *to the student.* From this criticism, the student learns how to analyze and interpret, and gains insight into the direction of his own work. Art instructors need to function as critics *during* the process of execution as well as at its conclusion. Decisions often result from a critical collaboration between instructor and student.

In the past students sought out teachers whose work they admired and wished to imitate. Few believed criticism could be based on standards other than those

JACKSON POLLOCK.
Untitled. c. 1936.
Collection Mrs. Lee
Krasner Pollock,
New York

embodied in a teacher's own art. The instruction which resulted might be valuable insofar as the teacher did not try to reproduce his artistic personality among his students. Certainly Robert Henri (1865–1929) was an inspiring teacher of this type; his instruction did not constitute a constricting influence on his students. Thomas Hart Benton (born 1889), on the other hand, from the force of his personality or the narrowness of his vision, succeeded in producing a host of "little Bentons," for example, Jackson Pollock, whose early work was touchingly Bentonesque.

The prevailing philosophy of pedagogical art criticism would seem to call for a certain modesty on the part of the artist-teacher. His function is to assist in the development of critical standards *within* the student—standards which are congenial to the *student's* artistic personality as it appears to be emerging. This objective constitutes a genuine challenge to critical sensitivity and teaching skill.

SCHOLARLY CRITICISM

Academic art criticism is the fully developed product of scholarship and critical sensibility. Its function is to provide the best analysis, interpretation, and evaluation of art which ample time, space, and evidence can make possible. Generally, it requires the sponsorship of universities. Scholarly criticism represents an approximation to "the judgment of history" for a living artist; it constitutes part of the changing judgment of history for an artist who is dead. Presumably, the scholarly critic, settled in the safety of academic tenure and undergirded by university traditions of scrupulous research and disinterested truth-seeking, is invulnerable to special interest. He can function as well as his critical equipment will permit. But as the university confronts contemporary life, it may lose its precious detachment and objectivity.

A useful function of academic critics is their re-examination of artistic reputations which have been categorized and set aside. Each era has its characteristic way of seeing; thus an artist who seemed unintelligible in his time may be discovered to have meaning for the present. Museums frequently function in this manner when they resurrect the reputation of a school or style of art which has fallen into disesteem. This was done, for example, by the Museum of Modern Art in its 1960 exhibition and scholarly catalogue devoted to Art Nouveau. Hitherto regarded as an art movement of only minor decorative value, Art Nouveau was shown to have had a significant influence on many of the leading painters, sculptors, architects, designers, and craftsmen whose work we regard as classics today.

POPULAR CRITICISM

Throughout this discussion, I have referred to popular art criticism, the judgments made by the large public which has no claim to critical expertness. Clearly, most citizens will continue to judge art whether qualified or not. Therefore, the existence of a large amount of popular critical opinion has to be considered in its effect on the total art situation. We must seriously entertain Mark Twain's view: "The public is the only critic whose opinion is worth anything at all."

As mentioned earlier, critical opinion influences what artists create. And this is true of popular as well as expert criticism. The concept of an avant-garde, of a body of artists working in advance of popular taste, assumes the existence of popular taste as a sort of huge, laggard collection of preferences. But if it were not for this popular taste, there would be no body of conventional preference for the avant-garde to rebel against! The idea of progress in art, of advanced and retarded preferences, is very misleading—a misapplication to aesthetics of the idea of progress in history.[38]

There will always be many people who judge art intuitively, who regard the possession of normal vision as adequate equipment for the conduct of art criticism. The number of such persons is so large, and their critical consensus so consistent, that their opinions and standards cannot be ignored by artists, scholars, or critics. Their desire for an art which is faithful to the visual facts has been discussed in connection with the style of objective accuracy. Of course, cinematic imagery may satisfy the desire for realism; it also creates the opportunity for art *to depart* from realism or naturalism. Nevertheless, each generation of artists works in a context partly determined by the public's preference for naturalism. We may hope, however, that aesthetic education will enable people to discriminate among types of realism. It should not be impossible to see the difference between a mechanical realism in art and a style which reveals the *character* of things. Popular criticism, in other words, can become discriminating within its own standards of fidelity to visual facts.

Kinds of Critical Judgment

What are the grounds on which a critic justifies his evaluations? Assuming the critic is knowledgeable, disciplined, and possessed of the appropriate temperament and sensibility, are there any final standards to which he can repair?

It would be enough if critics had the right credentials and practiced a method open to reason and discussion. This would enable them to carry on the work of description, analysis, and interpretation. But evaluation must take place in the light of ideas about excellence. Here we can examine some of the ideas of artistic and aesthetic value which underlie what critics and others say is good.

FORMALISM

Once we have abandoned the notion that excellence consists of accurate imitation, we can turn to what is called formalist criticism. Such criticism locates excellence in formal organization—in the relationships among the visual elements of the work, independent of labels, associations, or conventional meanings these elements may have in life.

For a formalist, successful relationships are designed; they result from calculation and planning by the artist rather than a viewer's subjective tendencies. Obviously, Cézanne or Mondrian would appeal to the formalist since they minimize accidental effects. There is no uncertainty on our part about the artist's means or method: it is to put together the work without permitting "extraneous" that is—nonartistic—considerations to enter.

Formalist excellence does not require a geometric or an abstract style. In the paintings of Poussin, representational imagery is combined with the simulation of figures and naturalistic space, but the entire composition is organized so that the masses, contours, and directions are related to each other with preci-

sion: they balance, or cancel out, like books audited by an accountant.

The formalist critic may find value in subject matter or the sensuous appeal of materials. However, he is willing to judge a work excellent only insofar as its *form,* its underlying organization, is responsible for his *perception* of meaning or sensuous quality. For example, he would admire the bronze-metal skin of Mies van der Rohe's Seagram Building, not because bronze is an inherently beautiful material, but because the bronze members have precisely the right dimensions and are located at the best intervals in relation to the tinted glass, the shapes, and the total spatial envelope of the building.

Formalist criticism takes an interest in craftsmanship, since putting things together soundly and working them to the "right" degree of finish invokes formal criteria of pleasing relationships. Craftsmanship is ultimately based on the logical use of tools and materials—utilitarian concerns which are not a primary focus of formalist criticism. But if we penetrate to the heart of formalism, we should find the wish that works of art depend for their effectiveness *solely* on the principle of *unity in variety,* with that unity achieved through the nonsymbolic, noncognitive properties of materials.

Formalism has had a healthy influence on art when it has been negative in its strictures; that is, when it has insisted on the elimination of literary elements as the principal vehicles of meaning. On the positive side, however, formalism experiences some difficulty in establishing just what its idea of excellence is. That is, how do we know which formal relationships are pleasing or significant? The formalist critics Roger Fry and Clive Bell never succeeded in defining the criteria of formal excellence; they merely associated it with the capacity to generate disinterested, aesthetic emotion.

If pressed, the formalist might say that an organization is best when it *embodies the ideal structural possibilities of the visual elements present in the work.* But how do we know whether the organization we see represents the *ideal* possibilities of its components? Here, the formalist must fall back on the quality of his perceptions—that is, he must rely on the conviction that his perceptions in the presence of the work are intrinsically satisfying. Bernard Berenson was relying on formalist ideas of aesthetic value when he employed the term "life-enhancing" to describe the characteristics of great art. This term (which is really an elegant way of saying "good") represents a viewer's belief that pleasure in aesthetic perception is based solely on the qualities of visual form.

This criterion of aesthetic value may not be as subjective as it appears. Qualities in the organization of an art object which elicit the designations "excellent," "beautiful," or "life-enhancing" are presumably the qualities a reasonably intelligent person would discover to be pleasing. That is, they approximate an *ideal standard,* or *norm,* which connects with whatever it is in people that seeks such norms.

THE FORMALIST AS PAINTER

First the formalist tries to capture nature within a measured, orderly framework (Poussin); next he tries to represent nature's vitality without losing control of its underlying structure (Cézanne); finally, he uses nature as a source of objects that can fit into his vision of the universe as a perfect machine (Léger).

NICOLAS POUSSIN.
Landscape with the Burial of Phocion. 1648.
The Louvre, Paris

PAUL CÉZANNE. *Lac d'Annecy.* 1896.
Courtauld Institute Galleries,
London

FERNAND LÉGER.
Nudes in the Forest. 1909–10.
Kröller-Müller Museum, Otterlo,
The Netherlands

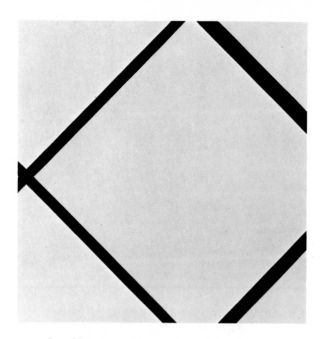

PIET MONDRIAN. *Painting I.* 1926. The Museum of Modern Art, New York. Katherine S. Dreier Bequest. An exceedingly subtle work that involves the formalist sensibility. The viewer is obliged to measure and compare forms: length, thickness, divergence, convergence, beginnings, endings, openings, closings. Then he must make adjustments in feeling that will bring him into harmony with what he sees.

We come, in effect, to a theory of communication which underlies the formalist's idea of excellence. He shares with the Platonist the view that there is an ideal or perfect embodiment of all things, and that art, when it is successful, reveals, represents, or *communicates* that ideal. The formalist and the Platonist might quarrel about whether the ideal embodiment exists *before* or *after* the work of art is created. But they agree that art approximates to a greater or lesser degree an idea or form of perfection. The normal person has, because of his biological and psychological makeup, the ability to recognize and to enjoy ideality of form. Thus, excellent form communicates itself to individuals, because, as normal persons, they cannot help responding to it.

These views about the foundations of aesthetic excellence are held by artists as well as laymen. Often, artists invoke formalist criteria as they create, particularly when faced with the problem of deciding when a work is finished. There is a strong artistic tendency to "perfect" the forms of a work, long after its theme has become visible. The artist continues to adjust and modify formal relationships until *he feels* they can be carried no further. In measuring the finish or perfection of the work against his ideal requirements, he is, in effect, proposing his own ideas of what is normative for the approval of reasonably sensitive and intelligent viewers, thus demonstrating

the formalist theory that universal norms and ideal possibilities communicate themselves among persons attuned to grasp them. Such persons, in turn, are those who possess the normal appetites and capacities in proper measure.

Many artists and critics are formalists without knowing it. Their criteria of excellence consist of feelings of sympathy with the organization of the art object, feelings derived from design qualities and communicated by affirmative signals received from the glandular, nervous, or muscular systems. This can only be suspected. Formalism provides us mainly with a guide to the values it rejects as aesthetically irrelevant: social, historical, and psychological description; literary and emotional association; imitation or representation of real objects. Beyond the *form preferences of the normal person,* it offers no certain rule of artistic excellence.

EXPRESSIVISM

Expressivist criticism sees excellence as the ability of art to communicate ideas and feelings intensely and vividly. It is at the opposite pole from formalism in its lack of interest in formal organization for its own sake. A good example of art admired by expressivist criticism is seen in the work of children. Children rarely possess the skill or the desire to arrive at perfect organizations of form. For them, the impulse to communicate, to objectify some inner need, is usually stronger than the desire to embellish or adjust forms so they will be "beautiful" as adults understand the word. The art of children may often be enjoyed for the delight afforded by its uninhibited color, design, and imagery. Yet the principal reason for its appeal seems to lie in the naivete of the child's *view* of the world. Some expressivist critics believe that children reveal a world of ideal possibilities, since they can see through to the "heart" of things without the cultural distortions that plague adult vision. This suggests that we are interested in the ideas and emotions expressed by child art more than their technical and organizational qualities.

Now, all art, regardless of style, communicates ideas or feelings to some extent. Consequently, expressivism must provide some way of deciding whether we are in the presence of something *beyond* the sharing of feelings and ideas. To meet this problem, expressivist criticism offers us the idea of *intensity of experience.* The best work arouses the most vivid feelings—feelings stronger than those we would experience in everyday life. Furthermore, we realize that an artist is responsible for the way we feel. For example, if a photograph presents a mechanical image of a catastrophe—an earthquake, a sea disaster, an air attack—we may respond with feelings of shock; but we tend to believe the event, not the photograph, is responsible for our feelings. When an artist deals with the same theme, we feel he has governed our intellectual and emotional responses.

WASSILY KANDINSKY. *Sketch I for Composition 7.* 1913. Collection Felix Klee, Bern. For Kandinsky, painterly forms constitute an independent language: they generate rather than echo experience.

It thus appears that the expressivist critic believes art should "have something to say," which implies that the artist should have something to say. This school of criticism, therefore, shares with many laymen a preference for art as a source of insight about life. It sees the artist as wise in a way that other wise men are not. That is, the artist has taken hold of some truths about life, and, through skill and imagination, has found a way to embody those truths. The *originality, relevance,* and *cognitive validity* of the ideas expressed by art become criteria for judgment. Although the expressivist critic recognizes the importance of technique and formal organization, he insists that they be associated with the communication of significant ideas.

It is not uncommon for expressivist critics to apply the criterion of truthfulness to life in judging art. The idea of art as a credible imitation of life survives in the

PAUL KLEE. *Shame.* 1933.
Paul Klee Foundation, Kunstmuseum, Bern

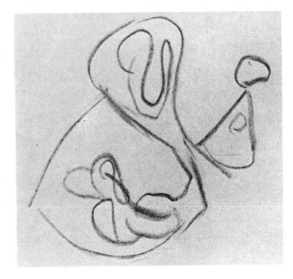

Drawing by a four-year-old child

What Klee found in child art was a combination of primal innocence and insight.
Like the expressivist critic, he prized psychological truth over formal beauty.

OTTO DIX. *Punishment*. 1934.
The Museum of Modern Art, New York.
Gift of Mr. and Mrs. Erich Cohn

GEORGE GROSZ. *Lens Bombed*. 1924.
Philadelphia Museum of Art. Gift of anonymous donor

Photograph of an air attack on a tank
during World War I

expressivist demand that art be *relevant* to life; works
of art need not look like objects, places, and persons,
but they must support ideas which have immediate
meaning for the reasonably perceptive person. We
come again to the normal individual, the mythical
person who sets the standard of emotional and in-

tellectual relevance for the expressivist critic as he set
the standard of satisfying structural relationships for
the formalist critic.

INSTRUMENTALISM

Instrumentalist theories conceive of art as a tool for
advancing some moral, religious, political, or psychological purpose. Thus artistic excellence is not based
primarily on the ability to solve problems inherent in
the use of materials—problems *internal* to the artistic
enterprise. Neither is excellence based on the expressivist criteria of vividness, credibility, and relevance
in the communication of ideas or the sharing of
feelings. The instrumentalist is concerned with the
consequences of the ideas and feelings expressed by
art. He wishes art to serve an end more important
than itself.

An ordinary illustration of the instrumentalist idea
of art is found in the background music that accompanies a film. The music should support the
dramatic action, heightening its meaning or anticipating climactic moments but never calling attention
to itself. The relation of art to social, political, or
moral ends thus should be the same as the relation of
background music to the visual and dramatic action
on the cinema screen.

In a sense, the history of art is the history of its

service to society's principal institutions and dominant classes. It has only been in the modern era that art has functioned to some extent as a free-floating activity, unattached and unpatronized by a single class or institution. More recently, modern museums, universities, and foundations have emerged as sponsors of art or of artists; but, for the most part, they have taken care not to alter the unattached character of artistic creativity. They have tried not to have their support seem contingent on any loyalty of the artist to the people who help him or the institution which feeds him. Certainly they have not endeavored to influence the *content* of art. Hence, the instrumentalist theory of art finds support mainly in the practices of the past. At present, instrumentalists must accept the independence of the artist, his detachment from institutions; but they can argue for the *usefulness of art*, the necessity that it serve some external purpose.

One difficulty with the instrumentalist interpretation of historic art—art, for example, in the service of the Church—is that today we admire that art for different reasons than it was created to serve. Romanesque sculpture was created to communicate the doctrines of the Church to people who could not read. But we *can* read; our religious indoctrination comes from other sources. Nevertheless, we admire Romanesque sculpture for the vigor of its forms, its human interest, and its technical achievement. For us, such sculpture is art *about* religion; for its contemporaries, it was *part of* the religious life.

A strong argument for the instrumentalist theory lies in its implied analysis of artistic creativity. The instrumentalist has to concede that art which formerly served purposes outside itself is now prized for formal or expressive qualities. These qualities are present, he believes, because they had to be "built into" the art object so that it would function adequately in the service of Church or state. In other words, the creation of great art requires strong motivation.

Is the instrumentalist really a formalist or expressivist critic, differing only in the requirement that art have extra-artistic motivation? This view would be incorrect since instrumentalist critics *derive artistic motivation* from the purposes art serves. Instrumentalists do not believe aesthetic values exist independently, that satisfactions or meanings in art can be experienced apart from their involvement in some larger purpose. They would argue that Michelangelo's *Pietà* is a great work not only because it illustrates a central religious event but also because it supports crucially important ideas about grief and maternal love. These ideas are the *purposes* for whose expression the forms were created. There is a clarity in the relationship between the visual organization of forms and the expressive function which provides the instrumentalist standard of judgment. Unlike the formalist, who must speculate about whether an organization has realized its ideal possibilities, the instrumentalist critic can readily discern the purpose of the work. Hence, he can direct his critical energies to the estimation of the artist's success in fulfilling this purpose.

There is a vulgar kind of instrumentalism which requires that art illustrate stereotyped political ideas. Thus, some Marxist critics want art to represent scenes of class struggle, the impoverishment of the masses under capitalism, the heroism of manual workers, and so on. At its best, Marxist thought can be convincing in its explanation of the social relations between creators and users of art, but it tends to be unsatisfactory in the formulation of criteria of artistic excellence. Consider Diego Rivera, himself a Communist, who was able to satisfy Marxist canons of taste. His murals dealing with the exploitation of the Mexican Indian masses were intended to provide the motivation for revolutionary change. It is likely, however, that Rivera's enduring reputation as an artist rests more securely on formalist than on instrumentalist grounds.

The efforts of the Soviet government to stimulate the creation of art which supports the regime's official views have been consistently productive of mediocrity. This result may not be due to instrumentalism, however. It is more likely due to bureaucratic rigidity or clumsiness, not to say ignorance. Citizens and politicians of many persuasions adhere to theories of vulgar instrumentalism: art is excellent when it illustrates officially proclaimed goals; it must never be

MICHELANGELO. *Pietà.* 1498–99. St. Peter's, Rome

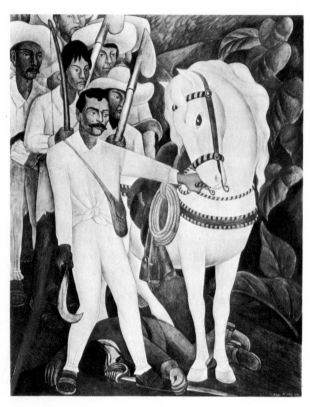

DIEGO RIVERA. *Agrarian Leader Zapata.* 1931.
The Museum of Modern Art, New York.
Abby Aldrich Rockefeller Fund

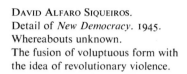

DAVID ALFARO SIQUEIROS.
Detail of *New Democracy.* 1945.
Whereabouts unknown.
The fusion of voluptuous form with
the idea of revolutionary violence.

JEAN METZINGER. *Tea Time.* 1911.
Philadelphia Museum of Art.
The Louise and Walter Arensberg Collection

DIEGO RIVERA. *Two Women.* 1941.
The Arkansas Arts Center, Little Rock.
Gift of Abby Rockefeller Mause, 1955

Rivera's affinity for Metzinger's almost decorative Cubism reveals the essentially
formalistic foundation on which Rivera built his "revolutionary" art.

HONORÉ DAUMIER. *The Connoisseurs.* c. 1840. Boymans-van Beuningen Museum, Rotterdam

GEORGE PRICE. *"I think you have something to say, all right, but I don't think you're saying it."* Cartoon. © 1960 The New Yorker Magazine, Inc.

PIETER BRUEGEL THE ELDER. *The Painter and the Connoisseur.* c. 1565. The Albertina, Vienna. What could better express the artist's awareness of the critic—looking over his shoulder, eagerly awaiting the birth of a masterpiece.

"negative" except in dealing with competitive economic and social systems.

Notwithstanding the vulgar application of instrumentalist theories—especially in old-fashioned censorship—instrumentalism provides useful grounds for the criticism of art. It encourages the critic to seek out the social, moral, or civic purposes art may serve. It emphasizes the legitimacy of art related to the dominant concerns of life and thus acts as a corrective to the artistic tendency to become excessively involved with purely personal and technical problems.

Conclusion

Other grounds for critical judgment could be mentioned in addition to those discussed here. I have tried to indicate the main types of argument used to justify assertions of aesthetic value. For the student, it is perhaps useful to know that these theories exist and can be relied on to support critical judgments. Some individuals may wish to develop justifications which place greater stress on the hedonic or pleasurable element in art; or they may stress the sensory, biological, and physiological foundations of art. In connection with the criticism of architecture, the crafts, and industrially produced objects, it may be useful to rely on theories of social utility, workmanship, and the expressiveness of processes of forming and fabrication. The kinds and purposes of art are so varied that no single critical theory is likely to be adequate for the evaluation of all works. Indeed, some theories rule out certain classes of objects as aesthetically irrelevant, thus confining consideration to the kinds of art where a certain set of critical principles must be applied. The person who says, "Such and such a work is not art," avoids the task of criticizing what he does not like or understand. Probably he knows no critical theory which will allow him to examine the object in question. But obviously, if we want to understand art and assess its value, theories which exclude certain works of art from consideration are not very useful. We would be wise to employ a definition of art which includes potentially everything that man makes. Then, equipped with a suitable critical apparatus, we can examine the merits of any work that presents itself for judgment.

DAVID SEYMOUR. Photograph of Bernard Berenson at the Borghese Gallery in Rome, 1955

Critics and connoisseurs: What makes it good? Is it better than something else? Can my opinion be defended? How?

17

THE CRITICAL PERFORMANCE

HAVING DISCUSSED THE QUALIFICATIONS OF A CRITIC, the purposes of his work, and the kinds of argument he can use to support his judgments—we can turn to a consideration of the critical performance itself. Throughout this book I have functioned informally as a critic. Indeed, any statement about art is likely to contain examples of critical performance, since it is difficult to talk about art without carrying out some of the operations of criticism. Now it would be appropriate to describe the critical performance in some detail.

My guiding assumption is that there is a systematic way of behaving like a critic, just as there is a systematic way of behaving like a lawyer. A lawyer has a method of offering evidence, of refuting adversaries, of citing precedents, of appealing to jurors, and so on. Art criticism may not have the form of legal debate, but it *does* have a form. We must become conscious of the form, process, or system we use in making critical statements.

I divide the art critical *performance* into four stages: Description, Formal Analysis, Interpretation, and Evaluation or Judgment. One could break down these categories further; to some extent they overlap. Nevertheless, they entail fundamentally *different* operations, and their *sequence* proceeds from the easiest operation to the most difficult—from the specific to the general. That is, we focus on particular visual facts before making inferences about their overall meaning and value.

Description

Description is a process of taking inventory, of noting what is immediately visible. We are interested at this

stage in avoiding inferences. We wish to arrive at a simple account of "what is there." In description, the language of the critic should be as "unloaded" as possible. That is, it should not contain hints about the meaning or value of what is described.

The reason for deferring inferences and value judgments is to make certain that the description, or inventory, is complete. If the critic made value statements at this stage, he might also try to justify these evaluations. This would prevent him from completing

GERALD GOOCH. *Hmmm.* 1968.
Hansen-Fuller Gallery, San Francisco

471

the description, from finding what is "there" to be discovered.

What are the things we wish to describe in a work of art? First, we should mention what is most obvious. If we are dealing with a realistic work, we can note the *names* of the things we see. We should use words which will minimize disagreement. For example, we might say that Picasso's *Les Demoiselles d'Avignon* contains the figures of five women. But, despite the title, it may not be apparent that one of the figures is a woman. Then, we should say the painting has five *figures*, four of which appear to be women. It would be better for the critic to *prove* that the fifth figure is a woman. Quite possibly, the uncertainty about the figures may be useful in forming an interpretation.

As works grow abstract, it becomes difficult to name objects, trees, persons, and so on. The subject matter we are accustomed to recognize disappears or becomes something else. We are obliged to describe the principal shapes, colors, and directions we see. A shape is ovoid or rectangular; the edge of a contour is hard or soft. But we should not say it is beautiful or grotesque, harmonious or harsh. Beyond describing forms, the critic should point out compositional features, and these, too, can be described without making value judgments. That is, the critic can readily recognize repetitions of shapes and colors; he can identify the directions forms seem to take. He can point to spatial characteristics which the viewer would not have found unaided.

Another necessary task is to call attention to characteristics of execution. We should know whether paint has been brushed out, how it has been mixed, whether a surface is made of transparent layers or applied in one coat. In architecture, features such as the use of cast-concrete or steel-frame construction should be considered. With handcraft or manufactured objects, the critic should describe the processes of fabrication: is a container turned, built up by hammering, stamped, welded, or cast? Are the marks of the tools or forming process visible or concealed? The answers to these questions affect our perceptions of an object, our understanding of its form, our feelings about its use.

For discussions of technique, viewers are dependent on the knowledge of the critic. Professor Vincent Scully provides a good example of such criticism at work: "Moreover, the Beinecke Library wall is actually a Vierendeel truss; it thus need be supported only at the four corners of the building. But the truss does not look structural to the eye, which therefore sees the building as small, since the span looks to be a little one. Yet the building is huge and therefore disorienting to the viewer."[39] The critic maintains that the engineering qualities of the span have been violated visually. Mr. Scully points to a difference between the way the building is constructed and the way it appears to be constructed. There should be a correspondence, he implies, and since there is none, the

SKIDMORE, OWINGS AND MERRILL.
Beinecke Rare Book and Manuscript Library,
Yale University, New Haven, Connecticut. 1963

Scully's reference to De Chirico is a *tour de force* of the critical imagination. Not only does he diagnose the technical difficulty in the building, but he also identifies the symbolic source of its aesthetic failure.

GIORGIO DE CHIRICO. *Delights of the Poet*. c. 1913.
Collection Helen and Leonard Yaseen, New York

building is "disorienting to the viewer." Thus we see, in a brief excerpt, how technical analysis leads to an aesthetic judgment, "disorientation," which this critic holds up to a standard of visual and structural correspondence. Then he concludes: "It all ends, I think, by creating an atmosphere of no place, nowhere, nobody, matched only by some of De Chirico's images of human estrangement and by a few similarly motivated Italian buildings of the Thirties and early Forties."

Professor Scully believes the building is unsuccessful, and he has given technical reasons for his view. He also endeavors to *persuade* us to this view by sharing his subjective impressions of the building, by citing an analogy to the forlorn imagery of Giorgio de Chirico, and by making a comparison with the generally condemned architecture of the Fascist era in Italy. The judgment, in short, begins as a conclusion and ends as an attack.

Whether or not we agree with his conclusions, this critic has earned the right to make them.

Formal Analysis

In formal analysis, we try to go "behind" a descriptive inventory to discover the relations among the things we have named. We may have identified five female figures in *Les Demoiselles*, but now we want to know how they have been organized as shapes, areas of color, and forms with particular contours, textures, and locations in space.

In *Les Demoiselles*, some of the figures are made of angular, flat planes of color, whereas the two central figures are more curvilinear, have gentler transitions of color, and seem less distorted. One of the central figures has white lines to delineate its shapes. Strangely, the outer figures have heads which are in marked contrast to their bodies. The central figures, while frontally posed, present the nose in profile; and one figure seems insecure, like a statue which might fall from its pedestal. Her torso is erect, but her feet are too far to the left to support her body.

My notion that the figure seems to be falling illustrates one of the sources of inferences about form: the erectness of human posture and the influence of gravity. No matter what style of art we examine, certain physical and biological assumptions about people are shared by artist *and* viewer. We cannot view a tilted representation of the human figure without feeling that it may fall. The expectation of collapse may be an important perception about the work.

Although the color in *Les Demoiselles* seems to model the forms, we have very little impression of depth. Instead there is a shallow space implied by the overlapping of the forms. There are no perspective devices, no changes in size, focus, color intensity, or sharpness of edge to suggest a representation of space deeper than the picture plane.

Notice that the drawing of the hand in the central figure involves some skill in foreshortening; it is more or less believable, but the other two hands in the painting are crudely drawn; one is childlike, while the other is schematic and stiff—part of an arm which resembles a carved substance more than flesh. But that arm, at the left of the canvas, is painted in the typical pink tones of European figurative art. Thus, there is a conflict, within the arm, between the drawing and color and the paint quality. Is this the type of conflict that Scully noted in his architectural critique, or is it an *intended conflict* which has relevance to an interpretation of the work?

We should also notice that there are three kinds of distortion in the heads of the three outer figures. In the head at the left, color shifts from pink to brown, the eye is much enlarged, and the planes of the nose are simplified as in African wood sculpture. The *shape* of the head remains naturalistic, however; it is conventionally illuminated. Moving to the upper-right head, we depart from logical representation. Very pronounced harsh green lines are used to indicate the nose plane in shadow; a rough, unfinished kind of execution characterizes the head. The breast has a squarish shape. At this point the painting begins to depart from the simple imitation of appearances as the goal of painting.

Nevertheless, the upper-right head has a normal attachment to the body. The head on the seated figure, however, is uncertain in its relation to the body. The nose has been flattened out; the convention of a shadow plane has been employed as a decorative element, or an element of pure form in what might be called a synthetic composition based on the head. The alignment of the eyes is illogical. A collection of forms based on different views of the head has been assembled and located where the head would be. From this head alone, we cannot deduce the sex, race, age, or any other distinguishing characteristic of the

PABLO PICASSO.
Les Demoiselles d'Avignon. 1907.
The Museum of Modern Art, New York.
Lillie P. Bliss Bequest

473

Details of
Les Demoiselles d'Avignon

figure. Only the hips and thighs, plus the title, confirm that the figure is a woman.

At the extreme left position of the canvas is a brown area which seems to be a close-up of a female figure, employing forms typical of African art. It is not one of the *demoiselles* but seems to be an echo of a woman's back carried out in the brown color of carved wood sculpture. Perhaps it is an announcement of the *leitmotif* of the painting, or an enlarged rear view of the figure at the left.

The idea of the viewer's expectation is very important in formal analysis. And the artist is usually aware of the viewer's conditioning. Picasso knows how to use linear perspective and he knows that viewers in the Western world expect perspectivist illusions to create the space for the *demoiselles*. Nevertheless, he deliberately breaks up any possibility of deep space. The still life in the bottom of the painting provides the

merest hint of a plane leading *into* the picture space. But the artist does not follow through on that spatial representation. Indeed, he locates the foot of the figure on the left in the same plane and at the same height as the still life. The foot must be on the floor, yet the floor cannot be at the same level as the table top on which the still life rests. Obviously, the expected logic of spatial representation is destroyed in this painting.

It is plain that in making a formal analysis, we have been accumulating evidence for an interpretation of the work and a judgment of its excellence. The breakdown of spatial logic might justify a conclusion that the work is unsuccessful. However, we must first ascertain whether a different logic has been created. Or perhaps a logic of spatial representation is irrelevant here. In the case of *Les Demoiselles*, it is enough to say that the activity of the forms takes place in a shallow space parallel to the plane of the picture. The

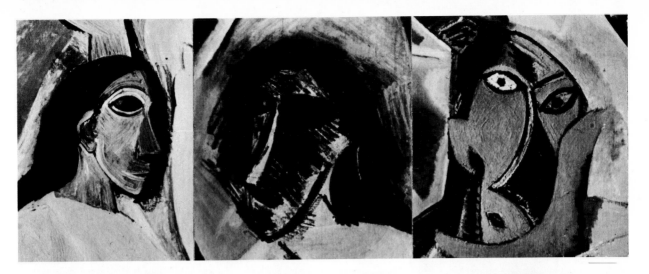

linear and coloristic clues keep us close to the surface. As soon as our eyes begin to penetrate inward, they are turned to one side. Picasso makes the viewer feel he must move to make sense of the profile view of the nose. A fixed position for the viewer will not let him deal with a front view of the face and a profile of the nose in the same head. *We must move imaginatively from left to right as we view the two central figures.* And this imaginative movement is in the same direction as the "falling" central figure. We encounter a reinforcement of our tendency to "read" everything in a clockwise direction. But there are numerous violations of our other expectations. By the time we reach the seated figure at the right, we may be willing to accept the joining of the shoulder, arm, forearm, and hip in a single continuous form, with emphasis shifted from the limbs to the *shape of the openings* they form.

Our formal analysis has begun to move from an objective description of forms to statements about the way we perceive them. We appear to be groping for a principle of organization, an idea or set of ideas which can account for the way the work is structured. As observations of the work increase, as information accumulates, it becomes increasingly difficult to defer the work of interpretation. However, we can undertake the task with certain modest feelings of security: we have *tried* to be objective in our description, we have tried *not* to overlook evidence, and we have endeavored to make assertions which would not in themselves be the subject of disagreement.

Interpretation

By interpretation in art criticism, I mean the process of expressing the meanings of a work the critic has

Guardian figure, from the Bokota area,
Gabon. 19th–20th century.
Ethnographic Collection of the University,
Zurich

An interesting transformation occurs here: the
dancer is adapted from a type of African funerary
figure which is usually armless. But Picasso has
broken the symmetry of the African model and has
added arms folded behind the staring face. Why?

PABLO PICASSO. *Dancer*. 1907.
Collection Walter P. Chrysler, Jr., New York

analyzed. I do not mean that the critic finds verbal
equivalents for the art object. Neither does he evaluate
the work. Obviously, we are not in a position to judge
a work until we have decided what it means, what its
themes are, what problems it has succeeded in solving.

Interpretation is tremendously challenging; it is
certainly the most important part of the critical enterprise. Indeed, if we have thoroughly interpreted a
work, the business of evaluation can often be omitted.
Explaining a work of art involves discovering its
meanings *and also* stating the relevance of these meanings to our lives and to the human situation in general.

Certain assumptions underlie critical interpretation. We assume that an art object, being a human
product, cannot escape some aspect of the value system of the artist. Just as a human being cannot go
through life without consciously or unconsciously
forming a set of values, an art object cannot avoid
being a vehicle of ideas. As critics, we are not particularly interested in whether these ideas are faithful to
the artist's views. That is, we are not interested in
using art to find out what an artist thinks. However,
an art object somehow becomes charged with ideas—
ideas which may be significant in more than a technical sense. They may be present in the work without
the conscious knowledge of the artist. But it is our
function as critics to discover what they are.

An important principle of criticism is that *the artist
is not necessarily the best authority on the meaning of
his work*. As critics, we are interested in what the
artist thinks about his work; we are interested in
anything he can tell us about it. But we regard his
views as material which requires confirmation by our
own methods of analysis and interpretation.

It may be felt that interpretation violates the
qualities of art which are not readily verbalized. How
can one talk about colors and textures and shapes
except in very imprecise terms? My reply is that art
criticism is not intended to be a substitute for aesthetic
experience. I realize that if the content of a work of
art could be expressed verbally, it would not be neces-

PABLO PICASSO. *Les Demoiselles d'Avignon.* 1907. The Museum of Modern Art, New York. Lillie P. Bliss Bequest. Can this work be explained wholly on the basis of what we see? Or must it be approached via the history of art? Must we know the Western conventions for dealing with the pose and composition of female nudes before we can adequately appreciate Picasso's departure from those conventions? The answer depends on whether we regard the work as one document in a continuing story or whether we see it as an independent, organic thing. It is possible, however, with agility in shifting one's perceptual gears, to understand the work through visual sensibility *and* scholarly intelligence. But that obliges us to discipline our seeing and knowing.

RAPHAEL. *The Three Graces*. 1500. Musée Condé, Chantilly, France. Raphael uses these ladies for a superb demonstration of classical equipoise: they are balanced on their feet, within the pictorial space and on the picture plane. Is it essential to remember this painting as we look at Picasso's?

PETER PAUL RUBENS. *The Judgment of Paris*. 1638–39. The National Gallery, London. With Rubens, flesh, display, and asymmetry govern. The ladies compete with one another—one even addresses herself to the viewer. Again, must we keep her in mind as we look at the central figures in *Les Demoiselles*?

JEAN-AUGUSTE-DOMINIQUE INGRES. *Venus Anadyomene.* 1848. Musée Condé, Chantilly, France. This Venus clearly aspires to a Raphaelite grace but somehow lacks nobility: a strange, almost insipid mixture of the sensual and the sentimental creeps in. Surely Picasso was reacting against her.

sary to make it in the first place. In critical interpretation we deal with sensuous and formal qualities of the art object by examining their *impact* upon our vision. As we perceive the work, its qualities seem to organize themselves into a kind of unity, and it is this unity which becomes the meaning of the work, the meaning we wish, however badly, to verbalize.

During description and analysis we *direct the attention* of viewers to *actual* colors and shapes in the art object, not to our language about them. Now variation in perception becomes troublesome because we are faced with the problem of making statements about art which others can accept without surrendering their individuality. In the following discussion, therefore, I shall deal with the subjectivity of perception as it affects critical interpretation.

FORMING A HYPOTHESIS

How do we begin the work of interpretation? Fortunately, during description and analysis, several possible explanations of the work have presented themselves spontaneously. Now we must attempt to formulate an explanation which will fit the evidence we have been assembling. The explanations which seemed to suggest themselves as we analyzed the art object were based on incomplete examination. Technically, they were explications—partial explanations of the work as it unfolds. Yet we can try one or more of them as hypotheses to see if they are satisfactory explanations of the whole.

For the purposes of interpretation in art criticism, *a hypothesis is an idea which seems to relate the material of description and formal analysis meaningfully.* And, just as in science, where more than one hypothesis can account for a given phenomenon, more than one hypothesis can explain a work of art. Changing social and cultural conditions change our perceptions, so we are justified in finding more than one satisfactory hypothesis to serve as the interpretation of a work.

If more than one hypothesis can explain a work, should the critic abandon the effort to furnish a single explanation? The answer depends partly on the public the critic believes he is serving. For example, the teacher of children may explain Seurat's *A Sunday Afternoon on the Island of La Grande Jatte* as a picture of people enjoying a day off by strolling, resting in the shade, watching fishermen, or playing social games. In other words, an adequate interpretation for small children might consist of little more than an account of the visible subject matter. For others, the quality of the picture's surface might be explained in terms of pointillist technique and the relation of this technique to the representation of light, the flattening of forms, and the control of contours. One could speak of the dignity, silence, and order of the painting as opposed to the noise and random movement which must have characterized an *actual* Sunday afternoon. Finally, we might offer the hypothesis that the picture is "really"

GEORGES SEURAT. *A Sunday Afternoon on the Island of La Grande Jatte.* 1884–86. The Art Institute of Chicago. Helen Birch Bartlett Memorial Collection

an abstract work which uses familiar objects to sustain the attention of viewers until they become aware of complex relationships of light and dark, silhouette, flat and deep space, atmosphere, and imitations of sunlight with pigment. Another hypothesis, not incompatible with the others, is that the picture is a *game* played by the artist with his viewers—a game employing the pictorial conventions of drawing, cast shadows, light and dark, perspective, and a new way of applying color. It induces recognition of familiar things in forms which are painterly inventions. The viewer is "taken in" by a few contours and perspective devices; he has been "fooled"—to his own advantage and delight.

Photograph of staff assistant and children before the *Grande Jatte* at the Art Institute of Chicago, 1970

How are hypotheses formed? A hint can be gained from the remarks people make about "experimental" works of art, works which seem "wild," "crazy," "far out." We know what people say when they are frustrated about a difficult work. Sometimes they express their frustration by trying to be funny. A free-form sculpture reminds someone of a "dog taking a bite out of a mailman's leg." The humor is questionable, yet amazingly recurrent. It probably indicates embarrassment as much as anything else. But it also reveals the normal impulse to use what might be called the "looks-like," "feels-like," and "reminds-me-of" reaction. The mind, confronted with material it cannot organize, struggles to find some correspondence between present, confusing perceptions and past experience which has already been organized and understood.

At a certain level, the sculpture may look like a watch-dog biting a mailman. But if we are satisfied with that hypothesis, we deny ourselves potential

SEYMOUR LIPTON. *Cerberus*. 1948.
Collection Mr. and Mrs. Alvin S. Lane, New York

meanings which are more valuable than the saga of dog and mailman celebrated in the adventures of Dagwood Bumstead. Consequently, we must employ the "looks-like" reaction at a more sophisticated level. What is there about a dog-bites-man episode that corresponds with the art object? Is it ridiculous for a noble creature like a man to become entangled in the low concerns of a creature far below him in moral and intellectual stature? Is the episode an "excuse" for an artist to create forms which play with dignity and animality? The idea of animality is explored by Seymour Lipton (born 1903) in *Cerberus*. Several hypotheses are suggested by a simple "looks-like" or "reminds-me-of" reaction. An analysis of the object enables us to select among them; we should modify our statement until it approaches an adequate explanation of the work.

INTERPRETING "LES DEMOISELLES"

Let us return to Picasso's *Demoiselles*. Perhaps it can be employed to illustrate interpretation. We can discard some hypotheses first. The work is not a celebration of female beauty. It *does* evoke references to works of that type, such as Rubens's *The Judgment of Paris* or Raphael's *The Three Graces*. The work does not display artistic virtuosity—that is, skillful drawing and brushwork, painterly modeling of forms and representations of light. Color and shape are not employed as a source of sensuous delight. In other words, this is not a work whose values lie in the optical enjoyment of its surface. Rather, the forms we have analyzed serve to designate or symbolize ideas. Indeed, it is possible for *Les Demoiselles* to express ideas which are original in a philosophical or historic sense. Let us build our hypothesis on the basis of the clue offered by the left-central figure, which *looks like* a statue on an insecure base. The figure seems to be falling, but, being a statue, maintains a serene expression; the statue does not *know* it is collapsing. *This work of art, I think, deals with the idea of collapse.*

We observed earlier that the artist used white lines to delineate forms in the central figure—a use of line which occurs in Greek vase painting, especially of the sixth century B.C. The faces of the two central figures also have the expressionless stare which is characteristic of archaic Greek female images. A more recent ancestor of the central figure might be found in a highly sentimental work, *Venus Anadyomene* by Jean-Auguste-Dominique Ingres (1780–1867). Even without this information, however, we sense the classical origins of the central figures. They symbolize conceptions of female beauty which originated in the cultures of the ancient Mediterranean world. They belong to a tradition which Picasso feels deeply. By contrast, the other standing figures are derived from non-Western sources—African or Pre-Columbian. And, as observed earlier, they employ angular as opposed to curvilinear shapes. These figures disappoint the expectations of Mediterranean pulchritude

PABLO PICASSO. *Head of a Woman.* c. 1909. The Art Institute of Chicago. The Charles L. Hutchinson Memorial Collection. In 1909, Picasso was still trying to come to terms with African sculpture. It was a question of adapting to its angularity and abrupt change of plane. But this was difficult for an artist who had absorbed the long European tradition of optical accuracy, linear perspective, chiaroscuro, tonal blending, and the careful geometries of Cézanne.

aroused by the central figures. The upper-right figure is aggressively "ugly." The leg of the left figure belongs to a human type which is not at home in Western cities. We have here a change of race along with a change of artistic treatment. Picasso has intentionally juxtaposed Western and non-Western racial and plastic types to express the *fall* of Western ethnocentrism. The classical beauty symbolized by the central figures is contrasted with the form ideas of the other standing figures and is synthesized in a new development which appears in the lower-right figure. Its head is based on non-Western plastic forms subjected to a type of Western cerebral play. In the *fall* of the classical figures we see the fall of a culture in which beauty is the object of serene contemplation. This ideal is displaced by ideals of activity, beauty as procreative power, and the victory of magic over rationality.

Historians tell us that Picasso originally intended to paint a brothel scene showing a sailor surrounded by nude women, fruit, flowers, and a symbolic intimation of death. The final version of the canvas does not, of course, carry out this plan. But it should be stressed that a defensible interpretation of the work need not follow Picasso's intent; indeed, the critic can be misled by the artist's plan, interesting though it may be. Our critical procedure is designed to get at meanings which can be visually confirmed in the work—meanings the artist may not have intended.

In 1907, well before World War I and the dissolution of European colonialism in Africa and Asia, Picasso's painting represented, at the very least, a remarkable anticipation of the political and cultural developments which emerged some forty years later. So, if this interpretation is correct, Picasso's painting has value for general history as well as the development of artistic style. The art of painting becomes, with this work, a means of dealing with a vast range of experience and meaning.

My interpretation of *Les Demoiselles* leads to an appraisal, or judgment. It should be plain that the work has enormous significance. In the following section on evaluation we shall try to deal with critical judgments of artistic value.

Judgment

Judging a work of art means giving it a rank in relation to other works of its type. This aspect of art criticism is much abused and may be unnecessary if a satisfying interpretation has been carried out. Nevertheless, for a variety of motives, human beings seem unable to avoid ranking art objects. And there are practical situations where ranking and appraisal are unavoidable. Museums are anxious to acquire works which are "important." Individuals are encouraged to buy what pleases them, but usually they like to feel that what pleases them also possesses substantial intrinsic value.

Certain kinds of art scholars are called connoisseurs—persons who "know" a great deal about matters of taste and artistic excellence. When dealing with older works, connoisseurship helps determine authenticity. Since the importance of an artist like Giorgione, for example, has already been established, connoisseurship involves deciding whether he did, in fact, execute a certain work; when in his career the work was done; whether other versions exist; whether it is a good example of his style; and so on.

In the case of contemporary art, somewhat different problems come up. Authenticity is not usually a problem. Most of the facts about the work are known. But many collectors and gallery owners desire to acquire works of art *before* their artists have become well known. They wish to exercise critical judgment in the form of a "bet." Such persons would like to identify artistic excellence before it is widely discovered. Hence, connoisseurship of contemporary art is related to the *prediction* of aesthetic values. The connoisseur must somehow know *what* people are going to like, which works are going to be "likable."

COMPARISONS WITH HISTORICAL MODELS

In making a critical judgment, it is important that a work be related to a wide range of comparable works. One of the errors made by young artists and critics is to form judgments with reference to a very recent or narrow context of artistic creativity. If we are to take critical judgments seriously, we need to know the range of objects in time and space which have been considered. Since we know examples of artistic creativity beginning over twenty thousand years ago and continuing to the present day, the range of relevant objects is enormous. I do not cite the long history of art to increase the difficulty of making critical judgments. But I wish to stress the necessity that the critic be acquainted with as many artistic styles and types as possible. Modern communication, the inexpensive dissemination of reproductions, and the wide display of original works greatly extend the known history of art. The critic who judges according to standards derived only from familiarity with the works of a certain "school," geographic location, or historical epoch is severely limited.

There may seem to be a paradox in our requirement that judging art calls for relating it to historical examples while we require it to express present needs and aspirations. But a comparison with the best work of the past does not imply *imitation* of the past. Historical examples are misused if they are reproduced; they are employed intelligently if they serve as bench

marks or touchstones of excellence. When we have to judge excellence, Shakespeare, Rembrandt, and Beethoven give us some ideas about the capacity of genius operating within specific historical and cultural contexts.

We can admire Max Beckmann's self-portrait as well as the *Portrait of a Young Man* by Agnolo Bronzino. Both works tell us something about their subject, of course. Bronzino, in addition to establishing the grace and self-confidence of the young man, takes pains to create a credible illusion of his skin, clothing, and architectural surroundings. The hand at the waist is magnificently drawn and modeled. Beckmann, contending with himself, portrays an older person with an experienced and cynical expression. Although the pose has a certain grace, the portrait is hardly a celebration of manly beauty. Despite the evening clothes and the nonchalance of the hands, we receive an ominous impression. In the Bronzino portrait, the element of psychological analysis is minimal. In the Beckmann portrait, psychological analysis dominates, especially in the grim set of the mouth, the dramatic lighting of the face, and the exaggerated sharpness of the facial planes. Bronzino's young man symbolizes an age. The book he holds suggests the intellectual interests of Renaissance men, just as Beckmann's cigarette symbolizes today's neurotic tendencies—the frantic wish to achieve poise and serenity through a weed.

The more we penetrate Beckmann's portrait, the more apparent it becomes that we are in the presence of a work of the highest order. Obviously its values are different from those of the Bronzino. Both pictures are of the same type or genre. It is this similarity

JOHN SLOAN.
Connoisseurs of Prints. 1905.
International Business Machines
Corporation, New York

AGNOLO BRONZINO.
Portrait of a Young Man. c. 1535–40.
The Metropolitan Museum of Art, New York.
The H. O. Havemeyer Collection.
Bequest of Mrs. H. O. Havemeyer, 1929

MAX BECKMANN.
Self-Portrait in a Tuxedo. 1927.
Busch-Reisinger Museum, Harvard University,
Cambridge, Massachusetts

which enables us to compare them, to seek a range of meaning and a power of expression in the modern work which is comparable to the range we find in the sixteenth-century work. We do not seek the *same values*, but the same *capacity to support values*. The flawless surface of the Bronzino is a vehicle of aesthetic expressiveness just as are the harshly manipulated planes in the Beckmann.

THE RELEVANCE OF TECHNIQUE

What is the role, for the purposes of art criticism, of craftsmanship, mastery of technique, skill and facility in the use of materials? To answer, let us begin with the proposition that *art is making*. It is what the Greeks called *technē*. Art is not an idea *followed by* its technical expression; it is idea *and* materials simultaneously united through the employment of technique. The notion of *technique* as subordinate to *idea* is a philosophic error that has bedeviled aesthetics and art criticism for hundreds of years. We cannot afford in criticism to ignore the *character* of making and forming. One *result* of making and forming is the embodiment of ideas through materials, and we

legitimately study those ideas, but we must also study the processes which brought them into being.

Technical analysis has been mentioned as an important tool of art criticism. We endeavor to find clues for the interpretation of a work by studying how it was executed. Now we wish to study execution with a view toward making judgments about artistic and technical excellence. Craftsmanship and technique are legitimate subjects for critical judgment because they are themselves supportive of aesthetic value. Technique is not merely a means toward an end; it is an end in itself. Conceivably, the roots of aesthetic pleasure in technique arise from our identification with the successful use of our hands or hand tools. The logical and effective use of tools is one of the most fundamental demonstrations of our mastery over the environment. Man is called, after all, a "tool-using animal."

How do we judge whether a work is technically successful? Some critics evaluate technique indirectly: if a work is expressive as a whole, then its technique is adequate. But this circular argument amounts to asserting that every effect has a sufficient cause. It does not consider the aesthetic values which inhere in

Stele of Aristion, from Attica. 510–500 B.C.
National Archaeological Museum, Athens

PABLO PICASSO.
Detail of *Les Demoiselles d'Avignon*. 1907.
The Museum of Modern Art, New York.
Lillie P. Bliss Bequest

The uncanny resemblance between these figures could be entirely fortuitous. Still, the critic may discover clues in their resemblance that help establish a hypothesis about Picasso's *Les Demoiselles*. Our problem is not to assign influence but to arrive at an interpretation by accounting for similarities and differences among archaic and modern forms apparently based on the same type.

technique, workmanship, skill. It avoids the fact that works of expressive power may be technically deficient, just as works of technical excellence may be expressively inferior. The modern era has seen many departures from traditional craftsmanship, departures from the rules and formulas of artistic technique which used to be taught academically and which were thought to be guarantees of excellence. Also, modern media and materials have been developed by technology so rapidly that a logic or tradition of using them has not had time to evolve. Consequently, contemporary art is frequently weak in craftsmanship, and contemporary criticism tends to focus on other matters.

In other eras, craftsmanship may have been chiefly a concern with the *durability* of whatever an artisan formed or fabricated. It may also have been a visible

sign of labor expended and hence a sign of its owner's power to command labor. But in modern times, craftsmanship or technical excellence means *logic in the use of tools and materials* and *correspondence between the appearance of an art object and its function*. Durability remains one of the meanings of excellent craftsmanship, but it is less prominent today because modern materials permit poorly executed works to survive. The evidence of much human effort is less valuable as a sign of status since some of the most costly things we possess are made by machines. Thus, the older meanings of technique have given way to the idea of a logic of materials and function.

The physical properties of materials tend to govern what may be done with them. Craftsmanship may consist of extracting the maximum of performance and meaning from materials without violating their

nature. Certain things that can be done with materials *ought not to be done*. Perhaps craftsmanship can be defined as the *morality* as well as the logic of technique. Plastics can be formed and treated to resemble a variety of materials from marble to wood, but we invariably feel cheated when we discover the deception. To be sure, our ideas about the "appropriate" use of tools and materials are not fixed forever. Engineers and designers are continually extending our ideas of the appropriateness of new materials or old materials used in new ways. An artist may also employ a *perverse* logic of materials so that a viewer's feelings in connection with his *anticraftsmanship* affect the meaning of the work.

Certainly this is the case with Pop art. In *Two Cheeseburgers, with Everything (Dual Hamburgers)* by Claes Oldenburg (born 1929) we have a "sculpture" of an everyday object. The oversized hamburgers are made of plaster painted in vivid, garish colors. Because of the crudely painted plaster, the distortion of scale, and a general lack of "finish," the feeling of vulgarity the artist is trying to achieve is heightened. Technique is employed to identify the object, and also to violate our sense of the logic of materials. There is enough accuracy to remind the viewer that he is looking at something meant to be eaten; then he becomes aware of sinking his teeth into painted plaster. The "aesthetic" reaction approaches physical revulsion. Anticraftsmanship becomes a positive instrument for achieving an aesthetic intent.

By *correspondence between appearance and function*, we mean the use of craftsmanship to suggest the meaning or operation of an object. Industrially produced art often violates our rule that objects should *look like* what they do. The desire to conceal the operational features of utilitarian objects may be a survival of the nineteenth-century aversion to machine imagery. Today craftsmen protest against the creation of objects with inferior materials on the inside which are covered with a gleaming "skin" on the outside. The principles of handcraftsmanship extended to the design and production of industrial art constitute an

WENDELL CASTLE. Double chair. 1968. When the creation of illusions is not an artistic objective the critic can attend directly to relationships among materials, forms, processes, and purposes.

487

STUART DAVIS. *Visa*. 1951. The Museum of Modern Art, New York. Gift of Mrs. Gertrude A. Mellon. Words constitute an integral part of the imagery of this work; the critic has to consider them from the standpoint of color, shape, size, and meaning—and even of sound.

ethical position while they also create an aesthetic foundation for art criticism. By "inferior materials" we do not imply that some materials are intrinsically superior to others. Materials become "inferior" only when they are employed improperly, from the standpoints of durability, honesty of appearance, and logic of forming or fabrication.

Craftsmanship is a somewhat more elusive problem in the criticism of painting, drawing, and graphic arts. This is because craftsmanship in painting and related arts has been closely associated with the capacity to create convincing illusions, whereas the crafts stress the operational results of technique. Another consideration of traditional pictorial art—resistance to cracking and fading—is also in decline. Technique in modern painting, therefore, is almost independent of its principal reasons for being: illusion and permanence. Thus, when examining contemporary art, we look for signs of *technical mastery* in the artistic *performance*. We study execution—the application of paint, the control of edges, the control of surface quality, the handling of color—to learn whether these aspects of performance have been managed successfully. Do they reflect the artist's understanding of the medium? The knowledgeable critic should be able to recognize technical incapacity; he should not confuse technical failure with aesthetic innovation.

One of the crucial decisions an artist needs to make is the decision to stop working. The process of execution is strewn with difficulties, but it also yields satisfactions which are only reluctantly set aside. A time arrives, however, when the artist's critical judgment overcomes the desire to embellish and tinker with a substantially completed project. Prudence suggests that further elaboration *may* enhance an effect but is more likely to imperil those already achieved. This is true of a book, especially one that tries to discuss the art of criticism. The author of such a book ought to cherish conciseness more than exhaustive explanation; he should exhibit critical discrimination if he has not always displayed scholarly depth. Perhaps he can demonstrate these virtues by knowing when it is time to stop.

NOTES TO THE TEXT

1. *Garden Cities of Tomorrow* (London: Swan Sonnenschein, 1902).
2. *The Living City* (New York: Horizon Press, 1958).
3. *Concerning Town Planning*, trans. Clive Entwistle (New Haven: Yale University Press, 1948), p. 118.
4. This point is made from a Jungian standpoint by de Riencourt: "The androgynous nature of all human beings is a biological fact that finds its counterpart in the realm of psychology. The psyche is bisexual, a fact that even Freud accepted under the spur of his doctor friend, Wilhelm Fliess . . ." *Sex and Power in History* (New York: David McKay Company, 1974) p. 60.
5. Commenting on the fact that women's noses are usually smaller than men's, John Brophy goes on to point out that "smallness is not enough: her nose must be elegantly shaped. This is to conform to the more delicate structure of the feminine face, as well as the softer and clearer texture of the skin." *The Human Face* (New York: Prentice-Hall, 1946) p. 16.
6. Consider the vast literature devoted to the inscrutability of the Mona Lisa's smile. According to John Brophy there is no particular mystery about it: "This smile... is confined to the left corner of the mouth, and in this it conforms to one of the social tricks cultivated by Renaissance ladies, who were told by advisors on beauty and deportment that it was an infallible recipe for charming the opposite sex." (*Op. cit.*) p. 127.
7. *Art, Artists and Society: Origins of a Modern Dilemma: Painting in England and France, 1750–1850* (Englewood Cliffs, N.J.: Prentice-Hall, 1963) p. 141.
8. It is a common misconception that because he painted so many ballet dancers, Degas was fascinated by feminine daintiness and grace. But an anecdote of Kenneth Clark's suggests just the opposite: "Monsieur Degas, why do you always paint such ugly women?" a lady asked him, to which he replied, "Madame, because women in general are ugly." *The Romantic Rebellion* (New York: Harper & Row, 1973) p. 326.
9. Vladimir Nabokov, *Lolita* (New York: McGraw-Hill, 1970).
10. Notice the virtually identical attitude of the man in Kokoschka's *The Tempest*.
11. According to Meyer Schapiro, "Cézanne, it is known, desired to paint the nude from life but was embarrassed by the female model . . . Renoir recalled a conversation with Cézanne in which the latter had said: 'I paint still-lifes. Women models frighten me.'" *Modern Art: 19th and 20th Centuries* (New York: Braziller, 1978) p. 30.
12. *Art, Artists and Society: Origins of a Modern Dilemma: Painting in England and France, 1750–1850* (Englewood Cliffs, N.J.: Prentice-Hall, 1963) p. 146.
13. For a pioneering historical study of this subject, see Ann Sutherland Harris and Linda Nochlin, *Women Artists: 1550–1950* (New York: Knopf, 1977).
14. The central importance of woman's role in the invention of the several Neolithic arts has not been sufficiently studied with respect to its contemporary aesthetic and stylistic implications. See V. Gordon Childe, *What Happened in History* (Harmondsworth: Penguin Books, 1942); and Jacquetta Hawkes, *Prehistory*, Vol. I, Part 1 (New York: Mentor Books, 1965) p. 436ff.
15. In addition, prejudice is a factor. As Francine du Plessix Gray points out: "In the literature of art as well as in its practice, bias still runs much more deeply against women artists than against [women] novelists or poets." "Women Writing About Women's Art," *The New York Times*, September 4, 1977.
16. There is a disturbing strain of violence in modern pornographic art, an emphasis on bound, bruised and maimed women. Andrea Dworkin calls it "the propaganda of sexual terrorism." See the news article "Woman, Pornography, Free Speech," in *The New York Times*, December 4, 1978, p. D10.
17. This image is related to the "femme fatale," a concept with exceedingly ancient roots, notably in the Biblical figures of Eve, Jezebel, Delilah, Judith and Salome. The revival of this deadly female type is analyzed in detail by Patrick Bade, *Femme Fatale* (New York: Mayflower Books, 1979).

18. Lucy Lippard rightly points out: "The overwhelming fact remains that a woman's experience in this society is simply not like that of a man . . ." But she may overstate the case when she adds: "and if this factor does not show up in women's art, only repression can be to blame." This conclusion seems too schematic, both from a social and psychological standpoint. After all, the formal language and the conventions of visual art can be mastered by women as by men; and these conventions have the capacity to transcend age, gender and class. *Women Choose Women* (New York: The New York Cultural Center and Fairleigh Dickinson University, 1973) p. 7.

19. See John Berger's discussion of the difference between male and female ways of looking at pictures of women, in *Ways of Seeing* (London: British Broadcasting Corporation and Penguin Books, 1972).

20. *Twentieth Century Engineering* (New York: Museum of Modern Art, 1964), unpaginated.

21. Gyorgy Kepes, *Language of Vision* (Chicago: Theobald, 1944), p. 13.

22. Allan Kaprow, "A Service for the Dead," *Art International*, January 25, 1963.

23. Quoted in Peter Selz, "Jesse Reichek," *Art in America*, September-October, 1968, p. 98.

24. "Writings," in *The New Art: A Critical Anthology*, ed. Gregory Battcock (New York: E. P. Dutton, 1966), p. 205.

25. Quoted in Douglas M. Davis, "The Dimensions of the Miniarts," *Art in America*, November-December, 1967, p. 86.

26. "The New Sculpture," in *Art and Culture* (New York: Beacon Press, 1961), p. 142.

27. *African Art* (New York: Macmillan, 1954), p. 132.

28. "Design for Culture in Washington," *Saturday Review*, May 23, 1964, p. 23.

29. Eduardo Torroja, *Philosophy of Structures* (Berkeley and Los Angeles: University of California Press, 1958), p. 273.

30. Roland Barthes, *Mythologies,* trans. Annette Lavers. (London: Jonathan Cape, 1972) p. 91.

31. James Agee, *A Way of Seeing: Photographs of New York by Helen Levitt*. (New York: Viking Press, 1965) p. 1.

32. Van Deren Coke, *The Painter and the Photograph: From Delacroix to Warhol*. (Albuquerque: University of New Mexico Press, 1964).

33. Bela Balazs, *Theory of the Film*, 1952. Reprint. (New York: Dover, 1970).

34. See Edward T. Hall, *The Silent Language* (New York: Doubleday, 1959).

35. For a more complete glossary, see James Monaco, *How to Read a Film* (New York: Oxford University Press, 1977).

36. *Going Steady* (Boston: Atlantic-Little Brown, 1970).

37. Michael J. Arlen, "The Air: The Tyranny of the Visual," *The New Yorker*, April 23, 1979, p. 132.

38. See John Bagnell Bury, *The Idea of Progress* (London: Macmillan, 1920).

39. "Architecture and Man at Yale," *Saturday Review*, May 23, 1964.

GLOSSARY

Cross references are indicated by words in SMALL CAPITALS.

ABSTRACT EXPRESSIONISM. A style of painting (mainly American, 1950s and 1960s) emphasizing spontaneous execution, large brushing gestures, bursts of muscular energy, and nonrepresentational imagery. See "ACTION" PAINTING.

ABSTRACTION. The essential form after superficial or changeable features have been taken away; sometimes used (incorrectly) to mean any image that does not resemble its model in reality.

ACADEMIC. The artistic approach taught in the eighteenth- and nineteenth-century art academies of Europe; a philosophy of art based on bland imitations of ancient CLASSICAL art; by extension, any systematic, traditional, anti-experimental type of art.

"ACTION" PAINTING. A style in which the meaning or content of a picture relies strongly on the implied activity of the painted surface, especially the signs of brushing, spattering and dripping paint; related to ABSTRACT EXPRESSIONISM.

AERIAL PERSPECTIVE. Creation of depth illusions in painting through the use of diminishing intensity of colors, the use of cooler colors for distant objects, softening of edges and blurring of focus.

AESTHETIC. Pertaining to art theory or matters of taste and appreciation in art; the beautiful as opposed to the good, true or useful; any vivid or intense experience. Also *an* aesthetic: an artistic or stylistic point of view; a philosophy of art.

ALLA PRIMA. Italian for "all at once"; DIRECT PAINTING; immediate achievement of final effects; the painting has one "skin" rather than many layers; the opposite of indirect painting.

ARABESQUE. Imagery that resembles the flowing interlaces of Islamic art; stylized ornamental motifs based on plants and flowers; intricate and fantastic decorative pattern of ORGANIC or geometric origin.

ARCHAIC. Primitive, antiquated or obsolete; Greek art before the seventh century B.C. Also, archaic smile: the expression, almost a smile, of Greek sculptured heads before the seventh century.

ARCHITECTONIC. Architectural. Paintings, sculptures or craft objects that exhibit the structural or textural traits of buildings.

ARMATURE. The skeleton or framework inside a wax or clay (usually) sculpture; it supports the work while it is being modeled.

ART NOUVEAU. French for "new art" (JUGENDSTIL in German); highly decorative style of the 1890s; emphasis on the whiplash curve, rich color, flat patterns, floral ornamentation, vertical attenuation.

ASSEMBLAGE. Creation of imagery by the aggregation of different materials, often fragments of other, recognizable images and objects.

AUTEUR THEORY. The view that the artistic quality of a motion picture is mainly the responsibility of the film director, who is the real cinema "artist."

AVANT-GARDE. French word for those who are advanced, "ahead of the times"; artists who point out the direction others will follow.

AXIS. The center line, real or imaginary, around which the parts of a work of art are composed and balanced.

BAROQUE. Art of the seventeenth century in Europe; characterized by irregularity of form, illusions of infinite space, theatricality of color and lighting, grandiose gestures, over life-size figuration.

BASILICA. Originally a Roman building used as a court of law or for public meetings; evolved under Christianity into the church, a building with a long, narrow NAVE, side aisles, and an apse at the end formerly occupied by the judge or emperor's representative.

BAUHAUS. The school of art and industrial design founded in 1919 by Walter Gropius to promote the unity of all the arts; closed by the Hitler regime in 1933.

BIOMORPHIC. Having the qualities of living form. See ORGANIC.

BROKEN COLOR. Painting technique typical of IMPRESSIONISM; short touches of bright color, often complementaries, placed side-by-side to create a vibrating effect.

BRUTALISM. An architectural style in the 1950s featuring exposed steel and large areas of coarse, undecorated concrete; the building treated almost like an Expressionistic sculpture.

BYZANTINE/BYZANTINE ICONS. The art and architecture, mainly religious, of the Byzantine Empire; icon paintings of sacred persons venerated in the Eastern Orthodox Church; style of strict frontality, little or no naturalistic modeling, rich decoration, other-worldly outlook. See MOSAICS.

CALLIGRAPHIC. Pertaining to the art of beautiful writing as in the scripts of Persia, China and Japan; an artistic style characterized by graceful, flowing curves.

CANTILEVER. The free part of a horizontal member that projects into space, seemingly without support, while its internal end is anchored in the main structure.

CAPITAL. The head or topmost part of a column or pier; because of its characteristic shape and decoration, it may be called Doric, Ionic, Etruscan, or Corinthian.

CARTOON. A full-scale preparatory drawing for a painting, MURAL or tapestry; a humorous sketch or caricature or series (as in a comic strip) usually made for a newspaper or magazine.

CHIAROSCURO. In painting, the MODELING of form with light and dark; any artistic treatment that stresses the contrast between light areas and shadows.

CHROMATIC. Pertaining to color, especially HUE. See also POLYCHROMATIC, MONOCHROMATIC.

CLASSICAL. The art of ancient Greece and Rome; any work exhibiting the traits of ancient Greek art; an art of formal order stressing simplicity, dignity, clearly defined intervals, mathematical proportion. A "classic" is, by extension, a work generally accepted as a masterpiece.

CLOSED FORM. The sense of unbroken space characteristic of CLASSICAL composition in painting, sculpture and architecture.

COLLAGE. From the French coller, to paste; any artistic composition made by gluing assorted materials (cloth, newsprint, wallpaper, wood veneers) to a flat surface, usually a canvas or a panel.

CONCEPTUALISM. An art movement (after 1960) emphasizing the transient character of the creative act rather than its outcome; art objects become the report, written or spoken, of an event; deemphasis of visual imagery. Related to Process Art.

CONNOISSEUR. Literally, one "who knows" and is therefore competent to offer critical judgments of art; an expert in a particular branch of art who can recognize certain techniques, establish dates, verify authenticity, estimate prices; a person of discriminating taste in art, cooking, etc.

CONSTRUCTIVISM. Twentieth-century nonrepresentational sculptural style, associated with the Russians Naum Gabo and Antoine Pevsner; theoretical foundations in modern physics, engineering and technology; an endeavor to treat volume with a minimum of mass.

CONTRAPPOSTO. A twisting of the human figure in such a manner that the head, chest, abdomen, hips, and thighs may face in different directions. The various directions create an opposition of forces within the figure which is felt as emotional tension by the viewer.

CRITICISM. The act of describing, analyzing, interpreting and judging works of art; informed talk about art; incorrectly used to mean censure or fault-finding.

CUBISM. A style of art originated by Picasso and Braque in Paris around 1907; emphasis on the geometrical foundations of form, the two-dimensionality of the picture surface, multiple views of the same objects, super-

imposition and interpenetration of forms. Intellectual phase is *Analytic Cubism* (1909–12); decorative, playful phase is *Synthetic Cubism* (1912–14).

DADAISM. Post-World War I style stressing accidental images and events, the "logic" of absurdity, irrationality in art, literature and morality. Related to SURREALISM.

DAGUERREOTYPE. An early photographic process (1839) named after L. Daguerre, employing silver salts, iodine and mercury vapor in developing a picture.

DIRECT PAINTING. See ALLA PRIMA. A technique that stresses spontaneity or the appearance of spontaneity in execution; a minimum of reworking; avoids transparent effects and "building up" a surface with several layers of paint.

DOCUMENTARY. A photographic, motion picture or television presentation of unposed or uncontrived events; a style of art that *seems* to report actual events.

EARTH SCULPTURE. The excavation of earth, the relocation of boulders, the digging of water channels, etc., to create pleasing or expressive aesthetic effects. Also Earthworks and ENVIRONMENTAL ART.

ECLECTICISM. Creating a form or style on the basis of many borrowings; the combination of recognizable elements from several styles to fashion something new.

ENCAUSTIC. A painting medium using hot wax to bind colors to a wood panel or a wall.

ENTABLATURE. The portion of a CLASSICAL building facade between its column capitals and its roof; it contains the *architrave*, *frieze* and *cornice*.

ENTASIS. A slight convexity or swelling in the shaft of a CLASSICAL column; it counteracts the optical effect whereby perfectly straight columns seem to be narrower in the center.

ENVIRONMENTAL ART. Any ordered arrangement or reconstruction of the natural or built environment; a garden, for example. See EARTH SCULPTURE and HAPPENINGS.

EXPRESSIONISM. A style of modern painting, originally Central European, emphasizing intense color, agitated brushwork and violent imagery to express painful emotions, anxiety and hallucinatory states.

EXPRESSIVISM. A term used here to describe the critical position that greatness in art results from the vivid, intense and convincing expression of emotion.

FAUVISM. From the French *fauve* (wild beast). An early twentieth-century painting style emphasizing the juxtaposition of extremely bright areas of color, arbitrary drawing unrelated to the color, and distorted linear perspective. Main aim is breakdown and reform of traditional pictorial structure; not as anguished as German EXPRESSIONISM, which it resembles.

FETISH. A charmed or magical object; often a sculpture regarded as the home or embodiment of a spiritual substance, much as the *ka* or soul of an Egyptian pharaoh is believed to reside in the many statues of him; a psychological obsession with an object or part of the body which results in an erotic response.

FORESHORTENING. The representation through drawing of three-dimensional forms on a flat surface to create the illusion of their depth, as of an arm and hand extended toward the viewer. See Siqueiros, *Self-Portrait*.

FORMALISM. A term used here to describe the critical position that greatness in art results from the ideal juxtaposition and treatment of the basic elements of visual form.

FRESCO. A type of MURAL or wall painting in which dry colors are mixed with water and applied to a wet plaster surface; *fresco* means "fresh" in Italian.

FRONTALITY. The full-face or head-on presentation of the human figure; planarity in the organization of forms, that is, emphasis on forms parallel to the frontal plane.

FUNCTIONALISM. The doctrine prominent in the early twentieth century that architecture, furniture and other useful objects should be designed to reveal their materials and process of making, to work well and to endure, and to express their practical purpose; the view that aesthetic excellence results from successful utilitarian design and performance.

FUTURISM. An Italian painting style (about 1910) derived from CUBISM; devoted to the celebration of speed, the representation of motion and the dynamization of civilized life.

GEODESIC. Word invented by R. Buckminster Fuller to describe his basically hemispherical domes, which rely for strength on a geometric grid of thin, straight members in tension and compression.

GESSO. The mixture of chalk or plaster and glue applied to wooden panels and (rarely) to canvas to serve as a ground for tempera painting.

GLAZE. A semitransparent film of pigment and oil or varnish used to color or model an underlying painting which is usually MONOCHROMATIC or limited in color range; imparts a lustrous effect.

GOTHIC. Originally applied to the art and architecture of France, then Europe, from the twelfth to the mid-sixteenth century; emphasis on vertical space, basilican plan, long, narrow NAVE, slender masonry construction, progressive enlargement of window area, ribbed groin VAULTS, flying buttresses, stained glass.

GRAPHICS. Also the graphic arts; from the Greek word for drawing or writing. Applied to engraving, etching, woodcut, lithography; any method of printmaking or communication through line, especially when reproduced in books, magazines, posters and by electronic transmission.

GUILDS. Free professional and social associations of medieval artisans, merchants and tradesmen, organized to protect their interests, to maintain standards of craft, to govern the training of apprentices and journeymen, the admission of members, the preservation of trade secrets and the control of business and work.

HAPPENING. A quasi-theatrical event staged or contrived in non-repeatable form, employing people, places and objects to make a visual-sculptural-satirical statement. See ENVIRONMENTAL ART.

HATCHING. A drawing and printmaking technique; a kind of shading in which fine lines placed close together create a tone that models form; in painting a series of parallel strokes (as in Cézanne) that create the appearance of planes or facets of form.

HEDONIC. Pertaining to pleasure; art created to generate agreeable sensations.

HUE. The name of a color, such as red, blue or yellow; the quality of light (wavelength) that separates one color from another.

ICONOGRAPHY. The conventional meanings of the images used to convey or symbolize ideas in works of art; an artist's distinctive use of visual SYMBOLS.

ICONOLOGY. The historical study and interpretation of visual SYMBOLS in art, with particular attention to their literary origins; the study of religious symbolism.

IDEALIZATION. Visual representations which omit defects or imperfect variations in a form; a type of ABSTRACTION; a type of STYLIZATION; representations that follow perfect models.

IMPASTO. From the Italian word for paste; paint applied in thick slathers or lumps.

IMPRESSIONISM. A late nineteenth-century (mainly French) style of painting; the extension of REALISM to the scientific analysis of color and light; stress on capture of transient atmospheric effects; use of BROKEN COLOR and color complementaries to render form; outdoor painting and direct observation of subjects emphasized.

INSTRUMENTALISM. A term used here to describe the critical position that greatness in art results from effectiveness in advancing the objectives of humanity usually as defined by one of a number of major social or economic institutions: family, church, state, GUILD, firm, political party, corporation.

INTENSITY. In color, a high degree of brightness; the fullest manifestation of a color's chroma, its freedom from black, white or gray. In AESTHETICS, high emotional excitement.

INTERNATIONAL STYLE. First applied to Gothic art; the style of architecture and utilitarian design developed in the 1920s by Walter Gropius, Mies van der Rohe and Le Corbusier; an outgrowth of the Bauhaus philosophy.

JUGENDSTIL. See ART NOUVEAU.

JUNK ART. The use of rubbish and trivial objects (by Schwitters, Duchamp, Dubuffet and others) to create images and objects; an extension of the COLLAGE idea.

KEYSTONE. The wedge-shaped stone in the center of a masonry arch.

KINETIC ART. Mainly three-dimensional or sculptural art which seems to move spontaneously in space (as in a Calder mobile) by the aid of a mechanism or through some naturally recurring force, like tide, wind or water.

KITSCH. Mediocrity in the highest degree. In aesthetics, pretentiously bad art; bad taste in art; cheap, mass-produced objects and images designed to arouse easy emotions.

LANTERN. An open cylindrical construction which lets light into the top of a dome. See also, OCULUS.

LINEAR. Pertaining to line. One of Wölfflin's categories stressing the creation of form by outlines or contour lines. Also a main trait of the graphic arts.

LINTEL. The horizontal member of the POST-AND-LINTEL structural device supporting the weight above an opening in a wall.

LOCAL COLOR. The natural or daylight color of an object, seen closely, as opposed to its OPTICAL COLOR as seen from a distance, or as influenced by reflections, weather or surrounding objects.

MANNERISM. A post-Renaissance, mainly sixteenth-century aristocratic style, characterized by elongation of the figure, artificial poses and gestures, strange distortions of the figure, forced perspective and strident color; affectedness in art as well as behavior.

MATTE. Having a dull, almost non-reflective surface; the opposite of glossy. Matte varnishes protect a painting without glossiness.

MEGALITHS. Immense stones such as were used in the construction of Stonehenge. Menhir: a single, uncut, prehistoric megalith.

MIMESIS. The Greek word for imitation or reproduction; the theory generally attributed to Aristotle that art is the imitation of human beings in action.

MINARET. The tall, slender tower attached to a mosque; it has one or more balconies from which the muezzin calls

493

Muslims to prayer.

MINIMALISM. A style of nonrepresentational art that restricts itself to very few visual elements organized as simply as possible.

MODELING. In sculpture, the direct forming of materials such as wax, clay, wood, stone. In painting, the creation of more-or-less sculptural illusions.

MODULE. A standard or unit for measuring and designing; in architecture a device for standardizing the sizes and proportions of building parts and furnishings. See Le Corbusier's *modular*.

MONOCHROMATIC. Pertaining to a single color or HUE; a composition organized around tonal variations of one color.

MONTAGE. A method of composition in photography, cinema and television; the technique of combining imagery from various sources to create a unified visual presentation; film editing: superimposition, intercutting, overlapping, etc.

MONUMENTALITY. The combined quality of dignity, grandeur and impressiveness, especially in architecture and sculpture, regardless of actual size.

MOSAICS. A surface decoration or picture made with pieces of colored glass, stone or ceramic (called TESSERAE) set into cement or mastic; typical of wall, apse and dome decoration of BYZANTINE churches.

MURAL. Any large wall painting. See FRESCO.

NAIVE ART. The art of untrained or self-taught artists; the art of preliterate peoples. See PRIMITIVE ART.

NATURALISM. The doctrine that art should consist of the exact transcription of visual appearances. See *The Style of Objective Accuracy*.

NAVE. The central part of a church used by the congregants, running from the main entrance to the altar; usually flanked by side aisles and bordered by piers and columns.

NEOLITHIC. Also New Stone Age; starting about 10,000 or 8,000 B.C.; beginnings of settled living: farming, animal husbandry, spinning and weaving, fired pottery.

NONOBJECTIVE ART. Literally, art without objects, wholly nonrepresentational art; an art whose images have no obvious models in physical reality. Should not be confused with abstract art.

NEO-PLASTICISM. A twentieth-century style of painting, mainly associated with Piet Mondrian and the De Stijl group in Holland; characterized by limited palette (black, white and the primaries) and restriction to absolutely vertical and horizontal forms.

OCULUS. The "eye" or circular opening at the top of a dome. See also, LANTERN.

OP ART. A style of painting which creates disorienting effects by juxtaposing vibrating colors, after-images, perspectival illusions, and subtle, progressive changes of repeated shapes.

OPTICAL COLOR. The perceived color of an object; color modified by intervening conditions. See LOCAL COLOR.

ORGANIC. Forms that resemble the structure of living things; shaped like the parts of plants and animals rather than machines; natural.

ORPHISTS. A school of abstract painters in Paris about 1912, grouped around Robert and Sonia Delaunay, combining Cubist form with bright, vivid color.

PALEOLITHIC. Also Old Stone Age; from 32,000 B.C. to about 8,000 B.C.; the period of the cave dwellers who employed tools of stone and bone and lived mainly by hunting and gathering.

PALETTE. The thin panel (often with a thumb hole) on which a painter mixes pigments; also the colors usually employed by an artist.

PAPIER-MÂCHÉ. A sculptural material made of pulped paper or strips of paper mixed with paste; can be pressed, molded or modeled when moist; dries hard.

PATINA. The mellow, greenish-brown film created on a copper or bronze sculpture either through natural oxidation or by applying chemicals and heat.

PEDIMENT. The triangular space formed by the gable end of a CLASSICAL building; the shape created by the sloping roof and the horizontal cornice; usually holds sculptured figures.

PENDENTIVES. The curved, triangular areas of masonry that support a dome resting on a square base.

PERSPECTIVE. A system for creating illusions of depth on a flat surface; usually a linear system is meant. See also, AERIAL or atmospheric PERSPECTIVE.

POLYCHROMATIC. Made of many colors, as in painted statuary or the multicolored ceramic sculpture of the Della Robbia family. See MONOCHROMATIC.

POP ART. A style of painting (and sculpture) originating in the 1960s, employing enlarged images and motifs from commercial art, road signs, comic strips and outdoor advertising.

POST-AND-LINTEL. The principal structural device of CLASSICAL Greek architecture employing two vertical members or posts, and a horizontal beam or lintel.

PRIMITIVE ART. The art of preliterate peoples; a slightly opprobrious term for untrained or unsophisticated art; mistakenly applied to European paintings before the Italian Renaissance. See NAIVE ART.

PROVENANCE. Also prevenience; origin or source, especially of a work of art.

REALISM. A nineteenth-century style of painting associated with Gustave Courbet and related to the novels of Zola; emphasis on a truthful account of human existence; opposed to idealized and academic art. See SOCIAL REALISM.

RENAISSANCE. Also Renascence. The fifteenth-century "rebirth" of art and letters, that is, the revival of CLASSICAL art in Italy and afterward throughout Europe. The Renaissance style displaced medieval GOTHIC and BYZANTINE art.

ROCOCO ART. A late form of BAROQUE architecture and decoration, but more intimate and secular; playful, witty and often erotic; ornate decor; light colors; irregular form; reflects the effeteness of the French court in the late eighteenth century.

ROMANESQUE. The art and architecture of Europe from the ninth to the twelfth century; characterized by heavy masonry construction, dark church interiors and mystical, restless sculptural forms.

ROMANTICISM. In art, an eighteenth- and nineteenth-century style emphasizing subjective feeling and the emotions associated with exotic life-styles, escape from the present, extreme danger, suffering, nostalgia, myth and historical evocation.

SERIAL ART. Also series painting, systems sculpture and "ABC art." A style of the 1960s and 1970s in which simple geometric configurations are repeated with little or no variation; sequence becomes important as in mathematics and linguistic theory.

SFUMATO. The soft, "smoky" treatment of contours, notably by Leonardo, to avoid edginess and to create an impression of rounded volume.

SHAMAN. Sorcerer, magician, medicine-man, priest of the Old Stone Age hunting cultures; he was probably responsible for the pictures of animals painted on the cave walls and ceilings.

SOCIAL REALISM. The style of art, allegedly Marxist, which is based on the doctrine that painting and sculpture should accurately represent the workers' experiences, especially their oppression by class enemies and their triumphs of production.

STYLING. As used in industrial or product design: superficial change. The stylist alters the appearance of a product for marketing rather than functional reasons.

STYLIZATION. The process of making visual representations conform to a conventional model. See IDEALIZATION.

SURREALISM. A literary and artistic style stressing the subconscious and nonrational sources of imagery; influenced by Freudian psychology. See also DADAISM and *The Style of Fantasy*.

SYMBOL. In art, an image employed to designate something else. Symbolism: the systematic use of visual symbols according to mythical, religious, literary, etc., traditions; see ICONOGRAPHY. Symbolist: a late nineteenth-century school of painters (including Gauguin) who used color especially to suggest ideas and emotions; also Synthetists.

TACTILE. Pertaining to the sense of touch; in painting, the use of textured materials or the treatment of surfaces to induce sensations of touch. "Tactile values": an expression of the connoisseur Berenson to designate the convincing or authentic qualities of a painting.

TECTONIC. Pertaining to architecture and construction; one of Wölfflin's categories meaning "closed-form," where it applies to painting and sculpture, too. Also, ARCHITECTONIC.

TEMPERA. A type of paint whose medium or binder is egg yolk, glue or casein; water soluble until it dries.

TERRA-COTTA. A reddish-brown baked clay used for earthenware, sculpture and building construction, as in terracotta tiles, pipes and fire insulation.

TESSERAE. Pieces of colored glass, stone or ceramic used in making MOSAICS.

TONAL BLENDING. In painting, modeling a form by changes in tones of a single color instead of changes in HUE.

TOTEM. The protecting creature, usually an animal or bird, to which a clan believes itself related; the emblem which represents a clan or family. Totem pole: a carved and painted wooden post showing figures of totemic protectors or ancestors.

TRANSEPT. The crossarm in a basilican church; it meets the NAVE at right angles, separating the NAVE from the apse; the main altar is usually under the crossing of NAVE and transept.

TROMPE-L'OEIL. "Fool the eye" in French; a highly illusionistic method of painting as in the works of Harnett and Peto; see also NATURALISM.

UNDERPAINTING. The first stage of indirect painting method; the establishment of the chief shapes, lights, darks and masses, usually with a limited palette or in monochrome.

UNITY. A coherent relationship among the parts or elements of a work of art.

VALUE. The lightness or darkness of a color. In aesthetics: any perceived quality; any source of appeal in a work of art; the artistic satisfaction of a human interest.

VAULT. A masonry, brick or concrete arched structure forming a ceiling or roof over a hall; *barrel* vault, *groin* vault, *ribbed* vault.

VEHICLE. The binder or glue that holds the coloring matter in pigment and makes it adhere to a surface.

VOUSSOIR. A wedge-shaped block used in the construction of a masonry arch. See KEYSTONE.

WASH. A thin, semitransparent film of paint, highly diluted with turpentine or water (as in watercolor painting) and applied with a broad, continuous sweep of the brush.

ZIGGURAT. The almost pyramid-shaped monument of the ancient Babylonians and Assyrians, consisting of four or five stages or stories stepped back to form terraces; outside stairways lead to temples and a shrine at the top.

ZONING. Partitioning a city or town by ordinance into specific areas or zones for manufacturing, recreation, and residence.

ZOOMORPHIC. Pertaining to animal art; ascribing animal forms or attributes to humans, especially to gods and goddesses.

TIME-LINES

*Please see Index for page numbers of specific
works of art mentioned below.*

PRIMAL, PREHISTORIC AND ANCIENT ART

TIME	PLACE	PERIOD OF CULTURE	SOCIAL ORGANIZATION	KEY EVENTS: POLITICAL, ECONOMIC, RELIGIOUS, TECHNOLOGICAL
No Date	Universal	All cultures	Any kind of human family	Discovery of fingers and thumbs as tools of expression; discovery of relationship between visual form and real world; ability to control reality through representation; beginning of separation of world from the self: people, places and things organized *around* the self. This art, or something very much like it, preceded the specimens of prehistoric art known to us
30,000–25,000 B.C.	Austria, Europe	Upper Paleolithic (Old Stone Age), Aurignacian culture	Nomadic hunting band, about 60 people; some division of labor between sexes; everyone forages; males hunt	Homo sapiens emerges; Cro-Magnon man drives out Neanderthal man; incest taboo establishes families; improved tools for hunting and fishing: better spears, harpoons; bow and arrow invented; animal trapping; burial of dead; red ochre a symbol of blood and life
No Date (probably 19th century)	Mali (Sudan), West Africa	Neolithic Metal Age, Dogon culture	Tribal, extended family; polygamous, exogamous (girls marry out); men hunt, women cultivate small plots; men's and women's societies act as check on power of chief, govern initiation of boys and girls	Settled agriculture, hoe cultivation, some hunting; ruling class descended from stock raisers, mounted warriors; local wars produce captives who become slaves; monopolies of metalwork (especially in gold) exercised by king's family and courtiers
400–600 A.D.	Chicama Valley, Peru, South America	Late Neolithic, Mochica (pre-Inca); (comparable to pre-Dynastic Egypt)	Warrior-hunter caste enslaves farmers; served by priests, artisans, dancers; close village life, some leisure; human sacrifice practiced	Copper, silver and gold work; textile manufacture; frequent wars; irrigation systems; maize-farming, ocean fishing; pyramids of adobe brick; worship of sun, moon, jaguars, serpents; no potter's wheel, no wheeled vehicles, no draft animals; no written language
2650 B.C.	Giza, Egypt	Old Kingdom, Fourth Dynasty	Matriarchal; brother and sister marriages in royal house; pharaoh (who could be a woman) is god-king and absolute ruler	Unification of Upper and Lower Egypt, 3100 B.C.; royal household governs through small group of priests and officials; hieroglyphic writing, 3000 B.C.; great pyramid construction (2570–2500 B.C.); Hyksos invasions (1730–1580) end isolation of Egypt
1900–1600 B.C.	Salisbury Plain, England Also Carnac, Brittany, Maltese Islands	Late Neolithic (Bronze Age), Megalithic, pre-Celtic	Egalitarian farming communes; tribal chieftains; some matriarchal survivals; fear of witches among herdsmen	Gold trade with Ireland; amber trade with Baltic countries; copper trade with Near East; flint mining; stone imitations of bronze weapons; wood, mud, reed houses; underground burial in gallery graves; cattle, sheep and swine raising to supplement low-yield agriculture
1600 B.C.	Knossos, Crete	Aegean, Late Minoan, Late Bronze Age	Mercantile aristocracy; luxury-loving leisure class; matriarchal customs survive in freedom, flirtatiousness of upper-class women	Palace civilization based on Mediterranean sea trade; "Linear A" writing; Hyksos invasions, earthquakes destroy palaces, 1720 and 1450; high style of fresco painting, no monumental art; elaborate dresses for women: full skirts, bared breasts
1350 B.C.	Thebes, Egypt	New Kingdom, Eighteenth Dynasty	Powerful priesthood and priestly bureaucracy control throne; drive out "subversives," including rebellious army officers	Akhenaton's monotheism challenges priesthood (1372–1358); his successor, 18-year-old Tutankhamen, restores priests and ancient cult; stonecutters obliterate name of one-God, sun-disk, Aton; priests interpret oracle, Amon, thus control politics; restoration of gigantic architecture and statuary

TYPICAL OBJECT, IMAGE, MONUMENT	MATERIAL, MEDIUM, PROCESS	MAKER, ARTIST	USER, SPONSOR, PATRON	FUNCTION, PURPOSE
Child's Drawing	Crayon and paper (any pointed instrument; any surface), 4″ high	Four-year-old girl	Autonomous creation; art sponsored by the artist	To overcome fear of outside world; to control environment through magic; to "name" things; to assert own existence
Venus of Willendorf	Limestone carving, 4 3/8″ high	Unknown shaman-artist	Child-bearing woman; mother cult (?); fecundity rites	Promote fertility, induce pregnancy; good-luck charm, amulet; sympathetic magic
Dogon Ancestor Figures	Wood carved with iron adze and knife; rubbed, charred and oiled, 26 1/4″ high	Tribal carver, village smith-medicine man (?)	Probably commissioned by secret society of male elders and priests	To preserve the spirits of ancestors; to guard and advise the family; to accompany genealogical accounts of clan's founding at annual feast; to express dualism of male and female principles
Portrait Jar (of ruler?) with stirrup-spout handle	Painted sun-baked clay, 4 3/4″ high	Unknown potter-portraitist	All classes use effigy jars decorated according to social status	Placed in boxlike grave; holds liquid believed to sustain life of deceased
Pharaoh Khafre (Chefren) with hawk-god Horus	Green Diorite carved, abraded and polished	Unknown temple sculptors	The pharaoh is sponsor and only beneficiary	To provide a permanent home for the *ka* or soul of the king in case his mummy is damaged or other heads stolen; hawk symbolizes sun (*Re*) and royal descent of Khafre
Stonehenge	Upright stones with lintels (about 13′ high, up to 50 tons) arranged in ritual circle or *cromlech*	Gangs of farmers and herdsmen supervised by priests and skilled stoneworkers	Bronze Age farming, herding-hunting community	Shrine for worship of "Great Mother" deity; possible observatory to sight solstices, plot moon's movement, predict sun's eclipse; mother goddess causes sunrise, return of Spring, renewal of earth's fertility; for rites connecting earth and sky gods
Snake Goddess (or priestess)	Faience (glazed multicolored pottery), 13 1/2″ high	Unknown sculptor-priestess (?)	Cult of mother goddess (?)	To worship woman as embodiment of fertility principle; snakes symbolize earth insemination (the male principle) controlled by the goddess
Throne of King Tutankhamen	Gold-sheathed wood, carved and inlaid with glass pastes and semi-precious stones	Unknown palace craftsmen under direction of priests of Amon	Commissioned by King for his tomb	To show King "Tut" as upholder of *Maat* (truth-justice) as evidenced by sun's rays bathing him and his queen

497

CLASSICAL AND MEDIEVAL ART

TIME	PLACE	PERIOD OF CULTURE	SOCIAL ORGANIZATION	KEY EVENTS: POLITICAL, ECONOMIC, RELIGIOUS, TECHNOLOGICAL
510–500 B.C.	Attica, Greece	Archaic Greek "Transitional"	Tribal aristocratic: gods, heroes, heroic dead, kings, noble families, free workers, peasant farmers, slaves; barbarians beneath everyone	Rule of *polis* (Greek town and surrounding pasture) by old Dorian clans; armored infantrymen (*hoplites*) replace horsemen; the phalanx (*hoplites* fighting in unison); military comradeship weakens tribal ties; egalitarianism of warriors extended to civic life; poor farmers enfranchised; more money spent on public building
450–440 B.C.	Argos, Greece	Classical Greek	Old aristocracy weakened by insurgence of mercantile class and prosperous laborers; *polis* becomes democratic city-state	Greek cities defeat Persians, 448 B.C.; Athenian fleet and merchants dominate Eastern Mediterranean and Black Sea; spread of Hellenism—Greek art, language and literature; emergence of Athens as model of an open society: free speculation unfettered by priests and tyrants, but for citizens only; Peloponnesian War (431–404 B.C.), Athens defeated by Sparta
c. 225 B.C.	Pergamum, Asia Minor	Early Hellenistic, Greek	Oligarchic control of Hellenistic cities; large estates; independent farmers disappear; emergence of small, rich leisure class living off land rents and slave labor	Alexandrian conquests (336–323 B.C.); Oriental colonization; spread of Greek culture (330 B.C.–100 A.D.) to Rome, Egypt, Syria, Asia Minor, Persia, India; imperial bureaucracy, standardized city-planning; great library in Alexandria, much prestige in philosophy; Roman conquest of Corinth (146 B.C.), Greece controlled by Rome
125 A.D.	Rome	Late Hellenistic, Roman	Imperial state; cosmopolitan capital city; large-scale importation of European slaves; laborers and artisans live in tenements	Growth of mystery religions, Zoroastrianism, Manichaeism, astrological cults; Roman economic exploitation of the provinces; death of Jesus (c. 30 A.D.); Jewish rebellion (60 A.D.); death of Paul (c. 65 A.D.); Christian underground; slave revolts; growth of large proletariat in Rome; free "bread and circuses" for urban masses
532–37	Constantinople (Istanbul)	Byzantine, First "Golden Age"	Absolute monarchy supported by urban aristocracy of merchants, monopolists, priesthood, civil service and army of spies; the commercial model for Venice	Roman legalization of Christianity in 313 A.D.; Constantine establishes new imperial capital at Byzantium, 330; Rome sacked by Goths, 410; Justinian and Theodora rule in Constantinople, 527–65; Gregory the Great becomes Roman pope, 590; birth of Muhammad c. 570; Muslim conquests begin, 632; Jerusalem taken, 638; Arabs defeated at Poitiers by Charles Martel in 732; Charlemagne becomes Holy Roman Emperor of the West, 800
c. 825	Oslo, Norway	Early Medieval, Northern Carolingian	Tiny kingdoms subsisting on farming, fishing, trapping and piracy; polygamy and primogeniture produce sons without property looking for loot	Viking sea raiders invade Ireland, England, France, Italy and Sicily, penetrating inland on shallow-draft ships (830–900); Central Asian nomads invade Europe, 890; feudal system in Europe; monastery at Cluny, France, founded, 910
c. 1095–1115	Poitou, France	Western Romanesque	Manorial feudalism and monasticism well-established; conversion of Roman estate slaves into serfs by victorious raiders who set themselves up as new nobility; employment of foreign artisans as builders	Norsemen and Huns become Christians, c. 1000; England conquered by William of Normandy, 1066; international pilgrimages to holy sites, veneration of saints' relics; schism between Roman Catholic and Eastern Orthodox Churches, 1054; Capetian dynasty in France under Louis VI guided by Abbot Suger (1081–1151); reconquest of Spain from Arabs begins, 1085
c. 1163	Chapel of the Grey Friars (Franciscan), Nancy, France	Romanesque	Restless and pugnacious nobility addicted to feuds, killings, destruction; higher clergy (abbots, bishops) chosen from their peaceful sons	St. Bernard preaches second Crusade, 1146; sends knights to fight Islam for possession of Jerusalem; European barbarians exposed to Middle Eastern wealth, learning and civilization; deeper-cutting plough opens northern European plains to agriculture, rotation of crops, more protein in diet; peasants more vigorous

TYPICAL OBJECT, IMAGE, MONUMENT	MATERIAL, MEDIUM, PROCESS	MAKER, ARTIST	USER, SPONSOR, PATRON	FUNCTION, PURPOSE
Stele of Aristion	Carved and chiseled Pentelic marble; color added	Aristocles	Family of Aristion or his fellow *hoplites*	Gravestone marker; memorial to aristocratic "warrior-gentleman"
Doryphorus (*Spear Bearer*)	Carved marble (Roman copy of bronze original, which was decorated with colored stones, pastes, gold and silver)	Polyclitus	Citizens of Athens	To symbolize the union of reason, action and correct proportion in the ideal Greek man, or god; to establish a perfect, i.e., geometrical, standard of physical beauty
Dying Gaul	Carved marble (Roman copy of bronze original)	Epigonus	General Attalus I	To celebrate victory over Celtic or Galatian invaders; to memorialize bravery of barbarians, their worthiness as men and foes
The Pantheon	Coffered dome on cylindrical base; brick, stone rubble, marble, granite, "cement" and gilded bronze	Unknown architects	Emperor Hadrian	Officially dedicated to the gods of the seven planets; to create a vast interior space symbolizing the cosmos; to glorify Hadrian
Cathedral of Hagia Sophia	Dome-on-pendentive construction; brick, stone rubble, marble, mosaics and fresco	Anthemius of Tralles and Isidorus of Miletus, architects	Emperor Justinian	To express the Eastern Christian idea of the unity of God and light in a great vertical space; announces Emperor is God's deputy on earth, Empress is God's wife
Animal Head from Oseberg ship-burial	Carved and drilled wood	Unknown carver-shipwright	Crew of Viking "longship"	Figurehead (dragon?) for sailing vessel-war-galley protects raiders, terrifies farmers and villagers; ship buried with chieftain
Nave, St.-Savin-sur-Gartempe	Hall church; barrel or tunnel vault construction; painted ceiling of nave, cut stone arcade; pillars painted to imitate marble	Unknown masons, craftsmen and painters	Religious community and people	To express the Latin Christian idea of salvation in a long, horizontal space culminating in the chancel, altar, reliquary and choir
Crusader and His Wife	Carved and painted limestone	Unknown stone-mason-carver	Count of Vaudemont and his wife, Anne of Lorraine	To celebrate faithfulness of Christian marriage and virtue of the feudal-warrior caste

RENAISSANCE AND BAROQUE

TIME	PLACE	PERIOD OF CULTURE	SOCIAL ORGANIZATION	KEY EVENTS: POLITICAL, ECONOMIC, RELIGIOUS, TECHNOLOGICAL
c. 1495–98	Refectory of Sta. Maria delle Grazie, Milan, Italy	Italian Renaissance, Florentine School	Italy's city-states ruled by feudal princes (dukes), bankers, landed aristocrats and mercenaries (condottieri); brief republic in Florence (1494–1512)	World exploration: Columbus (1492), Vasco da Gama (1498), Balboa (1513), Magellan (1519–22); Byzantine and Gothic styles repudiated; classical Greek and Latin texts published in Italy; intellectual life flourishes in ducal courts; artists emerge from artisan class
1500	Perugia (?), Italy	Italian Renaissance, Roman School	Roman popes and curia dominate regional dukedoms (except Venice)	Borgia popes and Julius II consolidate power of papacy; best artists go to Rome, now the world's financial center; Michelangelo paints Sistine Ceiling (1508) while Raphael works on frescoes for papal apartments in the Vatican; nominally religious art with strong pagan-classical flavor
c. 1507	Nuremberg, Germany	Northern Renaissance	Mercantile aristocrats in Nuremberg and Augsburg (the Fuggers) imitate Italian princes, patronize artists and scholars, resent flow of funds to Rome	Martin Luther posts his theses, 1517; Luther excommunicated, 1521; Luther publishes German Bible in 1522 with woodcuts by Lucas Cranach; Peasant Revolt in Germany (1524–25); iconoclasm, confiscation of ecclesiastical art and property (1520–40)
1546–64	Rome	Early Baroque	Papal household dominates Rome; cardinals and bankers compete in self-glorification	German army sacks Rome, 1527; artists scatter; Henry VIII breaks with Rome, 1534; Council of Trent (1540–63) fails to reconcile Protestants; Spain rules much of Italy through local surrogates; Michelangelo paints *Last Judgment* (1534–41)
c. 1580	Toledo, Spain	Mannerism	Feudal Spain is bankrupt; imperial Spain milks American colonies; nobility impoverished; intense otherworldly religious feeling	Muslims driven out of Spain, 1492; Jews expelled by Ferdinand and Isabella; Ignatius Loyola founds Jesuit Order, 1534; large infusions of American gold and silver weaken Spanish economy; Spanish naval power destroyed by English pirates; Armada defeated (1588) by Drake
1638–39	Antwerp, Flanders (Belgium)	Northern (Flemish) Baroque	Jesuits control art, education and architecture; sponsor devotional art for the masses, classical studies for sons of the rich	Holland gains freedom from Spain, 1609; Antwerp, Amsterdam, Augsburg and Ulm become major banking centers; French, English and Dutch settlements established in North America; Hudson's Bay Company organized, 1670; Spanish Habsburg influence lingers in Flemish art, education and upper-class behavior
1650	Rome, Italy	Spanish Baroque	Spaniards dominate Italian politics and religion; Roman Baroque dominates art of Europe	Galileo tried for heresy by the Inquisition, 1633; end of Thirty Years' War, 1648; Catholicism triumphs except in northern Europe; skepticism of Descartes (d. 1650) undermines intellectual authority of Rome; France becomes most powerful nation in Europe; French Academy established, 1648
c. 1648–50	Amsterdam, Holland	Northern (Dutch) Baroque	Dutch towns ruled by wealthy, conservative bourgeoisie supported by Calvinist clergy	Dutch East India Company (chartered 1602) monopolizes Southeast Asian trade; Harvey discovers circulation of blood, 1628; Rembrandt paints *Anatomy Lesson*, 1632; Dutch ruling class sponsors secular art, realistic style, everyday subject matter

TYPICAL OBJECT, IMAGE, MONUMENT	MATERIAL, MEDIUM, PROCESS	MAKER, ARTIST	USER, SPONSOR, PATRON	FUNCTION, PURPOSE
The Last Supper	Egg tempera plus oil glaze on stone wall covered with plaster and sealed with varnish	Leonardo da Vinci	Commissioned by Duke Ludovico Sforza for the monastery of Sta. Maria delle Grazie	To enable the prior and monks, while eating, to contemplate Jesus' last meal with his disciples; to psychologize Jesus and each of his disciples
The Three Graces	Oil on wooden panel, 6 3/4″ square	Raphael	Made for himself (?)	To express ideas drawn from ancient humanistic texts; to revive the classical ideal of beauty in the nude; to visualize perfection embodied in human form
Study for Adam	Pen and sepia wash on paper	Albrecht Dürer	Study for the artist	To master "the science of proportion" in preparation for his figure paintings and engravings; to represent nature truly, i.e., in the "new" Italian manner
St. Peter's	Stone, marble, mosaics; metal chains in dome fabric; fusion of central plan and basilican plan; 452′ high	Michelangelo (dome completed by Giacomo della Porta)	Pope Paul III	Initiated by Julius II to contain his tomb; to restore prestige of city of Rome after sack in 1527; to combine dome-of-heaven symbolism of the early Church with the longitudinal orientation of Latin Christianity
The Agony in the Garden of Gethsemane	Oil on canvas	El Greco	Church in Toledo (?)	To combine the qualities of Spanish religiosity with the aims of the Counter-Reformation; to render the Passion of Christ in terms of noble suffering and mystical transcendence
The Judgment of Paris	Oil on canvas	Peter Paul Rubens, his pupils and assistants	Private patron	To express the compatibility of Catholic courtly culture, Renaissance humanism, and the grandiose lifestyle of the aristocratic merchants of Flanders
Pope Innocent X	Oil on canvas	Velázquez	Painted for the Pope during Velázquez' trip to Italy (1649–51)	To emphasize the power and sagacity reposed in the head of the Roman Catholic faith
Christ Healing the Sick	Etching, 11 × 15″	Rembrandt	For sale by the artist through his dealer, Pieter de la Tombe; price: one hundred guilders	To render the miracles of Jesus according to the egalitarian ideals of Protestant Christianity and the realistic outlook of the prosperous Dutch burgher class

FROM ROCOCO TO MODERN

TIME	PLACE	PERIOD, STYLE, CULTURE	SOCIAL ORGANIZATION	KEY EVENTS: POLITICAL, ECONOMIC, RELIGIOUS, TECHNOLOGICAL
1752	Versailles (?) (now in Old Pinakothek, Munich)	Rococo	French aristocracy concentrated in royal court, loses governing function; people impoverished by royal wars and extravagance	Louis XIV rules France as absolute king (1643–1715); "Glorious Revolution" and English Bill of Rights, 1689; Hobbes (d. 1679) questions absolute monarchy; Locke (d. 1704) urges representative government; J. J. Rousseau (d. 1778) justifies revolution; Watt perfects steam engine, 1765; Adam Smith writes *Wealth of Nations,* 1776; American Revolution, 1776; French Revolution, 1789–94
c. 1816	Brussels, Belgium	Neoclassicism	Powerful entrepreneurial class struggles to control European society after revolutionary radicals are overthrown in France	Napoleon dominates French and European history (1799–1814); David is artistic dictator during French Revolution *and* under Napoleon; Goya paints Spanish resistance to Napoleonic invasions, 1814; Napoleon defeated at Waterloo, 1815; David exiled; French "Academy" reinstated, 1816
1861	Paris	Romanticism	Bitter alienation of artists from society; bohemianism; growing split between art and science; doctrine of art for art's sake	Revolution of 1830 in France and throughout Europe in 1848; Daguerre perfects photography, 1839; Marx's *Communist Manifesto,* 1848; Courbet paints *The Stone Breakers,* 1849; Baudelaire publishes *Fleurs du Mal,* 1857; Darwin publishes *Origin of Species,* 1859; serfs nominally freed in Russia, 1861; American Civil War, 1861–65
1886	Calais, France	Romanticism-Impressionism-Symbolism	Factory system establishes new managerial class; terrible exploitation of industrial workers; middle class firmly controls art, politics and education	Tolstoy writes *War and Peace* (1864–69); Marx writes *Das Kapital* (1867–94) in England; Edison invents light bulb, 1879; germ theory of disease demonstrated by Pasteur 1881; Roebling builds Brooklyn Bridge (1869–83); Manet paints Emile Zola (1868)
1890–92	Aix-en-Provence	Post-Impressionism	Industrial societies dominate the world; Western imperialism; strong belief in progress through education, science, technology, business enterprise	Monet paints haystack series, 1891; Spanish-American War (1898); U.S. emerges as world power; Chicago invents skyscraper (1885–1900); revolutions in China and Mexico begin, 1911; World War I (1914–18); Russian Revolution, 1917; League of Nations, 1919
1909	Chicago	International Modern Prairie style	Boom atmosphere in U.S.; massive immigration, powerful corporations; blacks and women still disenfranchised; culture essentially WASP	Freud publishes *Interpretation of Dreams,* 1900; Planck's quantum theory, 1900; Wright brothers' flight, 1903; Einstein's relativity theory, 1905; Ford assembly line, 1909; Futurist Manifesto, 1910; U.S. opens Panama Canal, 1914; Griffith directs *Birth of a Nation,* 1915; Americans in World War I, 1917
1937	Paris (on extended loan, Museum of Modern Art, New York)	Late Cubist-Expressionist	World-wide depression, unemployment, wild speculation destabilize capitalist societies; mass communication plus charismatic leaders result in mass-movement dictatorships	Mussolini's Fascists take over Italy, 1922; Surrealist Manifesto, 1924; Wall Street "Crash" and Great Depression, 1929; Hitler's Nazis take over Germany, 1933; Gropius and the Bauhaus (1919–33); F. Roosevelt and the New Deal, 1933; Spanish Civil War, won by Franco's Loyalists (1936–39); Hitler-Stalin non-aggression pact, 1939; World War II (1939–45)
1960	Museum of Modern Art, New York (self-destroyed)	Abstract Expressionism, kinetic "metamatic" art	Growing independence of "Third World" peoples; Protestant ethic strong in Asia; "loss of nerve" in Europe and America; backward Russia emerges as "superpower"	Atomic bombs dropped on Hiroshima and Nagasaki, 1945; United Nations formed, 1945; British leave India, 1947; State of Israel founded, 1948; Marshall Plan for Europe, 1949; Soviets explode atomic bomb, 1949; U.S. explodes hydrogen bomb, 1954; Soviets launch Sputnik, 1957; Cuban missile crisis, 1962; John F. Kennedy assassinated, 1963; Solzhenitsyn describes Gulag, wins Nobel Prize (1972), moves to U.S.

TYPICAL OBJECT, IMAGE, MONUMENT	MATERIAL, MEDIUM, PROCESS	MAKER, ARTIST	USER, SPONSOR, PATRON	FUNCTION, PURPOSE
Miss O'Murphy (*Nude on a Sofa*)	Oil on canvas, 23 5/8 × 25 3/8″	François Boucher	Louis XV	To portray the King's mistress as his plaything; to express a light-hearted, spontaneous approach to love; to join the idea of childlike innocence with eroticism
Man with a Hat	Oil on canvas	Jacques-Louis David	Portrait commission	A tribute to the elegance and fastidiousness of Europe's newly rich class of businessmen and industrialists; David integrates the noble form language of Neoclassicism with the naturalistic detail desired by his wealthy clientele
The Lion Hunt	Oil on canvas	Eugène Delacroix	Painted for Salon exhibition	Feeds French curiosity about "Oriental" exoticism; satisfies bourgeois appetite for a life of action and danger; substitutes exciting color and brushwork for controlled feeling of classical drawing and modeling
The Burghers of Calais	Bronze, 85 × 98 × 78″	Auguste Rodin	The people and town fathers of Calais	To dramatize the heroism of a group of ordinary citizens; to demonstrate the possibility of a democratic public monument; to analyze the emotions of men facing death by execution
The Card Players	Oil on canvas, 25 1/2 × 32″	Paul Cézanne	Painted for himself; later (1895) exhibited by the dealer Ambroise Vollard	To create a harmony of colors, shapes and their interrelations; to demonstrate the geometrical roots of form; to fix and record the artist's perceptions of objects in space
Robie House	Steel beams, wood, brick, glass, stucco; cantilever and masonry pier construction	Frank Lloyd Wright	Frederick D. Robie	To express the unity of the house with the land by emphasizing horizontality; to make the dwelling seem to belong "organically" to its site; to create decorative and textural effects by exposing natural building materials
Guernica	Black, white and gray oil paint on canvas, 11′6″ × 25′8″	Pablo Picasso	For Spanish Pavilion, Paris World's Fair	To protest Franco's bombing of civilians and to denounce Fascism; to create a form language which can describe the bombing and its emotional impact simultaneously; to relate modern war to ancient, subconscious memories of violence
Homage to New York	Piano, drums, wheels, gears, typewriter, electric motor, Coke bottles	Jean Tinguely	For audience in the garden of the Museum of Modern Art	To entertain; to ridicule mechanization; to dramatize the "suicide" of a machine; to condemn industrial civilization and the "machine aesthetic"

SELECTED BIBLIOGRAPHY

Following is a list of books and articles related to the major themes discussed in this volume. It is by no means complete. Rather the list is intended to be suggestive of the range of published material which can be consulted in connection with questions raised in the text. Specialized monographs and publications about individual artists have been omitted as much as possible. The listing of periodicals, too, has been kept to a minimum. World histories of art are not included, on the assumption that the reader is already familiar with them or has access to a bibliography of the outstanding works of comprehensive art history.

THE FUNCTIONS OF ART

Antal, Frederick. *Florentine Painting and its Social Background.* London: Routledge and Kegan Paul, 1948.

Dorner, Alexander. *The Way Beyond "Art."* New York University Press, 1958.

Feldman, Edmund B. "Homes in America." *Arts and Architecture*, October and November, 1957.

Hauser, Arnold. *The Philosophy of Art History.* New York: A. A. Knopf, 1959.

Huyghe, René. *Art and the Spirit of Man.* New York: Abrams, 1962.

Larkin, Oliver. *Art and Life in America.* New York: Rinehart, 1949.

Lommel, Andreas. *Shamanism: The Beginnings of Art.* New York: McGraw-Hill, 1968.

Morris, William. *On Art and Socialism.* London: Lehmann, 1947.

Read, Herbert. *The Grass Roots of Art.* New York: Wittenborn, Schultz, 1947.

THE STYLES OF ART

Ackerman, James. "Style," *Art and Archaeology*, Ackerman and Rhys Carpenter. Englewood Cliffs, N.J.: Prentice-Hall, 1963.

Hitchcock, Henry-Russell, and Johnson, Philip. *The International Style: Architecture since 1922.* New York: Norton, 1932.

Hunter, Sam. *Modern American Painting and Sculpture.* New York: Dell, 1959.

Myers, Bernard. *Expressionism in German Painting: A Generation in Revolt.* New York: Praeger, 1966.

Nochlin, Linda. *Realism.* New York and Baltimore: Penguin Books, 1971.

Ortega y Gassett, José. *The Dehumanization of the Arts.* Garden City, N.Y.: Anchor Books, 1956.

Panofsky, Erwin. *Meaning in the Visual Arts.* Garden City, N.Y.: Anchor Books, 1955.

Ritchie, Andrew C. *Abstract Painting and Sculpture in America.* New York: Museum of Modern Art, 1951.

Rubin, William S. *Dada, Surrealism and Their Heritage.* New York: Museum of Modern Art, 1968.

Schapiro, Meyer. "Style." In *Anthropology Today*, edited by A. L. Kroeber, University of Chicago Press, 1953.

Selz, Peter, ed. *Art Nouveau: Art and Design at the Turn of the Century.* New York: Museum of Modern Art, 1959.

Wölfflin, Heinrich. *Principles of Art History.* Translated by Mary D. Hottinger. New York: Dover, 1950.

Woods, Gerald. Philip Thompson and John Williams, editors. *Art Without Boundaries: 1950–70.* London: Thames and Hudson, 1972.

Worringer, Wilhelm. *Abstraction and Empathy: A Contribution to the Psychology of Style.* Translated by Michael Bullock. New York: International Universities Press, 1953.

THE IMAGE OF WOMAN IN MODERN PAINTING

Bade, Patrick. *Femme Fatale.* New York: Mayflower Books, 1979.

Berger, John. *Ways of Seeing.* London and Harmondsworth: British Broadcasting Corporation and Penguin Books, 1972.

Clark, Kenneth. *The Nude: A Study in Ideal Form.* New York: Pantheon Books, 1957.

DeRiencourt, Amaury. *Sex and Power in History*. New York: David McKay Company, 1974.

Fine, Elsa Honig. *Women and Art*. Montclair/London: Allanheld & Schram/Prior, 1978.

Harris, Ann Sutherland and Nochlin, Linda. *Women Artists: 1550–1950*. New York: Knopf, 1977.

Pelles, Geraldine. *Art, Artists and Society*. Englewood Cliffs, N.J.: Prentice-Hall, 1963.

Petersen, Karen and Wilson, J. J. *Women Artists*. New York: New York University Press, 1976.

Tuchman, Gaye. Arlene Kaplan Daniels and James Benet, editors. *Hearth and Home: Images of Women in the Mass Media*. New York: Oxford University Press, 1978.

THE STRUCTURE OF ART

Anderson, Donald M. *Elements of Design*. New York: Holt, Rinehart and Winston, 1961.

Arnheim, Rudolph, *Art and Visual Perception*. Berkeley and Los Angeles: University of California Press, 1954.

Gombrich, E. H. "How to Read a Painting." *Saturday Evening Post*, July 29, 1961.

Hill, Edward. *The Language of Drawing*. Englewood Cliffs, N.J.: Prentice-Hall, 1966.

Itten, Johannes. *Design and Form: The Basic Course at the Bauhaus*. New York: Reinhold, 1964.

Kepes, Gyorgy. *Language of Vision*. Chicago: Theobald, 1944.

Klee, Paul. *Pedagogical Sketchbook*. New York: Praeger, 1953.

Moholy-Nagy, László. *The New Vision*. 4th rev. ed. New York: Wittenborn, Schultz, 1949.

Raphael, Max. *Prehistoric Cave Paintings*. New York: Pantheon Books, 1945.

Wölfflin, Heinrich. *The Sense of Form in Art: A Comparative Psychological Study*. New York: Chelsea, 1958.

PAINTING

Arnason, Harvard H. *History of Modern Art*. New York: Abrams, 1968.

Doerner, Max. *The Materials of the Artist*. Translated by Eugen Neuhaus. New York: Harcourt, Brace, 1949.

Haftmann, Werner. *Painting in the Twentieth Century*. 2 vols. New York: Praeger, 1960.

Henri, Robert. *The Art Spirit*. Philadelphia: Lippincott, 1923.

Hitchcock, Henry-Russell. *Painting Toward Architecture*. New York: Duell, Sloan and Pearce, 1948.

Hunter, Sam. *American Art of the 20th Century*. New York: Abrams, 1972.

Janis, Harriet, and Blesh, Rudi. *Collage: Personalities, Concepts, Techniques*. Philadelphia: Chilton Book, 1962.

Read, Herbert. *A Concise History of Modern Painting*. New York: Praeger, 1959.

Seitz, William C. *The Art of Assemblage*. New York: Museum of Modern Art, 1961.

Selz, Peter. *New Images of Man*. Prefatory note by Paul Tillich. New York: Museum of Modern Art, 1959.

Williams, Hiram. *Notes for a Young Painter*. Englewood Cliffs, N.J.: Prentice-Hall, 1963.

SCULPTURE

Giedion-Welcker, Carola. *Contemporary Sculpture: An Evolution in Volume and Space*. New York: Wittenborn, Schultz, 1955.

Read, Herbert. *A Concise History of Modern Sculpture*. New York: Praeger, 1964.

Rickey, George. *Constructivism: Origins and Evolution*. New York: Braziller, 1967.

Ritchie, Andrew C. *Sculpture of the Twentieth Century*. New York: Museum of Modern Art, 1952.

Rodin, Auguste. *On Art and Artists*. New York: Philosophical Library, 1957.

Schmalenbach, Werner. *African Art*. New York: Macmillan, 1954.

Seuphor, Michel. *The Sculpture of This Century*. New York: Braziller, 1960.

Tucker, William. *Early Modern Sculpture*. New York: Oxford University Press, 1974.

Wittkower, Rudolf. *Sculpture: Processes and Principles*. London: Allen Lane/Penguin Books, 1977.

ARCHITECTURE

Andrews, Wayne. *Architecture, Ambition and Americans*. New York: Harper, 1955.

Arnheim, Rudolf. *The Dynamics of Architectural Form*. Berkeley: University of California Press, 1977.

Burchard, John, and Bush-Brown, Albert. *The Architecture of America*. Boston: Little, Brown, 1961.

Conrads, Ulrich, and Sperlich, Hans. *The Architecture of Fantasy: Utopian Building and Planning in Modern Times*. New York: Praeger, 1962.

Giedion, Sigfried. *Space, Time and Architecture: The Growth of a New Tradition*. 3rd rev. ed. Cambridge: Harvard University Press, 1954.

Jeanneret-Gris, Charles E. [Le Corbusier]. *New World of Space*. New York: Reynal and Hitchcock, 1948.

Norberg-Schulz, Christian. *Meaning in Western Architecture*. New York: Praeger, 1975.

Rasmussen, Steen Eiler. *Experiencing Architecture*. Cambridge: Massachusetts Institute of Technology Press, 1959.

Rudofsky, Bernard. *Architecture Without Architects: An Introduction to Non-Pedigreed Architecture*. New York: Museum of Modern Art, 1964.

Salvadori, Mario, and Heller, Robert. *Structure in Architecture*. Englewood Cliffs, N.J.: Prentice-Hall, 1963.

Scott, Geoffrey. *The Architecture of Humanism: A Study in the History of Taste*. London: Constable, 1914.

Scully, Vincent J. *American Architecture and Urbanism*. New York: Praeger, 1969.

Torroja, Eduardo. *Philosophy of Structures*. Translated by Milos and J. J. Polivka. Berkeley and Los Angeles: University of California Press, 1958.

CITY PLANNING

Bacon, Edmund N. *Design of Cities*. New York: Viking Press, 1967.

Blake, Peter. *God's Own Junkyard: The Planned Deterioration of America's Landscape*. New York: Holt, Rinehart and Winston, 1964.

Goodman, Paul and Percival. *Communitas: Means of Livelihood and Ways of Life*. New York: Vintage Books, 1960.

Holland, Lawrence B., ed. *Who Designs America?* Garden City, N.Y.: Anchor Books, 1966.

Jacobs, Jane. *The Death and Life of Great American Cities*. New York: Random House, 1961.

Lynch, Kevin. *The Image of the City*. Cambridge: Technology Press and Harvard University Press, 1960.

Moholy-Nagy, Sibyl. *Matrix of Man: An Illustrated History of Urban Environment*. New York: Praeger, 1968.

Mumford, Lewis. *The City in History*. New York: Harcourt, Brace, 1961.

Rosenau, Helen. *The Ideal City: Its Architectural Evolution*. New York: Harper & Row, 1972.

Rudofsky, Bernard. *Streets for People: A Primer for Americans*. New York: Doubleday, 1969.

Tunnard, Christopher, and Pushkarev, Boris. *Man-Made America: Chaos or Control; An Inquiry into Selected Problems of Design in the Urbanized Landscape*. New Haven: Yale University Press, 1963.

Zucker, Paul. *Town and Square*. New York: Columbia University Press, 1959.

THE CRAFTS AND INDUSTRIAL DESIGN

Banham, Reyner. *Theory and Design in the First Machine Age*. New York: Praeger, 1960.

Drexler, Arthur, and Daniel, Greta. *Introduction to Twentieth Century Design*. New York: Museum of Modern Art, 1959.

Giedion, Sigfried. *Mechanization Takes Command*. New York: Oxford University Press, 1948.

Gropius, Walter and Ise. *Bauhaus, 1919–1928*. Edited by Herbert Bayer. New York: Museum of Modern Art, 1938.

Klingender, Francis D. *Art and the Industrial Revolution*. London: Royle Publications, 1947.

Mumford, Lewis. *Technics and Civilization*. New York: Harcourt, Brace, 1934.

Pevsner, Nikolaus. *Pioneers of Modern Design from William Morris to Walter Gropius*. New York: Museum of Modern Art, 1949.

Read, Herbert. *Art and Industry*. London: Faber & Faber, 1934.

PHOTOGRAPHY

Braive, Michael F. *The Photograph: A Social History*. New York: McGraw-Hill, 1966.

Coke, Van Deren. *The Painter and the Photograph*. Albuquerque: The University of New Mexico Press, 1972.

Kahmen, Volker. *Art History of Photography*. New York: The Viking Press, 1973.

Levitt, Helen. *A Way of Seeing: Photographs of New York*, with an essay by James Agee. New York: The Viking Press, 1965.

Lucie-Smith, Edward. *The Invented Eye*. New York: Paddington Press Limited, 1975.

Mozley, Anita Ventura. *American Photography: Past into Present*. Seattle: Seattle Art Museum, 1976.

Newhall, Beaumont. *The History of Photography*. New York: The Museum of Modern Art, 1964.

Pollack, Peter. *The Picture History of Photography*. New York: Abrams, 1969.

Scharf, Aaron. *Art and Photography*. London: Allen Lane The Penguin Press, 1968.

Schuneman, R. Smith, ed. *Photographic Communication*. New York: Hastings House Publishers, 1972.

Sontag, Susan. *On Photography*. New York: Farrar, Straus and Giroux, 1977.

Szarkowski, John. *The Photographer's Eye*. New York: The Museum of Modern Art, 1966.

FILM AND TELEVISION

Arnheim, Rudolph. *Film as Art*. Berkeley and Los Angeles: University of California Press, 1958.

Kael, Pauline. *Deeper into Movies*. New York: Bantam Books, 1971.

Kracauer, Siegfried. *Theory of Film: The Redemption of Physical Reality*. New York: Oxford University Press, 1960.

MacGowan, Kenneth. *Behind the Screen: The History and Techniques of the Motion Picture*. New York: Delacorte Press, 1965.

Monaco, James. *How to Read a Film*. New York: Oxford University Press, 1977.

Newcombe, Horace, ed. *The Critical View: Television*. New York: Oxford University Press, 1976.

Nilsen, Vladimir. *The Cinema as a Graphic Art*. New York: Hill and Wang, 1959.

Spottiswoode, Raymond. *Film and Its Techniques*. Berkeley and Los Angeles: University of California Press, 1966.

Tyler, Parker. *The Three Faces of the Film*. Cranbury, N.J.: Barnes, 1967.

Whitaker, Rod. *The Language of Film*. Englewood Cliffs, N.J.: Prentice-Hall, 1970.

Williams, Raymond. *Television: Technology and Cultural Form*. New York: Schocken Books, 1975.

ART CRITICISM

Boas, George. *A Primer for Critics*. Baltimore: Johns Hopkins University Press, 1937.

Feldman, Edmund B. "The Critical Act," *The Journal of Aesthetic Education*, Vol. I, No. 2, Autumn, 1966.

Greene, Theodore M. *The Arts and the Art of Criticism*. Princeton University Press, 1947.

Jacobs, Jay. "What Should a Critic Be?" *Art in America*, No. I, 1965.

Margolis, Joseph. *The Language of Art and Art Criticism*. Detroit: Wayne State University Press, 1965.

Panofsky, Erwin. *Studies in Iconology*. New York: Oxford University Press, 1939.

Pepper, Stephen C. *The Basis of Criticism in the Arts*. Cambridge: Harvard University Press, 1949.

Stolnitz, Jerome. *Aesthetics and Philosophy of Art Criticism: A Critical Introduction*. Boston: Houghton Mifflin, 1960.

Venturi, Lionello. *History of Art Criticism*. New York: E.P. Dutton, 1936.

INDEX

A page number in *italic type* refers to an illustration, with colorplate page numbers preceded by an asterisk (*).

Decalcomania, 293, 294

De Chirico, Giorgio, 205, 472, 473; *Great Metaphysician*, 205; *Delights of the Poet*, 472

Degas, Edgar, 116, 134, 136, 151–53, 323, 432; *Développé en avant*, 270; *Glass of Absinthe*, 151, *151*; *Two Laundresses*, 119, *120*, *123*

Deitrick, William H., 96; J. S. Dorton Arena (Raleigh, N.C.), 96, *96*

De Kooning, Willem, 41, 57, 116, 134–35, 167, 273, 295; *Black and White, Rome D*, 295, *296*; *Two Women*, *162*; *Woman, I*, 57, *58*; *Woman, II*, 135, *293*

Delacroix, Eugène, 43, 276–78; *Liberty Leading the People*, 43, *43*–44; *Lion Hunt*, 277; *Lion Hunt*, sketch for, 277, *277*; *Portrait of Chopin*, *285*

De La Tour, *see* La Tour, Georges de

Delaunay, Robert, 171; *Eiffel Tower*, 171, *171*; *Homage to Blériot*, *175*

De Lempicka, Tamara, 137, 138; *Reclining Woman in Pink*, 137, *138*

Della Robbia, Luca, *Madonna and Angels*, 322

De Maria, Walter, *Mile Long Drawing*, 368

Demuth, Charles, 171; *My Egypt*, 171, *171*

Depth, photographic, 433, 434, 439

Derain, André, 246; *London Bridge*, *177*, 246

Der Blaue Reiter, 246

De Rivera, José, 38; *Construction "Blue and Black,"* 38, *38*–39; *Homage to the World of Minkowski*, 361

Description, in criticism, 471–73

Design (*see also* City planning; Domestic architecture; Industrial design), 251–66; balance in, 256–58; principles of, 251–52; proportion, 262–65; rhythm in, 258–62; unity, 252–56

Despair, and anxiety, in art, 131–32, 196–99

De Stijl, 311

"Dick Cavett Show," Photograph from a, *446*

Diebenkorn, Richard, *Ocean Park, No. 22*, *174*

Die Brücke, 246

Dionysiac tendency in art, 167

Direct painting, 274–80, 296; brushwork, 276, 277, 278, 279, 293, 294, 296

Distortion: emotion and, 194–99; Expressionism, 199; objective accuracy and, 147, 149, 153, 155–56; photographic, 194, 422; proportion and, 265; in satire, 196

Dix, Otto, 149; *My Parents*, 149, *149*; *Punishment*, 466

Documentary films, 444

Domes, 182, 272, 395, 396–97, 406, 411; coffers in, 396; geodesic, 406, 408; oculus or lantern in, 396; pendentive, 396–97; squinches of, 396, 397

Domestic architecture (*see also* City planning), 70–83; apartment houses, 72–73, 80–81, 82; appliances and labor-saving devices, 71–72; climate control, 72–73; family and home interaction, 70–71; furnishings, 70–71; interior decoration, 74–75, 82; Le Corbusier's

work and influence, 77–80; materials and techniques, 71–73; Mies's work and influence, 75–77; modern, 81–82; ornament, 74, 76, 82; site, 72, 81; space, 77, 81; Wright's work and influence, 73–75

Dominance in design, 252–56

Dorazio, Piero, *Janus*, 257

Douglas, Melvin, 30

Dove, Arthur G., *Critic*, 458; *That Red One*, *211*

Dramatic enactment in painting, 294–95

Drawing, *see* Line

Dreams, expression in art (*see also* Fantasy), 205–8, 213; cinematic media and, 447–48; Surrealism and, 205–8

Drexler, Arthur, 202

Dreyfuss, Henry, 112

Duble, Lu, 197; *Cain*, *196*, 197

Dubuffet, Jean, 41, 295, 299, 310, 317; *Corps de Dame*, 299; *Leader in a Parade Uniform*, *189*; *My Cart, My Garden*, 299; *Sea of Skin*, 250

Duchamp, Marcel, 216, 262, 295, 299, 347, 355; *Boîte-en-valise (The Box in a Valise)*, 355, *355*; *Bride*, 216, *216*; *Nude Descending a Staircase, No. 2*, 262, *263*, 442

Duchamp-Villon, Raymond, 171; *Horse*, 171, *171*

Durability: and craftsmanship, 486; of paintings, 271, 272–74

Durante, Jimmy, 318, 350

Dürer, Albrecht, *Painter's Father*, 281; *Study for Adam*, 264

Dwellings, *see* Domestic architecture

Dying Gaul (Pergamum), 35, *36*

Eakins, Thomas, 32, 153, 262; *Agnew Clinic*, 32, *32*, *152*, 153; *Gross Clinic*, *152*, 153; *Multiple Exposure Photograph of George Reynolds, Pole Vaulting*, 262, *263*

Eames, Charles, 112, 319; Chaise longue, *111*; Eames House, 82; Lounge chair, *110*; *Solar Toy (Do Nothing Machine)*, *104*

Earth sculpture, 367–69

Echaurren, *see* Matta

Eckhardt, Wolf van, 375

Eclaboussage, 294

Economics, industrial design and, 108, 112

Edgerton, Harold E., Stroboscopic study of motion: swirls and eddies of a tennis stroke, *442*

Egg tempera (*see also* Tempera painting), 271, 275, 276

Egyptian art, 185; architecture, 373–74, 376, 389; sculpture, 24, 320, 329, 330, 333–34, 371

Ehrenzweig, Anton, 311

Eiffel, Gustave, 382, 384, 409; Eiffel Tower, 384, *384*, *385*

"Eight, The," 47–49

Eisenstein, Sergei, *Potemkin* (film still from), *445*

Ekkehard and Uta (Naumberg Cathedral, Germany), *328*

El Greco, 241, 272, 273, 280; *Agony in the Garden of Gethsemane*, *240*, 241, 280; *Fray Felix Hortensio Paravicino*, 283

Emery, Lin, *Homage to Amercreo*, 363, *363*

Emotion, as art style, 186–201; anxiety and despair, 131–32, 196–99; in architecture, 200–201, 410, 415–16; brushwork and, 278–79; criticism and, 186, 459; distortion and, 194–99; emotional perception theory, 186; Expressionism, 199; joy and celebration, 199–201; organizational sources and, 186; Romanticism, 188, 194; in sculpture, 188, 197, 319; thematic sources and, 186, 188

Employment and women, 119, 129–30

Encaustic painting, 276

Engineering: and art, 69, 171, 409, 410, 411; domestic architecture, 73; suspension, 78, 382–83, 391

Ensor, James, 133

Environments, 298, 303–10

Epstein, Jacob, 19, 114, 158, 160, 321; *Head of Joseph Conrad*, *159*, 160; *Madonna and Child*, 19, *19*

Epstein & Sons, Sara Lee Administration Building (Deerfield, Ill.), 95, *95*

Erni, Hans, *Atomkrieg Nein (Atom War No)*, 44

Ernst, Max, 204, 293–94, 295, 299, 303; *Capricorne*, *338*; *Eye of Silence*, 294; *Joy of Living*, 213; *Swamp Angel*, 294

Eroticism in art, 19–24, 116, 117, 118, 314–17

Escobar, *see* Marisol

Estes, Richard, *Store Front*, 165

Estève, Maurice, *Rebecca*, *173*

Etching (Exhibition of Painters and Sculptors at Louvre), 455

Etienne-Martin, *Grand Couple*, *339*

Etruscan art: Sarcophagus (Cerveteri), *327*

Evans, Walker, 425, 434; *Frank's Stove, Cape Breton Island*, 430; *Graveyard in Easton, Pennsylvania*, 434, *434*

Expressionism, 28, 288–92; Abstract, 57–59, 295, 301, 312, 347; color, 246; distortion, 199; emotion and, 199; German, 49, 133

Expressivism, critical, 464–66

Face, female, and sexual dimorphism, 114–15, 141

Factories, 93, 95, 390

Fairfield and Dubois and F. C. Etherington, Central Technical School (Toronto), *412*, 413

Fantasy, as art style, 202–17; advertising art, 207; architectural, 202; dreams, 205–8; hallucinations, 205–8, 213; illusionism, 215–17; myths, 202–5, 213; primitive art, 208, 213; scientific, 214–15; sculptural, 188, 207; Surrealism and, 205–8, 214–16; Utopianism, 202

Fashion drawing, 265

Faulkner, Ray, drawing, *Art Today*, 389

Fauves, 246

Feininger, Andreas, 434; *Cemetery in New York City*, 434, *434*

Feininger, Lyonel, 169; *Church of the Minorites (II)*, 169, *169*

Fellini, Federico, *La Dolce Vita* (film stills from), *450*, *451*

Female form, treatments of (*see also* Human form; Women), 19–20, 113–42

PHOTO CREDITS

The author and publisher wish to thank the libraries, museums, galleries, and private collectors named in the picture captions for permitting the reproduction of works of art in their collections, and for supplying the necessary photographs. Photographs from other sources are gratefully acknowledged below.

Alinari (including Anderson and Brogi), Florence: 70 below, 71 below right, 166, 167, 272, 273, 276 above right, 282 above, 284 below left, 322 left, 353 above right, 398 below; American Airlines, New York: 83 above; American Crafts Council, New York: 108 above; Copyright A.C.L., Brussels: 284 above right; Amigos de Gaudi, Barcelona: 232 below left; Wayne Andrews, New York: 97 above; George A. Applegarth, San Francisco: 183 below; Art Institute of Chicago: 481 below; Australian News and Information Bureau, New York: 261 above; Ronald Baldwin, New York: 446; Bank of Hawaii, Honolulu: 409 right; H. Baranger, Paris; 414 above right; Welton Becket & Assoc., Los Angeles: 390 below; Ken Bell Photography Ltd., courtesy of University of Toronto Public Relations Department: 97 center; Bethlehem Steel Corporation, Bethlehem, Pa.: 79 above right; Oscar Bladh, Stockholm: 87; Blue Ridge Aerial Surveys, Leesburg, Va., courtesy of Gulf Reston, Inc.: 83 below; Grace Borgenicht Gallery, New York: 348 above right; Bowdoin College Museum of Art, Brunswick, Maine: 397 below left; Office of E. H. Brenner, Lafayette, Inc.: 405; Bulloz, Paris: 136 left; Rudolph Burckhardt, New York: 99 left, courtesy of Leo Castelli Gallery, 105 above, 139 above, 317 below, courtesy of Sidney Janis Gallery; R. D. Burmeister, Clovis, New Mexico: 300 below; California Division of Highways, Sacramento: 89 center, 388 above right; California Institute of Technology, Pasadena: 411 below left; Canadian Consulate General, New York: 406; Ludovico Canali, Rome: 378, 401 above; Leo Castelli Gallery, New York: 313 below; Central Technical School, Toronto: 412 below; Ron Chamberlain, Warwick, N.Y.: 351 below right; Victor Chambi, Cusco, Peru: 375 below; Chase Manhattan Bank, New York: 297 center, 409 left; Geoffrey Clements, New York: 60 below, 139 below, 159 above left, 293, 312, 318 right, 351 above right, 362 above; Colorado Highway Commission: 89 below; CBS Television Network, New York: 30 above right; Commonwealth United Entertainment, Inc., Beverly Hills, Calif.: 450 above, 451; Community Service Society, New York: 52 center; Cordier & Ekstrom, New York: 298; Craft Horizons, New York: 110 above right, 363 left; Craftsmen Photo Company, New York: 447 left; Thomas Y. Crowell, Inc., New York: 104 below, from Primitive Art by Irwin

O. Christensen; George Cserna, New York: 182 above right, 407 below right, courtesy of Harrison & Abramovitz; Cunningham & Walsh, Inc., New York: 370 above left; Design M—Ingo Maurer, Munich: 253 right; Deutscher Kunstverlag G.m.b.H., Munich: 114; Dumas-Satigny, Orléans, France: 331 above left; Dwan Gallery, New York: 365 above left, 368 above, 368 center; John Ebstel, New York: 416 below; Edholm & Blomgren Photographers, Lincoln. Neb.: 265 below; Foto ENIT, Rome: 93 above right, 397 above left; Michael Fedison, courtesy of Western Pennsylvania Conservancy: 74 above; Fischbach Gallery, New York: 357, 359 above right; Courtesy Fischer Fine Art, Ltd., London: 133; Ford Motor Company, Dearborn, Mich.: 106 above, 364 above right; French Government Tourist Office, New York: 92 above right, 384 right; Copyright Buckminster Fuller, Carbondale, Ill.: 72; Copyright David Gahr, New York: 365 above right; Roger Gain, Paris: 112; General Instrument Corporation, Microelectronic Division, New York: 235 above left; German Information Center, New York: 415 above; John Gibson, New York: 368 center; Giraudon, Paris: 120 above right, 478; Alex Gotfryd, New York: 63 below left; Greater London Council: 415 below right; Pedro E. Guerrero, New York: 82 above left; Solomon R. Guggenheim Museum, New York: 182 below right; Paul R. Hanna, Stanford, Calif.: 74 below right; Office of Zvi Hecker, Montreal: 88 above; Hedrich-Blessing, Chicago: 74 below left, 96 above, from Bill Hedrich, 76 above left, 76 above right, 412 above, from Bill Engdahl, 380 above; Lucien Hervé, Paris: 78 center, 81 above left, 78 below, 79 above left, 79 below, 85, 232 above, 402 above; John T. Hill, New York: 75 above; Hans Hinz, Allschwil: 128; Hirmer Verlag, Munich: 333 left; Michael Holford, London: 332 above; Martin Hürlimann, Zurich: 397 above right; Illinois Institute of Technology, Chicago: 76 above left; Intourist, Moscow: 374 above; Alexander Iolas Gallery, New York: 294; Office of Philip Johnson, New York: 77; S. C. Johnson & Son, Inc. , Racine, Wis.: 78 above, 94 above left, 94 below left; Luc Joubert, Paris: 295 below; Office of Louis I. Kahn, Philadelphia: 404 above; Kitchens of Sara Lee, Deerfield, Ill.: 95 above; Knoedler Gallery, New York: 320; Alicia B. Legg, New York: 352 below; Library of Congress, Washington, D.C.: 383 above right; Terry S. Lindquist, Miami: 309 below; Roger Lucas, New York: 367 above; Edward B. Luce Studios, Worcester: 126 below; Magnum Photos, Inc., New York: 71 below left, 470; Manhattanville College, Purchase, N.Y.: 375 above; Michael Maor, Jerusalem: 382 left; Foto Marburg, Marburg/ Lahn: 393 below left; Marlborough Fine Art, Ltd., London: 39 below right, 197 above right; Maryville College, Maryville, Tennessee: 386 above; Foto MAS, Barcelona: 155, 232 below right, 353 below; Pierre Matisse Gallery, New York: 67 below; Ministerio de Informacion y Turismo, Madrid: 411 below right; Ministry of Information, Baghdad: 377 left; Ministry of Works, London, Crown Copyright: 372; Monkmeyer Press Photo Service, New York: 84 below right, from Hugh Rogers; Peter Moore, New York: 262 below; Riccardo Morandi, Rome: 414 above left; André Morisseau, Saintes, France: 387 above; Morley, Baer, Berkeley: 414 below right; Municipality of Bat-Yam, Israel: 410 above; Museum of Modern Art, New York: 76 below right, 227 below, 299 below, 353 center, 386 below, 390 above, 390 center; Museum of Modern Art Film Stills Archive, New York: 203 below, 204 above right, 441 right, 441 below, 445 above; Museum of New Mexico, Sante Fé: 88 below; Museum of Pre-Columbian Art, Dumbarton Oaks, Washington, D.C.: 410 below right; National Aeronautics and Space Administration, Washington, D.C.: 345 below; National Film Archives, London: 443 left, 443 right; National Gypsum Company, Buffalo, N.Y.: 382 above right; Studio Nervi, Rome: 384 left, 413 above; New York Times: 71 above right, 89 above, 249, from Gene Maggio, 309 above; New York Zoological Society: 231 left; Sydney W. Newbery, London: 225 above; Irving J. Newman, Greenwich, Conn.: 201 below; Niedersächsische Landesgalerie, Hanover, Germany: 304 above; Nordness Gallery, New York: 197 left; North Carolina Department of Conservation & Development, Raleigh: 96 center; Perls Galleries, New York: 193 below right; Philadelphia Museum of Art: 184 right; Studio Piaget, St. Louis: 33 left; Pictorial Parade, Inc., New York: 44 below left, 57; John Pitkin, New York: 160 above, 274 right; Planair Photography, Edinburg: 86; Eric Pollitzer, New York: 310, 352 above, 354 left; Portland Cement Association, New York: 415 below left; Dorothy Prather, Mitchell, S. D., courtesy of Mitchell Chamber of Commerce: 398 above; Progressive Architecture, New York: 413 below, from Jan C. Rowan; Nathan Rabin, Chicago: 356 below; Rapho-Guillumette, New York: 42, from Marc and Evelyn Bernheim; John Reed, East Hampton, N.Y.: 299 above; George Rickey, East Chatham, N.Y.: 362 below right; Rijksmuseum, Amsterdam: 254 below; Harry W. Rinehart, New York: 96 below, 321; Rockefeller Center, Inc., New York: 379; Rodin Museum, Paris: 159 above right; Morris Rosenfeld & Sons, New York: 233 above right; Bruce Rosensheet, Toronto: 369 above; Jean Roubier, Paris: 393 above right, 395 below, 396; Office of Paul Rudolph, New York: 416 above; Walter Russell, Courtesy The Forum Gallery, New York: 132 below; Lucas Samaras, New York; 353 below right; Sandak, Inc., New York: 31 above, 63 above left, 207 above, 392, 394 above, courtesy of Lamar Dodd; Oscar Savio, Rome: 36 above; SCALA, New York: 328 left; Barry Schein, New York: 224 below right; John D. Schiff, New York: 165; Hans Schiller, Mill Valley, Calif.: 415 below; Schipporeit-Heinrich, Inc., Chicago: 387 above left; Der Senator für Bau- und Wohnungswesen, Berlin; 388 below; Walter Seng, North Versailles, Pa.: 367 below; Bob Serating, New York: 330, courtesy of Lincoln Center for the Performing Arts; Service Photographique des Musée Nationaux, Paris: 126 above; Julius Schulman, Los Angeles: 81 below, 82 above right, 388 below, courtesy of Perry Neuschatz and Gary Call, 407 below right; Edwin Smith, London: 395 above, 397 below right; Office of Smith & Williams, Pasadena, Calif.: 374 below; Jerry Spearman, New York: 381 above; Standard Oil Co., New Jersey: 93 below; Stilnovo, Milan: 371 right; Dr. Franz Stödtner, Düsseldorf: 75 below left, 75 below right, 394 below; Ezra Stoller Assoc., New York, ©ESTO: 94 above right, 94 below right, 96 center, 169 right, 185 above, 383 below, 393 below right, 403 below, 404 below, 408; Allan Stone Galleries, Inc., New York: 303 above; Straits Times, Malaysia: 412 center; Eric Sutherland, Minneapolis: 332 below; Taylor & Dull, Inc., New York, courtesy of Finch College Museum of Art: 206 above; Thames & Hudson, Ltd., London: 274 left; Frank J. Thomas, Los Angeles: 311; Thomas Airviews, New York: 92 below; Enrique Franco Torrijos, Mexico City: 91 below, 407 center; Travelers Corporation, Hartford, Conn.: 380 below; Turkish Tourist and Information Office, New York: 399 above, 399 below; Turner Ltd., New York: 82 below; TWA, New York: 402 below; Charles Uht, New York: 216 right, 361 above; UNESCO Photographic Service, Paris: 35; United Nations, New York: 376 right; United Press International, New York: 195 below left, 376 left, 466 below; United States Steel Co., Pittsburgh: 414 below left; University of California Press, Berkeley: 385 below left, from Eduardo Torroja, Philosophy of Structures; University Properties, Inc., Seattle, Wash.: 411 above right; Upjohn Pharmaceutical Company, Kalamazoo, Mich.: 195 above left; Victoria & Albert Museum, London: 385 below right; John Waggaman, La Jolla, Calif., courtesy of Lamar Dodd: 383 above left; Morris Warman, New York, courtesy of Lincoln Center for the Performing Arts: 93 above left; Watts Towers Committee, Los Angeles: 308 right; John Webb, London: 123 below; John Weber Gallery, New York: 369 below; Etienne Bertrand Weill, Paris: 230; Cole Weston, Carmel, Calif.: 182 above right; Myron Wood, Colorado Springs: 353 center; World Color Slides-Cutler J. Coulson, Rochester, N.Y.: 381 below; Yale University News Bureau, New Haven: 80 below.